Dear Reader,

Thank you for choosing *Mastering Autodesk® Revit® Architecture 2013*. This book is part of a family of premium-quality Sybex books, all of which are written by outstanding authors who combine practical experience with a gift for teaching.

Sybex was founded in 1976. More than 30 years later, we're still committed to producing consistently exceptional books. With each of our titles, we're working hard to set a new standard for the industry. From the paper we print on, to the authors we work with, our goal is to bring you the best books available.

I hope you see all that reflected in these pages. I'd be very interested to hear your comments and get your feedback on how we're doing. Feel free to let me know what you think about this or any other Sybex book by sending me an email at nedde@wiley.com. If you think you've found a technical error in this book, please visit http://sybex.custhelp.com. Customer feedback is critical to our efforts at Sybex.

Best regards,

Neil Edde
Vice President and Publisher
Sybex, an Imprint of Wiley

Justine: You're a peace-loving Kiwi and mother who insists on handgun lessons and a concealed carry permit. I don't understand all the contradictions in the previous sentence, but the upside is I get to have friends like Eddy and James.

Harrison: High school is upon you. The most amazing careers haven't even been created yet. The trick? Studying in order to become an entrepreneur — not just an employee.

Millicent: As soon as Carol Bartz pens her biography, we're going to stand in line to buy it. Until then, there's always Ayn Rand and Jane Austen — neither of whom would ever suggest you settle for the 99%.

Jasper: Stubbornness is a virtue, and the world certainly needs more people who refuse to believe in the impossible (such as airplanes, atom splitting, and personal computers). But arguing about bedtime isn't one of those things.
— Phil

For Angiela, with whom all things are possible.
— Eddy

To Stephen, Christopher, Arianna, and Joey for being constant sources of inspiration, laughs, and love.
— James

Acknowledgments

Ah, acknowledgments. While all the glory of writing a book is consumed by the authoring team, it takes so many more people than the three of us to actually make this happen. Just like building design, the process of writing and publishing a book is truly a team sport — and without the hard work, dedication, and willingness to put up with the authoring team, this book would have never have happened.

First of all, we'd like to thank the staff at Autodesk® Revit®. Without their fine work, this would be a very empty book. With that, we'd also like to thank Phil Bernstein for taking the time to write such an inspiring foreword and helping to mold the software that helps to reshape our industry.

Second, a big thanks to our technical team. They dot our i's, cross our t's, and belittle us every time we turn in something late. Their work and effort ensures that we as authors can produce something that you the reader can actually comprehend. So thank you to Dick Margulis, duke of content and baron of flow; to copyeditor Judy Flynn for taking our broken grammar and slang sentences and making them into something readable; and to production editor Christine O'Connor for putting all the pieces together and keeping the project going. Thanks also to Pete Gaughan for watching the schedule. We're so very grateful for using you as an excuse for not visiting our in-laws on Sundays. To Tony DiMartino, the technical editor, who checks all of our Revit work and lives solely off of meat, and to our excellent support team at Sybex who helped us develop this foxy content. And always, a big Thank You to Willem Knibbe because without his continuous support, we wouldn't be motivated to keep working evenings and weekends.

We would like to express our sincerest gratitude to our friends, the architects who generously shared their work, allowing us to inspire you with it: University of Kansas, el dorado Architects, LakeFlato, Open Studio, SOM, HOK, and AECOM.

The building image on the cover was provided by NBBJ. Thank you, Sean. The building is NBBJ's competition-winning entry for the design of a new world-class, patient-centered hospital, approximately 1.6 million square feet, in Eastern Asia. NBBJ is a global architecture, planning, and design firm with offices in the North America, Asia, and Europe. Its approach is based on the belief that design can support and enhance organizational performance. The folks at NBBJ customize their solutions based on each client's enterprise, using an engaging process of discovery, design, and delivery. NBBJ is a leader in architecture for civic, corporate, commercial, health care, research, retail, science and education, and sports and entertainment. For more information, visit www.nbbj.com.

About the Authors

Phil Read is the founder of Arch | Tech as well as one of the driving forces behind the original Revit software. He's also a blogger, a speaker, a tweeter, and a popular presenter at Autodesk University. After working in both civil engineering and architecture, he downloaded Revit version 1.0 (at the suggestion of an ArchiCAD reseller) and was hooked. Less than a year later, he began working for Revit Technology and then Autodesk as a project implementation specialist, where he had the honor and pleasure of working with some of the most remarkable people and design firms around the world. He relishes the role of change agent as long as it makes sound business sense. Phil holds degrees in communications and architecture as well as a master's degree in architecture.

Eddy Krygiel is a senior project architect, a LEED Accredited Professional, and an Autodesk Authorized Author at HNTB Architects headquartered in Kansas City, Missouri. He has been using Revit since version 5.1 to complete projects ranging from single-family residences and historic remodels to 1.12-million-square-foot office buildings. Eddy is responsible for implementing BIM at his firm and also consults for other architecture and contracting firms around the country looking to implement BIM. For the last four years, he has been teaching Revit to practicing architects and architectural students in the Kansas City area and has lectured around the nation on the use of BIM in the construction industry. Eddy has also coauthored several other titles on Revit and sustainability.

James Vandezande is a registered architect and a principal at HOK in New York City, where he is a member of the firm-wide BIM leadership and is managing its buildingSMART initiatives. After graduating from the New York Institute of Technology in 1995, he worked in residential and small commercial architecture firms performing services ranging from estimating and computer modeling to construction administration. In 1999, he landed at SOM and transformed his technology skills into a 10-year span as a digital design manager. In this capacity, he pioneered the implementation of BIM on such projects as One World Trade Center, aka Freedom Tower. James has been using Revit since version 3.1 and has lectured at many industry events, including Autodesk University, VisMasters Conference, CMAA BIM Conference, McGraw-Hill Construction, and the AIANYS Convention. He is a cofounder of the NYC Revit Users Group (http://nyc-rug.com) and has been an adjunct lecturing professor at the NYU School for Continuing and Professional Studies as well as the Polytechnic Institute of NYU.

Contents at a Glance

Contents

Foreword

As I write these notes, we are fast approaching the 10th anniversary of Autodesk's acquisition of Revit Technologies in April 2002. One of my earliest presentations after joining Autodesk in 2000 posited that the building industry takes approximately 10 years to understand and absorb any innovation, and the uptake of Revit, and with it the concept of building information modeling (BIM), in some ways is proof of that concept, but in other more important ways, perhaps I missed the real point. When we decided to make that acquisition more than a decade ago, we were convinced that the building industry was poised to make an important transition in the means of representation — a shift from exclusively drafting-based paradigms to something much more efficient. But who could have anticipated the sorts of changes, and the emerging potential transformations, that Revit has driven the BIM revolution?

Of course, everyone knew that parametric modeling could be the basis of better technical drawings of all sorts and that poorly coordinated documents were the plague of the industry. But Revit's early competitors touted those capabilities. What was really interesting about 2002 and the decade to follow was the convergence of a number of ideas: realization that productivity in the industry was stunted, that sustainable design was no longer optional, that new business structures could create systemic change, and that ever-more-powerful computers brought the reality of modeling to the architect's desktop. Lots of work and investment by the AEC industry — software providers, individual customers, academics, and consultants — created the technology platform for transformation that has changed the very nature of design, construction, and building operation on the basis of BIM — and with Revit at the forefront. But for the tool to have had such an impact across a broad spectrum of critical industry issues, it needed advocates, fierce critics, and contributors to its success.

Three such contributors to that momentum are the authors of this book — Phil Read, Eddy Krygiel, and James Vandezande. Each is a technical virtuoso in his own right, but what separates them from the many who understand and advocate on behalf of Revit is their very public enthusiasm for innovation and their uncanny ability to explain the implications of the use of tools in the furtherance of the design and construction professions. Although each has trod a different path, they come together regularly to collect, synthesize, and, most important, memorialize and transmit their enormous skills and insights so the entire community of architects can benefit from their know-how. The text that follows this foreword, the fifth iteration of the *Mastering Autodesk Revit Architecture* series, is testimony to their insight and dedication and is a necessary companion for anyone traveling the BIM path.

More than ten years into this project to improve the built environment by empowering designers and builders with new tools, we have reached a point where BIM — as enabled with potency with Autodesk Revit — is no longer speculation but rather the emerging reality of modern practice. Hundreds of thousands of copies deployed and in use testify to that shift. Assuring that practitioners are properly equipped to both understand and exploit the power of these tools is what Phil, Eddy, and James have done so well during their careers. It's been a pleasure to watch their progress, share in our mutual successes, and be assured that they continue to work tirelessly and advocate for the profession through technology. This text is just another in a long line of their contributions toward that end. I am sure its readers will benefit accordingly.

—*Phil Bernstein, FAIA*

Vice President, Strategic Industry Relations, Autodesk
Lecturer in Professional Practice
Yale School of Architecture

Introduction

Architecture is the process of turning a thought into space. While it's so simple to convey that in the written word, the actual act of doing so is much more than it is possible to write. It's glory, it's torment, it's frustration, it's freedom, it's the realization that one miscalculation means a complete redesign, like blowing on a house of cards, and it's the 3 a.m. epiphany when you realize that the new design was what you were meant to get to in the first place. With all of that, it's also the burning desire to work relentlessly to make something better one step at a time.

Autodesk® Revit® Architecture software is one of the many tools we employ to help us through this organic process. It's one tool in the toolbox, but it can be much more than that. It can be the workflow that helps to empower a team. That team is the designers, the contractors, and ultimately the owners who are all looking to speak the same language.

We hope that in the process of using this book, you'll experience a bit of the struggle to realize a bit of the satisfaction of finding the solution. We hope what you learn in this book helps inspire you to your own bit of greatness. Because what's most important is that architecture isn't about buildings. It's about what we are able to accomplish with what little time we have. This is the elegant essence of Revit.

All the tutorial files necessary to complete the book's exercises plus sample families are hosted online at www.sybex.com/go/masteringrevit2013. To download the trial version of Revit Architecture, go to http://usa.autodesk.com/revit-architecture, where you'll also find complete system requirements for running Revit.

Who Should Read This Book

This book is written for architects and designers who have had some exposure to Revit and are eager to learn more. It's for architects of any generation — you don't need to be a computer wizard to understand or appreciate the content within. We've designed the book to follow real project workflows and processes to help make the tools easier to use. The chapters are full of handy tips to make Revit easier to leverage in your day-to-day world.

This book is also for the entire range of architects, from those who are fresh out of school to seasoned project managers. We have endeavored to include content for all walks of the profession so that regardless of your role on a project, you can learn how BIM changes both workflow and culture within a project team. With that, a basic understanding of Revit will make it easier to work through the book. Revit is a very robust tool requiring more than one project iteration to master.

For BIM managers, the book offers insights into the best practices for creating good project or office templates; these managers should also take a sneak peek into the powerful world of building content and Revit families. We've added many timesaving and inspiring concepts to the book, supported by examples from our own projects and the rest of the real world, to help motivate and inspire you on your journey through building information modeling.

What You Will Learn

This book will help you take the basics of Revit and BIM that you already know and expand on them using real-world examples. We will show you how to take a preliminary model and add layers of intelligence to help analyze and augment your designs. We'll show you how to create robust and accurate documentation, and then we'll help you through the construction process.

We go beyond introductory topics. To that end, we won't be starting a project from scratch or teaching you how to build a simple BIM model. If you are interested in learning at that level, we strongly recommend you pick up *Introducing Autodesk Revit Architecture 2013* (Wiley, 2012) before plunging headlong into this book. Instead, our book begins with a brief overview of the BIM approach. As you are already aware, BIM is more than just a change in software; it's a change in architectural workflow and culture. To leverage the full advantages of both BIM and Revit in your office structure, you will need to make some changes to your practice. We've designed the book around an ideal, integrated workflow to help you make this transition.

Starting with the project team, standards, and culture, we'll discuss how BIM changes your project approach and how to best build your team around a newer workflow. From there, we'll delve into conceptual design and sustainability studies, continuing through best practices for design iteration and refinement. You'll learn how to use powerful modeling techniques, how to design documentation best practices, how to make compelling presentation graphics, and how to take advantage of parametric design with the Family Editor. We'll explore workflow topics like tracking changes and worksharing as well as some strategies that move beyond traditional concepts of BIM. The book concludes with an appendix on troubleshooting and best practices so you can avoid common pitfalls. Throughout the book we've shared our practical experience with you, particularly in the form of real-world scenario sidebars.

Whether you're studying Revit on your own or in a class or training program, you can use the "Master It" questions in the section called "The Bottom Line" at the end of each chapter to test your mastery of the skills you've learned.

Also featured is a color project gallery containing inspirational Revit projects from friends and colleagues who were generous enough to share their good work with the rest of the world.

The Mastering Series

The Mastering series from Sybex provides outstanding instruction for readers with intermediate and advanced skills, in the form of top-notch training and development for those already working in their field and clear, serious education for those aspiring to become pros. Every Mastering book includes the following:

- Real-world scenarios, ranging from case studies to interviews, that show how the tool, technique, or knowledge presented is applied in actual practice

- Skill-based instruction, with chapters organized around real tasks rather than abstract concepts or subjects

- Self-review test questions, so you can be certain you're equipped to do the job right

Contacting the Authors

In all, we welcome your feedback and comments. You can find the three of us on our blog, www.architecture-tech.com, or email us at MasteringRevit@architecture-tech.com. We hope you enjoy the book.

Part 1

Fundamentals

Although this book is focused on helping you *master* Autodesk® Revit® Architecture software, we recognize that not everyone will know how to find every tool or have a complete understanding of the workflow. The chapters in Part 1 will help you build a foundation of essential knowledge and may even give the veteran Revit user some additional insight into the basic tools and concepts of building information modeling (BIM).

- ◆ **Chapter 1: Introduction: The Basics of BIM**
- ◆ **Chapter 2: Principles: UI and Project Organization**
- ◆ **Chapter 3: The Basics of the Toolbox**

Introduction: The Basics of BIM

In this chapter, we cover principles of a successful building information modeling (BIM) approach within your office environment and summarize some of the many tactics possible using BIM in today's design workflow. We explain the fundamental characteristics of maximizing your investment in BIM and moving beyond documentation with an information-rich model.

In this chapter, you'll learn to:

♦ Leverage the model

♦ Know how BIM affects firm culture

♦ Focus your investment in BIM

Leveraging the Model

CERT
OBJECTIVE

According to the National Institute of Building Sciences (www.nibs.org), a building information model (BIM) is defined as "a digital representation of physical and functional characteristics of a facility" that serves as a "shared knowledge resource for information about a facility forming a reliable basis for decisions during its life cycle from inception onward." While this is the definition of the noun used to represent the electronic data, the verb form of building information *modeling* is equally important. BIM is both a tool and a process, and one cannot realistically exist without the other. This book will help you to learn one BIM tool — Revit Architecture — but we hope that it will also teach you about the BIM process.

Building information modeling implies an increased attention to more informed design and enhanced collaboration. Simply installing an application like Revit and using it to replicate your current processes will yield limited success. In fact, it may even be more cumbersome than using traditional CAD tools.

What is Revit? It is a BIM application that utilizes a single, parametric, 3D model to generate plans, sections, elevations, perspectives, details, and schedules — all of the necessary instruments to document the design of a building. Drawings created using Revit are not a collection of 2D lines and shapes that are interpreted to represent a building; they are live views extracted from what is essentially a virtual building model. This model consists of a compilation of intelligent components that contain not only physical attributes but also functional behavior familiar in architectural design, engineering, and construction.

Elements in Revit are managed and manipulated through a hierarchy of parameters that we will discuss in greater detail throughout this book. These elements share a level of bidirectional associativity — if the elements are changed in one place within the model, those changes are visible in all the other views. If you move a door in plan, that door is moved in all of the elevations, sections, perspectives, and so on in which it is visible. In addition, all of the properties and information about each element are stored within the elements themselves, which means that most annotation is merely applied to any view and is transient in nature. When contrasted with traditional CAD tools that store element information only in the annotation, Revit gives you the opportunity to more easily extract, report, and organize your project data for collaboration with others.

Planning for BIM

As architects or designers, we have accepted the challenge of changing our methodology to adapt to the nuances of documentation through modeling rather than drafting. We are now confronted with identifying the next step. Some firms look to create even better documents, whereas others are leveraging BIM in building analysis. As we continue to be successful in visualization and documentation, industry leaders are looking to move BIM to the next plateau. As BIM did a decade ago, many of these new possibilities represent new workflows and potential changes in our culture or habits, which require you to ask a critical question:

What kind of firm do you want, and how do you plan to use BIM?

As the technology behind BIM continues to grow, so does the potential. A host of things are now possible using a building information model; in fact, that list continues to expand year after year. Figure 1.1 shows some of the potential opportunities.

FIGURE 1.1
Design opportunities supported by BIM

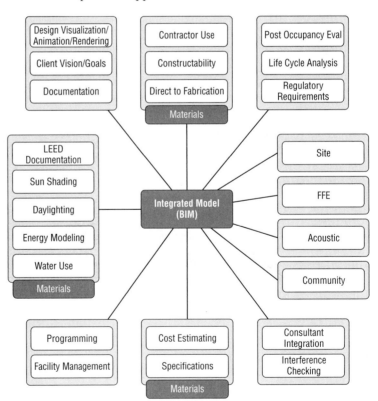

When moving to the next step with BIM — be that better documentation, sustainable analysis, or facility management — it's important to identify your priorities in three primary categories for your use of BIM:

- Visualize
- Analyze
- Strategize

Understanding these areas, specifically how they overlap within your firm, will help you define your implementation strategy for BIM. We'll first define each of these areas individually and then discuss what it means to begin combining them in practice.

VISUALIZE

Creating documentation using BIM gives you the added advantage of being able to visualize the project in 3D. Although this was initially conceived as one of the "low-hanging fruits" of a BIM workflow, this benefit has led to an explosion of 3D graphics — perspectives, wire frames, renderings, and animations — within the industry as a means to communicate design between stakeholders on a project.

This digital creation of the project has given us a variety of tools to communicate aspects of the project. It becomes "architecture in miniature," and we can take the model and create a seemingly unlimited number of interior and exterior visualizations. The same model may be imported into a gaming engine similar to an Xbox for an interactive virtual experience. Clients no longer need to rely on the designer's pre-established paths in a fly-through — they can virtually "walk" through the building at their own pace, exploring an endless variety of directions. The same model again can then be turned into a physical manifestation either in part or in whole by the use of 3D printers (known as rapid prototyping), creating small models (Figure 1.2) in a fraction of the time it would take to build one by hand. Many types of visualization are currently possible with BIM.

FIGURE 1.2
An example of rapid
prototyping using
BIM data
Source: HOK

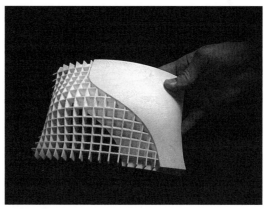

Source: HOK

If we consider a complete spectrum of representations from tabular data to 2D documentation and then to 3D visualization, tremendous opportunities exist to transform the notion of traditional design deliverables. Schedules give you instantaneous reports on component quantities and space usage, whereas plans, sections, and elevations afford you the flexibility to customize their display using the information embedded in the modeled elements. For example, the plan in Figure 1.3 shows how color fills can be automatically applied to illustrate space usage by department.

FIGURE 1.3
Even 2D views can evolve to illustrate and analyze spatial properties.

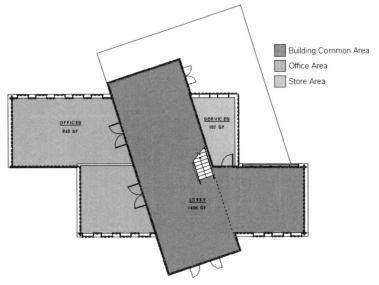

Expanding 2D documentation to include 3D imagery also gives you the ability to clearly communicate the intent of more complex designs. It may even have a positive effect on construction by transcending possible language barriers with illustrative documentation rather than cryptic details and notations. Figure 1.4 shows a basic example of a drawing sheet composed of both 2D and 3D views generated directly from the project model.

FIGURE 1.4
Construction documentation can begin to transform from 2D to 3D.
Source: HOK

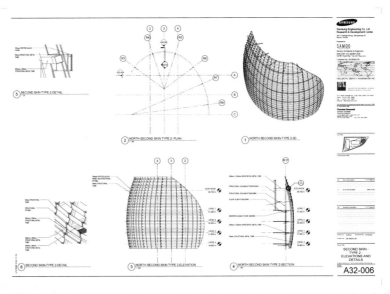

The obvious benefit to creating a complete digital model of your building project is the ability to generate a wide variety of 3D images for presentation. These images are used to not only describe design intent but also to illustrate ideas about proportion, form, space, and functional relationships. The ease at which these kinds of views can be mass-produced makes the rendered perspective more of a commodity. In some instances, as shown in the left image of Figure 1.5, materiality may be removed to focus on the building form and element adjacencies. The same model is used again for a final photo-realistic rendering, as shown in the right image of Figure 1.5.

FIGURE 1.5
Two different meth-
ods of utilizing 3D
presentation views
Source: HOK

By adding materiality to the BIM elements, you can begin to explore the space in color and light, creating photo-realistic renderings of portions of the building design. These highly literal images convey information about both intent and content of the design. Iterations at this level are limited only by processing power. The photo-realism allows for an almost lifelike explo-ration of color and light qualities within a built space even to the extent of allowing analytic brightness calculations to reveal the exact levels of light within a space.

The next logical step is taking these elements and adding movement. In Figure 1.6, you can see a still image taken from a phasing animation (commonly referred to as a 4D simulation) of a project. These simulations not only convey time and movement through space, they also have the ability to demonstrate how the building will react or perform under real lighting and atmospheric conditions. All of this fosters a more complete understanding of the constructabil-ity and performance of a project before it is realized.

FIGURE 1.6
A still from an ani-
mation showing
accurate physical
conditions for the
project

ANALYZE

As with visualization, the authoring environment of a BIM platform isn't necessarily the most efficient one to perform analysis. Although you can create some rendering and animations within Revit, a host of other applications are specifically designed to capitalize on a computer's RAM and processing power to minimize the time it takes to create such media. Analysis is much the same way — although some basic analysis is possible using Revit, other applications are much more robust and can create more accurate results. The real value in BIM is the interoperability of model geometry and metadata between applications. Consider energy modeling as an example. In Figure 1.7, we're comparing three energy-modeling applications: A, B, and C. In the figure, the striped bar reflects the time it takes to either import model geometry into the analysis package or redraw the design with the analysis package. The gray bar reflects the amount of time needed to add data not within Revit, such as loads, zoning, and so on. The white bar represents the time it takes to perform the analysis once all the information is in place.

FIGURE 1.7
BIM environmental analysis time comparison

BIM Environmental Analysis Time Comparison

◼ Geometry Manipulation ◻ Adding Load Data ◻ Simulation

A

B

C

In A and B, we modeled the project in Revit but were unable to use the model geometry in the analysis package. This caused the re-creation of the design within the analysis tool and also required time to coordinate and upkeep the design and its iterations between the two models. In application C, you can see we were able to import Revit model geometry directly into the analysis package, saving nearly 50 percent of the time needed to create and run the full analysis. Using this workflow, you can bring analysis to more projects, perform more iterations, or do the analysis in half the time.

The same workflow is true for daylighting (Figure 1.8) and other types of building performance analysis. With the ability to repurpose the Revit model geometry, we are able to move away from anecdotal or prescriptive design solutions and begin to rely on calculated results. Using Revit also ensures consistency because the model is the sole source for design geometry.

FIGURE 1.8
Daylighting overlay from Autodesk®
3ds Max® Design
software

Building analysis can reach beyond just the design phase and into facility management. Once the building has been constructed, the use of BIM doesn't need to end. More advanced facilities management systems support tracking — and thereby trending — building use over time. By trending building use, you can begin to predict usage patterns and help anticipate future uses. This strategy can help you become more proactive with maintenance and equipment replacement because you will be able to "see" how equipment performance begins to degrade over time. Trending will also aid you in providing a more comfortable environment for building occupants by understanding historic use patterns and allow you to keep the building tuned for optimized energy performance.

STRATEGIZE

To maximize your investment in a BIM-based workflow, it's necessary to apply a bit of planning. As in design, a well-planned and flexible implementation is paramount to a project's success. By identifying goals on a project early on in the process, it allows BIM to be implemented efficiently to reach those objectives. A good BIM strategy answers three key questions about a project:

- What processes do we need to employ to achieve our project goals?

- Which people and team members are key to those processes?

- What technology or applications do we need in place to support the people and process?

Ask these questions of your firm as a whole so you can collectively work toward expertise in a given area, be that sustainable design or construction or something else. Ask the same questions of an individual project as well so you can begin building the model in early stages for potential downstream uses. In both cases (firm-wide or project-based), processes will need to change to meet the goals you've established. Modeling techniques and workflows will need to be established. Analysis-based BIM requires different constraints and requirements than a model used for documentation or clash detection. If you're taking the model into facilities management, you'll need to add a lot of metadata about equipment but a lower level of detail than if you were performing daylighting studies. Applying a new level of model integrity during a design phase can be a frustrating and time-consuming endeavor. Regardless of the goal, setting and understanding those goals early on in the project process is a prerequisite for success.

Setting Firm Goals for BIM

Combining visualization, analysis, and strategy will help you define your implementation methodology and direction. It's important to note that no matter where you fall or how these elements are combined, there is no wrong answer. Identifying a direction is the critical piece so you can better plan for the success of your projects. BIM ultimately is a communication tool. It can aid in analysis and documentation, but the primary goal is to communicate design ideas and concepts to the team in all the various states of the project's life cycle.

The adoption curve isn't really much of a curve. We'll discuss the process of moving beyond basic documentation with the use of three concentric circles. Each circle represents one of the primary elements we discussed in the previous sections. Figure 1.9 shows two of the iterations possible with the curve. The combination on the left shows a late adopter and one where the elements — visualization (V), strategy (S), and analysis (A) — are separate from each other. The other iteration shows almost a complete integration of these tools.

FIGURE 1.9
Two extremes of
adoption

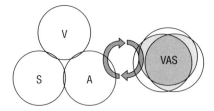

Although the graphic shows a balanced use of each of these tools, they can be used in any combination, depending on your goals and uses for BIM. To better understand where you fall into any of the possible iterations, we'll discuss three examples and what those possible workflows will look like to your projects: late adopters (the image on the left), intermediate adopters, and early adopters.

LATE ADOPTERS

Late adopters, shown with the configuration in Figure 1.10, see each of these tools as distinct efforts. There is little overlap between the systems, and any of them can be taken and removed from a process without negatively impacting any of the others. Late adopters typically come to new technologies after others have demonstrated successful use of new tools and processes. In late adoption, the *I* in *BIM* is not critical. Information within the model will be used for documentation (e.g., door schedules), but analysis will probably be done using different model sources.

FIGURE 1.10
Late adoption

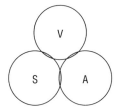

INTERMEDIATE ADOPTERS

Intermediate adopters, as shown in Figure 1.11, tend to assume a much stronger relationship between visualization, analysis, and strategy. These elements are seen in a more concurrent workflow and are more dependent on each other for their individual successes. For intermediate adopters, the *I* in *BIM* is very important, and a more robust level of data is pulled from various model resources. Intermediate adopters see the changes in technology as a means to help improve current processes and make them more efficient and effective. These changes in technology are used to explore new markets and help create new opportunities for growth.

FIGURE 1.11
Intermediate
adoption

Early Adopters

Early adoption, shown in Figure 1.12, focuses on a combination of all these elements in a dependent relationship. Early adopters create new tools, technologies, and workflows to implement new processes and opportunities that did not previously exist in the marketplace. In each of these cases, there is a significant development investment and a perception that higher risk can equal higher reward. It is not nearly enough to have the best or most advanced applications available on the marketplace, but there is a need to create the "next best thing." To early adopters, the *I* in *BIM* becomes a core part of their strategy for project success. They do not wait to follow markets but instead work to create new ones, which they can then lead.

FIGURE 1.12
Early adoption

How BIM Affects Firm Culture

In understanding where you are and where you want to be in this adoption curve, it's also important to understand that moving between any of the iterations of this curve requires a shift in your internal firm culture. As anyone who's adopted BIM can tell you, the difficulties you might experience do not come from learning a new application but from understanding how that application affects your workflow — and managing that change. The ability to adapt and accept that change within an organization will in some way determine where you fall on the adoption curve.

Predictability vs. Innovation

To understand the process of any change, think about it as a product of happiness over time, as shown in Figure 1.13. The process of any change, be it adoption of a new workflow or tool within your office or for personal use, such as with a new cell phone, can be described by this curve.

FIGURE 1.13
Happiness vs. time
in technological
adoption

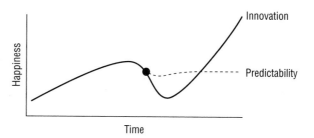

Let's use the simple example of a new cell phone. When you first get the new cell, there is an increase in your happiness. The new device might have a color screen, or it might allow you to send and receive emails, play games, or find the nearest Starbucks. As you gain familiarity with these features, your happiness goes up. At some point, there is an initial pinnacle to your happiness. You briefly plateau. This occurs when you are asked to do something within a limited timeframe or utilize a new feature that is outside your comfort zone — and things don't proceed as planned.

In our cell phone example, this could occur the first time you try to synchronize your phone with the office email server, and instead of performing correctly, it duplicates or shuffles your contacts. Now the names are no longer associated with the proper phone numbers or email addresses, and the system you've come to rely on is now unpredictable. In a BIM-based example, this could mean you have a schematic design deadline or you need to create a wall section or model a set of ornate stairs in a limited amount of time. You might know that the task is technically possible, but you have yet to ever perform that task personally.

There comes a point as your stress level goes up that your happiness begins to decline (shown as a dot on the graph in Figure 1.13). At this point, you perceive a crossroads: Do you go back to the previous technology (the old phone) and choose a path of predictability, or do you muscle forward and push for mastering the change in the hope of achieving innovation? No matter how inefficient any system may be, if it is predictable, there will be a certain amount of comfort associated with the existing system. As you try to find your way along the adoption curve, understand that part of what you are trying to manage — either personally or for your project team — is this nexus of predictability versus innovation while trying to maintain a level of happiness and positive morale.

Evolution vs. Revolution

While you're in the process of trying to manage the amount of change you're willing to endure, you also need to consider the speed at which that change will affect your project teams. Progress and innovation are iterative, and it can take several cycles to perfect a technique or workflow. The process of change and creating new methodologies using BIM is an evolution, not a revolution.

Figure 1.14 shows two bicycles. The image on the left is the penny-farthing bicycle taken from *Appleton's Cyclopaedia of Applied Mechanics* of 1892. Although not the first bicycle (which was invented in 1817 in Paris), it does demonstrate many of the rudimentary and defining features of a bicycle today: two wheels, a handlebar, and pedals to supply power. The image on the right is the 2006 thesis design of Australian University student Gavin Smith. The bike was designed to assist people with disabilities or those with impaired motor skills in riding a bike unaided. The basic concept is that the bike would supply its own balance at low speeds and the wheels would remain canted. As the bike moves faster and wheel speed increases, the wheels become vertical and the rider is able to ride at faster speeds while balancing mostly on their own. As the bike slows, the wheels cant back in again, giving the rider the necessary balance needed at lower speeds. The bike on the right still possesses all of the distinguishing characteristics of what we define as a bicycle and is thusly an evolution of the bike over many, many iterations. A similar evolution will occur with your use of BIM — the more often you iterate the change, the more comfortable and efficient affecting change will become.

FIGURE 1.14
Understanding
replication vs.
innovation

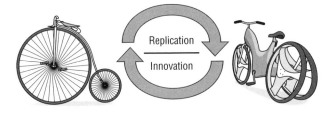

Replication

Innovation

Focusing Your Investment in BIM

One of the common assumptions is that larger firms have a better opportunity than smaller firms in their capacity to become early adopters, take on new technologies, or innovate. Although larger firms might have a broader pool of resources, much of the investment is proportionally the same. We have been fortunate enough to help a number of firms implement Revit over the years, and each has looked to focus on different capabilities of the software that best express their individual direction. Although these firms have varied in size and individual desire to take on risk, their investments have all been relatively equal. From big firms to small, the investment ratio consistently equates to about 1 percent the size of the firm. If you consider a 1,000-person firm, that equals about 10 full-time people; however, scale that down to a 10-person firm, and that becomes 1 person's time for five weeks.

The key to optimizing this 1 percent investment is focusing your firm's energy and resources on the most appropriate implementation objectives. The following list highlights many of the expanded uses that are currently possible using Revit and other BIM tools. Some of these things are core precepts of what BIM is and does, such as 3D visualization; some, like energy modeling, are emerging technologies; and others, such as facility management, are truly cutting edge.

- Construction documentation
    - Coordinated documentation
    - Automated keynoting
    - Consultant coordination (integrating multiple models)
    - Design visualization
    - Scheduling systems/materials/quantities
    - Specifications
    - Furniture, finishes, and equipment (FF&E)
    - Tracking/logging/procurement
- Spatial program validation
- Construction
    - Constructability analysis
    - Clash detection
    - Quantity takeoffs
    - Cost analysis/estimating
    - Direct to fabrication
- Traffic studies
- Building performance analysis
    - Rainwater reclamation
    - Photovoltaic potential

- ◆ Energy analysis
- ◆ Lighting analysis
- ◆ Solar impact studies
- ◆ Computational fluid dynamics simulations
- ◆ LEED documentation
- ◆ Programming
- ◆ Facilities management
  - ◆ Asset tracking
  - ◆ Trending

Identifying the importance of visualization, analysis, and strategy to your process will help guide you in selecting areas of implementation within your own practice. If your investment (regardless of scale) is focused and well planned, it will yield strong results. When choosing areas of implementation or how much focus to give to these areas, there are no wrong answers. Just choose a path that reflects the comfort level of your firm while maintaining focus on achieving success.

We elaborate on most of these topics throughout the remainder of this book. Using real-world examples, we illustrate a variety of techniques to visualize, analyze, and strategize using Revit.

The Bottom Line

Leverage the model. Understanding the level of risk your firm is willing to take in new technologies will help you establish goals for your future use of BIM.

Master It Using the three areas of firm integration (visualization, analysis, and strategy), define how those areas overlap for your firm or project.

Know how BIM affects firm culture. Not only is the transition to BIM from 2D CAD a change in applications, it's also a shift in workflow and firm culture. Understanding some of the key differences helps to ensure project and team success during the transition.

Master It What are some of the ways that BIM differs from CAD, and how does this change the culture of an office or project team?

Focus your investment in BIM. One of the key elements to understanding BIM beyond documentation is simply to have an awareness of the possibilities. This allows you to make an educated decision as to what direction your firm or project would like to go.

Master It List some of the potential uses of a BIM model beyond documentation.

Chapter 2

Principles: UI and Project Organization

After more than a decade in the architecture, engineering, and construction (AEC) industry, Autodesk® Revit® software continues to be unique in its "whole-building BIM" approach to design integration. Sure, other BIM-ish tools allow you to design in 3D. And 10 years ago, 3D might have been a differentiator, but today 3D is a commodity!

Whole-building BIM is the ability to design, manage, and document your project information from within a single file, something that no other building information modeling (BIM) software will allow you to do. In a workflow with any other software, you'd have to design your project across multiple files — not just across disciplines but within the same discipline! Imagine the dysfunctional workflow of having separate files for the building shell, roof, and each interior level for a modest 50-story building. That means you'll be managing at least 50 files just for the architecture. Count on another 50 files for the mechanical, electrical, and plumbing (MEP) and structural design and now your team has to juggle more than 150 separate files that have to be manually linked together. Then you will have to export your files to separate sheets and views for documentation.

So, now your building has been smashed up into 2D information. And when you have changes, expect to go back to the model and repeat the process because you can't risk making changes in 2D when they're not bidirectionally associative. No thanks!

How would you complete the same project in the Revit environment? Well, worst case is that you're probably looking at *three* files for the same building (architecture, structure, and MEP) because design is a team sport and you're not all in the same office or geography. So everyone does their work and links each other's projects. Three files!

As for documentation, it's all in the same file as the respective project — no exporting required. It's a completely bidirectional, multiuser, working environment, so if you're trying to compare Revit functionality to what you're used to in other 2D CAD or 3D BIM tools, stop now. This chapter provides an overview of the user interface as well as the key aspects of a project.

In this chapter, you'll learn to:

◆ Understand the user interface

◆ Understand project organization

Understanding the User Interface

The user interface (UI) has continued to evolve since it was redesigned in 2010, and it now displays real finish and elegance. Persistence of tool location is one of the keys to increased usability. Even though tools remain contextually exposed or hidden depending on what you're working on, the majority of them can be found in the same place.

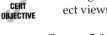

Figure 2.1 shows the Autodesk® Revit® Architecture 2013 UI. To illustrate some different project views, we've tiled four view types: plan, elevation, 3D, and sheet.

FIGURE 2.1

The Revit Architecture 2013 user interface

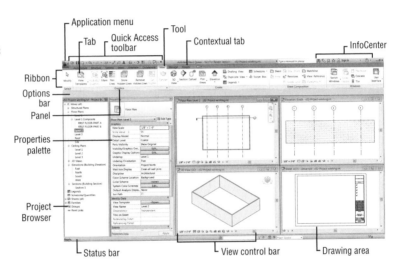

Application Menu

Clicking on the big *R* in the upper-left corner of the UI opens the Application menu (Figure 2.2) and allows you to access commonly used commands: New, Open, Save, Print, and so on. You can also export your project to a number of 2D and 3D formats from this menu. This menu is also where you manage licensing information. The Publish option lets you upload RFA files to Autodesk Seek (seek.autodesk.com) or utilize a Buzzsaw® connection to share project documents with your team. Use the Close command to quickly close a project or family without the necessity of closing every open view.

New for Revit 2013 software is the ability to access all three disciplines of the Revit software — Architecture, Structure, and MEP — provided you have licenses to use each.

Quick Access Toolbar

The Quick Access toolbar (QAT) allows you to keep frequently used tools at your fingertips (Figure 2.3).

FIGURE 2.2
Application menu

FIGURE 2.3
Quick Access
toolbar

Right-click any button in one of the ribbon tabs and you will find the command Add To Quick Access Toolbar. By clicking the small, down-facing arrow to the far right of the QAT, you'll find that tools may be further customized, grouped, and removed from the toolbar (Figure 2.4). You also have the option to show the QAT below the ribbon.

FIGURE 2.4
Customizing the
QAT

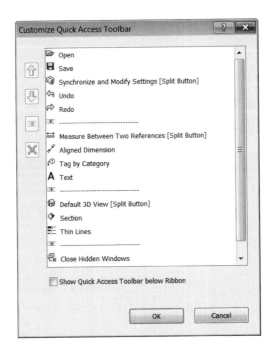

InfoCenter

To the far right of the QAT is the InfoCenter (Figure 2.5).

From left to right, you have the ability to search for help solutions, access the Subscription Center, open the Communication Center, show Favorites (saved articles and solutions from the Communication Center), sign in to other Autodesk services (such as cloud rendering), and open the help service (wikihelp.autodesk.com/revit).

FIGURE 2.5
InfoCenter

Ribbon

The ribbon contains all of the tools for designing and documenting your project (Figure 2.6). Throughout this book, we will refer to the ribbon frequently, so you should be familiar with its basic parts: tabs and panels.

FIGURE 2.6
The ribbon

TABS

Tabs are used to select from among the various groups of functionality. There are up to 11 tabs along the top of the ribbon shown in Figure 2.6. We'll take a moment to briefly describe them:

Home   If you are using Revit Architecture, the Home tab contains all the basic tools you will need to create architectural elements. You will also find other common tools such as datum objects, rooms and areas, and work planes.

Architecture, Structure, and Systems   If you are using Revit you have access to the tools for all three design disciplines. The Architecture, Structure, and Systems tabs are used to create or place content specific to each design discipline. You can control the visibility of these tabs from the Options dialog box (accessed from the Application menu). If you don't need structural or systems content, simply remove these tools from the User Interface options (Figure 2.7).

FIGURE 2.7
Setting the User
Interface options

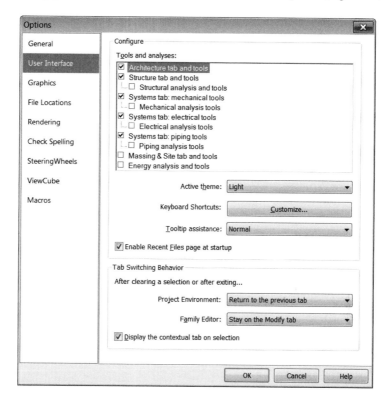

Insert   The Insert tab is used to link external files (2D, 3D, image, and other RVT files) as well as search for external content via Autodesk Seek (Figure 2.8).

FIGURE 2.8
Insert tab

Annotate   The Annotate tab contains many of the tools necessary to annotate, tag, dimension, or otherwise graphically document your project (Figure 2.9).

FIGURE 2.9
Annotate tab

Analyze The Analyze tab contains the tools necessary to modify energy analysis settings and to run an energy simulation via Green Building Studio® (Figure 2.10).

FIGURE 2.10
Analyze tab

Massing & Site The Massing & Site tab contains the tools necessary to add massing- and site-related elements such as toposurfaces and property lines (Figure 2.11).

FIGURE 2.11
Massing & Site tab

Collaborate The Collaborate tab contains the tools that you'll use to coordinate and manage the project within your own team as well as across other teams and their linked files (Figure 2.12).

FIGURE 2.12
Collaborate tab

View The View tab contains the tools that you'll use to create all your project views, 2D and 3D, as well as schedules, legends, and sheets. You can also modify your user interface from this tab, including your keyboard shortcuts (Figure 2.13).

FIGURE 2.13
View tab

Manage The Manage tab contains all your project standards and other settings (Figure 2.14). You will also find the Design Options and Phasing tools on this tab.

FIGURE 2.14
Manage tab

CERT
OBJECTIVE

One of the most important settings that you'll use during your project is Object Styles on the Manage tab. Selecting this option will allow you to manage the global visibility settings for just about everything in your project: how it projects, how it cuts, and its associated color and pen weight.

Modify The Modify tab contains the tools you'll use to manipulate the content that you're creating in your project (Figure 2.15). You'll find tools like Cut, Join, Split, Move, Copy, and Rotate among many others.

FIGURE 2.15
Modify tab

Contextual Modify   Contextual Modify tabs are revealed as an extension to the Modify tab when specific elements are selected. As an example, the Modify | Walls contextual tab (Figure 2.16) is displayed when a wall is selected. Throughout this book we will refer to this as the *contextual tab*.

FIGURE 2.16
Contextual Modify
tabs

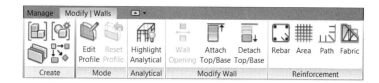

PANELS

Panels identify areas of grouped functionality in the Ribbon. They can also be pulled out of tabs and arranged so that functionality is persistently exposed. To relocate a panel, drag the panel out of the Ribbon using your mouse pointer on the panel title bar (Figure 2.17).

FIGURE 2.17
Panels identify
areas of grouped
functionality.

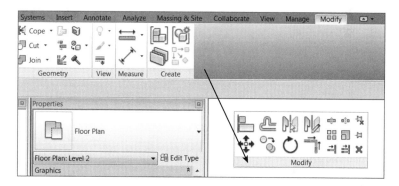

The panels will snap together if you hover over a previously placed panel. To return a panel to the Ribbon, click the down arrow in the upper portion of the right gray bar in the floating panel.

On some panels, you will find a flyout menu or a link to open another dialog box. In Figure 2.18, the small arrow on the Text panel will open the Text Types dialog box. Clicking the down arrow on the Tag panel exposes Loaded Tags and Keynoting Settings commands.

FIGURE 2.18
Special panel
features

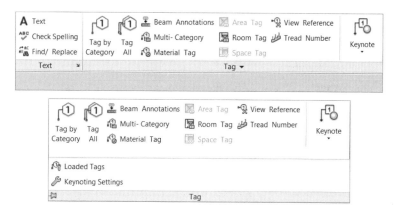

**CERT
OBJECTIVE**

Options Bar

The Options bar is located directly below the Ribbon and is a contextually sensitive area that gives you feedback as you create and modify content. In Figure 2.19, you see the options available when the Wall tool is active.

FIGURE 2.19
Options bar

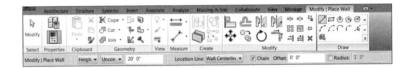

Properties

The Properties palette contains the instance parameters of whatever you're currently working on. In this palette, you will find the Type Selector, a selection filter, and the Edit Type button (Figure 2.20). You'll learn more about filtering selected objects in Chapter 3, "The Basics of the Toolbox."

FIGURE 2.20
Properties palette

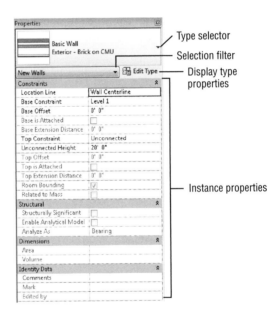

Project Browser

The Project Browser (Figure 2.21) is a hierarchical listing of all the views, legends, schedules, sheets, families, groups, and links in your project. You can collapse and expand the project tree by selecting the + or – icons.

**CERT
OBJECTIVE**

The Project Browser can also be filtered and grouped into folders based on a number of user-defined parameters. To access the type properties of the Project Browser, right-click the Views portion at the top of the palette (see Figure 2.22). You can also select and edit these settings from the Browser Organization dialog box, found in the View tab under the User Interface flyout button.

FIGURE 2.21
Project Browser

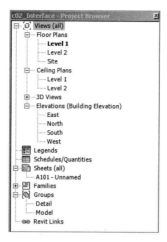

FIGURE 2.22
Project Browser's
type properties

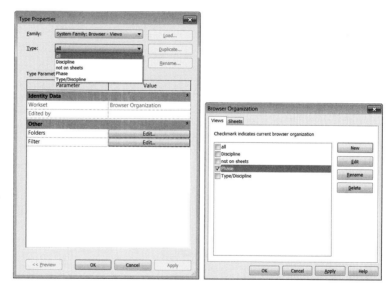

Status Bar

The status bar at the bottom of the UI provides useful information about selected objects and active tools (Figure 2.23). When you start a tool, the status bar will display prompts about the next step required of the tool. It is also useful when you are using the Tab key to toggle between object snap points or when selecting chains of elements.

FIGURE 2.23
Status bar

Click to select, TAB for alternates, CTRL adds, SHIFT unselects.   Workset1   ▼ &:0   Main Model   ▼   ☐ Editable Only ☑ Press & Drag ▽ 4

Toward the middle of the status bar, you will find toolbars for worksets and design options. At the far right end, you will see a filter icon next to a number. When you select objects in a view window, the number of selected objects will be displayed here. Click the filter icon to open the Filter dialog box and refine the selection set.

Drawing Area

The drawing area is the window into your design space. In this example, we've tiled four view windows: plan, elevation, 3D, and sheet (Figure 2.24). Rather than jump between expanded drawing areas that obscure each other, it's sometimes helpful to tile many views in the same area.

FIGURE 2.24
Drawing area

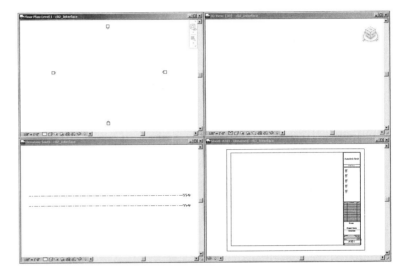

When you do this, you'll be able to zoom into only the extents that are defined by the drawing area. If you want to get around this limitation, here's a helpful tip:

Create a new sheet, but then delete the sheet border. This is your "working" space for any view of the project. Now you can create duplicate views of any of your project views and assemble them in this working space (Figure 2.25). Zooming in and out is much more fluid, and you're not limited to the extents of one drawing area. You can create a keyboard shortcut to activate and deactivate views, which is helpful as well.

FIGURE 2.25
Working sheet view

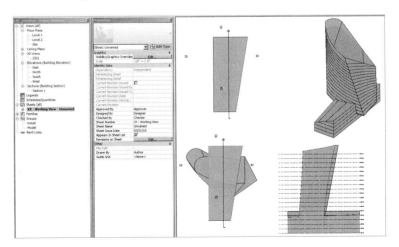

View Control Bar

The view control bar is at the bottom of every view and changes slightly depending on the type of view (Figure 2.26). For example, sheet views only have three buttons and perspective views don't have a scale option.

FIGURE 2.26
View control bar

Some of the buttons in the view control bar are just shortcuts to view parameters that are also available from the Properties palette. Scale, Detail Level, Crop View, and Crop Region Visible are found in both locations. The Visual Style button allows you to select from a short list of graphic display modes that can be customized in detail with the Graphic Display Options in the Properties palette.

Other buttons in the view control bar are unique commands. One example is the Temporary Hide/Isolate command. When you select an object in a view window, use this button to select from various tools to hide or isolate either the selected objects or the entire category of objects. Temporary visibility states do not affect printing, and the view window will display with a turquoise border until the temporary visibility is reset. Next to the Hide/Isolate button is the Reveal Hidden Elements button. Use this tool to highlight any elements that are hidden in the current view, either temporarily or through other methods.

The last button is available only on projects where worksharing is enabled. Worksharing visibility can be enabled and configured in any view to illustrate Owners, Checkout Status, Model Updates, and Worksets.

Graphic Display Options

Selecting the Graphic Display Options from the Properties palette opens a dialog box that lets you completely customize the graphic settings for the current view (Figure 2.27), such as adding silhouette edges and real-time shadows.

There are many new graphic options available in the 2013 version of Revit Architecture software, including customized backgrounds, photographic exposure, and a transparency slider. Experiment with a variety of the settings to see which ones meet your presentation and documentation needs.

Work Plane Viewer

A Viewer option is located on the Work Plane panel of the Architecture tab. This viewer is available from all model views when you're in the project environment. By default, the work plane is based on the active work plane of the last active view. But when you enter Sketch mode, the active work plane is that of the sketch (Figure 2.28). So even if the project window shows a 3D view, the viewer shows the plane of the sketch — and you can sketch directly in the work plane viewer! This is useful for working on sloped surfaces such as roofs.

ViewCube

You'll find the ViewCube® in 3D views (Figure 2.29). You can use the ViewCube as an alternative method for navigating in 3D. Click on any face of the cube to orient the view to that face or click on a corner of the cube to orient to an axonometric angle. Press and hold the left mouse button while hovering the mouse pointer over the ViewCube to orbit the view freely. Press and hold the left mouse button while hovering over the compass and the view will rotate as if it were on a turntable.

FIGURE 2.27
Graphic Display
Options dialog box

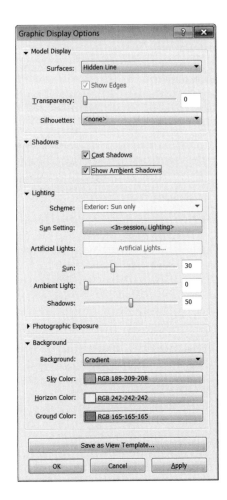

FIGURE 2.28
Sketch mode with
active work plane

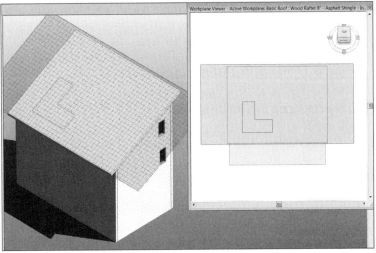

FIGURE 2.29
ViewCube context
menu

Hovering over the ViewCube with your mouse pointer reveals the Home option (the little house above the ViewCube), which you click to return to your home view. Right-clicking the ViewCube opens a menu that allows you to set, recall, and orient your view (see Figure 2.29).

Selecting Options from the context menu takes you directly to the ViewCube options in the Options dialog box (see Figure 2.30). You can also access this dialog box from the application menu.

Steering Wheel

Another method of navigation that is unique to Autodesk software is the Steering Wheel. This tool can be activated by pressing the F8 key, by pressing Shift and W, or from the Navigation Bar. The Steering Wheel will follow your mouse pointer as you move about a view and will stop when the mouse movement slows, allowing you to hover the mouse pointer over one of the command areas on the wheel. As you hover the mouse pointer over a navigation command, press and hold the left mouse button while moving the mouse to activate the corresponding navigation method. This is easier to demonstrate than explain in text, so feel free to try the various modes of the Steering Wheel as you continue through this book.

Navigating with the Mouse

As with most modern design applications, the mouse can also be used to navigate in any view. You are not constrained to using the ViewCube, Steering Wheel, or Navigation Bar. Pressing the left mouse button is the default method for selecting objects. Press the Ctrl key while clicking to add objects to a selection and press the Shift key to remove objects. The right mouse button is primarily used to access contextual menus.

FIGURE 2.30
ViewCube options

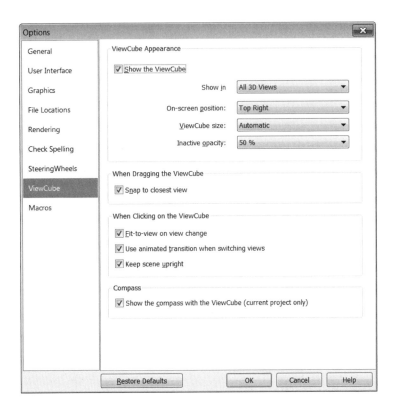

Press and hold the wheel button to pan in any view. Hold the Shift key and use the wheel button on the mouse to orbit a 3D view.

The mouse wheel can be used to zoom in and zoom out of any view, but the zooming will be somewhat choppy. Hold the Ctrl key and press the wheel button while moving the mouse forward to zoom out (pushing the model away) or backward to zoom in (pulling the model toward you). In camera views, zooming works a bit differently. Scrolling the mouse wheel zooms in and out but includes the view's crop region. To adjust the view within the crop region, only the Steering Wheel and the ViewCube can be used.

In addition to a traditional mouse, you can also use a 3D navigation device such as the Space Navigator™ from 3Dconnexion (www.3dconnexion.com) as shown in Figure 2.31. A 3D mouse allows you to navigate in multiple directions simultaneously using joystick-like motions. Simply attach the device to your computer, install the 3Dconnexion software, and a 3Dconnexion button will be displayed on the Navigation Bar. The 3D mouse will automatically navigate in any 2D or 3D view, but the Navigation Bar button allows you to toggle between modes.

FIGURE 2.31

The Space
Navigator 3D mouse
from 3Dconnexion

Project Organization

If you have experience with 2D computer-aided drafting (CAD) software, you're familiar with many of the terms and concepts, but not all of them have exact similarities in Revit software. You may be comfortable with thinking in terms of what needs to be drawn and coordinated: plans, sections, elevations, details, schedules, and so on. Such information is likely stored in a plethora of separate files that have to be linked together in order to reference other parts of a building design. For teams collaborating on design, you are also likely accustomed to allowing only one person in one file at a time. And finally, maintaining all your project settings and standards is a struggle across so many disconnected files.

Working in the Revit environment affords you much more control and efficiency in managing the aforementioned issues. Allow us to posit the four key components of a holistic and efficient design process as *relationships*, *repetition*, *representations*, and *restrictions*. These concepts are respectively managed in Revit software as *datum objects*, *content*, *views*, and *project management*. And they are managed from within a single, bidirectional database.

Figure 2.32 shows what we like to think of as a Revit organization chart, which should give you a visual description of these four top-level categories and the kinds of things these categories contain. In the following sections, we'll discuss each of these categories and describe their particular role in your Revit project environment.

Datum Objects (Relationships)

Data (plural) are sometimes referred to in Revit software as *datum objects* and consist of references, grids, and levels (Figure 2.33). Datum objects establish geometric behavior by controlling the location and extents of your content (the building, stuff that goes in a building, and the stuff you need to document your building).

FIGURE 2.32
Revit organization
chart

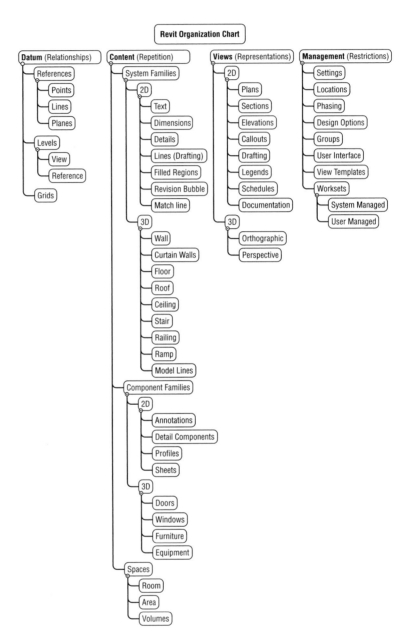

Reference planes can be created in any 2D view from the main Ribbon tabs (Architecture, Structure, or Systems), but once created, they may not be visible in 3D. After you add reference planes to your project, they can be set and seen from the Work Plane panel. This will allow you to work with respect to the desired work plane.

Grids are used to locate structural elements in your project. You are not required to include grids in your project, but they are quite useful in managing structural walls and columns. Like reference planes, grid lines can be added to any 2D view. Keep in mind that grids can only be perpendicular to levels. Furthermore, grids are only visible in views that are perpendicular to the grid. So if the grid is in a north–south orientation, you'll be able to see it only in plan and from the east–west orientation.

FIGURE 2.33
Datum objects

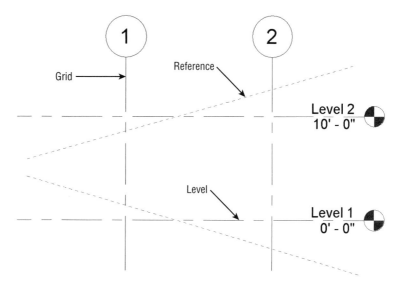

Levels are datum objects that are parallel to the ground plane. They serve several purposes. First, they are the main method for placing and managing the elevation (or Z-location) of content. Virtually all content placed in a Revit model has a Level parameter. You can even move objects from one level to another simply by changing this property in the Properties palette. Levels also function as constraints for objects such as walls and columns. These objects have top and bottom constraints that can be set to levels so that they will automatically update if the levels are adjusted. Levels may be seen and created only in elevation and section views; therefore, you can't create levels in plan, and they can't be diagonal to the ground plane.

Creating any datum is easy. Simply select the desired tool from the Architecture tab and then pick two points to define the start and end location. Despite their two-dimensional appearance, all datum objects have three-dimensional extents that help you manage their appearance throughout a project. You will explore this further in the section "Analytic and Graphic Datum Extents" later in this chapter.

CREATING AND DUPLICATING LEVELS

In the previous section, we discussed the overall purpose of datum objects; however, there are special conditions related to the creation of levels. First, you should understand that a level does not always require an associated plan view. Levels that have plan views will have a blue graphic symbol at the end (double-click it to go to that view), whereas those that don't will have a black graphic symbol. When you create a new level, you have the option to create a corresponding plan view by using the Make Plan View option from the Options bar.

Copying an existing level will not create the corresponding plan views. This is useful if you are working on a larger project, such as a high-rise, and you want to quickly configure multiple levels without creating them one at a time. You might also want to use levels just as a reference for content, but not for a specific plan, such as for an intermediate landing or mezzanine.

While it is easy to create many levels by copying or arraying, only create the levels that are necessary to manage major parts of your project. You don't need to create a level for every slab, stair, or floor offset. Too many levels can have a negative impact on your project's performance.

Let's explore the creation and duplication of levels with an exercise. First, download and open the file c02-Project-Start.rvt from this book's website at www.sybex.com/go/master-ingrevit2013. Then follow these steps:

1. Open the c02-Project-Start file and activate the South elevation view. You will see two levels that are usually present when you create a new project using the default template.

2. From the Architecture tab in the ribbon, find the Datum panel and click the Level tool. In the Options bar, ensure that the Make Plan View option is selected.

3. From left to right, draw a new level exactly 10'-0" above Level 2. When you hover the mouse pointer anywhere near either endpoint of the existing levels, you will see alignment guides (dashed lines) that help keep the extents of the datum objects consistent.

4. Click the Modify button or press the Esc key and you will notice that the new level has a blue target. Double-click on the target for Level 3 and the Level 3 floor plan will open.

5. Return to the South elevation view and select Level 3. From the Modify tab in the Ribbon, click the Copy tool. In the Options bar, select the Multiple option.

6. Create two copies of Level 3; one that is 2'-0" above Level 3, and one that is 8'-0" above that one, as shown in Figure 2.34.

FIGURE 2.34
Create multiple copies of levels.

7. Rename the first copied level **Level 2B** and then rename the uppermost level **Roof**.

As we stated earlier, plan views are not created for levels that are copied or arrayed. This gives you the flexibility to quickly generate levels for taller buildings without all the associated views that may increase your project file size unnecessarily. While this workflow may be beneficial for you in early design phases, what do you do when you need all those floor plans and ceiling plans for that high-rise design?

If you want to convert a level that doesn't have a view to one that does, find the Create panel on the Views tab and then select the Plan View command. This opens the dialog box shown in

Figure 2.35. You can select among all the levels without corresponding views in your project. Note that only the levels you copied in the previous exercise steps are listed in the dialog box.

FIGURE 2.35
Adding views to levels

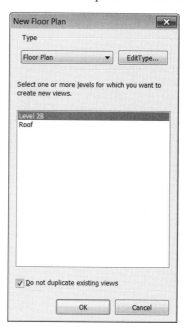

You can also use this command to create duplicate views of existing levels. Clear the Do Not Duplicate Existing Views option at the bottom of the dialog box (Figure 2.36) to see all the levels in your project.

FIGURE 2.36
Creating duplicates of views

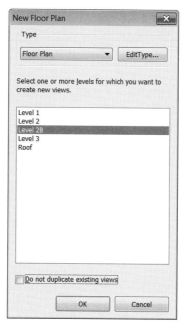

Select the Roof level and click OK. A floor plan will be created for the Roof level and that floor plan will be opened. It is important to note that every plan you create with this method will be opened as you complete the command. Remember to use the Close Hidden Views tool (available in the Quick Access toolbar) to avoid slower performance in your work session.

ANALYTIC AND GRAPHIC DATUM EXTENTS

Datum objects — specifically grids and levels — have two types of extents: analytic (3D) and graphic (2D). These extents are expressed as grips that are shown at the endpoints of the grids and levels in plans, sections, and elevations. The analytic grips control the extents of the datum across the entire project and all views. The analytic grip is shown as an open circle and the indicator will display as 3D, as shown in Figure 2.37.

FIGURE 2.37
Controlling the analytic extents of datum

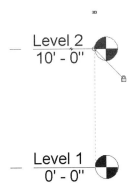

If you want to adjust the graphic extents of your datum in only the current view, click the 3D icon and it will change to 2D. You can then modify the graphic extents of the datum but not the analytic extents. We will explore this further in an exercise later in this section.

Datum objects are visible only in views that intersect their analytic extents. The elevation in Figure 2.38 shows four grids and four levels. Grid lines 3 and 4 are not visible on Levels 3 and 4 because their analytic extents are not intersecting those levels.

You can use the analytic and graphic extents to your liking in any view. In Figure 2.39, for example, the analytic extent (3D) of grid line 1 crosses both Level 1 and Level 2, but the graphic extent (2D) is above Level 2. This means that the grid datum would still be visible in both levels, even though it looks like it doesn't intersect the levels.

When you move a datum object, one way or another, content is going to respond. If you move a level, walls and furniture are going to move accordingly. If you move a grid, structural elements are going to relocate. And if you move references, the elements associated with them update. As a matter of fact, you'll often constrain or pin datum objects in order to restrict their movement as your project is starting to develop.

FIGURE 2.38
Analytic (3D) extents affect visibility of datum objects.

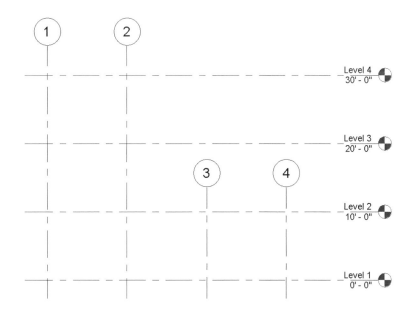

FIGURE 2.39
Customizing graphic and analytic extents

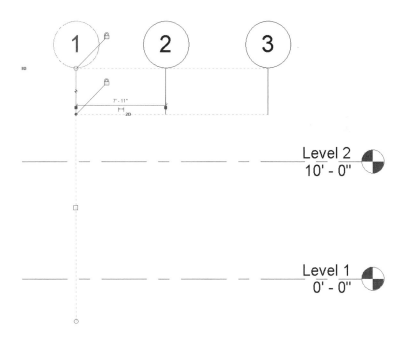

Let's continue with the exercise from the section "Creating and Duplicating Levels" and edit the graphic (2D) extents for one of the levels you copied. Remember that although this exercise utilizes levels, these methods can be applied to grids as well. Here are the steps:

1. Open the South elevation view again and you'll notice that the label for Level 2B is slightly overlapping the label for Level 2 because they are relatively close. You'll need to adjust the graphic extent of Level 2B.

2. Select Level 2B and you'll see two items at the right endpoint with which you'll need to interact: the 3D indicator and the lock symbol. First, click the lock symbol to "unlock" the right endpoint. This will allow you to move the endpoint for the selected level without affecting all the other levels.

3. Click the 3D indicator so that it changes to 2D. Now you are ready to modify the graphic extents of the level.

4. Click the graphic extents grip (the solid circle) and drag it to the right. The result should look like the image shown in Figure 2.40.

FIGURE 2.40
Adjusting the graphic extents of a level

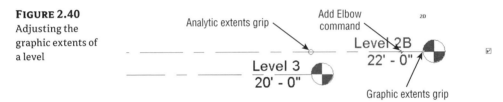

5. As a final option, you can choose to break the end of a level or grid line so that the tag or label will clearly display. Click the Add Elbow symbol near the label at the right endpoint of Level 2B. We have indicated the location of this symbol in Figure 2.40.

6. Use the additional line grips to adjust the level endpoint so that it resembles the image shown in Figure 2.41.

FIGURE 2.41
Adding an elbow to a level

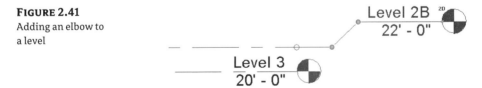

PROPAGATING EXTENTS

Quite often you will adjust the extents of datum objects that need to be replicated in several other views. Fortunately, there is a tool to help you accomplish this — Propagate Extents. While the premise of this tool is simple, you must be aware of the subtleties in applying it to a three-dimensional model.

The Propagate Extents tool pushes any modifications you apply to a datum object from one view to other parallel views of your choosing. This tool does not work well on levels because the parallel views are essentially mirrored views of each other. For example, the orientation of the South elevation is the opposite of the North elevation; therefore, if you make a change to the extents at the right end of a level in the South elevation, those changes would be propagated to the left end in the North elevation.

The best way to apply the Propagate Extents tool is with the graphic (2D) extents of grids. Why only the graphic extents? Because changing the analytic (3D) extents affects the datum object throughout the project, independent of any specific view. Let's examine this behavior with a quick exercise:

1. In the c02-Project-Start file, activate the Level 1 floor plan. You will see four levels.

2. Select grid number 3 and click the 3D indicator at the bottom endpoint. Notice that the lock symbol turns off automatically, allowing you to immediately adjust the graphic extents of the grid.

3. Drag the graphic extent of grid 3 up toward the top. Repeat this process for grid number 4 so that the result looks like the image shown in Figure 2.42. Note that the line weight of the grid lines has been increased for clarity.

FIGURE 2.42
Adjusting the graphic extents of grids

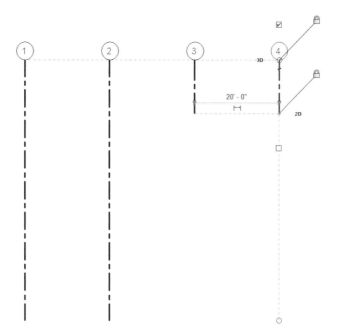

Before you continue, open the Level 2 and Level 3 floor plans and observe that grids 3 and 4 look like their original configuration — the lower extents of all four grids are aligned. If you had adjusted the analytic (3D) extents of the grids in Level 1, those changes would already be reflected in the other views. We're using this method because we want to maintain the analytic extents but modify the graphic extents.

4. Return to the Level 1 floor plan and select grids 3 and 4. Click the Propagate Extents button in the ribbon and the dialog box will appear as shown in Figure 2.43.

FIGURE 2.43
Propagating extents
to other views

5. In the Propagate Datum Extents dialog box, select the floor plans for Level 2, Level 3, and Roof.

6. Click OK to complete the command and then activate the Level 2 floor plan. Observe that the graphic extents of grids 3 and 4 now match the modifications you applied in Level 1.

RESETTING OR MAXIMIZING 3D EXTENTS

Two commands you might need when adjusting datum object extents are commands that give you the ability to reset or maximize the 3D extents. These commands are available in the right-click context menu when you have a datum object selected (Figure 2.44).

FIGURE 2.44
Extent commands
in the right-click
menu

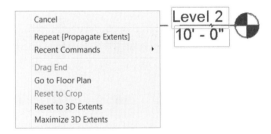

The Reset To 3D Extents command allows you to reset any graphic extent modifications back to the analytic extents. Let's apply this command in the continued exercise file:

1. In the c02-Project-Start file, return to the Level 1 floor plan. Right-click grid number 3 and select Reset To 3D Extents from the context menu. Repeat this step for grid number 4.

2. You will see the grid lines return to their original condition; however, this has been changed only in the current view (Level 1 floor plan). Activate other floor plans to observe this behavior.

3. Return to the Level 1 floor plan and select grids 3 and 4. Click the Propagate Extents button in the ribbon and select the floor plans for Level 2, Level 3, and Roof.

4. Click OK to close the dialog box and the reset graphic extents will be applied to the grids in the other views.

The other command in this pair serves a similar purpose in dealing with datum objects. Maximize 3D Extents is most often used if your levels or grids are exhibiting strange behavior. There are various reasons this happens, but you'll realize it when it does. You can use this command to set the analytic extents of a datum object to the outer boundaries of your project geometry.

Continuing in the exercise file, return to the Level 1 floor plan and notice that grid line C seems to be displayed as all the other grids. Now activate Section 1 from the Project Browser or by double-clicking on the section head shown in the floor plan. You'll notice that grid line C is not visible in the section view. This is because someone mistakenly pulled the analytic (3D) extents far to the left in plan while the graphic (2D) extents remained consistent with the other grids. Let's continue the exercise and repair this problem.

5. Activate the Level 1 floor plan and select grid line C. Right-click, and from the context menu, choose the Maximize 3D Extents command.

6. It may not seem like anything happened but activate the Section 1 view and you'll now see that grid line C is visible.

7. Return to the Level 1 floor plan, select grid line C again, and then click the 2D indicator at the right endpoint so that it indicates 3D.

Using Reference Planes

Objects in the Revit model are able to maintain relationships with other objects; however, you may not always have other model elements (like walls, floors, and roofs) to relate to other geometry. This is why datum objects are so important.

If you've been using Revit for a reasonable amount of time, it seems obvious that levels and grids would control content, but reference planes aren't often appreciated. Here's a simple exercise to demonstrate this special kind of relationship between reference planes and walls:

1. Start a new project using the default template. Go to a plan view and create a series of concentric walls, as shown in Figure 2.45.

FIGURE 2.45
Concentric walls

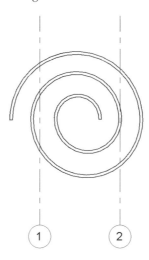

2. Go to the South elevation view. From the Architecture tab in the Ribbon, click the Reference Plane tool and add two angled planes (dashed lines) as shown in Figure 2.46. If you move Level 1, you'll notice that the walls all move with it. You don't have to select the walls; it's in the properties of the walls to maintain a relationship to the Level 1 datum. You could make the top of the walls maintain this same kind of relationship to Level 2.

FIGURE 2.46
Reference planes and levels shown in elevation

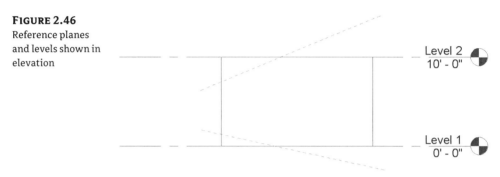

Level 2
10' - 0"

Level 1
0' - 0"

3. You can also create a relationship to the reference planes. To do so, simply select all the walls (just hover your mouse over one wall and then press and release the Tab key to select the chain of walls) and then click the Attach Top/Base button in the ribbon. Note that Attach Wall ➢ Top is the default selection in the Options bar, so first pick the upper reference plane. Click the Attach Top/Base button again, make sure Attach Wall ➢ Base is selected in the Options bar, and then pick the lower reference plane.

Figure 2.47 shows the results in a section view, once you've attached the top and bottom of the walls to the upper and lower reference planes.

FIGURE 2.47
Finished walls

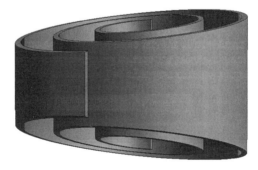

Try moving and rotating the reference planes and notice that the walls will maintain their relationships to the planes. This is shown in a section view of the walls in Figure 2.48.

While you can use levels, grids, and reference planes to customize model elements, there may be situations where you need to establish relationships with nonplanar geometry. You can find video tutorials on custom wall constraints posted on our YouTube channel at www.youtube.com/user/MasteringRevit.

FIGURE 2.48
Section view

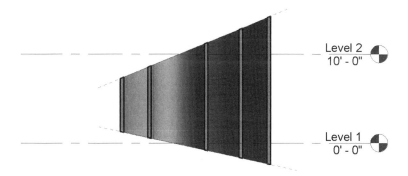

Content (Repetition)

Effective use of content is all about repeated elements in a hierarchy (project, family, type, instance) that you put in your Revit project to develop and document your design. Content can often maintain relationships with other content, but more important, content maintains relationships to datum objects. As you can see from the Revit organization chart shown earlier in Figure 2.32, content includes system families, component families, and spaces.

System families (also called *host families*) are content that is part of the Revit project environment. These families are not created and stored in external files (RFA) — they're found only in the RVT project file. If you need another type of a system family, you'll duplicate an existing type from within the project. System families can be 3D elements such as walls, floors, roofs, ceilings, stairs, and railings or 2D elements such as text, dimensions, revision bubbles, and insulation.

Component families are created in the Family Editor and are either 2D or 3D content. This means that you'll have to create and load these kinds of families outside the Revit project environment as RFA files. When you start to create a component family, you'll need to select an appropriate family template (Figure 2.49). By selecting the right family template, you'll be certain that the component that you're creating is going to behave, view, schedule, and (if necessary) export properly.

FIGURE 2.49
Selecting a family template

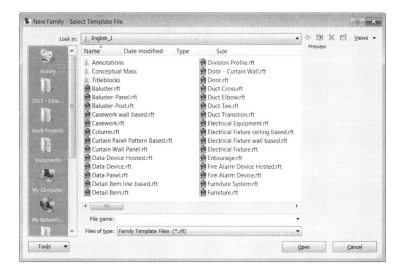

While most system families help shape the physical aspects of a building, the occupied voids within are critical to a successful design. These elements are *spaces*, which take the form of rooms and areas. Spaces maintain relationships to datum objects, but also to model elements including floors, walls, ceilings, and roofs. In addition to spatial properties, rooms are used to document finishes within your project. Take a look at the properties of a room and you'll find Floor Finish, Base Finish, Wall Finish, and Ceiling Finish.

TYPE AND INSTANCE PARAMETERS

All content in a Revit project has *parameters*, which are simply the information or data about something. Parameters can affect many different aspects of an object, such as visibility, behavior, size, shape, and material. Parameters can be assigned to elements in various ways (Figure 2.50).

FIGURE 2.50
Types of parameters

CERT OBJECTIVE

To develop a fundamental understanding of parameters, you must note that there are two kinds of parameters: *type* and *instance*. Type parameters control information about every element of the same type. So, for example, if the material of a piece of furniture is designated as a type parameter and you change it, the material for all the furniture of that type will change. Instance parameters control only the instances that you have selected. So if the material of the piece of furniture that you've selected is an *instance* parameter, you'll be editing only the selected elements.

Instance parameters can be constantly exposed in the Properties palette. Selecting something initially displays the instance parameters. Figure 2.51 shows the instance parameters of a wall that control the relative height, constraints, and structural usage.

By clicking the Edit Type button, you expose the type parameters (Figure 2.52). These parameters control values such as the structure, graphics, and assembly code.

FIGURE 2.51
Instance parameters of a wall

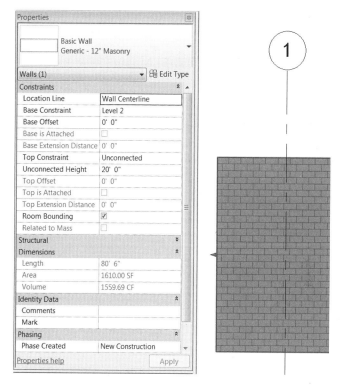

FIGURE 2.52
Type parameters of a wall

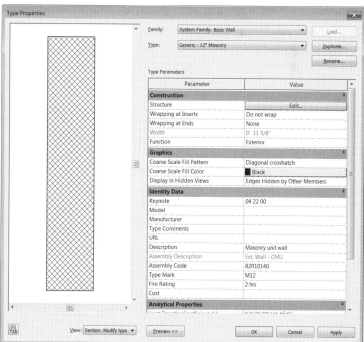

Views (Representation)

Views are the means in which you will interact with and document the project. As you can see in the Revit organization chart shown earlier in Figure 2.32, there are both 2D and 3D views. Two-dimensional views are oriented to specific coordinates like plan, elevation, section, and so on. Although we list schedules as 2D views in our organization chart, they represent project information in a tabular format. Three-dimensional views are either orthographic or perspective (camera view) in nature. Views also have type and instance parameters that control properties such as name, scale, detail level, phase filter, and graphic display options.

Common Properties of Views

Let's first review, in detail, some of those properties that apply to most views:

Crop region   With the exception of schedules and drafting views, the extents of all views can be limited using crop regions. The visibility of the crop region itself can be turned off, but note that you can choose to hide all crop regions in the Print Setup dialog box when using the Print command. Although you might feel the need to keep crop regions visible to allow easier editing, you can use the Reveal Hidden Elements tool in the View Control Bar to temporarily show hidden crop regions.

View scale   The scale of a view automatically controls the relative weight of line work as well as the size of annotation such as text, dimensions, and tags.

Visibility/graphics   The Visibility/Graphic Overrides dialog box (Figure 2.53) allows overrides of elements in two essential ways: visibility (turn object categories on/off) and graphics (customize line thickness, color, and fill pattern).

FIGURE 2.53
Visibility and graphic overrides for an elevation

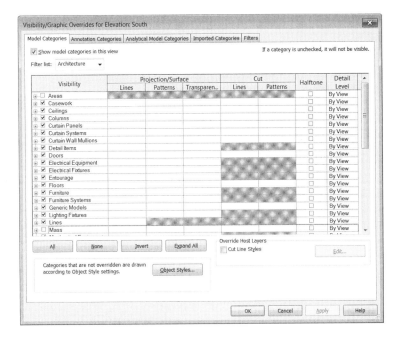

Detail level   The Detail level parameter can be set to one of three predefined choices: Coarse, Medium, or Fine. This setting depends on how families are constructed, but it can help improve model performance and avoid cluttered views by limiting the visibility of smaller model elements.

View templates   As an aid to standardization, view templates can help you organize common view settings and apply them to groups of views throughout your project and other projects within your office or firm. View templates are covered in detail in Chapter 4, "Configuring Templates and Standards."

CREATING AND DUPLICATING VIEWS

You can create views in various ways in order to work with your project in a manner that meets your needs. Although creating views is quick and easy, you should avoid populating your project file with too many unnecessary views. An overabundance of unused views will increase the size of your project file and cause it to perform poorly. Let's review the procedures to create different view types and how to control their extents after they're created.

New views can be generated from the Create panel on the View tab of the Ribbon (Figure 2.54) and the process is quite simple. Click one of the buttons and a new view is activated and stored in the Project Browser.

FIGURE 2.54
Creating new views
from the Ribbon

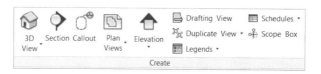

CERT
OBJECTIVE

Another quick way to create new views is to right-click a view name in the Project Browser and select one of the Duplicate View commands (Figure 2.55). You can also duplicate the current view by using the Duplicate View button in the Create panel of the Ribbon.

FIGURE 2.55
Duplicating views
from the Project
Browser

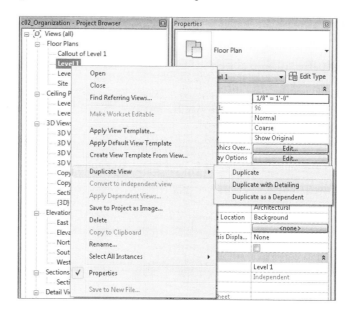

As you can see in Figure 2.55, there are three choices in the Duplicate View flyout command: Duplicate, Duplicate With Detailing, and Duplicate As A Dependent. Let's take a quick look at what each of these options means:

Duplicate This command will create a copy of the selected view but will not replicate any of the annotation in the view. Use this command when you need a fresh copy of a view in which you will create new annotation for a different documentation purpose.

Duplicate with Detailing As its name suggests, this command will create a copy of the selected view with all of the annotation in the view. We don't recommend this command too often because replicated annotation is often a sign of an inefficient production process.

Duplicate as a Dependent This command allows you to create a series of partial views that assume the properties of one parent view. Using dependent views does not mean that you can have a parent view with a larger scale like 1:100 and then create dependent views at larger scales such as 1:50. The parent view has all the same properties as the dependents, but you can manage the crop regions and settings from the parent view.

Floor plans and ceiling plans As you learned in the section "Creating and Duplicating Levels" earlier in this chapter, when you create a level in an elevation or section view, you have the option to create a plan view for that level in the Options bar. If you have levels without corresponding plan views, you can also use the Plan Views tool from the Ribbon to create a plan view.

The vertical extents of plans and ceiling plans are controlled by the View Range settings. The View Range settings, as shown in Figure 2.56, define the vertical range of the view.

FIGURE 2.56
View Range dialog box

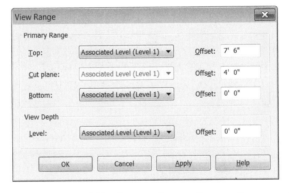

The view range properties can be difficult to understand, so we have created a diagram to illustrate the principles. In Figure 2.57, you will see that the primary range is the zone you usually see in a default floor or ceiling plan. If an object crosses the cut plane, the object's Cut values are used. If the object is below the cut plane but above the bottom, the object's Projection values are used.

For most views, the Bottom and View Depth parameters are set to the same plane. As such, objects below the bottom of the view range simply wouldn't appear. So, what happens if you need to show objects on a lower terrace for reference in the current view? When you set View Depth to Level Below or Unlimited, objects that are below the bottom of the view range but within the view depth will be overridden with the <Beyond> line style.

Perhaps you only need to apply a different view range setting to isolated areas of a view. This can be accomplished with the use of the Plan Region tool. You can find this tool in the Create panel of the View tab along with the other Plan View tools. The Plan Region tool allows you to sketch a boundary within which the View Range dialog box will be available to make specific changes. This method can be utilized for areas such as windows that might be placed in a wall above the cut plane but need to be shown on the plan for documentation.

FIGURE 2.57
View range properties explained

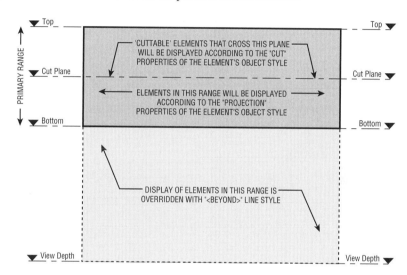

Another useful property of plans is known as an underlay. While this property may function more like a tool, it is found in the Properties palette along with the other view properties. An underlay allows you to use any other level as a reference in the current view. You can use the underlay to display ceiling soffits in a floor plan, to display furniture layouts in a ceiling plan, or to use another level as a reference for replicating partition layouts.

ELEVATIONS

Selecting the Elevation function on the View tab creates elevations of various types. You'll also notice that as you place an elevation tag, they automatically orient to walls (Figure 2.58). If there's no host element nearby to reference, they'll automatically orient to the west.

FIGURE 2.58
Elevation tag orientation

Selecting the center of the tag will allow you to create additional elevation views (more typically done for interior elevations) by selecting the unchecked boxes that surround the elevation tag (Figure 2.59).

FIGURE 2.59
Creating additional elevations

If you select the nose of the elevation tag, you'll see a blue line that defines the beginning of the cut plane for the elevation as well as a dashed line that defines the side and rear extents (Figure 2.60). This allows you to control the analytic extents of the elevation without moving the graphic tag, which is useful if you want the tag in a particular location but you want the cutting plane to start somewhere else.

FIGURE 2.60
Elevation extents

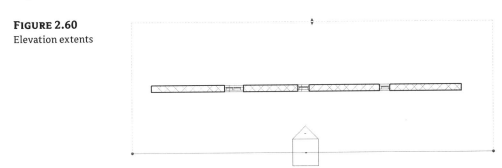

Finally, there are three types of elevations in a Revit project: exterior, interior, and framing. Their differences are more than graphic. *Exterior elevations* by default don't have an active crop boundary, only a starting cut plane. *Interior elevations* have their crop boundary on by default and attempt to find boundaries of host elements, like walls, floors, and ceilings. *Framing elevations* can be placed only along a grid line, and their cut plane corresponds to the respective grid.

SECTIONS

Selecting the Section function on the View tab creates sections. By default, there are three types of sections available from the Type Selector: Building, Wall, and Callout Detail (Figure 2.61). This allows them to be grouped with better clarity in the Project Browser, but there are also other important properties.

FIGURE 2.61
Section types in the
Type Selector

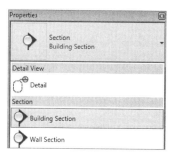

Unlike with elevations, the cutting plane of a section must correspond with its graphic line. Figure 2.62 shows the instance properties of a Building section. The far and side cut planes of a section can also be controlled. This goes for both Building and Wall sections.

FIGURE 2.62
Section properties
and extents

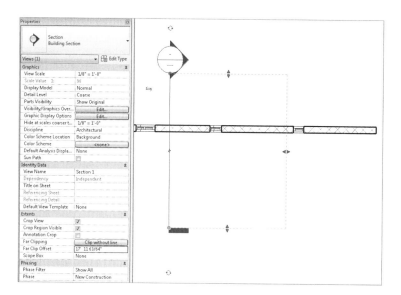

Building and Wall sections must be created in a perpendicular orientation with respect to levels. But after you create them, they can be rotated in elevation. However, doing so would lead to confusion in your project because once rotated, the section wouldn't be displayed in plan.

This is where the Detail section is such a great help. A Detail section that's created in plan not only can be seen in corresponding views, it will also assume different graphic conventions.

For example, look at the two Detail sections in Figure 2.63 that are to the right of the Building section. When you create a Detail section, it will look like Detail Section 1. But when you view it in referring views, it will look like Detail Section 2.

CERT OBJECTIVE

The other thing that you should note is the color of callout and section heads in Figure 2.63. These blue icons act as hyperlinks to the other views in your project. The great thing about them is they are automatically coordinated numerically when you place the views on sheets in your document set.

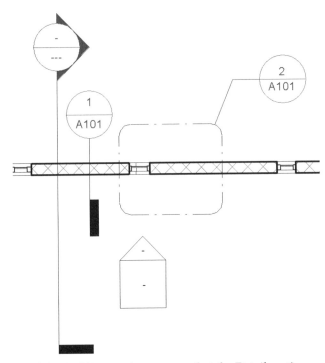

If you go to the view of the Building section, you see that the Detail sections are graphically the opposite of what you've seen in plan view (Figure 2.64).

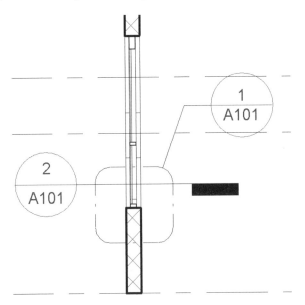

CALLOUTS

There are two types of callouts available in the Type Selector: Detail and Floor Plan (Figure 2.65). Although detail callouts may look like detail sections graphically, they're not visible inside other perpendicular views. So a callout created in plan view will not be visible in elevations or sections like a detail section.

FIGURE 2.65
Callout types

It's probably best to think of a Detail callout as an enlarged view. Its Far Clip settings are by default the same as the parent view. Detail callouts will be filed under Detail Views in the Project Browser. They also have the ability to be displayed in intersecting views, while Floor Plan callouts do not. In other words, a Detail callout placed in a plan view will appear as a detail section in an intersecting view such as a Building or Wall section.

You can think of a Floor Plan callout as another plan view but with associated callout graphics. Floor Plan callouts also have all the same view controls as a regular plan view, such as Depth Clipping and View Range (Figure 2.66). Take a moment to note the line and control arrows around the border of the view. By modifying the location of these arrows, you're modifying the extents of the view. Of course, more than plan views can have their extents modified; elevations, sections, and callouts can all have their view extents modified in the same way.

CERT OBJECTIVE

FIGURE 2.66
Floor Plan callout

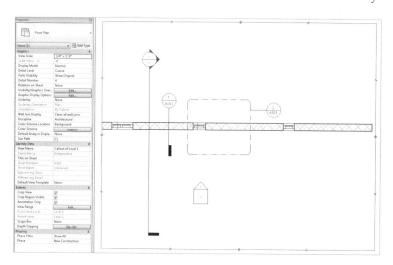

DRAFTING VIEWS

Drafting views give you the ability to draw without first creating a reference to something in your project. They may contain Detail and Repeating Detail components and any other annotation content. Drafting views are great for quickly documenting typical conditions that don't require an actual model geometry.

Once you've created a drafting view, you can refer to this view when creating an elevation, section, detail, and so on that would normally rely on an actual view of the model. As you start to create a standard project view (Figure 2.67), simply select the Reference Other View option and then you'll be allowed to select a reference view from all the other like views in your project as well as any drafting views.

FIGURE 2.67

Drafting view reference

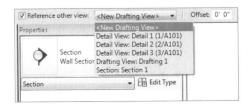

LEGENDS

Legends are views in which you can display samples of model elements that won't affect schedules and quantity takeoffs. There are two types of legends: legends and keynote legends. Regular legends are used to assemble analytic views of content in your project, graphics, geometry, tags, and so on — anything that lives in your project. Legends may contain Detail, Repeating Detail, and Legend components — which are live representations of 3D model elements.

A Legend component (Figure 2.68) is a special live representation of a system or component family that may appear only in legend views (not drafting views). If you make a change to an element in your project, the representation of that element in the legend will change as well. When you are creating a legend view, the Legend Component tool is located in the Component flyout button on the Detail panel of the Annotate tab in the ribbon.

FIGURE 2.68

Legend components

Keynote legends are special schedules. When creating a keynote legend, you'll be prompted much the same way as you are when creating a schedule (Figure 2.69). These types of legends are meant to be placed on either one sheet or multiple sheets. If the legend is placed on every sheet in which keynotes are used, the Filter By Sheet option should be selected on the Filter tab of the Keynote Legend Properties dialog box. With this option selected, only those keynotes that appear in views placed on a sheet will appear in the sheet's keynote legend.

FIGURE 2.69
Creating keynote
legends

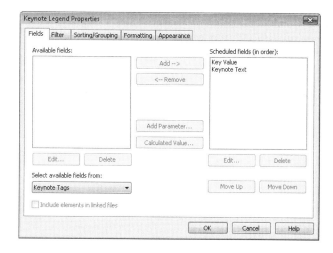

SCHEDULES

All model elements have information about their properties such as size, material, and cost. You can report and interact with this information in tabular views known as schedules. There are six types of schedule views that can be accessed from the Create panel in the View tab of the ribbon: Schedule/Quantities, Graphical Column Schedule, Material Takeoff, Sheet List, Note Block, and View List.

Schedule/Quantities   This is the most commonly used schedule type, allowing you to list and quantify all the element category types. You would use this type to make door schedules, wall schedules, window schedules, and so on. These schedule types are usually limited to scheduling properties within the same category; however, you can create a multicategory schedule or use some fields from other elements. For example, many model elements can refer to the properties of the room in which they are placed.

Graphical Column Schedule   This schedule is different from the other schedule types and is commonly used by structural engineers. Structural columns are displayed according to their grid intersections, indicating top and bottom constraints as well as offsets.

Material Takeoff   This type of schedule lists all the materials and subcomponents of any family category. You can use a material takeoff to measure any material that is utilized in a component or assembly. For example, you might want to know the volume of concrete within the model. Regardless of whether the concrete is in a wall or floor or column, you can tell the schedule to report the total amount of that material in the project. Material takeoffs will report material properties across multiple categories.

Sheet List   This schedule allows you to create a list of all the sheets in the project.

Note Block   This tool creates a unique schedule that lists the properties of a generic annotation symbol used in a project.

View List   This schedule shows a list of all the views in the Project Browser and their properties. A view list can be a valuable tool to help you manage your project's views efficiently.

SHEETS

You will use sheets to organize views and other annotation for the purpose of issuing printable (physical or digital) documents. Sheet borders can be customized, but the important fact to realize is that sheets are always scaled at 1:1. The important thing to remember is that you're not going to select a scale when you print a sheet; it's really more like printing than plotting. If you need your sheet to be smaller or fit on the desired page, these options are available, and using them is little different than printing from a word processing application.

You will learn more about creating sheets in Chapter 18, "Documenting Your Design."

3D VIEWS

Two kinds of 3D views are supported: orthographic and perspective. The Default 3D view is orthographic, while Camera and Walkthrough views are in perspective. You can't change one to another after they are created, so select carefully (Figure 2.70). We'll also cover 3D views in more detail in Chapter 12, "Visualization."

FIGURE 2.70
3D view types

Orthographic views will always show parallel edges along Cartesian x-, y-, and z-axes. Orthographic views are best if you need to show model information to scale. A lot of people don't realize that it's possible to dimension and detail in Revit software from a 3D orthographic view. For a more thorough explanation of annotating a 3D view, refer to Chapter 20, "Presenting Your Design."

Create Camera views by placing the start and end points of a camera (typically from a plan view). It should be noted that the first point you select in plan is the point from which the view will be taken, but the second point is also the rotation origin for the view (Figure 2.71). This is important because if you select a second point that is far beyond your view, when you open the view and attempt to modify it, it will rotate around a target that doesn't seem to make sense. That's because the target location of the view is off in the distance.

FIGURE 2.71
Setting camera and
target origin

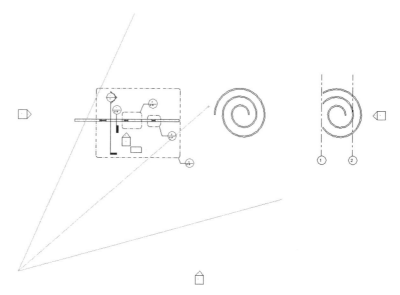

A perspective view will not be to scale, but it can be made relatively larger or smaller by selecting the view's crop region and then selecting the Size Crop button from the Modify | Camera tab (Figure 2.72). Once you do this, you'll have the option to change the view size and field of view (proportionally or nonproportionally). You can also simply drag the nodes of the bounding box.

FIGURE 2.72
Modifying the view
size and field of
view

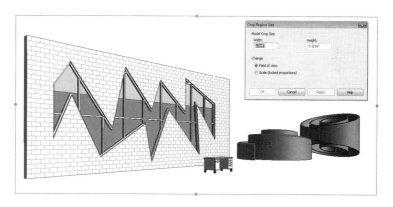

Camera extents are defined by the Far Clip Offset option, accessed in the Properties palette for the view. If the Far Clip Offset is too low, the view may resemble the image shown in Figure 2.73. Geometry that you'd expect to see will be "clipped" in the view.

FIGURE 2.73
The far clip offset is
too shallow.

FIGURE 2.73
The far clip offset is
too shallow.

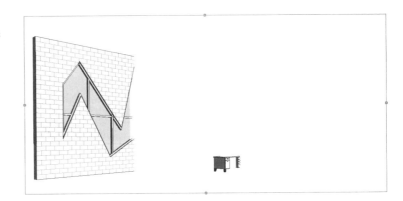

Simply increase the Far Clip Offset value to show more of the model. You may also do this graphically by returning to a plan view, right-clicking the Camera view in the Project Browser, and then selecting Show Camera. Once the camera is shown in your plan view, you can select the node at the far end of your clipping plane and manually drag the node to extend the far clip offset of your view (Figure 2.74).

FIGURE 2.74
Extending the far
clip offset

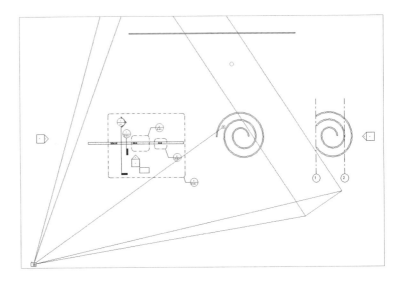

Finally, the extents of 3D views (even walkthroughs) may be customized with the use of section boxes. You can find the Section Box option in the Properties palette for a 3D view (Figure 2.75). This will allow you to control how much of the project is shown and is helpful for creating cutaway visualizations in real time or in renderings.

FIGURE 2.75

Section box applied
to a 3D view

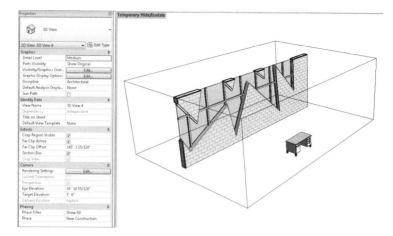

Once a section box is enabled in a 3D view, you can select it in order to stretch or rotate it according to your needs. The section box is not considered a crop region, and therefore it is not affected when you use the Crop Region Visible command. If you want to hide a crop region, select it and then select Hide Elements from the View panel in the ribbon.

Project Management (Restrictions)

Project management involves all the project settings that control (and therefore restrict) any number of project variables. Returning to the organization chart in Figure 2.32, we'll examine some of the crucial management options in the rest of this chapter. The two most important parts of project organization to discuss are *worksets* and *settings* because these topics involve workflow and how the team comes together to work on the project simultaneously. Worksharing (the process that utilizes worksets) is covered in more detail in Chapter 6, "Understanding Worksharing," but we'll cover this topic here at a high level as it relates to overall workflow.

Worksets represent an additional layer of control that enables multiple users to access a single model file. They can be used to divide a project and only load those elements that are needed by each team member at the time of opening a project file. Most of the system elements such as views, family definitions, and settings within a project are automatically managed. Modeled elements are assigned to user-defined worksets.

The other key aspect to project management is settings — specifically, many of the tools found in the Manage tab. Beginning with Object Styles, these are the project-wide definitions for each of the model element categories (Wall, Floor, Door, and so on). In the Object Styles dialog box (Figure 2.76), you will find graphic options similar to those in the Visibility/Graphic Overrides dialog box, only the Object Styles apply to the entire project.

Also within the Manage tab, you will find the Additional Settings flyout button, which gives you access to many other important project-wide settings. Open the Line Weights dialog box and you will see how the simple sequential line weight assignments are translated to scale ranges for model elements (Figure 2.77).

FIGURE 2.76
Object Styles dialog box

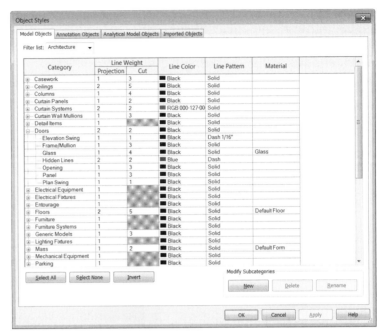

FIGURE 2.77
Line Weights dialog box

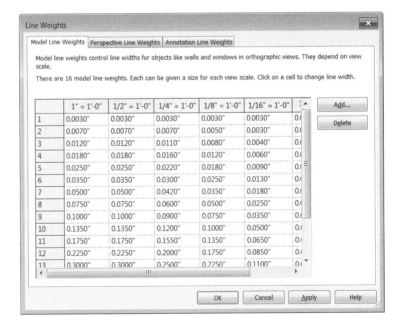

Phasing is another important group of settings that brings the element of time to all modeled elements in a project. The Phasing dialog box allows you to define project phases as well as the graphic overrides for model elements as they interact with view phases (Figure 2.78).

FIGURE 2.78
Phasing dialog box

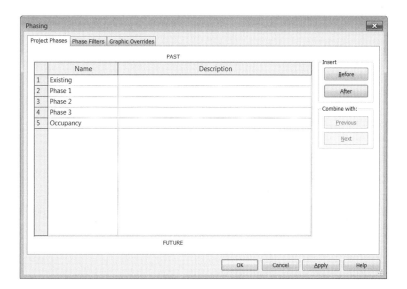

The Bottom Line

Understand the organization of the user interface.   In addition to understanding how your project is organized, to use Revit software well you must understand how the user interface is organized. Once you grasp both of these concepts, you'll be ready to move ahead.

Master It   The "big" areas of the user interface are the ribbon, the Properties palette, the Project Browser, and the drawing area. How do these areas work together, and what tabs correspond to an iterative design process?

Understand project organization.   Revit software has been available for about 10 years, and yet after a decade, it remains unique in its approach to "whole-building BIM." The compelling advantage of being able to design, document, and manage your project across multiple disciplines — the architect, structural, and mechanical disciplines — is something that you can do only in Revit software, and understanding project workflow is key to getting off on the right foot.

Master It   Thinking back to the Revit organization chart shown in Figure 2.32, what are the main components of a Revit project, and how can you apply them to your design process? How do these categories directly affect your design workflow?

Chapter 3

The Basics of the Toolbox

The road to mastering Autodesk® Revit® Architecture software will always include reinforcement of fundamental skills. Just as an accomplished musician will practice her scales, we will "practice" by reviewing the fundamental selection and editing tools throughout the Revit Architecture program. There are many tools in Revit software that can assist you in refining your models and project designs. Some are simple geometry editing functions, whereas others possess more powerful capabilities. In this chapter, we'll review these tools and provide some exercises for you to remain productive.

In this chapter, you'll learn to:

◆ Select, modify, and replace elements

◆ Edit elements interactively

◆ Use other editing tools

Selecting, Modifying, and Replacing Elements

Knowing how to efficiently select, modify, and replace elements is fundamental to working productively in Revit software. These interface operations are the foundation on which you will build skills to create and edit your project models. In the following sections, we will review methods for selecting, filtering, and modifying properties.

Selecting Elements

Revit was one of the first programs that had the ability to highlight elements as you hovered the mouse pointer over them before actually clicking to select. Not only does this give you a clear idea of what you are about to select, it displays information about that object in the status bar and in a banner near the mouse pointer. When you hover over an element, it highlights in blue; click the highlighted element and it turns blue, indicating that it is selected.

Once an element is selected, the ribbon changes to Modify mode where consistent editing tools are located in the left side, and context-sensitive tools appear to the right. Notice the subtle differences in the ribbon, as shown in Figure 3.1, when a roof, stacked wall, and floor are selected.

FIGURE 3.1

The right end of the Modify tab changes based on the element that is selected: (a) the Roof Modify tab; (b) the Stacked Wall Modify tab; (c) the Floor Modify tab

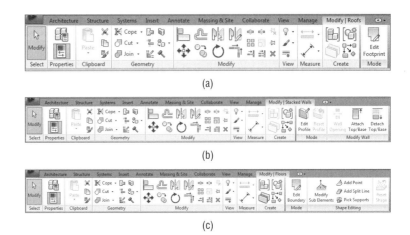

(a)

(b)

(c)

CHANGING SELECTION COLORS

Note that you can change the Revit default colors for selection, highlighting, and alerts to your own color palette. To do this, click the Application menu and select Options. In the Options dialog box that opens, switch to the Graphics option on the left to edit the settings for colors.

You can select elements in many different ways:

Add or subtract You can build a selection of individual elements by using the Ctrl and Shift keys on your keyboard. Hold down the Ctrl key while picking to *add* elements, and hold down the Shift key while picking to *remove* elements. Notice that the mouse pointer will indicate a plus (+) when you hold the Ctrl key and a minus (–) when you hold the Shift key while clicking elements.

Window To select large amounts of elements in a view window, you can click and drag the mouse to form two different types of selection windows. Click and drag from left to right and only the elements completely within the window will be selected — this implied window is displayed as a solid line. Click and drag from right to left and any element within or crossing the window will be selected — this implied window is displayed as a dashed line. Note that to activate either window selection tool, you must begin by clicking in a blank area (not on an element) within the View window.

Chain Chain-select is an intelligent method for selecting connected elements. To activate this mode, hover your mouse over (but don't click) one wall that is connected to several other walls. While the element is pre-highlighted, press the Tab key once and the connected elements should be selected. When selecting objects, note that the Tab key is used to cycle through all available objects near your mouse pointer. If a floor edge happens to be near the edge of a wall you are trying to chain-select, you can skip the chain of walls and select the floor. Be sure to look at the status bar; it will indicate "Chain of walls or lines" when you have selected correctly.

Selection count   Whenever you select any number of objects, the count of selected objects is displayed at the right end of the status bar. Clicking the filter icon next to the selection count opens the Filter dialog box, allowing you to further refine the elements you want to modify.

Select Previous command   A little-known feature allows you to select elements you had previously selected. Either right-click and choose Select Previous from the context menu or press Ctrl and the left arrow key on your keyboard.

Filtering Your Selection

Once you have elements selected, you can filter the selection by object categories using the Filter tool. This tool allows you to select large numbers of elements and then focus your selection by removing categories you don't need, as shown in Figure 3.2. For example, if you box-select an entire floor plan, you will have a selection set of many different categories. Using the Filter tool, you can limit the selection to just the Doors category — or perhaps Doors and Door Tags.

FIGURE 3.2
Use the Filter dialog box to fine-tune your selections.

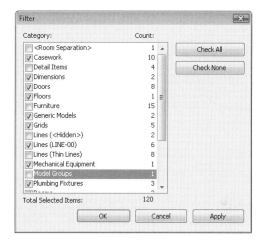

Note that the Filter tool in the ribbon appears only if you have elements from multiple categories selected. If you have elements of only one category selected, you can still open the Filter tool by clicking the filter icon in the status bar. You can use the Properties palette as a filter as well; see the section "Using the Properties Palette" later in this chapter for more information.

Selecting All Instances

Another fast and powerful method for selecting objects is the Select All Instances function. When you right-click a single object in the drawing area or right-click a family in the Project Browser, the Select All Instances tool gives you two options: Visible In View or In Entire Project. Selecting the Visible In View option will select only those items you can see in the current view. This will *not* select elements that have been either temporarily or permanently hidden in the view.

Use the In Entire Project option carefully because you can modify elements in many places that you did not intend to change. Always remember to look at the selection count in the status bar when you use Select All Instances. Here are some common situations where you might use this tool:

◆ View titles — when updating graphics

◆ Walls — when switching from generic to specific types

◆ Title blocks — moving from design to detail documents

◆ Viewports — useful when trying to purge unused viewports

Note that Select All Instances does not work on model lines or symbolic lines. This limitation exists because lines are not only drawn in project views; they are integral parts of other objects such as filled regions and shaft openings.

Using the Properties Palette

The Properties palette is a floating palette that can remain open while you work within the model. The palette can be docked on either side of your screen, or it can be moved to a second monitor. You can open the Properties palette by using one of the following methods:

◆ Clicking the Properties icon in the Properties panel of the Modify tab in the ribbon

◆ Selecting Properties from the right-click context menu

◆ Pressing Ctrl+1 on your keyboard (as in Autodesk® AutoCAD® software)

As shown in Figure 3.3, the Properties palette contains the Type Selector at the top. When placing elements or swapping types of elements you've already placed in the model, the palette must be open to access the Type Selector.

FIGURE 3.3
The new Properties palette contains the Type Selector and is used to set view properties.

Properties	⊠
Basic Wall Exterior - Brick on Mtl. Stud	
New Walls	Edit Type
Constraints	⌃
Location Line	Wall Centerline
Base Constraint	Level 1
Base Offset	0' 0"
Base is Attached	☐
Base Extension Dista...	0' 0"
Top Constraint	Unconnected
Unconnected Height	20' 0"
Top Offset	0' 0"
Top is Attached	☐
Top Extension Distance	0' 0"
Room Bounding	☑
Related to Mass	
Structural	⌃
Structurally Significant	☐
Enable Analytical Mo...	☐
Analyze As	Bearing
Dimensions	⌃
Area	
Volume	
Identity Data	⌃
Comments	
Mark	

When no elements are selected, the Properties palette displays the properties of the active view. If you need to change settings for the current view, make the changes in the Properties palette and the view will be updated. For views, you do not even need to use the Apply button to submit the changes — simply move the mouse out of the Properties palette and the changes will automatically be accepted.

Finally, you can also use the Properties palette as a filtering method for selected elements. When you select elements from different categories, the drop-down list below the Type Selector displays the total number of selected elements. Open the list and you will see the elements listed per category, as shown in Figure 3.4. Select one of the categories to modify the parameters for the respective elements. This process is different from the Filter tool in that the entire selection set is maintained, allowing you to perform multiple modifying actions without reselecting elements.

FIGURE 3.4

Use the Properties palette to filter selection sets.

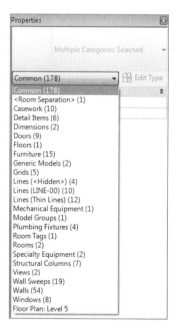

Matching Properties

Located on the Modify tab of the ribbon under the Clipboard panel, the Match Type Properties tool allows you to select one element and apply its type and instance properties to other elements of the same category. Once you select one element, the brush icon near the mouse pointer appears filled. Each subsequent pick on elements of the same category will replace the selected element with the properties of the first element picked. Clicking in an open space will clear the brush icon and allow you to pick a new source object without restarting the command.

Be careful when using this tool with walls because not only does it change the wall type, it also changes the top and bottom constraints of the walls being matched. One best practice for changing wall types without affecting height constraints is to use the Type Selector.

Using the Context Menu

The context menu that appears when you right-click in the View window contains several options. You can activate the last command or select from a list of recent commands, as shown in Figure 3.5.

FIGURE 3.5
Run recent commands from the context menu.

In addition to the other right-click commands listed throughout this chapter (such as Create Similar), zoom commands including Previous View are on the context menu. There are also useful commands when you right-click views in the Project Browser. For example, activate a plan view and then try right-clicking a 3D view in the browser. Select Show Section Box and you can edit the extent of the 3D view's section box while in a floor plan.

Editing Elements Interactively

Revit provides a range of options to interactively edit elements in the model. The most obvious is selecting elements to drag onto the screen, or use the blue control grips to extend walls, lines, shape faces, and region boundaries; however, you often need more precise ways of moving and copying objects. Let's look at some ways to do this.

Moving Elements

You can move elements in several ways, ranging from choosing traditional tools to using intelligent dimensions that appear on the fly when you select elements. Become familiar with each method and determine what is best for your workflow.

Using Temporary Dimensions

You have likely noticed by now that dimensions appear when elements are selected or newly modeled. These dimensions are called temporary dimensions and are there to inform you of the location of the elements relative to other elements in the model, as well as to help you reposition them. Clicking the blue dimension value makes it an active and editable value. Type in a new value and the selected element will move relative to the element from which it is dimensioned. Remember that when you are editing the position of an element via the dimensions, it will always be the selected element that moves. You can't change a dimension value if nothing is selected.

If a temporary dimension isn't referencing a meaningful element, you can choose a different reference by dragging the small blue dot on the dimension's witness line to a new parallel reference, which will highlight when the mouse moves over them (Figure 3.6). For example, if you want to position a door opening at a specific dimension from a nearby wall, you will need to drag the grip of the temporary dimension that references the center of the door to the side of the opening. Then you can edit the value of the dimension as required. When you are dragging the grip of a temporary dimension, you can also use the Tab key on the keyboard to cycle through available snapping references near the mouse pointer.

FIGURE 3.6

Drag or click the blue grip to change the reference of the temporary dimension.

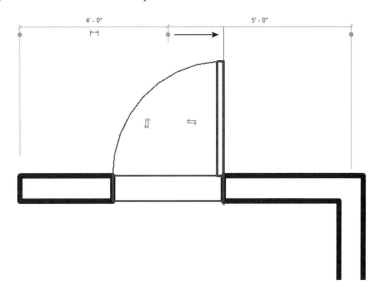

If you click a blue grip, it cycles to the next possible reference in the element. For example, clicking the grip of a dimension to a door or window cycles between the left and right openings and the center reference. The same applies to walls: Try clicking the grip on the temporary dimension extending from a wall and see how the dimension cycles through the various references in the wall (interior face, centerline, exterior face). Note that when you drag a temporary dimension reference to a different position, the new reference is remembered when you return to the element for future editing.

You can also change the default behavior of temporary dimensions using the Temporary Dimension Properties dialog box, shown in Figure 3.7 (on the Manage tab, click Additional Settings and then selecting Temporary Dimensions). Here you can specify how temporary dimensions will independently reference walls, doors, and windows.

You can modify the font size and transparency of temporary dimensions in the program options. To customize these values, click the Application menu and select Options. In the Options dialog box that opens, switch to the Graphics tab and locate the Temporary Dimension Text Appearance settings. Adjust the text size and transparency according to your needs.

If you have many elements selected at the same time or select an element within the proximity of a large number of other elements, temporary dimensions sometimes don't appear. Check the Options bar for the Activate Dimensions button; clicking it will make the temporary dimensions appear in the view.

FIGURE 3.7
The Temporary
Dimension
Properties dialog
box lets you define
default behaviors
based on your
modeling needs.

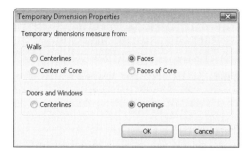

BEHAVIORS FOR MODIFY TOOLS

You have the option to activate the tools without any elements selected. If you choose this method, you must press the Enter key after selecting the objects you intend to modify.

You can also switch between any of the Modify panel tools while you have elements selected. For example, if you initially chose Mirror – Pick Axis and selected an element during the command, you can simply activate the Mirror – Draw Axis command without reselecting the elements.

USING THE MOVE TOOL

Use the Move tool to relocate elements with more precision rather than simply dragging them. The tool allows you to type in values or use temporary dimensions as helpers.

Moving elements is a two-click process: First, you define a start point, and then you click to define a destination. If you know you need to move something a specific distance, it doesn't matter where your two picks take place. All that matters is that the distance between the two clicks is the specified distance. Alternatively, you can type the desired value after picking the first point and guide the mouse pointer in the desired direction of the move.

There are a few options on the Options bar to be aware of when the Move command is active:

Constrain   When this option is selected, it constrains movement to horizontal and vertical directions. Deselecting it allows you to move the element freely as long as the element is not hosted. Hosted elements, such as windows or doors, always move in a constrained manner parallel to their host's axis.

Disjoin   Hosted elements can't change hosts and move to another host without being explicitly disjoined from their original host — for example, moving windows from one wall (host) to another wall, or moving walls between levels that host them. This option lets you disconnect inserts from their hosts and move them to new hosts. For example, if you need to move a door from one wall to another, select the door and activate the Move tool. Select the Disjoin option and move the door to another host. Similarly, you can use the Disjoin option to move one wall away from another without maintaining the join between the two elements.

Multiple   The Multiple option is not active for the Move tool. This option is available only when you switch to the Copy tool.

NUDGING ELEMENTS

Nudging is a simple way to push things around quickly, as you would in software programs such as Adobe Photoshop. When elements are selected, you can use the arrow keys on the keyboard to move the elements horizontally or vertically in small increments. Each press of an arrow key nudges the element a specific distance based on your current zoom factor. The closer you zoom, the finer the nudge. Note that your snap settings do not affect the nudging distances set by the zoom level.

MOVING WITH NEARBY ELEMENTS

A simpler way to constrain freestanding elements is to use the Moves With Nearby Elements option. This setting is designed to capture logical relationships between elements without establishing an explicit constraint. When furnishing a space, for example, you probably want to align the bed or dresser with an adjacent wall. If you change the design of the space, you want the furniture to follow the wall to the new location. For this purpose, select the furniture and then select Moves With Nearby Elements in the Options bar, as shown in Figure 3.8.

By setting this option, you create an invisible relationship between the bed and the wall so that each time you move the wall, the bed moves with it. To clarify the difference between this approach and other constraint relationships, you could create a wall-hosted family, but that would limit your placement options and would subject instances to deletion if the host is deleted. You could align and constrain the family to its host, but too many explicit constraints will adversely affect model performance.

Copying Elements

The Copy tool is another modifying tool that is nearly identical to the Move tool, but it makes a copy of the selected element at the location of the second pick. This tool doesn't copy anything to the clipboard; it copies an instance of an element or selection of elements in the same view. If you change views while using this tool, your selection is lost.

To activate this tool, either choose elements you want to copy and then select the Copy tool in the Modify tab in the ribbon or activate the Copy tool first, select elements you want to copy, and then press the Enter key to start the copy process. Using the Options bar, you can choose to make multiple copies in one transaction by selecting the Multiple option.

An alternative to using the Copy tool is to use standard Windows accelerator keys to copy elements. To quickly copy a single element without the precision of the Copy tool, click and drag an element while pressing the Ctrl key on your keyboard. This technique is useful for quickly populating a quantity of elements in a design without the required precision of the multiple picks of the Copy tool.

FIGURE 3.8
Once an object is selected, it can be set to move with nearby elements:
(a) Select the furniture, and then select the Move with Nearby Elements tool;
(b) Note that the elements keep their relationships.

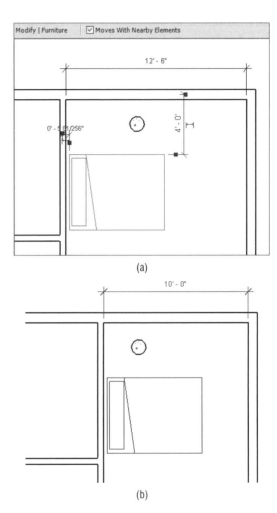

(a)

(b)

Rotating and Mirroring Elements

CERT
OBJECTIVE

When refining or expanding your building design, you will likely find a frequent need to rotate or mirror one or more objects. Just as with moving or copying, there are a few methods for these types of interactive operations. The quickest way to rotate elements in 90-degree increments is by pressing the spacebar on your keyboard. For more precision, you can use the Rotate tool to rotate elements to any specific angle you require.

Using the Spacebar

You can use the spacebar to rotate an element, both at the time of initial placement and after it has been placed. In addition to rotating an object in 90-degree increments, pressing the spacebar will locate any nearby diagonal references (walls, grids, or reference planes) as rotation candidates. This is a great timesaving command to become familiar with because you can forgo the necessity of using an additional tool, such as Rotate And Mirror after placing an object. Here are a few examples:

Doors and windows If you have a door with its swing in the wrong direction, select it and press the spacebar. You can cycle through all four possible orientations of the door using the spacebar. The same holds true for windows; however, many window families are built to only let you flip the window from inside to outside because many windows are symmetrical in elevation. If you are creating an asymmetrical window family, be sure to add flip controls to the window family during its creation. These controls allow the spacebar to work on hosted elements.

Walls If you select a wall, pressing the spacebar flips the element as if it were being mirrored about its length. Walls flip based on their location line, which often isn't the centerline of the assembly. If you aren't sure which direction your wall is facing, select it and look for the flip-control arrows. These are always located on the exterior side of walls (Figure 3.9).

FIGURE 3.9
The flip arrow is another way to reorient an element. For walls, it is always found on the exterior side.

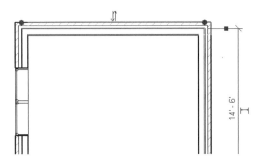

Freestanding elements If you select a freestanding element, the spacebar rotates the element about the center reference planes defined in the family. Depending on how the family was built, the rotation origin may not make the most sense. If you decide to edit a family in order to change the location of the geometry relative to the center reference planes, be careful: When the family is loaded back into a project, all instances of the family will jump to a new location based on the change you made relative to the reference planes.

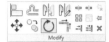

USING THE ROTATE TOOL

To rotate an element, select it and click the Rotate tool. Remember, you can also activate the Rotate tool first, select one or more elements, and then press Enter to begin the operation. This is a two-click operation similar to the Move and Copy tools. Alternatively, you can enter numeric values for the desired rotation angle. The software locates the geometric center of the selected elements and uses that as the default center of rotation; however, you will most likely want to designate a more meaningful center.

To choose a new center of rotation, you have a couple of options. First, you can select the elements you want to rotate and drag the center icon to a new location before clicking to set the starting reference angle. Note that you might have to zoom out in order to find the center icon. Once the center is established, begin rotating the element using the temporary dimensions as a reference or by typing in the angle of rotation explicitly. The second option is to select elements you want to rotate and then use the Place option to locate the origin without dragging.

You'll notice that while moving the center of rotation, you lose the ability to pan and zoom the view. To overcome this, drag the center into the Project Browser and release the mouse button; then move the mouse pointer back into the view. The mouse pointer changes to a rotation icon, and you can freely zoom and pan to the desired location. The next click you make places the origin, and you can continue with the rotation operation. Note that you can also use keyboard snap shortcuts to refine the location of the center of rotation while dragging it. For example, type **SE** to snap to an explicit endpoint while dragging.

USING THE MIRROR TOOL

The Mirror tool allows you to mirror elements across an axis in order to create a mirror image of an element or multiple elements. You can either pick an existing reference in the model with the Mirror – Pick Axis tool or draw the axis interactively using the Mirror – Draw Axis tool. In Figure 3.10, the centerline of the plumbing chase wall was picked as the axis for mirroring the plumbing fixtures.

As with the other Modify tools you have seen so far, the Mirror tools have the option to create a copy of the selected elements or to simply mirror the selected elements to a new position. You can find the Copy option in the Options bar after you activate either of the Mirror tools.

Modify	Multi-Select	☑ Copy

BE CAREFUL WHEN MIRRORING

The Mirror tools should be used carefully on any type of freestanding elements that may be asymmetrical in design. While you can use the Mirror tools on any object, performing this operation to suit a design may distort a product component. For example, if an asymmetrical chair family was loaded into your model and you decide to mirror it to fit a space layout, the mirrored version of that chair may not be a viable product offered by the manufacturer. Remember that although an object can be scheduled, the schedule cannot determine if the object has been mirrored.

FIGURE 3.10
The sink, toilet, and bath fixtures are mirrored about the centerline of the chase wall: (a) selecting the axis; (b) the mirrored elements.

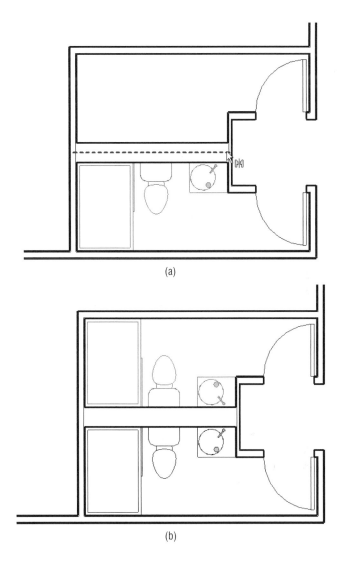

(a)

(b)

Arraying Elements

An array allows you to copy instances of an element with equal spacing between the instances. You have the option to create intelligent arrays that can be grouped and associated for further refinement, as well as one-off, unassociated arrays. Like the other tools we've reviewed in the Modify tab of the ribbon, the array options are presented on the Options bar.

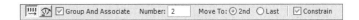

You can create two types of arrays: linear and radial. *Linear* arrays are set as the default because they're the most common. As you would expect, a linear array creates a series of elements in a line. Each element in the array can be given a defined distance from the previous element (Move To 2nd option) or can be spaced equally based on a defined overall array length (Move To Last option). Figure 3.11 shows a linear array where the Move To 2nd option was selected to define a fixed distance between each instance in the array. Think of this type of array as additive and subtractive: If you change the number, the length of the array increases or decreases.

FIGURE 3.11
The Move to 2nd option is used in the Array tool to set a fixed distance between instances: (a) setting the array distance; (b) changing the number of elements in the array.

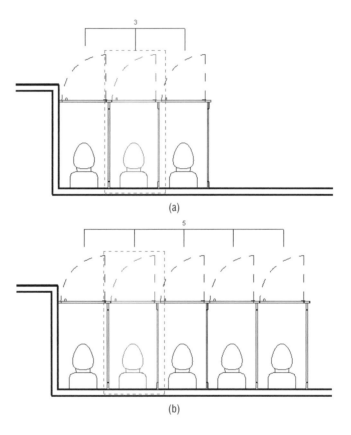

If you want to arrange elements in a fixed space and the exact spacing between elements is less important, use the Move To Last option. Figure 3.12 shows an array where the location of the last element in the array was picked and the elements were placed equally between the first and last elements. With this option, the length is fixed and the array squeezes elements within that constraint as the number changes.

A *radial* array uses the same options as a linear array, but it revolves around a center point. The Move To 2nd and Move To Last options function as angles instead of distances in a radial array. You can specify the instance angle or overall array angle with two picks, or you can enter a specific value. With this type of array, elements auto-rotate so that each element faces the center of the array, as shown in Figure 3.13.

FIGURE 3.12
This array uses the Move To Last option and fills instances between the first and last instances: (a) creating an array first to last; (b) adding more elements to this array to keep the end element in the same location but add more in between.

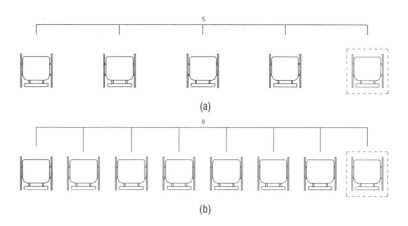

FIGURE 3.13
Elements will auto-rotate in a radial array.

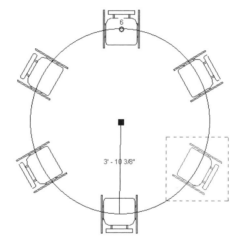

The radial array is a little trickier than a linear array. Here is how to achieve the example shown in Figure 3.13:

1. Before starting the radial array, draw a detail line to help locate the intended center of the array.

2. Select the element and activate the Array tool from the Modify tab in the ribbon. Select the Radial option button, change Number to **6**, and choose the Move To Last option.

3. Drag the center of rotation off the element and to the endpoint of the detail line you drew in step 1.

4. Click the mouse to define any starting point. An exact starting point is not important because you will be defining a complete circle in the next step.

5. Do not click a second time; instead, go to the Options bar, type **360** in the Angle option, and press Enter on the keyboard.

Enabling the Group And Associate option allows you to treat an array as a group that can be modified later to adjust the number and spacing of the array. If this option is unchecked, the array is a one-off operation and you have no means of adjusting it after it is created.

As shown in Figure 3.11 and Figure 3.12, when an element in a grouped array is selected, a control appears, indicating the number of elements in the array. Editing that number changes the number of elements in the array. This tool comes in handy when you're creating certain families because the array number can be associated with a parameter or driven by a mathematical formula. See Chapter 15, "Family Editor," for a detailed exercise.

GROUPING ARRAYS OF DATUM ELEMENTS

When developing a project for a multistory building, you may find that using the Array tool is a quick and easy way to generate many levels and grid lines. We recommend not using the Group And Associate option when arraying datum elements. Maintaining grids and levels inside groups can cause problems with elements that refer to those data.

Scaling Elements

The Scale tool lets you scale certain lines and graphic elements in 2D that are appropriate for scaling, such as imported raster images and 2D line shapes. While not an obvious option, the Scale tool can be used in Sketch mode for any type of sketch-based element in a project or for solid and void geometry sketches in the Family Editor.

Keep in mind that you are working with a model made out of real-world objects, not abstract primitive forms. You cannot scale most elements because it's not practical or meaningful and may cause dangerous errors in scheduling and dimensions. For example, you can't scale the size of a door, wall, or sink because they represent real assemblies and scaling them would mean resizing all their components. This would lead to impractical results, such as a sink being displayed as a fraction of its actual manufactured size.

Aligning Elements

If you've been using Revit software for any amount of time, you have likely discovered the power of the Align tool. It has the ability to supplant the need to use many of the tools we've already discussed. The Align tool lets you line elements up in an efficient way that works on almost all types of objects.

With this tool, you explicitly align references from one element to another regardless of the type of either object. For example, you can align windows in a façade so their centers or openings are all in alignment. To use the Align tool, activate it from the Modify tab in the ribbon and first select the target reference — a reference to which you want to align another element. Next, select what you want to align to that reference — the part or side of the element whose position needs to be modified. The second element picked is the one that always moves into alignment. This selection sequence is the opposite of the other editing tools we've discussed so far, so remember: *destination first*, then the element to align.

As soon as you make your second pick and the aligned element is moved, a lock icon appears, allowing you to constrain the alignment. If you click the icon, thereby constraining the alignment, the alignment is preserved if either element moves. Figure 3.14 illustrates the use of the

Align tool to align multiple windows in an elevation view using the Multiple Alignment option on the Options bar.

FIGURE 3.14

You can use the Align tool for lining up edges of windows in a façade.

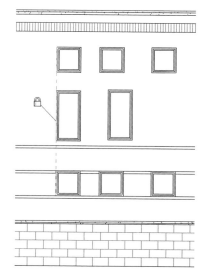

The Align tool also works within model patterns, such as brick or stone on surfaces of model objects. Select a line on an object such as the edge of a wall, and then select a line in the surface pattern. Use the Tab key if you cannot get surface patterns selected with the first mouse click. Note that the Align tool will also rotate elements in the process of aligning them to objects that are not parallel. This is a real time-saver compared to moving and rotating.

CERT
OBJECTIVE

Trimming or Extending Lines and Walls

You can trim and extend lines and walls to one another using the Trim/Extend tools on the Modify tab of the ribbon. In older versions of Revit Architecture, this function was assigned to a single button with three options in the Options bar. In the latest version, there are three separate tools in the ribbon: Trim/Extend To Corner, Trim/Extend Single Element, and Trim/Extend Multiple Elements. With the Trim/Extend tools, you first activate the tool and then operate on elements in the model, selecting two lines or walls that need to meet in a corner or as a T intersection.

The Trim/Extend tools are used frequently for editing sketches of floors and roofs because it's easy to end up with overlapping lines that need to be trimmed to form a closed loop. Keep in mind that with the Trim/Extend tools, you are selecting pairs of elements to *remain*, not to remove. While the Single Element and Multiple Elements tools are similar to the Extend command in AutoCAD, the behavior of the Trim/Extend To Corner tool in Revit Architecture is more like that of the Chamfer or Fillet command rather than its Trim command.

The Trim/Extend tools for extending a single element or multiple elements function in a slightly different way than Trim/Extend To Corner. To extend a wall or line, first select a target reference; then select the element you want to extend to that target (Figure 3.15). Using the Multiple Elements tool, you first select the target reference; then each subsequent pick extends the selected element to the target reference.

FIGURE 3.15
Extend walls to references by picking the target (a), then the wall to extend (b).

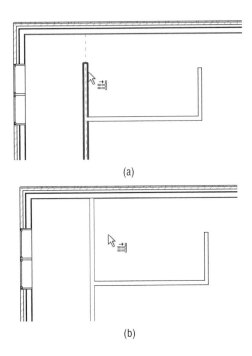

USE TRIM/EXTEND ON LINE-BASED COMPONENTS

You can use the Trim/Extend tools on line-based families that are either model or detail components. Try this using a line-based detail component for batt insulation or gypsum wallboard. The Trim/Extend tools will help make your detailing process much more efficient and fun!

Splitting Lines and Walls

The Split tool operates on walls and lines and lets you divide an element into two pieces. To cut an element, activate the Split tool from the Modify tab in the ribbon and place the mouse pointer over the edge of a wall or line. Before you click, you'll see a preview of the split line. The split line will automatically snap to any adjoining geometry.

The Options bar displays a nice feature called Delete Inner Segment that removes the need to use the Trim tool after a splitting operation. In the example in Figure 3.16, the middle section of a wall needs to be removed so that you end up with a clean set of wall joins. Using the Split tool with the Delete Inner Segment option checked, you can accomplish this with two clicks and get a clean condition without having to return with the Trim command.

FIGURE 3.16
Using the Split tool with the Delete Inner Segment option checked

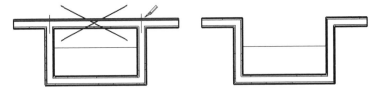

Split With Gap

The Split With Gap tool allows you to specify a gap distance and pick a single point on a wall. Although the wall is divided into two separate segments, the gap distance is maintained with an automatic constraint. To use Split With Gap, follow these steps:

1. Go to the Modify tab, and from the Modify panel, select Split With Gap.

2. Specify the Joint Gap distance in the Options bar. Note that this distance can only be set between 1/16" [1.6 mm] and 1'-0" [300 mm].

3. Move the mouse pointer over a wall and click to place the gap.

Once you have successfully split a wall with a gap, select the wall and notice the constraints (locks) on the gap and between the two parallel wall segments. Try to drag either of the wall ends separated by the gap and you will see that the gap distance is maintained. Try to move the wall in a direction perpendicular to the wall segments and you will notice that the two wall segments remain aligned.

If you'd like to rejoin walls that have been split with a gap, follow these steps:

1. Select a wall split with a defined gap.

2. Click the constraint icon in the gap to unlock the dimension constraint.

3. Right-click the end grip of one wall segment and select Allow Join.

4. Select the other wall and repeat step 3.

5. Drag the wall end grip of one wall segment to the end of the other segment. The walls should join.

Note that on walls with smaller gaps, the segments may automatically join as soon as you select Allow Join; however, rejoined segments may not form a single segment. If you have trouble joining two parallel wall segments into one, try to drag one of the wall ends away from the other and release the mouse button; then drag the segment back to the other end.

CERT OBJECTIVE

Offsetting Lines and Walls

Offset is similar to the Move and Copy tools in that it moves and makes a copy of an element by offsetting it parallel to an edge you select. You can find the Offset tool in the Modify tab of the ribbon. You can also specify an offset distance as an option in the Options bar when you are sketching lines or walls.

This tool is especially useful in the Family Editor when you're making shapes that have a consistent thickness in profile, such as extruded steel shapes. The Offset tool has a Copy option available in the Options bar that determines whether the offsetting operation generates a copy of the selected elements or simply moves them.

Remember that you can Tab-select a chain of elements and offset them in one click, as shown in Figure 3.17.

FIGURE 3.17
Use Offset with
Tab-select to copy a
chain of elements.

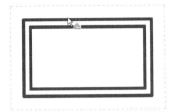
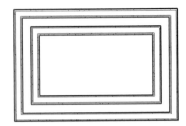

Keeping Elements from Moving

In some cases, you may want to make sure some elements in the model never move. An example of this is when you work on a renovation to an existing building. For obvious reasons, you would not like to move walls that are in the model and already built in reality. Other examples include imported drawings, grids, levels, and exterior walls. There are two ways to deal with this and lock certain elements, thus preventing them from moving.

PINNING ELEMENTS

You can restrict an element's ability to move by pinning it with the Pin tool. Use this tool to lock down critical elements that need to remain fixed for long periods of time. As one example, this is an important tool to use on imported CAD files because it's easy to accidentally select an import and drag it or move it. This kind of accidental modification can lead to coordination problems, even in a BIM environment. Use pins to lock down grid lines because you certainly don't want to accidentally relocate those either.

This tool is located in the Modify panel of the Modify tab in the ribbon. Select one or more elements for which you want to prevent movement, and click the Pin tool. If you try to move the element, nothing will happen — you won't even get a preview of a potential move. To unpin an element, select it and click the Unpin tool, which is also located in the Modify panel. You can also unpin an element by clicking the pin icon that appears near a pinned element when it is selected.

DELETING PINNED ELEMENTS

Pinned elements can be deleted. This unfortunately is misunderstood by users who believe that a pinned element is safe from deletion. You will receive a warning after a pinned element is deleted, so pay close attention to these types of alerts.

CONSTRAINTS

Constraints aren't as rigid as the Pin tool, but they do allow you to create dimensional rules in the model so that elements remain fixed relative to other elements. You can create a constraint using dimensions or alignments, and then click the lock icon that appears upon creation of a dimension or completion of an alignment operation.

A simple example of using constraints is maintaining a fixed distance between a door and a side wall. If the wall moves, the door will also move. If you try to move the door, the software will not let you move it. Look at Figure 3.18; the door has been constrained to remain 4" [10 cm] from the wall face.

FIGURE 3.18

A door constrained to a wall can't be moved independently of the wall.

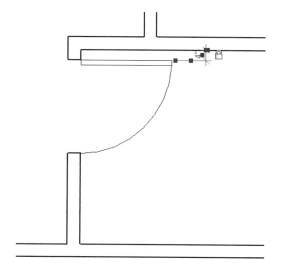

This type of constraint is accomplished by placing a dimension string between the side of the door and the face of the wall, and then by clicking the lock icon on the dimension. Note that the dimension can be deleted while preserving the constraint. If you delete a constrained dimension, an alert will appear giving you the option to unconstrain the elements or simply delete the dimension while maintaining the constraint (Figure 3.19). Note that you can determine where constraints were by creating new dimensions; constrained relationships will still display with the lock icon. You can also view these relationships when a constrained element is selected. Simply hover the mouse pointer near the constraint icon and you will see the dimension constraint represented as a dashed dimension string.

FIGURE 3.19

Deleting a constrained dimension generates an alert.

Autodesk Revit Architecture 2012

Warning - can be ignored

A Dimension with Lock and/or EQ Constraints is being deleted, but the elements will still be constrained. Push "Unconstrain" to remove the Constraints or "OK" to leave elements constrained.

Show   More Info   Expand >>

Unconstrain   OK   Cancel

Exploring Other Editing Tools

A range of other editing tools are available, and we'll cover them in subsequent chapters when they're used in specific operations; however, there are a few tools you should know about now because they are generic tools you can put to immediate use on any project.

Using the Join Geometry Tool

Joining walls to floors and roofs creates clean-looking drawings, and Rivet will attempt to create these joins automatically; however, in some cases, elements don't look right until they are explicitly joined. This is where the Join Geometry tool comes into play. This tool creates joins between floors, walls, ceilings, roofs, and slabs. A common use for this tool is in building sections, where floors and walls may appear overlapped and not joined. Figure 3.20 shows a floor intersecting with some walls that aren't joined. Using the Join Geometry tool, you can clean up these conditions nicely.

FIGURE 3.20
Intersections at Level 2 have been joined: (a) unjoined; (b) joined.

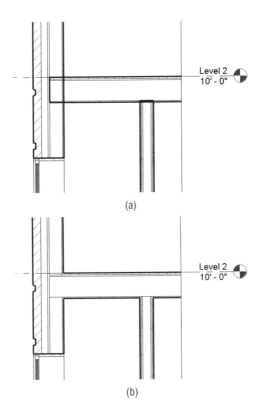

You might notice that some joins — especially in a view set to the Course detail level — contain a thin dividing line between two elements. This is usually because the two elements you joined consist of differing materials. Ensuring consistent material application will give you increased graphic quality in your project views.

You should also be aware that joining large host elements to many other elements may cause degraded model performance. One way to avoid this is to apply a black solid fill to elements in the cut plane of your course view sections and avoid overall manual joining; then selectively join for medium and fine views. This can be easily done by selecting the element in question (wall, floor, and so forth) and choosing Edit Type from the Properties palette. By default, the Course Scale Fill Pattern is set to blank. Set this to Solid Color; in all your course views, your elements will show as solid black.

Using the Split Face and Paint Tools

Occasionally you may need to apply a thin material to the face of an object without making a new type of element. You may also need to divide an overall surface into smaller regions to receive different materials. You can use the Paint tool to apply materials and the Split Face tool to divide object surfaces. With the Paint tool, you can apply alternative materials to the exterior faces of walls, floors, roofs, and ceilings. This material has no thickness, but you can schedule it with a material takeoff schedule and annotate it with a material tag. A typical use case for these two tools is the application of a carpet or thin tile to a floor. See Chapter 14, "Floors, Ceilings, and Roofs," for a detailed exercise on this topic.

Copying and Pasting

Copying and pasting is a familiar technique used in almost all software applications, and Revit software provides the basic features you'd expect (Ctrl+C and Ctrl+V). It also has some additional time-saving options that are specific to working on a 3D model.

To copy any element or group of elements to the Clipboard, select them and press Ctrl+C. To paste, press Ctrl+V. In the majority of cases, the software pastes the elements with a dashed bounding box around them. You then determine where to place the elements by clicking a point to define its final position. In the Options bar you will find a Constrain option that when clicked will only let you define the location of the pasted content orthogonally to the original elements.

EDIT PASTED

Immediately after you select a point for the location of the pasted content, you will find a new panel in the ribbon called Edit Pasted (Figure 3.21). You can click Finish to complete the pasting action or start another command. If you are unsatisfied with the pasting action, select Cancel.

FIGURE 3.21
Additional actions
are available when
pasting elements.

If you select Edit Pasted Elements, a special mode will be started with the Edit Pasted tools appearing at the top left of the active window (Figure 3.22). In this mode, only the pasted elements are editable. You can use the Select All or Filter button to refine those elements within the pasted selection. When your edits are completed, click the Finish button.

FIGURE 3.22
Edit Pasted mode
allows additional
modification of
pasted elements.

PASTE ALIGNED

If you need to paste elements with greater location control, Paste Aligned offers options to make the process simple and efficient. These options allow you to quickly duplicate elements from one view or one level to another while maintaining a consistent location in the x-coordinate and y-coordinate plane. After selecting elements and copying them to the clipboard, find the Paste button in the Clipboard panel, as shown in Figure 3.23.

FIGURE 3.23
Paste Aligned
options

Five options, in addition to the Paste From Clipboard option, are available when you click the Paste drop-down button. Depending on the view from which you copy and what kinds of elements you copy, the availability of these options will change. For example, if you select a model element in a plan view, you won't have the Aligned To Selected Views option. These options are as follows:

Aligned To Selected Levels This is a mode you can use to quickly paste copied elements to many different levels simultaneously. When you select this option, you choose levels from a list in a dialog box. This is useful when you have a multistory building design, you want to copy a furniture layout that repeats on many floors, and selecting level graphics in a section or elevation would be too tedious.

Aligned To Selected Views If you want to copy view-specific elements, such as drafting lines, text, or dimensions, this option allows you to paste them by selecting views from a list of views in a dialog box. In the list available for selection, you don't see levels listed but rather a list of parallel views. For example, if elements are copied from a plan view, all other plan views are listed. Likewise, if you copy from an elevation view, only elevation views are listed.

Aligned To Current View   This option pastes the elements from the Clipboard into the active view in the same spatial location. For example, if you copy a series of walls in one view, switch to another view in the Project Browser and paste with the Aligned To Current View option, the software pastes the walls to the same x-coordinate and y-coordinate location in the view you switched to.

Aligned To Same Place   This option places elements from the clipboard in the exact same place from which they were copied or cut. One use for this tool is copying elements into a design option; see Chapter 11, "Designing with Design Options and Groups," for an explanation of design options.

Aligned To Picked Level   This is a mode you can use to copy and paste elements between different floors by picking a level in a section or elevation. Although you can cut or copy elements from a plan view, you must be in an elevation or section to paste using this option. You might use this paste option to copy balconies on a façade from one floor to another.

Using the Create Similar Tool

Rather than hunting through a list of families or making copies you'd have to edit later, try using the Create Similar tool to add new instances of a selected element to your model.

This tool is available in the Create panel of the Modify tab of the ribbon when an object is selected or from the right-click context menu. To use this method, select an existing instance of the same type of element you'd like to create and click the Create Similar tool and you will immediately be in a placement or creation mode according to the type of element. For example, if you use Create Similar with a floor selected, you're taken directly into Sketch mode, where you can start sketching the boundary for a new floor.

Using Keyboard Shortcuts (Accelerators)

To increase your productivity even further, you may like to use keyboard shortcuts to speed up common commands and minimize interruptions to your workflow. When you hover your mouse pointer over any tool in the ribbon, the keyboard shortcut is indicated to the right of the tool name, as shown here.

You can customize the keyboard shortcuts assigned to all commands. To access this tool, go to the View tab in the ribbon, find the Windows panel, and select User Interface ➤ Keyboard Shortcuts. When the Keyboard Shortcuts dialog box appears (Figure 3.24), you can search for commands in the Search box. Once you find a command to which you'd like to assign a shortcut, select it and type the shortcut in the Press New Keys box. Click the Assign button and you will see the new shortcut added to the selected command. Click OK to close the dialog box and the keyboard shortcuts will be ready for immediate use.

FIGURE 3.24
Customize keyboard shortcuts for commonly used Revit commands.

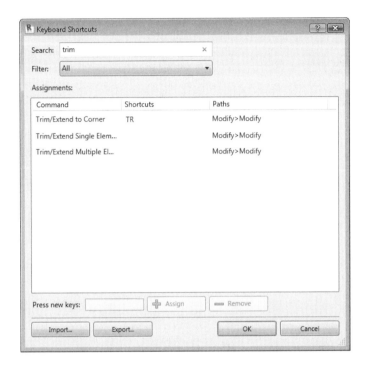

Modeling Site Context

In the previous sections of this chapter, you learned about the fundamental tools for editing and modifying model elements. Another set of tools you should become familiar with are the site tools. They allow you to create a context within which your building models can be situated. For example, a toposurface will create a hatched area when you view your building in a section, and it will function as a hosting surface for site components such as trees, shrubs, parking spaces, accessories, and vehicles (Figure 3.25).

The Revit site tools are intended for use only in the creation of basic elements, including topography, property lines, and building pads. Although editing utilities are available to manipulate the site elements, these tools are not meant to be used for civil engineering like the functionality found in Civil 3D® software.

In the following sections, you'll learn about the different ways to create and modify a toposurface, how to generate property lines with tags, and how to model a building pad within a toposurface.

Using a Toposurface

As its name suggests, a toposurface is a surface-based representation of the topography context supporting a project. It is not modeled as a solid; however, a toposurface will appear as if it were solid in a 3D view with a section box enabled (Figure 3.26).

FIGURE 3.25
A toposurface can host components such as trees, people, vehicles, and other entourage.

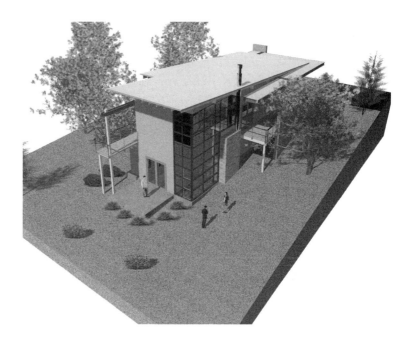

FIGURE 3.26
Toposurfaces will appear as a solid in a 3D view only if a section box is used.

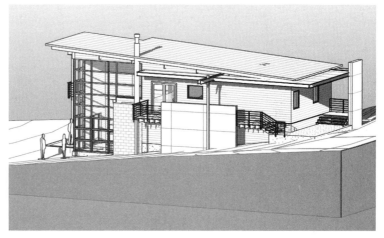

You can create a toposurface in three different ways: by placing points at specific elevations, by using a linked CAD file with lines or points at varying elevations, or by using a points file generated by a civil engineering application. We'll examine these techniques in the following exercises.

CREATING A TOPOSURFACE BY PLACING POINTS

CERT OBJECTIVE

The simplest way to create a toposurface is by placing points in your Revit project at specific elevations. To create a clean outer edge for your toposurface, we suggest drawing a large rectangle using detail lines in your site plan. When you are creating a toposurface by placing points, there are no line-based geometry tools; however, points can be snapped to the detail lines. The following exercise will show you how to create a toposurface by placing points:

1. Begin by opening the file c03-Site-Tools.rvt, which can be downloaded from this book's companion web page at www.sybex.com/go/masteringrevit2013.

2. Activate the floor plan named Site and you will see a rectangle created from detail lines.

3. Go to the Massing & Site tab, and from the Model Site panel, click Toposurface.

TURNING ON AND OFF TABS

New to Revit Architecture 2013 is the ability to turn on and off the tabs on the ribbon. If this is the first time you've opened Revit, you probably don't see the Massing & Site tab. To turn this on, just navigate to the Application button and choose Options. From there, select the User Interface tab. Here you can turn on and off any of the tabs from the ribbon.

Notice in the contextual tab in the ribbon that the default tool is Place Point.

4. Notice the Elevation value in the Options bar. Set the value of the points you are about to place.

Modify | Edit Surface   Elevation   20' 0"   Absolute Elevation ▼

Also note that the elevation values are always related to the Revit project base point. They do not relate to the elevation of any shared coordinates.

5. With the Elevation value set to 0'-0" [0 mm], place a point at each of the left corners of the rectangle.

6. Change the Elevation value to 20'-0" [6000 mm], and then place a point at each of the right corners of the rectangle. You will notice the contour lines of the surface begin to appear after the third point of the surface is placed.

7. In the contextual tab of the ribbon, click Finish Surface (green check mark) to complete the toposurface. Activate the Default 3D view and you will see the sloping surface, as shown in Figure 3.27. And keep in mind that this will be a thin surface, not a solid. Notice that the 3D view in this project already has the section box property enabled. To adjust the section box, activate the Reveal Hidden Elements tool in the View Control bar.

8. Save the project file; we'll use it in subsequent exercises.

CREATING A TOPOSURFACE FROM IMPORTED DATA

CERT
OBJECTIVE

A common workflow you may encounter involves the use of CAD data generated by a civil engineer. In this case, the engineer must create a file with 3D data. Blocks, circles, or contour polylines must exist in the CAD file at the appropriate elevation to be used in the process of generating a toposurface in Revit.

FIGURE 3.27
A simple toposurface created by placing points

In the following exercise, you will download a sample DWG file with contour polylines. You must link the file into your Revit project before creating the toposurface:

1. Create a new Revit project using the `default.rte` or `DefaultMetric.rte` template. If you're selecting from the New Project dialog box, choose Architectural Template.

2. Download the file `c03-Site-Link.dwg` from this book's web page.

3. Activate the Site plan in the Project Browser.

4. Go to the Insert tab in the ribbon and click the Link CAD button. Select the `c03-Site-Link.dwg` file and set the following options:

   ◆ Current View Only: Unchecked

   ◆ Import Units: Auto-Detect

   ◆ Positioning: Auto-Center To Center

   ◆ Place At: Level 1

5. Click Open to close the dialog box and complete the insertion of the CAD link. Open a Default 3D view to examine the results (Figure 3.28).

FIGURE 3.28
Linked CAD file as seen in a 3D view

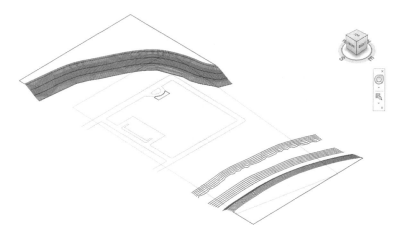

6. From the Massing & Site tab in the ribbon, click the Toposurface button. In the Tools panel of the Modify | Edit Surface tab on the ribbon, select Create From Import, and then Select Import Instance.

7. Pick the linked CAD file and the Add Points From Selected Layers dialog box will appear (Figure 3.29). Click the Check None button and then select the layers C-TOPO-MAJR and C-TOPO-MINR.

FIGURE 3.29
Select only the layers containing 3D contour information.

8. Click OK to close the dialog box. It may take a few seconds to generate the points based on the contour polylines in the linked file, but they will appear as black squares when they have all been placed.

9. If you would like to use fewer points to define the toposurface, click the Simplify Surface button in the contextual ribbon and enter a larger value such as 1'-0" [250 mm].

10. Click the Finish Surface button in the contextual ribbon tab to complete the toposurface. Change the visual style of the view to Consistent Colors to examine your results.

CREATING A TOPOSURFACE FROM A POINTS FILE

CERT OBJECTIVE

A less common method for creating a toposurface, although equally effective when using linked CAD data, is using a points file. A points file is a text file that is usually generated from a civil engineering program. It must be a comma-delimited file (TXT or CSV format) in which the x-, y-, and z-coordinates of the points are the first numeric values in the file. In the following exercise, we have provided a sample points file that was exported from Civil 3D using the XYZ_LIDAR Classification (comma-delimited) format setting:

1. Open the file c03-Site-Points-Start.rvt, which can be downloaded from this book's web page.

2. Download the file c03-Points.csv from this book's web page to your local computer.

3. Activate the Site plan in the Project Browser.

4. From the Massing & Site tab on the ribbon, click the Toposurface button. In the Tools panel of the Modify | Edit Surface tab, select Create From Import and then choose Specify Points File.

5. Navigate to the c03-Points.csv file and click Open. Note that if you were using a TXT format file, you'd change the Files Of Type option to Comma Delimited Text.

6. In the Format dialog box, select Decimal Feet. It is important to understand the units of the values in the points file to ensure that the toposurface will be created at the correct scale. Click OK to close the dialog box.

7. Click the Finish Surface button in the contextual ribbon to complete the toposurface. Open the Default 3D view to examine your results. You may have to use the Zoom All command to see the extent of the new toposurface.

8. Save the project file for use in subsequent exercises.

In the following sections, you can continue to use this file to explore the tools available for modifying a toposurface, or you can download the completed version of the project, c03-Site-Points.rvt.

Modifying the Surface with Subregion

The points file example in the previous exercise represents a section of terrain across Lake Mead, Nevada. If you wanted to define an area of the toposurface with a different material but not change the geometry of the overall surface, you would use the Subregion tool. In the following exercise, you will use this tool to create a region that will represent the water of the lake:

1. Using the c03-Site-Points.rvt file, activate the Site plan from the Project Browser. In this view, there are dashed detail lines that represent the edge of the water.

2. Go to the Massing & Site tab in the ribbon and click the Subregion tool.

3. Switch to Pick Lines mode in the Draw panel of the contextual ribbon.

4. Hover your mouse pointer over one of the dashed detail lines on the left side of the surface, Tab-select the chain of lines, and then click to select them. You will see a purple sketch line appear.

5. Repeat step 4 for the dashed detail lines at the right side of the surface.

6. Switch to Line mode in the Draw panel of the contextual ribbon and draw a line connecting each open end of the water edge lines, as shown in Figure 3.30.

7. Click Finish Surface in the contextual ribbon to complete the subregion.

8. Activate the Default 3D view and select the subregion you created in the previous steps.

9. In the Properties palette, locate the Material parameter and click the ellipsis button to open the Materials dialog box. Locate and select the material named Water. Note that you can easily find this material by typing **Water** in the search field at the top of the dialog box.

FIGURE 3.30
The sketch boundary for a subregion must be a closed loop but can overlap the edge of the toposurface.

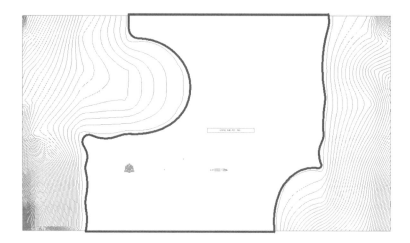

10. Click OK to close the Materials dialog box; you will see the results in the 3D view, as shown in Figure 3.31.

FIGURE 3.31
The subregion is assigned a different material for visualization purposes.

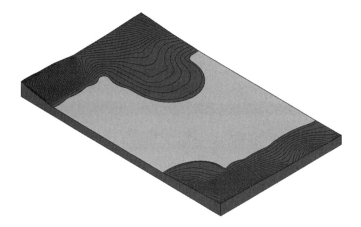

When you use the Subregion tool, the geometry of the original surface remains unchanged. If you no longer need the subregion, you can select it and delete it. Be aware that topographic surfaces cannot display surface patterns assigned to materials.

Using the Split Surface Tool

If you need to divide a topographic surface into separate parts for the purpose of editing the geometry, you can use the Split Surface tool. With this tool, you can sketch a single line along which the surface will be divided into two editable entities. These separate entities can be recombined later using the Merge Surfaces tool. In the following exercise, you will split a topographic surface and edit some of the points. Remember that you can also use Split Surface to delete a portion of a topographic surface. Here are the steps:

1. Open the file c03-Site-Tools.rvt you saved earlier.

2. Activate the Site plan in the Project Browser.

3. Go to the Massing & Site tab in the ribbon and click the Split Surface tool. Remember that you should use the Subregion tool if you plan to only assign a different material to the split region of the original surface.

4. Select the topographic surface and you will enter Sketch mode. Using the Line mode in the Draw panel of the contextual ribbon, draw two lines that overlap the edges of the surface, as shown in Figure 3.32.

FIGURE 3.32
Sketch lines that overlap the edge of the topographic surface

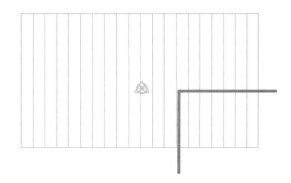

5. Click Finish Edit Mode in the ribbon and you will see the split surface highlighted in blue.

6. Activate the Default 3D view and turn off the Section Box option in the Properties palette.

7. Select the split surface and click the Edit Surface tool in the Modify | Topography tab of the ribbon.

8. Select the point at the outer corner of the topographic surface and change the elevation value in the Options bar from 20'-0" [6000 mm] to 10'-0" [3000 mm].

9. Click Finish Surface in the contextual ribbon and you will see the result shown in Figure 3.33.

FIGURE 3.33
A split region after editing the elevation of a corner point

10. To illustrate the difference between a split surface and other topographic surface edits, select the main surface and click Edit Surface in the contextual ribbon. Select the point at the upper corner opposite from the split region and change the elevation value to 10'-0" [3000 mm]. Notice the difference in how the surface slope is interpolated between the other points on the surface (Figure 3.34).

FIGURE 3.34
Compare the difference between an edited split region (left) and an edited point directly on the surface (right).

Creating a Building Pad

A *building pad* in Revit terminology is a unique model element that resembles a floor. It can have a thickness and compound structure, it is associated with a level, and it can be sloped using slope arrows while you're sketching its boundary. The building pad is different from a floor because it will automatically cut through a toposurface, defining the outline for your building's cellar or basement.

The process to create a building pad is virtually identical to that of creating a floor. Let's run through a quick exercise to create a building pad in a sample project:

1. Open the file c03-Site-Pad.rvt, which can be downloaded from this book's web page.

2. Activate the floor plan named Site in the Project Browser. You will see an existing topographic surface and property line. Notice that reference planes were created to demarcate the required zoning setbacks from the property line. Foundation walls have been created within these reference planes.

Note that you don't have to create a property line and walls before creating a building pad. You might create a building pad before any other building elements. Just realize that you can utilize the Pick Walls mode to associate the boundary of the building pad with the foundation walls.

3. Activate the Cellar floor plan from the Project Browser.

4. Go to the Massing & Site tab in the ribbon and click the Building Pad button. In the Properties palette, change the Height Offset From Level value to 0.

5. Switch to Pick Walls mode in the Draw panel of the contextual ribbon, and then pick the inside edges of the four foundation walls. You can use the Tab-select method to place all four lines at once.

6. Click the Finish Edit Mode button in the contextual ribbon to complete the sketch and then double-click the section head in the plan view to examine your results. Notice that the top of the building pad is at the Cellar level and the pochè of the topographic surface has been removed in the space of the cellar (Figure 3.35).

FIGURE 3.35
This section view illustrates how the building pad adjusts the extents of the topographic surface.

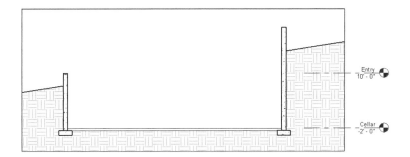

ADJUSTING THE SECTION POCHÉ FOR TOPOGRAPHIC SURFACES

If you would like to customize the settings for the fill pattern and depth of pochè, locate the small arrow at the bottom of the Model Site panel in the Massing & Site tab of the ribbon. Clicking it will open the Site Settings dialog box, shown here.

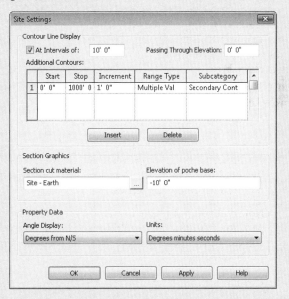

As you can see in this dialog box, you can change the Section Cut Material and the Elevation Of Poché Base settings. Note that the elevation value is in relation to the Revit project base point. You can also adjust the display format of contour lines shown on topographic surfaces, as well as the units displayed by property lines.

Generating Property Lines

Property lines are used to delineate the boundary of the lot within which your building will be constructed. These special types of lines are different from simple model lines or detail lines because they can be tagged with standard property line labels that will display segment lengths along with bearings. The property line object can also report its area in a special tag.

You can create a property line in one of two ways: by sketching lines or by entering distances and bearings in a table. In the following exercise, you will create a simple property line by sketching and converting the sketched property line into a table of distances and bearings for comparison:

1. Start a new project using either the `Default.rte` or `MetricDefault.rte` template file and activate the Site plan in the Project Browser. If you're selecting from the New Project dialog box, choose Architectural Template.

2. Go to the Massing & Site tab and click the Property Line button. When prompted by the Create Property Line dialog box, choose Create By Sketching.

3. Switch to the Rectangle tool in the Draw panel of the contextual ribbon and draw a rectangle measuring 120' × 70' [36 m × 21 m].

4. Click the Finish Edit Mode button in the contextual ribbon to complete the sketch.

5. With the property line still selected, click the Edit Table button in the Modify | Property Lines tab of the ribbon. You will be prompted with a warning that you cannot return to Sketch mode once the property line has been converted to a table of distances and bearings. Click Yes to continue.

6. You will now see each vertex of the property line expressed as a distance and a NE bearing, as shown in Figure 3.36.

FIGURE 3.36
A property line can be defined in a table of distances and bearings.

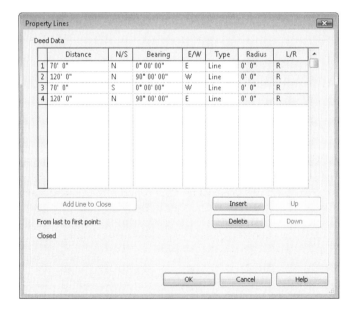

Tagging Property Lines with Area

In standard construction documentation, it is customary to annotate each vertex of a property line with its distance and bearing. There are two different types of tags you can use to annotate property lines. In the following exercise, you will load these two types from the Revit default library and tag each segment of the property line, as well as display the area contained within it.

1. Go to the Insert tab of the ribbon and click the Load Family button. Navigate to the Revit default library; double-click the `Annotations` folder and then the `Civil` folder.

2. Locate the following files and select them both by pressing the Ctrl key (the equivalent Metric library families are shown in parentheses):

    ◆ `Property Line Tag.rfa` (M_Property Line Tag.rfa)

    ◆ `Property Tag - SF.rfa` (M_Property Tag.rfa)

3. Click Open to load both families.

4. Go to the Annotate tab of the ribbon and click Tag By Category, and then uncheck the Leader option in the Options bar.

5. Click on each segment of the property line to place the tags indicating the distance and bearing, as shown in Figure 3.37.

FIGURE 3.37
Tags are applied to display the distance and bearing of each segment of the property line.

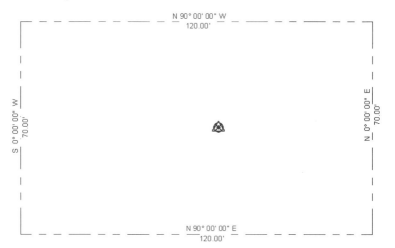

Now that you have tagged the individual vertices of the property line, it is time to display the area within the property line. This process is not the same as applying an area tag because an area object doesn't exist for the property line. Instead, the annotation family `Property Tag - SF.rfa` (M_Property Tag.rfa) is designed to apply to the property lines when all its segments are selected.

You can try this with the property line you created earlier. Go back to the Annotate tab in the ribbon and click Tag By Category. Instead of picking a single vertex of the property line, hover your mouse pointer over one segment and use Tab-select to highlight the entire chain of property line segments. Click to place the property area tag. Click the question mark above the area to change the name of the property line, as shown in Figure 3.38.

FIGURE 3.38
Use Tab-select to place a property area tag for all segments.

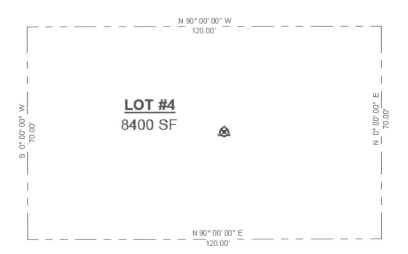

Cut and Fill Schedules

As we mentioned earlier, Revit site tools are not meant to replace civil engineering software programs. We have shown you how to create a topographical surface in a variety of ways as well as some methods of modifying these objects. There is also a way to quickly quantify how much earth is displaced by proposed changes to existing topography. This is commonly referred to as a cut/fill schedule.

One easy way to demonstrate the use of a cut/fill schedule is through the creation of a building pad that automatically modifies the topographic surface. Let's go through a quick exercise to examine this process:

1. Open the file c03-Site-Cut-Fill.rvt, which can be downloaded from this book's web page.

   In this file, notice that the topographic surface has been assigned to the Existing phase.

2. From the View tab in the ribbon, click Schedules and then select Schedules/Quantities to open the Edit Schedule dialog box.

3. From the Category list, choose Topography and then click OK.

4. In the Fields tab of the Schedule Properties dialog box, choose Name, Projected Area, and Net Cut/Fill, clicking Add after each one.

5. Activate the Cellar plan from the Project Browser and create a building pad in the same way you created one earlier in this section.

   After you complete the creation of the building pad and the topographic surface is modified, notice that the Net Cut/Fill values in the topography schedule still have a value of 0. This is because the Graded Region tool must be used on a surface to generate the differences required to calculate what volume must be cut versus filled in the proposed design.

6. Tile the open Revit windows so you can see both the Default 3D view and the topography schedule.

7. From the Massing & Site tab, click the Graded Region tool and then select the topographic surface. When the Edit Graded Region dialog box appears, choose the option Create A New Toposurface Exactly Like The Existing One. This effectively creates overlapping existing and proposed surfaces, which will allow the software to schedule the differences between the two.

8. When you select the surface, you will see the volume values in the topography schedule update to reflect how the excavation for the building pad affected the overall soil. Note that this type of calculation does not account for various construction methods, such as backfilling.

Try selecting the building pad and changing the Height Offset From Level value. Observe how the Net Cut/Fill values change as the pad helps define the scope of excavation on the site.

You can also make the topography schedule easier to read by assigning descriptive information to each topographic surface. Select the surface and enter a value in the Name field in the Properties palette. Change the name of the main surface to **Existing Grade** and then locate the surface where the building pad is. Change its name to **Pad Area** and observe the topography schedule once again.

The Bottom Line

Select, modify, and replace elements.   There are many fundamental interactions supported by Revit software to select just what you need and to modify elements efficiently.

Master It   How can you quickly select only the door tags in a plan view and switch them to another type?

Edit elements interactively.   The editing tools in Revit are similar to those found in other CAD and BIM software programs. Tools such as Move, Copy, and Trim are available on the Modify tab of the ribbon.

Master It   How do you create a parametric repetition of an element?

Use other editing tools.   Beyond the basic editing tools are more advanced commands to help you consistently and intelligently populate a building model with content.

Master It   How do you copy model elements in the same location for a multistory building?

Creating site context for your Revit project.   The site tools allow you to create context for your building models, including topographic surfaces, graded regions, and property lines.

Master It   Describe the different methods used to create a topographic surface.

Part 2

Understanding the Workflow

In Part 1, you became familiar with the Autodesk® Revit® Architecture user interface and editing tools. Now we'll take a look at what makes a Revit project tick. Part 2 sets you on the path toward using Revit software on a team or throughout your firm.

- ◆ **Chapter 4: Configuring Templates and Standards**
- ◆ **Chapter 5: Managing a Project**
- ◆ **Chapter 6: Understanding Worksharing**
- ◆ **Chapter 7: Working with Consultants**
- ◆ **Chapter 8: Interoperability: Working Multiplatform**

Configuring Templates and Standards

In this chapter we discuss how to configure and manage graphic standards through the development and use of a project template. Such templates can be rich with information that goes beyond the out-of-the-box content provided by Autodesk. We will present proven methods for establishing template settings and content as well as explain how the reuse of work will increase productivity with each successive project.

In this chapter, you'll learn to:

◆ Define settings for graphic quality and consistency

◆ Organize views for maximum efficiency

◆ Create custom annotation families

◆ Start a project with a custom template

◆ Develop a template management strategy

Introducing Project Templates

Like many other applications, the Autodesk® Revit® Architecture application allows you to start with a basic template and then evolve your own custom templates to suit specific needs. As your knowledge of the software progresses, you'll begin to create new and reusable content such as wall types, roof types, ceilings, stairs, tags, and other families in order to meet your design and documentation needs. This is also the case with regard to the graphical language that you or your firm has established and needs to implement within Revit. How you graphically present elements such as text, dimensions, annotations, keynotes, and hatch patterns defines your graphic style of design documentation. In reality, the architectural profession tends to develop stylized graphics to convey design intent, and Revit respects this by enabling the customization of almost all aspects of the project template.

Revit project templates are configured by one or more of the following methods:

◆ Defining all project settings to meet graphic requirements

◆ Preloading model and annotation families

◆ Defining standard system families

We'll explain these methods in greater detail throughout this chapter. For now, know that you can save the completed settings as a new project template (with the filename extension .rte) and use these templates whenever you start a new project. You can create templates by using a completely blank project, by saving an existing project as a template, or by using one of the default templates provided with the Revit installation. To start from scratch, click the Application menu and choose New ⯈ Project. In the New Project dialog box, shown in Figure 4.1, choose None for the Template file option, and choose Project template for the Create new option. Once you click OK, you'll be asked to choose a default unit of measurement—imperial or metric. Note that this dialog box does *not* appear when you press Ctrl+N or click New in the Recent Files window.

Starting a new project template without a base template requires you to develop *all* common content such as levels, grids, sections, callouts, tags, and model elements. If you have only custom graphics and system families, this approach would be appropriate; however, if much of your graphic style is similar to the defaults, we suggest you start with one of the default templates and edit it as necessary. You can find these templates by clicking Browse in the Template File area of the New Project dialog box. By default, the template files are installed in the root folder of the templates directory: C:\Documents and Settings\All Users\Application Data\Autodesk\RAC 2012\Imperial Templates.

FIGURE 4.1
Starting a new project template from scratch

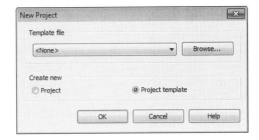

Customizing Project Settings for Graphic Quality

One of the most common complaints from teams implementing Revit software on their first projects is poor graphic quality of printed documents. When you first install the software, only some default settings are defined to approximate a standard graphic appearance of architectural drawings. For example, walls cut in sections are thicker than those shown in projected views and callout boundaries are dashed; however, all annotation categories are set to a line weight of 1. Fortunately, you can easily overcome these problems with some basic configuration.

Object Styles

The primary means of controlling graphic consistency throughout a project is through *object styles*. To access these settings, switch to the Manage tab and choose Object Styles from the Settings panel. As shown in Figure 4.2, the dialog box is divided into four tabs: Model Objects, Annotation Objects, Analytical Model Objects, and Imported Objects. Settings for Line Weight, Line Color, Line Pattern, and Material are established for each category.

FIGURE 4.2
The Object Styles dialog box gives you graphic control of all Revit categories and their subcategories.

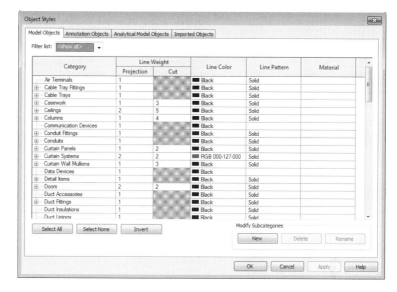

Model Objects The Category column on the Model Objects tab lists all available categories and subcategories of model elements. It is important to note that the subcategories for model and annotation objects are created in families, which are loaded into the project or template. This will be discussed in greater detail in Chapter 15, "Family Editor."

The next two columns, under Line Weight, define the line weight used when the elements are displayed in projection or cut modes. In some categories, the Cut setting is unavailable; these element categories will never be cut in plan or section views, regardless of the location of the view's cut plane. For categories that enable Cut display, element geometry in the Family Editor can be set to follow that rule or not, as shown in Figure 4.3.

FIGURE 4.3
Customizing the cut display of geometry in a family

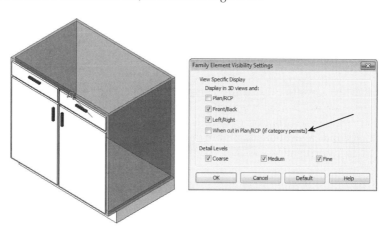

Line Color and Line Pattern allow you to customize the display properties of each category and subcategory, but remember that printing a Revit view is WYSIWYG (what you see is what you get)—colors will print as colors unless you override them to print as grayscale or black in the Print Setup dialog box. The last column, Material, allows you to define a default material to be associated with the category or subcategory in case family components in that category don't have materials explicitly defined. If a family has materials set to By Category, it references the material set in Object Styles.

Annotation Objects   The Annotation Objects tab is similar to the Model Objects tab except there are no material definitions. There is also only one column for line weight (Projection) because lines do not have three-dimensional properties like model objects and cannot be "cut."

Analytical Model Objects   This tab allows you to color the various physical conditions in the building that correspond to the building's structural components.

Category	Line Weight		Line Color
	Projection	Cut	
⊞ Analytical Beams	4		▓ RGB 255-128-064
⊞ Analytical Braces	4		▓ RGB 210-210-000
⊞ Analytical Columns	4		░ Cyan
Analytical Floors	4		▓ RGB 128-064-000
Analytical Foundation Slabs	4		▓ RGB 128-064-000
Analytical Isolated Foundations	4		░ RGB 128-255-000
⊞ Analytical Nodes	1		■ Black
Analytical Wall Foundations	4		▓ RGB 255-106-000
Analytical Walls	4		▓ RGB 000-128-000
Boundary Conditions	1		■ Black
⊞ Structural Load Cases	1		■ Black

Imported Objects   You can control the graphic appearance of layers (DWG) and levels (DGN) within linked or imported CAD files throughout the project on the Imported Objects tab of the Object Styles dialog box; however, we will cover this in greater detail in Chapter 8, "Interoperability: Working Multiplatform."

ASSIGNING LINE WEIGHT 1

You may want to avoid assigning line weight 1 to objects because this is the weight used by most fill patterns. Reserving its use will help object profiles stand out compared to their patterns.

Line Settings

You can use lines in a variety of ways. Some lines relate to obvious tools, such as detail lines and model lines, whereas you can place others with filled regions and by using the Linework tool. Lines also relate to the graphic representation of model and annotation elements, as previously discussed. Achieving the desired graphic quality requires a review of Revit line weights, patterns, and styles.

SETTING LINE WEIGHTS

To open the Revit line weight settings, click the Manage tab and choose the Additional Settings flyout from the Settings panel. Click the Line Weights button ▤ Line Weights on this menu. The dialog box shown in Figure 4.4 manages the printed line weights relative to a numbered assignment from 1 to 16. For model objects, heavier line weights vary between view scales. If you require more granular control between scales, click the Add button to insert another scale value column and edit the line weights as required.

FIGURE 4.4
Model line weights vary depending on the view scale.

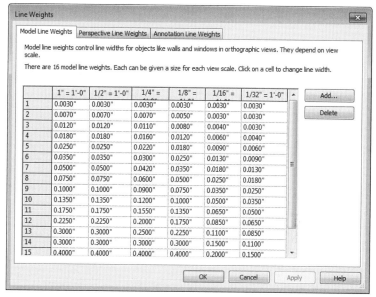

We recommend that you first customize the graphic appearance of model and annotation elements with object styles before trying to manipulate any of the information in this dialog box. You should attempt to refine the line weight settings only with a rigorous investigation of printed views in multiple scales because changes in one area can have an impact on several others.

SETTING LINE PATTERNS

Line patterns are created from a repetitive series of line segments, spaces, and points. To edit or create line patterns, switch to the Manage tab and choose Additional Settings ➢ Line Patterns. The Line Patterns dialog box, shown in Figure 4.5, displays a list of existing line patterns in the project.

FIGURE 4.5
This dialog box displays all line patterns in the project.

To edit an existing pattern, click the Edit button, or click New to create your own. You create patterns by specifying dash and space lengths, which will form a repeating sequence, as shown in Figure 4.6. For dots, a length value isn't required.

FIGURE 4.6
Line patterns consist of dashes, spaces, and dots.

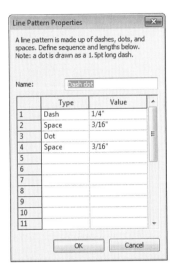

USE CAUTION WHEN DELETING LINE PATTERNS

Before deleting a line pattern from the Line Patterns menu located in the Additional Settings panel on the Manage tab, you must verify that it hasn't been used anywhere in your project. You can do so only by manually checking Object Styles, Line Styles, and Visibility/Graphic Overrides. If you fail to do so, all line styles using the deleted pattern will be assigned as Solid.

Frequently, a line pattern is required to include a symbol or text for elements such as fence lines, piping, or underground utilities. In Autodesk® AutoCAD® MEP software, shape definitions could be used within linetype definitions to achieve the desired results. These special lines can be created as line-based detail components. A sample of this type of custom line can be found by downloading the file c04-Lines.rvt from this book's companion web page at www.sybex.com/go/masteringrevit2013.

CREATING A NEW LINE PATTERN

Follow these steps to create a new simple line pattern:

1. Switch to the Manage tab and choose Additional Settings ➢ Line Patterns.

2. In the Line Pattern dialog box, click New.

3. Give the new line pattern a name.

4. Define the sequence, as shown here.

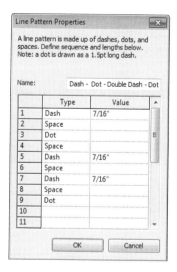

5. Confirm by clicking OK.

The resulting line pattern looks like this.

SETTING LINE STYLES

Now that we have discussed the basic components of lines—color, weight, and pattern—the three are combined to create *line styles* for use in detail lines, model lines, filled regions, and masking regions. They are also available when the Linework tool is used to override a part of a model element. You will find the button that opens the Line Styles dialog box (shown in Figure 4.7) on the Manage tab under Additional Settings.

FIGURE 4.7
Line styles consist of weight, color, and pattern.

Category	Line Weight Projection	Line Color	Line Pattern
Lines	1	RGB 000-166-000	
<Area Boundary>	6	Magenta	
<Beyond>	1	Black	Solid
<Centerline>	1	Black	Center
<Demolished>	1	Black	Demolished
<Hidden>	1	Black	Hidden
<Overhead>	1	Black	Overhead
<Room Separation>	1	Black	
<Sketch>	3	Magenta	
<Space Separation>	1	Black	
Axis of Rotation	6	Blue	Center
Hidden Lines	1	RGB 000-166-000	Dash
Insulation Batting Lines	1	Black	Solid
Lines	1	RGB 000-166-000	
Medium Lines	2	RGB 000-000-127	
Thin Lines	2	Black	
Wide Lines	2	Blue	

In the Line Styles dialog box, notice that some of the style names are bracketed—for example, <Hidden>. These are internal, "system" types of lines that cannot be renamed or deleted; however, their weight, color, and pattern can be modified.

USE CAUTION WHEN DELETING LINE STYLES

If you delete a line style used in a project, any elements utilizing the deleted style will be unable to reference that style anymore. The lines assigned to the deleted style will be reassigned to a common style such as Thin Lines—possibly producing undesirable results.

Establishing the best styles for your templates will be completely up to you, but we will offer some proven examples for inspiration. First, realize that the application already uses common line styles such as Thin Lines, Medium Lines, and Wide Lines. If you are creating a complete array of customized line styles for your colleagues to use, rename the common styles to fit into your graphic standard.

One common approach is to create line styles organized by their weight number along with any variable to their appearance, such as (3) Gray Dashed. Note that the parentheses (or the use of any special characters at the beginning of the line's name) keep your custom line styles sorted to the top of the list in the Line Styles dialog box as well as in the Type Selector when you're using a line-based tool. This approach has proven to be effective and efficient when creating details in drafting views or generating fill or masking regions.

Another approach reserves certain line styles for special circumstances where lines represent aspects of a building in a plan, elevation, or section and must be assigned to a specific layer when views are exported in CAD format. For example, the crossing lines typically used to indicate an area in plan that is "Open to Below" may need to be assigned to the CAD layer "A-FLOR-BELW." This is difficult if you used a line style based solely on weight and pattern such as (2) Dashed. You cannot separately assign that line style to A-FLOR-BELW for the floor plan export and A-DETL-THIN for all other exports. Here are some examples of line styles you could create:

- Open to Below
- ADA Circles
- Curbs
- Fire Rating

In summary, take care to understand the different settings when you are beginning to customize graphic settings for lines in the Revit template. To change the displayed weight of an element in a project, changes should not be made in Line Weights but rather through the Object Styles dialog box. For example, if you want to increase the cut line weight of a wall already set to (5), do not increase the value of (5) in the Line Weight dialog box. You would change this value by selecting (6) or (7) as the cut weight of a wall in the Object Styles dialog box.

Materials

CERT OBJECTIVE

Defining materials in your project template is another important task that can help maintain graphic consistency in many other areas. Materials drive the graphic representation of elements, not just in a rendered view, but also in hidden line, 2D or 3D views. They are also responsible for cleanups because materials can merge with one another when elements of the same material are joined. A material can define how an element is annotated within the model and how an element's surface looks in shaded views, when cut in plan or section, and when seen in 3D views. In Figure 4.8, the surface patterns are all derived from the material used in the element.

FIGURE 4.8
Materials define the surface and cut patterns, color, and render material of the elements.

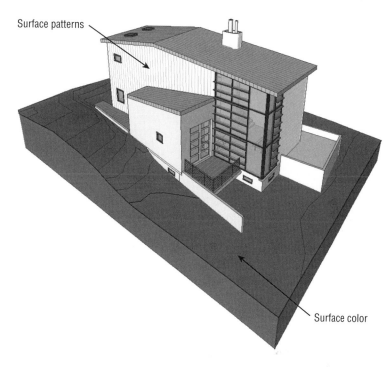

Surface patterns

Surface color

To access the Material Editor (Figure 4.9), switch to the Manage tab and choose Materials on the Settings panel. Right-click on the material name to access (A) basic editing commands such as Duplicate, Rename, and Delete. At the upper right (B) is a search bar for quickly locating specific materials in the project, and all material properties are found at the right side (C) of the dialog box.

MATERIAL PROPERTIES

Double-click the material name to open the Material Editor. The material properties are divided into five different values: Identity, Graphics, Appearance, Physical, and Thermal.

Identity Defines schedule values and keynotes for materials. Specifying correct identity data for your standard or typical materials will increase efficiency when you're using annotation such as material tags as well as facilitate quality management by aligning model data such as manufacturer, model, and mark with your project specifications. In Figure 4.10, some sample identity data have been entered. Notice how the Material Class field can be customized to group project materials. Keywords can be entered for use with the Search bar and cost data have been entered for use in a Material Takeoff schedule. The use of material identity data in project annotation and detailing is discussed in greater detail in Chapter 19, "Annotating Your Design."

FIGURE 4.9
Manage material
properties using the
Material Editor.

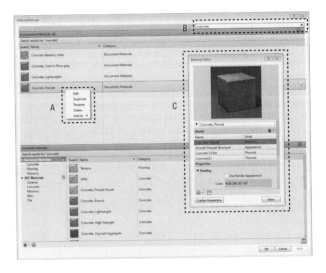

FIGURE 4.10
Use identity data
to classify, find,
tag, and schedule
materials.

Graphics   Defines shading color, surface patterns, and cut patterns:

Shading   Defines the color and transparency of a material when the view is set to Shaded, Shaded With Edges, or Consistent Colors display mode. Note that the color can be dependent on the material's render appearance. If the Shading option is selected, the color and transparency are adopted from the Render Appearance settings and the shading controls will be disabled.

Surface Pattern   Allows the selection of a *model pattern* to be displayed on the faces of elements in elevation, plan, and 3D views. Note that a material's surface pattern does not appear in rendered views; a pattern can be defined in the Render Appearance tab.

Cut Pattern   Allows the selection of a drafting pattern to be displayed when an element is cut in a model view. Some elements can't be cut, as discussed earlier in this chapter; in these cases, this setting has no effect on the graphic display and the pattern will not be displayed.

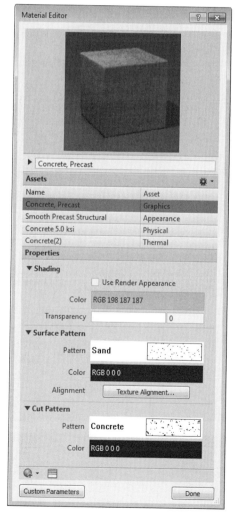

Appearance Defines rendering attributes. Click the Render Appearance tab to view render properties. These properties will become visible only when you render a view and will not affect construction documentation graphics.

Physical Defines physical properties of a material for analysis.

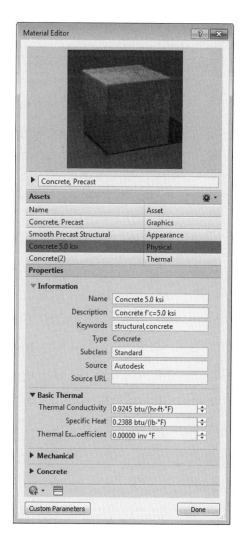

Thermal   Defines thermal properties of a material for analysis.

MATERIAL STRATEGIES

It may seem impossible to imagine all the materials you'll need in a project, making building a template seem daunting. Think of the basic materials you're likely to use—wood, brick, concrete, glass, and so on—and build from those. Remember, a template is just a starting point, and you can always expand it. If you end up making a lot of nice materials over the course of a project, use the Transfer Project Standards function to move materials back into your templates.

When you start to organize materials by name, there are many prevailing theories too numerous to list here, but here are a few suggestions:

By type Each material is prefixed with a descriptor such as *Metal*, *Paint*, *Carpet*, *Wood*, and so on.

By use Each material is prefixed with a description of its application, such as *Cladding*, *Interior*, *Exterior*, *Site*, and so on.

Alphabetical Materials have no prefixes.

By CSI division Each material is prefixed with a MasterFormat numerical descriptor corresponding to its specification section.

By mark Each material is prefixed with the designation of its Mark annotation parameter (for example, WD01-Wood-Cherry).

CREATING A SIMPLE EXTERIOR GLAZING MATERIAL

In the early phases of design, you may want to keep the level of detail to a minimum. In fact, guidelines for modeling levels of development may be established as part of a BIM execution plan (see AIA E202 BIM Protocol Exhibit at www.aiacontractdocuments.org/bim or the model progression specification at www.ipd-ca.net). To simplify the creation of exterior enclosures such as a curtain wall, try creating a glass material with a surface pattern approximating the layout dimensions of a curtain wall system (such as 5″×12″). Then create a generic wall type using this material, and you will have a much lighter wall type to explore design options with great ease.

Fill Patterns

Materials are often represented with simple hatch patterns. For any material used, you can define a *surface pattern* and a *cut pattern*. For simple parallel hatches and crosshatches, you can use the patterns already supplied or you can make your own patterns.

For more complex patterns, you need to import an external pattern file (with the filename extension .pat). Such pattern definitions can be imported from pattern files used by AutoCAD—a process we explain later in this chapter. To create, modify, or view an available fill pattern, switch to the Manage tab and choose Additional Settings ➤ Fill Patterns (see Figure 4.11). On the left side of the Fill Patterns dialog box, you can view the names and small graphic previews of the patterns. Below those are the Pattern Type options, where you choose what type of patterns to create and specify what type of pattern you wish to edit (Drafting or Model).

FIGURE 4.11
Fill patterns are defined separately for drafting and model representations.

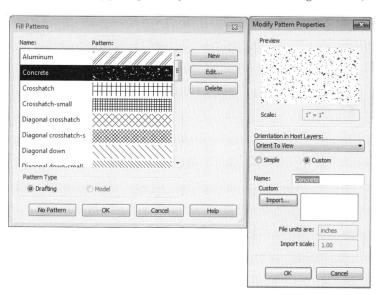

Model patterns are used to convey real-world dimensional patterns to represent a material, whereas *drafting patterns* are intended for symbolic representations. For example, a model pattern is used to show a brick pattern in 3D and elevation views, whereas a brick drafting pattern is used to represent the material in plan and section. Figure 4.12 shows how concrete masonry units (CMUs) are represented with a running bond pattern (model) as well as a crosshatch (drafting).

FIGURE 4.12
The CMU wall has both a drafting pattern (cut) and a model pattern (surface) defined.

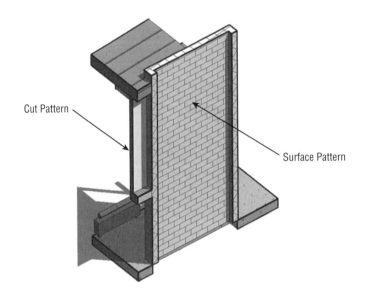

Cut Pattern

Surface Pattern

Model and drafting patterns have specific behaviors. In this example, you have a CMU wall with blocks that measure 16" × 8" [400 mm × 200 mm], regardless of the view scale. With a drafting pattern, the opposite is true: The pattern adjusts with the view scale, so the pattern looks identical in all scales.

CREATING A NEW DRAFTING PATTERN

To create a new pattern, first choose either Model or Drafting, and then click the New button. A generic pattern appears in the New Pattern dialog box. You can then design your pattern and assign behaviors.

The option Orientation In Host Layers is particularly useful when you're making drafting patterns. This option allows you to specify how a pattern orients itself relative to host elements such as walls, floors, roofs, and ceilings when they're represented as cut. Note that the option isn't available for model pattern types. As shown in Figure 4.13, the orientation options are Orient To View, Keep Readable, and Align With Element.

FIGURE 4.13
From left to right: Orient To View, Keep Readable, and Align With Element

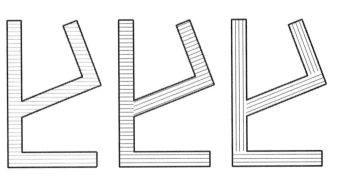

Orient To View When this orientation is applied, the patterns used in the project all have the same orientation and the same origin. They're always perfectly aligned with the origin of the view.

Keep Readable   This orientation will maintain alignment with the view (i.e., horizontal lines will remain horizontal) but will be adjusted relative to angled host elements.

Align With Element   This orientation ensures that the pattern orientation depends on the orientation of the host element. Patterns essentially run parallel with the element.

You can choose to make either simple or custom patterns with this dialog box, using the radio button options. Figure 4.14 illustrates some examples of each option:

FIGURE 4.14
From left to right: simple fill pattern, simple fill pattern with the crosshatch option selected, and a custom fill pattern

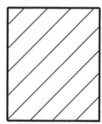

Simple   These patterns are generated with parallel or crosshatch lines that can have different angles and spacing. With both the crosshatch and parallel options, you can specify only one angle for the entire pattern. Using crosshatch, you can set two spacing values.

Custom   To create a more complex custom pattern, you have to import a pattern (PAT) file from an external source. This is often necessary because of the current limitation in creating natively complex patterns. Your office may have a set of established patterns that have been used for years, and the Custom option allows you to import and reuse them without having to make them again from scratch. Custom patterns let you import a PAT file from anywhere on your hard drive or on a network and use it as a base pattern for a new fill pattern. The next section shows best practices for importing a PAT file.

CREATING A CUSTOM COMPLEX PATTERN

Custom patterns require an external file that contains the definition of the pattern. The filename extension of that pattern should be .pat, which is what you'll make in this exercise by editing an existing AutoCAD PAT file. An advantage of specifying patterns in the template file is that the PAT file won't need to be installed on each computer where the application is installed; patterns are stored internally in each template or project.

Before modifying PAT files, always make a copy of the original PAT file you intend to use as a base; you don't want to risk messing up other files that might already be using that original PAT file. PAT files can be edited with Notepad, but any text-editing application will also do. For this exercise, you'll choose the AutoCAD pattern called Grass, which you can find in acadiso.PAT (in metric units) or acad.pat (imperial units) located on this book's web page.

IMPORTING A CUSTOM PATTERN

Follow these steps to make a custom fill pattern by importing an existing pattern definition:

1. Using Notepad, open the file acadiso.PAT or acad.PAT.

2. Highlight the lines that define the pattern, and select them:

```
45, 6.35, 0, 4.49013, 4.49013, 1.5875, -5.80526, 1.5875, -8.98026
*GRASS, turfed surface
```

```
90, 0, 0, 17.9605, 17.9605, 4.7625, -31.1585
45, 0, 0, 0, 25.4, 4.7625, -20.6375
135, 0, 0, 0, 25.4, 4.7625, -20.6375
*GRATE, grid
0, 0, 0, 0, 0.79375
```

3. Choose Edit ➢ Copy.

4. Open a new text file, and paste the selection. (You can also open the PAT file located in `C:\Program Files\Autodesk\Revit Architecture 2012\Data`, in which all Revit patterns are already saved. In that case, you can paste the selected text in that file.)

5. This is the important part: In the new text file where you pasted the selected text, add the two lines shown boldfaced here:

```
;%UNITS=MM
*GRASS, turfed surface
;%TYPE=DRAFTING
90, 0, 0, 17.9605, 17.9605, 4.7625, -31.1585
45, 0, 0, 0, 25.4, 4.7625, -20.6375
135, 0, 0, 0, 25.4, 4.7625, -20.6375
```

The first line that you write before the pattern text, `;%UNITS=MM`, can appear only once in the text file. It defines the value for the units used in the pattern. In the example, the units are millimeters (MM); if you wanted to work in imperial units, it would be `;%UNITS=INCH`. (If you use the option in step 4 to collect all patterns in the master PAT file, then this line already exists and you don't need to add it.)

The second statement, `;%TYPE=DRAFTING`, helps define whether you're creating a drafting or model pattern. In this example, the pattern is the Drafting type.

6. Save your text file with a `.pat` filename extension.

7. On the Manage tab, choose Additional Settings ➢ Fill Patterns.

8. In the Fill Patterns dialog box, verify that the Drafting option is selected, and click New.

9. In the New Pattern dialog box, select the Custom option. The lower part of the dialog box offers new options.

10. Click Import.

IMPORTING PAT FILES

It's important to know that when you import a new pattern, the type of pattern needs to be the same as the new type of pattern you're making. In other words, if you're making a new model pattern, you can't import a drafting pattern. If you try to do so, you'll see a warning message like the one shown here:

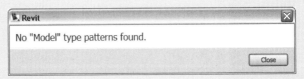

11. Navigate to the place on your hard drive or network where you saved the PAT file, and click Open.

12. In the list that appears to the right of this button, you can see the name of the pattern you created: GRASS, as shown in Figure 4.15. (If you have a PAT file with many patterns defined, you see all the other drafting patterns available in that list.) The name of the pattern automatically becomes the name of your fill pattern, but you can change that if you like.

FIGURE 4.15
The New Pattern dialog box displays the imported PAT file in the Custom group.

13. If necessary, you can adjust the scales of the imported pattern. The Preview window displays the graphic of the pattern, always in 1:1 scale. This informs you if you need to scale the pattern up or down. You'll know that you need to scale the pattern if the preview appears as a solid black box—that means the pattern is too dense.

14. If you're happy with the result, confirm by clicking OK.

Color Schemes

The use of color schemes in project documentation will be covered in greater detail in Chapter 20, "Presenting Your Design"; however, for now, just know that you can preconfigure them in project templates for a variety of scenarios. For example, an architect may perform many projects for a single client who utilizes the same department names in all of its program design requirements. The architect would like to ensure that an identical color scheme is used in the colored plans in all projects for this client. In the following steps, you will create a new color fill legend with some predefined department values and associated colors to be saved in a custom project template:

1. On the Annotate tab, go to the Color Fill panel and select the Color Fill Legend tool.

2. Place a legend in any available floor plan view and you will see the Choose Space Type And Color Scheme dialog box, shown in Figure 4.16. Set Space Type to Rooms and Color Scheme to Department. (These choices can be modified later.)

FIGURE 4.16
Select criteria for assigning a color scheme to a view.

Edit
Scheme

3. Select the color fill legend you placed in the previous step and find the Edit Scheme icon at the right end of the ribbon. The Edit Color Scheme dialog box, shown in Figure 4.17, will appear.

FIGURE 4.17
Edit color schemes to add predefined values, colors, and fill patterns.

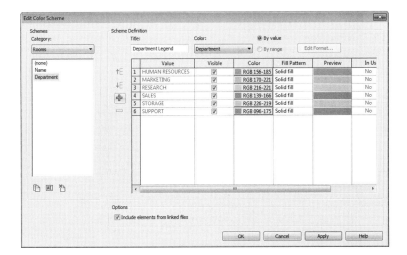

4. As shown in Figure 4.17, click the Add Value icon to populate the list of departments in the Scheme Definition area. Choose colors and fill patterns according to your graphic requirements.

5. Click OK to close the dialog box.

6. Open the floor plan, Level 1 and use the Wall tool to create some walls that are bound on all sides (so you can drop room elements into them). Now, from the Architecture tab, choose the Room button and add rooms to the plan. You won't want to let these remain in the template, but it will help to better visualize the color schemes if you can see them collocated.

7. When rooms are placed, you can either type values for departments that match the pre-defined values in the color scheme or select the values in the element properties of the room, as shown in Figure 4.18.

FIGURE 4.18
Select from pre-defined values in the Properties dialog box of a room.

As shown in Figure 4.19, the department values utilized in every project started with your project template will have the same colors and fill patterns according to those specified in the original color scheme. You also have a predefined list of your client's department names.

FIGURE 4.19
Color-filled plans can utilize pre-defined values in templates.

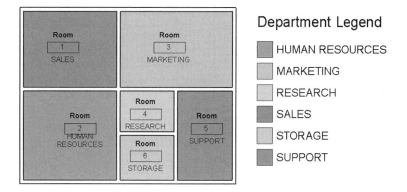

You can download the sample file c04-AreaPlans.rvt from this book's web page.

Efficient View Management

Once you've customized the settings for graphic quality, you can use several other tools and techniques to increase efficiency and ensure that your visual standards are applied consistently throughout your projects. The properties of all views can be used to your advantage in creating a browser organization that meets the needs of your teams. You can apply filters to views for generating graphic overrides based on model element parameters. You can manage and deploy these settings and more in view templates that can be applied to many views simultaneously.

Organizing Views

Maintaining a clear and consistent organization of views within a Revit project can generate measurable increases in project productivity. Especially in larger projects, a Revit file can have more than 1,000 views, which can easily cause confusion and wasted time if the right view cannot be found in the Project Browser when needed. The default project template contains a few simple browser organization types that can be copied and/or customized—except for the type named All. To access these settings, switch to the View ribbon, find the Windows panel, click the User Interface drop-down button, and select Browser Organization, as shown in Figure 4.20.

FIGURE 4.20
Accessing browser organization settings in the ribbon

Select any one of the listed types in the Browser Organization dialog box and click the Edit button. Remember, you can't edit or delete the type named All.

In the Browser Organization Properties dialog box (Figure 4.21), there are two tabs called Folders and Filter. Folders allow you to group views together based on selected view parameters, whereas the Filter tab will give you the opportunity to display only views that pass selected criteria.

FIGURE 4.21
Use view parameters to create folders in the Project Browser.

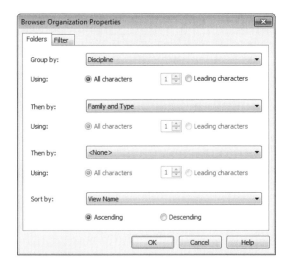

Choose the Folders tab to specify up to three levels of "folders" to be shown in the Project Browser. Here are some examples:

♦ Family and Type, Discipline, Scale

♦ Phase, Discipline, Family, and Type

♦ Detail Level, Family, and Type

To further organize the views in your project, you can create additional parameters and assign them to views and sheets. The following is one example of adding custom text parameters to views for more refined organization:

1. On the Manage tab, find the Settings panel, and click Project Parameters.

2. In the Project Parameters dialog box, click Add.

3. In the Parameter Properties dialog box, create a parameter named **Custom View Type**; for Type Of Parameter, specify Text. Select the Instance option; then find and check the Views category, as shown in Figure 4.22.

FIGURE 4.22
Create custom project parameters for additional view organization options.

4. Repeat steps 2 and 3 and create another text parameter named **Custom View Sub-Type** assigned to the Views category. Remember to set the Type Of Parameter option to Text.

5. Click OK to close the window.

6. Return to the Browser Organization dialog box and click New. Name the new type **Custom Type/Sub-Type**, and click OK.

7. Set the following values on the Folders tab in the Browser Organization Properties dialog box:

   ◆ Group By: Custom View Type

   ◆ Then By: Custom View Sub-Type

8. Check the box to make this view setting current and click OK to close the open dialog box. The Project Browser is now ready to support the use of the custom view parameters you created earlier.

It is now up to you to assign values to the custom view parameters created in the previous exercise. These values can be assigned directly to the view properties in the Properties palette or by adding them to view templates. Views that do not have values for these parameters will be found under the folders listed as ??? (three question marks). Figure 4.23 illustrates this scenario in which plans and elevations have been assigned to the Custom View Type and Custom View Sub-Type parameters, but the 3D view was not.

FIGURE 4.23

Customized browser organizations can make larger projects easier to navigate.

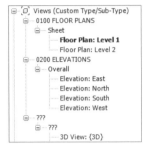

Creating and Assigning Filters

Filters are another view configuration and customization tool that can be developed and deployed in Revit project templates. They are similar to the filters available in schedules in that they can either display or hide elements matching user-specified criteria. But view filters can also override the graphic appearance of such elements affected by them. The possible combination and application of view filters is virtually limitless, so let's take a look at a few real-world examples.

First, we'll review the steps to create and assign a view filter. The fundamental steps are as follows:

1. Create a named filter.

2. Assign it to object categories.

3. Assign data criteria.

4. Add to the Visibility/Graphic settings of a view.

5. Define graphic overrides.

In the following example, you will create view filters to identify fire-rated walls with different colors. You can download the sample file c04-Sample-Building.rvt from this book's web page. Here are the steps:

1. Open the file c04-Sample-Building.rvt. Switch to the View tab, find the Graphics panel, and click Filters.

2. Add a new named filter by clicking the New icon at the bottom of the Filters zone at the left side of the dialog box. Name the first new filter **Walls-Fire 1** and click OK.

3. Find Walls in the center zone and check the category.

4. In the Filter Rules zone at the right side, define the criterion to filter by Fire Rating Equals 1 HR.

5. Click Apply. With the Walls-Fire 1 filter still selected, click the Duplicate icon twice and Walls-Fire 2 and Walls-Fire 3 should be created.

6. Select Walls-Fire 2 and change the value in Filter Rules to **2 HR**.

7. Select Walls-Fire 3 and change the value in Filter Rules to **3 HR**, as shown in Figure 4.24.

FIGURE 4.24
Filter rules applied to walls for fire ratings

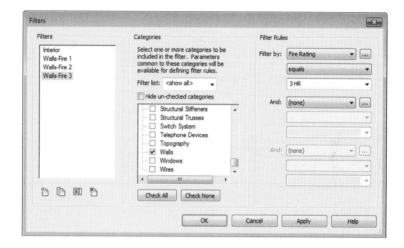

8. Click OK to close the window.

9. Activate the Level 1 floor plan, open the Visibility/Graphic settings, and select the Filters tab.

10. Click the Add button, select all three Walls-Fire filters, and click OK.

11. Click the Override button in each filter row under Cut-Lines and change the line color as follows:

♦ Walls-Fire 1 = Green

♦ Walls-Fire 2 = Yellow

♦ Walls-Fire 3 = Red

12. Click OK to close the Visibility/Graphic Overrides dialog box.

With the filters now applied to the floor plan, walls that have been assigned a fire rating value will appear with the color overrides you had assigned to the respective filters. You can create more filters to define graphic styles for specific model elements such as furniture by owner, interior walls, secure doors, or equipment not in contract.

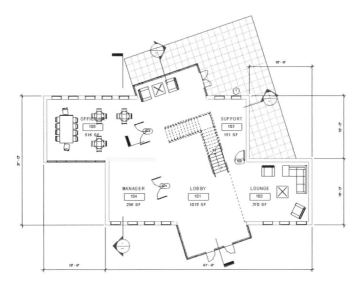

Applying View Templates

After you have defined your desired settings in as many view types as possible, you can use view templates to manage these settings and apply them to other views of the same type. They will be described in greater detail in Chapter 18, "Documenting Your Design," but we will discuss their importance to the project template in this section. Let's begin by opening the View Templates tool:

1. On the View tab, find the Graphics panel and select View Templates ➢ View Template Settings .

2. In the View Templates dialog box (Figure 4.25), you will find icons to duplicate, rename, or delete view templates below the list on the left. On the right are the view properties that can be applied when the view template is applied to a view.

3. Notice the column named Include. This column allows you to include or exclude various view properties when you're applying the view template. In Figure 4.25, notice that View Scale and Detail Level are not included. This would allow you to apply this template to plans of multiple scales and detail levels, while applying settings such as visibility of Object Styles, Phase Filter, and View Range. On a more granular level, you can also choose to include View Scale and Detail Level for more specific views that are replicated.

   Also notice in Figure 4.25 the two custom view parameters: Custom View Type and Custom View Sub-Type, which we described earlier in this chapter. These values can be applied with the view template, which will have the effect of cataloging the views in your standardized folders within the Project Browser.

4. Click OK to close the window.

FIGURE 4.25
View Templates
dialog box

FIGURE 4.25
View Templates
dialog box

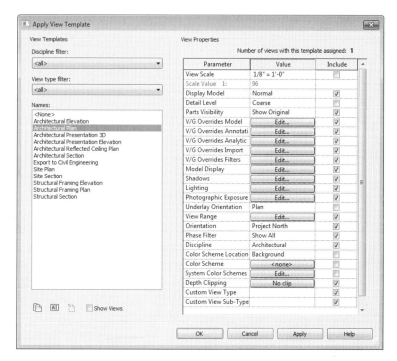

Changes to view templates are not automatically reflected in the views to which they have been applied; however, the software has a method for making these updates easy to maintain. When a view template is applied to a view for the first time, it becomes the default view template for that view. Subsequent view template applications will not change a view's default view template; rather, it can be changed only in the view properties.

When you apply a template as the Default view template, it is easy to update all views prior to publishing sheets. Simply select the sheets you are about to print or publish from the Project Browser, right-click, and select Apply Default View Template to All Views, as shown in Figure 4.26.

FIGURE 4.26
Reapplying default
templates to views
on sheets

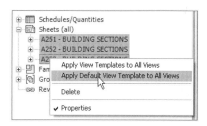

Including view templates in your project template will give your teams the ability to quickly apply your standard view settings. It will also support continued consistency as each building project grows in scope and size. Remember that view templates are easily shared between projects using the Transfer Project Standards tool, which we will discuss later in this chapter in the section "Strategies for Managing Templates."

Creating Custom Annotations

We are avid supporters of global graphic standards for architecture and engineering such as the US National CAD Standard (www.nationalcadstandard.org), but each architect or designer will likely have their own set of standards that will need to be implemented in their Revit projects. Placing customized annotation families in your project template will save time when you're starting new projects and ensure maximum compliance with your firm's standards. You can load tag families into the template using several methods:

◆ Switch to the Insert tab, and in the Load Library panel, select Load Family.

◆ Using Windows Explorer, select RFA tag families and drag them into the Revit project environment with the template open. If you try to drag more than one family at once, you are prompted to either open each of those files in an independent window (so you can modify them) or load them all in the current project. Choose the second option.

◆ Use the Loaded Tags tool available in the Annotate tab when you expand the Tag panel (Figure 4.27). This tool allows you to preview all loaded and preset tags that will be used for respective element categories.

FIGURE 4.27
The Tags dialog box shows loaded annotation families assigned to selected categories.

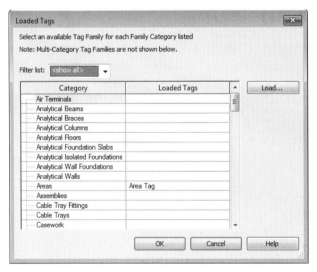

In the following sections, we'll walk you through creating some common element tags and customizing system annotation.

ARCHIVING AND MANAGING CUSTOM CONTENT

Many new users are unsure where to store custom-created families. It isn't advisable to save them in the system folders created during the installation of Revit because you may lose track of them or inadvertently delete them when you reinstall the software. Reinstalling the application erases just about any folder and its entire contents. It is thus advisable to keep your personally created content elsewhere, under a separate independent folder; if you are not a single user, store that folder on a shared network drive.

You should also keep your templates up-to-date as you add more content; that way, you only need to maintain a few template files rather than dozens of separate family files. It's even better if you can establish a template manager as a role within the office so everyone isn't making graphical changes to your templates.

Tag Family Fundamentals

Before you begin to customize annotation families or create your own, it is important to review the fundamental difference between text and labels:

Text   In the Family Editor, placing text in an annotation or title block means you're defining text that will always be the same and is unchangeable when that annotation is placed in the project environment. Figure 4.28 shows the words *AREA* and *VOLUME* as text. Regardless of where this room tag is placed, the text will always say AREA and VOLUME. Section tags work the same way: If you add static text, that text appears exactly the same for all section marks. This technique isn't typically used for sections because each section is a reference to a unique view, and you want that information to be dynamic and parametric. That's where label functionality comes into play.

FIGURE 4.28
A custom room tag showing room name, number, area, and volume

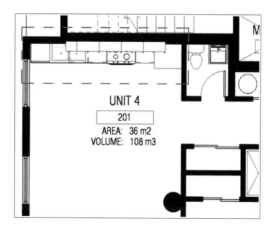

Labels Like static text, a label offers textual information; however, it's a live reference to a parameter value of an element in the project. For example, if you add an Area label, it will pull the value of the area of the room; if you add a Sheet Number label in a Section Head family in the Family Editor environment and then use that section head in a project, the label will automatically display the actual sheet number on which the section is placed in the project. If you move the section from one sheet to another, the label will automatically report the new sheet number.

In Figure 4.28, Unit 4 is a label of the room name; the number 201 is a label of the room number. The label behaves as dynamic text and is always fully coordinated with the value of the parameter it represents.

Creating a Custom Door Tag

FIGURE 4.29
Custom door tag
with parametric
label

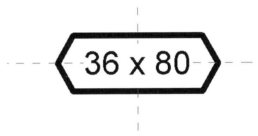

As an example of creating custom tags for a basic model element, use the following steps to create the custom door tag shown in Figure 4.29:

1. Click the Application menu, and select New ➤ Annotation Symbol.

2. In the Select Template File dialog box, select the family template called `Door Tag.rfa` or `M_Door Tag.rfa`, and click Open.

   The Family Editor opens in a view with two crossing reference planes, the intersection of which represents the origin of the tag. To avoid problems later, don't move these planes.

3. On the Create tab, find the Text panel and select Label. Click the intersection of the two planes to position the label.

4. In the Edit Label dialog box that opens, select Width from the column on the left, and click the Add Parameter To Label icon between the Category Parameters and Label Parameters fields, as shown in Figure 4.30. Then do the same for Height.

The Width and Height parameters will be concatenated in a single label, which will display the actual size of the door in the tag. In the subsequent steps, you will customize the display of the label.

FIGURE 4.30
Adding more than one parameter to a single label

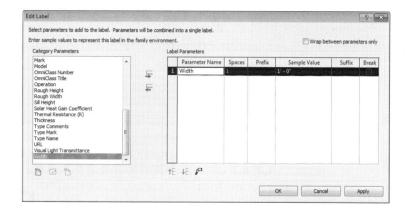

5. Add a space and the letter *x* in the Suffix column of the Width parameter and change the number in the Sample Value column to 36 [in] or 1000 [mm]. Change the sample value of the Height parameter to 80 [in] or 2000 [mm].

6. With the Width row selected, click the Edit Parameter's Units Format icon. In the Format dialog box, uncheck the Use Project Settings option and set the following:

   ♦ Units: Decimal Inches or Millimeters

   ♦ Rounding: 0 decimal places

   ♦ Unit Symbol: None

7. Repeat the previous step for the Height parameter.

8. Click OK in all open dialog boxes.

9. On the Home tab, activate the Masking Region tool and sketch a six-sided polygon, as shown in Figure 4.29.

   Remember to finish the sketch by clicking the green check in the Mode panel.

10. Save your tag and load it into your project template. Make sure that it is specified as the default tag for doors in the Tags dialog box and use the Tag By Category or Tag All Not Tagged tool or place new doors with the Tag On Placement option. Using concatenated parameters in tag labels allows a great deal of flexibility while utilizing actual parametric values. In this example (Figure 4.31), the actual width and height parameters driving the door size become the text displayed in the tag.

FIGURE 4.31
The custom tags
applied to doors
comprise actual
door sizes.

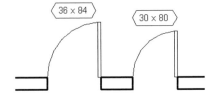

SET SOME DEFAULTS

To aid the users of your custom templates, take some time to establish default values for common elements, such as doors, windows, rooms, grids, sheets, and levels. Create one of each element and change the Mark value to a number just below the value at which you'd like your users to begin. Unfortunately, this approach does not work for letters because nothing comes before *A*.

View Tags

Section, callout, and elevation tags are graphic indicators that reference (link to) other views in your project. The graphics for these elements can be customized to meet most scenarios. To create a custom section tag, for example, you have to first create a custom section tag family and load it into a template or project. You must then associate it with a section tag system family type, which is then assigned to a section type. Switch to the Manage tab, and choose Additional Settings ➤ Section Tags; you will see the application of separate section head and tail families in a section tag system family type, as shown in Figure 4.32.

FIGURE 4.32
Section tag system
family properties

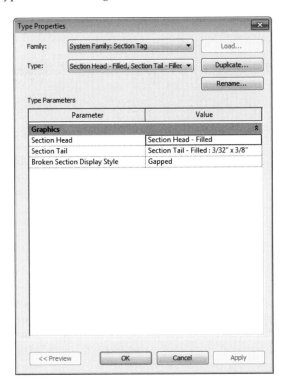

In simple terms, view tags are organized in the following hierarchy:

◆ System Family: Section

    ◆ System Family: Section Tag

    ◆ Annotation Family: Section Tag/Tail

By default, there is a predefined view tag for each view type. The graphics can vary depending on the language version of Revit you have installed on your machine. The tags shown in Figure 4.33 are displayed and available by default in the US English version.

FIGURE 4.33
Samples of graphic content as supplied by Autodesk

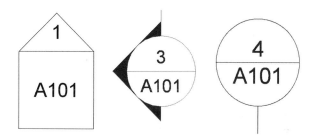

CREATING A CUSTOM SECTION TAG

In the next exercise, you will create a section tag that looks like the one shown in Figure 4.34. You'll first need to create a section tag family using the Family Editor before loading the section tag family into the template.

FIGURE 4.34
Custom section tag

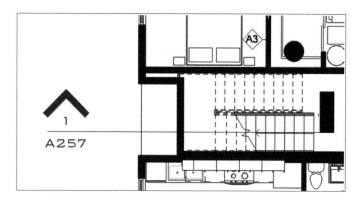

To begin, follow these steps:

1. Click the Application menu, and select New ➤ Annotation Symbol.

2. In the Open dialog box, select the family template called `Section Head.rft` or `M_ Section Head.rft`, and click Open.

3. The Family Editor environment automatically opens, and the drawing area shows a view in which three green reference planes (two vertical and one horizontal) have already been drawn. Do *not* change the position of either the horizontal reference plane or the vertical reference on the right. In some templates, this is indicated with help text in red (which you can later remove).

The intersection of horizontal and right reference planes defines the connection location with the section line. This means your annotation will be located in between the two intersections points.

A proposed geometric shape is drawn for the annotation: a circle (two arcs) and a horizontal line. You're free to delete this default geometry and create your own tag shape. The default shape is there to help you visually understand where to begin drawing your new tag geometry.

4. Select the arcs that create the circle (use the Ctrl key for faster selection), and delete them.

5. On the Home tab of the Text panel, click the Label button. Position your cursor between the two vertical reference planes and below the horizontal plane, and click to position the start of the label.

6. In the Edit Label dialog box, select Sheet Number. Click the Add Parameter(s) To Label button. In the Sample Value column, you can enter a value; the default is A101.

The label is placed and displays blue grips when selected. These let you change the length of the label text field. The length is important because any value that is added (in a project) that is longer than the length of this box will begin to wrap and could cause undesirable results.

7. Following the same principle, place the label Detail Number above the horizontal reference but still between the vertical references, as shown in Figure 4.35.

FIGURE 4.35
Place labels for
Detail Number and
Sheet Number.

8. You can reposition a label by selecting it and using the Move button to move it around. For more precise positioning, use the arrow keys on your keyboard to nudge elements in small increments. You can also help yourself by zooming in for a better view. (Note that zooming in refines the increment for the nudge tools.)

9. On the Detail panel of the Home tab, click the Filled Region button. You'll be put into Sketch mode. Using the Line tool, draw the shape shown in Figure 4.36. In the Region Properties dialog box, check that Color is set to Black and Cut Fill Pattern is set to Solid Fill. Make sure the lines form a closed loop (no gaps or overlapping lines).

FIGURE 4.36
Draw the outline of the filled region to form the section arrow.

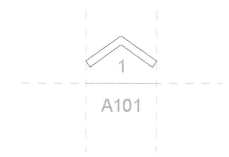

10. Click Finish on the Mode panel of the Modify | Create Filled Region Boundary tab.

11. Save the tag you just created as `Custom Arrow.rfa` on your hard drive or network and you're ready to use it in the template or a project. To load it into your project, click the Load Into Projects button located in the Family Editor panel. Choose the project in which you want to use the symbol, and click OK.

Next, you'll assign this tag to a section mark system family type in the context of a project or template.

CREATING A SECTION TYPE WITH A CUSTOM HEAD/TAIL GRAPHIC

To create a section type that utilizes the section head family you created previously, you need to load the created section head in the template file (if you've already loaded the custom arrow family in the previous exercise, skip to step 3):

1. If the family isn't already loaded, switch to the Insert tab, and on the Load From Library panel, choose Load Family.

2. In the Load Family dialog box, find the `Custom Arrow.rfa` section head you created previously, select it, and click Open.

3. Switch to the Manage tab and select Additional Settings ➢ Section Tags.

4. In the Type Properties dialog box, click Duplicate.

5. In the Name dialog box, name the new type **Custom Filled Arrow,** and click OK.

6. In the section head's Type Properties dialog box, click the drop-down menu for Section Head and select Custom Arrow. For Section Tail, click <none>. This means the other end of the section line will not use a symbol. Click OK.

   The final step is to create a customized section type, which will utilize the new section tag type you created in the previous step.

7. Switch to the View tab, and on the Create panel, select Section.

8. On the Properties tab, select the Edit Type button.

9. In the Type Properties dialog box, select Duplicate.

10. Name the new type **Custom Arrow - No Tail**, and click OK.

11. Once your new tag is created, there's one more step to apply it to the section marker. Highlight the section marker and choose Type Properties from the Properties palette. Here you can use the drop-down menu to change the default arrow to the one you just created.

You can now place a section in your drawing area and see the results shown in Figure 4.37.

FIGURE 4.37
Custom section mark after the section is placed on a sheet

The custom section tag exercise can also be applied to the creation of custom callouts, as shown in Figure 4.38.

FIGURE 4.38
Custom callout annotation (left); custom callout annotation associated with callout boundary (right)

CREATING A CUSTOM ELEVATION TAG

Now you can create custom elevation tags. You are no longer limited to either a circle or square tag. Here's how it works:

1. Click the Application button, and select New ➢ Annotation Symbol.

2. In the Open dialog box, select the family template called `Elevation Mark Body.rft` or `M_Elevation Mark Body.rft`, and click Open.

3. Using steps similar to those in the section tag exercise, place the Sheet Number label and draw lines as shown in Figure 4.39.

FIGURE 4.39
Define the custom line work and sheet number for the elevation mark body.

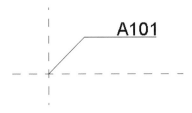

4. Make sure the properties Keep Readable and Fixed Rotation are checked for the label.

5. Save the family as **Custom Elev Head.rfa**.

6. Click the Application menu, and select New ➤ Annotation Symbol.

7. In the Open dialog box, select the family template called `Elevation Mark Pointer.rft` or `M_Elevation Mark Pointer.rft`, and click Open.

8. Using methods similar to those in previous steps, place labels for the Detail Number and Reference Label parameters. Draw a diamond with lines and a small triangular-filled region, as shown in Figure 4.40.

FIGURE 4.40
Custom elevation pointer composed of lines, filled region, and labels

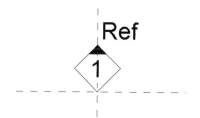

9. Again, remember to make sure the properties Keep Readable and Fixed Rotation are checked for the labels.

10. Save the family as **Custom Elev Pointer.rfa** and load it into the `Custom Elev Head.rfa` family.

11. Place four instances of the Custom Elev Pointer family around the intersection of the visible reference planes, as shown in Figure 4.41.

FIGURE 4.41
The nested pointer family is placed four times in the head family.

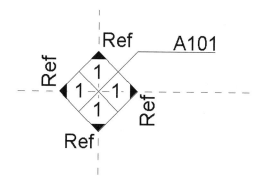

When this custom elevation tag family is loaded into a project and associated with an elevation type, it will function much like standard elevation symbols.

After the views are placed on a sheet, you get a preview of the completed elevation symbol, as shown in Figure 4.42.

FIGURE 4.42
A customized eleva-
tion tag for interior
elevations

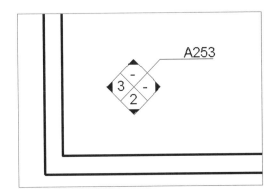

Starting a Project with a Custom Template

Now that we have covered many areas of customization within project templates, you can configure Revit to use your new template. To do so, follow these steps:

1. Click the Application menu, and at the bottom of the menu click Options.

2. In the Options dialog box, select the File Locations tab. The first option in the dialog box
   lists the default template location.

3. Click the Browse button to choose a new path to your default template file (see
   Figure 4.43).

FIGURE 4.43
Change the path
to your default
template.

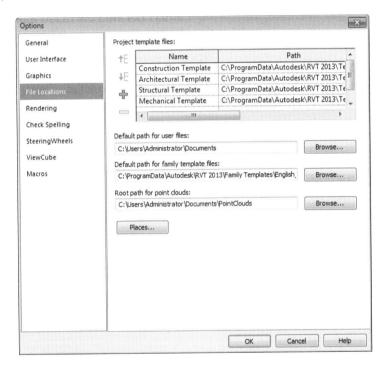

Strategies for Managing Templates

During implementation, you can take one of two approaches when managing project templates: additive or subtractive. An *additive* approach, as shown in Figure 4.44, assumes that more than one project template will be developed to manage standards and content for a single project. Typically, a "base" template is used to start a project with a minimum amount of settings, whereas content and settings from "supplemental" templates are appended based on region, project type, or project style. In this scenario, each template file is lighter, but managing the templates becomes more difficult because changes in common settings or families must be applied to all templates.

FIGURE 4.44
Additive template approach

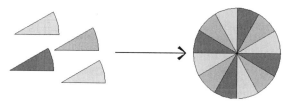

In contrast, the *subtractive* approach, shown in Figure 4.45, uses a single master template that contains all standard settings and content and relies on the project teams to remove and purge unused content. Although these templates tend to be heavier, graphic settings are easier to manage within a single file.

FIGURE 4.45
Subtractive template approach

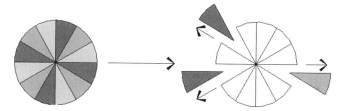

Aggregating Template Data

Whether you are managing the settings between templates or developing a project with multiple templates in an additive approach, you have useful tools to help share data between projects, such as Transfer Project Standards, Insert Views From File, and Insert 2D Elements From File.

TRANSFERRING PROJECT STANDARDS

You can easily share Revit families between project files by loading their RFA files; however, most other types of content can be transferred with the Transfer Project Standards command. Types of elements commonly transferred with this command include, but are not limited to, the following:

- Materials
- System family types (Walls, Floors, Roofs, and so on)
- Text and dimension styles
- Grid and level types
- Line styles and patterns
- Object style settings
- Viewport types

Real World Scenario

USING PROJECT TEMPLATES TO REDUCE REDUNDANT WORK

Based on a survey conducted by Robert Manna for an Autodesk University class, the majority of responders indicated that they develop two to five project templates primarily to differentiate between project types and/or market sectors. For example, if you work for an architectural firm that is usually contracted to perform work on large transportation sector projects, you might need to create a Revit file just to manage the site data for every project.

In that case, you would use a specific template as a site project template. Within such a template, you could use the following settings to reduce the amount of redundant work every time different teams attempt to establish a site model to which other building models are linked:

♦   Name levels Sea Level and First Floor Reference.

♦   Set default view scales to larger sizes.

♦   Change default project units to reflect civil engineering.

♦   Add a Cut/Fill schedule.

♦   Create dimension types useful for large drawings.

♦   Pad types including "gravel."

More information on template management, including results of the survey, can be found on Robert Manna's website at http://revit.krarchdesign.net. His Autodesk University content can be found at http://au.autodesk.com.

Transfer
Project Standards

To use this command, you must first have both the source and target Revit files open (or the source file linked into your target file); then make the target file the active project. Switch to the Manage tab, and select Transfer Project Standards on the Settings panel. In the Select Items To Copy dialog box (Figure 4.46), choose as many item categories as you'd like to transfer, and then click OK.

FIGURE 4.46
Select categories
to be transferred
between projects.

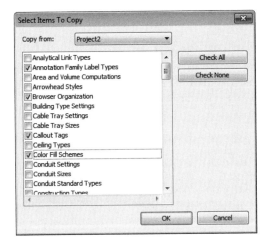

If you choose an element category containing some of the same types that already exist in your current project, you will be prompted with the option to overwrite the existing types or import the new types only (New Only), as shown in Figure 4.47.

FIGURE 4.47
Transferring project standards with duplicate types

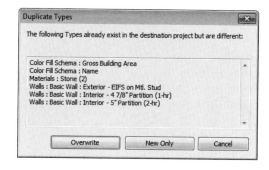

INSERTING VIEWS FROM A FILE

The Insert Views From File command is useful for sharing drafting views of standard or typical details with other Revit project files. It can also insert entire sheets with all attached drafting views and associated properties. You can use the Insert Views From File command with the following view types:

◆ Drafting views

◆ Sheets

◆ Schedules

Switch to the Insert tab, and choose Insert From File ➤ Insert Views From File in the Import panel.

Browse to a Revit project file (with the filename extension .rvt), and you will see the Insert Views dialog box (Figure 4.48). In the left pane, all eligible drafting views, sheets, and schedules will be listed. If necessary, use the drop-down list above to filter the choices.

If one or more sheets are selected in the Insert Views dialog box, all eligible drafting views placed on those sheets will be inserted into the current project as well. Note that repeating this process will not update the drafting views in the project but instead will create new renamed drafting views and sheets. Also note that any custom view parameters are maintained during the transfer and can fit right into your customized Project Browser organizations, as we discussed earlier in this chapter.

INSERTING 2D ELEMENTS FROM A FILE

Similar to Insert Views From File, the Insert 2D Elements From File command imports the 2D elements of the selected view as a detail group into the active view in the current project instead of the entire view. For best results, make sure you have a drafting view active before using this command. On the Insert tab, find the Import panel, choose Insert From File ➤ Insert 2D Elements From File, and then navigate to a project file.

FIGURE 4.48
Insert Views can
be used to transfer
an entire sheet of
drafting views into
your project.

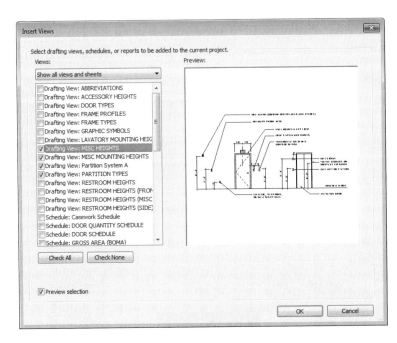

Choose one of the available drafting views in the Insert 2D Elements dialog box (Figure 4.49).

FIGURE 4.49
Insert 2D Elements
dialog box

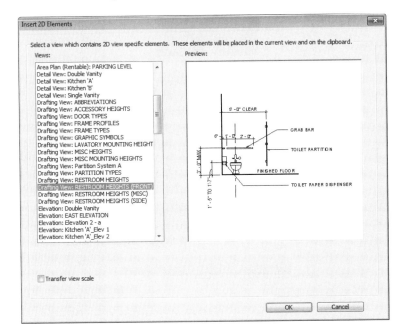

For consistency, be sure to select the Transfer view scale option to convert the scale of the active drafting view to that of the view you are inserting. You can move the elements into position using the Move command, and after placing the 2D elements, be sure to click Finish in the Edit Pasted panel or double-click anywhere outside the elements to complete the command.

DUPLICATE TYPES WHEN INSERTING

When using Insert Views From File or Insert 2D Elements From File, be sure to watch for warnings about duplicate types being renamed, as shown here. You may be able to use the Purge Unused tool to remove any renamed styles; however, some types may need to be manually modified.

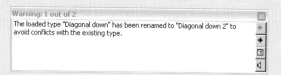

If duplicated types cannot be removed with Purge Unused, you will need to swap the duplicated types with the originals. Find the duplicated family types in the Project Browser, right-click on the duplicate type, and choose Select All Instances. Doing so selects all instances of that type throughout the entire project. Open the Properties palette and select a different type. You will then be able to remove the duplicated type with Purge Unused or by right-clicking on it in the Project Browser and choosing Delete. Note that the Select All Instances method does not work on line styles.

The Bottom Line

Define settings for graphic quality and consistency.   The fundamental building blocks for any template are the customized settings to object styles, line styles, fill patterns, materials, and more.

Master It   How can a complex custom fill pattern be imported?

Organize views for maximum efficiency.   The project template can be used to capture a framework supporting your visual and organizational standards.

Master It   How can you customize the Project Browser to support your business needs?

Create custom annotation families.   Developing a graphic style to match your standards will usually require you to edit some annotation families or create them from scratch.

Master It   Can a single label display more than one parameter? How are custom view tags loaded into a project?

Start a project with a custom template.   Making your custom template available for new projects ensures that all future projects will maintain the same level of graphic quality and efficiency you expect.

Master It   How do you set your own custom project template to be the default for new projects?

Develop a template management strategy.   Organizing your standards, content, and settings while using Revit tools to transfer content will make your effort more efficient.

Master It   How do you insert your standard details from one Revit project to another? How do you transfer settings such as materials?

Chapter 5

Managing a Project

Understanding Autodesk® Revit® Architecture software and how to use it is not a difficult challenge. The real challenge in understanding Revit and BIM is determining how it changes your organization's culture and your project's workflow. Revit software gives you more than just a different way to draw a line. In this chapter, we'll focus on what those changes are and provide some tools, tips, and tricks on how to manage the changes.

In this chapter, you'll learn to:

◆ Understand a BIM workflow

◆ Staff a BIM project

◆ Work in a large team

◆ Perform quality control on your Revit model

Understanding a BIM Workflow

Regardless of the design and production workflow you have established in the past, moving to BIM is going to be a change. In Chapter 1, "Introduction: The Basics of BIM," we discussed some of those changes and tried to help define your place in the process of managing that change. Regardless of where you fall on the adoption curve, you'll still need some tools to help transition from your current workflow to one using Revit software. To begin, we'll cover some of the core differences between a CAD-based system and a BIM-based one.

Moving to BIM is a shift in how designers and contractors approach the design and documentation process throughout the entire life cycle of the project, from concept to occupancy. In a traditional CAD-based workflow, represented in Figure 5.1, each view is drawn separately with no inherent relationship between drawings. In this type of production environment, the team creates plans, sections, elevations, schedules, and perspectives, and must coordinate any changes between files manually.

In a BIM-based workflow, the team creates a 3-D, parametric model and uses this model to automatically generate the drawings necessary for documentation. Plans, sections, elevations, schedules, and perspectives are all by-products of creating an embellished BIM model, as shown in Figure 5.2. This enhanced documentation methodology not only allows for a highly coordinated drawing set, but also provides the basic model geometry necessary for analysis, such as daylighting studies, energy, material takeoffs, and so on.

FIGURE 5.1
A CAD-based
workflow

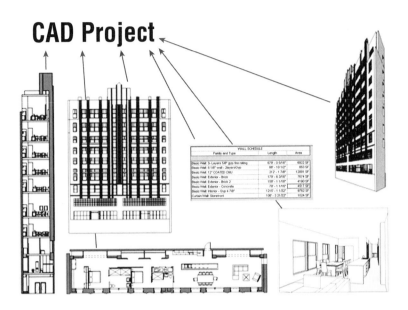

FIGURE 5.2
A BIM workflow

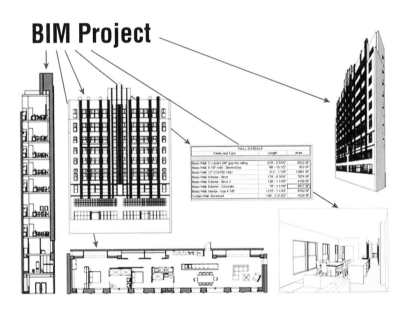

Using BIM becomes more than a change in software; it becomes a change in workflow and methodology. To better address the impacts and nuances of this change in process, let's look at the existing paradigm. A traditional design and documentation workflow can be diagrammatically expressed, as shown in Figure 5.3.

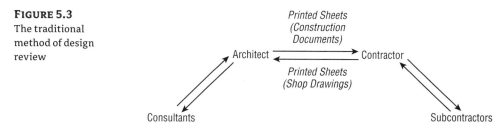

Design is a cyclical process and one of continual refinement. As you share ideas and coordinate information with the entire project team, you can make adjustments to your own portion of the project. A standard architectural project might go something like this:

1. The architect draws a building design and shares this information with consultants.

2. Various consultants, working separately, will reuse parts of the architect's drawings to create a new series of their own drawings specific to their discipline.

3. The consultant's drawings will be shared with the architect, who will need to use them to further coordinate their own work. Portions that affect the architectural drawings, such as building structure or mechanical ductwork, are in large part redrawn within the architectural set.

4. At a certain point in the project process, all of the drawings (typically in printed form only) are shared with a contractor or builder. The contractor disseminates the drawings to various subcontractors who will need to utilize their specialties to embellish the information in the original drawings.

5. The contractor will create new sets of drawings with added detail related to the execution of the work but all based on the original set of documents.

With all of these separate teams making their own sets of drawings, a system of checks and balances is needed to ensure that the information is communicated accurately and effectively. In our traditional model shown earlier, the subcontractors will send their drawings back to the contractor to verify the work. The contractor will create multiple copies of the drawings (based on the number of parties needed to review) and pass them to the architect. The architect will review their own set while giving the other copies to various consultants to do the same. All these changes will be manually transcribed to one set before being sent back to the contractor to be passed back to subcontractors for further revisions and clarifications.

This entire chain of manual information sharing has many opportunities for communication errors. Much of the information is redundantly reproduced as a way of error checking, which can just as easily create its own errors. If you can utilize the advantages inherent in a BIM-based method (Figure 5.4), you can eliminate many of the redundant efforts, improve communication, and focus more time on improving the design and expediting construction.

FIGURE 5.4

An integrated
approach to design
review

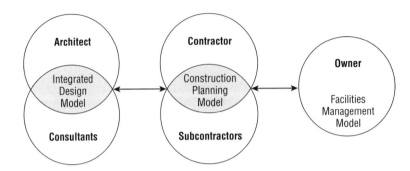

In an ideal BIM-based system, the following occurs:

1. The architect and consultants would work together on a single building model. This might be one model or a model consisting of interconnected parts.

2. After this model reaches a stage of refinement, it is passed on to the contractor and building team to further embellish with information specific to their trades and expertise.

3. As they construct the physical building, the BIM model can be adjusted to reflect the changes that happen in the field.

4. The revised model can then be shared with the owner and facilities operator. The model can contain the necessary product information about the systems installed to aid the owner's facility operator in maintaining the building. The model can also be used for future personnel moves or even building additions.

As various design specialists interact and create the building model (Figure 5.5), you can see how structure, mechanics, energy, daylight, and other factors inform design direction. You can also draw relationships between some of these elements that might not have been as obvious in a more traditional approach. Although some of these specialties (such as structure and mechanics) are historically separate systems, by integrating them into a single design model, you can see how they interact in relation to other systems with a building. Analysis, such as daylighting, can inform your building orientation and structure. Depending on your glazing, it can also affect your mechanical requirements (as solar gain). You can see some of these effects through a computational fluid dynamics (CFD) model (used to calculate airflow). Geographic information system (GIS) data will give you your relative location globally and allow you to see how much sunlight you will be receiving or what the local temperature swings will be during the course of a day. As you can see, all of these variables can easily affect building design.

As with any methodological change, you'll have success if you address all the factors. Project success happens on more than a financial or chronological level. It is also determined by a team's ability to replicate successful results. A difficult aspect of transitioning to BIM is predictability. Any system or method, even if it is inherently inefficient, is at some level successful if the system is predictable. If you can say that x effort + y time will yield z result, there is an established comfort level with that system even if it is an inefficient system. When you move to BIM, the system automatically becomes unpredictable because team members need to experience the new system to establish a comfort level with the given results. No longer does x effort + y time yield z; instead, the result is unknown.

FIGURE 5.5
The integrated
design model

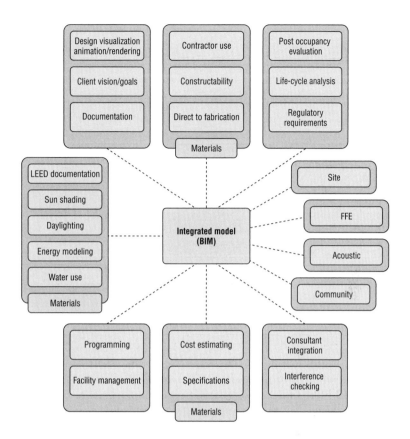

Eventually, you reach a point of temporary diminishing returns. The amount of effort you need to put into understanding the new process feels like it has begun to exceed the value you derive from the change, and happiness plateaus or slightly declines. At a point during this plateau, you're put in a position where you need to perform a task in a given amount of time using the new technology. It might be represented by needing to get a schematic-level design sent out to a contractor or create something as simple as a stair. Regardless, the process is a foreign one and by its nature is unpredictable in time. You'll be faced with a decision to forge ahead using an unpredictable method or revert to a more familiar yet inefficient process.

Here your path can split. By regressing to your previous process, you'll enjoy an immediate increase in happiness with the familiarity and predictability of the former method, but this will only level out and never reach any greater heights than it did before you contemplated the initial change. If you stay the course with the new process, happiness will decrease (and frustration increase) as you struggle with the change. However, as the new method eventually becomes more predictable and comfortable, your happiness can achieve greater value.

Although this might be an oversimplification of a process change, the core meaning is critical. Change can be challenging; however, to realize greater goals and adapt to an ever-changing environment, both professionally and globally, you will need to rethink your process in order to achieve success. Moving to BIM is acknowledging a change in workflow and process — from abstraction to virtualization (Figure 5.6). As you transition from a traditional workflow to a BIM-based one, keep in mind the change in culture. It will help you manage expectations, time, and team members' stress levels.

FIGURE 5.6

From abstraction to virtualization

Staffing for BIM

As you rethink the process of design and documentation, one of the fundamental changes you will need to address is staffing. A common misconception of project management when teams are first moving from CAD to BIM is that staffing the project will be the same in both workflows. This couldn't be further from the truth. When the workflow changes, staffing allocations, the time to complete tasks, and the percentage of work by phase are all affected as a result of the changes.

Several years ago, Patrick MacLeamy, FAIA, set out to illustrate the fundamental benefit to more informed design that happened to be a byproduct of building information modeling. The graph, which has come to be known as the MacLeamy Curve (Figure 5.7), is not intended to imply a simple shift in labor earlier in the design process; rather, it stresses the importance of being able to make higher-value decisions before it becomes too difficult to make changes to a design. The x-axis of the chart represents project phases from conceptual design through occupancy, whereas the y-axis represents the amount of effort in each phase.

Another way to think about this shift is as a diagram of leverage, as shown in Figure 5.8. Implementing BIM in earlier phases of a project gives you the greatest opportunity to add value to the overall compilation of building information delivered for a facility. When you begin BIM earlier, you may need to increase staff to build a better model or to perform energy analysis or preliminary quantity takeoffs; however, using a better tool like Revit software will not necessarily translate to the same labor used in a CAD-based project. You will find how this affects your team effort after a few BIM projects.

FIGURE 5.7
Staffing in BIM

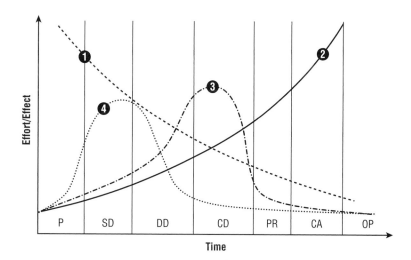

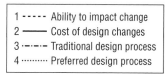

	Ability to impact change
1 - - - -	Ability to impact change
2 ———	Cost of design changes
3 ·—·—·	Traditional design process
4 ·········	Preferred design process

FIGURE 5.8
BIM provides the most leverage when it is implemented earlier in the design.
Source: Based on a graphic created by Lee Miller, HOK

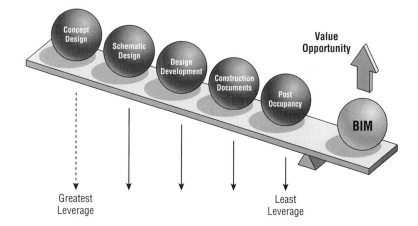

Project Roles

With such a significant change in the effort behind a BIM-based project flow, it's also important to understand how this change affects the various roles and responsibilities for the project team. Project managers need to be able to predict staffing and time to complete tasks throughout the project phases and have relied on past precedent of staff and project types to do this. Since a BIM-based project can significantly alter the project workflow, many of the historic timetables for task completion are no longer valid. However, a BIM-based project can be broken down into a few primary roles that will allow you some level of predictability through out the various project phases. Although the specific effort and staffing will vary between offices (and even projects), there are some general roles that will need to be accounted for on every project.

There are three primary roles on every BIM project:

Architect Deals with design issues, code compliances, clear widths, wall types, and so on

Modeler Creates content in 2-D or in 3-D

Drafter Deals with annotations, sheet layout, view creation, and detail creation

These roles represent efforts and general tasks that you need to take into account on any Revit project. On a large project, these roles could also represent individual people, whereas on a smaller project they might be all the same person or one person might carry multiple roles. We'll now cover each of these in a bit more detail and discuss how these roles interact with the project cycle.

ARCHITECT

The role of the architect is to deal with the design and technical issues of the project. As the model is being created, you will naturally have to solve issues like constructability and wall types, set corridor widths, deal with department areas, and deal with other issues involving either codes or the overall architectural design. This role will be the one applying standards to the project (as in wall types, keynotes, and so on) and organizing the document set. This role will need to be present on the project from the beginning to ensure consistency of the virtual building creation and isn't necessarily limited to only one person. This role also might or might not be a "designer." Although it is possible to do early design in Revit software, many project teams prefer to utilize other tools such as Google SketchUp or even a pencil and trace paper. The job of the architect is steering the creation of the building within the Revit environment. This role includes the following tasks:

◆ Leading the creation of architectural elements and building from within the model

◆ Designing around code requirements and other building logistics

◆ Constructability and detailing aspects of the design

MODELER

The role of the modeler — in some firms referred to as the BIM coordinator — is to create and manage the 3D families and detail components needed in the project, which includes all the parametric families for things such as windows, doors, casework, wall types, stairs, railings, furnishings, and so on. Typically, this role is the responsibility of less-experienced staff who might not be able to fulfill the role of architect. These roles tend to have longer periods of undisturbed time, making them better suited to deal with some of the longer, more-involved tasks in modeling content. Finally, they also tend to have some 3-D experience coming out of school. They might not have worked with Revit software directly but possibly with Autodesk® 3ds Max® software or Google SketchUp and are thereby familiar with working in a 3-D environment. This role includes the following tasks:

◆ Creating model content and families

◆ Creating drafting components

◆ Managing system families within the project

DRAFTER

The role of the drafter is to create sheets and views and embellish those views with annotations or other 2-D content. This role will be doing the bulk of the work needed to document the project. In earlier stages of the project, this role is typically assumed by either the architect or the modeler, but as documentation gets moving into high gear, this can quickly become the role of multiple people on a larger project. The following tasks are among those for this role:

- Keynoting
- Dimensioning
- Setting up sheets and views
- Creating schedules

Now let's apply these roles to the project timeline. It's important to understand how these roles can be best integrated into the typical project workflow. If you look at a typical project process, outlined in Figure 5.9, you see Time on the x-axis and Effort/Effect on the y-axis. Superimposed on this chart is the curve that represents the effort in a BIM workflow demonstrating labor intensity at various times of the project cycle. We have also taken the roles of architect, modeler, and drafter and shown them in the graph represented by the numbers 1, 2, and 3, respectively.

FIGURE 5.9
Roles over the project cycle

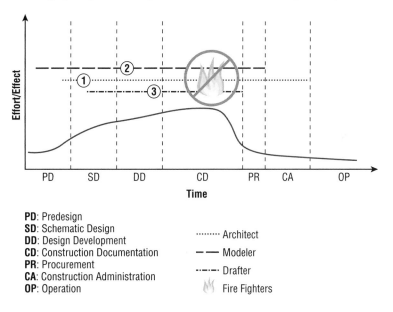

PD: Predesign
SD: Schematic Design
DD: Design Development
CD: Construction Documentation
PR: Procurement
CA: Construction Administration
OP: Operation

········· Architect
— — Modeler
··—··—· Drafter
 Fire Fighters

From a work planning purpose, we are demonstrating the ideal times to bring in some of these various roles. At the inception of a project design, a modeling role will be of the best use. This person can help create building form, add conceptual content, and get the massing for the building established. If you're using the conceptual modeling tools (covered in Chapter 9, "Advanced Modeling and Massing"), the modeler can even do some early sustainable design calculations (covered in Chapter 10, "Conceptual Design and Sustainability").

Once the project begins to take a more established form and you complete conceptual design, you'll need an architect role to step into the project. As in a typical project, you'll have to mold the form into building by applying materials, applying wall types, and validating spatial requirements and the owner's program.

During schematic design, you'll need to include the role of the drafter to begin laying out sheets and creating views. These sheets and views don't have to be for a construction document set as of yet, but you'll need to establish views for any schematic design submittals. If these views are set up properly, they can be reused later for design development and construction document submittals as the model continues to gain a greater level of detail.

You should avoid adding staff to your project during the construction documentation phase. In a BIM/Revit workflow, this can sometimes cause more problems than it solves and slow down the team rather than get work done faster.

Establishing a Work Plan

Another proven technique of managing larger Revit projects is to assign work according to elements of the building rather than by drawing a series. For example, one person would be responsible for building enclosures, another for structure, interior partitions, furniture, vertical circulation, and so on. This strategy encourages each team member to develop their portion of the design more collaboratively because the modeling for each component must be coordinated with the surrounding systems.

Even though your team won't be assigned work through a series of sheets, each person should be tasked with overseeing each sheet series. The annotation related to each building system is the responsibility of the respectively assigned team member, but someone else will be responsible for reviewing each series of sheets to ensure that they are appropriately maintained for presentation or distribution. On smaller projects, the project architect would likely be the person supervising the entire sheet set.

This dual responsibility is an important aspect of team management that will keep your BIM projects on track. Spending the majority of time working in the model and thus neglecting the preparation of properly annotated sheet views becomes very alluring.

Adding Team Members to Fight Fires

In many projects, there might come a time when the schedule gets tight and project management wants to add more staff to meet a specific deadline. When in a 2-D CAD environment, new team members would be added to help meet a deadline and would have the burden of trying to learn the architecture of the building, the thoughts behind its design, and how its various systems interact. In a Revit project, they have that same obligation, but they have the additional task of learning how the *model* has been configured. The model will have constraints set against various elements (such as locking a corridor width) and various digital construction issues (such as how floors and walls might be tied together, what the various family names are, or workset organization). New team members can need additional time to "ramp up."

Regardless of planning, deadlines still escape the best of architects and project managers. It's a good idea to know when and how you can "staff up" to be sure to meet those deadlines. Keeping in mind that your team members new to the project have to learn about both the design and the model, here are some task ideas to both help production and make sure they don't accidentally break anything:

Content creation   You will find that you will be making model families or detail components until the end of the project. This will help get the new team members engaged in a specific part of the project and also isolate them enough until they learn a bit more about how the model has been configured.

The drafting role   Even if this isn't their ultimate role, having new team members help create views and lay out sheets will get them familiar with the architecture while still allowing the team to keep progressing on the document set.

Working on detailing   Every project can always use someone who knows how to put a building together. If you have someone new to the project and possibly even new to Revit software, let them embellish some of the views already created and laid out on sheets with 2D components, linework, and annotations.

Working in a Large Team

A Revit model is a single-file environment. This single file can be used by one person, or it can be tapped by multiple people using a feature built into Revit called *worksharing*. Worksharing allows more than one user to access the Revit file at a time, which lets a team of designers work on the same model simultaneously. The concepts and use of worksharing are covered in depth in Chapter 6, "Understanding Worksharing," so in this chapter, we'll just touch on how you would manage and plan a large project in the Revit environment. In a large-project environment — when you have half a dozen or more people working in one Revit file — it takes some additional coordination and planning for successful BIM implementation.

Breaking Up a Model

Although a multiuser workflow is supported, because of the nature and workflow inherent to design, it is possible to have too many people working in a model at the same time. The threshold will vary based on the size of the model and what team members are working on, but it will become obvious when the model is overburdened. Save times will be slow, there will be frequent occurrences of team members asking others to Synchronize With Central (SWC) so they can acquire permission over elements, and saving work to get everyone an updated model will become a time-consuming process. As a general rule of thumb, the maximum number of people you should have working simultaneously seems to be anywhere from six to eight users.

When this happens, it's a good idea to discuss the option of breaking up the model into multiple models that can be linked back to each other. For example, you might have a project that will document a Shell and Core package followed later by an Interiors package. If the project is a large one or you're planning on more than a half dozen people working on each set, it would be wise to divide those sets into distinct Revit files. Because the second package is going to need to show elements of the first, it's a simple matter of linking the Shell and Core Revit file into the Interiors file.

As another example, let's say you are working on a campus project and your project has multiple buildings on a site. In this case, each building can easily become a separate Revit file.

A note of caution: You can split your model apart at any time in the project process, but once it is split, it is difficult to recombine it. Trying to recombine a model will also mean that you will be able to merge only model elements. Two-dimensional information and content from one model cannot be readily combined into another.

Within this workflow are some things that you'll want to make sure are consistent across all the files:

You need your drawing sheets consistent between Revit files.   This can easily be addressed either by using the same template file for both projects or by exporting the Revit sheet family from one model and importing it into the other.

Your building plans and elevations need to show the context of the other file.   This can easily be fixed by linking one file into another. This method can be used to display the building site as well. Create the site in a separate Revit file and link it on its own workset.

You are planning to do some renderings in the Revit environment and need consistent materials for multiple models.   When you are working across multiple files, don't think that your building model has to be the source for all of your content. If you are creating walk-throughs or renderings, typically you are populating the view you are rendering with all kinds of entourage, including people, trees, or vehicles. You might also be constantly tweaking materials and lighting to get the view to render or look just right. In your construction document set, you don't want to see these elements appearing in your sheets or accidentally getting printed as part of your building sections. Create a separate Revit file for this sort of presentation work and link your building geometry into it. In this file, you can perform all your renderings, add entourage, and adjust materials without the worry of interfering with the production of construction documents. You'll also get updates to the design every time you Synchronize With Central (SWC).

You have details that need to be consistent in multiple document packages.   Any details you create within the Revit environment can be moved from one file to another. By right-clicking the view in the Project Browser, you can use Save As to save the view and it will be saved to a separate file. This file can then be imported as a group into your other file or files and used again. The process of reusing details between Revit projects is explained with greater detail in Chapter 18, "Documenting Your Design."

Using Worksets

Worksets, which are part of the worksharing process, allow you to divide up portions of the model along logical building divisions. Don't think of these as layers; think of them more as building assemblies and components. Whereas in 2-D CAD you might have doors and walls as separate layers, in Revit you might have Building Skin, Building Core, and Interior Walls as separate worksets.

Worksets on a large project give team members a way to manage what goes into the active RAM on their individual workstations. Each workset can be selected to load or not load when you open a project. In Figure 5.10, you can see how we have chosen to open only selected worksets. To open this dialog box and change this, click the Workset button on the Collaborate tab.

Choosing to leave a workset off means that you won't load that information into the active memory of the computer, making the model easier to manipulate and manage. It will be "lighter" and more responsive. Views will open quicker. And when you need to see your work in context with the other worksets, simply turn them back on. Figure 5.11 shows the same view with the Shell workset turned off and then turned back on. Just don't forget to turn them back on before you print your set; otherwise, you might be wondering where some of the walls have gone.

FIGURE 5.10
Turning worksets on and off

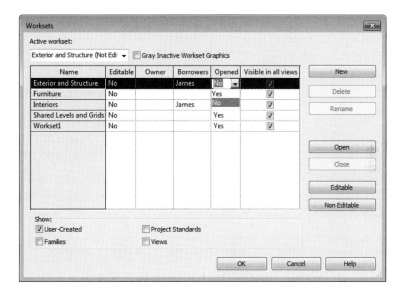

FIGURE 5.11
The Shell workset turned off (left) and turned on (right)

🌐 Real World Scenario

SETTING NAMING STANDARDS

When working on a large team, one of the problems you eventually run into is trying to find families in the Project Browser or the Type Selector. As the project grows in size and more people are added, everyone seems to self-stylize their own family-naming conventions. When inserting casework, you don't know if you're looking for Base-Cabinet-2 door or Cabinet-Base or Casework. Since both the family list and the Type Selector sort alphabetically, it can be quite a challenge to find the family you want to insert when the list grows long.

On a recent, very large project we worked on where the architectural model alone consisted of five separate files, we needed a family-naming convention that would allow people to move back and forth between models and still be able to insert families easily. We settled on a naming convention that would utilize the first four digits of a material's MasterSpec number as the prefix to the family name. Instead of having Cast In Place Concrete in one location and Precast Concrete further down the list, the families were renamed to 0330 Cast in Place Concrete and 0345 Precast Concrete. This sorted them numerically before sorting alphabetically and allowed all the families to be located quickly. The short prefix was also useful so the description wouldn't be too truncated in the Type Selector.

Quality Control and BIM

In any project process, you should always maintain a level of quality control to ensure a solid workflow. When working in a BIM environment, good model maintenance is an imperative part of the process. A well-maintained model will open quickly and be responsive when you're changing views or manipulating content. A model that is not well maintained can have a very large file size, take a long time to open or save, or even become corrupted. Letting the quality of your model suffer can negatively impact the team's overall production and lead to frustration because they cannot be as efficient as they'd like to be. The model size will grow, it will take a long time to save locally or SWC, and the file can suffer corruption or crashes.

Maintaining a good, healthy model is not a hard thing to accomplish. It takes about as much effort as regularly changing the oil in your car. The important thing, as with your car, is actually doing the regular maintenance so you don't have to fix a big problem that could have been avoided. In the following sections, we'll cover some simple things you can do using the tools already built into Revit software.

Keeping an Eye on File Size

The size of your file is a good metric for general file stability. A typical Revit file size for a project-in-construction will be between 100 MB and 250 MB — 250 MB is really on the high side of file sizes. Beyond that, you will find that the model will be slow to open and hard to rotate in 3-D views. Other views, such as building elevations and overall plans, will also be slow to open.

Should your file become large or unwieldy, you have several ways you can trim your file down and get your model lean and responsive again.

PURGING UNUSED FAMILIES AND GROUPS

On the Manage tab is a command called Purge Unused. This command removes all the unused families and groups from your model by deleting them. There are many times in a design process when you will change window types or wall types or swap one set of families for another. Even if those elements are not being used in the project, they are being stored within the file, and therefore, when the file is opened, they are being loaded into memory. Depending on the stage of your project, you should periodically delete these elements from the model to keep your file size down. Don't worry — if you find you need a family you've removed, you can always reload it.

Select the Manage tab and choose Purge Unused from the Settings panel. Depending on the size of your model and how many families you have loaded, it might take the software a few minutes to complete this command.

After the software is done thinking, it will provide you with a list of all the families and groups in the file that are not actively within a view (Figure 5.12). At this point, you have the option to select the elements you want to delete or keep, and remove the rest. You can select either entire families or just unused types. Notice that some of the families cannot be selected for deletion because they are either nested in another family or there are other types of that family already being used in your project.

FIGURE 5.12
The Purge Unused
dialog box

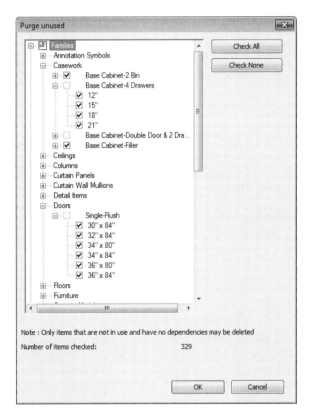

In addition to families, unused materials and property sets can be removed using the Purge Unused command. Imported categories can be purged as well; however, you don't have the option to choose which ones to delete.

We don't recommend that you use this command in the early stages of design because your file size won't be that large early on, and purging would eliminate any preloaded families that you might have included in your template. During schematic design and design development, you are typically going through design iteration and will likely be adding and removing content regularly. It can become a hassle to have to constantly load or reload families into the model. If your model is not suffering from performance issues or the file size isn't unruly, it's not necessary to perform a Purge Unused.

CUTTING DOWN ON THE NUMBER OF VIEWS

The ability to quickly create views within a model is one of the benefits of using Revit; however, this ability can be a detriment if it is not managed. Beyond the simple hassle of sorting through many views to find the one you need, too many views can also negatively affect your performance and file size.

Obviously, a number of views are needed within the model to create the construction documentation. Beyond those views, you will find yourself creating views to study the design, deal with model creation, or simply view the building or project from a new angle. These types of "working views" will never make it to the sheet set, and some will be used for only brief periods.

Before you go through the effort of counting all your unused views, let's remember that a Revit model is a database. You can use this feature to let the software perform the counting for you using schedules. To create a schedule that will track unused views, open the c05-Jenkins-Central.rvt model from the book's web page at www.sybex.com/go/masteringrevit2013. Select the Schedules flyout from the View tab and choose View List.

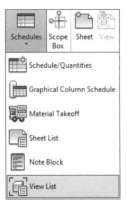

HOW MANY WORKING VIEWS IS TOO MANY?

How many working views is too many to have in your model? The obvious answer is that when performance begins to suffer, you need to start looking at ways to make the model lean and speed up response times. We had a project team new to Revit software, and they were complaining about the file being slow to open and manipulate. When reviewing their model, we saw their file size was around 800 MB! We were surprised they were even able to do any work at all.

One of the first things we did to get the file size down to something more reasonable was look at all the views that were not on sheets. We found they had more than 1,200 views not being used. Deleting those views paired with a File ➤ Save (with the Compress box checked) brought the file size down to 500 MB. Although the size was still high, this example demonstrates the impact too many views can have on your file size.

Doing so opens the View List Properties dialog box and allows you to select the fields you want to have in your schedule. For your View List schedule, select the following fields (in order):

◆ Sheet Number

◆ View Name

◆ Title On Sheet

Use the Add button to move those fields from the left column to the right one and sort them in the order listed (Figure 5.13).

FIGURE 5.13
Selecting fields for your View List

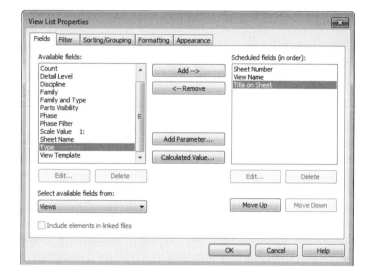

If you were to click OK right now, you'd create a schedule of all the views you have within the model. Since you want to see only the views that are not on sheets, you have a bit more formatting to do. By selecting the next tab, Filter, you can choose to see only the views not placed on sheets. In the Jenkins model, there are two sheet types: those that begin with an *A* and ones that begin with a *K*.

1. On the Filter tab, choose to filter the sheets by sheet number.

2. From the drop-down menu, choose Does Not Begin With as a filter type.

3. Finally, in the text field, enter a capital **A** (Figure 5.14).

Remember that since these are database functions, they are also case sensitive. Before moving on to the next tab, choose to add another filter selection. Copy the one you just created to filter A sheets, but now filter out all the K sheets.

As a last bit of formatting, select the Sorting/Grouping tab. On this tab, from the drop-down menu select Sheet Number. Should you have missed a sheet number type (for instance, if you have G sheets in your list), it would appear at the top. Be sure to have the Grand Totals check box selected and the Itemize Every Instance box selected (Figure 5.15). Click OK when you're done.

FIGURE 5.14
Filtering out views
on sheets

FIGURE 5.15
Sorting the sched-
ule by sheet name

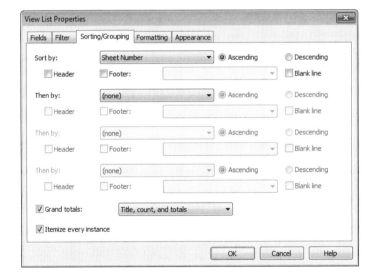

The result of this exercise will be a schedule that looks similar to Figure 5.16; it shows a list and the total of all the views not on sheets in your model. You can see that in our model we have 36 views not currently on sheets. You can add this schedule to your office template where it will keep a running list of views not on sheets that you can refer to at any time in the project process.

FIGURE 5.16
The finished schedule

Sheet Number	View Name	Title on Sheet
	Basement	
	Basement	
	Level 1	
	PARAPET	
	ROOF	
	Level 5	
	Level 1	
	Level 3	
	Level 2	
	Level 4	
	Level 6	
	Level 7	
	Level 8	
	Mezzanine	
	ROOF	
	PENTHOUSE ROOF	
	PENTHOUSE	
	PENTHOUSE ROOF	
	Level 2	
	Mezzanine	
	Level 3	
	Level 4	
	Level 5	
	Level 6	
	Level 7	
	Level 8	
	Section 1	
	Solar Array	
	3D View 1	
	3D View 2	
	West Elevation	
	3D View 3	
	Section 2	
	3D View 4	
	exterior worm-eye {3D}	

Grand total: 36

Using Schedules

As you saw in the previous example, using schedules is a great way to utilize tools already in the software to perform quality control on your projects. Don't think that all schedules need to be placed on sheets. There are several uses for schedules as a quality assurance measure. In the previous example using views, you used schedules to help troubleshoot poor model performance; however, you can use schedules to help you control quality for all kinds of things. The following sections highlight two more examples.

MULTICATEGORY SCHEDULES

An excellent way to monitor the contents of your building model is through the use of multicategory schedules. For the purpose of quality control, you might not be too concerned with extensive quantity takeoffs. As such, you will need to create a schedule with a limited number of fields, organized in a way that doesn't list each and every object instance in the project. We'll show you how to do this in the following exercise:

1. Continuing with the c05-Jenkins_Central.rvt file, go to the View tab in the Ribbon, click the Schedules flyout, and select Schedule/Quantities.

2. Choose <Multi-Category> at the top of the Category list and change the name to **Multi-Category QA Schedule**.

3. In the Fields tab of the Schedule Properties dialog box, add the following fields (in order) to the Scheduled Fields list:

   ◆ Category

   ◆ Assembly Code

   ◆ Assembly Description

   ◆ Family and Type

   ◆ Count

4. Switch to the Sorting/Grouping tab and set the first sorting parameter to Category and select the Header option. For the second sorting parameter, choose Assembly Code and set the third sorting parameter to Family and Type. Finally, uncheck the Itemize Every Instance option at the bottom of the dialog box (Figure 5.17).

FIGURE 5.17
Specify the sorting and grouping options for the multicategory schedule.

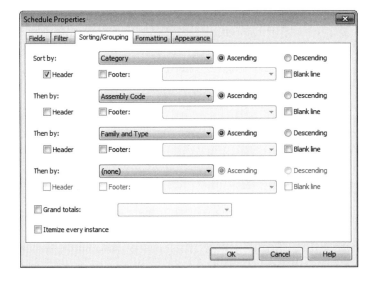

5. Switch to the Formatting tab and select the Category field. Check the box to make it a hidden field and then click OK to view the results (Figure 5.18).

FIGURE 5.18
The multicategory schedule shows all elements in the project

Multi-Category Schedule			
Assembly Code	Assembly Description	Family and Type	Count
Casework			
		Bookshelf 48 wide: Booksh	2
		Family1: cash counter 1	2
		Framed_artwork_2189: 24"	2
		single vanity: single vanity	25
		stool01: stool01	14
C1030400	Fabricated Cabinets & Counters	Counter Top no sink: 24" D	28
C1030400	Fabricated Cabinets & Counters	Counter Top no sink: 36" d	9
C1030400	Fabricated Cabinets & Counters	Counter Top no sink: dining	2
C1030410	Cabinets	5 high 24 base cabinet: 24	8
C1030410	Cabinets	Base Cabinet-4 Drawers: 1	41
C1030410	Cabinets	Base Cabinet-Single Door:	70
C1030410	Cabinets	upper cabinet: 18"	48
Curtain Panels			
		System Panel: Glazed	16
		System Panel: Level1 Store	68

With this type of schedule, you can manage the entire scope of contents actively placed in your model. Objects that don't have the proper assembly codes can be corrected right in this schedule. For other issues such as family or type naming conventions, you will need to make those adjustments in the Project Browser. In addition to verifying that the correct content has been utilized throughout your project, you can check the Count field for rows where a small number of elements have been placed — perhaps indicating that a family has been placed in error.

DISCOVER A BUNDLE OF SCHEDULES

Did you know that there are some valuable elements hidden in project templates provided by Autodesk? If you create a new project file using the Construction-Default template, you will find many schedules related to quality assurance (qa) or quantity surveying (qs). There is also a sheet named 000 - Temporary Schedule Sheet from which you can copy any number of schedules and then paste into your own project.

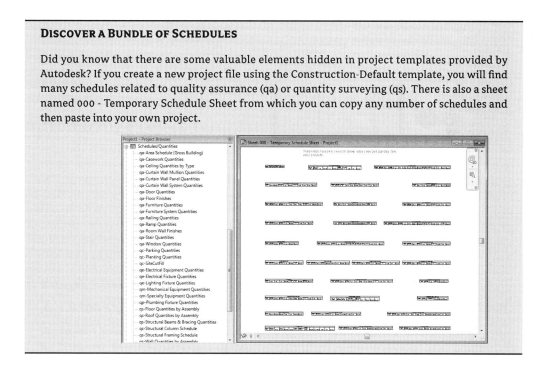

KEYNOTES

As a final example illustrating the use of schedules to manage the consistency of a project, we'll discuss how to use keynotes in the construction document process. Regardless of whether you use numerical keys or text-based keys, you will invariably need to use one of them to add annotations to your project. Although the software can easily produce both types of annotation, for the sake of ease and consistency we will refer to them as *keynotes* for the remainder of this section because that is the name of the Revit command.

If you are keynoting a project, you are adding annotations that call out specific materials or conditions within your details. Those notes not only need to be consistent across multiple details, but they will also link directly back to the project specifications — a separate set of documents published outside of the Revit environment. Historically on a project, to maintain any sort of consistency between notes in different views, you needed to manually coordinate all the notes and manually check them. When you are talking about hundreds of sheets in a drawing set and thousands of notes, there is plenty of room for error. In a manual process, you can have notes on one sheet that read "Cast-in-Place Concrete" while on another sheet they read "CIP Concrete" and on a third sheet "Cst in Place Conncrete" (note the typos).

The Keynote tool has some built-in checks and balances to ensure a level of consistency when it is being used, and we'll explore the tool further in Chapter 19, "Annotating Your Design." However, it should be pointed out that a keynote legend is another good way for the project manager to maintain a level of oversight throughout the project. A keynote legend will give you a running list of what notes are being used in a project — even though it is intended to be placed on sheets to complement your documentation. This overall list can also be cross-checked against the specifications so you can ensure that everything you've added to the model has a corresponding section.

To create a keynote legend, follow these steps:

1. On the View Ribbon, select the Legends drop-down, and choose Keynote Legend.

2. The fields for a keynote legend are limited to Key Value and Keynote Text.

3. Switch to the Filter tab and you will notice an option unique to this type of legend. Check the box labeled Filter By Sheet if you want the legend to display only the keynotes shown within the same sheet on which the legend is placed. Remember you can place a legend on as many sheets as necessary.

4. In the Sorting/Grouping tab, you have one additional option to help you review the keynotes used in your project. If you select the Footer option and choose the Count And Totals option (Figure 5.19), you can view how many times each keynote is used throughout your project. Remember that this option will also affect the instances of the keynote legend already placed on sheets. Use this option sparingly and disable it after your quality control tasks.

FIGURE 5.19
Use the Footer option to show a count of each keynote

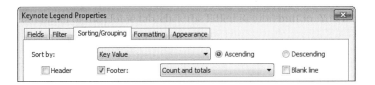

The finished schedule will look like Figure 5.20. If you look at the elements displayed in the schedule, you'll notice that it is organized by CSI division, and every note will be listed so you can verify the spelling and accuracy of each item.

FIGURE 5.20

The Keynote Legend view

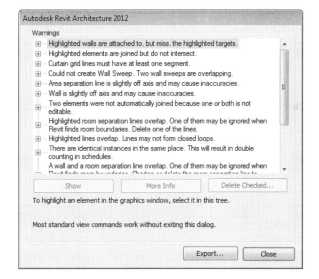

Keynote Legend	
Key Value	Keynote Text
03 53 00.A8	3" Concrete Topping
06 11 00.A8	Double Top Plate
11 13 00.A1	16" Horizontal Dock Bumper

Reviewing Warnings

CERT OBJECTIVE

A seemingly obvious place to troubleshoot your model is the Review Warnings tool. Although this technique will do very little to affect your overall file size, the Warnings dialog box will alert you to problems within the model that should regularly be addressed to ensure file stability. To locate this dialog box, go to the Manage tab in the Ribbon, find the Inquiry panel, and click the Warnings button.

Selecting this tool will give you the dialog box shown in Figure 5.21, which lists all the warnings still active in your project file.

FIGURE 5.21

The Warnings dialog box

Warnings are notifications of all types of issues the software has resolving geometry, conflicts, or formulas that do not equate. Things that will appear in this dialog box are instances where you have multiple elements sitting directly on top of each other, thereby creating inaccurate schedule counts; wall joins that do not properly clean themselves up; wall and room separation lines overlapping; stairs that have the wrong number of risers between floors; and so on. This dialog box shows you all the times the yellow warning box appeared at the bottom-right corner of the screen and you did not take action to solve the problem. Warnings that go unchecked not only can compound to create other errors but can lead to inaccurate reporting in schedules or even file corruption. You'll want to check the Warnings dialog box regularly as part of your periodic file maintenance and try to keep the number of warnings to a minimum. You might also notice that the dialog box has an Export feature. This feature exports your warning list to an HTML file, allowing you to read it at your leisure outside the model environment (Figure 5.22). Pulling this list into a Microsoft Word or Excel document allows you to distribute the warnings across the team for them to be resolved.

In the example shown in Figure 5.22 using the c05-Jenkins.rvt model, we have 261 warnings in the file. How many warnings in a file are too many? That depends on your model, computer capabilities, what the warning types are, and your deliverable. For instance, if you are delivering a model to your client or to the contractor, you might have a zero warning requirement. In that case, all warnings must be resolved prior to delivering the model. If you are still actively in the design phase of the project, however, you will always have some warnings — it is an inescapable part of the process of iteration. As you refine the drawings, problems will be resolved, and as you add new content to the model that is in need of resolution, new ones will be created. If you are not worried about a model deliverable, you can get away with having fewer than 1,000 warnings in the project without too much trouble. That said, the cleaner the model, the smoother it will run.

FIGURE 5.22
Exporting the warnings

Jenkins-Central Error Report	
Error message	**Elements**
Highlighted walls are attached to, but miss, the highlighted targets.	Exterior and Structure : Floors : Floor : CIP Concrete : id 263090 Exterior and Structure : Walls : Basic Wall : 12" COATED CMU : id 613698
Highlighted walls are attached to, but miss, the highlighted targets.	Exterior and Structure : Floors : Floor : CIP Concrete : id 263090 Exterior and Structure : Walls : Basic Wall : Exterior - Brick 2 : id 693453
Highlighted walls are attached to, but miss, the highlighted targets.	Exterior and Structure : Floors : Floor : CIP Concrete : id 269226 Interiors : Walls : Basic Wall : Interior - Gyp 4 7/8" : id 605102
Highlighted walls are attached to, but miss, the highlighted targets.	Exterior and Structure : Walls : Basic Wall : Exterior - Brick 2 : id 325781 Exterior and Structure : Floors : Floor : CIP Concrete : id 334468
Highlighted walls are attached to, but miss, the highlighted targets.	Exterior and Structure : Walls : Basic Wall : Exterior - Brick 2 : id 325861 Exterior and Structure : Floors : Floor : CIP Concrete : id 334468
Highlighted elements are joined but do not intersect.	Exterior and Structure : Walls : Basic Wall : Exterior - Brick 2 : id 327689 Interiors : Walls : Basic Wall : Interior - Gyp 4 7/8" : id 660103
Curtain grid lines must have at least one segment.	Exterior and Structure : Curtain Wall Grids : Curtain Wall Grids : Grid Line : id 741235
Curtain grid lines must have at least one segment.	Exterior and Structure : Curtain Wall Grids : Curtain Wall Grids : Grid Line : id 741873

Another option for finding and resolving warnings is available in the contextual tab of the Ribbon. When you select one or more objects that have warnings associated with them, you will see the Show Related Warnings button at the end of the Ribbon. Click this tool to display the warning dialog box and only the warnings related to the selected elements will be displayed. This is a good way to resolve model issues as you and your team develop a project. Being proactive about model quality will save you time in the long run. As Benjamin Franklin once said, "An ounce of prevention is worth a pound of cure."

The Bottom Line

Understand a BIM workflow.   Understand how projects are completed in BIM and how the use of Revit software on a project can change how information within a project is created.

Master It Explain one of the primary differences between a more traditional 2-D CAD-based workflow and producing documents using Revit.

Staff a BIM project. Since using Revit software is a change in workflow, it is also important to understand the change in staffing and who is needed to perform what roles on a project.

Master It What are the three primary roles in a Revit project and what are the responsibilities of those roles?

Work in a large team. Many projects require multiple team members. Some require having a very large team assembled on a project. Working with a large team in the Revit environment is a matter of collectively managing a series of smaller models. Know how to manage these smaller models.

Master It How many people is too many to have working in a single Revit file? What do you do when you reach that limit?

Perform quality control on your Revit model. Since you have several people using one file to create possibly hundreds of drawing sheets, it's important to keep a model clean of errors and functioning well. Performing regular maintenance on your model is essential to maintain file stability and functionality. Should a file happen to become corrupted, you stand to lose the work of the entire team. Understand how to maintain a model and how to regularly check under the hood.

Master It There are several ways to keep an eye on the model so it stays responsive and free of corruption. List some of these ways.

Chapter 6

Understanding Worksharing

Most projects involve more than one person working together at any given time. It's common in design for many people to work collaboratively to meet deadlines and create a set of construction documents. Autodesk® Revit® Architecture software has tools that allow for a collaborative design and documentation process while giving multiple people simultaneous access to its single-file building model. Keeping with the theme of "whole-building BIM," Revit software allows for this workflow without breaking apart the model. A complex model can be edited by many people at once using a feature called *worksharing*.

In this chapter, you'll learn to:

- ◆ Understand key worksharing concepts

- ◆ Use worksharing in your project

- ◆ Manage workflow with worksets

- ◆ Understand element ownership in worksets

Understanding Worksharing Basics

CERT OBJECTIVE

Worksharing refers to the use of *worksets* to divide a model for the purpose of sharing project work among multiple people. A workset is a customizable collection of building elements that can be used to manage project responsibilities. By associating these various building elements with worksets, the design team has additional control over visibility and element ownership, and several people can collaborate and work within the same file. By default, worksharing is not enabled when you start a project because it is assumed you are in a single-user environment.

Worksharing is commenced when worksets are enabled and a project file is saved as a *central file* located on a network drive. This central file becomes the repository where all the design team's work is saved. Each team member then creates a local copy of the central file in which they will work as usual. The local copies of the model remain connected to the central file (Figure 6.1).

The only information that flows instantly between the local copies and the central file is permissions. Edits to model elements or settings are not transferred among the project team members because this would significantly decrease performance and it would be distracting to your workflow to see the model constantly changing on the screen. In other words, the only way another team member knows you are editing something is by seeing that you own the element. Even though worksets are established to break a model into manageable chunks, permissions for a worksharing-enabled project are managed at the object level. This means that you could have a workshared project with only one workset. Remember, a project file is essentially a database. As you are working on elements within the model, you're automatically obtaining permission to edit elements from the central database. Once permission to modify an element is granted, no one else can make changes to that element until the changes are reconciled with the central file. This occurs when you use the Synchronize With Central (SWC) command on the Collaborate tab to save changes you've made back to the central file and simultaneously update your local file with any other changes that have been published to the central file by other team members.

FIGURE 6.1
The worksharing concept

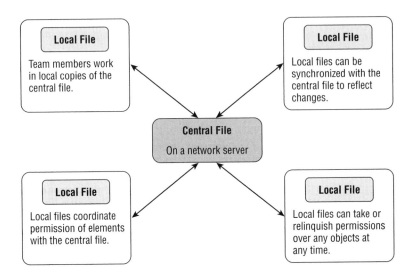

THE LIBRARY WORKSHARING ANALOGY

Another way to understand worksets and how they relate to object permissions is to think of a workset as a shelf of books in a library and the model objects as individual books on the shelf. If you are working on a paper about beavers, you can go to the library and do one of two things: check out the entire shelf of books about animals or check out the book about beavers. Checking out an entire shelf of books within a certain category is the same as making an entire workset editable — no one else can do their animal research paper because you have all the animal books. You have become the *owner* of that workset and there can be only one owner per workset.

As an alternative, you would likely borrow only the book on beavers so that your fellow students can access other animal books to complete their papers. You have become an element *borrower* and there can be many borrowers within each workset. Of course, the teacher probably made a mistake if she assigned two students to complete a report on the same animal. This mistake may also hold true when your team is working in Revit. The same model object cannot be edited simultaneously by more than one person. After all, you probably shouldn't be working on the same model area as your teammate anyway, right?

The actual use of worksets can vary greatly from project to project. Quite frankly, creating more worksets beyond the defaults is technically not necessary; however, you can use worksets to take advantage of other benefits:

◆ Use worksets to control the visibility of groupings of building components such as building skin, core, interior walls, and so on without the need to use temporary view settings or control visibility manually.

◆ Close worksets as needed to remove those parts of your project from active memory, thus improving performance.

◆ Use workset ownership to prevent others from editing a part of the project you are currently designing.

Using Worksharing in Your Project

The worksharing feature can be enabled in any Revit project file. You can commence worksharing during any stage of the project, create and remove worksets, or move elements between worksets.

WORKSHARING IN THE PROJECT PROCESS

When you choose to enable the worksharing feature, make sure the team is aware of the change to the file and that it is planned within the project process.

To follow along with the text in this chapter, you can download the Jenkins Music Building project file from this book's companion website at www.sybex.com/go/masteringrevit2013. One version of the project does not have worksets, while the other has retained worksets but is not configured for worksharing. The worksharing tools are found on the Worksets panel of the Collaborate tab, as shown in Figure 6.2.

FIGURE 6.2
The Collaborate tab

Worksets

You can initiate worksharing by clicking the Worksets button. It will initially be the only active button on the panel. Selecting this tool opens the Worksharing dialog box alerting you that you are about to enable worksharing for your project (Figure 6.3). Two worksets are automatically created within your project: Shared Levels and Grids, to which any existing levels and grids in your project will be assigned, and Workset1, to which all other building elements will be assigned. You can rename these worksets; however, we recommend not renaming Workset1 because you can never delete that workset — even if it has been renamed. You'll read about an alternative way to use Workset1 in the section "Organizing Worksets" later in this chapter.

FIGURE 6.3
Activating
worksharing

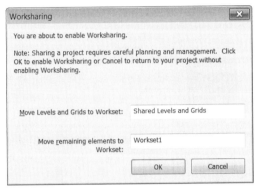

Click OK to confirm that you want to enable worksets. Depending on the size of your model and your processor speed, this process can take a few minutes to complete. Once it is done, the Worksets dialog box opens (Figure 6.4).

FIGURE 6.4
The Worksets dialog
box

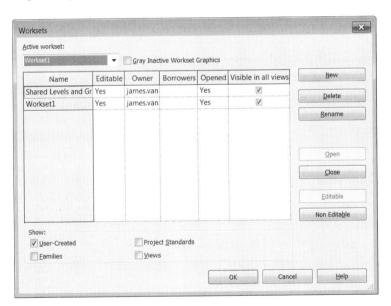

In the Worksets dialog box, you can create as many user-defined worksets as necessary; however, we offer some tips in the section "Organizing Worksets" later in this chapter. By default, when a new workset is created, it does not contain any model elements or components. You can add model elements to worksets as you build them or reassign existing elements to worksets. The Worksets dialog box also lets you take and relinquish permissions over existing worksets. First, you should understand the different types of worksets illustrated by the options in the Show box at the bottom of the Worksets dialog box, shown in Figure 6.4.

Types of Worksets

There are four types of worksets in any project: user-created, families, project standards, and views. User-created worksets such as Shared Levels and Grids and Workset1 are shown by default, and you have the option to list the others by selecting the check boxes at the bottom of the Worksets dialog box:

User-created worksets   In addition to the two worksets automatically generated when you first enable worksharing, all of the worksets you add in the Worksets dialog box will fall under this category. All building elements, spaces, and datum objects you place in the project are assigned to user-created worksets. Only elements in user-created worksets can be moved to other user-created worksets.

Families worksets   For each family loaded in the project, a workset is automatically created. When editing the properties of a family, you will automatically take ownership over that family.

Project standards worksets   The project standards workset type is dedicated to all the project settings, such as materials, dimension styles, annotations, tags, line styles, and so on. Any time you need to edit a project standard, such as modifying the type properties of dimensions, you will be taking ownership of the element's workset.

Views worksets   Every view created in a project has its own workset. The views workset type controls ownership of the view properties and any view-specific elements such as annotations, dimensions, tags, detail lines, and so on. You can take ownership of a particular view workset by selecting it from the workset list and clicking the Editable button, but this is not necessary to start working in a view. You can also take permission of a view by right-clicking the view in the Project Browser and choosing Make Workset Editable from the context menu. This can be a helpful shortcut in construction documents when much of the effort on the project is more view specific. Regardless of ownership, any team member always has the ability to *add* annotation elements to any view — you just can't *change* any existing view-specific elements when another user owns a view workset.

Organizing Worksets

When dividing your project into worksets, it's important to think about the larger building systems rather than trying to isolate its individual components. A good way to think about dividing up worksets is to consider the building elements and the number of people working on each of these elements. A basic breakdown of a project's elements might include the following:

◆ Exterior skin

◆ Core

◆ Interior partitions (in a larger building, by floor)

◆ Site

◆ Furniture, fixtures, and equipment (FF&E)

This breakdown mirrors some of the roles and responsibilities on the project as well. There might be a small group working on exterior skin design and detailing, another group working on interior partitions, and a third working on FF&E. And for larger projects where you have linked files (possibly from other disciplines like mechanical, electrical, and plumbing [MEP] or structure), it's helpful to associate those linked files with their own worksets.

How Many Worksets Do You Need?

A good rule of thumb is that you should have one or two worksets for every person working on the project (besides Shared Levels and Grids). On a small project with two or three people, you might only have three or four worksets. On larger projects, you could have a dozen or so.

Also keep in mind that once you have six to eight people working in a project, Revit's performance slows somewhat, not to mention that you spend a bit more time saving local files because each person actually saves twice (once to save changes to central and another to download everyone else's changes). If your project is large enough to warrant more than six to eight people concurrently in the model, consider dividing the model into multiple files, as we discussed in Chapter 5, "Managing a Project."

For the Jenkins Music Building, we have divided the model into five worksets, as follows:

Exterior and Structure This workset contains all the exterior skin of the building as well as the elevator, stair, slabs, and columns.

Furniture This workset contains all the furniture, fixtures, casework, and appliances.

Interiors This workset contains all the interior walls and doors.

Shared Levels and Grids This workset contains the level and grid information from the model, as was originally established when worksharing was enabled.

Workset1 Why keep Workset1? Well, it's a great holding place when new users need to work on the project but they aren't certain to which workset they should assign the new elements they create. Tell them not to worry! Simply ask them to make Workset1 their active workset. After they've finished their work, they can isolate all the elements they've created and then assign them to the right workset later (maybe with some oversight). You can even have a 3D view with only Workset1 visible.

The worksets we've set up demonstrate how a typical breakdown might occur in a project of this size, but creating, defining, and assigning worksets is by no means limited to this scheme. Depending on how you structure work in your office, the worksets might be quite different.

Managing Workset Structure

Worksets are groupings of elements logical to a three-dimensional, virtual building. One of the biggest challenges facing teams new to Revit is conceptualizing the difference between layers in 2D CAD as compared to worksets. These teams typically want to try to manage worksets as they managed layers in 2D CAD, which can result in worksets named Doors, Windows, Walls, and so on. Although this is effective management in a 2D CAD environment, you don't want to create all of this structure for worksets. Not only is it time consuming, it doesn't provide any benefit.

Much like layers, the workset is a standard that the team will need to understand and follow to use it successfully. Worksets should be structured by a team's BIM manager or a project manager familiar with a BIM workflow. Ultimately, though, it is up to the team members to place elements on the proper worksets and ensure that project standards are being followed.

Moving Elements between Worksets

If you are applying worksharing to an existing model, you'll need to assign the existing model elements to the worksets you've created. The easiest way to move elements between user-defined worksets is by using a customized 3D view. The following exercise will walk you through moving elements from Workset1 to the worksets we have established using a subtractive method to reassign the model geometry. Note that this should be done by a single person who owns all the elements to ensure that there are no permissions issues when elements are being moved between worksets. Follow these steps:

1. Open the Default 3D view so you can see the entire model. By selecting a 3D view, you can't accidentally select view-specific elements (like elevation or sections) or datum — you'll be selecting only elements that can be assigned to user-defined worksets. Now open the Visibility/Graphic Overrides dialog box and choose the Worksets tab. Choose to hide all the worksets except for Workset1 (Figure 6.5), and click OK. This will turn off any elements that are visible on those worksets and allow you to "subtract" elements from this view as you move them to the nonvisible worksets.

FIGURE 6.5
Isolating Workset1
in Visibility/
Graphic Overrides

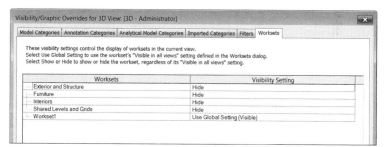

2. Now, depending on your model size, you have a few options:

   ◆ For a smaller model, select a comfortable number of elements and click the Element Properties button (if it is not active in your Project Browser). What constitutes a "comfortable" number of elements depends on your computer capabilities. Then use the Filter tool located to the far right of the contextual ribbon to filter out all the elements that are in opposing worksets. As an example, if we select a series of elements in our Jenkins Music Building model, we can choose to keep the furniture and casework active and uncheck the remaining items. Click OK. Finally, in the Properties palette, choose a new workset (Figure 6.6).

FIGURE 6.6
Moving objects
between worksets

◆ For a larger model, it might first be necessary to select some individual components and move them separately. Although the process remains the same (select elements, change the workset in the Properties palette), the selection system can vary. Another example of moving elements by selection would be to highlight an exterior wall and use the Tab key to select a chain of exterior walls. Those exterior walls can be moved to the Exterior and Structure workset.

3. Using the same technique, you can move the remainder of the site elements to their respective worksets. When the Default 3D view is empty, you'll know that all the elements have been reassigned to new worksets.

At any point in this process, you can check your work by opening the Workset tab in the Visibility/Graphic Overrides dialog box and clearing all the boxes but one to see what is in each workset. Figure 6.7 shows the Furniture workset with all its elements.

FIGURE 6.7
The Furniture
workset

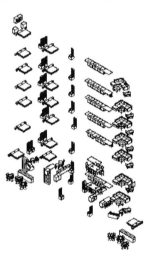

MOVING EVERY INSTANCE OF AN ELEMENT

A quick way to move every instance of an element type to a new workset is to use the Select All Instances option from the context menu. For example, select a chair in the model and right-click it. From the context menu, choose Select All Instances ➤ In Entire Project. This selects all the family elements in the entire model, allowing you to quickly move them all to the same workset in the Properties palette.

Another way to select all instances of an element is to right-click the family name in the Project Browser under the Family node. Simply navigate to your family in its proper category.

Managing Workflow with Worksets

Once worksharing is enabled, there is always a single central file that is used to manage element permissions and create local files. This is the file that will collect all the work done by your team members and allow the team to see regular updates of changes being made to the model or documents. After initializing worksharing, there are a few more steps to complete before all the team members can begin working in a multiuser environment.

BENEFITS OF LOCAL FILES

Using a worksharing environment allows you to do something your IT department typically asks you *not* to do: work directly on your workstation's hard drive. Although working off a network file is typically a good idea, there are several reasons why a local copy offers additional benefits:

◆ It allows more than one user to make changes to the central file by editing local files and synchronizing those changes with the central file.

◆ Your local copy will be more responsive than a networked local file because your access speed to your hard drive is much faster than it is across most networks.

◆ If anything bad happens to your network or your central file, such as file corruption, each local file is basically a backup that can be used to create a new local file by performing a Save As operation.

Creating a Central File

Now that you've activated worksharing, you'll establish this file as the central file. To do this with the default settings, save the central file on your network; then create the local files that the team will be using. From the Application menu, select Save. You'll be presented with a warning telling you that this is the first time the file will be saved since worksharing was enabled. Select Yes to make it the central file and save the file in its current location.

As an alternative, we recommend using the Save As ➤ Project command from the Application menu. When you click this button instead of Save, the Save As dialog box will appear (Figure 6.8).

FIGURE 6.8
Save As dialog box and options

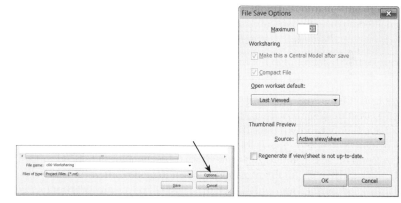

If you want to modify the default settings when saving the central file, click the Options button in the Save As dialog box to access the options in the File Save Options dialog box, shown to the right in Figure 6.8. This dialog box contains some important settings. At the top, you can set the number of backups the file will keep in the folder history after saves. The default value is 20. Depending on the storage availability on your network, how often your network is backed up, and the number of people working in the model (remember, local files are also backups), you might want to reduce this number. Also note that the Make This A Central Model After Save check box is selected and grayed out. This is because we've activated worksharing in this file and Revit assumes that we will be making a central file on the next save. You can also specify default settings for opening the project file (discussed in the section "Creating the Local File" later in this chapter) as well as the thumbnail preview image. Click OK to exit the dialog box.

Back in the Save As dialog box, choose a network location that everyone on the team has access to for your central file. Be sure that when you are naming your new central file, you choose a new name. Do not save over the existing Revit project file. There are two reasons for this. First, it automatically gives you a backup of your file as it existed before worksharing was enabled. Second, saving over an open Revit file can sometimes cause corruption, even if it is the same model. It's also a good idea to name the file with some clarity that helps identify it as a central file, such as `MyProject-Central.rvt`.

Once you've entered a new name for the file, click the Save button to save the file. Now that your file is saved to the network, close all the open view windows. As one final step, you need to make sure you don't accidentally retain any rights over the objects and elements within the central file, thereby prohibiting anyone from editing those elements.

To do this, go to the Collaborate tab, find the Synchronize panel, and click the Synchronize With Central button. Note that this button is a flyout button that contains two commands: Synchronize And Modify Settings and Synchronize Now. You'll want to use Synchronize And Modify Settings in this case. In the Synchronize With Central dialog box, shown in Figure 6.9, make sure you select any available check boxes in the middle portion to relinquish owner-ship of all worksets. You can also add a comment to identify the action taken during this synchronization.

FIGURE 6.9
Synchronizing with central to relin-quish permissions

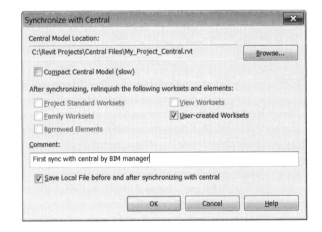

Yes, it might seem odd to use the Synchronize With Central command when you're actually in the central file, but this method is an easier way to relinquish all worksets and complete the setup of the central file.

Selecting a Starting View

On the Manage Project panel in the Manage tab of the ribbon, you can select the starting view for a project by first clicking the Starting View option (Figure 6.10, left). Once you click this option, you can select any project view (Figure 6.10, right). Because 3D views take longer to regenerate when your project opens, we recommend you select a 2D view to speed this process; you can even create a drafting view that contains the project name and image as the starting view.

FIGURE 6.10
Selecting the start-ing view

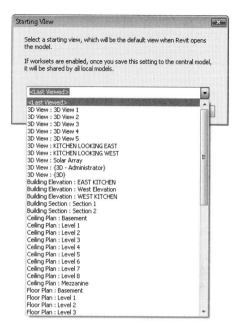

Another use for the starting view is as a project bulletin board. Simply create a drafting view for the starting view and keep it populated with project standards, modeling action items, and other notes your team might need to know.

Creating the Local File

Now that you've made a central file, you'll need to create a local copy of it in which you will continue your design and documentation. There are several ways to perform this action. One option is to simply open the network location of the central file and copy the file from the network to your Desktop or anywhere on your hard drive. Be careful not to *move* the file — only copy it. It's also a good idea to rename the file to something that identifies it as a local file, such as `***-Local.rvt`.

Another method of creating a local file is to utilize a script or macro. There are so many variations of this method, so we won't discuss them in detail here. We believe the simplest example of a script is to use common Windows commands in a BAT file. You can create a BAT file in any simple text editor such as Windows Notepad, and you will find a command-line reference in Windows Help and Support on your computer (search for *commands*). You can also find a free tool on David Baldacchino's blog at:

`http://do-u-revit.blogspot.com/2008/03/streamlining-local-file-creation.html`

The last and most predictable method for creating a local file is to use the functionality integrated with the Open command. Using any common method to open a file, you will get to the Open dialog box (Figure 6.11). Navigate to the central file, and when it is selected, you will have the option to create a new local file at the bottom of the dialog box.

FIGURE 6.11
Create a new local
file from the Open
dialog box

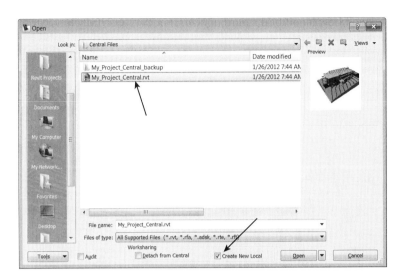

The local file is created in the location specified as the default path for user files. This setting can be found in the application options, under the File Locations settings. The default location for this setting is the My Documents folder. If you choose this method, the local file will be appended with your workset username. If you have already created a local file with this method, you will be prompted with a warning the next time you attempt to create a new local copy from the central file (Figure 6.12). You have the option to either overwrite the existing local copy or append a time stamp to the existing file.

FIGURE 6.12
Overwriting exist-
ing local files

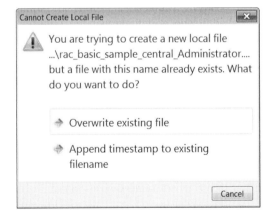

Before you proceed to open the file, you can change the way you interact with worksets. If you click the small arrow to the right of the Open button, you will see a list of options as shown in Figure 6.13.

FIGURE 6.13
Workset options
when opening a file

The default setting for opening worksharing files is Last Viewed, but each of the available settings is helpful to your workflow. Let's review these settings in detail:

All   This setting opens all available user-created worksets.

Editable   Only opens those worksets that you have previously made editable. If you didn't retain ownership of any worksets the last time you worked on a local file, none of the user-created worksets will be opened. To retain ownership of worksets when you close a file, you will be prompted with the alert shown in Figure 6.14. Choose the option to keep ownership of elements and worksets. Note that we do not recommend this workflow because it restricts others on your team from working on elements for which you retain ownership.

FIGURE 6.14
Closing a file while
retaining owner-
ship of worksets

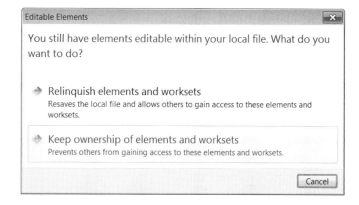

Last Viewed   The file will be opened with the Last Viewed worksets configuration. If you use this option when opening a new local file for the first time, all worksets will be opened.

Specify   We highly recommend this option because it will give you the most flexibility when opening a local file. When Specify is selected, you will be presented with the Worksets dialog box immediately after you click the Open button. You can then choose the worksets you'd like to open or close before the file is loaded into memory.

Once you've chosen a method to open the local file, click the Open button. The first time any local file is opened, you'll see a warning message alerting you that you are opening a local file (Figure 6.15). This warning will be displayed only if you didn't use the Create New Local option in the Open dialog box. All this means is that you've made a local file and you'll be the owner of the local file. Click Close to dismiss the warning and continue the file-opening process.

FIGURE 6.15
Opening a local file
for the first time

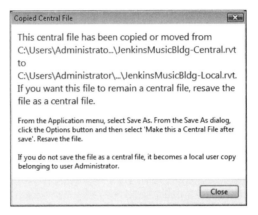

Copied Central File

This central file has been copied or moved from
C:\Users\Administrato...\JenkinsMusicBldg-Central.rvt
to
C:\Users\Administrator\...\JenkinsMusicBldg-Local.rvt.
If you want this file to remain a central file, resave the file as a central file.

From the Application menu, select Save As. From the Save As dialog, click the Options button and then select 'Make this a Central File after save'. Resave the file.

If you do not save the file as a central file, it becomes a local user copy belonging to user Administrator.

Close

Each local file is owned by the local machine and username, and once it's opened, Revit will pair the local machine and username with that local file. By default, your Windows login name is used as your worksharing username. That user would then become the owner of the local file. In this case, the local login is Administrator, which you can see in the Owner column of Worksets dialog box (Figure 6.16).

FIGURE 6.16
Workset and ele-
ment ownership

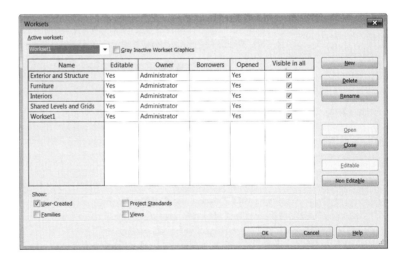

It can be a good idea to adjust this naming convention to help team communication and identification of who owns what on a project. In a smaller office, it might not be as necessary, but in a larger office, or if you're working across multiple offices, clarification of ownership is vital. A good workflow is to change this name to a first name, last name, and phone extension. This way, team members can quickly identify and contact you if they need you to relinquish permission over a given element. To make this modification, follow these steps:

1. First, close all your open projects. You can change the default username only when no workshared projects are open (you can't change your username while it's active in open projects). After you change your workset username, you'll need to create new local files because the old local file is associated with a different username.

2. From the Application menu, choose Options at the bottom.

3. In the Options dialog box, select the General tab.

4. In the Username field, enter a new value (Figure 6.17). Click OK to exit.

FIGURE 6.17
Changing the default username

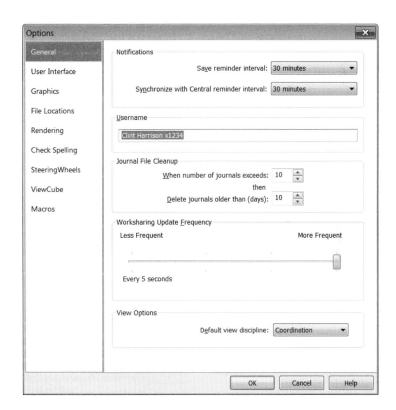

Working in a Worksharing Environment

Now that you have created a local copy of the central file, it's time to get to work. Do you need to do anything special to commence working in a project that's enabled with worksets? No. You can simply start adding or editing content in your project because permissions are being automatically managed as you work. Just remember that you can't edit any elements (2D or 3D) that someone else is already editing.

You don't have to make any worksets editable unless you want to prevent other team members from editing certain parts of your project until you have completed some work. Remember the library analogy earlier in this chapter.

DON'T WORK IN THE CENTRAL FILE

Make sure that you *never work directly within the central file*. Doing so will change the file attributes on the server and prohibit anyone with a local file from being able to synchronize with the central file. The possibility of losing a lot of work and effort from team members exists, so it is safer to err on the side of caution by simply never opening the file.

The most important thing to remember when you use worksharing is that every element in the file and added to the file belongs to a workset. To make sure you are placing elements in the proper workset while working, there are a few tools to ensure that the right workset is selected.

One such location is on the Collaborate tab, where you originated worksharing to begin with. As shown in Figure 6.18, our active workset is Exterior and Structure. Note that this also tells us that the Exterior and Structure workset is not editable. What this means is that as a user, we have not taken ownership of this workset. However, as we mentioned earlier, you don't need to own a workset to add elements to it. It just needs to be active in this window.

FIGURE 6.18
Changing the active workset

The second location is in the status bar at the bottom of the application (Figure 6.19). The drop-down menu on the left serves the same function as the Active Workset drop-down in the Collaborate tab, but it allows you to verify that the proper workset is active without the need to bounce between tabs in the ribbon and interrupt your workflow. From this location you can also change the active workset and even open the Worksets dialog box using the small button to the left of the drop-down menu.

FIGURE 6.19
Changing the active workset from the status bar

A helpful tool located on the Collaborate tab is the Gray Inactive Worksets button. This dims all the elements that aren't active, helping you identify what elements are in your current, active workset. This is a temporary view state and will not affect any printing or other output.

Additionally, you can always view an object's workset assignment by hovering your mouse pointer over the object and viewing its workset in the status bar (Figure 6.20). This location will also display an object's family and category. In the example shown here, the chair is in the Interiors workset, in the Furniture category, and its type is Armless Chair.

FIGURE 6.20
Workset assignment displayed in status bar

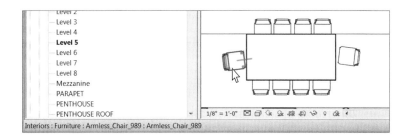

Saving Work

It will eventually become necessary to save your work and share your progress with others in the model. There are three ways to both save your work and view the work of others: Save, Synchronize And Change Settings, and Synchronize Now.

Save The Save button saves the work you've done to your local file only; the work isn't shared or published back to the central file. This can be a useful step if you're in the middle of a process and want to make sure your work is saved but aren't ready to share the changes with the rest of the team. You can find the Save tool either by choosing Application ➤ Save or by clicking the Save icon on the Quick Access toolbar (QAT).

Synchronize With Central ➤ Synchronize And Modify Settings When you are ready to publish your work for the rest of your team to see, you have two command choices to synchronize with the central file. The first of two synchronizing commands is known as Synchronize And Modify Settings. You can access this command in a couple of ways. The first is on the Collaborate tab in the Synchronize panel, as shown in Figure 6.21. The Synchronize With Central flyout button is located on the left of this panel.

FIGURE 6.21
Synchronize With Central command on the ribbon

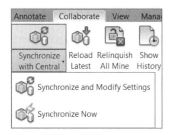

Alternatively, you can use the Synchronize With Central button located on the QAT. Both buttons perform the same action and will open the Synchronize With Central dialog box (Figure 6.22). This dialog box gives you some additional tools to assist your workflow:

◆ The Compact Central Model check box allows you to compact the model to save on disk space. It will take some additional save time, but it can temporarily decrease your file size significantly. This should not be seen as a permanent solution to managing a large file, however. Compaction will decrease the file size, but use of the file will expand the compacted elements. Reducing file size is discussed in Chapter 5.

FIGURE 6.22
Synchronize With
Central dialog box

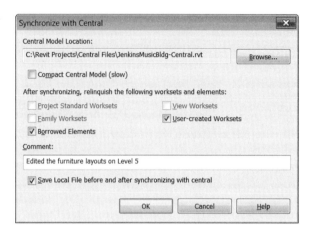

◆ There are five additional check boxes that will be available (depending on what work you've done to the file) to allow you to relinquish or keep permission over the elements you've previously edited. Unchecking these boxes means that you will retain ownership over all the elements you currently own with the model. This can be useful if you are planning to continue working on the same elements and want to publish only recent changes of the model.

◆ You can add comments to the synchronization that can be useful for tracing potential model conflicts later in the production process.

◆ A final check box, Save Local File Before And After Synchronizing With Central, allows you to save your changes locally, get any new changes from the central file, and then save locally again, ensuring that your local copy is up-to-date. This is the save option that takes the longest, and you might choose to uncheck this periodically if you're pressed for time or have a large file that typically takes longer to save.

Synchronize With Central ⋗ Synchronize Now The second command choice to publish your changes is called Synchronize Now. Choosing this option allows you to bypass the Synchronize With Central dialog box and simply sync your file immediately. With this option, you'll be relinquishing all your permissions over any elements you have borrowed; however, you will remain the owner of any worksets you have made editable in the Worksets dialog box.

Saving at Intervals

You will be prompted to save your work at regular intervals. Once worksharing is enabled, you will receive an additional reminder to synchronize with the central file as well as to save your work (Figure 6.23). You can dismiss these dialog boxes by clicking Cancel at the lower right, but remember, it's a good idea to save regularly so you don't lose any work.

FIGURE 6.23
Changes Not
Synchronized
dialog box

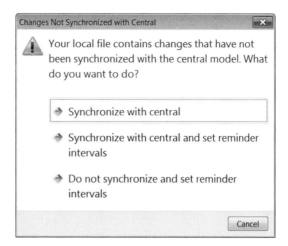

If the Changes Not Synchronized dialog box appears, you'll have three options to choose from:

◆ Synchronize With Central, which will perform a save operation identical to that of the Synchronize Now command

◆ Synchronize With Central And Set Reminder Intervals, which will synchronize your file and then pull up the Options dialog box, allowing you to set the intervals in which you receive this message

◆ Do Not Synchronize And Set Reminder Intervals, which will cancel all future reminders for the remainder of your Revit session

You can modify the reminder time shown in the dialog box at any time by clicking the Application button, selecting Options, and then choosing the General tab.

Loading Work from Other Team Members

It is possible to update your model and load work from other team members without publishing your own work back to the central file. This process, called Reload Latest, basically downloads the latest changes from the central file to your local file. Since you are only downloading content from the central file and not uploading, this process takes only a portion of the time a full SWC does. To do this, click the Collaborate tab on the ribbon, and choose Reload Latest from the Synchronize panel. The default keyboard shortcut for this command is RL.

Worksharing Visualization

Sometimes it helps to have the ability to graphically display worksets and their status in the project. With worksharing visualization, you can visualize four different values: ownership status, individual ownership, updated elements, and workset assignment. You can open the settings from the view control bar (Figure 6.24). To display any of the values, select the desired setting. When any value is selected, the temporary view condition is indicated by colored highlighting around the edges of the view window.

FIGURE 6.24
Workset
visualization

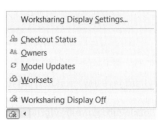

Select the Worksharing Display Settings menu item to customize the graphic appearance of the visualization overrides. The Checkout Status tab of the Worksharing Display Settings dialog box shows three values: what is owned by you, owned by others, or not owned at all (Figure 6.25).

FIGURE 6.25
Checkout Status tab

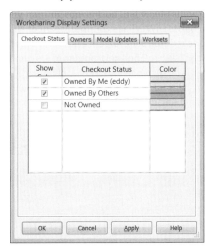

The Owners tab of the Worksharing Display Settings dialog box illustrates which elements are owned by the users in your project. If there are users listed who do not have any enabled elements or worksets, you can remove them from the list by selecting their username and clicking the Remove User icon at the lower left (Figure 6.26).

FIGURE 6.26
Owners tab

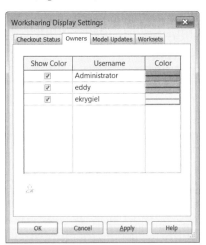

The Model Updates tab of the Worksharing Display Settings dialog box indicates changes to the central file that may not be apparent until you have synchronized with the central file (Figure 6.27).

FIGURE 6.27
Model Updates tab

The Worksets tab allows you to color-code the model based on the workset assignment of all the building elements. Color-coding is also helpful for keeping track of your active workset (Figure 6.28).

FIGURE 6.28
Worksets tab

Finally, how often the display settings update in your project is up to you. To modify these settings, choose Application ➢ Options to modify the Worksharing Update Frequency option

(Figure 6.29). Moving the slider to the far left will set the description below the Updates slider to Manual Updates Only and the update will occur when you use Reload Latest or Sync With Central. Slide just a bit to the right and you'll see that the display will update every 60 seconds. Slide it all the way to the right and your display will update every 5 seconds.

FIGURE 6.29
Modifying the settings for Worksharing Update Frequency

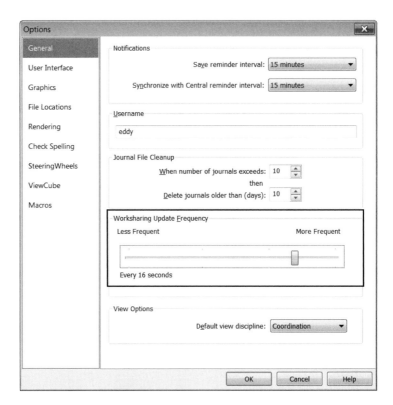

Workset Visibility in View Templates

As we've described in the section "Moving Elements between Worksets," worksets can be used as a different way to visualize your project using the Visibility/Graphic Overrides dialog box. Workset visibility can also be managed as part of a view template. To modify these settings, go to the View tab, locate the Graphics panel, and select View Templates ➢ Manage View Templates. In the View Templates dialog box (Figure 6.30), select V/G Overrides Worksets to modify the visibility settings in any view template. Refer to Chapter 4, "Configuring Templates and Standards," for more information on view templates.

FIGURE 6.30
Workset settings in
view templates

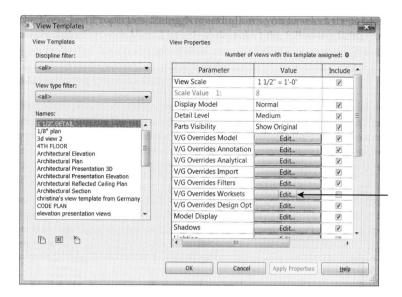

Closing Revit

Eventually, you will need to close your project and leave for lunch or go home for the day. Don't worry — the project will still be there tomorrow. But in the meantime, it's important to understand how to close the project correctly so you don't accidentally retain permission over any elements. This situation — where a team member has accidentally left the office and not closed the project file or relinquished permissions — leaves the other team members without a way to edit elements with which the team member had permission or even request permission. So that you are not the unfortunate victim of their wrath upon your return, make sure you close the application properly.

The most thorough way to close the file is to simply quit the application completely. You can do this by clicking the X at the upper right or clicking Exit Revit from the Application menu. You'll be presented with a dialog box in which you can choose to synchronize with central, save your changes locally, or discard the changes (Figure 6.31). Obviously, the best choice is to synchronize with central, allowing your changes to be published and any objects you own to be relinquished; however, you might be in the middle of a design study and not ready to share your changes. In that case, you may choose to save locally and retain ownership of certain elements.

FIGURE 6.31
Saving options
when closing a local
file

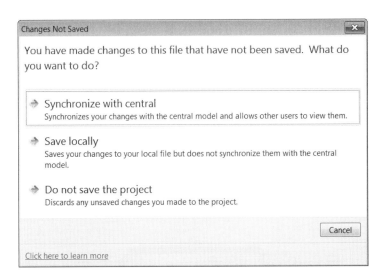

What if you were only reviewing the model, making some minor changes, and you don't want to save the changes? Close the file or application with any of the methods previously mentioned and select Do Not Save The Project from the Changes Not Saved dialog box. You will then be presented with another dialog box with two choices concerning borrowed elements (Figure 6.32). In the Close Project Without Saving dialog box, you can either relinquish any borrowed elements and worksets or retain ownership of them. Clearly, the best choice is to relinquish all elements and worksets.

FIGURE 6.32
The Close Project
Without Saving
dialog box

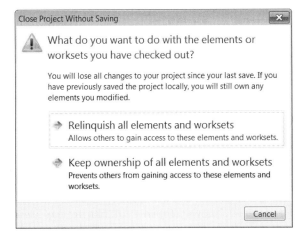

Disabling Worksharing

In a few cases, you might decide that you've enabled worksharing too soon, or after enabling worksharing you'd rather go back. Prior to the 2012 version, doing so was not possible. Now worksharing may be disabled as part of the Detach From Central functionality. This option can be found at the bottom of the Open dialog box. When you elect to detach a copy of the central file, you have the option to discard worksets, as shown in Figure 6.33.

FIGURE 6.33
Disabling worksharing

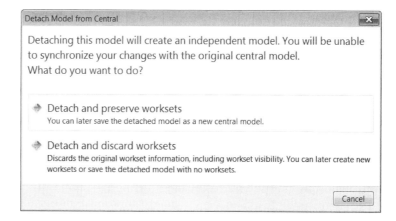

If you choose to preserve worksets, the worksharing functionality remains in the file. This allows you to maintain any visibility configurations you've established that depend on worksets. Although this file retains the worksharing capability, it can no longer be synchronized with the original central file because it will become a new central file as soon as you save it after detaching. If you elect to discard worksets, you will lose any visibility settings established from worksets. You will also need to create all new worksets from scratch if you decide to enable worksharing again in the future.

Understanding Element Ownership in Worksets

One of the fundamental concepts in a model enabled with worksharing is the ownership of elements. When you directly edit an element in a project, you automatically take ownership of that element — as long as no one else owns it. Determining whether you own an element is fairly easy. Simply select it. If you do not own it, you will see a worksharing icon, as shown in Figure 6.34.

FIGURE 6.34
The worksharing icon on a selected element

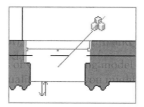

By borrowing elements, team members can take ownership of only portions of a workset, leaving the remainder of the workset to be edited by someone else. Taking ownership of elements in this style creates a more "take what you need" approach to editing and usually results in less overlap between team members.

Besides automatically borrowing elements when they are edited, there are a few other ways you can obtain ownership of an element or group of elements:

◆ In the Worksets dialog box, you can make any workset editable. You then become the owner of the workset instead of borrowing elements within one.

◆ Select any element or series of elements and take permission of them by clicking the worksharing icon.

◆ You can right-click any element in the Project Browser under the Family node. In the context menu that appears, you can take ownership of families, groups, or views.

◆ You can right-click any element in a view and choose Make Elements Editable from the context menu (see Figure 6.35). Note that you also have the ability to make editable the entire workset to which the selected object is assigned.

FIGURE 6.35
Making an element editable using the context menu

Using any of these options, if the selected element is already owned by another team member, Revit will alert you and you will not be able to modify the element or make it editable.

🌐 Real World Scenario

ACCIDENTS HAPPEN

It's human nature: Eventually an accident will occur on a project, and elements will get modified or deleted unexpectedly. It's important to know how to recover when these accidents occur.

On one project we worked on, someone new to Revit software and new to the team was working on window details in a three-sided building. In the detailing process, he somehow deleted one of the walls in the project. By deleting the wall, he also deleted the elevation as well as all the wall sections associated with that wall, along with the details in plan and section. When the new team member deleted the element, he wasn't aware of the mistake and then performed Synchronize With Central, publishing all the deletions to other team members. Fortunately, we caught the mistake before everyone performed a Synchronize With Central, and we did not have to resort to restoring the model from the previous night's backup. We were able to use another team member's local file to create a new central file, thereby minimizing the loss of work. Once everyone on the team made a new local copy, we were back in business.

Had the deleted elements been more isolated (like a conference room layout), recovery would have been much less invasive. In such a case, you simply create a group from all the elements you would like to save, then right-click the group in the Project Browser. You'll have the option to save the group out of the file, which can then be inserted into a different project file and ungrouped again.

Editing Requests

When working in a worksharing project, it is not always necessary to take ownership of an entire workset in order to begin editing elements. As we discussed earlier in this chapter, it is possible to take ownership of individual model elements. This process is referred to as *borrowing*. Remember, there can be only one owner of a workset but multiple borrowers of elements within a workset.

If you need to work on elements that already belong to someone else, you will receive an alert that you cannot edit the elements until the other person relinquishes them, and you'll be given the option to place an editing request.

Understanding the editing request workflow is critical for multiuser teams; it allows users to transfer permission of objects without having to constantly save all their work to the central file and relinquish all worksets. Let's look at this interchange of permissions in more detail.

Placing an Editing Request

Imagine you are happily working away on your model in a worksharing environment and you try to edit an element that someone else owns. What do you do? When that situation occurs, you will be presented with a dialog box that allows you to request permission to edit the element from the other user (Figure 6.36).

FIGURE 6.36
Placing a request for permission

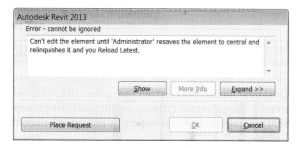

Looking at the dialog box, you have two options:

◆ You can click Cancel and not take permission of the element, and then focus your efforts on another part of the design.

◆ You can click Place Request to ask your team member to relinquish permission over the element in question. When you click Place Request, the dialog box shown in Figure 6.37 opens.

FIGURE 6.37
Editing Request
Placed dialog box

Once you have placed your request, you're in a bit of a holding pattern. You cannot continue to edit this element until the other user has granted permission over it, and you cannot continue working on other portions of the project. Note that this situation applies only if you were editing an element and you needed to make an editing request related to that element. If you simply wanted to request permission of an element and not edit it right away, you could close the request confirmation box and continue working on other elements in your project.

The recipient of an editing request will see a pop-up notification appear at the bottom of the application, as shown in Figure 6.38. The notification gives the recipient instant information about the element in question, who made the request, and buttons to grant or deny the request. It also provides a Show button that finds the element in a view so you can determine the most appropriate response to the request.

FIGURE 6.38
Editing request
notification

If you happen to miss or accidentally close the request notification, there is also a small visual indicator on the status bar at the bottom of your screen. It indicates whether there are any outstanding requests (both to and from you). Clicking this icon opens the Editing Requests dialog box (Figure 6.39).

FIGURE 6.39
The Editing
Requests dialog box

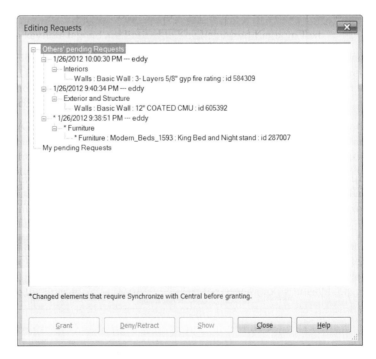

Granting an Editing Request

Let's now observe the other side of this scenario. If you are the recipient of an editing request and you are ready to grant it, one of two things will happen. If you haven't changed the element, you can simply click Grant and the permission for the element will be transferred to the requesting team member.

If you have modified the element or one that is dependent on or hosted by the element in question, you will be alerted that you'll need to SWC before the request can be granted. Your team member on the other end will subsequently need to use the Reload Latest command or SWC to receive the recent changes, and then they can edit the most recent version of that element. Permission requests that require an SWC are flagged in the Editing Requests dialog box by an asterisk next to the request (refer to Figure 6.39).

After your editing request has been granted, you will receive a notification similar to those shown in Figure 6.40. If the request didn't require an SWC from the other team member (as indicated in the left image in Figure 6.40), you can continue the editing command that prompted the request. Otherwise, you will need to Reload Latest before you can continue the editing command. If you need to return to a view of the element or elements related to the editing request, you can click the Show button. Click the X to close the notification box.

FIGURE 6.40

Notifications of a granted editing request

GETTING PERMISSION FOR SOMEONE ELSE'S OBJECTS

Inevitably it happens on a project; someone leaves their desk for a meeting or goes home without relinquishing permission over all their elements and worksets, leaving the rest of the team in the lurch. The best solution is to contact the person and gain their network password and just synchronize their file with central. Doing so ensures that all their changes as well as permissions are synchronized and no work is lost. If that is not possible, there is a workaround for this problem. Note that the workaround will result in the loss of the work by the missing team member, but it will clear up all the permissions issues.

If the immediate team needs outweigh the potential loss of the missing person's work, follow these steps:

1. Open a new session of Revit.

2. Click the Application menu, select Options, and choose the General tab in the resulting dialog box.

3. Change the name listed in the Username field from your username to the person's whose permissions you are looking to release.

4. Create a new local file of the project and open it. Now simply SWC, and all their elements will be available to the team to edit. Then close the file.

5. Before closing Revit, be sure to go back to the Application menu, click Options, and select the General tab so you can change the username back to your own.

Relinquishing Permission

It is not always necessary to wait for a request from another team member to relinquish permission over your elements. Fortunately, there is a tool to do just that. On the Synchronize panel of the Collaborate tab is a button called Relinquish All Mine (Figure 6.41). This feature returns the permissions for any elements you have not edited back to the central file so they are available to the rest of your team.

FIGURE 6.41
Relinquish All Mine

The Bottom Line

Understand key worksharing concepts.   Once the team has created local files, it is necessary to understand how to keep both the local files and the central file up-to-date as changes occur on the project. Doing so ensures that everyone is working from an updated and recent copy of the model at all times.

> **Master It**   Once you've begun working in your local file, how do you publish your changes to the central file? How do you download changes from the central file to your local file?

Use worksharing in your project.   Knowing how to activate and utilize worksharing is indispensable to working in a team environment using Revit.

> **Master It**   How do you transition a single-user Revit file to a multiuser environment using worksharing?

Manage workflow with worksets.   Once the central file has been created, you'll need to organize and structure the model into logical worksets to maintain workflow with Revit.

> **Master It**   How do worksets differ from layers in 2D CAD? What are some logical ways to create worksets within a model?

Understand element ownership in worksets.   Editing elements in a central file means you have sole ownership over further changes to those elements. Understanding the permissions is critical to working in a team.

> **Master It**   How do you edit an element in the model if someone has already taken ownership of it in a worksharing environment?

Chapter 7

Working with Consultants

Whether you work on large or small projects — on residential, commercial, or industrial building types — collaboration is an almost certain aspect of the workflow you will encounter when implementing BIM. This chapter discusses important considerations for interdisciplinary coordination as well as the tools within Autodesk® Revit® Architecture software to help you manage the process. This chapter covers aspects of collaboration solely utilizing the Revit Architecture platform, and Chapter 8, "Interoperability: Working Multiplatform," focuses on collaborating with other software programs.

In this chapter, you'll learn to:

◆ Prepare for interdisciplinary collaboration

◆ Collaborate using linked Revit models

◆ Use Copy/Monitor between linked models

◆ Run interference checks

Preparing for Collaboration

Working alone in the Revit environment will deliver measurable increases in productivity, quality, and consistency; however, the true benefit of building information modeling (BIM) is the ability to effectively collaborate between design disciplines with contractors and deliver useful data to facility operators.

Social BIM

The difference between these working paradigms has been described as *lonely BIM* vs. *social BIM* by John Tocci of Tocci Building Corporation (www.tocci.com), which is a forward-thinking construction company headquartered in Woburn, Massachusetts. Lonely BIM can also be referred to as the use of "isolated BIM techniques for targeted tasks," whereas social BIM is the underpinning for the goals set forth by organizations such as the buildingSMART Alliance of the National Institute of Building Sciences (NIBS), according to Penn State's BIM wiki at:

    http://bim.wikispaces.com/BIM+Project+Execution+Planning+Project

The ability to support information exchanges, such as the facility life cycle helix concept shown in Figure 7.1, necessitates the proper use of 3D models and nongraphic data in a highly collaborative environment. Furthermore, the buildingSMART Alliance and the National BIM Standard (NBIMS) stress the need for platform-neutral, open interoperability *between* applications, not just within a program such as Revit.

FIGURE 7.1
BIM data exchanges
according to NBIMS

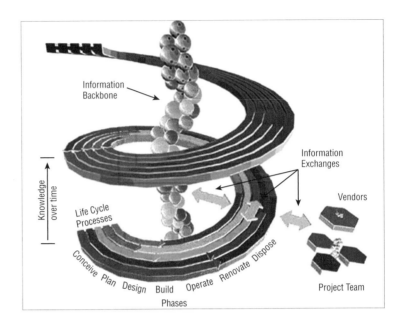

BIM EXECUTION PLAN

Once a project team decides to participate in social BIM — either through desire or the requirements of a client — they must decide how to distribute the BIM execution plan in a useful way to all constituents throughout the project life cycle. Whether your client requires it or not, you should develop a BIM *execution plan* to define the goals, exchanges, and results related to the use of BIM.

The buildingSMART Alliance (www.buildingsmartalliance.org) — in an effort sponsored by the Charles Pankow Foundation, the Construction Industry Institute, Penn State Office of Physical Plant, and the Partnership for Achieving Construction Excellence (PACE) — has created a BIM Execution Planning Guide and template for a BIM Execution Guide. You can find the two guides at the Penn State Computer-Integrated Construction (CIC) website: www.engr.psu.edu/ae/cic/bimex.

One of the most critical parts of a BIM execution plan is the definition of the goals and uses of BIM. If you are just beginning your implementation of Revit software, perhaps you are using it because it is the latest parametric program to enter the AEC industry, or perhaps you are attempting to increase your drafting productivity. Defining clear and concise reasons for implementing BIM on each project will help you define where to concentrate your modeling efforts. According to the buildingSMART Alliance, "[A] current challenge and opportunity faced by the early project planning team is to identify the most appropriate uses for Building Information Modeling on a project given the project characteristics, participants' goals and capabilities, and the desired risk allocations." A listing of the common uses of BIM along with potential value opportunities and required resources is also available on the Penn State CIC website.

According to the American Institute of Architects's (AIA's) "Integrated Project Delivery: A Guide," a BIM execution plan "should define the scope of BIM implementation on the project, identify the process flow for BIM tasks, define the information exchanges between parties, and describe the required project and company infrastructure needed to support the implementation." To be clear, the development of such a plan does not imply the application of integrated project delivery (IPD). IPD is "a project delivery approach that integrates people, systems, business structures and practices into a process that collaboratively harnesses the talents and insights of all participants to optimize project results, increase value to the owner, reduce waste, and maximize efficiency through all phases of design, fabrication, and construction." For the purpose of this chapter, we will consider only the collaboration and coordination between members of a project design team, not the interactions with a client or contractor.

For additional reading on IPD, refer to these sources:

◆ IPD and BIM white papers by Ted Sive: `www.tedsive.com`

◆ Integrated Practice/Integrated Project Delivery: `www.aia.org/ipd`

◆ buildingSMART Alliance: `www.buildingsmartalliance.org`

◆ McGraw-Hill Construction, BIM Special Section: `bim.construction.com`

Coordination

The coordination process in a Revit environment begins with linking multiple files together to form a composite view of your building project. A project can be divided in many different ways to meet a variety of workflow requirements. Most often each discipline will develop at least one separate Revit project file, and many of these project files will be linked into each other for reference. Because there are several workflow possibilities, this chapter will focus on the coordination among a traditional design team consisting of the following:

◆ Architect

◆ Structural engineer

◆ Mechanical, electrical, and plumbing engineers

FIGURE 7.2
The relationships of interdisciplinary coordination

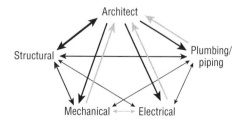

The workflow within a traditional design team is more complex than you might assume. If you were to graph the dependencies and coordination between these parties (Figure 7.2), you would see a web of primary relationships (architect to/from structure, architect to MEP) and secondary relationships (structure to/from mechanical and piping).

In addition, these relationships can be further parsed into physical and logical relationships. If we use mechanical and electrical as an example, you can see that a physical relationship means making sure a light fixture is not hitting the bottom of a duct, whereas a logical relationship means making sure the electrical design properly accounts for the load of the heating coil in a variable air volume (VAV) box (being designed by the mechanical engineer).

It is the complexity of these possible workflow scenarios that makes this process prone to errors and a major source of coordination between the traditional design team. So, what are the tools that can be used for collaboration between Revit products? Three distinct tools are typically used in a collaboration scenario:

Linked models   Linking models together using the Revit Link tool provides full visual fidelity of the referenced content, showing the complete context of the other disciplines' data, fostering a complete understanding of their geometry. The data can also be controlled and shown in any manner appropriate to the use. You can turn it on or off, half-tone the data, or enhance it with color or line pattern overrides. Linking also provides support for the Interference Check and Coordination Monitor tools.

Copy/Monitor   Copy/Monitor is a powerful tool available in all products built on the Revit platform and is considered the most intelligent of the coordination tools. It offers several benefits. It lets you link Revit files from other team members (structural engineers or MEP engineers) and copy key elements from their model into yours. Once that link is created, you can monitor that relationship and know if the element has moved or changed when you receive updated models from your team members. A basic example of using this tool would be copying the structural grid into your architectural file. If the grid moves or changes with subsequent updated models, you'll be instantly alerted to the change. The following other benefits are also included:

>   **Intelligent bond**   Using Copy/Monitor, you can choose items from another model that you want to monitor for change and the degree to which you want to monitor them.

>   **Multiple modes**   Many people do not realize that there are two distinct modes of this tool: Copy and Monitor. Using the correct mode can provide additional functionality flexibility.

>   **Geometry creation**   When this tool is used in Copy mode, you can create geometry in the source file based on objects in the linked file. In this mode, you will also establish a monitor relationship.

Interference Check   In many cases, the only workflow requirement is to verify that items from another discipline are not interfering with your items. The Interference Check tool can be used to check between categories within a single model or between linked models.

INDIANA UNIVERSITY BIM REQUIREMENTS

In 2009, the University Architect's Office at Indiana University (www.iu.edu) announced that it would require the use of BIM on all projects with a capital value of over $5 million. Accompanying the announcement was the release of the IU BIM Standards and Project Delivery Requirements, which included a BIM execution plan template and IPD template — developed under the guidance of Autodesk and SHP Leading Design (www.shp.com/leadingdesign). Although the university's BIM requirements may seem new, the desire to ensure the maximum reuse of information has been evolving at IU for several years, beginning with its implementation of integrated GIS tools for campus and facility management in 1996.

One important excerpt from these requirements focuses on the organization of the interference checking (aka clash detection) process. Within the IU BIM Standards & Guidelines for Architects, Engineers, & Contractors, rules have been established for classifying clashes between modeled elements. Level One clashes are considered critical and include ductwork and piping clashing with ceilings, rated walls, or structure; equipment clearances interfering with structure are included in Level One as well. Level Two clashes are less critical but include casework clashing with electrical fixtures and structure vs. specialty equipment. Finally, Level Three clashes are still important but are a lower priority. These include casework clashing with walls and plumbing interfering with mechanical equipment.

These requirements may be defined differently by other clients, but it's critical to understand the importance of using interference checking tools for logical groups of model elements. Checking for clashes throughout an entire model will yield a plethora of unusable data and will limit the effectiveness of model-based coordination.

For more information, visit the IU BIM site at www.indiana.edu/~uao/iubim.html or read a review of these standards at the Arch | Tech blog at:

www.architecture-tech.com/2009/11/indiana-university-requires-bim.html

Given the range of available Revit tools for collaboration, they are not necessarily applicable to all interdisciplinary relationships. As shown in Figure 7.3, only the most appropriate tools should be applied to each collaborative situation. Note that these situations are merely suggestions based on the experience of the authors. The needs for your collaborative workflows may vary.

FIGURE 7.3
Suggestions for collaboration tools to be used between disciplines

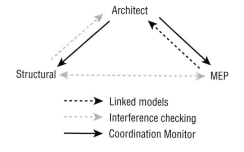

Architect to structural engineer The relationship between the architect and structural engineer is becoming closer as we strive for lighter structures and more innovative design. In many respects, structural engineers may be affecting the building aesthetic as much as the architects. As such, this workflow may be considered the most crucial and should be bidirectional.

Architect to structural engineer: Coordination Monitor By using Copy/Monitor, the structural engineer is able to create a strong, intelligent link between the structural and architectural models. In doing so, he can easily track the changes in the architect's model that will affect the structural design. He is also able to create geometry in his model using these tools, which can be directly or indirectly related to architectural elements such as walls and floors.

Remember that coordination of relationships for datum (grids and/or levels) should be established at the beginning of a project. For example, does the architect "own" the levels and the grids — or will the structural engineer? Conflicts due to a lack of proper planning will negatively impact the effective use of the Copy/Monitor tools on your projects.

Structural engineer to architect: Interference Check The architect's primary requirement for the structural model is to include the structure in context and to know if the structure is interfering with any architectural elements. For this workflow, it is recommended that the architect link in the structural model and use interference checking. The rules governing what clashes are considered critical may be established by a client's BIM standards and protocols.

Architect to MEP engineer The relationship between architecture and MEP is not quite as dynamic as that between architecture and structure but represents specific opportunities to benefit from collaboration.

Architect to MEP engineer: Coordination Monitor The MEP engineer needs to link in the architect's model to have the architectural model for context and positional relationships for ceiling-based items and the avoidance of clashes. Copy/Monitor is used to copy and monitor the architects levels and rooms. These room objects take on the additional properties, such as light levels and airflow. Note that levels are required to copy or monitor the rooms.

MEP engineer to architect: linked models The architect's primary benefit from linking in the MEP model(s) is the ability to reference this geometry within the context of the architectural model and drawings. There is not usually a compelling reason to use the Coordination Monitor from MEP to the architectural project, although interference checking may be required under certain circumstances.

Structural to MEP engineer This relationship is almost always best served by cross-linked models using interference checking. The most important aspect of collaboration between these disciplines is the early detection and correction of clashes.

Linked Models

The first rule governing all Revit-to-Revit coordination situations is that all linked project files must be generated with the same Revit platform version. For example, the architecture model must be generated with Revit Architecture 2013, the structure model must be generated with Revit®

Structure 2013, and the MEP model must be generated with Revit® MEP 2013. In a worksharing environment, it is also important to ensure that the computers of all team members working on a project have the same Revit version installed (Figure 7.4). As discussed earlier in this chapter, a BIM execution plan should include an agreement on all modeling and coordination software to be used on a project, including the versions of each listed program.

FIGURE 7.4
Linked files must use the same platform version, and all worksharing team members should use the same build.

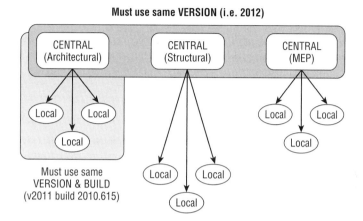

You can find the build information for your Revit product by clicking the Help drop-down button and selecting About. As shown in Figure 7.5, the build appears at the upper right of the About Autodesk Revit Architecture 2013 dialog box.

FIGURE 7.5
Click the Help button flyout and select About to find the build of your Revit software.

SHARED POSITIONING

In the collaborative process of sharing information via linked models, the coordinated positioning of each model is of paramount importance. Agreement on a common coordinate system and origin must be included in every project's BIM execution plan to ensure accuracy. This section will help you develop a fundamental understanding of the coordinate systems within Revit so you can configure and manage them in your projects. For a more complete history of coordinate systems and various examples of using them within the Revit environment, we recommend the following class material from Autodesk University 2009, available at www.autodesk.com/au:

◆ *AB118-3 Finding Your Way Around Shared Coordinates,* by Teresa Martin, Ideate Inc.

◆ *AB9114-1 Autodesk Revit Collaboration: Shared Coordinates for Projects Big and Small,* by Steve Stafford, AEC Advantage, Inc.

There are two coordinate systems in a Revit project: *project internal* and *shared*. Each system has essential features and limitations.

Project internal   Every Revit project has an internal coordinate system referred to in several places as Project. You can find this reference in the type properties of datum-measuring objects such as levels and spot coordinates, as well as in the settings for exporting CAD files. The project coordinate system cannot be changed, and your model should be constructed within a *one-mile radius* of the project origin. The true origin in Revit is referred to as the Project Start Up Point, and the Project Base Point can be reset to this point by setting it to Unclipped, right-clicking on the icon, and selecting Move To Start Up Location.

A complementary component of the project internal coordinate system is the view orientation of Project North. This setting is the default and can be found in the View Properties of any plan. We strongly recommend that your model be created in an orthogonal relationship to project or as you expect the plans to be oriented on a typical sheet. Your project's actual relation to true north will be established via shared coordinates.

Shared coordinates   According to Ideate's Teresa Martin, "[S]hared coordinates are simply a way for the project team to utilize the same definitive work point." In other words, the shared coordinate system consists of a single origin and true north orientation that can be synchronized between models and even Autodesk® AutoCAD® drawings. In the diagram shown in Figure 7.6, you will see an architectural model and structural model linked together. Each model was created using a different project base point (not the recommended method), but their shared coordinates were synchronized.

FIGURE 7.6
Diagram of the relationship between project base points and shared coordinates in linked models

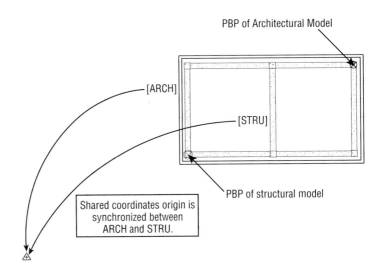

LIMITATIONS ON USING SHARED COORDINATES FOR EXPORTING

Although you can use either Project Internal or Shared as the setting for Coordinate System Basis when exporting CAD formats, there are some limitations. If you are exporting sheet views, the plan data will always use the project internal coordinate system. Using the Xref Views On Sheets option during export does not change this limitation. We recommend using views — not sheets — for issuing 2D CAD backgrounds to project participants not using Revit.

The shared coordinates are also not supported if you export your project to IFC format. Only the project internal coordinates are used. If you are planning to utilize IFC exported data in tools such as Solibri Model Checker, BIMServer, or TOKMO, you will have to either manually transform the coordinates between linked models after export or make sure that each linked model in your project has the same relation to the project internal origin before beginning the project. Refer to Chapter 8 for more detailed information on exporting.

ACQUIRING OR PUBLISHING COORDINATES

When you attempt to synchronize shared coordinates between linked projects, there are two tools to achieve this: Acquire Coordinates and Publish Coordinates. A simple way to understand the difference between these tools is to think of them in terms of pulling versus pushing:

◆ Acquire = Pull

◆ Publish = Push

It is important to understand the situations in which you would pull or push coordinates between linked files. A typical workflow for establishing a synchronized, shared coordinate system on a single building project would be as follows:

1. A site model is generated in which the survey point in the Revit project is coordinated with geodetic survey markers or station lines. The site model is linked into the architectural Revit model. This file can be placed manually, and then moved and rotated into a position relative to the building. *Do not move or rotate your building to the linked site model!*

2. From the Manage tab, select Coordinates, then Acquire Coordinates. Pick the linked file and the origin of the shared coordinate system and the angle of true north in your Revit model will be synchronized with those in the linked file.

3. All engineers or consultants using Revit should obtain a copy of the site model and repeat steps 1 and 2. When linking other project models that have already been synchronized with the site model, they can be placed using the Auto–By Shared Coordinates option.

Acquiring Coordinates from a CAD File

A common scenario in a project workflow begins with the architect commencing a design model and receiving a 2D survey file in DWG format from a civil engineer. The survey is drawn in coordinates that are geospatially correct but may not be orthogonal to true north. The architect should create the model close to the internal project origin; however, the architect will need to ensure that the building and survey coordinates are synchronized for properly oriented CAD exports and for coordination with additional linked Revit models from engineers in later phases of the project.

The architect will link the 2D CAD file into the Revit model but will first manually place it — moving and rotating the CAD file to be in proper alignment with the building model. Once the link is in place and constrained (or locked), the architect will acquire the coordinates from the DWG survey by switching to the Manage tab, selecting Coordinates ➤ Acquire Coordinates from the Project Location panel, and then clicking the DWG link. This will not affect any views that are oriented to Project North — only those set to true north will display the orientation established by the coordinates acquired from the survey file.

For a campus-style project in which you might be creating multiple instances of a linked building model, you would most likely use Publish Coordinates to push information from a site model into the linked building model. Here's how that would work in a hypothetical scenario:

1. Assuming a site model and building model were created in Revit, you would begin by opening the site model and linking the building model into the site.

2. Adjust the position of the first instance of the linked building model to location A.

3. From the Manage tab, select Coordinates from the Project Location panel, and then click Publish Coordinates and pick the linked model.

4. The Location Weather And Site dialog box will open and you will create a duplicate location named Location A, as shown in Figure 7.7.

FIGURE 7.7
Creating multiple locations for a single linked model

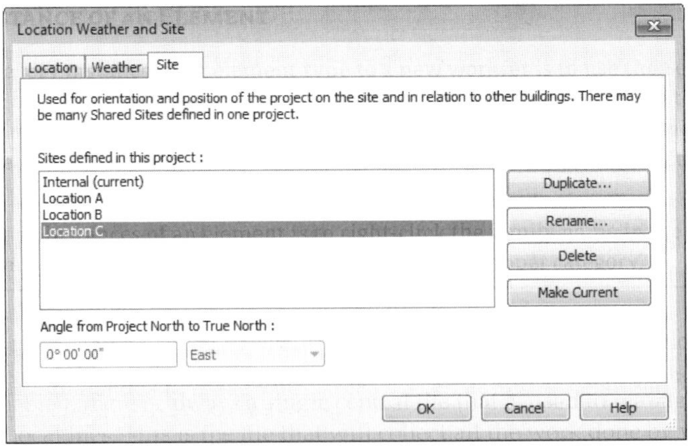

5. Copy the linked building model as required for each subsequent location. Repeat steps 2 through 4 for each copy.

6. When you close the site model and open the building model, you can link the site model to the building using any of the named location references you *pushed* into the building model.

Using Project Base Point and Survey Point

In prior versions of Revit, locating the project origin or shared coordinate point was only accomplished by using an imported AutoCAD file or by using spot coordinates and moving elements as required. Revit now provides two objects to identify these points: the *project base point* and the *survey point*. In the default templates, these points are visible in the floor plan named Site; however, they can also be displayed in any other plan view by opening the Visibility/Graphic Overrides dialog box, selecting the Model Categories tab, and expanding the Site category, as shown in Figure 7.8.

FIGURE 7.8

The project base point and survey point are found under Site in Visibility/Graphic Overrides.

Project Base Point   The project base point (PBP) defines the 0,0,0 point of the project. Notice that we are not calling it the *origin*. Using that term, you might confuse the PBP with the Revit internal project origin. The unclipped PBP *can* be moved in relation to the internal origin, thus creating a secondary reference point for spot coordinates, spot elevations, and levels — as long as the measuring control is set to Project in the respective type properties. Moving the clipped PBP icon is the equivalent of using the Relocate Project tool, moving the project relative to the shared coordinates system.

Unless your project requires the use of a secondary point of reference other than the survey point, we recommend that you do not adjust the PBP and that you do make sure your building model lies within a close reference of this point, such as the corner of a property line or intersection of column grids A and 1.

Survey Point   The survey point is the equivalent of a station pin or geodetic survey marker in a civil engineering drawing (Figure 7.9). This is the point that will be coordinated to real geospatial coordinates. For coordination with Autodesk® Civil 3D® software, the survey point is used when a Revit project is exported to the ADSK file format.

Note that specifying a particular location for the survey point based on civil engineering data is not a requirement. For smaller projects, the survey point and shared coordinates may never be used at all; however, they are critical in the use of analytical tools for daylighting and solar analysis.

FIGURE 7.9
The survey point can be considered similar to a real-world geodetic survey marker.

Survey Point - Internal
Shared Site:
N/S   0' 0"
E/W   0' 0"
Elev 0' 0"

To further expand your understanding of these points and what happens when they are modified, we have created a sample file for your reference. Open the file c07-Shared-Points.rvt from this book's companion web page (www.sybex.com/go/masteringrevit2013). In this file you will find three copies of the floor plan Level 1. One view is configured to display the project coordinates, another view displays the shared coordinates, and the third view displays a combination of the two. There are also two types of spot coordinates: one indicating project coordinates in which the values are prefixed with the letter p and the other indicating shared coordinates with the prefix of s. You can open these three floor plans and tile the windows (click the View tab, select the Window panel, and choose Tile or type the keyboard shortcut WT) to get a better sense of how these points affect one another (Figure 7.10).

In this sample file, you can explore the effects of moving the project base point and survey point on your model's coordinates. When selected, the project base point and survey point have paperclip icons that determine the behavior of the points when you move them. Clicking the paperclip icon changes the state from clipped to unclipped and back to clipped.

FIGURE 7.10
Using tiled windows helps you examine the effect of project and shared coordinates.

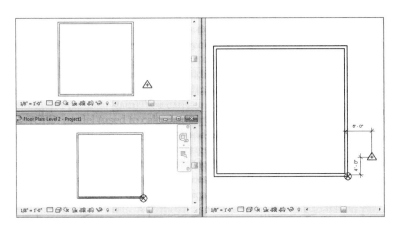

The following is a list of the possible point modifications and explanations of how they affect the project. Note that in most cases you shouldn't have to move the survey point or project base point if you are using a linked Civil file (2D or 3D) and acquiring the coordinates from the linked file.

Project Base Point (PBP): Clipped

◆ Move the PBP.

◆ PBP values change.

◆ Project-based spot coordinates don't change.

◆ Model elements "move" relative to shared coordinates.

Moving a clipped PBP is the same as using Relocate Project. That is, the model elements maintain their relationship to the PBP, but the relationship of the PBP to the survey point is changed.

Project Base Point: Unclipped

◆ Move the PBP.

◆ PBP values change.

◆ Project-based spot coordinates change.

◆ Model elements don't move.

Unclipping the PBP essentially *detaches* it from the internal project origin. Moving the unclipped PBP is only used to affect the values reported in spot coordinates set to the project origin base. It does not have any effect on exported files.

Survey Point (SP): Clipped

◆ Move the SP.

◆ SP values don't change.

◆ Shared spot coordinates change.

◆ Model elements don't move.

The clipped survey point represents the origin of the shared coordinate system. Moving it is the equivalent of setting a new origin point. Use caution if you must move the shared coordinates origin if linked models already exist in which the shared coordinates have already been synchronized. In such a case, each linked model must be opened and manually reconciled with the model in which the origin has changed.

Survey Point: Unclipped

◆ Move the SP.

◆ SP values change.

◆ Shared spot coordinates don't change.

◆ Model elements don't move.

Moving an unclipped survey point essentially doesn't do anything. It doesn't affect spot coordinates and it doesn't affect the origin of exported files.

USE PINNING TO PROTECT COORDINATE ORIGINS

An excellent way to prevent accidental modification of your project's coordinate systems is to pin them. To do so, you must first make sure the survey point and project base point are visible in a view (as we discussed earlier in this section). Next, select each point and click the Pin button from the Modify panel when the Modify | Project Base Point Or Modify | Survey Point ribbon appears.

ATTACHMENT VS. OVERLAY

Linked Revit models utilize what we will call a *portability setting* that is similar to the way Xrefs are handled in AutoCAD. Although this setting is not exposed when you initially link a Revit model, you can modify the setting by switching to the Insert tab and selecting Manage Links. Change the setting in the Reference Type column as desired (Figure 7.11).

FIGURE 7.11
Determining the reference type of linked Revit models

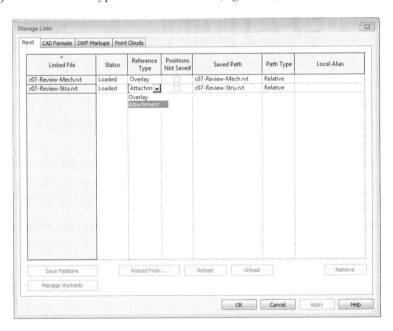

Attachment   The Attachment option ensures that the linked model will be included if the host model is subsequently linked into other hosts. For example, if Project A is linked into Project B as an *attachment*, when Project B is linked into Project C, Project A will automatically be included as well.

Overlay   The Overlay option prevents linked models from being included if the host model is subsequently linked into other hosts. For example, if Project A is linked into Project B as an *overlay*, when Project B is linked into Project C, Project A will not be included.

LINKS WITH WORKSHARING

If you are utilizing linked Revit models where one or more of the project files have worksharing enabled, there are a few guidelines to follow as well as some tangible benefits. Be sure to read more about worksharing in Chapter 6, "Understanding Worksharing."

The first guideline is to ensure that the files received from consultants are set up as central files within your own domain. Even though you may not have direct access to your consultants' servers, the software will attempt to reconcile the location of each project model's central file location. We recommend opening each received Revit file and using the following steps to set up a copy as a central file:

1. From the Application menu, select Open ➢ Project.

2. In the Open dialog box, make sure you have the worksharing-enabled project selected and check the Detach From Central option (Figure 7.12).

FIGURE 7.12
Open a worksharing project detached from its central file.

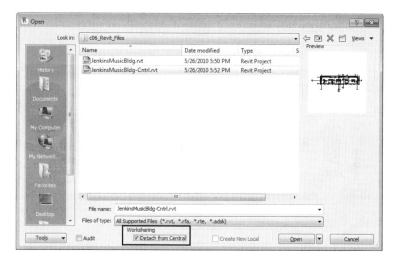

3. After the file opens, return to the Application menu and select Save or click the save icon on the Quick Access toolbar (QAT). Note that the Detach From Central option has created an unnamed project.

4. Save the project to a new location. When a worksharing project is detached from its central file, the first save will automatically consider the project a new central file. If you did not use the Detach From Central option when you opened the file, you must click the Options button in the Save dialog box and choose the option Make This A Central File After Save (Figure 7.13).

FIGURE 7.13
Save option to
establish a new
central file

5. Finally, click the Synchronize And Modify Settings button in the QAT, and in the Synchronize With Central dialog box, be sure to check the option to relinquish all user-created worksets before clicking OK to complete the process (Figure 7.14).

FIGURE 7.14
Relinquish all user-
created worksets
when saving a
file that has been
detached from
central.

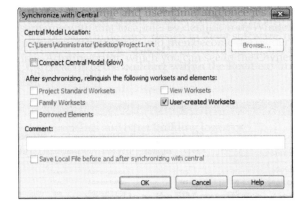

When the host model is enabled for worksharing, we recommend that you create and reserve a workset for each linked Revit model, such as Link-RVT-Structure or Link-RVT-HVAC. This simple step will allow your team members to choose whether they would like any, all, or none of the linked models to be loaded when working on a host model. To enable this functionality, use the Specify setting in the drop-down options next to the Open button.

When the Worksets dialog box appears, select the worksets reserved for the linked models and set their Open/Closed status as you desire. The benefit of using worksets to manage linked Revit models is the flexibility it offers a project team. When a team member closes a workset containing a linked model, the linked model is unloaded only for that person — it does not unload for the entire team.

Additional flexibility can be leveraged with the Workset parameter in both the instance and type properties of a linked model. In a large and complex project that consists of multiple wings where some of the wings are identical, each wing may consist of multiple linked models: architecture, structure, and MEP. Figure 7.15 shows a simplified representation of such a design where Wings A, D, and E are identical, as are Wings B, C, and F.

FIGURE 7.15
Schematic representation of a complex project assembled with multiple linked models

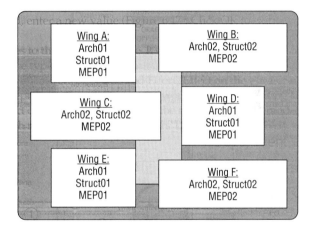

In Figure 7.15, there are two Revit models that represent wing design 01 and 02 for each discipline (Arch01, Arch02, and so on). Note there are three instances of each linked model. For each instance of a linked model, you can specify the Workset parameter so that the workset instance property represents the wing and the type property reflects either the entire discipline or one of the discipline models, as in this example:

◆ Instance workset: Wing A

◆ Type workset: Link-Architecture01 or simply, Link-Architecture

Using this example, you can choose to open the Wing A workset, which would load all the discipline models, but only for Wing A, or you could choose to open the Link-Architecture workset, which would load only the architectural models but for all the wings. Note that you can modify the workset-type properties only after placing a linked model in your project. Access this setting by selecting an instance of a linked model and opening the Properties palette, and then click Edit Type. Although this functionality can offer a variety of benefits to your project team, it should be used with care and proper planning because it can adversely affect model visibility if you are using worksets for visibility manipulation.

Worksharing-enabled linked models also afford you the flexibility to adjust the visibility of project elements for the entire project, without relying on individual settings per view or maintenance of view templates. For example, grids and levels are not usually displayed from linked models because their extents are not editable in the host model and the graphics may not match those in the host model. Without worksets, the owner of the host model would have to establish visibility settings for the linked model within all views and hopefully manage those settings in view templates. Assuming the owner of the linked model maintains the levels and grids on an agreed-upon workset such as Shared Levels And Grids, you will be able to close that workset in one place, thus affecting the entire host project. To modify the workset options for linked Revit models, follow these steps:

1. Open the Manage Links dialog box and switch to the Revit tab.

2. Select one of the linked files and click the Manage Worksets button.

3. In the Linking Worksets dialog box, select the worksets you would like to unload, click the Close button, and then click Reload.

4. Click OK to close the Manage Links dialog box.

RELATIVE PATHS OF LINKED MODELS

If your team is working in a situation where your project file(s) is regularly transferred between multiple locations throughout the design process, you may find it difficult to maintain linked files (they are unloaded when the file is returned), even if you are using relative paths. To alleviate this problem, try keeping the linked models and CAD files within subdirectories of the central file. For example, if your central file is saved in W:\Architecture\BIM, try keeping linked CAD files in W:\ Architecture\BIM\Links-CAD and linked Revit models from consultants in W:\Architecture\ BIM\Links-RVT.

BENEFITS AND LIMITATIONS

To summarize using linked Revit models, let's review some of the benefits and limitations. You should carefully consider these aspects not only when preparing for interdisciplinary coordination, but also when managing large complex projects with linked files.

The following list highlights some of the benefits:

Tagging elements in linked files Most model elements (not rooms) from a linked model can be tagged in a host model. Linked views can also be utilized if the annotation exists in the linked model and needs to be displayed in the host.

Scheduling elements in linked files In the Fields tab of the Schedule Properties dialog box, check the option Include Elements In Linked Files.

Copying/pasting elements from linked files In a host model, use the Tab key to select any individual element within a linked file and you can use standard copy and paste techniques to create a copy of the element in the host model.

Hiding elements in linked files In addition to having full control of a linked model's visual fidelity through object styles, you can use the Tab key to select an individual element in a linked file and use the Hide In View commands as you would on any element within the host model.

The following list highlights some of the limitations:

Joining walls Walls cannot be joined between linked Revit models. Consider alternative graphic techniques such as using coarse-scale black solid fill to mask unjoined walls.

Opening linked models   You cannot have a host model with loaded linked models open in the same Revit session as the linked model files. Either separate Revit sessions must be launched or the host file must be closed before opening a linked model.

EXERCISE: USING LINKED MODELS

Before beginning the exercises in this chapter, download the related files from this book's web page. The project files in each section's exercise should be saved because the lessons will build on the data. In this exercise, you will do the following:

- Link the architectural model to a blank project.
- Establish shared coordinates.

Note that the structural model is essentially a blank project with a few element types specifically built for this chapter's lessons. Let's get started working with shared coordinates:

1. Open the sample project file c07-1-Structure.rvt.

2. Switch to the Insert tab and select Link Revit.

3. Navigate to the file c07-2-Architecture.rvt.

4. Set the Positioning option to Auto – Center To Center and click Open.

5. Activate the South elevation view and use the Align tool to bring the linked model's Level 1 down to align with Level 1 in the host model if necessary.

Remember, linked files should be adjusted to keep the geometry in the host model as close to the host's internal project origin as possible.

6. Switch to the Manage tab and from the Project Location panel, select Coordinates ➢ Acquire Coordinates. Pick the linked model.

Notice that the elevation value displayed in the level within the current file has changed to match the shared elevation in the linked file. This is because the Elevation Base parameter of the level's type properties has been set to Shared.

7. Save the project file for subsequent exercises in this chapter.

MODIFYING ELEMENT VISIBILITY IN LINKED FILES

Once you have linked one or more Revit files into your source project file, you may want to adjust the visibility of elements within the linked files. By default, the display settings in the Visibility/Graphics Overrides dialog box are set to By Host View for linked files, which means model objects in the linked files will adopt the same appearance as the host file. In the following exercise, we'll show you how to customize these settings to turn the furniture off in the linked file and then display the room tags:

1. Continue this exercise with the file c07-1-Structure.rvt that you saved with the linked architectural model.

2. Activate the Level 1 floor plan from the Project Browser.

3. Go to the View tab in the ribbon, locate the Graphics panel, and select Visibility/Graphics. In the Visibility/Graphics Overrides dialog box, select the Revit Links tab.

You will see the linked architectural model listed as an expandable tree. Click the plus sign next to the name of the linked file and you will see a numbered instance of the link. This allows you to customize the visibility for each instance of a linked file if you have multiple copies of the link in the host file.

4. In the row displaying the name of the linked file, click the button in the Display Settings column that is labeled By Host View. Doing so opens the RVT Link Display Settings dialog box.

5. To begin customizing the display of elements in the linked file, you must first choose the Custom option in the Basics tab, as shown in Figure 7.16. This enables all the options in each tab of the RVT Link Display Settings dialog box.

FIGURE 7.16
Enable all custom display settings for a linked RVT file.

6. Select the Model Categories tab and choose <Custom> in the drop-down list at the top of the dialog box, as shown in Figure 7.17.

FIGURE 7.17
Enable custom display settings for model categories of a linked RVT file.

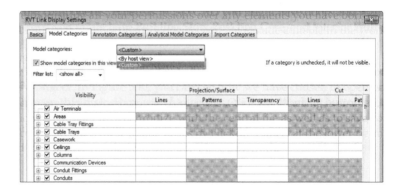

7. Clear the checks from the following categories: Casework, Furniture, and Furniture Systems.

8. Click OK to close all open dialog boxes.

You should observe that all the furniture and casework from the linked architecture file are no longer visible in the Level 1 floor plan. In a standard architecture-to-structure collaboration scenario, the structural engineer is likely to have a view template in which typical architectural elements are already hidden. In such a case, the default By Host View settings would be sufficient. The previous exercise illustrates a scenario where additional visual control is required.

Whereas the previous exercise focused on the display of model elements, a slightly different approach is required to utilize annotation elements from a linked file. In the following exercise, we will show you how to display the room tags from the linked architectural model. Note that many other tags can be applied to linked model elements in Revit 2013 products. Here are the steps:

1. Continue with the `c07-1-Structure.rvt` file saved from the previous exercise and make sure you have activated the Level 1 floor plan.

2. Open the Visibility/Graphics dialog box and select the Revit Links tab.

3. The button in the Display Settings column should be labeled as Custom based on the previous exercise. Click the Custom button to open the RVT Link Display Settings dialog box.

4. Select the Basics tab and click the Linked View drop-down box. You will see the floor plans available for reference in the linked file. Only view types similar to the current view in the host file will be available for use as a linked view.

5. Select the linked view named Level 1-A-Anno.

6. Click OK to close all open dialog boxes.

After completing these steps, you should see the room tags from the linked architectural file in the host file. Remember that you can tag other model elements in linked files. Try using the Tag By Category tool to place some door tags on the linked architectural model.

Coordination Tools

Once you have established the configuration of linked Revit models for your project, the next step is to create intelligently bound references between specific elements within the models. In the past, CAD users might have referenced files containing grid lines or level lines to establish a level of coordination between one user's data and another's. Note that these elements in CAD are merely *lines* — not datum objects as they are in a Revit model. If these referenced elements were modified in a CAD setting, the graphic appearance of the referenced lines would update, but there would be no additional automated response to the geometry. It would be the responsibility of the recipient to update any referring geometry in their host files.

Revit coordination tools — Copy/Monitor and Coordination Review — allow a project team to ensure a high degree of quality control while achieving it at an increased level of productivity. These tools can function on datum (levels and grids) as well as model elements such as columns, walls, and floors. The Copy/Monitor command is used first to establish the intelligent bonds between linked elements and host elements, whereas the Coordination Review command automatically monitors differences between host and linked elements that were previously bound with the Copy/Monitor command.

Although these tools are indeed powerful and have no similar discernable similarities to CAD workflows of the past, it is important to employ proper planning and coordination with your design team. The familiar adage of "quality over quantity" holds true for the implementation of coordination tools. It may not be necessary to create monitored copies of all structural elements within the architectural model. How would these affect project-wide quantity takeoffs for the sake of minor improvements in graphic quality?

Again, we reiterate the necessity of developing a BIM execution plan to determine important aspects of the collaboration process. When using specific coordination tools such as those in Revit, teams might plan on issues such as these:

- Who is the "Owner" of grids and levels?

- Who is the "Owner" of floor slabs?

- Are structural walls copied, monitored, or just linked?

- How often are models exchanged?

- How are coordination conflicts resolved?

A seemingly powerful BIM tool will not replace the need for professional supervision and the standard of care implicit to respective disciplines in the building industry. As such, there is no substitution for the most important part of effective collaboration: *communication*. Without open and honest communication, the coordination tools will discover conflicts, but the results may be ignored, dismissed, or overwritten to the detriment of the team's progress.

COPY/MONITOR

CERT
OBJECTIVE

The Copy/Monitor command allows you to create local copies of linked elements for better graphic control of the elements while maintaining an intelligent bond to the linked elements. If the linked element changes in a subsequent iteration of the project file, the changes are detected in the Coordination Review tool, which will be discussed later in this chapter.

With the project file saved from the previous exercise, switch to the Collaborate tab and select Copy/Monitor ➢ Select Link. Pick the linked architectural model and the ribbon will change to Copy/Monitor mode. Click the Options icon to open the dialog box shown in Figure 7.18; note that the options seen in the Copy/Monitor tool in Revit Architecture are slightly different from those in the Structure and MEP products. For the purpose of this book, we will focus only on the options available in Revit Architecture.

As shown in Figure 7.18, the Copy/Monitor Options dialog box in Revit Architecture is divided into five tabs representing the elements available to be copied and/or monitored. For each element tab, there is a list called Categories And Types To Copy. As shown in Figure 7.19, the Floors tab lists the available floor types in the linked model in the left column and host model floor types in the right column. Notice that any of the linked types can be specified with the option Don't Copy This Type. This feature can be used for quality control if your project's

BIM execution plan states that certain elements are not to be copied. For example, if walls are not to be copied, switch to the Walls tab and set all linked wall types to Don't Copy This Type.

FIGURE 7.18
Element tabs available for Copy/Monitor in Revit Architecture

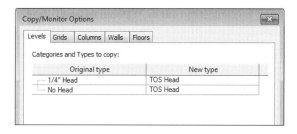

FIGURE 7.19
The Copy/Monitor Options dialog box allows customization for intelligent collaboration.

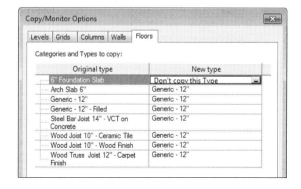

At the bottom of the Copy/Monitor Options dialog box, you will find a section called Additional Copy Parameters for each element tab (Figure 7.20). Note that the additional parameters are different for each element category. For example, when levels are copied and monitored, an offset and naming prefix can be applied to accommodate the difference between the finish floor level in a linked architectural model and the top of steel level in the host structural model.

FIGURE 7.20
Additional copy parameters can be applied to each element category.

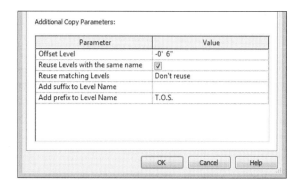

Let's take a closer look at each of the element category options available for the Copy/Monitor tool:

Levels   In most cases, the difference between the location of a structural level and an architectural level may lead to the presumption that you would not want to copy levels between files. However, maintaining an offset between linked and host levels can be quite desirable. Keep in mind the offset will apply to all copy/monitor selections. Thus, if a structural level needs to be offset by a different value, create the level in the host model and use the Monitor command to create the intelligent bond to the linked model's level. The difference will be maintained through any modifications in the linked model.

Grids   Copying in the grids is usually a strong workflow. You can use the options on these tabs to convert the grid bubbles used by the architect into those used by the structural engineer. It is also possible to add a prefix to the grid names. For instance, you could add the value S- in the prefix field and then grid A from the architectural model will come into the structural model as S-A.

Columns   The structural engineer can choose to replace any column — architectural or structural — in the architectural model with an appropriate structural column; however, this implies that the architect will maintain an understanding of where differentiating column types would exist. Realistically, the structural elements should only exist in the structural engineer's model and then link into the architectural model. The architect may then choose to either copy/monitor the linked structural columns with architectural columns (which act as finish wrappers) or place architectural columns along the monitored grid lines. In the latter option, architectural columns will move along with changes in grid line locations but would not update if structural columns are removed in the linked model.

Walls and Floors   Similar to columns, structural walls that are important to the coordination process may be better managed in the structural model and linked into the architectural model. If you decide to use a copy/monitor relationship for these types of elements, it is best to create uniquely named wall types for structural coordination. Name such wall types in a manner that makes them display at the top of the list in the Copy/Monitor Options dialog box. You can do so by adding a hyphen (-) or underscore (_) at the beginning of the wall type name.

Finally, make sure you select the check box Copy Windows/Doors/Openings for walls or Copy Openings/Inserts for floors so that you also get the appropriate openings for those components in the monitored elements.

EXERCISE: USING COPY/MONITOR

Continue with the project file saved in the previous exercise in this chapter. In this exercise, you will do the following:

◆   Use Copy/Monitor to establish new levels and grids.

◆   Use Copy/Monitor to create floors.

◆   Link the new structural model back to the architectural model.

◆   Use the Monitor option for grids in the architectural model.

These steps will establish the intelligent bonds between elements in the host file with the related elements in the linked model. With the file c07-1-Structure.rvt open (saved from the previous exercise), activate the South elevation view. Then follow these steps:

1. Switch to the Collaborate tab and select Copy/Monitor ➤ Select Link. Choose the linked model.

2. On the Copy/Monitor tab, click the Options button.

3. Select the Levels tab and enter the following options under Categories And Types To Copy:

   ◆ **1/4″ [6 mm] Head = TOS Head**

In the Additional Copy Parameters section, set the following options:

   ◆ Offset Level: **-0′ 6″ [15 cm]**

   ◆ Add the prefix to Level Name: T.O.S.

4. Select the Grids tab and enter the following options under Categories And Types To Copy:

   ◆ 1/4″ [6 mm] Bubble = 1/4″ [6 mm] Square

5. Select the Floors tab and enter the following options under Categories And Types To Copy:

   ◆ Arch Slab 6″ [15 cm] = LW Concrete on Metal Deck

   ◆ Set all other entries under Original Types to Do Not Copy This Type.

In the Additional Copy Parameters section, set the following option:

   ◆ Copy Openings/Inserts: Yes (checked).

6. Click OK to close the Copy/Monitor Options dialog box.

7. From the Copy/Monitor ribbon, choose the Copy button.

8. Select the Level 2 and Roof levels in the linked model. Levels in the host model should be created 6″ [15 cm] below the linked levels with the prefix *T.O.S.* (Top Of Structure).

Note that there is already a Level 1 in the host model. You will need to use the Monitor tool to establish a relationship to the Level 1 in the linked model.

9. From the Copy/Monitor ribbon, choose the Monitor button and select the Level 1 in the host model. Note that you can only select levels in the host model for the first pick.

10. Select Level 1 in the linked model to complete the monitored relationship.

11. Activate Section 1 and return to Copy mode by clicking the Copy button in the Copy/Monitor ribbon.

12. Select the floor in the linked model at Level 2.

13. Activate the Level 1 floor plan and make sure the Copy tool is still active. Check the Multiple option in the Options bar.

14. Select all the visible grids using any selection method you prefer.

15. Click the Finish button in the Options bar to complete the copy process for the grids. Do not click the Finish icon in the Copy/Monitor ribbon without finishing the multiple selection mode first.

16. Click the Finish icon in the Copy/Monitor ribbon to exit Copy/Monitor mode.

If you now select any of the grids or levels in the host file, you will see a monitor icon near the center of the element. This icon indicates that the intelligent bond has been created between the host and the linked element and will evaluate any modifications in the linked file whenever the file is reloaded.

Save and close the file c07-1-Structure.rvt and then open the file c07-2-Architecture.rvt. Using the procedures you have learned earlier in this chapter, link the structural file into the architectural model. Placement should be done in the Level 1 floor plan using Auto – By Shared Coordinates positioning.

Use the Copy/Monitor tools in Monitor mode to establish the relationships of the grids between host and linked models. Doing so will ensure that changes to grids in either model will be coordinated.

COORDINATION REVIEW

After intelligent bonds have been established between elements in linked models, it is the purpose of the Coordination Review tool to support the workflow when datum or model elements are modified. This tool was designed to allow the recipient of linked data to control how and when elements in host models are modified based on changes in the linked models.

When a linked model is reloaded — which will happen automatically when the host model is opened or when you manually reload the linked model in the Manage Links dialog box — monitored elements will check for any inconsistencies. If any are found, you will see a warning message that a linked instance needs a coordination review.

The Coordination Review warning is triggered when any of the following scenarios occur:

◆ A monitored element in the linked model is changed, moved, or deleted.

◆ A monitored element in the host model is changed, moved, or deleted.

◆ Both the original monitored element and the copied element are changed, moved, or deleted.

◆ A hosted element (door, window, opening) is added, moved, changed, or deleted in a monitored wall or floor.

◆ The copied element in the host file is deleted.

To perform a coordination review, switch to the Collaborate tab and select Coordination Review ➤ Select Link. After picking one of the linked models, you will see the Coordination Review dialog box, which lists any inconsistencies in monitored elements (Figure 7.21).

FIGURE 7.21
The Coordination Review dialog box lists inconsistencies in monitored elements.

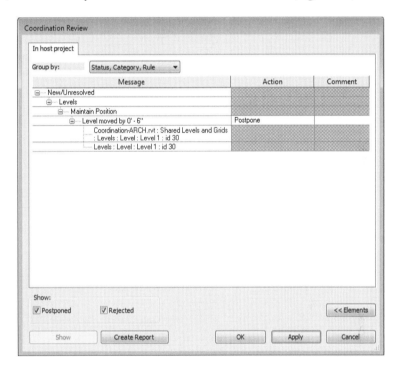

For each of the changes detected in the Coordination Review dialog box, one of the following actions can be applied. Note that actions resulting in changes to elements will be applied only to the host model; they do not modify elements in a linked model. Also note that not all options are available for all monitored elements.

Postpone   Takes no action on the monitored element and changes the message status so that it can be filtered out or considered later.

Reject   Select this action if you believe the change made to the element in the linked file is incorrect. A change must then be made to the element in the linked file.

Accept Difference   Accepts the change made to the element and updates the relationship. For example, if a pair of grids was 200 mm apart and one was moved to 300 mm away, the change would be accepted and the relationship would now be set to 300 mm.

Modify, Rename, Move   The command name changes based on the action. If the name of the monitored element has changed, the command reads Rename. If a column or level is moved, the command is Move. If a grid is changed or moved, the command is Modify.

Ignore New Elements   A new hosted element has been added to a monitored wall or floor. Select this action to ignore the new element in the host. It will not be monitored for changes.

Copy New Elements   A new hosted element has been added to a monitored wall or floor. Select this action to add the new element to the host and monitor it for changes.

Delete Element   A monitored element has been deleted. Select this action to delete the corresponding element in the current project.

Copy Sketch   The sketch or boundary of a monitored opening has changed. Select this action to change the corresponding opening in the current project.

Update Extents   The extents of a monitored element have changed. Select this action to change the corresponding element in the current project.

As you can see, Coordination Review can be a powerful tool to support the collaboration process. Remember that such a tool may not be appropriate for all elements at all times. For example, instead of copying and monitoring columns and grids, it may be sufficient to copy and monitor only grids because the columns placed in your host model will move with the grids anyway.

EXERCISE: USING COORDINATION REVIEW

In this exercise, you will utilize two files that have already been linked together with monitored elements between both files. You can download the files c07-Review-Arch.rvt (architectural model) and c07-Review-Stru.rvt (structural model) from this book's web page. In this exercise, you will do the following:

♦   Modify elements in the architectural model.

♦   Use Coordination Review to address these changes in the structural model.

Remember that you can't have a host model and a linked model open in the same Revit session. To make this lesson easier, you can launch a second Revit session. Open c07-Review-Arch.rvt in one session and c07-Review-Stru.rvt in the other. Then follow these steps:

1. In the architectural model, activate the Level 1 floor plan and make the following modifications:

   ♦   Move grid line F to the north by 2'-0".

   ♦   Rename grid 6 to 8.

2. Save the architectural model and switch to the structural model. Open the Manage Links window, select the linked architectural model, and click Reload. Once the file is done reloading, you are presented with the Coordination Review warning. Click OK to close the dialog box.

3. In the structural project, switch to the Collaborate tab and choose Coordination Review ➢ Select Link. Select the linked architectural model.

4. When the Coordination Review dialog box opens, you will see changes to monitored elements detected in the reloaded architectural model (Figure 7.22). You may need to expand some of the statuses and categories to reveal the detected change and the drop-down list under the Action column.

FIGURE 7.22
Coordination
Review detects
changes to moni-
tored elements.

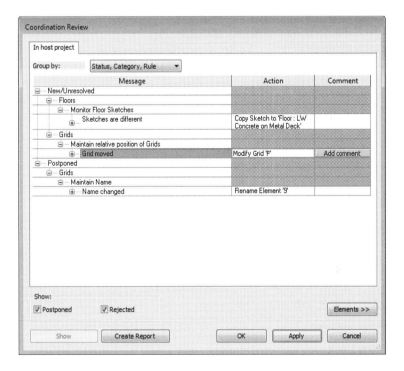

5. Apply the appropriate modifying action to each of the detected changes. (Copy the sketch of the changed floor, modify the moved grid, and rename the numbered grid.)

6. Click Apply and OK to close the dialog box.

In the previous exercise, you might have noticed the appearance of a monitored floor sketch. Why did a floor sketch change if you only moved a grid and renamed another? The answer lies in constraints and relationships. The exterior wall in the architectural model was constrained to be 2'-0" offset from grid line F. When it was moved, the exterior wall was moved to maintain the offset. The sketches of the model's floor slabs were created using the Pick Walls tools, creating an intelligent relationship to the wall. The modified grid affected the wall, which modified the floor, and the Coordination Monitor tools ensured that all changes were detected and presented to you for action.

Interference Checking

In addition to asset management, digital fabrication, and cost estimation, 3D coordination is one of the most important components of building information modeling. It has enormous potential to reduce the costs of construction through the computerized resolution of clashing building elements as well as exposing opportunities for alternate trade scheduling or prefabrication. The key component to achieving 3D coordination is interference checking, also known as *clash detection*.

 **Real World Scenario**

INDIANA UNIVERSITY DEFINES CLASHES

As we mentioned earlier in this chapter, not only are some building and facility owners requiring BIM processes and deliverables for new projects, they are defining how these processes are to be utilized. When you focus on interference checking, the myriad of potential clashes can be distilled into a prioritized grouping of building elements. Borrowing from Indiana University's BIM Standards & Guidelines for Architects, Engineers, & Contractors, the following is an intelligent approach to the organization of potential interferences. (Always remember that the priorities listed here are based on the requirements of one organization. The needs of your firm and those of your clients may vary.)

LEVEL ONE CLASHES

Clashes in these categories are considered the most critical to the coordination process. They usually relate to systems or construction techniques that are more costly to delay or reschedule.

◆ Mechanical Ductwork and Piping vs. Ceilings

◆ Mechanical Ductwork and Piping vs. Rated Walls (for coordination of dampers and other mechanical equipment needs)

◆ Mechanical Ductwork and Piping vs. Structure (columns, beams, framing, etc.)

◆ All Equipment and Their Applicable Clearances vs. Walls

◆ All Equipment and Their Applicable Clearances vs. Structure

◆ Mechanical Equipment and Fixtures vs. Electrical Equipment and Fixtures

◆ Mechanical Ductwork and Piping vs. Plumbing Piping

LEVEL TWO CLASHES

These categories of clashes are considered important to the design and construction process but are less critical than those designated as Level One.

◆ Casework vs. Electrical Fixtures and Devices

◆ Furnishings vs. Electrical Fixtures and Devices

◆ Structure vs. Specialty Equipment

◆ Structure vs. Electrical Equipment, Fixtures, and Devices

◆ Ductwork and Piping vs. Electrical Equipment, Fixtures, and Devices

◆ Ductwork vs. Floors

LEVEL THREE CLASHES

These clashes are considered important to the correctness of the model; however, they will usually change on a regular basis throughout the design and construction process.

◆ Casework vs. Walls

◆ Plumbing Piping vs. Electrical Equipment, Fixtures, and Devices

◆ Plumbing Piping vs. Mechanical Equipment, Fixtures, and Devices

◆ ADA Clear Space Requirements vs. Doors, Fixtures, Walls, Structure

TOOLS FOR INTERFERENCE CHECKING

The Revit Interference Check tool is a basic tool supporting 3D coordination. You can use it within a single Revit project model or between linked models. You can also select elements prior to running the tool in order to detect clashes within a limited set of geometry instead of the entire project.

For more powerful clash detection capabilities, Autodesk offers Navisworks® Manage (`www.autodesk.com/navisworks`), which is a multiformat model-reviewing tool with various modules supporting phasing simulation, visualization, and clash detection. Figure 7.23 shows an example of a model in Navisworks Manage comprising Revit, Tekla Structures, and AutoCAD MEP components. Some of the benefits of using Navisworks for interference checking over Revit include automated views of each clash, grouping of related clashes, enhanced reporting, clash resolution tracking, and markup capabilities. Although many other 3D model formats can be opened directly in Navisworks, Revit models can be exported directly to Navisworks format with an exporter add-in.

FIGURE 7.23
3D coordination model in Navisworks Manage

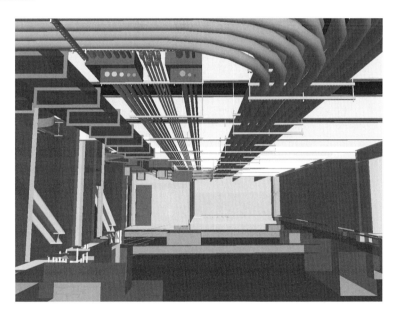

EXERCISE: RUNNING AN INTERFERENCE CHECK

CERT OBJECTIVE

Let's take a look at the Revit interference checking process. For this exercise, you will need to download three sample files to your computer or network: `c07-Interference-Arch.rvt`, `c07-Interference-Mech.rvt`, and `c07-Interference-Stru.rvt`. You can download these files from this book's web page. The sample files are already linked into each other using relative paths so be sure to place all three files in the same folder. Then follow these steps:

1. Open the file `c07-Interference-Mech.rvt` and activate the 3D view named Coord-STR-MEP. You should see some ductwork in the host model and the linked structural model. The architectural model has been turned off in this view.

2. Switch to the Collaborate tab, find the Coordinate panel, and choose Interference Check ➢ Run Interference Check.

3. When the Interference Check dialog box appears, choose c07-Interference-Stru.rvt from the Categories From drop-down list in the left column. Select Structural Framing in the left column and Ducts in the right column (Figure 7.24).

FIGURE 7.24
Select categories to be included in an interference report.

4. Click OK to close the dialog box.

5. The Interference Report window will appear, listing all clashes detected between the categories you selected. The list can be sorted by either Category 1 or Category 2, representing the left and right columns in the Interference Check dialog box, respectively. In Figure 7.25, one interference condition has been selected and the corresponding element is highlighted in the 3D view.

Note that you can navigate in the 3D view using any method (mouse, ViewCube®, or Navigation Wheels) while keeping the interference report open. This facilitates resolution of the clashing items. The results of the interference check can also be exported to an HTML format report. Click the Export button and specify a location for the report. You can then share this report with other members of your design team for remedial actions on linked models.

FIGURE 7.25
Results of an interference check are displayed in the Interference Report window.

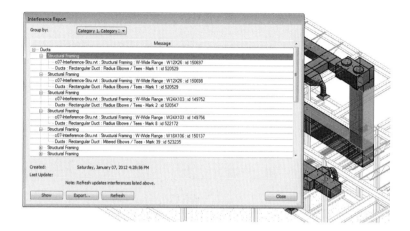

The Bottom Line

Prepare for interdisciplinary collaboration. Proper planning and communication are the foundation of effective collaboration. Although only some client organizations may require a BIM planning document, it is a recommended strategy for all design teams.

> **Master It**   What are the key elements of a BIM execution plan?

Collaborate using linked Revit models. The most basic tool for collaboration is the ability to view consultants' data directly within the context of your own model. Project files from other disciplines can be linked and displayed with predictable visual fidelity without complex conversion processes.

> **Master It**   How can worksharing complement the use of linked Revit models?

Use Copy/Monitor between linked models. The Coordination Monitor tools establish intelligent bonds between elements in a host file and correlating elements in a linked model. They also support a workflow that respects the needs of discrete teams developing their own data, perhaps on a different schedule than that of other team members.

> **Master It**   How can grids in two different Revit projects be related?

Run interference checks. Interference checking — also known as *clash detection* — is one of the most important components of building information modeling. It is the essence of virtual construction and has the greatest potential for cost savings during the physical construction process.

> **Master It**   How do you find interfering objects between two linked Revit models?

Chapter 8

Interoperability: Working Multiplatform

In the previous chapter, we discussed working with others in an environment in which all parties use Autodesk® Revit® Architecture software; however, often you'll need to work with data from other software platforms. For example, you may need to coordinate data from other disciplines, reuse legacy data, or integrate disparate design platforms. There are several ways to use external data within your Revit Architecture model in both 2D and 3D. We will discuss not only the methods of importing and exporting data but also when to use each method and the reasons for using specific settings. In this chapter, you'll learn to:

- ◆ Use imported 2D CAD data
- ◆ Export 2D CAD data
- ◆ Use imported 3D model data
- ◆ Export 3D model data
- ◆ Work with IFC imports and exports

The BIM Curve

Based on a 2004 study, the National Institute of Standards and Technology (NIST) reported annual losses of $15.8 billion in the building industry due to insufficient interoperability. This study underscores a problem that building information modeling as a whole is designed to address. Adequate interoperability will help rectify the problem illustrated in Figure 8.1, sometimes known as the *BIM curve*.

In Figure 8.1, the downward spikes in the lower line at the end of each project phase represent a loss of knowledge and acquired data. This loss usually occurs when a project is exported from BIM to a 2D CAD format or is printed to paper. Project data is then gradually reconstructed in another software platform. The upper line represents a more ideal paradigm where data and knowledge are gradually increased throughout the life of the project — a paradigm supported by BIM and full interoperability.

While full interoperability between BIM platforms is the ideal scenario, we realize that you are likely to be working with constituents who are using 2D CAD software or non-BIM 3D modelers. This chapter will show you not only how to export data and use imported data in a variety of ways but also when and why to apply different settings to ensure the best results.

FIGURE 8.1:
The BIM curve shows loss of data without interoperability at project milestones.

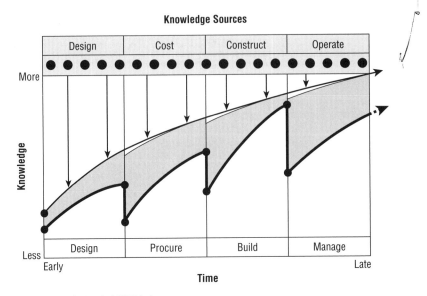

Source: P. Bernstein, Autodesk AEC Solutions

Overview of Importing

Although Revit software provides ample means to generate 2D documentation based on a rich multidimensional (3D, 4D, 5D, and so on) model, there are a few real-world scenarios in which CAD data must be integrated with the building information model. Such scenarios might include the following:

◆ Using CAD details developed within your firm

◆ Coordinating with other firms using CAD software

◆ Converting projects from CAD to a Revit model

◆ Using external modeling tools for conceptual massing

◆ Using complex component models from other software

Import Settings

When you are importing data from a DWG or DXF file, layers within the file are assigned a Revit line weight based on the weight assigned to each layer. If the layer line weights are set to Default in the CAD file, they will follow a translation template you can configure that maps the layer colors to Revit line weights. To access these settings, select the Insert tab and click the shortcut arrow at the bottom right of the Import panel. Doing so opens the Import Line Weights dialog box, shown in Figure 8.2.

FIGURE 8.2

Defining settings for imported DWG/DXF line weights

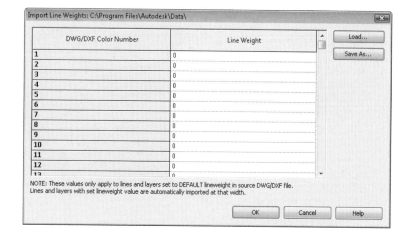

As you can see in the title bar of this dialog box, these settings are stored in a text file (TXT) in C:\Program Files\Autodesk\Data. There are several predefined text files based on international CAD standards for layer color:

◆ AIA (American Institute of Architects)

◆ BS1192 (British Standard)

◆ CP83 (Singapore Standard)

◆ ISO13567 (International Standards Organization)

Click the Load button to import one of these predefined line weight import templates or your own. Based on the unique needs of some projects, you might also consider creating customized import setting files and storing them along with the rest of your project data.

IMPORTING THE LINE WEIGHTS SETTING IN REVIT.INI FILES

The file location for the imported line weights map is stored in the Revit.ini file under the following category:

```
[Directories]
ImportLineweightsNameDWG=< Full path to TXT file >
```

If you are using any kind of automation scripts to set up standards, your import line weights template file location can be written into the Revit.ini file for all your users. Doing so ensures consistency if several team members are linking CAD data into your Revit project.

FONT MAPPING

Another important aspect for imports and links is the ability of Revit to map shape-based fonts to TrueType fonts. Usually a remnant of older CAD standards based on graphic performance, CAD files may contain fonts such as Simplex, RomanS, or Monotxt that do not have matches in standard Windows fonts. The shxfontmap.txt file tells Revit which TrueType font to substitute for each specified SHX font. You can find this text file at C:\ProgramData\Autodesk\RAC 2013\UserDataCache.

If your firm frequently uses imported CAD data as an integrated part of your final documentation, the shxfontmap.txt file should be configured to map your standard CAD fonts to your standard Revit fonts. This file should then be copied to the workstations of all team members using Revit. Failure to do so may result in undesirable results when utilizing linked CAD files in a worksharing environment.

Importing vs. Linking

You can bring CAD data into the Revit environment in two ways: importing and linking. Each method has advantages and disadvantages.

Importing Similar to the using the Insert command in Autodesk® AutoCAD® software, importing data integrates the CAD data into the Revit project but does not allow the imported data to be updated if the original CAD file is modified. In such a case, the imported data would have to be deleted and reimported. It also does not give you an easy way to purge the layers, linetypes, and hatch patterns of the imported file after it has been deleted.

Importing is the only method supported for accurate representation of 3D model geometry. The method for integrating external model data will be discussed later in this chapter in the section "Importing 3D Data."

Linking A linked CAD file in a Revit project is analogous to an external reference (Xref) in an AutoCAD project. When the original CAD file is modified, its reference is automatically updated in the Revit environment. Linking also allows you to easily unload or remove a file when it is no longer needed, which will leave no trace of the file's contents after removal.

Linked data cannot be modified in a Revit project unless it is converted to an import in the Manage Links dialog box (Insert ➤ Manage Links) and then exploded.

Linking is the preferred method for external data integration; however, too many linked files will make it slower to open a Revit project. Although ceiling plan fixture layouts may change with every design iteration (where linking is preferred), static standard details that all share a minimal amount of standardized layers, linetypes, hatch patterns, text, and dimension styles might be better suited as imports.

COLLECT CAD LINKS IN A LINKED REVIT FILE

Another option to manage many CAD references in larger projects is to create a separate Revit project containing only the linked data. If the CAD data is placed with the Current View Only option, you must use linked views between Revit models. If the linked data does not use this option, it will be visible as any other modeled element in a linked Revit model.

Options During Importing/Linking

After you have configured the necessary settings for inserted CAD data and decided on whether to import or link, you will need to understand certain options during the import/link process. We'll discuss the preferred settings for each of the options based on real-world situations in the sections "Importing 2D Data" and "Importing 3D Data." To place your first CAD file into a Revit project, switch to the Insert tab and select either the Link CAD or the Import CAD button. No matter which tool you use, there will be several important options at the bottom of the command dialog box, as shown in Figure 8.3.

FIGURE 8.3
Options available for import/link

Let's examine the meaning of the settings in this situation:

Current View Only   When this option is selected, the linked or imported file can be seen only in the view in which it was inserted and is thus considered a view-specific element. In a worksharing-enabled project, this data will be assigned to the view's workset. More often than not, you will want to choose this option to limit the number of views in which the referenced data will appear. If you need this data in other views, you can copy and paste it from one view to another.

If the option is not selected, the linked file can be seen in all views, including 3D, elevations, and sections. In a worksharing-enabled project, this data will be assigned to the active workset. A benefit to using links in a worksharing environment is the ability to create a workset specifically for linked data and uncheck its Visible In All Views option. The CAD file(s) placed in this manner will not appear in every view but are available when you need them by adjusting the workset visibility in the Visibility/Graphic Overrides dialog box.

Colors   Colors don't matter for linked CAD files being used for model conversion; however, using Invert or Preserve may help distinguish the CAD data from the modeled elements during the conversion process.

Layers   These options allow you to import or link all the layers, only the layers visible when the CAD file was last saved, or a selected group of layers you choose from the linked file in a separate dialog box. (Layers is a DWG-based term. Revit software supports the same functionality with levels from DGN files.)

Import Units   For CAD files generated in an original program (that is, DWG from AutoCAD or DGN from MicroStation), the Auto-Detect option works well. If you are linking CAD data that has been exported from a different program, such as DWG exported from Rhino, you should specify the units to the respective CAD file.

Positioning   To maintain consistency in a multilevel project during a CAD-to-Revit coordination or conversion process, you should use Auto – Origin To Origin or Auto – By Shared

Coordinates. Origin To Origin will align the world coordinates origin of the CAD file with the project internal origin. Although Autodesk claims Auto – By Shared Coordinates is only for use with linked Revit files, it can be used with CAD files if rotation of true north becomes inconsistent using the Origin To Origin option.

Place At   This option is available only if Current View Only is not selected; it specifies the level at which the inserted data will be placed.

Correct Lines That Are Slightly Off Axis   New to Autodesk Revit Architecture 2013 is a command that automatically corrects lines that are slightly off axis when you import or link CAD geometry. This option is selected by default and will help keep your Revit elements (such as walls or linework) that tie to CAD lines from being askew.

Manipulating Linked Data

Once you have data imported or linked into a Revit project, you have several ways of manipulating the data to suit your needs:

Foreground/Background   This setting applies only to linked or imported CAD files placed with the Current View Only option. With the inserted file selected, a drop-down menu will appear in the Options bar so you can adjust whether the data appears above or below your modeled Revit content.

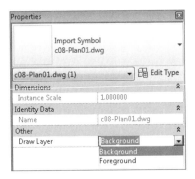

Pay close attention to this option when integrating 2D CAD data with an existing Revit model — sometimes linked or imported CAD data may not appear at all until you set the option to Foreground because of floors or ceilings obscuring the 2D data.

Visibility of layers/levels   The layers or levels within a linked or imported CAD file can be accessed in two ways, the easiest of which is the Query tool. First, select a linked or imported CAD file, and you will see a special Modify panel appear at the right end of the ribbon. Select the Query tool and then pick an object in the CAD file.

You will see the Import Instance Query dialog box (Figure 8.4). Using this tool, you can hide the layer or level by clicking the Hide In View button. Note that the Query tool will remain active even after you click any of the command buttons in the Import Instance Query dialog box, and you must press the Esc key or click the Modify button.

FIGURE 8.4

Querying objects within a linked CAD file

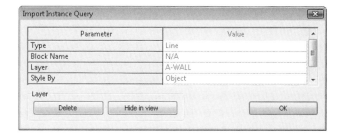

The second way to make layers or levels in imported or linked CAD files invisible is to use the Visibility/Graphic Overrides dialog box by switching to the View tab and selecting Visibility/Graphics from the Graphics panel. Once the dialog box opens, select the Imported Categories tab, as shown in Figure 8.5. Every imported or linked CAD file in the project will be listed. Expand any listed file to expose the list of layers/levels within that file, and use the check boxes to customize visibility of the link within the current view. Note that this method is the only way to restore visibility of layers/levels that were hidden with the Query tool.

FIGURE 8.5

Controlling visibility of layers within imported objects

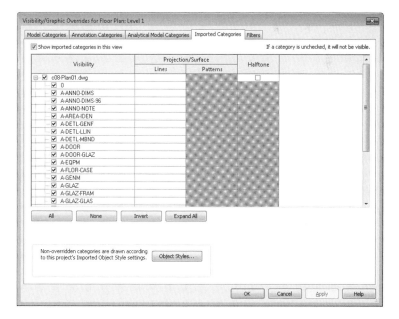

IMPORTED DATA IN FAMILIES

Remember that 2D and 3D data imported into Revit families will be listed under the Imports In Families category in both the Visibility/Graphic Overrides and Object Styles dialog boxes. They will not appear as separately listed files.

Graphic overrides If you need to change the appearance of the content within a linked or imported CAD file, you can accomplish that at the project level or within an individual view. To change a CAD file's appearance throughout the project, select the Manage tab on the ribbon, and click Object Styles in the Settings panel. Select the Imported Objects tab (Figure 8.6) and expand any of the imported or linked CAD files to change the color, line weight, line pattern, or material of the layers/levels within the referenced file. Note that changing these properties in the row of the filename does not affect the contents of that file. You can also apply these settings in a specific view using the Visibility/Graphic Overrides dialog box.

FIGURE 8.6
Changing the graphic appearance of imported layers via object styles

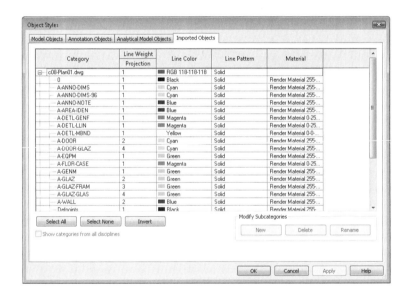

Exploding Although we do not recommend exploding CAD data within a Revit project, you can do it to facilitate the modification of such data. Linked content must first be converted to an import in order to be exploded. You do this by selecting the Insert tab on the ribbon, choosing Manage Links from the Link panel, choosing a listed link, and clicking the Import button. To explode the imported file, select it, and choose Explode ➤ Full Explode or Partial Explode from the special Modify tab in the ribbon. The lines, text, and hatch patterns will become new line styles, text types, and fill regions in your Revit project. Remember that these types of objects cannot be removed from your project via the Purge Unused command; you must remove them manually.

TIPS ON IMPORTING CAD FILES

To minimize the adverse impact of unnecessary styles and types carried into the Revit environment via exploding imported CAD data, we recommend removing extraneous data in the CAD file *before* importing it. Here are some general tips for this workflow:

◆ If your import contains hatches or annotations not intended for use in the Revit project, delete them before importing.

◆ Consider consolidating data within the CAD file to a minimum number of layers or levels. Doing so will ease the process of converting to standard Revit line styles if the file is exploded as well as facilitate graphic overrides.

◆ Revit doesn't allow line segments shorter than 1/32". While it might seem like you wouldn't have a lot of lines that length, many manufacturer's details, small fillets in sections and plans, and the like will fall into this range. Take care when exploding CAD details with very small line segments because they will be removed upon exploding.

Importing 2D Data

In the following sections, we will discuss how to import 2D CAD data from platforms such as AutoCAD (DWG) and MicroStation (DGN), or in the generic Drawing Exchange Format (DXF). You can also use files from other software platforms, but only if they are DWG, DGN, or DXF format. Most commercially available CAD programs are able to export in DWG or DXF format.

There are two fundamental ways 2D CAD data can be used with respect to a building project's floor plans, ceiling plans, or site plans:

◆ Using 2D data as backgrounds for BIM conversion

◆ Integrating 2D data with the model

Backgrounds for BIM Conversion

In this situation, we will assume that 2D CAD data will be linked into the Revit model to be converted into building elements. Although the positioning of the files is important, the color and line weights of the imported data are not.

To begin the next exercise, you will need the files c08-Plan01.dwg and c08-Start.rvt. You can download these files from this book's companion web page. After downloading, open the c08-Start.rvt file, and activate the Level 1 floor plan. Then follow these steps:

1. Switch to the Insert tab and select Link CAD from the Link panel. Browse to the file c08-Plan01.dwg.

2. In the Link CAD Formats dialog box, set the following options:

   ◆ Current View Only: Selected

   ◆ Colors: Invert

   ◆ Layers: All

   ◆ Import Units: Auto-Detect

   ◆ Positioning: Auto – Origin To Origin

LINKING LARGE CAD DATA

Use caution when attempting to link or import CAD files with vector data very far from the origin. Revit software has distance limitations on imported vector data that — if exceeded — may result in a warning, as shown here:

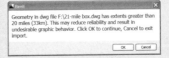
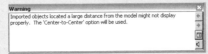

Notice in the warning message that the software will automatically use Center To Center positioning if the distance limitations are exceeded. This will preclude you from using the origin of the linked file for Origin To Origin placement. If you must link data that is physically larger than a 20-mile cube — which may occur in projects such as airports or master plans — you should separate the data into smaller portions before linking. If the data is smaller than the 20-mile cube but is located farther than 20 miles from its origin, an alternate origin should be coordinated with your project team, and the data should be moved closer to the origin.

Coordination

If you need to use 2D CAD data as an integrated component of your team coordination, different settings become important. Here are a few examples of these types of scenarios:

◆ Showing light fixture layouts from a lighting designer

◆ Integrating landscape design into a site plan

◆ Reusing existing CAD data for a renovation project

Most of the settings and procedures for conversion apply to the coordination process; however, color and the placement visibility will be different. Because this data will be included in the Revit output, you will always want the color option to be set to Black And White in the options during linking. It is also likely that some sort of background plans will be exported from the Revit model for use in coordination by one or more consultants using a CAD-based program. The data returned in this process may still contain the background information originally exported from Revit; thus, we recommend agreement on a standard that establishes unique layers for the consultants' content. This will help you select layers to be loaded when linking your consultants' files into the Revit project.

Use these options when linking CAD files into a Revit project for plan-based coordination:

◆ Current View Only: Selected if data is needed in one view; unselected if data is needed in many views

◆ Colors: Black And White

◆ Layers: Specify (choose only designated layers to isolate consultants' content)

◆ Positioning: Auto – By Shared Coordinates

If Current View Only is not selected, the 2D CAD data will be visible in all other views. This could be a nuisance in views such as sections and elevations; however, you might find it useful to visualize the data alongside the Revit model, as shown in Figure 8.7.

FIGURE 8.7
Existing CAD data integrated with the Revit model

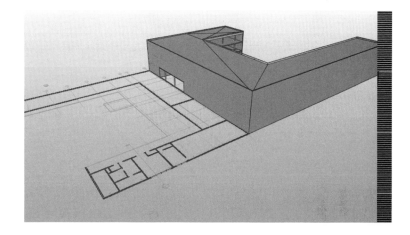

Details

Your company's CAD detail library does not need to go to waste when you implement a Revit environment. External CAD data can be linked into drafting views, allowing you to leverage the powerful view coordination tools within Revit. Entire sheets of CAD details can be inserted to reduce the number of linked files you have to reconcile; however, we recommend linking one detail into each drafting view and utilizing the software's ability to automatically manage the view references with callouts, sections, and detail views. You may also want to name these drafting views with a unique prefix to help keep track of where any linked CAD data might reside. For example, a drafting view might be named CAD-Roof Detail 04. Also refer to Chapter 4, "Configuring Templates and Standards," for additional information on view organization.

In this exercise, you will create a drafting view into which a single CAD detail will be linked. This view can be referenced throughout your Revit model using a section, callout, or elevation view with the Reference Other View option selected in the Options bar, as shown in Figure 8.8.

FIGURE 8.8
Creating a view as a reference to a drafting view

To begin this exercise, open the c08-Jenkins.rvt file. You can download this file and the associated CAD file (c08-Detail.dwg) from the book's web page.

1. Switch to the View tab and select Drafting View from the Create panel.

2. Name the new drafting view **CAD Wall Detail 1**, and set the scale to 1-1/2"=1'-0".

3. Switch to the Insert tab and select Link CAD.

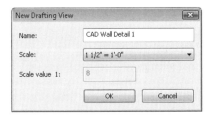

4. In the Link CAD Formats dialog box, navigate to the c08-Detail.dwg file and set the following options:

♦ Colors: Black And White

♦ Layers: All

♦ Units: Auto-Detect

♦ Positioning: Auto – Center To Center

5. Click Open to complete the command. If you don't see the linked detail in the drafting view, use Zoom To Fit (ZF on the keyboard) in order to reset the extents of the view.

6. Open the Section 2 view from the Project Browser, and zoom to a portion of the view where a floor meets an exterior wall.

7. From the View tab, select Callout from the Create panel, and select Reference Other View in the Options bar (similar to Figure 8.8). Choose Drafting View: CAD Wall Detail 1 from the drop-down list. You'll see the result shown in Figure 8.9.

FIGURE 8.9
Callout created to reference a drafting view containing a linked CAD detail

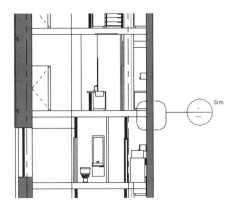

8. Double-click the callout head, and you will be taken to the drafting view with the CAD detail linked in the previous steps.

Importing 3D Data

Now that we have discussed using 2D reference data, we will cover how to use 3D model data within your Revit project. There are many valid reasons for modeling outside of the Revit environment, including software expertise, the availability of content or generation, and optimization of complex geometry. The following sections will explore some situations in which model data can be shared between programs:

♦ Imported data as a mass

♦ Imported data as a face

♦ Imported data as an object

Imported Data as a Mass

In Chapter 9, "Advanced Modeling and Massing," you will learn more about harnessing the impressive modeling toolset in the Revit conceptual massing environment; however, the fast and flexible process of design may lead architects to a tool in which they have more expertise or comfort. This type of massing design workflow is supported in the Revit environment under the following conditions:

♦ Masses require volumetric geometry to calculate volume, surface area, and floor area faces.

♦ Finely detailed complex geometry should be avoided because the Host By Face tools may not be able to generate meaningful objects.

Refer to the Revit Architecture help system for even more details on using imported geometry in a mass family.

This example demonstrates the process of creating an in-place mass by linking an external model — in this case, a SketchUp model. You can download the file `c08-Mass.skp` from the book's web page.

1. Start a new Revit project. From the Massing & Site tab (don't forget to turn the tab on under Application button ➢ Options ➢ User Interface), select In-Place Mass from the Conceptual Mass panel.

2. Name the new mass family **SKP Mass** and click OK.

3. Switch to the Insert tab and select Link CAD from the Link panel; be sure to switch your file type filter to `*.skp` files.

4. Navigate to the SKP file downloaded from the book's web page and set the following options:

   ♦ Current View Only

   ♦ Colors: Invert

   ♦ Layers: All

   ♦ Import Units: Auto-Detect

   ♦ Positioning: Auto – Center To Center

   ♦ Place At: Level 1

5. Click Open to complete the link process.

6. Click Finish Mass in the In-Place Editor panel.

Now that a new mass has been created, you can assign mass floors and begin to see calculated results in schedules of masses and mass floors. (Refer to Chapter 9 for more information on these processes.) Calculation of volumes, perimeters, and mass floor areas will work well in this workflow, but be careful when using imported model geometry with the By Face tools because face updates will likely be more difficult for the software to maintain than with native Revit massing.

Using linking instead of importing enables continued iteration of the form in the original software. In the case of this example, you may edit the original file in Google SketchUp, which is available as a free download from `http://sketchup.google.com`, or you can download the file `c08-Mass-2.skp` from the book's web page.

If you modify and save the original SKP file yourself, save, close, and reopen the Revit project. Alternatively, open the Manage Links dialog box, select the SKP file, and click Reload. If you want to use the alternate file downloaded from the book's web page, use the following steps:

1. Open the Manage Links dialog box from the Insert tab.

2. Select the SKP file and click Reload From.

3. Navigate to the file `c08-Mass-2.skp` and click Open.

4. Click OK to close the Manage Links dialog box.

With the modified mass loaded, notice the changes in the Mass Schedule and Mass Floor Schedule.

Imported Data as a Face

Similar to the data as mass workflow, externally modeled data can be used as a driver for more complex forms. An example might be the need to generate a complex curved roof surface. We will demonstrate this workflow using Rhino by McNeel (`www.rhino3d.com`) to generate a shape, link the shape into the project, and create a roof by face on the shape.

As shown in Figure 8.10, a complex surface is generated in Rhino from drawing two curves and using the Extrude Curve Along Curve tool. Note that some reference geometry was exported from a Revit model to DWG and linked into this study in Rhino.

FIGURE 8.10
Curves for a complex surface in Rhino

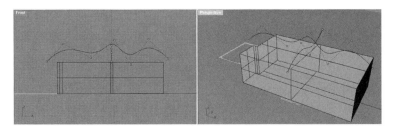

A flat surface model is enough to generate a roof by face; however, it may be difficult to see the imported surface, so use the Extrude Surface tool to give it a thickness. Once the surface is complete (Figure 8.11), select only the double-curved geometry, choose File ➤ Export Selected Objects, and choose the `.sat` filename extension. SAT will generate the cleanest geometry for curved solids and surfaces.

FIGURE 8.11
Completed complex
surface in Rhino

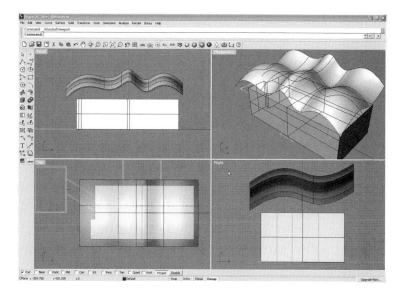

You can download the Rhino file (c08-Roof-Face.3dm) and SAT export (c08-Roof-Face
.sat) from this book's web page. You can also download the sample Revit project and continue
the process as follows:

1. Open the file c08-Roof-by-Face.rvt and make sure you are in the 3D view named 00-Start.

2. On the Massing & Site tab, choose In-Place Mass and name it **Rhino Roof**.

3. Switch to the Insert tab and select Link CAD. Switch to filter your file type to *.sat and
   navigate to the c08-Roof-Face.sat file downloaded from the book's web page.

4. Set the placement options as follows:

   ◆ Positioning: Auto – Origin To Origin

   ◆ Place At: Level 1

   ◆ Import Units: Inch

5. Click Open to complete the link and close the dialog box, and then click the Finish Mass
   button in the ribbon. The mass should be seen above the tops of the walls in the Revit
   model, as shown in Figure 8.12.

FIGURE 8.12
Complex surface linked as
an in-place mass

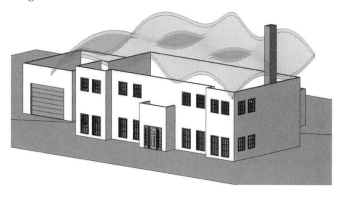

6. Return to the Massing & Site tab and select the Roof tool from the Model By Face panel. Choose the Basic Roof: Generic 12" from the Type Selector, and click the top face of the mass created in the previous steps. Click the Create Roof button in the ribbon to complete the command and the roof will be generated along the mass surface, as shown in Figure 8.13.

FIGURE 8.13
Roof By Face applied to the mass with linked SAT geometry

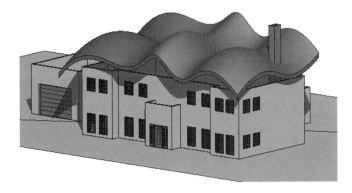

7. Select all the perimeter walls — using the Tab key or Ctrl to add individually to the selection.

8. Select the Attach Top/Base tool from the Modify | Walls tab, set the Top option in the Options bar, and pick the roof by face created in step 6. The walls will connect to the underside of the complex roof shape, as shown in Figure 8.14.

FIGURE 8.14
Completed roof with tops of walls attached

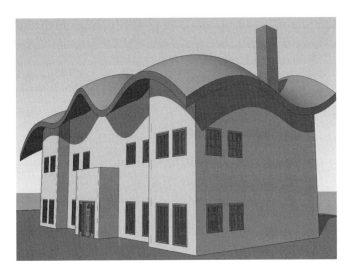

The original shape can be edited in the originating software and will update via the link if the original exported SAT file is overwritten. To update the roof based on the newly modified massing geometry, select the roof and click the Update To Face button in the Modify | Roofs tab.

Imported Data as an Object

Yet another derivation of the reference data workflow supports the use of linked model geometry for specific instances of building components. Examples of this scenario might include a complex canopy structure being designed in SolidWorks or a building's structural framing being modeled in Bentley Structural Modeler. The workflow is again similar to that of using imported data as a mass or face; however, the file format will help you control the component's visualization. In the previous exercise, we used an SAT format to transfer complex curved geometry from Rhino to Revit; however, a limitation of an SAT file is that the geometry contains only one layer, making it impossible to vary material assignments for different components of the design. We recommend using a solids-based DWG, DGN, or DXF file format, which will maintain a layer structure in most cases.

In the following example, you will create an in-place structural framing component that will act as a placeholder for a consultant's structural model created in Bentley Structural Modeler. You will be using the file c08-Framing.dgn, which you can download from the book's companion web page: www.sybex.com/go/masteringrevit2013.

1. Launch the Revit application and start a new project using the default.rte template.

2. Switch to the Home tab and choose Component ⊳ Model In-Place. Set the category to Structural Framing. For other scenarios, remember that some categories cannot be cut.

3. Name the new in-place model **DGN Structure**.

4. From the Insert tab, select Link CAD.

5. Change the Files Of Type option to DGN Files (*.dgn) and navigate to the downloaded file.

6. Set the following options and click Open:

   ◆ Current View Only: Unselected

   ◆ Colors: Black and White

   ◆ Layers: All

   ◆ Positioning: Auto – Origin To Origin

   ◆ Place At: Level 1

7. Click Finish Model in the In-Place Editor panel to complete the process.

Switch to a 3D view, and you should see the entire contents of the DGN model (Figure 8.15). Because the linked content was created as a structural framing model, the linked data will be displayed similarly to any other structural framing element. Examine the linked model in different plans and sections to observe this behavior.

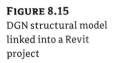

FIGURE 8.15
DGN structural model linked into a Revit project

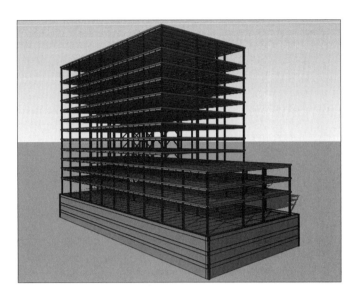

Utilizing linked models in DWG, DGN, or DXF format also allows you to modify the graphic representation of the elements within the Revit environment. To adjust these settings, do the following:

1. Select the Manage tab, click Object Styles, and switch to the Imported Objects tab.

2. Find your linked file, expand it to expose the layers or levels included in it, and modify the graphic settings as desired.

When you are using linked model data for custom components, the consistency of the data you bring into Revit software from other programs depends on the ability of that software to generate organized information. Some programs utilize layers, and some don't. Recognizing this difference will give you the best opportunity for success in coordination through interoperability.

Overview of Exporting

Of equal importance to importing external data is the ability to export Revit data for use by others. We will now examine various processes for exporting data from your Revit project to other formats. To achieve your desired results when exporting, remember that exporting from Revit is essentially a WYSIWYG (what you see is what you get) process. For example, exporting a 3D view will result in a 3D model, exporting a floor plan will result in a 2D CAD file, and exporting a schedule will result in a delimited file that can be used in a program such as Microsoft Excel.

We will first review the process for preparing a set of files to be exported. This method is similar for almost all exports and will be referred to in subsequent sections.

There have been a number of significant improvements in Revit Architecture 2013 software. For instance, exporting of lines has been improved so that in the DWG Export settings you can map a Revit line pattern to use a different linetype in the resulting DWG file. To access this new functionality choose Export ➤ CAD Formats ➤ DWG Files from the Application menu. Click Export Setup and select the Lines tab. The available linetypes are loaded from the LIN file selected in the Load DWG Linetypes column. Any custom settings can be saved as well.

As with lines, exporting of hatch patterns has been modified. You can map a different hatch pattern to the one that was used in the Revit environment. To access this new functionality, select Export ➤ CAD Formats ➤ DWG Files from the Application menu. Select Export Setup and choose the Patterns tab. The available patterns are loaded from the `acdb.pat` file located in the `Program\ACADInterop` folder.

Text and fonts can now be mapped and exported to a different font than was used in Revit. To access this new functionality, select Export ➤ CAD Formats ➤ DWG Files from the Application menu. Select Export Setup and choose the Text & Fonts tab. The fonts available from the drop-down are loaded from your operating system's `Fonts` folder. Keep in mind that only fonts supported by Revit will be shown in the list.

Dimensions can now be mapped to a dimensional style-based DWG dimension. In other words, the dimension text is controlled by the text style. But the tick mark is controlled by the arrow properties in the DWG file.

Preparing for Exports

The first step to any export is to establish the set of files to be exported. The following steps will walk you through the process:

1. You can find all exporting commands by clicking the Application menu and clicking the Export flyout. As shown in Figure 8.16, check the bottom of the flyout menu for additional commands available for use.

FIGURE 8.16
Export commands accessed by clicking the Application menu

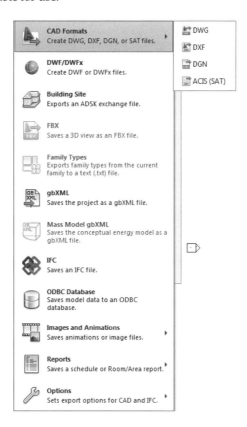

2. Beginning an exporting command such as DWF/DWFx, you will first see the typical Export Settings dialog box, as shown in Figure 8.17. Notice that in the View/Sheet tab, the Export value is usually set to <Current View/Sheet Only>.

FIGURE 8.17

First view of Export Settings dialog box

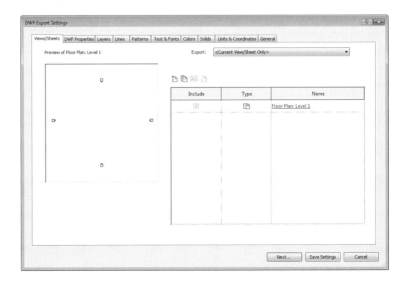

3. Begin to create your own list of views and/or sheets to export by picking <In Session View/Sheet Set> from the Export drop-down list, as shown in Figure 8.18. Note that the listings "Export Set 1" and "Export Set 2" are predefined lists we created for the purposes of this tutorial.

FIGURE 8.18

Viewing available export sets in the model

4. From this point, you can either use a temporary in-session set or create your own named set. We will continue these steps by creating a new set. Click the New icon above the view list, shown in Figure 8.19, and name the set **Export Set 3**. Click OK to close the dialog box.

USING IN-SESSION LISTS WITH WORKSHARING

Be careful when using an in-session list for printing or exporting on a worksharing-enabled project. If two or more team members working on the same Revit project attempt to use the in-session set, you may receive errors about the workset not being editable. Instead, always try to use predefined lists for exporting and printing on worksharing projects.

FIGURE 8.19

Create a new export list.

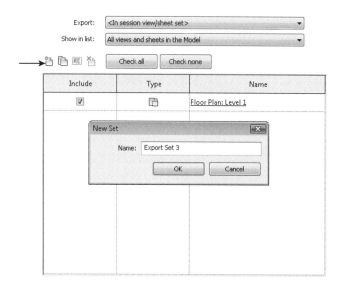

5. To begin adding views and/or sheets to your new export set, make sure the Show In List drop-down is set to Views In The Model, Sheets In The Model, or All Views And Sheets In The Model (see Figure 8.20).

FIGURE 8.20

Showing all views and sheets in the model

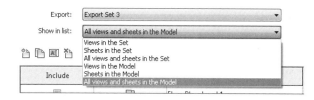

6. Select the views and/or sheets you need to export by checking the boxes next to the listed views in the Include column. Remember, you can sort the list by clicking any of the list headers (Figure 8.21).

7. If you are done creating your list of views to export and don't want to continue exporting, click the Save Settings button; otherwise, click Next.

The subsequent steps in the exporting process are slightly different based on each export format. You will usually see a Save To Target dialog box that allows you to specify automatic or manual naming conventions for multiple exported files. Exporting FBX files or images simply requires a file location and name.

FIGURE 8.21

Adding views/sheets to the export list

Export Layer Settings

We recommend that, in addition to creating and maintaining lists of views for various exporting tasks, you create at least one standardized layer mapping file for CAD format exports. Revit software stores these settings in a text file (with the filename extension *.txt) that can be loaded from any location on your computer or network. To access the layer mapping, select the Application menu and click the Export flyout on the DWG Properties tab. Then click the ellipsis button next to the Layers And Properties option (Figure 8.22).

FIGURE 8.22

Accessing export layer settings on the DWG Properties tab

Several exporting templates based on the industry-standard layering guidelines are included (Figure 8.23) with the Revit Architecture application and can be applied by clicking the Standard button in the Export Layers dialog box. Similarly, to import settings, you may want to create customized layer export templates and save them with your project data for future reference. Note that export templates will inherit all layer names of linked CAD files in your active project. Because of this, we recommend saving a copy of your export templates in a ZIP archive in case you need to return to the original template.

FIGURE 8.23
Industry-standard lay-
ering conventions can
be applied to export
settings.

Layer names and colors can be customized by directly editing the values in the Layers tab in the DWG Export Settings dialog box (Figure 8.24). Each category and subcategory is capable of independent color and layer names.

FIGURE 8.24
Exported layer
names and colors
can be customized
for any standard.

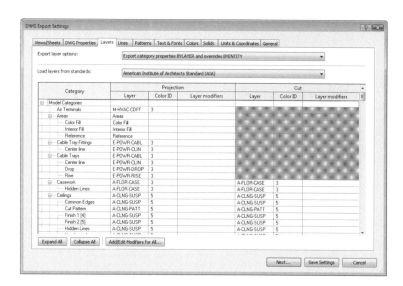

Special layer suffixes can be assigned to Revit model objects that are subject to graphic over-rides from phasing. The standard phasing overrides (Existing, Demolished, and Temporary) are listed as object styles in the Export Layers dialog box and can be customized as required. These settings are applied to the end of the specified layer for a given Revit object. For example, if a new wall was set to export to A-WALL, a wall displayed as demolished in a Revit view would be exported to the A-WALL-DEMO layer.

Exporting 2D CAD Data

When collaborating with others who require 2D CAD, planning a strategic workflow will allow you to share your Revit data more efficiently and consistently. We highly recommend that you determine and document the scope of data to be shared, the schedule by which it will be shared, and the software platforms to be used on a project. These aspects should be compiled in a BIM execution plan as explained in Chapter 7, "Working with Consultants."

To facilitate the setup and ultimate export of plan data, you can create copies of floor plans and ceiling plans with a standardized naming convention in your Revit project. These should be easy to recognize yet help in building the export list. Figure 8.25 shows a series of duplicated plans that have been created and named with the EXP- prefix. The rest of the view name conforms to the naming convention specified by the United States National CAD Standard (www.nationalcadstandard.org).

FIGURE 8.25
View organization for plans to be exported

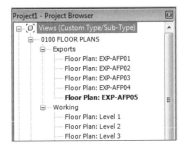

When it is time to export floor plans or ceiling plans, make sure you are using the most appropriate settings according to the conventions your team has established in the BIM execution plan. You can find these settings in the DWG Export Setup dialog box, as shown in Figure 8.26. Each setting is organized under its own tab, and these settings can be saved and used across multiple projects.

FIGURE 8.26
DWG properties for exporting

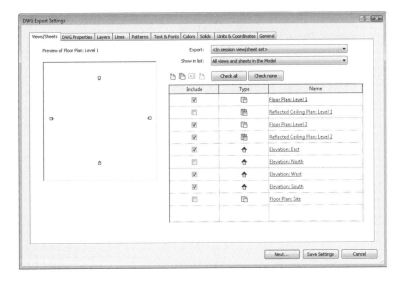

DWG Settings for Export

The following are the default DWG settings for exporting for each tab in the DWG Export Settings dialog box:

DWG Properties "Export category properties BYLAYER and overrides BYENTITY" will maintain the most visual fidelity to what you see in the Revit user interface. If you anticipate that the recipient of your CAD file will use scripts or macros to enforce their own graphic standards, select the "Export all properties BYLAYER" option and don't export overrides (Figure 8.27).

FIGURE 8.27
DWG properties
for exporting

Layers The Layers tab lets you designate export layer options as well as load layers from other standards (Figure 8.28).

FIGURE 8.28
Layer properties for
exporting

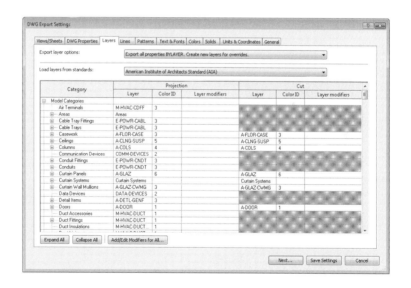

Selecting the Layer Modifiers button opens a further dialog box that lets you customize select layer properties (Figure 8.29).

Lines The Lines tab lets you carefully control how lines are generated (Figure 8.30), and the default setting lets the software automatically generate them to match what is shown.

But if you want to deviate from the automatically generated linetype, you can make a selection from the Linetypes In DWG drop-down menu (Figure 8.31).

FIGURE 8.29
Modifying layer
properties for
exporting

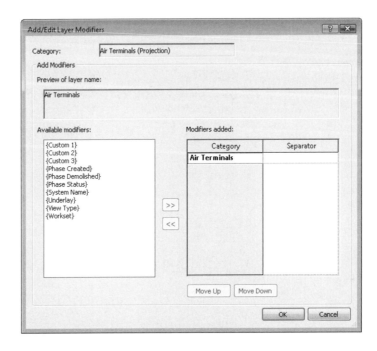

FIGURE 8.30
Lines properties for
exporting

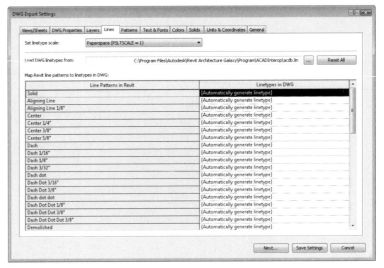

FIGURE 8.31
Custom line
properties for
exporting

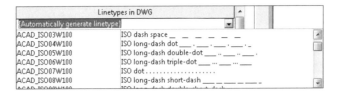

Patterns The Patterns tab allows you to control how patterns are exported (Figure 8.32). By default, Revit automatically generates them to match what is shown in your Revit file.

FIGURE 8.32
Pattern properties for exporting

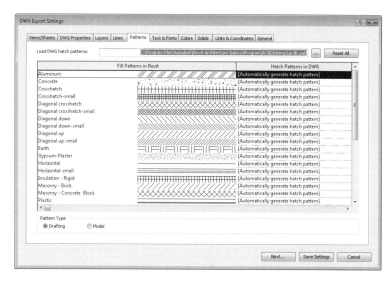

If you need to generate patterns that differ from what is shown in your Revit files, select from the Hatch Pattern In DWG drop-down menu (Figure 8.33).

FIGURE 8.33
Custom pattern properties for exporting

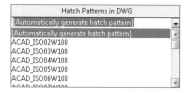

Text & Fonts The Text & Fonts tab allows you to control mapping of fonts and text from Revit to AutoCAD. The default selection generates fonts to match what is shown within the Revit environment (Figure 8.34).

To export a text or a font that is different from what is shown in the Revit interface, select from the Text Fonts In DWG drop-down menu (Figure 8.35).

Colors The Colors tab allows you to export colors based either on the Color ID specified on the Layers tab or as an RGB value from the Revit view (Figure 8.36).

Solids The Solids tab has two options for exporting, either Polymesh or ACIS Solids (Figure 8.37). You can select either option only if you have selected a 3D view for export. Otherwise, the options are grayed out and you can't select either.

Units & Coordinates The Units & Coordinates tab lets you select the units for export (imperial or metric) as shown in Figure 8.38. You can also select the coordinate system; either the Revit internal coordinate system or a user-defined system.

FIGURE 8.34
Text and font properties for exporting

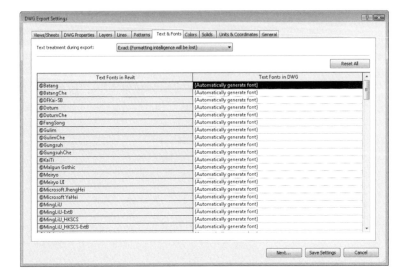

FIGURE 8.35
Custom text and font properties for exporting

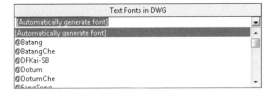

FIGURE 8.36
Color properties for exporting

FIGURE 8.37
Solid properties for exporting

FIGURE 8.38
Unit and coordinate properties for exporting

General   The General tab gives you control over the export of room and area lines (Figure 8.39). Select this option if you want the lines to export as a single polyline that you can query from your AutoCAD file.

FIGURE 8.39
Unit and coordinate properties for exporting

DWG Export Settings

| Views/Sheets | DWG Properties | Layers | Lines | Patterns | Text & Fonts | Colors | Solids | Units & Coordinates | General |

Room and area boundaries:

☐ Export rooms and areas as polylines

Exporting 3D Model Data

You can also export your Revit model as a 3D model in several formats for use in other modeling software. A frequent destination for such data is Autodesk® 3ds Max® software for its enhanced rendering and daylighting analysis capabilities. This workflow is supported by the FBX export format, which includes not only model geometry but materials, cameras, and lights as well. More generic exports in DWG, DGN, DXF, or SAT formats can provide numerous opportunities for you to become more creative with the presentation of your designs.

Studies in Google SketchUp

Earlier in this chapter we discussed using Google SketchUp for conceptual building massing studies. These studies were imported directly into the Revit environment for further development of a true building information model. Revit model data can also be exported via 3D DWG to Google SketchUp, where visualization studies can be conducted on an entire project or even a simple wall section. In the following exercise, we will export a wall section study from the Revit environment to Google SketchUp using files you can download from the book's web page:

1. Open the file c08-Sketchup-Wall-Study.rvt.

2. Activate the Default 3D view and enable the Section Box option in the Properties palette for the view.

3. Set the detail level of the view to Medium or Fine.

4. Activate the section box in the properties of the 3D view and shape handles will appear on each face. Grab the shape handle of one side of the section box parallel to the vertical edge of the wall sample and drag toward the wall until the section box intersects the wall, as shown in Figure 8.40. You should see the layers of the wall structure exposed.

5. With the section box still selected, right-click and choose Hide In View ➢ Elements, as shown in Figure 8.41. This will prevent the section box from being exported.

FIGURE 8.40
Using the section box to expose the layers of the wall

FIGURE 8.41
Hide the section box to prevent it from exporting.

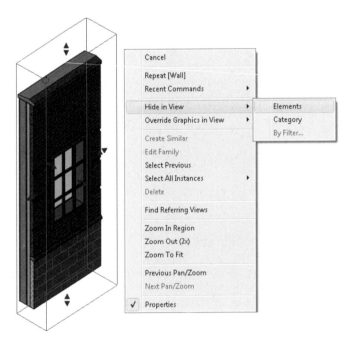

6. Click the Application menu and select Export ➤ CAD Formats ➤ DWG Files.

7. In the DWG Export Setup dialog box [...] , switch to the DWG Properties tab and set the Solids option to Export As Polymesh.

8. Click Next and save the DWG file to a location on your computer or network.

9. Launch Google SketchUp, and choose File ➤ Import.

10. Switch the Files Of Type option to AutoCAD Files, navigate to the file saved in step 8, and click Open.

11. Switch to the Select tool, select the entire DWG import, right-click, and choose Explode. This will allow you to directly edit the elements in the SketchUp environment. Note that other components within the exploded model may need to be exploded again.

Once the DWG model is loaded in Google SketchUp, you can use the Paint Bucket tool to apply materials to individual components, use the Push/Pull tool to hide or expose layers of the wall construction, and use the line tools to customize the profile of the revealed layers, as shown in Figure 8.42.

FIGURE 8.42
Completed wall study in Google SketchUp

IFC Interoperability

According to Wikipedia, "Industry Foundation Classes (IFC) is a data model based on a neutral and open specification that is not controlled by a single software vendor or group of vendors. It is an object-oriented file format with a data model developed by the buildingSMART Alliance (International Alliance for Interoperability, IAI) to facilitate interoperability in the building industry." The IFC model specification is registered by the International Standards Organization

(ISO) as ISO/PAS 16739 and is currently in the process of becoming the official International Standard ISO/IS 16739. Because of its focus on ease of interoperability between BIM software platforms, some government agencies are requiring IFC format deliverables for publicly funded building projects.

Understanding the limitations of the IFC file format is essential to fully utilizing them in a Revit workflow. Some scenarios where IFC exchange may apply and facilitate data exchange include, but are not limited to, the following:

◆ Linking Autodesk® AutoCAD® MEP software into a Revit project

◆ Using Solibri Model Checker

◆ Coordination between Revit projects and Nemetschek Allplan, VectorWorks, or ArchiCAD

You can export the Revit model quite effectively to the IFC 2x2, 2x3, or BCA ePlan Check formats by clicking the Application menu and selecting the flyout menu. The resulting IFC file (Figure 8.43) can be viewed in a number of programs that can be downloaded at no cost from any of the following websites:

◆ DDS CAD Viewer from Data Design System (www.dds-cad.net)

◆ Nemetschek IFC Viewer (www.nemetschek.com/ifc)

◆ IFC Engine Viewer (www.ifcbrowser.com)

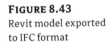

FIGURE 8.43
Revit model exported
to IFC format

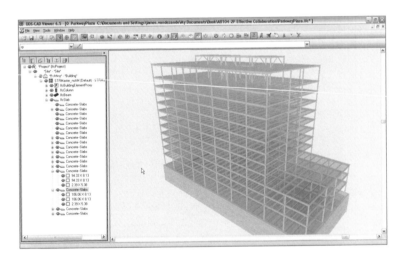

Importing IFC data into the Revit environment is similar to the process for importing 3D CAD geometry; however, the data generated is intended to be more intelligent and editable. Although this method has great potential, the accuracy of the Revit IFC import is highly dependent on the software used to generate the IFC output. We recommend the use of one of the free

IFC viewers listed previously to inspect IFC data prior to importing into a Revit project. (Note that only some tools, such as DDS CAD Viewer, have the ability to measure objects in an IFC format file.)

VIEWING THE CONTENTS OF AN IFC FORMAT FILE

Did you know that an IFC file can be viewed in a text editor such as Notepad? Download a sample file from the book's companion web page and check it out! Right-click an IFC file, select Open With, and choose Notepad.

Once you've reviewed the contents of the IFC file, you can open it in the Revit interface and integrate it into your coordination process as follows:

1. Click the Application menu, and select Open ➤ IFC.

2. Navigate to the c08-Structure.ifc file and click Open.

3. Save the file as a Revit project file (*.rvt).

4. Start a new Revit project using the default template. You will link the saved RVT file into a blank project to simulate the process for a host project model.

5. On the Insert tab, select Link Revit from the Link panel.

6. Navigate to the file saved in step 3, and click Open.

If an updated IFC file is received, repeat steps 1 through 3 and overwrite the RVT file created in step 3. When the host project file is reopened, the linked RVT file containing the imported IFC content will be updated.

3D EXPORTS BY LEVEL

Effective coordination between Revit Architecture and AutoCAD MEP frequently relies on the exchange of 3D DWG files of limited scope with respect to the overall project. MEP engineers using AutoCAD MEP will usually manage their BIM with one model file per level. Even though the entire architectural model can be exported to a single DWG model, they may not be able to reference such a large model efficiently. The good news? Your Revit project can be set up to achieve this by creating 3D views with section boxes for each level.

Begin by creating a series of floor plans designed for exporting (discussed earlier in this chapter). In the View Range settings for these plans, set the Top value to Level Above, Offset: 0 and the Bottom value to Associated Level, Offset: 0. Create a 3D view for each level required in the project and rename the views according to your standards. In each duplicated 3D view, right-click the ViewCube®, select Orient To View ➤ Floor Plans, and choose the corresponding floor plan with the adjusted view range. This series of 3D views can be saved in an export list and batch-exported to 3D DWG when needed for collaboration, as shown here:

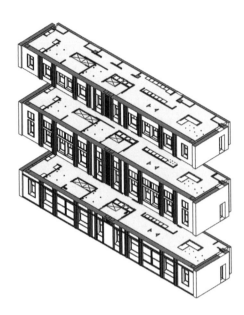

The Bottom Line

Use imported 2D CAD data. CAD data can be integrated into your Revit project in a number of ways: as plans of existing conditions, as fixture layouts from consultants, or as standard details from your company's library.

Master It How can CAD details be used in a Revit project?

Export 2D CAD data. The ability to deliver quality 2D information to other constituents involved in your project is as important as importing it into the Revit environment. Appropriately formatted views, standardized layer templates, and proper coordinate settings will result in happy team members and a smooth coordination process.

Master It Does Revit software comply with the National CAD Standard?

Use imported 3D model data. Model data generated outside of the Revit environment can be integrated into your projects as whole building systems, massing studies, or unique components.

Master It How can a building's structural model created with Bentley Structure be integrated into a Revit project?

Export 3D model data. Your modeled elements don't have to remain in the Revit environment forever. Data can be exported to 3ds Max, Google SketchUp, AutoCAD MEP, and more.

Master It How can I coordinate my architectural Revit model with an engineer using AutoCAD MEP?

Work with IFC imports and exports. Industry Foundation Classes (IFC) is a vendor-neutral model format designed to support interoperability in the AEC industry. It is widely used by some major BIM platforms available around the world.

Master It How is an IFC model integrated into a Revit project for coordination?

Part 3

Modeling and Massing for Design

In Part 2, we covered the topics that help you define important project standards when using Autodesk® Revit® Architecture software — within your team as well as across external Revit teams and with other consultants. In this section, we'll delve into the use of Revit from the earliest design stages to analysis, iteration, and finally, visualization.

- ◆ **Chapter 9: Advanced Modeling and Massing**
- ◆ **Chapter 10: Conceptual Design and Sustainability**
- ◆ **Chapter 11: Working with Phasing, Groups, and Design Options**
- ◆ **Chapter 12: Visualization**

Advanced Modeling and Massing

Nothing is more frustrating than building a design project in Autodesk® Revit® Architecture software only to find out the building you've created is too big and somehow the client's program still doesn't fit. You think you've done everything right — walls, floors, rooms, schedules — but somewhere, something is wrong. And you have no idea where to begin to change your design to get the building to fit the client's program.

Massing is a great tool for avoiding this kind of scenario. By creating the "big" design idea at a macro level, as a mass, you're able to quickly and easily quantify and analyze the results. This allows you to confidently work from general to specific as your design progresses, without starting with actual building elements (which would be too specific too soon anyway).

In addition, massing allows you to create forms and containers to control more granular components. Complex walls, curtain walls, curtain panels, and other elements would be incredibly difficult to make (much less update) without some underlying form to establish and drive their design. Massing is essential for this kind of design and design iteration.

Even though your overall design might not be represented by a complex massing form, it's very likely that somewhere in a more conventional design, massing is essential to the success of your project.

In this chapter, you'll learn to:

◆ Create and schedule massing studies

◆ Know when to use solid and surface masses

◆ Use mathematical formulas for massing

Massing UI and Functionality

You might not think that you need to use massing tools when you first begin using Revit software if you tend to design conventional or rectilinear buildings. But you'll quickly find that even though you don't create complex buildings, a lot of buildings you do create contain complex features or parts that require a firm understanding of the massing tool.

Massing is certainly used to create *masses* — that is, forms with geometric substance (solids and voids). But the massing tool is also used to create complex surfaces that can be used to create relationships with other host elements. Without these mass- or surface-based relationships, it would be hard to create and reiterate system families such as walls and curtain walls. Massing allows you to create a lightweight design idea, evaluate it, and then associate some real-world building elements with the massing element. To change the real-world building element, you change the lightweight design idea first.

Another important thing to know about massing is that masses can be created in both the project environment and the Family Editor. There's a lot of overlap of functionality in each case, but there's also a lot of important functionality missing. So what's the difference?

The main difference as to whether you create massing in place or in the Family Editor doesn't depend on the kind of shape or surface you want to create. Solid and surface forms can be created in both the project and Family Editor environments. Rather, it depends on *how* you want to create the massing and how you want to *change* the mass once it's been created.

Intuitive and Formula Mass Creation

Generally speaking, there are two ways to create form. The first approach tends to create masses more *intuitively*; the second approach tends to create masses more *formulaically*. Intuitively created masses could be created right in the project environment as in-place masses, but if the shape you're trying to create needs to be driven by formulas, you're better off opening the Family Editor and creating the shape there.

When using the intuitive method, you can model just about anything in the project environment, both host and component families. We strongly recommend that you don't model component families in-place unless the condition is unique and exceptional because the moment you need to create another just like it, you will have created a copy. If you have to change both of them, you'll have to change them both manually. It's best to model component families in the Family Editor.

In-Place Masses

Figure 9.1 illustrates a wall created using the intuitive method. This wall wasn't created by starting with a mass; the blend was created in place in the Wall category. Notice how the top and base of the wall are not consistently thick. It's narrower in some places and wider in others as it moves from bottom to top.

FIGURE 9.1
Complex in-place
wall

But if the wall was meant to be consistently wide, it would be more appropriate to make the mass or surface first and then assign the wall to the form (Figure 9.2). Notice how the top and bottom of the wall are the same width overall.

FIGURE 9.2
Wall created from
in-place mass
surface

At the end of the day, the previous two figures were created in the project environment through intuitive decision-making. There were no formulas, parameters, or rules; we just created the shape directly — in the moment, so to speak.

Family Component Masses

The other way to create a form is to first start to think about the rules that will govern the geometry of the form you're trying to accomplish. Figure 9.3 illustrates this kind of form.

FIGURE 9.3
Massing created in
the Family Editor

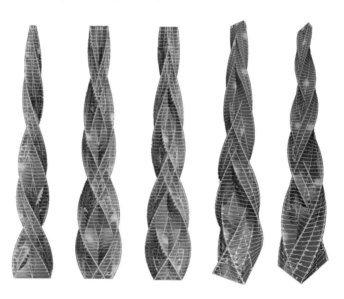

The rules that were created resulted in a form that would programmatically rotate and narrow depending on its relative elevation. Later, geometry was assigned to this form along the edges. Creating this kind of form as an in-place object would be tedious, and modifying it would be extremely time-consuming.

Now we'll talk about creating massing both in place and using the Family Editor.

Floor Area Faces and Scheduling Masses

Whether you create masses in place or in the Family Editor, you're able to generate floor faces (not the actual floors) and schedule important metadata before you've even begun to assign actual geometry to the masses. This is important to do early in the design process because the masses will be "light" in your project — they won't have a drastically negative impact on performance. Use them to establish your overall design idea.

In-place mass forms can be both solid- and surface-based forms. You can start them two ways. The first way is to select Component ➢ Model In-Place from the Architecture tab (Figure 9.4).

FIGURE 9.4
Selecting Model
In-Place

When you select this option, the dialog box in Figure 9.5 appears. Be sure to select the Mass category.

FIGURE 9.5
Selecting the Mass
category

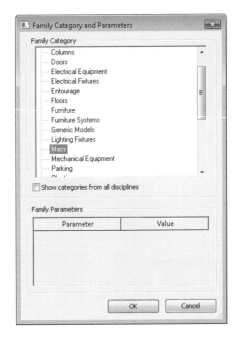

The other way to create an in-place mass is by selecting the Massing & Site tab, as shown in Figure 9.6. From the Conceptual Mass panel, select In-Place Mass. In either case, when you start to create the mass, you'll want to have the Mass category visible (it's turned off by default in all views).

FIGURE 9.6
Massing & Site tab

Rather than confuse you by allowing you to create objects that wouldn't be visible, the software prompts you to turn the category on (Figure 9.7). This warning only appears when you create an in-place mass via the Massing & Site tab. If you're using Autodesk Revit rather than Autodesk Revit Architecture, you'll need to turn on the Massing & Site tab. You can do this by selecting the Application button and choosing Options from the bottom of the menu. On the User Interface tab, you can turn on the Massing & Site tab.

FIGURE 9.7
Enabling the Show
Mass mode

Once you close this dialog box, you'll be given the opportunity to name your in-place mass. In this case, you're going to name the mass **Cube** (Figure 9.8).

FIGURE 9.8
Naming the mass

SIMPLE MASS CREATION

After you've named the mass from the previous steps and clicked OK, you'll be shown the contextually specific Massing toolset. The Create tab contains the tools that you'll use to create solid and void geometry as well as surface-generated masses, as shown in Figure 9.9.

FIGURE 9.9
Massing
functionality

When you're finished creating your mass, you'll have to select Finish Mass (or Cancel Mass) to return to the regular project environment.

Figure 9.10 shows three masses that we've created: cube, pyramid, and sphere. All three of these shapes have been created as separate masses.

FIGURE 9.10
Cube, Pyramid, and
Sphere

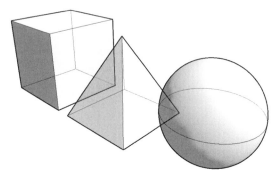

As each form was finished, the mass was completed, and the process was repeated for each mass. The difference is that in your Family Browser, each mass will show up as a separate line item (Figure 9.11).

FIGURE 9.11
Separate masses in
the Family Browser

Starting with the cube, its dimensions are 100′ × 100′ × 100′ (about 30 m × 30 m × 30 m). The base of the pyramid is the same size as the cube with equal sides tapering to the same height. And the sphere is the same width as the cube.

FLOOR AREA FACES

Once each shape is complete, it's important to understand how to create floor area faces. Keep in mind that the process for in-place masses would be the same as those created in the Family Editor.

To create floor area faces, follow these steps:

1. Create more levels in an elevation view above the two default levels by using the Level tool found on the Architecture tab. Do this as shown in Figure 9.12. This will give you a total of 10 levels.

FIGURE 9.12
Intersecting levels

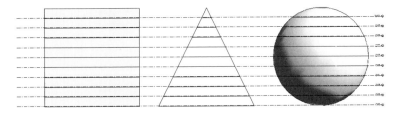

2. Now select all the masses and click the Mass Floors button in the contextual Model panel (Figure 9.13).

FIGURE 9.13
Mass Floors
command

3. Select all the levels, as shown in Figure 9.14.

FIGURE 9.14
Selecting all levels

Floor faces will intersect the solid masses, as shown in Figure 9.15. Now the masses and floor faces can be calculated and scheduled.

FIGURE 9.15
Floor area faces

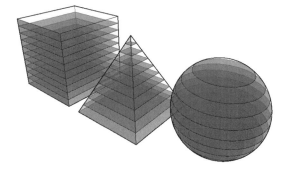

SCHEDULING MASSES

Select Schedules from the View tab and you'll be given the option to schedule both Mass and Mass Floor (Figure 9.16). In this case we'll schedule the masses so we can do a comparative analysis between the different mass types.

FIGURE 9.16
Creating a schedule

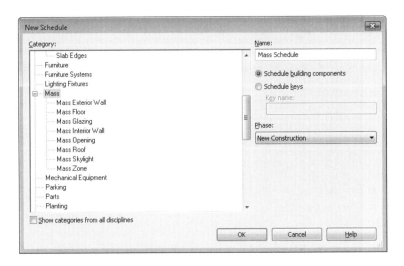

Select the categories as shown in Figure 9.17 and add them to the scheduled fields.

FIGURE 9.17
Scheduled fields

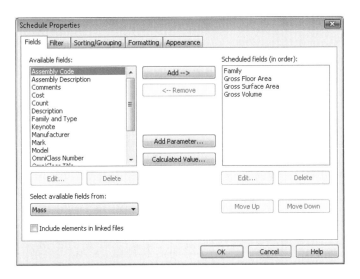

For this example, we'll also show you how to create two calculated values. This will allow you to calculate the overall volume compared to the floor area as well as the overall surface area compared to the floor area. Schedules like this will be helpful during the early design process to help you understand how efficient the space of your design is compared to the volume and surface area required to contain that space. Follow these steps:

1. Select the Calculated Value button in the Fields tab of the schedule properties to create the volume-to-floor ratio. Note the formula as shown in Figure 9.18. To keep the

units consistent, you divide the gross volume by 1′ before dividing by the gross floor area.

FIGURE 9.18
Volume-to-floor ratio

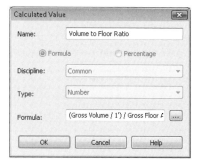

2. Create the calculated value to compare the surface-to-floor ratio, as shown in Figure 9.19.

FIGURE 9.19
Surface-to-floor ratio

3. Finish both calculated values and finish the schedule. You'll see the mass schedule as shown in Figure 9.20. Notice that proportionally, a sphere and a cube have efficient floor areas compared to their required surface area and volume.

FIGURE 9.20
Completed schedule

Family	Gross Floor Area	Gross Surface Area	Gross Volume	Volume to Floor Ratio	Surface to Floor Ratio
Cube	100000 SF	60000 SF	1000000.00 CF	10	0.6
Pyramid	38500 SF	32361 SF	333333.33 CF	8.658009	0.840537
Sphere	51837 SF	31416 SF	523598.68 CF	10.100858	0.606052

On the other hand, the pyramid mass will require significantly more surface and volume to create the same relative surface area as a cube or a sphere; as a result, it takes far more surface area than a cube to contain the same space. Perhaps this is why pyramids aren't a common building mass — it's too expensive.

You can download the finished file from the book's companion website, www.sybex.com/go/MasteringRevit2013. It's in the Chapter 9 folder and is named c09_Mass_Schedules.rvt.

CREATING MASSES

How you create masses (surface or form) differs significantly from the user interface used to create other standard content. When you're creating standard project content, you tend to think of the form that you're creating and then start to create that form in a discrete mode that isolates you from doing anything else until the form making is complete (Figure 9.21). In some ways, this is a Noun-Verb approach: You know the form that you want to create and then you create it.

FIGURE 9.21
Non-massing form
creation

Creating massing still requires that you know the form that you intend to create, but you're not required to select a particular noun type to get started. Rather, you simply start by creating the sketch-based elements that would define your shape. Then you select them as a group and choose the Create Form option (Figure 9.22). This will allow you to create both solids and voids.

FIGURE 9.22
Create Form option

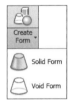

In the event that you don't select enough information for the Create Form command to make sense, you'll get the warning shown in Figure 9.23.

FIGURE 9.23
Create Form
warning

Both solid and surface may be created from model lines or reference lines (Figure 9.24). But the differences are important. Keep in mind that your ability to further iterate the form that you create depends on whether you use model or reference lines to generate the form, even though the forms created may at first look exactly the same.

FIGURE 9.24
Draw panel for both
model and refer-
ence lines

If your intent is to simply create a form that is not likely to require further iteration or rule-based parameterization, using model lines is fine. But if you intend to parameterize the form with formulas and other rules, it's best to start with reference lines. Figure 9.25 shows the subtle graphic difference between the two line types. The model line is on the left, and the green reference line is on the right.

FIGURE 9.25
Model lines and reference lines

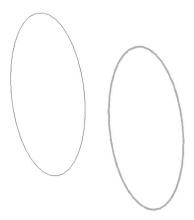

Since the difference is so subtle on the screen, we recommend that you give your reference lines more thickness and lighten the default green color so that they stand out better. You can do so using the Object Styles settings (Figure 9.26).

FIGURE 9.26
Object styles for reference lines

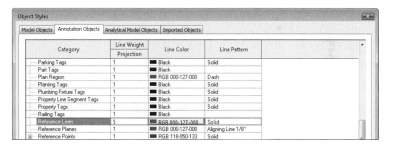

Because reference lines allow for more flexibility, we recommend that you use them (even when you don't think you need to). Another reason is that you can create faces from closed loops if you use reference lines (Figure 9.27). This option isn't available when you select model lines. Selecting a closed loop of model lines will create only a form (solid or void), never a face.

Massing Surfaces

All of the shapes that you'll create in this chapter are going to be done using reference objects. Figure 9.28 shows a number of linetypes: Spline Through Points, Spline, Curve, and Line.

FIGURE 9.27
Option to create
face or solid from
reference lines

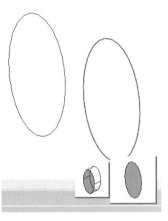

FIGURE 9.28
Reference line seg-
ment types

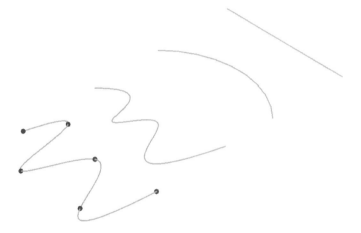

As you can see in Figure 9.29, each of these reference lines has different control points that allow for further control.

Since these are not closed loops, the form that will generate from each of these segments will only be face or surface (Figure 9.30). You generate the form by selecting each of the lines (one at a time, not together) and then selecting Create Form.

You can also create surface-based forms from more than one line at a time. The result is a surface that can be controlled in more complex ways than a single line.

Take the Spline Through Points line, for example. The form on the left in Figure 9.31 creates a face that is controlled by a single reference line, whereas the form on the right is a face controlled by two (and it could be more) reference lines.

FIGURE 9.29
Reference line control points

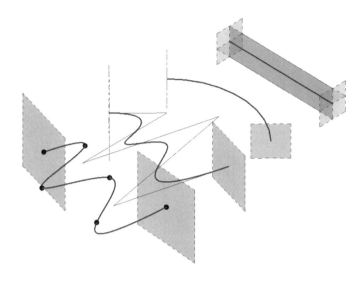

FIGURE 9.30
Surface forms

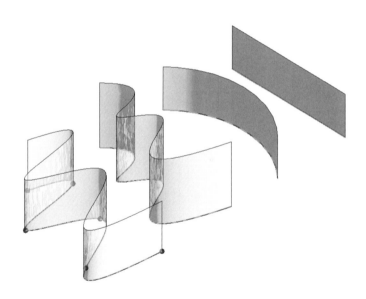

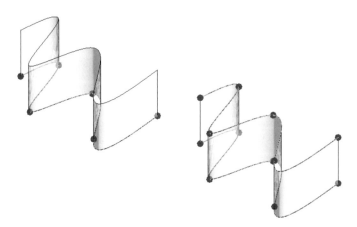

Moving the location of the control points on the form on the left maintains a consistent height to the top of the surface previously generated, whereas moving the control points of the surface on the right will create a surface that varies in height (Figure 9.32).

FIGURE 9.32
Single and multi-
spline surfaces

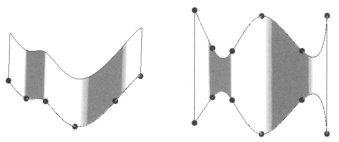

After a surface is generated, it's also possible to add more profiles, as illustrated by Figure 9.33.

FIGURE 9.33
Adding a profile

After the profile was added, it was moved to create a bulge in the surface (Figure 9.34).

FIGURE 9.34
Moved profile

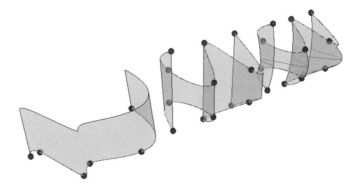

The fourth iteration of the form was created by selecting the surface and then selecting the Dissolve tool (Figure 9.35). This removed the surface (or solid form) but left us with all the references used to create the form.

FIGURE 9.35
Using the Dissolve tool

Once the face was dissolved, another reference called Spline Through Points was added between the upper and lower reference splines. The result is shown in Figure 9.36.

Selecting all three references and then selecting the Create Form tool stitched them all into a new single surface form (Figure 9.37).

FIGURE 9.36
Additional spline
added

FIGURE 9.37
New surface form

Selecting the points within the middle reference allowed for even more complex surface control (Figure 9.38).

Keep in mind that selecting all the splines and then creating the surface will result in very different forms than if you were to sequentially select only adjacent splines (Figure 9.39). The result is that the surface form isn't interpolated as smooth between the upper and lower splines. Instead, a distinct edge is created between the two splines.

As you can see, it's easy to create complex surface forms using reference lines. Now let's begin to create complex forms using reference planes.

FIGURE 9.38
Edited center spline

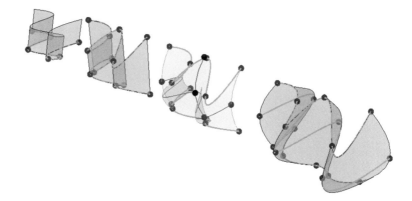

FIGURE 9.39
Spline-based
surfaces

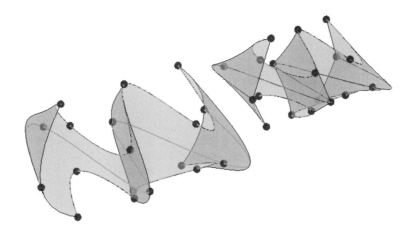

MASSING FORMS

As discussed earlier, you don't create solid masses by creating a particular type of form and then entering Sketch mode. Creating the necessary references and then evoking the Create Form tool creates mass forms.

First, you don't have to create solid forms. You can also create surfaces, not only from lines but also from closed loops. Figure 9.40 illustrates this.

Even if you create a surface, you'd still have the option to convert it into a solid mass (Figure 9.41) by selecting the surface and using the control arrows to pull the surface into a three-dimensional shape.

Now let's create each of the reference shapes necessary to create each of the familiar forms (Figure 9.42). From left to right, these shapes will create Extrusions, Blends, Sweeps, Revolves, and Swept Blends.

FIGURE 9.40
Surface or form
option

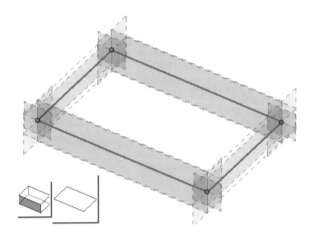

FIGURE 9.41
Creating a solid
from a surface

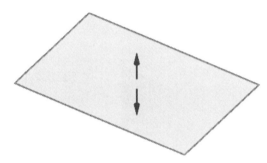

FIGURE 9.42
Using reference
shapes to create
forms

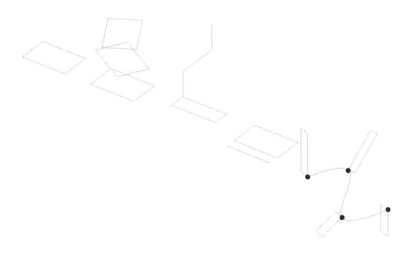

Figure 9.43 shows the resulting forms that are created from each of the references. You could also create voids from the same reference shapes. If you want to download this file for further investigation, it's named c09_Massing_Types.rvt.

FIGURE 9.43
Resulting mass
forms

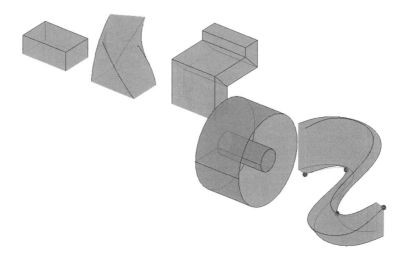

Each mass form contains parameters and controls relative to its form. We'll now explain how to create surface and solid forms intuitively in the project environment.

Intuitive Massing

Because we will now explain how to create an intuitive mass form, we'll cover how to create a surface and then assign host elements to the surface. This is a great way to create complex walls and roofs, for example. Then we'll explain how to assign patterns to the surface. Start by opening a new project using the default Architecture template, and then add a third level, as shown in Figure 9.44. You'll use these levels as controls for the Spline Through Points that will generate our first surface.

FIGURE 9.44
Creating an addi-
tional level

Select In-Place Mass and go to a top 3D view. Then create a Spline Through Points as shown on Level 1 (Figure 9.45). Although this might seem like a simple shape, the resulting form will be quite complex — just be patient!

FIGURE 9.45
Spline Through
Points

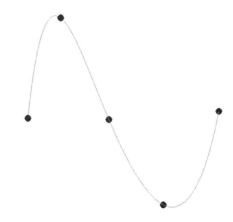

In-Place Surface

Now create another Spline Through Points using Level 3 as a reference, as shown in Figure 9.46. Since you're working in a 3D view, you'll be able to see both splines at the same time.

FIGURE 9.46
Second Spline
Through Points

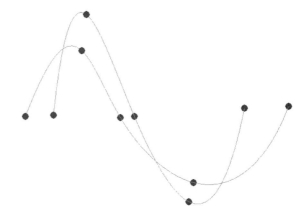

Now rotate the view so that you can see both splines separately. Select them both and then select Create Form, as shown in Figure 9.47. Figure 9.48 shows the resulting surface.

FIGURE 9.47
Selecting Create
Form

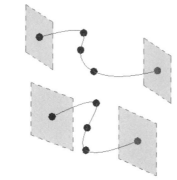

FIGURE 9.48
Resulting surface

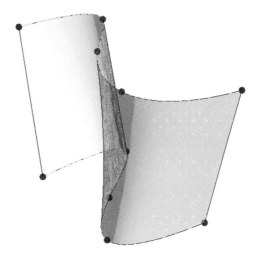

WALL BY FACE

Once you've selected the Finish Mass button, you'll be able to create a wall by face and assign it to this form. Go to the Architecture tab and select Wall By Face, as shown in Figure 9.49.

FIGURE 9.49
Wall By Face

Figure 9.50 shows the resulting wall. The mass surface has been turned off in order to show only the wall.

FIGURE 9.50
Resulting wall

Now let's return to the in-place mass and change the references. To do this, you select the mass and then click the Edit In-Place button. But before starting, you may want to hide the wall so that only the mass and its references are shown.

By selecting each of the controls, you'll notice you can move them in X, Y, and Z directions. Adjust the controls as shown in Figure 9.51.

Now finish the mass and unhide your wall in the view. Select the wall and then choose the Update To Face option (Figure 9.52).

FIGURE 9.51
Modified surface

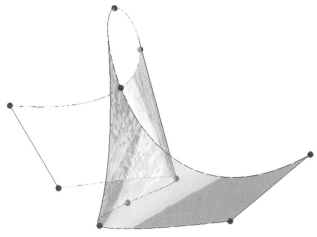

FIGURE 9.52
Update To Face

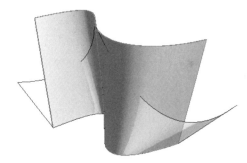

The wall will update to conform itself to the modified face, as shown in Figure 9.53.

Now hide the wall, select the mass surface, and return to editing in place. Add another Spline Through Points using Level 2 as a reference, as shown in Figure 9.54.

FIGURE 9.53
Updated wall

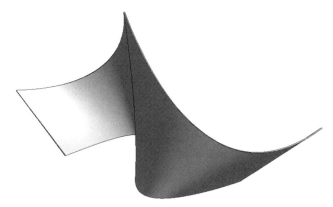

FIGURE 9.54
Adding another
Spline Through
Points

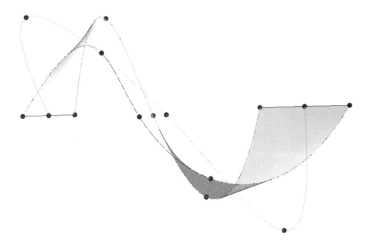

Select the surface and you have the option to dissolve it (Figure 9.55) in the Form Element panel of the ribbon. Go ahead and select this button. Then select all three splines and re-create the surface.

FIGURE 9.55
Dissolving the
surface

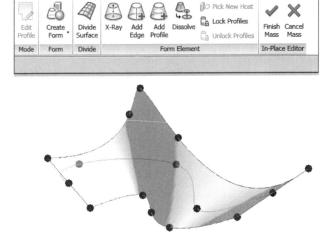

Once the surface has been revised, finish the mass and update the wall as done previously. Your updated wall will not look exactly like Figure 9.56. What's important is that you grasp the principles and the process. If the changes you made were so complex that the wall can't be updated to match the new face, just delete it and re-create it.

FIGURE 9.56
Finishing the family
and updating the
wall

PATTERN-BASED SYSTEM

Three steps are involved in assigning a pattern to a mass surface. First you divide the surface, then you assign a pattern to the surface, and finally, you assign a component to the pattern. Here are the steps:

1. Rather than start from scratch, create a copy of the surface previously created by selecting the pattern and choosing Duplicate from the Type Properties dialog box. Now select the mass surface and select Edit In-Place from the Modify menu. Delete the wall from the copied mass. We want to use only the surface itself. With the wall removed, select the surface.

2. While in Sketch mode and with the surface selected, choose Divide Surface from the contextual Divide palette (Figure 9.57).

FIGURE 9.57
Divide Surface tool

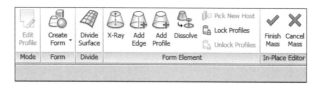

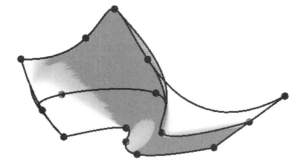

The default divided surface will look like Figure 9.58.

FIGURE 9.58
Divided surface

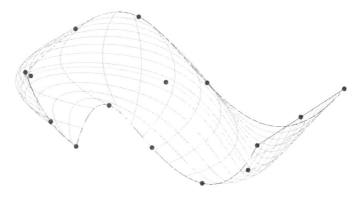

3. Once the surface has been divided, you can assign a pattern to it. The pattern will not contain any geometry; it's a lightweight method of resolving the eventual surface and giving it a graphical look and feel.

4. Select the surface and you'll see in the Type Selector that no pattern has been applied (Figure 9.59). Experiment with assigning different patterns from the Properties dropdown list to see the different visual effects you can apply to the shape.

FIGURE 9.59
Selecting No
Pattern

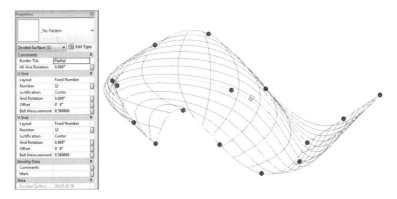

5. When your exploration is complete, select the Triangle (Flat) pattern (Figure 9.60).

6. The resulting surface will be faceted with an analytic triangular pattern (Figure 9.61).

7. Take a moment to investigate the edge conditions of your analytic surface. There are three options: Partial, Empty, and Overhanging. Select the surface and select Edit In-Place from the context menu to enter Sketch mode to investigate these three options.

The Partial option allows the triangulated surface to align with the edge of the mass surface (Figure 9.62).

FIGURE 9.60
Selecting the Triangle (Flat) surface pattern

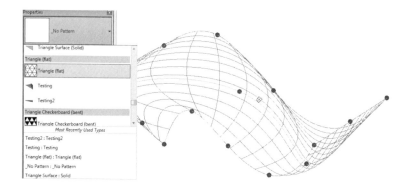

FIGURE 9.61
The result of choosing the Triangle (Flat) pattern

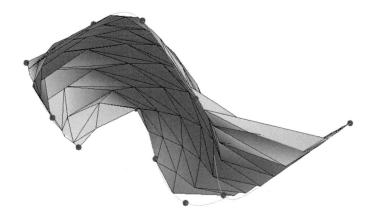

FIGURE 9.62
Partial option

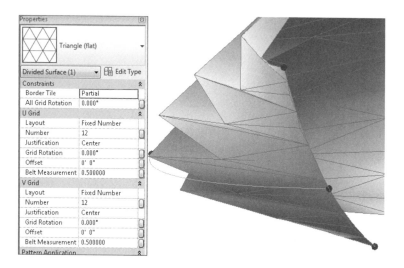

With the Empty option selected, the partial panel can't be created (Figure 9.63).

FIGURE 9.63
Empty option

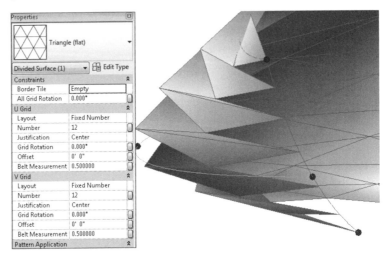

The Overhanging option completes the partial panels to extend beyond the mass surface (Figure 9.64).

FIGURE 9.64
Overhanging option

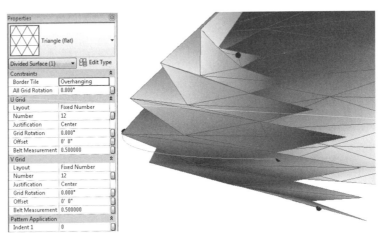

8. Select the Overhanging option. Now exit Edit In-Place mode.

PATTERN-BASED PANEL

Now you're going to create a pattern-based panel. Start a new family component by selecting the Application button, choosing New ➢ Family, and then choosing the Curtain Panel Pattern Based family template (Figure 9.65).

FIGURE 9.65
Curtain Panel
Pattern Based
template

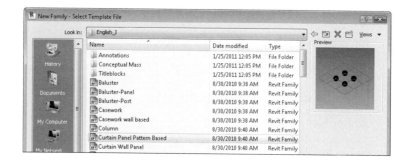

Then follow these steps:

1. To keep things simple, every pattern-based family that you'll need to create is in this family template. Just select the grid that contains the reference lines and you'll be able to select from all the panel options in the Properties palette (Figure 9.66).

FIGURE 9.66
Panel options in the
Properties palette

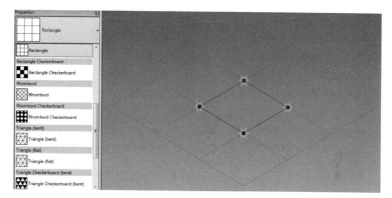

2. Select a few different options from the drop-down menu and you'll notice that the patterns change accordingly. Eventually you'll want to select the Triangle (Flat) type, as shown in Figure 9.67.

FIGURE 9.67
Triangle (Flat)
template

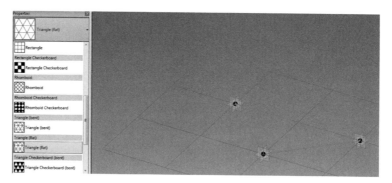

3. Apply the template and then update the panel in your project by reloading it into your project. This process is important because if something breaks, you'll know which step to reconsider.

4. Select the reference planes and then select Create Form. Again, create only the surface, not the geometry (Figure 9.68). Save the family (we've called it Testing.rfa) and then load it into your massing project.

FIGURE 9.68
Creating only the surface form

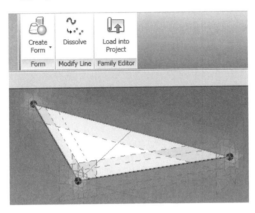

5. To assign the panel that you just created to the massing form, you need to select the mass and enter Edit In-Place mode. Once you've done this, select the mass again and open the Properties drop-down menu for your mass surface. Notice that in addition to the options for assigning a pattern, you now have options to assign geometry (Figure 9.69).

FIGURE 9.69
Options for assigning geometry

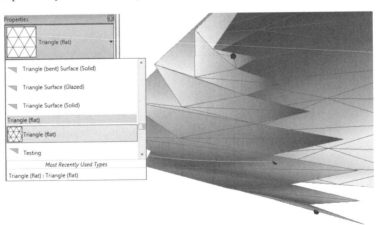

6. Assign this component to the mass. Then exit Edit In-Place mode. Now hide the mass so that only your panel will display (Figure 9.70).

FIGURE 9.70
Panel assigned to
mass surface

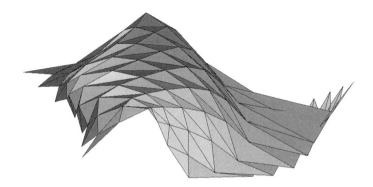

7. Return to the panel family. It's about to get very interesting!

Select all three reference points and copy above the work surface, as shown in Figure 9.71. You can use graphic display options to turn off the gradient background.

FIGURE 9.71
Copying the three
reference points

8. Go to a top view and move the points as shown in Figure 9.72.

FIGURE 9.72
Moving the refer-
ence points

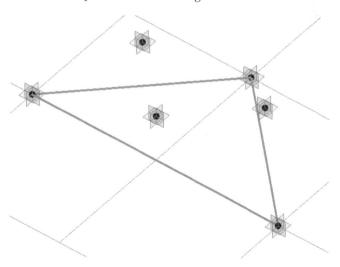

9. Join the reference points with new reference lines, as shown in Figure 9.73.

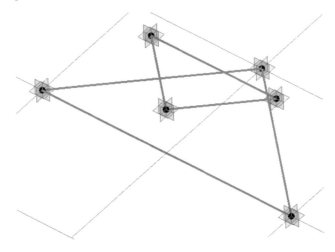

10. Select all the reference lines and create a new form. This will result in a blended form, as shown in Figure 9.74.

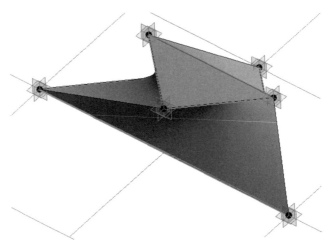

11. Reload the family into the project. Your components will update, creating a surprisingly complex form (Figure 9.75).

By revisiting the family and updating in the project, you can create interesting and complex forms. The panels in Figure 9.76 were created by associating a simple extrusion with a series of reference lines that were offset from the original sketch.

FIGURE 9.75
The updated components, resulting in a complex form

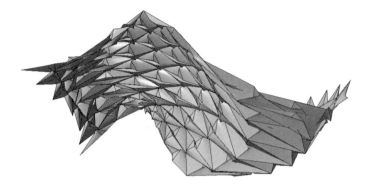

FIGURE 9.76
Voided blended panels

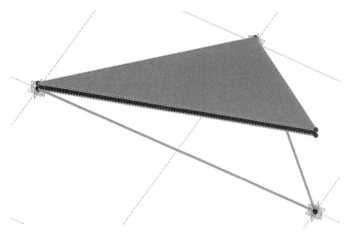

Figure 9.77 shows the resulting family, which has been assigned to a newly created blended surface. If you want to further investigate this project, download the c09_Intuitive_Massing_ Surface.rvt file in the Chapter 9 folder found on the book's companion website, www.sybex .com/go/masteringrevit2013.

FIGURE 9.77
Revised form

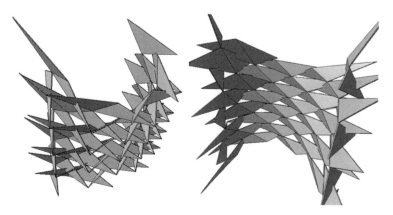

Of course, creating complex form-driven systems isn't for everyone or every project. But we think that CNC and other forms of rapid prototyping are going to make mass customization increasingly approachable over the next few years.

If you are interested in generative form making, head over to Zachary Kron's blog. He works for Revit Factory as a software analyst. His blog is at `http://buildz.blogspot.com` and his YouTube channel is `www.youtube.com/user/zachkron`. He's a great source of geometry, rule-based customization, and in some cases, API-driven customization.

In-Place Solids

Creating in-place mass solids is quite easy once you understand the process of creating and modifying the various forms. Let's start by entering in-place massing mode and selecting a rectilinear shape created from model lines (Figure 9.78). You should also select the option to make a surface from the closed loops that are being created. The other option would be to not make a closed loop, but you're creating a simple extrusion (initially), so this will save a step.

FIGURE 9.78
Rectilinear form

1. Sketch a form similar to the one shown in Figure 9.79. Specific dimensions are not important; it's more about the proportions.

FIGURE 9.79
Plan view of sketch

2. Open the Default 3D view and select the face of the surface that you just created. When you select this surface, controls become available that allow you to pull the surface into a solid (Figure 9.80).

FIGURE 9.80
Creating a solid
form

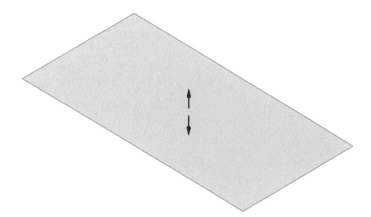

3. Pull the surface up until it resembles the form shown in Figure 9.81. Again, it's more about proportion than dimensions.

FIGURE 9.81
Resulting form

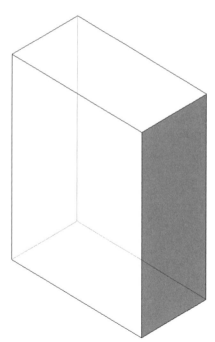

There are a number of shape handles that allow you to modify each face, edge, and intersection. Simply hovering over each face, edge, and vertex will highlight the appropriate control. You may also find it useful to tab through to select the desired control.

If you select a face, you'll be given the control shown in Figure 9.82.

FIGURE 9.82
Face control

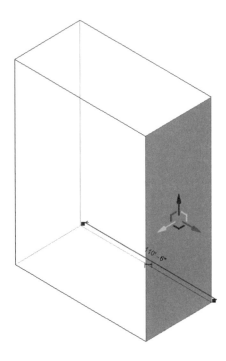

Selecting an edge will give you the ability to modify the edge of a form (Figure 9.83).

FIGURE 9.83
Edge control

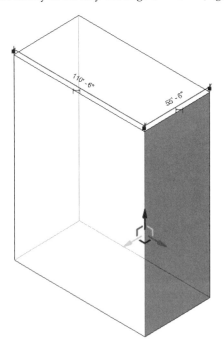

Selecting the intersection allows you to modify the location of a vertex (Figure 9.84).

FIGURE 9.84
Vertex control

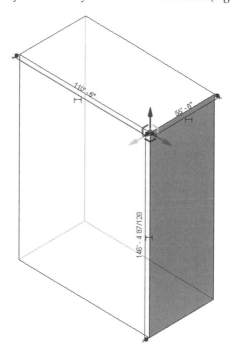

The control arrow allows you to modify the selected element parallel to the direction of the arrow, while the angled indicators of the same colors as their corresponding arrow will allow you to modify the location of the selected element perpendicular to the arrow (Figure 9.85).

FIGURE 9.85
Parallel and perpen-
dicular control

Turn on X-Ray mode so you can see any of the profiles and controls (Figure 9.86). X-Ray mode is helpful for seeing all the controls that are available as well as the trajectory control of the extrusion.

Now that X-Ray mode has been enabled, look at the options that Revit provides for turning a rather simple, extruded form into something complex. An edge (Figure 9.87) may be added to an existing form from vertex to vertex or parallel with the trajectory of the form (shown as a dotted line from the upper to the lower face).

FIGURE 9.86

X-Ray mode

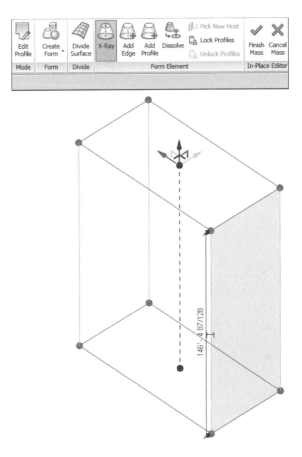

Once the edge has been added, you may push or pull the face adjacent to the new edge, as shown in Figure 9.87 and 9.88.

You may also push or pull the edge that has just been created, which will stretch both adjacent faces (Figure 9.89).

Pushing or pulling the edge that is perpendicular to the edge previously created will create curved and warped surfaces (Figure 9.90). This is fine because the form that you're creating can be rationalized later when you are adding a pattern to the surface.

FIGURE 9.87
Adding an edge

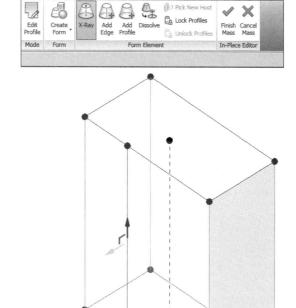

FIGURE 9.88
Pushing the face

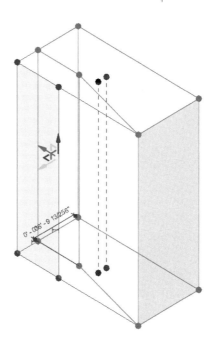

FIGURE 9.89
Pushing the edge

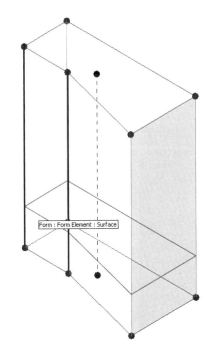

FIGURE 9.90
Pulling the edge

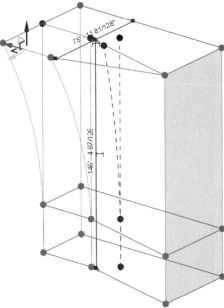

You can rationalize the form (and in doing so remove any warped surfaces), and then add another edge from vertex to vertex, as shown in Figure 9.91. Doing so will force the faces to become triangulated and planar because three points define a plane.

FIGURE 9.91
Adding more edges

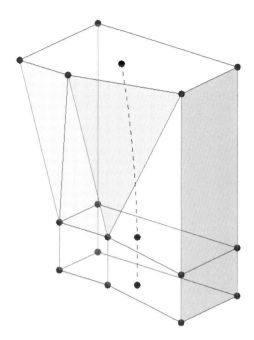

Pulling the top edge away from the vertical plane of the form results in a more dramatic form, as shown in Figure 9.92. Again, it's not necessary to maintain the exact dimensions; it's about trying to keep the proportions appropriate. This is what intuitive form making is all about!

FIGURE 9.92
Pulling the upper
edge

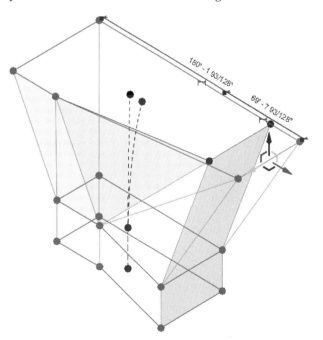

Using the Dissolve function (Figure 9.93) will remove the mass solid and leave behind the analytic profiles that define the solid. The dot in the center of each plane is a control that will allow you to edit the elevation, rotation, and location of the shape.

FIGURE 9.93
Using Dissolve to remove the mass solid

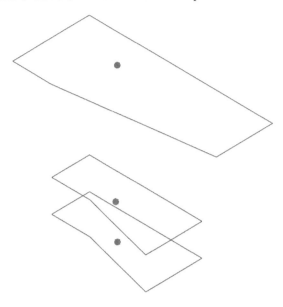

Selecting the profiles together and then choosing the Create Form command will stitch the form back together in a way that interpolates the shape as more of a lofted blend (Figure 9.94). You could also add more profiles to the shape.

FIGURE 9.94
Making a lofted blend from three profiles

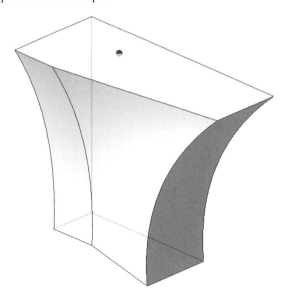

If you select only two profiles at a time, then the following occurs (see Figure 9.95). This form was created by first selecting the bottom and middle profiles and then creating the form. Then the middle and upper profiles were selected and another form was created. The result is straight — rather than curved — interpolation between the profiles.

FIGURE 9.95
Making a blend
from two profiles

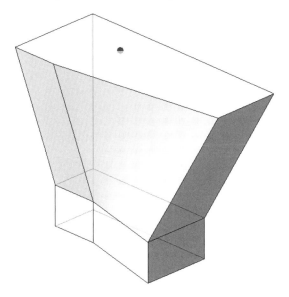

Rather than select either of the two previous options, you can alter the front edge of all three profiles. Start by deleting the existing edge (you'll have to tab to select just this edge), as shown in Figure 9.96.

FIGURE 9.96
Deleting the edge

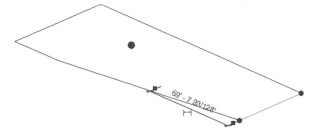

Now you'll want to draw a fillet arch to rejoin the two remaining edges. To do so, you'll have to set the work plane of the shape as shown in Figure 9.97. Just tab through until the horizontal work plane is highlighted and then select it.

Once the work plane is selected, you'll be able to draw additional model lines. In this example, you're using a fillet arch to connect the lines (Figure 9.98). You'll do the same thing for the other two shapes.

FIGURE 9.97
Selecting the work
plane

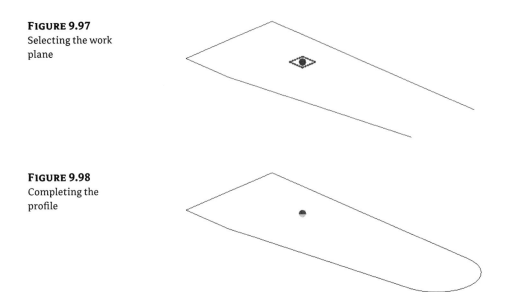

FIGURE 9.98
Completing the
profile

Now select the lower two profiles and choose Create Form. Then do the same with the upper two profiles. Finally, you'll want to remove any blends by adding an edge to the opposing edges.

Creating additional mass solids is easy. You can select an existing face, as shown in Figure 9.99, and then select the Create Form command.

FIGURE 9.99
Creating the form

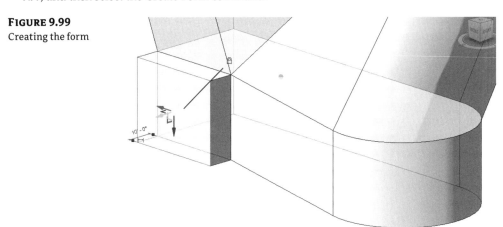

The same Create Form command was used to create the form shown in Figure 9.100.

In Figure 9.101, we've extended both faces considerably from their initial depth after using the Create Form option. Notice the locked relationship, which will allow only the faces of the form, not the edges or vertices, to be manipulated. In other words, you wouldn't be able to push or pull the top of the form up. You can remove this restriction by clicking the lock icon.

FIGURE 9.100
Creating another form

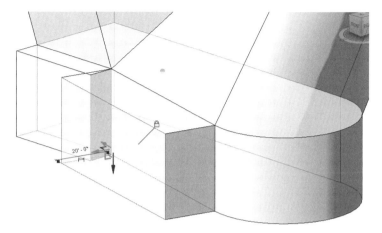

FIGURE 9.101
Unlocking a reference

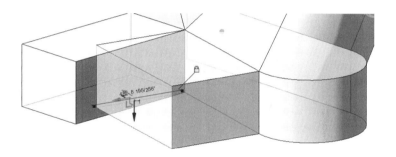

Once unlocked, the edge of the face is easily moved down to give a slope to the edge at the front of the form (Figure 9.102).

FIGURE 9.102
Modifying the edge

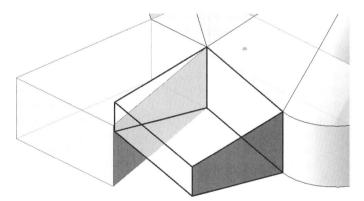

There will be many cases when creating existing geometry from an existing face will give you more mass than you need in your model. In these cases, it's simply a matter of drawing more model lines on the surface of the existing form. Then you'll be able to quickly and easily push and pull the faces, edges, and vertices of the resulting form (Figure 9.103).

FIGURE 9.103
Adding a profile

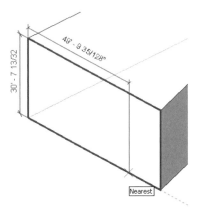

The in-place solid mass is finished, and the masses from Figure 9.102 have been joined so that the edge between the two masses is now visible (Figure 9.104). Finish the in-place solid mass and return to the regular project environment.

FIGURE 9.104
Completed mass

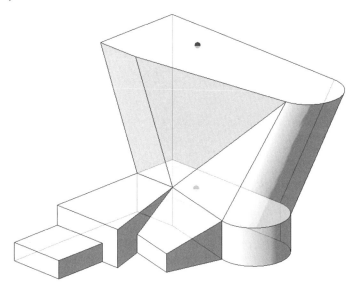

Once you're out of In-Place Massing mode, you'll notice that if you select the model, many shape handles simultaneously appear in the form of solid blue arrowheads (Figure 9.105). You can use shape handles to push and pull your solid mass, but you won't be able to modify edges or vertices without reentering In-Place Massing mode.

FIGURE 9.105
Using shape
handles

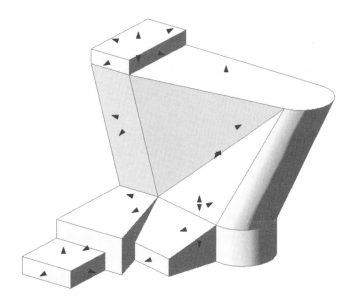

Figure 9.106 shows the finished mass in a perspective view. Both solids and voids can be used to complete a mass form. Whereas solids will add more geometry, voids will remove geometry from your mass.

FIGURE 9.106
Finished form

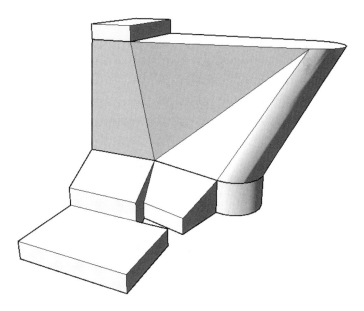

To demonstrate this, we'll return to In-Place Massing mode and create another face on the top of the existing form (Figure 9.107).

FIGURE 9.107
Adding a solid

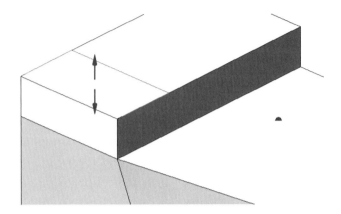

STARTING VOIDS AS SOLIDS

If you create the void as a void, it will immediately cut the solid mass and become invisible. This can be really annoying when you're trying to resolve your design and want to selectively cut after you've intuitively resolved a design idea. Fortunately, there's a better way.

Follow these steps:

1. Rather than create a void, start by creating a solid of a different color and category (if necessary) to keep things clear during your design iteration.

2. Select the solid mass and convert it to a void, as shown in Figure 9.108.

Figure 9.109 shows the result of the void cutting the solid. Keep in mind that if you want to convert the void back to a solid, you'll have to uncut any geometry that was being cut by the void. But the nice thing about this technique (converting solids to voids and then cutting) is that you've selectively cut only the solids that you wanted to cut. Had you originally modeled the void as a void, you would have found that the void was cutting many solids and you'd have to uncut solids that weren't even overlapping with the void!

Overall, creating solid masses intuitively is a great way to establish, analyze, and visualize your overall design idea. As you saw earlier in the chapter, mass floors allow you to even quantify gross floor areas before you've committed to geometry.

Furthermore, it's possible to put different intuitive massing ideas inside different design options (covered in Chapter 11, "Designing with Design Options and Groups") so that many ideas can live in a single Revit project file. Simply initiate worksharing and create worksets for each study mass. Multiple team members will be able to see one another's work at the same time and in context with their design ideas. This is the holistic kind of team approach to design information that makes massing a unique and valuable design tool. If you'd like to investigate this file further, you can download the file c09_Intuitive_Massing_Solid.rvt from the Chapter 9 folder of the book's companion website.

Next we'll investigate parametric and formulaic solid mass creation in the Family Editor.

FIGURE 9.108
Converting a solid to a void

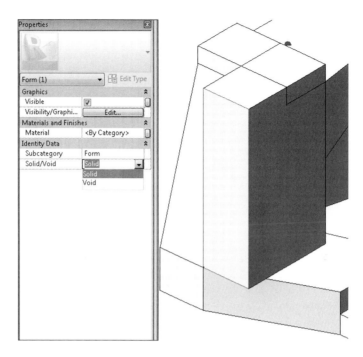

FIGURE 9.109
Cutting the void

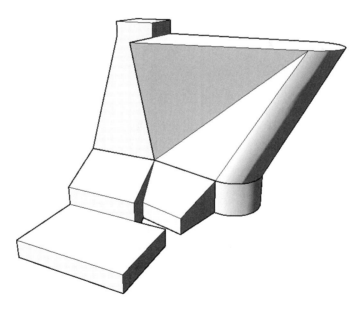

Formula-Driven Massing

Formula-driven massing can be done in the project environment, but the challenge is that you have to work in the context of the project, and all the parameters, formulas, reference planes, and lines can start to get in the way. Therefore, having the option of creating form-driven masses in the Family Editor without the clutter of the project environment can help you focus on what you're trying to accomplish.

You'll want to make sure that you open the right family template. The Mass template is in the Conceptual Mass folder (Figure 9.110). Don't start with a generic model or some other template.

FIGURE 9.110

Starting with the Mass template

Also, turn off the gradient background that's on by default in the graphic display options (Figure 9.111). You can keep this option on if you like, but the images will print better with it turned off.

FIGURE 9.111

Graphic display options

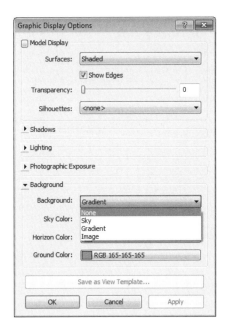

Overall, the UI is not too dissimilar from the project environment. It's like you're creating masses in place — except that you're not in the project environment, you're in the Family Editor. One significant difference that you can see is that there is a single level and two reference planes, which also define the origin for a massing family (Figure 9.112). So keep in mind that when you reload this family into your project, it will update relative to the origin in the family.

FIGURE 9.112
Massing user
interface

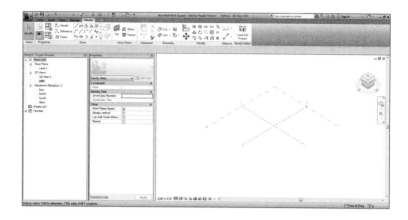

Simple Mass Family

In this example, you'll start by creating a simple mass and then add parameters and test the results. Follow these steps:

1. Create this simple mass using model lines on Level 1. You can save an extra step by selecting the Make Surface From Closed Loops option (Figure 9.113).

FIGURE 9.113
Selecting the Make
Surface From
Closed Loops option

2. Once you've created the surface in plan, go to the Default 3D view and then pull the surface, as shown in Figure 9.114. Again, don't worry about the actual dimensions. Just get the overall proportions close to how they look in the image.

FIGURE 9.114
Creating the mass

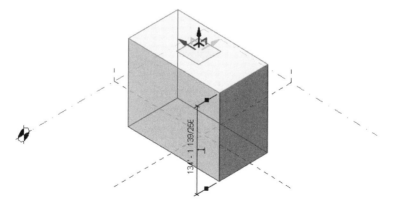

3. Now dimension the form. Be sure to maintain a relationship to the insertion point of the mass template by using a continuous dimension string. Set this string to "equal" by clicking on the blue EQ letters you'll see when you select and highlight the dimension string. Then dimension the overall dimensions in X, Y, and Z directions as shown in Figure 9.115.

FIGURE 9.115
Adding dimensions

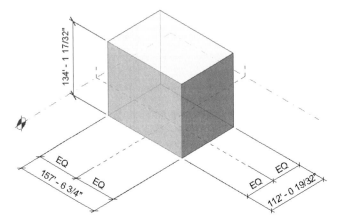

4. Now you'll add parameters to the overall dimensions. Simply select a dimension and you'll be shown a context menu that allows you to associate a parameter with the dimension you've just selected (Figure 9.116).

FIGURE 9.116
Associating
parameters

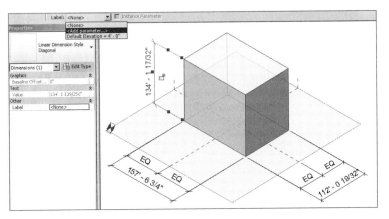

5. Label this dimension **Height** by selecting the dimension and choosing the Label pull-down from the Options bar. Select <Add Parameter…> and click the radio button to make it an instance parameter (Figure 9.117). If you had many massing elements of the same type loaded into your project and you wanted to control all of them with the same value, you would want to use a type parameter. For this example, though, an instance parameter is fine.

FIGURE 9.117
Creating
parameters

Once you have all your dimensions associated with parameters, your project should look similar to Figure 9.118. That's because as you associate parameter values with your dimensions, the parameter name will display along with the dimension.

FIGURE 9.118
Completed
parameters

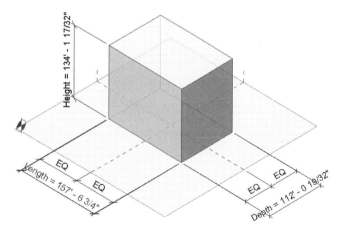

With the groundwork done, now it's going to start to get interesting. Rather than maintain independent instance parameters for each dimension, you're going to associate formulas with the Length and the Depth values. To do this, open the Type Parameters dialog box by clicking the Family Types button in the Properties palette. With the dialog box open, enter the following formulas, making sure to adhere to the proper case (formulas are case sensitive). Go ahead and do this, as shown in Figure 9.119:

Length = **Height / 2**

Depth = **Length / 2**

FIGURE 9.119
Creating formulas

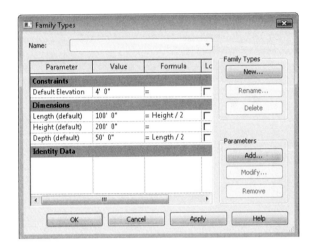

Now your entire mass family can be proportionally controlled simply by adjusting the Height parameter (Figure 9.120).

FIGURE 9.120
Proportional form

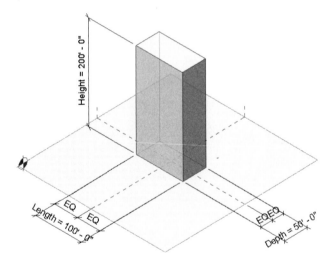

This proportional control can be accomplished in one of two ways. First, you can select the height dimensional value and change the dimension by keying in a new value (Figure 9.121). This is desirable when you want to edit a value to an exact amount.

In many cases, you'll still want to intuitively control the shape of the form first and then, when you get an idea of what looks right, set the resulting dimensional value to a more reasonable figure. You do so by selecting the top face of the form and pushing or pulling the control arrows until you get it close (Figure 9.122). Notice that each time you release the arrow, the form adjusts in all dimensions (since the other dimensions are being controlled by formulas related to the height dimension).

FIGURE 9.121
Adjusting the
height numerically

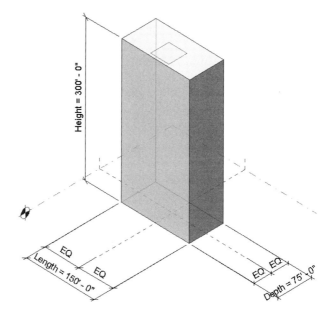

FIGURE 9.122
Adjusting the
height intuitively

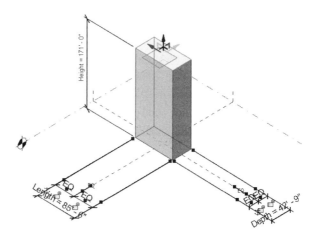

By doing the following, you can experiment further by creating more geometry at the base of the initial mass:

1. Dimension the form, as shown in Figure 9.123.

FIGURE 9.123

Adding a second form

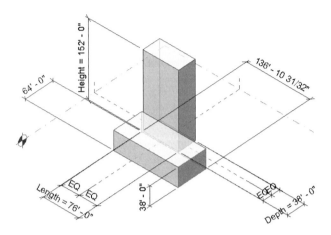

2. Associate the dimensions of this second form to the dimensions that you already created (Figure 9.124). What's terrific about this is that as you change a single value, the overall form will proportionally grow or shrink.

FIGURE 9.124

Associative parameters

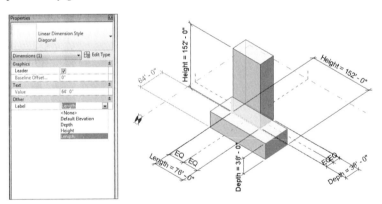

Ultimately this technique of associating parameters with other parameters is a great way to quickly and easily maintain important and interesting formal relationships between masses. Notice how the two masses in Figure 9.125 are barely intersecting near the base of the horizontal form.

When you modify the height of the vertical element, both forms grow accordingly (Figure 9.126). The intersection becomes much more noticeable, and if you continued to increase the height of the vertical mass, the intersection would eventually move beyond the face of the horizontal mass. If you want to download this family, look in the Chapter 9 folder on the book's companion website for the file c09_Parametric_Massing_Simple.rfa.

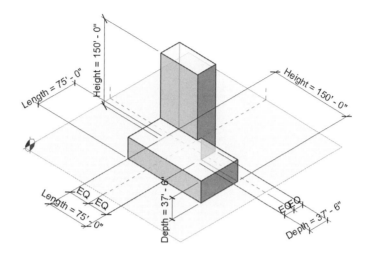

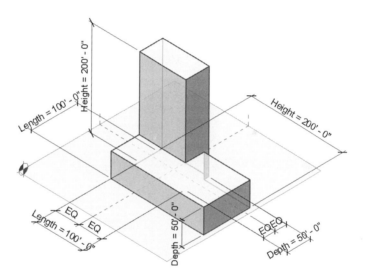

Generic Model Mass Family

A lot of users really miss the ability to use the old geometry tools to create masses from pre–Revit 2010. Although it's possible to create parametric generic forms in the Family Editor, when you place them in the project, they're still generic elements. You can assign standard walls, curtain walls, and roofs to the faces, but you can't add patterns, create mass floors, or even schedule the results as a mass. So, if you like the old tools, here's how to use them to create project masses:

1. Open a Generic Model template (Figure 9.127). You're going to create a flexible, parametric form and then "trick" the software into thinking that this generic family is a mass.

FIGURE 9.127
Generic Model
template

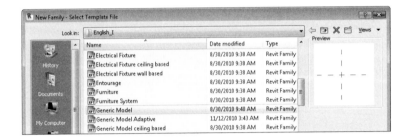

You won't be able to trick it by creating a generic model family and then converting it to a mass by changing the family category (Figure 9.128).

FIGURE 9.128
Message box
explaining you can't
change the category

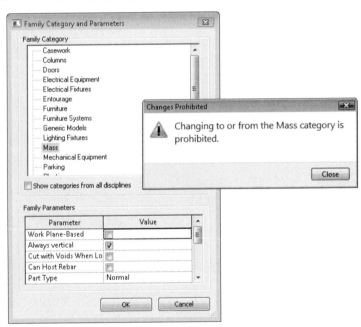

2. Go to a floor plan reference level view in your family. Begin by creating a reference line (not a reference plane), as shown in Figure 9.129. Note that the reference line is drawn from the intersection of the reference planes in an upward direction.

3. Draw another reference line in a downward direction (Figure 9.130). These reference lines will control the angular "twist" in your eventual family.

FIGURE 9.129
First reference line

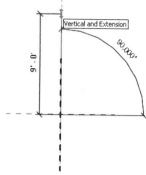

FIGURE 9.130
Second reference
line

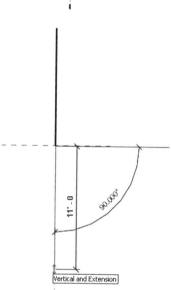

Now you're going to create a blend (Figure 9.131) by selecting the Create tab and choosing the Blend tool from the Forms panel. You want to associate this with the reference lines you just created. The bottom of the blend will be associated with the first reference line and the top of the blend will be associated with the second reference line.

FIGURE 9.131
Creating a blend

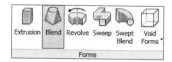

4. Start with the bottom blend. You're going to make a square 15′ (4.5 m) on each side. Start by selecting the Blend tool, and then you'll need to pick your workplane. Choose the Set button from the Work Plane panel and choose the first reference line you drew (Figure 9.132).

FIGURE 9.132
Setting the work plane

5. Sketch a form, as shown in Figure 9.133. Make sure the dimensions are equally distributed between the reference lines. You also want to give parameters to the overall dimensions. We've called the instance parameter BW (for bottom width) and assigned the parameter to both the overall dimensions (length and width).

FIGURE 9.133
Bottom with dimensions

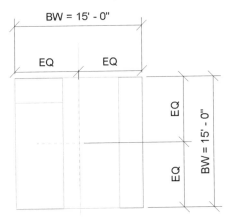

6. When you add the parameter, using the Label drop-down menu as you did earlier in this chapter, use the following settings (Figure 9.134):

   ◆ Enter **BW** in the Name text box.

   ◆ Select the Instance radio button.

   ◆ Leave the other parameters as their default settings.

   Make sure you set the bottom reference line as the work plane. Doing so allows you to control the angular twist of the blend when it's complete.

7. Select Edit Top from the Mode panel (Figure 9.135) to sketch the top of the blend.

FIGURE 9.134
The instance parameters for the bottom of the blend

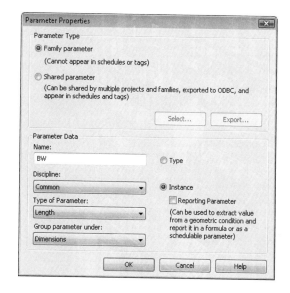

FIGURE 9.135
Switch to edit the top of the blend

8. Essentially you're going to repeat the previous step for the lower sketch for this upper sketch. Equally distribute the overall dimensions and create the parameters as you did previously, changing the name to **TW** (Top Width), as shown in Figure 9.136.

FIGURE 9.136
Top width parameters and sketch

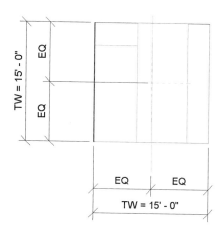

9. Now that the base and top width parameters have been set, and you're still in Sketch mode editing the top, you can add parameters to control the height of the blend. Do this by selecting the button to the right of the Second End constraints in the Properties palette (Figure 9.137).

FIGURE 9.137
Adding the height parameter

10. Add a parameter **H** (for height) as another instance parameter, as shown in Figure 9.138. Click OK to create the parameter. Now select Finish Family (the green check) to complete the blended form.

FIGURE 9.138
Instance parameter for the height

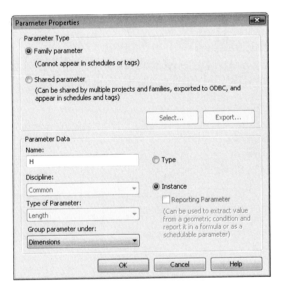

11. You should take a moment to test that the reference lines control the top and bottom sketch of the blend (Figure 9.139). Simply select the reference line to highlight it and then move the end of the reference line. The other end remains associated with the intersection of the insertion point, and the top and bottom sketch rotate.

FIGURE 9.139
Twisting the blend with reference lines

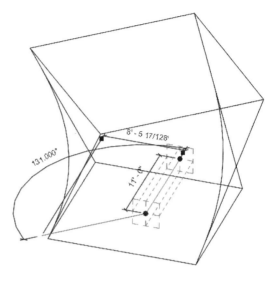

12. From a plan view, move the reference lines so that they're no longer on top of the reference planes. Now you can add angular dimensions between the reference line and the reference plane (Figure 9.140). Furthermore, you can add parameters to control the top and bottom angles of the blend. We've called these instance parameters BA and TA (for bottom angle and top angle, respectively). Figure 9.140 also shows all the parameters that control this blend. Go ahead and test them by adding angles and clicking the Apply button. The forms should rotate and twist.

FIGURE 9.140
Angular parameters

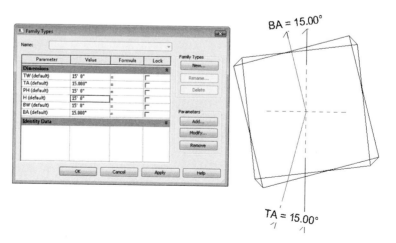

13. You're going to use the edges of this blend to drive the geometry that you're going to create, but since you don't want to see this blend, turn it into a void. With the blend selected, use the Solid/Void drop-down in the Properties palette (Figure 9.141). The resulting void will change color to a yellow-orange.

FIGURE 9.141
Turning a solid into a void

14. Now begin to create the sweep that will create your building mass in the project environment. Select the Sweep function from the Forms tab (Figure 9.142).

FIGURE 9.142
Selecting the Sweep function

15. Now select Pick Path (not Sketch Path) to select the edges of the blend previously created.

16. Pick the edges of the blend, as shown in Figure 9.143. Note the location of the sketch plane along the lower rear edge. This is because it is the first edge selected.

17. Once you have selected the edges of the blend, click the Select Profile option and select Edit Profile (Figure 9.144). Doing so allows you to sketch the profile in direct context of the selected edges.

18. You're going to sketch a profile 5'-6" (1.7 m) × 4'-6" (1.4 m). After you've sketched the profile as shown, be sure to add parameters to the profile width and height as you've done previously in this exercise. We've called the instance parameters PW (profile width) and PH (profile height), respectively (Figure 9.145).

19. Finish the sketch and the sweep, and the profile will generate as shown in Figure 9.146.

FIGURE 9.143
Selecting the edges
of the blend

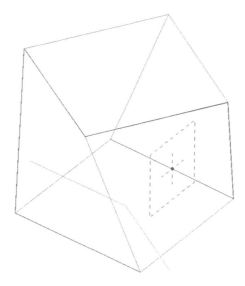

FIGURE 9.144
Selecting the Edit
Profile option

FIGURE 9.145
Adding parameters
to the profile width
and height

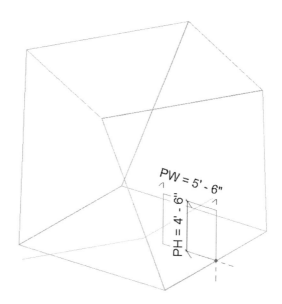

FIGURE 9.146
Finished mass

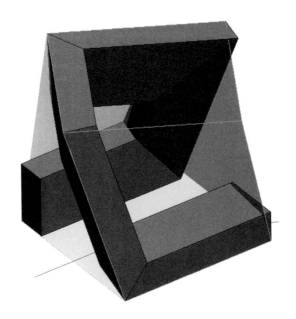

You'll use this generic model family in the project environment and the software will think it's a mass:

1. Open a new project using the default Architecture template and begin by creating an in-place mass from the Conceptual Mass panel of the Massing & Site tab. We've named the mass Generic Model Mass.

2. While still in the In-Place Mass Sketch mode, toggle back to the mass family you just created and load the generic model into your project environment. Place the generic family as a component into your project.

3. Select the mass you just inserted, and notice in the Properties palette that all of the attributes you gave to the mass are available for you to edit. Using these, flex the parameters as shown in Figure 9.147. What started as a small parametric form the size of a room is now over 100′ (30 m) tall!

4. Now finish the in-place mass by clicking the green check mark, which is the Finish Mass button. Even though this is a generic model family, because you've placed it during In-Place Mass mode, the software treats it as a mass.

5. Add the levels as shown in Figure 9.148 so that there are levels that extend across the entire elevation of your massing.

6. Select the mass and choose the Mass Floors button from the Model panel of the Modify | Mass context tab. You'll be able to associate each level represented in the project to the mass as a "floor."

FIGURE 9.147
Changing param-
eter values

FIGURE 9.148
Adding levels that
extend across the
elevation of your
massing

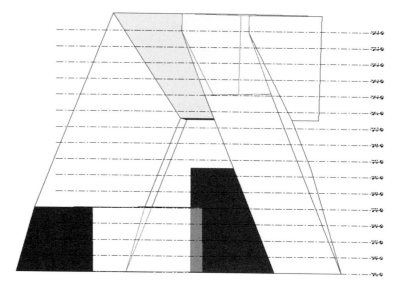

With the mass selected, click the Mass Floors button and add floors for each of the levels. You'll notice we've added some additional levels in our model. You can always go back to add more levels and reselect this tool at any stage in the process.(Figure 9.149).

7. Hover over the face and tab to select it. You'll also be able to associate patterns and pattern-based components with your generic massing family (Figure 9.150). This is because the software is now treating it as a massing element in the Mass category.

FIGURE 9.149
Floor area faces

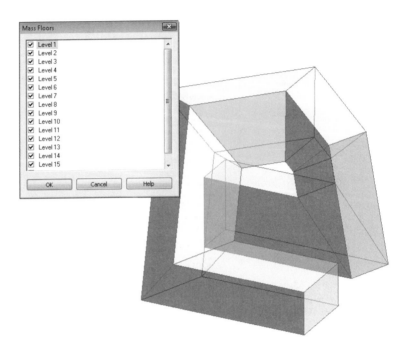

FIGURE 9.150
Adding pattern-based components

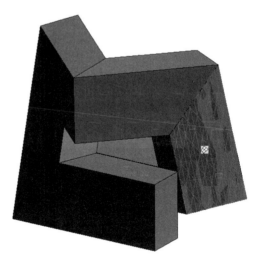

Figure 9.151 shows four perspective views of the completed massing study, all created with the familiar geometry toolset.

We've also rendered the model as shown in Figure 9.152. The results are quite interesting, and you'll still have the ability to modify the underlying parametric family and then rehost the faces. You'll also be able to schedule the volume, surface, and floor area of the mass.

FIGURE 9.151
Perspective views

FIGURE 9.152
Rendering of the
generic massing
project

You can download and further investigate the files that were used to create this exercise in the `Chapter 9` folder of the book's companion website. Download the project file `c09_Parametric_Generic_Massing.rvt`, which contains the in-place massing and the loaded generic element.

Now let's begin to investigate how to create parametric massing in the Family Editor using the conventional massing tools.

Complex Mass Family

Start by opening a conceptual massing family template. Click the Application button and choose New ➤ Conceptual Mass ➤ Mass.rfa.

In the past, the ability to parametrically control objects in the massing editor was done using reference planes and reference lines. The Revit team introduced reference point elements in 2010, which add another level of control to model elements. Point elements allow for Cartesian X, Y, Z, as well as rotational control.

With all complex and parametrically controlled families, we think it's best to understand complex families to get the basic rules down first. In this case, the rules are the parameters and formulas that will control a twisting, tapering tower.

To begin, start a blank Revit project. Select the In-Place Mass button from the Conceptual Mass panel of the Massing & Site tab. Next, open the Family Types dialog box and enter the values and formulas shown in Figure 9.153. Alternately, you can download the starting file, `c09_Parametric_Massing_Complex_Project_Start.rfa`, from the book's companion website, `www.sybex.com/go/masteringrevit2013`. This is a conceptual mass family. We've added these parameters for you to give you a starting point.

You're going to create the first rectilinear form on the first reference level (Level 1). As you do this, be sure to use reference (not model) lines.

Dimension the sketch twice, being sure to use the EQ function to evenly distribute the sketch at the center of the reference lines at the origin. When finished, associate both overall dimensions with the W0 parameter that you've already created (Figure 9.154). W0 is shorthand for the width dimension on the 0 level.

FIGURE 9.153
Family Types dialog box

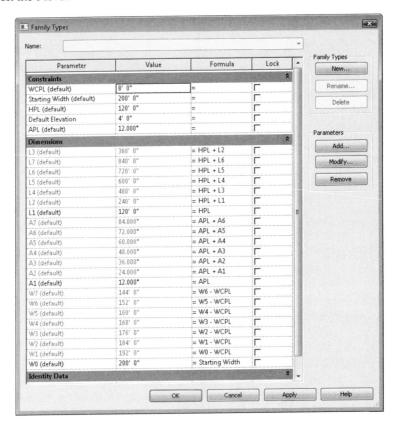

FIGURE 9.154
Dimensioned refer-
ence lines

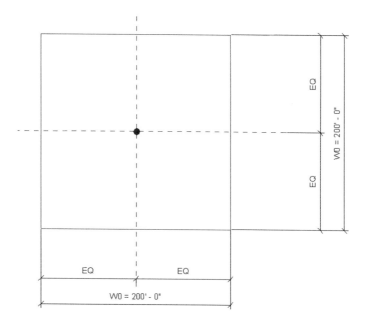

While in the same view, place seven point elements at the intersection of the default
reference places. Each time you place a point element, you'll get a warning about
overlapping point elements. You can ignore these warnings.

Now open the South elevation and select just one of the point elements that you
placed in plan. You can elevate it manually by dragging the up arrow to move it away
from the other overlapping point elements (Figure 9.155).

FIGURE 9.155
Moving the point
element

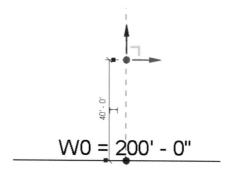

When you select the arrow, you'll also have the option to parametrically associate the point
element with one of the seven instance parameters that you've just created (Figure 9.156). This
is done by choosing the small button in the Properties palette for the Offset parameter. The L
parameters refer to the level number of each of your point elements. The first point element is L1
because it is reference Level 1. When you associate a parameter to this value, you'll notice that
the button fills with a small equal sign.

FIGURE 9.156
Adding a parameter
to the point element

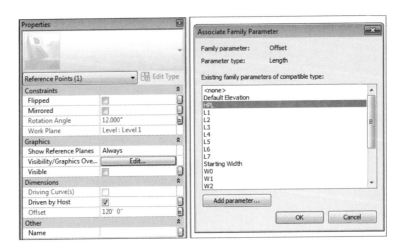

Now do this for all your point elements, elevating each to another level higher than the previous one. When you are finished, the South elevation will look similar to Figure 9.157.

FIGURE 9.157
The South elevation
will look like this.

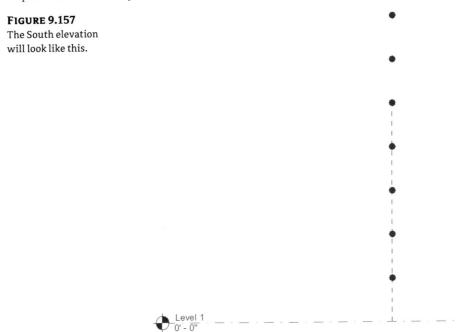

Right now the point elements are just spherical nodes. Their reference planes are not visible. Let's change that by selecting all of them and then selecting Always next to the Show Reference option in the Graphics panel of the Properties dialog box (Figure 9.158).

FIGURE 9.158
Selecting Always
next to Show
Reference

The reference planes of your point elements will now be visible, as shown in Figure 9.159.

FIGURE 9.159
The reference
planes will now be
visible.

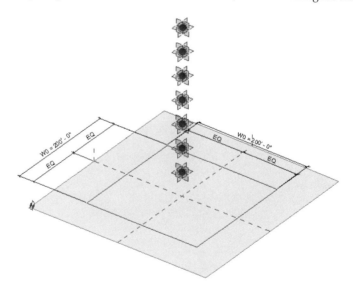

Select the lowest point element and associate it with the parameter that will control its rotation angle in the Properties palette (Figure 9.160). Select the button next to the rotation angle and associate it with the A1 instance parameter.

Now set the active work plane to the point element, as shown in Figure 9.161, by selecting the point element and then selecting the Set button from the Work Plane panel on the Modify tab.

FIGURE 9.160
Setting the rotation
angle

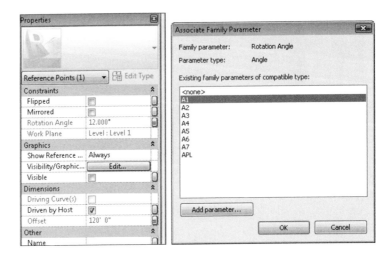

FIGURE 9.161
Associating the
work plane

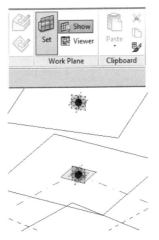

Then sketch a rectilinear shape using reference lines, as shown in Figure 9.162. Dimension it just as you did for the sketch at Level 0. Dimension both directions with an overall dimension as well as an EQ dimension. Finally, associate the overall dimensions with the W1 parameter, which will control the width of the sketch.

Systematically do this for each of the point elements, being sure to set the respective reference plane before you sketch the shape with reference lines. When you have finished this for all seven point elements that you created, your view will resemble Figure 9.163.

FIGURE 9.162
Creating the second
sketch

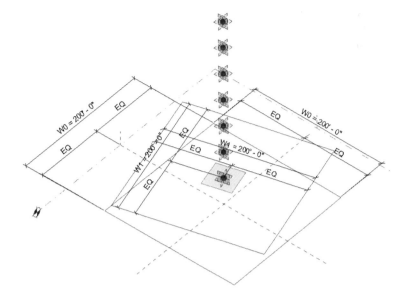

FIGURE 9.163
Reference lines and
point elements

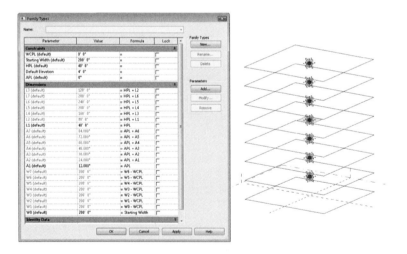

For clarity, we've hidden the dimensions in this image view so that you can see all the reference lines and point elements.

Select all the reference lines and select Create Form from the Form panel. Although this will look like a simple extrusion, it's actually a blend with many profiles. Open the Family Types dialog box and begin to test the results before loading the family into the project (Figure 9.164).

FIGURE 9.164
Testing the form
and instance
parameters

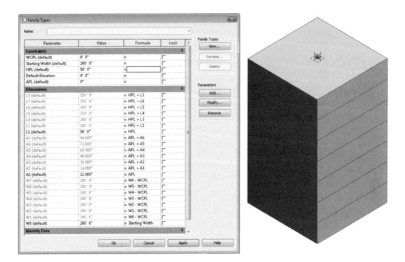

Test the parameter that controls the distance between levels by increasing the HPL instance parameter (which stands for height per level).

Now test the ability of the shape to taper (Figure 9.165). Do so by increasing the WCPL instance parameter (which stands for width control per level).

FIGURE 9.165
Increasing the
WCPL instance
parameter

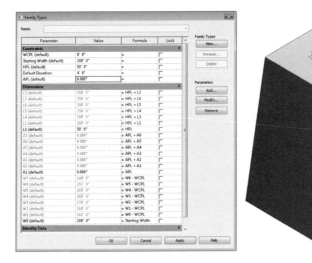

Next, test the parameters that control the amount of angular twist per level (Figure 9.166). Do so by increasing the APL parameter (which stands for angle per level).

Now that you've tested the massing in the family environment, open a new project and start to create a new, in-place mass from the Conceptual Mass panel of the Massing & Site tab. Then place this family into the project while in In-Place Mass Sketch mode. When you select the massing family, you'll be given access to all of its parameters in the Properties dialog box, as shown in Figure 9.167. You can quickly and easily test the massing parameters to significantly increase the height, width, taper, and incremental rotation of the massing family.

FIGURE 9.166
Increasing the APL
parameter

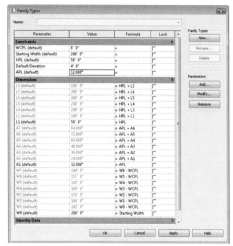

FIGURE 9.167
Flexing the
parameters

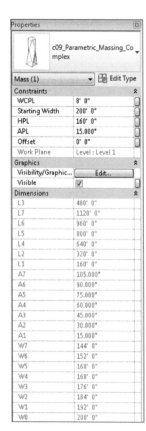

Adding patterns to the face of your mass should be second nature if you've been doing all the exercises in this book. Simply tab to select the face, and then apply the pattern as shown in Figure 9.168.

FIGURE 9.168
Adding patterns to the face of your mass

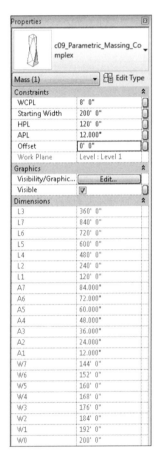

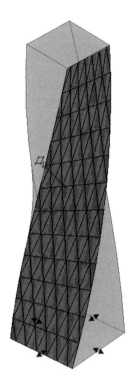

Floor area faces are another simple matter. Provided you have enough levels in your project, select the mass and then select the levels that you want to associate with the floor faces (Figure 9.169).

Creating interesting and complex massing studies that can be parametrically controlled isn't just a skill developed over time. The rules that you develop to make and reiterate your design are also carefully considered aesthetic choices to make decisions rather than blobs! To see this file, go to the Chapter 9 folder and download c09_Parametric_Massing_Complex_Project. rvt. Be sure to turn on Show Mass if it's not turned on when you open the file.

FIGURE 9.169
Floor area faces

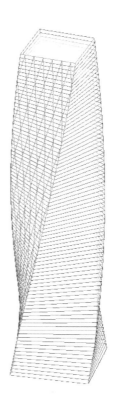

The Bottom Line

Create and schedule massing studies.   Starting the design process with actual building elements can lead to a lot of unexpected frustration. Walls lead to rooms, which get room tags and are eventually scheduled. But if you've failed to fulfill the client's program, you'll wonder where to start over!

Master It   You're faced with creating some design studies of a large hospital complex. How would you go about creating a Revit project that would allow you to create a massing study and schedule it against the client's program?

Know when to use solid masses and when to use surface masses.   While solid masses and surface masses can both be used to maintain relationships to host geometry like walls and roofs, surface masses can't be volumetrically scheduled or contain floor area faces.

Master It You've been asked to create a complex canopy system for the entry to a hotel project. The system will consist of a complex wave of triangular panels. What kind of mass would you create?

Use mathematical formulas for massing. Not all massing is going to involve intuitive, in-the-moment decision-making. By discovering the underlying rules that express a form, it is possible to create the formulas that can iterate and manipulate your massing study. So rather than manually manipulating the mass, you manipulate the formulas related to your mass.

Master It What's the best way to discover and create these formulas?

Chapter 10

Conceptual Design and Sustainability

In this chapter, we will take a further look at the Autodesk® Revit® Architecture Conceptual Design tool and how you can leverage it for sustainable design analysis. We'll also explore a few other tools, some of which use BIM geometry to support sustainable design analysis.

A number of Revit tools support sustainable design processes and analysis, ranging from accurate material takeoffs to energy analysis and daylighting studies. As you move from a more traditional design workflow to a Revit workflow, you will see more opportunities to engage environmental simulations within the Revit model. This ability to see the model from different points of view makes a BIM project perfect for exploring sustainable design strategies. We will explore how Revit software can help support those strategies.

In this chapter, you'll learn to:

♦ Embrace sustainable design concepts

♦ Leverage schedules

♦ Use sunshading and solar paths

♦ Prepare and export your model for energy analysis

♦ Analyze your project for daylighting

Sustainable Design Concepts

Environmentally thoughtful design strategies have been around for millennia, but the practice of sustainable design has seen substantial growth over the past few years. Sustainable design practices can help address many issues, among them energy use, access to natural daylight, human health and productivity, and resource conservation. One of the principal goals of sustainable design is to reduce a building's overall resource use. This can be measured in the building's carbon footprint (http://greenfootstep.org), or the net amount of carbon dioxide emitted by a building through its energy use.

An important factor in sustainable design is the large effect that the construction industry has on the environment. The United States, for example, uses 25 percent of the world's energy, and the US building industry uses 40 percent of global energy. Buildings, taken together, are the largest single resource consumer in the world. To solve the problem of global warming, you need to look at the low-hanging fruit of the architecture, engineering, and construction (AEC) industry and work toward a more efficient, more sustainable building practice.

Before we delve into discussing any specific workflows involving BIM and sustainability, it's important to recognize that many concepts are both interdependent and cumulative. The more sustainable methodologies you can incorporate into a project, the "greener" the project becomes.

Take the example of building orientation, glazing, and daylighting. Rotating your building in the proper direction, using the right glass in the correct amount and location, and integrating sunshading into the project to optimize the use of natural light all build upon each other. Using these three strategies together makes a building operate more efficiently while allowing occupants access to plenty of natural light. The amount of usable daylight you might capture will be greatly reduced with the application of highly reflective glass or if the building faces the wrong orientation. The appropriateness of any of these individual strategies and the benefits depend on building type and climate.

Revit software has similar characteristics. Because it is a parametric modeler, all the parts are interrelated. Understanding and capitalizing on these relationships typically takes numerous iterations that span multiple projects. Optimizing the integrated strategies and technologies for a high-performance, green design requires an understanding of how they work together to deliver the best potential. That is where Revit comes in — allowing the ability to iterate and analyze faster than in a more traditional process. The process is built on the following methodology for reducing the energy consumption of buildings:

1. Understand climate.

2. Reduce loads.

3. Use free energy.

4. Use efficient systems.

BAD MODELING HAS BAD DOWNSTREAM EFFECTS

Like poor ecology, poor modeling can have a negative impact downstream on team members and project stakeholders. If you are choosing to use your model for sustainable design analysis, remember that the more accurate you are in your modeling, the more accurate your results will be.

Conversely, a poorly assembled model will deliver inaccurate results. If you do not establish the proper materials in a daylighting model, for instance, you will not get the right reflectivity and therefore your daylighting study results will be inaccurate. If rooms and volumes are not established properly within the Revit model, your energy performance will be off. These faulty results may prompt you to make changes in your design that are incorrect or unnecessary.

It is a good idea to establish early on in your modeling process which sustainable design analyses you will be performing based on your Revit model geometry. It is much easier to set the model up for successful analysis when you begin than it is to go back and have to make significant changes to the model to perform analysis.

Using Schedules

You can repurpose many Revit tools for other uses. Schedules are a great example of this. In Chapter 5, "Managing a Project," we discussed how to use schedules to perform quality control within your model. Schedules are also a useful tool in sustainable design because they can help track the amount of recycled materials used in the design of a project. If one of your design objectives is to achieve a Leadership in Energy and Environmental Design (LEED) certification (www.usgbc.org/leed), one of the possible points is for the use of recycled materials. Based on how LEED calculates its recycled content requirements (by volume and cost), some of the key materials for recycled content tend to be steel and concrete. Although the schedules created in a Revit project can't be used for LEED credit submissions in this case, knowing how to calculate recycled content within a project can help steer the project goals during the design phase.

Calculating Recycled Content

In this section's project, let's assume you want to use fly ash, a by-product of steel manufacturing, in your project as recycled content in the concrete mix for your building's structure. Fly ash was first used as a concrete additive in 1929 in the Hoover Dam and can reduce the reliance on quarried materials such as sand. If you want to understand how much recycled fly ash would be used based on the overall volume of concrete in your project, a schedule can keep track of these quantities. We'll show you how to create a schedule that reports the quantity of concrete as well as a calculated value to determine the recycled content as a percentage of the overall volume.

To begin creating this schedule, open the c10-Jenkins.rvt file. You can download this file from the book's companion website (www.sybex.com/go/masteringrevit2013). Then follow these steps:

1. Select the View tab, choose the Schedules flyout, and then select Material Takeoff.

2. In the New Material Takeoff dialog box, rename the default schedule **Concrete Takeoff**. Make sure the Category selection is set to <Multi Category>.

3. Now you want to add a couple of fields. Choose Material: Name and Material: Volume from the list on the left. Using the Add button, add them to the column on the right (Figure 10.1).

FIGURE 10.1
Adding fields to the schedule

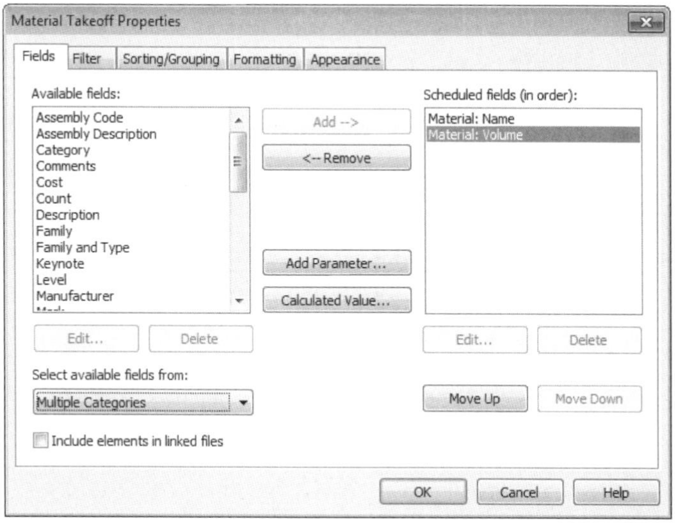

4. Now, still on the Fields tab, click the Calculated Value button. Clicking this button opens the Calculated Value dialog box, which allows you to add custom fields that contain equations. Not only can you leverage some of the features of the Revit database structure, you can also create fields in your schedules that are formulaically based on other content. In this dialog box, name the value **Recycled Content** and change the type to Volume.

   At the bottom of the Calculated Value dialog box is a blank field for the formula. This field directs the software on how to perform the calculations. In this project, you want to calculate the volume of fly ash in the model. So, in Revit terminology, you want to create a formula using the Material: Volume field and multiply that against the amount of fly ash you want to use in the construction.

5. To create this formula, you can either type the parameter names directly in the Formula field or select the fields you want to perform calculations against using the field selection button. If you choose to type your formula in directly, remember that schedules are case sensitive and the parameters will need to be entered that way. For this example, choose the selection button. This will open another dialog box, allowing you to choose fields you have already added to the schedule. Select the Material: Volume field and click OK.

6. For this project, your goal is to include 25 percent fly ash in your concrete mixture. Since you have just selected the Material: Volume field, you need to finish the equation. To do this, multiply by 0.25 so your final formula will look like the one in the Formula text box in Figure 10.2. Click OK.

FIGURE 10.2
Finishing the calculated value

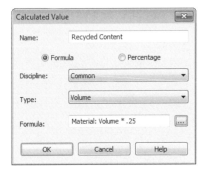

Now that you have your fields defined, you need to visit the rest of the tabs to define your schedule. The next tab is the Filter tab. So far, you haven't defined what materials you want to see in your schedule — you are currently showing all of them. In this example, you want to filter out all but concrete as a material.

7. Switch to the Filter tab, and in the Filter By field, select Material: Name. In the drop-down next to that, select Begins With, and in the field below Material: Name, type **Concrete**. Your filtered schedule should look like Figure 10.3.

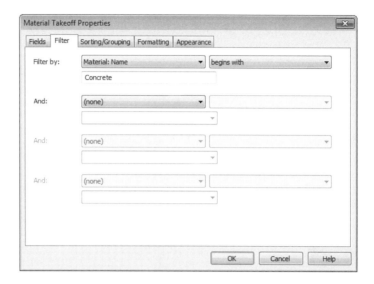

FIGURE 10.3
Adding filters to the
schedule

This filter will schedule only materials that begin with the name Concrete. Filtering in this way can be more effective than filtering for an exact name because it allows for some variety in the material names. If you are working on a project team and one team member has called the material Concrete – Cast in Place and another team member has created a material called Concrete – CIP, this schedule will include both.

8. After you complete the Filter tab, select the Sorting/Grouping tab. In this tab, choose to sort by Material: Name and make sure the Itemize Every Instance option is unchecked. You also want to select the Grand Totals check box at the bottom of this tab and set the Grand Totals drop-down to Totals Only.

9. The last tab in which you'll need to adjust settings is the Formatting tab. Select this tab and highlight Material: Volume in the column on the left. From the Alignment drop-down, choose Right and choose the Calculate Totals check box. Repeat these settings for the Recycled Content field, both right justification and calculating the totals.

   Also realize that you can change the unit format of schedule fields that use measured values. If you click the Field Format button, you can change the display units, rounding, or the unit suffix. In this example, try changing the units of the Material: Volume field to Cubic Yards and the rounding to 0 decimal places.

10. Now that you've completed all of the formatting and calculations, you can see the results of the schedule. Click OK, and the schedule will generate a single line, as shown in Figure 10.4. The new Concrete Takeoff schedule shows the name of the material, the cubic feet of concrete in the project, and how much fly ash would be (calculated in cubic feet) if you use 25 percent of the volume of the concrete. This schedule will continue to dynamically update as you add or subtract concrete from the overall design, giving you an up-to-date amount of fly ash.

FIGURE 10.4

The Concrete Takeoff schedule

Concrete Takeoff		
Material: Name	Material: Volume	Recycled Content
Concrete - Cast-in-Place Concrete	905 CY	6106.09 CF
	905 CY	6106.09 CF

Calculating the Window-to-Wall Ratio

The window-to-wall ratio (WWR) is the percent of glazing you have on any given façade versus the amount of unglazed area. Knowing this percentage can help determine the ideal amount of glazing you will want on each façade to maximize the efficiency of your HVAC system. The desired ratio will vary depending on your building use, latitude (north-south position matters), and façade orientation. Working directly with your mechanical consultant, you can arrive at a target percentage for each primary building façade.

As a general rule of thumb in the northern hemisphere, it's best to minimize east/west exposure and maximize the north/south exposure if the building site allows. With south exposures, it's easier to control the amount of daylight entering the building with the use of sunshading. In the northern hemisphere, north-facing walls have limited, if any, direct solar exposure. Since the sun rises and sets on the east/west sides of the building, there is a full arc of daylight (from the peak of the azimuth to the horizon) over the course of the day, making those exposures the most challenging to moderate.

In the sample Jenkins building project, you have an adjacent building proposed next to the existing one. In this scenario, you have been modeling a proposed new building form in Revit conceptual massing. While doing so, let's assume you've been working with your mechanical engineer to establish the ideal WWR for your primary façade. You now need to calculate the amount of façade you have per floor so you can begin to add glazing to the design.

During conceptual design, the focus was more on the building form than the exact locations of the floors relative to the existing building. Since the form was created as a conceptual mass, the only datum established was the ground plane. To view the sample building addition, open the c10-JenkinsAddition.rfa file located on the book's companion website. Open the Jenkins Building model and you'll notice the JenkinsAddition mass family has already been placed to the right of the primary façade (Figure 10.5).

Now you're ready to create a quick schedule to run these calculations:

1. The first thing you might notice is that the mass isn't visible in each of the views. You need to turn on the visibility of the mass so you can see it in all the views. On the Massing & Site tab in the ribbon, click the Show Mass button. The button will highlight in blue (and stay highlighted until it's turned off) and allow you to see the inserted mass family in all the views.

   This command represents a unique feature for masses; activating this button will allow you to see the masses, but remember that if you don't select the Mass category in the Visibility/Graphic Overrides dialog box, it won't show up when you print the views, even though you'll see it on the screen.

   Since you didn't add any levels to the mass, you need to project the levels of the original building into the addition and create floors. You want to ultimately create a schedule showing WWR by floor so you have more control over glazing areas. But first you need the floors projected into your mass.

2. Select and highlight the mass. The Modify | Mass tab will appear. Click the Mass Floors button.

FIGURE 10.5
Adding the conceptual mass to the Jenkins model

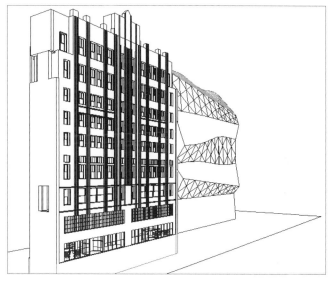

3. Selecting this tool will open the Mass Floors dialog box. Since you want one floor in the addition for each floor in the main model select Levels 1 through 8, as shown in Figure 10.6. In addition, you're choosing to incorporate a double-height lobby space so do not select the mezzanine level.

FIGURE 10.6
Selecting floors

4. Click OK and you will see the horizontal planes that are the mass floors. Select the mass and it will be more apparent because the object will become temporarily transparent, similar to Figure 10.7.

FIGURE 10.7
Mass floors have been added to the mass

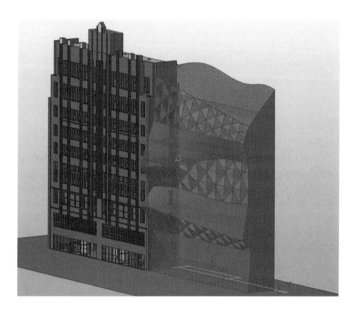

5. Now that mass floors are established, you can create a schedule that will report some key information about the mass, including the ability to list it by level. You can use scheduling to help you find not only the wall-to-floor ratio (so you can establish WWR) but also the actual area of each new floor plate. To start this, choose Schedules and then Schedule/ Quantities from the View tab in the ribbon.

6. From the list of schedule categories, choose Mass Floor and click OK to move to the next step.

7. Similar to the last schedule you created, you need to select some fields to populate the schedule. Choose the following fields (in order):

   ◆ Level

   ◆ Floor Area

   ◆ Exterior Surface Area

   You also want to create a new calculated value. Click the Calculated Value button and name the new field **Exterior Surface Area** %. Select Percentage from the radio buttons and from the Of drop-down and select Exterior Surface Area (Figure 10.8).

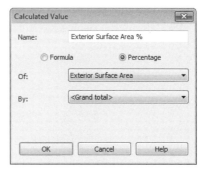

FIGURE 10.8
Creating the new
calculated value

8. Select the Sorting/Grouping tab and choose Level from the Sort By drop-down.

9. As a final adjustment to your schedule, select the Formatting tab. For the following fields, change Alignment to Right and select the Calculate Values box.

♦ Floor Area

♦ Exterior Surface Area

♦ Exterior Surface Area %

10. The finished schedule for this mass will look like Figure 10.9. You were able to quickly calculate the floor area available by level in the mass as well as the exterior wall area. The Exterior Surface Area % tells you how much of the existing wall area each floor occupies. Using this, you can work with your mechanical consultant to better determine how much glazing you should have by façade and floor.

FIGURE 10.9
The finished schedule

Mass Floor Schedule			
Level	Floor Area	Exterior Surface Area	Exterior Surface Area %
Level 1	1800 SF	5476 SF	19%
Level 2	1632 SF	3286 SF	12%
Level 3	2202 SF	3880 SF	14%
Level 4	1847 SF	2667 SF	9%
Level 5	2017 SF	2624 SF	9%
Level 6	1950 SF	2622 SF	9%
Level 7	2015 SF	3150 SF	11%
Level 8	1654 SF	4561 SF	16%
Grand total: 8	15118 SF	28266 SF	100%

Sunshading and Solar Paths

Good sustainable design optimizes the use of natural daylight within the building, thereby minimizing the need for artificial lighting. While letting in the natural daylight, it's good to mitigate the amount of direct light coming into the building because sunlight directly entering a building becomes heat and that heat then needs to be conditioned or taken into account for HVAC loads.

You can see even in this project the difference in direct sun exposure on the glazing at different times of year. Figure 10.10 shows the sun striking the building at noon on the equinox, while Figure 10.11 shows the sun hitting the building façade during the summer solstice. The deeper windows in this façade help to add some shading to the glazing.

FIGURE 10.10
The Jenkins building during the equinox

Creating a Solar Study

Sun studies are views that can be stills or animated and that help you visualize the solar exposure and sunshading on the building. These views can be created in interior or exterior conditions and help to demonstrate the course of the sun over a period of time. By creating camera views at key locations within your model, you can see the impact of solar exposure on your project. In Figure 10.12, you can see the difference in the sun between the summer and winter solstices (June 21 and December 21, respectively) at 4:00 p.m.

Remember that once the views are established, you will be able to revisit those same views as the design evolves so you can regularly see how the sun affects the building from the same angle.

FIGURE 10.11
The Jenkins building
during the summer
solstice

FIGURE 10.12
Summer solstice (left)
and winter solstice
(right)

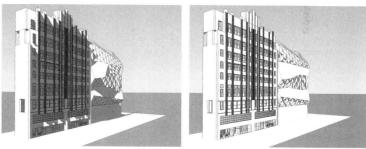

Let's create a few views to study the sun on a building's interior and exterior. Open the c10-Jenkins.rvt building model you used in previous exercises in this chapter. Remember, the file can be downloaded from the book's companion website. First, you need to establish a view in which to see the building:

1. Activate the Level 3 floor plan from the Project Browser. From the View tab in the ribbon, click the 3D View pull-down and select Camera. In the plan, click on the lower left, then on the upper right. This will create a camera view with a view angle similar to that of the images shown in Figure 10.12. Name the view **Solar Study — North**.

2. Before you activate the sun, you need to make the mass visible. Open the Visibility/ Graphic Overrides dialog box by pressing **VG** on the keyboard, and on the Model tab, select the Mass check box. This will allow you to see both the existing building and the new mass form.

3. By default, this view will look like a colorless perspective. You will adjust this as you add shade and shadow to the perspective. Now that you have a view established, click the Graphic Display Options button in the Properties palette for the view.

4. In the dialog box that opens (Figure 10.13), you're going to adjust some of the settings. To get started, click the button next to Sun Setting.

FIGURE 10.13
The Graphic Display
Options dialog box

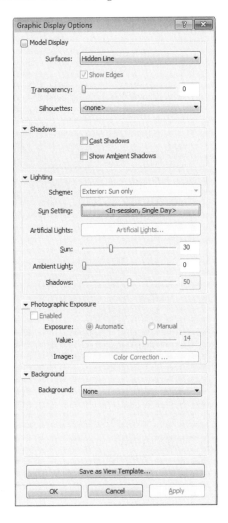

Doing so opens a new dialog box that contains sun settings (Figure 10.14). Here, you can control time of day, direction of the sun, and location of your project (longitude and latitude), among other settings. You can also specify if you want to see the sun placed at a single time of day or multiple times over a day, week, or year in an animation. There are four settings to choose from:

◆ Still casts the sun at a specific time of day based on the parameters you choose.

◆ Single-Day allows you to animate the sun and export the animation to an AVI file to show it over the course of a single day.

◆ Multi-Day casts the sun in the same position (same time of day) over the course of multiple days and can also be exported to an AVI.

◆ Lighting uses Revit lighting families. The previous three settings are sun based and will not activate any inserted lighting.

FIGURE 10.14
The Sun Settings dialog box

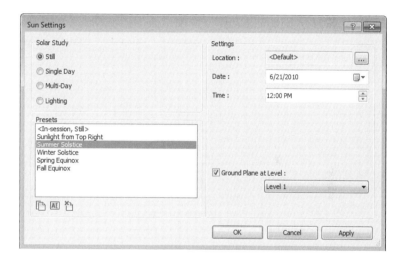

Let's start with a still view first. You're going to choose to see the sun and shadows on the summer solstice to begin.

5. Click the Still radio button.

6. Choose Summer Solstice from the Presets. All of the settings won't be correct, but once you put them in place, it will be set correctly for our location.

7. For the building location, you must specify the address or city. Click the field selection button next to Location to open the Location Weather And Site dialog box (Figure 10.15). Type **Kansas City, MO** as the project address and click Search. The Internet mapping service will find the city location for you. Click OK to accept the location and close this dialog box.

FIGURE 10.15
Set your project's location in the Location Weather And Site dialog box.

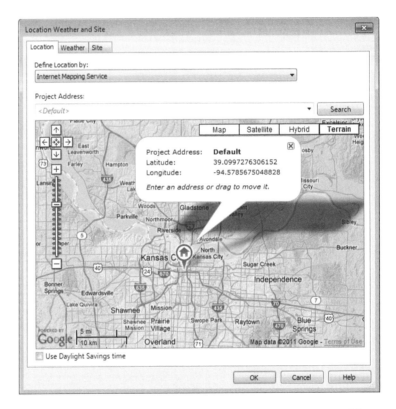

The building location doesn't automatically synchronize with the project address in Project Information (which can be modified from the Manage tab in the ribbon). You must enter the location for your solar studies in these dialogs for correct shading results.

KNOW YOUR TRUE NORTH

Make sure your Revit project has been set to the correct True North orientation before commencing any solar studies or energy analyses. Take a look at the view properties for any plan view and find the Orientation property. If it is set to True North, then the building in plan should look exactly the way it would if you were looking at it on a map. In other words, true north will be up, in the 90-degree direction.

You can set your project's True North orientation in several ways. If you have an accurate site plan from a civil engineer, you can link the file in and use Acquire Coordinates from the Manage tab (under the Coordinates button). You can also acquire the coordinates from another linked Revit model. If you don't have a reference model or drawing, you can use the Rotate True North command from the Manage tab under the Position button.

---

8. The default date and time for the solstice is June 21 at 12:00 p.m. Change the time of day to 4:00 p.m.

9. By default, no ground plane is selected. Without a ground plane, there's nowhere for the shadows to fall on the ground (sometimes you might not want to see those shadows if you are only concerned about the shadows on or in your building). For this setting, select the check box and choose Level 1 from the drop-down list. Click OK.

Note that if you have an accurate toposurface in your model, you don't need to select a ground plane in the Sun Settings dialog box. Shadows will be cast directly onto such surfaces.

10. Now you are back in the Graphic Display Options dialog box. There are a couple more options you'll want to select. First, select the Cast Shadows check box. This will turn the shadows on and they will fall based on the settings you just established. The other setting you want to specify is the background. Choose Gradient Background from the Background drop-down list. This controls the color of the ground plane and the horizon in 3D views and helps to add a bit of visual depth to the images. Once this is done, click OK to close the Graphic Display Options dialog box.

The finished view will look like Figure 10.16. After you create these settings, you can quickly toggle the shadows on and off using the Shadows button from the view control bar at the bottom of the view. Remember, turning the shadows off will allow the view to render more quickly if you are in the midst of making modifications to the model.

FIGURE 10.16
The finished camera view with Still sun settings applied

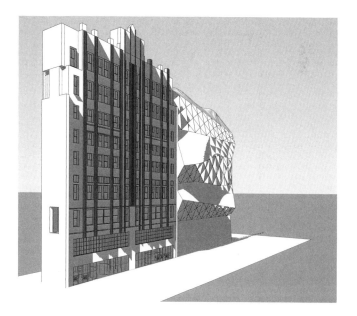

Once this view is complete, it's quick work to make other views using the same settings and visualize the building shading from various angles. Activate the Level 2 floor plan and create another exterior camera view from lower right to upper left (Figure 10.17). Zoom into the Living/Dining space toward the right side of the building and create another camera view inside the space, placing the camera at the upper left and then dragging the point of view to the lower right (Figure 10.18).

FIGURE 10.17
Exterior view from the south looking north

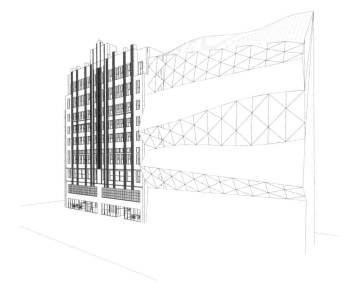

FIGURE 10.18
View from inside the Living/Dining area

Adding shading to the view is not much easier to do. Since you've already applied the settings to a previous view, all you need to do is edit the graphic display options from the Properties palette. Select the Cast Shadows option, set Sun to the Still setting named Summer Solstice, and set a gradient background.

Apply this same setting to the interior view and it will deliver some odd results — your windows won't be clear; they'll be solid. Whenever you are working in Revit views, it's important to know what phase you are working in as well as how phasing will affect visibility. Since the original building was created in an Existing phase, those materials render as solid in 3D views. To change this, scroll down in the Properties palette to the Phasing properties. Change Phase Filter to Show Complete and click Apply.

This will put all the materials shown within the view in the same state (a current or finished one). Now the finished view should have transparent glazing and look like Figure 10.19. You can see that even in this view, sunlight inside the space at this time of day is somewhat limited.

FIGURE 10.19
Interior view with sun and phase settings applied correctly

Creating an Animated Solar Study

Creating a solar study is a great tool to visualize the effects of the sun at various times of day on a building, but what about being able to watch the progress of the sun over the course of the day, week, or year? Fortunately, Revit has the ability to animate the solar studies so you can see the progress of the sun and its impact on the building. Any view with Shade and Shadows turned on can be animated to show the sun over time. To access these settings, edit the graphic display options in the Properties palette.

Using the same method you used for the still solar study, choose Sun Settings in the Graphic Display Options dialog box. This will bring you back to the Sun Settings dialog box you used for the still. This time, let's select one of the other options. You can choose one of the following:

Single Day   Create single-day studies with the settings on the Single-Day tab. These settings will show the effect of sun on a specific day at various intervals (15, 30, 45, or 60 minutes). By setting the date and checking the Sunrise To Sunset box, you'll be able to animate the effect of sun on your model based on the estimated sunrise and sunset times for the selected day.

Multi-Day   The settings on the Multi-Day tab are just like the settings on the Single-Day tab, but the interval is days, weeks, or months, and you can see the effect of sun over the course of an entire year. To create a multiday sun study, we will follow steps very similar to a single-day study.

For this exercise, let's choose the single-day study. We'll work with the summer solstice again, but you need to modify some of the settings from the last solar study:

1. Choose the Single Day radio button and select the Single Day Solar Study from the Presets list.

2. Set the date and time for the solstice as June 21, 2011, and select the Sunrise To Sunset check box.

3. Set Time Interval to 15 minutes and set Ground Plane to Level 1.

4. Click OK to close both the Sun Settings and Graphic Display Options dialog boxes.

PREVIEWING A SOLAR STUDY

Your solar study will now look like a still; however, you will have a new tool available in the view control bar. Select the Sun Path button and you'll see a new option: Preview Solar Study (Figure 10.20). Selecting this will give you tools for video playback, similar to your DVR or iTunes, under the ribbon.

FIGURE 10.20

Access the Preview Solar Study command by selecting the Sun Path button.

Using this method, playback will be choppy because the software will need to render each of the frames. A more fluid way to view the animation is to export it as an AVI and view the complete animation.

EXPORTING THE ANIMATION

The solar study is easy and quick to export. To do so, click the Application menu and select Export ➢ Images And Animations ➢ Solar Study. This option will first present a Length/Format dialog box (Figure 10.21). Let's look at these settings in a bit more detail.

This dialog box gives you the option to export all the frames or just partial frame sets. You might want to include partial frames if you're looking for a visualization that is only summer months or only the afternoon in a single-day sequence. You also have the ability to change the frame rate. By default, the frame rate is set to 15 frames per second. This is a good frame rate for video but tends to move pretty fast for a sunshading animation. We recommend reducing the frame rate to 4, which will allow you more time to absorb how the shading changes across the building over time but it still moves quickly enough so the video isn't stagnant. Note that changing the frame rate from 15 to 4 increases the total time from 3 seconds to 8.

FIGURE 10.21
Length/Format dialog
box

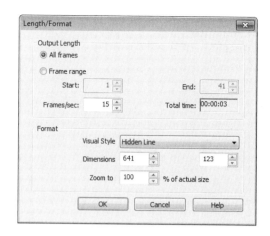

FIGURE 10.21
Length/Format dialog
box

The other element you can edit in this dialog box is the format. You can change the output of the video size and how it is rendered. Rendered video options are similar to the view settings (Shaded, Hidden Line, etc.).

Change the Frames/Sec setting to 4 and the Visual Style setting to Shaded With Edges. Then click OK.

Specify a folder location and filename for your animation and click Save. You'll be presented with one last set of options before the video exports: the Video Compression dialog box (Figure 10.22). This dialog box allows you to use a variety of video codecs available on your computer to compress the video for a smaller file size. Once you've chosen the appropriate compressor, click OK.

FIGURE 10.22
Choose a video
wcompression codec.

For the highest-quality results but largest file size, you should choose the Full Frames (Uncompressed) option. You can always experiment with each video compressor to find the codec that gives you the results you need with the most reasonable file size.

The size of the animation can also be adjusted, and you can adjust it in one of two ways: You can specify the width and height in pixels in the Length/Format dialog box, or you can change the size of the 3D view itself. To do so, select the crop region in the 3D view and click the Size Crop button in the contextual tab of the ribbon. In the Crop Region Size dialog box (Figure 10.23), choose the Scale option and then modify either the Width or Height value. The proportion of the view will not change, but the changed size will affect image and animation exports.

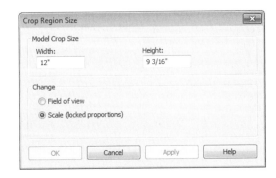

You'll see the Revit model reappear and render its way through the various animation times. Depending on the speed of your computer and the number of frames you're rendering, this process could take several minutes. Once it's finished, you'll be able to view your final animation. Since it's not possible for us to embed a copy of the video within this book, you can download a copy of this animation from the book's companion website.

Creating a Solar Path

You can also visualize the path of the sun across the model's sky directly in your project model. To activate this feature, continue with the c10-Jenkins.rvt model and open the Default 3D view.

In the view control bar at the bottom of the view, click the Sun Path icon and select Sun Settings. Choose the Single Day option and select Single Day Solar Study from the list of presets.

The settings here should reflect the single-day animation you completed in the previous section. Leave these settings for now and click OK to close this dialog box. Click the Sun Path icon and choose Sun Path On. You'll see a sun shown as a yellow ball placed in the sky and a compass rose placed under the building. The sun's arc will display the path across the sky, reflecting its position at the day you chose, and you'll see nodes on this path, reflecting the time intervals you had preset (Figure 10.24).

FIGURE 10.24
Activating the sun path

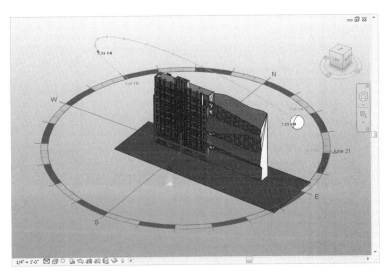

Click and hold on the sun; this will activate the entire solar path across the range of the entire year (Figure 10.25). You can now drag the sun to any position within this solar range. Note that the time will be reflected just above the sun itself, and the date ranges are shown next to the compass rose.

FIGURE 10.25
Dynamically modifying
the sun path

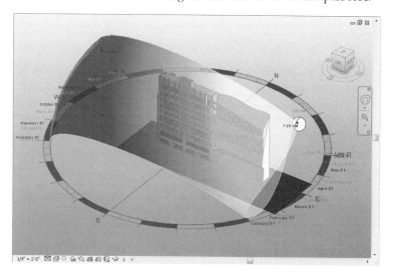

Energy Modeling

Understanding a building's energy needs is paramount to helping the project become more sustainable. According to the US Energy Information Administration (www.eia.doe.gov), buildings in the United States account for 30 percent of the world's energy and 60 percent of the world's electricity, making the United States the primary consumer of energy in the world (Figure 10.26). This reality will hopefully inspire you to build responsibly and to think about your design choices before you implement them.

FIGURE 10.26
Energy use in the
United States

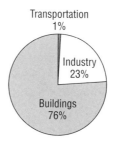

Transportation
1%

Industry
23%

Buildings
76%

U.S. Electrical Energy Consumption

Source: US Energy Information
Administration

The energy needs of a building depend on a number of issues that are not simply related to leaving the lights on in a room that you are no longer using, turning down the heat, or increasing the air-conditioning. Many of the components and systems within a building affect its energy use. For instance, if you increase the windows on the south façade, you allow in more natural light and lower your need for electric lighting. However, without proper sunshading, you are also letting in additional solar heat gain, with those larger windows increasing your need for more air-conditioning and potentially negating the energy savings from lighting.

In exploring the use of energy in a building, you must consider all related energy issues, which is a good reason to use energy simulation tools. These computer-based models use climate data coupled with building loads, such as the following:

◆ The heating, ventilation, and air-conditioning (HVAC) system

◆ Solar heat gain

◆ The number of occupants and their activity levels

◆ Sunshading devices

◆ Daylight dimming

◆ Lighting levels

The energy model combines these factors to predict the building's energy demands to help size the building's HVAC system. It also combines the parameters of other components properly so you are not using a system larger than what you need, and so you can understand the impact of your design on the environment. By keeping the energy model updated with the current design, you can begin to grasp how building massing, building envelope, window locations, building orientation, and other parameters affect energy demands.

There are two ways you can use Revit Architecture software for energy analysis — by analyzing mass forms directly in the model or by exporting a more detailed model to other application using the gbXML format. For either choice, you must first have accurate location and true north settings. Once you have those established, you can approach either analysis with confidence. Let's first take a look at the process for generating a conceptual energy analysis.

Conceptual Energy Analysis

One of the primary benefits of using BIM tools is the ability to make informed design decisions earlier in the process of developing your project. The Revit massing tools were developed precisely for this purpose. Before you even think of adding walls, doors, floors, and windows to your design, you can generate a conceptual model and assess the environmental impact of the overall proportions, orientation, and general construction assumptions.

A conceptual energy analysis (CEA) tool was added to the software as a Subscription Advantage Pack in late 2010. This tool creates a link to the online analysis service known as the Green Building Studio® service (www.autodesk.com/greenbuildingstudio) using the massing geometry in your project. The results will indicate such information as the life cycle and annual energy costs. In our opinion, it is wise to use the CEA tool only to determine which results are better or worse than others. If you convince your clients that these are the actual costs and they turn out to be too low when the building is constructed, will you be held responsible for the discrepancy?

In the following exercise, you will use a sample project with two different design options for massing. There are three basic tools for configuration, analysis, and comparison of results in the Analyze tab of the ribbon (Figure 10.27).

FIGURE 10.27
The Analyze tab in the ribbon

NOTE You will need an Autodesk Subscription account to access the Green Building Studio service and utilize the CEA tools.

Follow these steps:

1. Begin by opening the file `c10-Masses.rvt` from this book's website.

2. On the Analyze tab, click Energy Settings. The first step is to establish the correct location of your project. Click the Selection button next to the right of the Location parameter to open the Location Weather And Site dialog box (Figure 10.28). Type **Brisbane, Australia** in the Project Address field and click Search. Click on one of the closest weather stations in the list or directly on the map.

FIGURE 10.28
In Energy Settings, first specify the location and weather station.

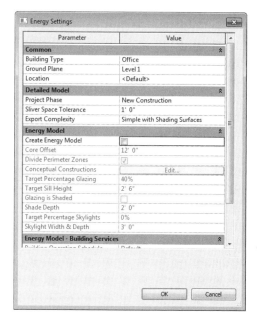

3. For this exercise, we will assume that the building type is an office. You may choose to change this assumption for your own project at the top of the Energy Settings dialog box.

4. Select the Create Energy Model check box and click the Conceptual Constructions edit button. The dialog box that appears (Figure 10.29) allows you to specify various assumptions for the construction of your building design.

5. Leave the initial conceptual construction assumptions and click OK to close the dialog box.

    Remember that this type of analysis is based on assumptions only and uses the overall size, location, and orientation of your proposed design. After you start analyzing the results, you can examine different massing configurations with the same construction and systems assumptions.

FIGURE 10.29
Specify assumptions for
the construction type
based on your mass
model.

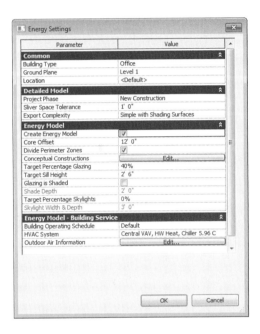

6. Click the Analyze Mass Model button on the ribbon to start the analysis. Name this analysis run **Tower Default** (Figure 10.30). The software will start to communicate with the Green Building Studio service.

FIGURE 10.30
Name each analysis run
for easy comparison.

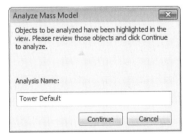

7. Click the Results and Compare button to view the progress of the upload. If you don't have the Results And Compare dialog box open, an alert will appear in the lower-right portion of the Revit window informing you that the analysis is complete. Once it is complete, you will see the run listed under the name of the model you are analyzing, as shown in Figure 10.31.

FIGURE 10.31
The Results And
Compare window

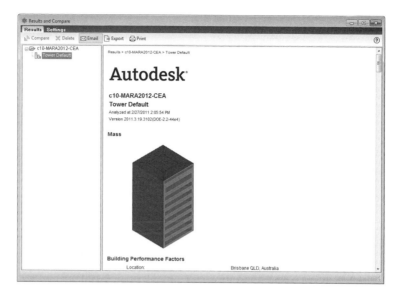

The next step will be to change some of the assumptions and run the analysis again to determine the impact of the changes on the energy usage. We are showing you only a small number of options, but again realize that you can explore many alternatives of building size, orientation, glazing percentages, and more.

8. Go back to the main Revit application and click the Energy Settings button again. Select the Glazing Is Shaded property and set the Shade Depth value to 2'-0" [500 mm].

9. Click the Conceptual Constructions edit button and change the Mass Glazing setting to **Double Pane Clear - High Performance, LowE, High Tvis, Low SHGC**. Click OK to close both dialog boxes.

10. Click the Analyze Mass Model button again and name this run **Tower with Shaded LowE Glazing**.

11. After the run has completed, return to the Results And Compare window and select both the Tower Default and Tower with Shaded LowE Glazing runs by pressing the Ctrl key. Click the Compare command.

You will see the results of the two analysis runs side by side. Notice that the second run has a lower monthly electricity consumption and lower fuel consumption. Be careful when reading the graphs because the values in each graph may be different. Take a look at the Monthly Cooling Load graphs. Notice that the values for Window Solar are lower for the second run; however, the values for Light Fixtures are slightly higher. This is due to the addition of the shading, which requires more electric lighting power.

In this exercise, we showed you how to change overall assumptions for the building; however, you can also select parts of the energy model or mass in a 3D view and override the energy settings for specific parts of your building. For example, you might want to add shading to the south façade only or perhaps customize the glazing percentage on each building face.

As you can see, generating a sustainable design for your projects is a process of testing a variety of options and comparing the results. We have shown you a simple example to give you familiarity with the basic process. It is up to you to explore these options further in the context of your own designs.

Detailed Energy Modeling

Later in the design process, you may want to use your building model to perform more detailed energy modeling. For this process to be successful, you first need a solid, well-built model. This does not mean you need all the materials and details figured out, but you do have to establish some basic conditions. To ensure that your model is correctly constructed to work with an energy modeling application, there are a few things you need to do within the model to get the proper results. Some of this might sound like common sense, but it is important to ensure that you have the following elements properly modeled or you can have incorrect results:

◆ The model must have roofs and floors.

◆ Walls inside and outside need to touch the roofs and floors.

◆ All areas within the analysis should be bound by building geometry (no unbound building geometry allowed).

To perform an energy analysis, you need to take portions of the Revit file and export them using gbXML to an energy analysis application. The following are the energy modeling applications commonly used within the design industry. They vary in price, ease of use, and interoperability with a gbXML model. Choosing the correct application for your office or workflow will depend on a balance of those variables.

IES <VE>   IES <VE> (www.iesve.com) is a robust energy analysis tool that offers a high degree of accuracy and interoperability with a BIM model. The application can run the whole gamut of building environmental analysis, from energy and daylighting to Computational Fluid Dynamics (CFDs) used to study airflow for mechanical systems. Cons to this application are its current complexity for the user and the relatively expensive cost of the tool suite.

Autodesk® Ecotect® Analysis software   This application (www.autodesk.com/ecotect-analysis) has a great graphical interface and is easy to use and operate. The creators of this application also have a number of other tools, including a daylighting and weather tool. While the program is easy to use, it can be challenging to import model geometry depending on what application you are using for your BIM model. For example, SketchUp and Vectorworks can import directly, whereas applications like Revit can be more of a challenge.

eQuest   The name stands for the Quick Energy Simulation Tool (www.doe2.com/equest). This application is a free tool created by the Lawrence Berkeley National Laboratory (LBNL). It's robust and contains a series of wizards to help you define your energy parameters for a building. As with Ecotect, it can be a challenge to import BIM model data smoothly, depending on the complexity of the design, although it will directly import SketchUp models by using a free plug-in.

Exporting to gbXML

Before you can export the model to gbXML and run your energy analysis, you need to create several settings so you can export the proper information. The order in which these options are set isn't important, but it is important to check that they are set before exporting to gbXML. If the information within the model is not properly created, the results of the energy analysis will be incorrect.

PROJECT LOCATION

As we mentioned earlier in this chapter, the physical location of the project on the globe is an important factor in energy use analysis. You can give your building a location in a couple of ways. One is to choose the Manage tab and click the Location button. Another way to get to this same dialog box is through the Graphic Display Options dialog box you used for solar shading earlier in this chapter.

BUILDING ENVELOPE

Although this might seem obvious in concept, you cannot run an accurate energy analysis on a building without walls. Although the specific wall or roof composition won't be taken into account, each room needs to be bound by a wall, floor, or roof. These elements are critical in creating the gbXML file and defining the spaces or rooms within the building. These spaces can in turn be defined as different activity zones in the energy analysis application. Before you export, verify that you have a building envelope free of unwanted openings. This means all your walls meet floors and roofs and there are no "holes" in the building (Figure 10.32).

FIGURE 10.32
Make sure your building envelope is fully enclosed.

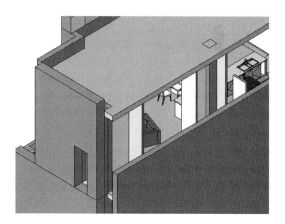

ROOMS AND VOLUMES

When Revit exports to a gbXML file, it is actually exporting the room volumes because they are constrained by the building geometry. This is what will define the zones within the energy analysis application. There are several things you will need to verify to make sure your rooms and room volumes are properly in place:

Ensure that all spaces have a room element.   Each area within the Revit model that will be affected by the mechanical system will need to have a room element added to it. To add rooms, select the Room tool from the Architecture tab. Rooms placed within the model will look like Figure 10.33.

FIGURE 10.33
Placing rooms

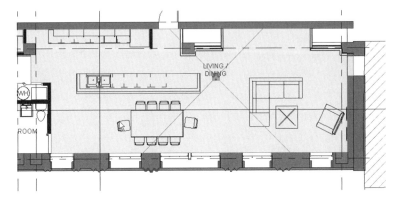

Set room heights.   Once all the rooms are placed, each room's properties should be redefined to reflect its height. The height of the room should extend to the bottom of the room above (in a multistory building), or if it is the top/only floor of a building, the room must fully extend through the roof plane. When you extend the room through the roof plane, the software will use the Roof geometry to limit the height of the room element and conform it to the bottom of the roof. Rooms should never overlap either in plan (horizontally) or vertically (between floors) as this will give you inaccurate results.

An easy way to set the room heights is to open each level and select everything. Using the Filter tool (Figure 10.34), you can deselect all the elements and choose to keep only the rooms selected. In this way, you can edit all the rooms on a given floor at one time.

FIGURE 10.34
Use the Filter tool to select only the rooms.

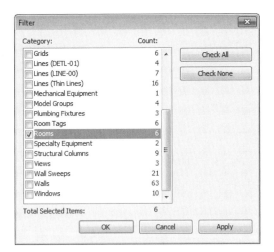

Once the rooms are selected, go to the Properties palette and modify the room heights. By default, rooms are inserted at 8'-0" high. You have the option to set a room height directly, or you can modify the room height settings to go to the bottom of the floor above. This second option is what you have set for the rooms in the exercises in this chapter and is shown in Figure 10.35. Note that you'll need to set Upper Limit to the floor above and delete the value (10'-0" [3000 mm] by default) in the offset. Repeat this same workflow for every floor of the building.

FIGURE 10.35
Modifying the room height

Turn on room volumes.   Now that all the heights are defined, you have to tell the application to calculate the volumes of the spaces. By default, Revit does not perform this calculation. Depending on the size of your file, leaving this setting on can hinder performance. Make sure that after you export to gbXML, you return to this dialog box from the Room & Area panel on the Home tab and change the setting back to Areas Only.

To turn on room volumes, select the flyout menu from the Room panel on the Architecture tab (Figure 10.36) and click Area And Volume Computations.

FIGURE 10.36
Opening Area And Volume Computations

Doing so opens the Area And Volume Computations dialog box. There are a couple of simple settings here that will allow you to activate the volume calculations (Figure 10.37). You'll want to select the Areas And Volumes radio button so that the software will calculate in the vertical dimension as well as the horizontal for your room elements.

The second setting tells the software from which to calculate rooms. If you choose Wall Finish, the software will not calculate any of the space a wall actually takes up with the model. Arguably, this is also conditioned space. Technically, what you would want is to calculate from the wall centers on interior partitions and the interior face of walls on exterior walls. However, you do not have that option, so choose to calculate from At Wall Center. Once you've modified those settings, click OK.

FIGURE 10.37
Enabling volume calculations for rooms

EXPORTING TO GBXML

Now that you have all the room settings in place, you're ready to export to gbXML. To start this process, click the Application menu and select Export ➢ gbXML. A dialog box that looks like the one in Figure 10.38 will open.

FIGURE 10.38
Exporting gbXML settings

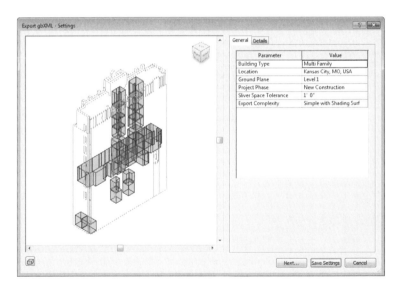

There are a few things to take note of in this dialog box. First, you'll see a 3D image of the building showing all the room volumes and bounded by the exterior building geometry. You can see in our building visualization that the boundary for the building is not completely full of room elements and that some of the room elements do not visually extend to the floor above. This would be your first clue that all your rooms do not have room elements placed or set properly, and you'll want to dismiss this dialog box to change those settings.

Second, you'll notice the ViewCube® feature at the upper right of the 3D view window. This window will respond to all the same commands as a Default 3D view will directly in the Revit interface, allowing you to turn, pan, and zoom the visualization.

There are also two tabs on the right of this dialog box. The General tab contains general information about your building (building type, postal code [zip code], ground plane, and project phase) and you'll want to verify that it is filled out properly. These settings will help determine the building use type (for conceptual-level energy modeling) and the location of your building in the world. There are two other settings: Sliver Space Tolerance and Export Complexity. Sliver Space Tolerance will help take into account that you might not have fully buttoned up your Revit building geometry. This will allow you a gap of up to a foot, and the software will assume that those gaps (12" or less) are not meant to be there. The Export Complexity setting allows you to modify the complexity of the gbXML export. There are several choices (Figure 10.39) based on the complexity of your model and the export.

FIGURE 10.39
Exporting complexity settings

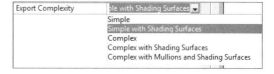

The Details tab will give you a room-by-room breakdown of all the room elements that will be exported in the gbXML model. Figure 10.40 shows the expanded Details tab. This is an important place to check because, as you'll also notice, this dialog box will report errors or warnings with those room elements.

FIGURE 10.40
The Details tab allows you to examine any errors or warnings.

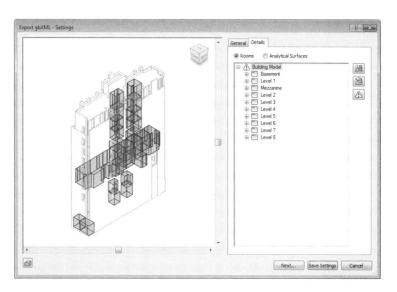

If you expand any of the levels and select a room, clicking the warning triangle will give you a list of the errors and warnings associated with that room (Figure 10.41). You'll want to make sure your gbXML export is free of any errors or warnings before completing the export.

Figure 10.41
Clicking the warning triangle will display the problems related to the selected room.

Once you're ready to finish the export, click Next. This will give you the standard Save As dialog box, allowing you to locate and name your gbXML file. Depending on the size and complexity of your building, a gbXML export can take several minutes and the resulting file size can be tens of megabytes.

You're now ready to import the gbXML file into your energy analysis application to begin computing your energy loads.

Daylighting

Daylighting is the use of natural light for primary interior illumination. This reduces your need for artificial light within the space, reducing internal heat gain and energy use. Natural light is the highest quality and most efficient light source available today, and the source is free.

An effective daylighting design relies heavily on proper building orientation, massing, and envelope design. The proper combination of these strategies allows you to optimize your building's use of natural resources and minimize your dependency on artificial lighting. A fully integrated daylighting system can enhance the visual acuity, comfort, and beauty of a space while controlling external heat gain and glare.

Here are some common terms that are associated with daylighting:

◆ *Footcandle* is a measure of light intensity. A footcandle is defined as the amount of light received by 1 square foot of a surface that is 1 foot from a point source of light equivalent to one candle of a certain type. Depending on the sky conditions, daylight can produce anywhere from 2,000 to 10,000 footcandles.

◆ *Illuminance* is the luminous flux per unit area on an intercepting surface at any given point, expressed in footcandles. It's commonly described as the amount of light on a surface.

◆ *Luminance* is the luminous intensity of a surface in a given direction per unit of projected area, expressed in footcandles. It's commonly described as the amount of light leaving a surface.

◆ *Glare* is the sensation produced by luminance that is within the visual field and sufficiently annoys, causes discomfort, or visual difficulty.

Not only does natural daylight help to light our workplaces and homes, it also supplies us with a connection to the outdoors. Providing occupants with natural light and ties to the outside has been proven in a number of cases to have a positive effect on human health and productivity. Studies have shown that buildings with good daylighting design have positive effects on their occupants, including:

◆ Increased productivity levels

◆ Low absentee rates

◆ Better grades

◆ Retail sale increases

◆ Improved dental records

◆ Healthier occupants

For more information on the concept of daylighting and how to incorporate it into your designs, visit the Whole Building Design Guide at www.wbdg.org/resources/daylighting.php.

Revit itself does not perform daylighting analysis. To get accurate daylighting results, you need to use other applications in the same way you did with energy analysis. Daylighting, however, is much easier to evaluate for accurate results and doesn't require several years of training to perfect. There are several tools on the market that will do daylighting analysis:

DaySIM   DaySIM is a free application supported by the US Department of Energy. It is built from the Radiance engine, one of the most accurate and trusted daylighting calculating tools currently available, but it requires a working knowledge of the Radiance engine to be properly proficient. Information can be found at the following location:

http://apps1.eere.energy.gov/buildings/tools_directory/software.cfm/ID=428/
pagename=alpha_list

Ecotect Analysis   Ecotect offers its own flavor of daylighting analysis (www.autodesk.com/ecotect-analysis). Ecotect is powerful as a one-stop shop for sustainable design analysis (because it also performs energy analysis as well as other building analysis) but has been noted to be clunky and difficult to use.

Autodesk® 3ds Max® Design software   3ds Max Design is a rendering application (www.autodesk.com/3dsmax) that in 2008 added a daylighting package. The daylighting engine is based on Radiance but is easy to use and will directly import Revit model geometry through the use of an FBX translator.

For the purposes of this exercise, we'll focus on 3ds Max Design because we think this product allows the most speed and versatility for daylighting analysis.

Setting Up for Daylighting Analysis

As in energy modeling, you must perform several steps to successfully analyze a building for daylight. If all the steps are not performed, your analysis will be inaccurate and not trustworthy. Let's step through the specific settings needed to perform daylighting. In this analysis, we will use the same Jenkins model we used for other exercises in this chapter to better emulate a real-life workflow.

BUILD A GOOD MODEL

As in energy modeling, if the building model is missing walls or has holes in the exterior (that aren't supposed to be there), it will leak light into the space and invalidate your results. Make sure your model is properly created; that there are roofs, floors, and walls in place; and that those elements meet properly in their corners.

Proper building phasing is also important. Your building model will be exported from a perspective or 3D view. Make sure you have the view phase set to Show Complete.

MATERIALS

Materiality is an important part of daylighting because the nature of the materials will allow light transmittance (in the case of glazing) or allow light reflectance (in the case of flooring, wall paint, etc.). You'll want to have all your materials properly defined in the view from which you want to create the daylighting simulation. To set your materials, navigate to the Manage tab and choose the Materials button. It will open the Materials Browser (Figure 10.42). All of your elements within the model, even generic elements (such as generic walls), should have materials defined. Let's look at some of these materials in more detail.

FIGURE 10.42
Materials browser and editor box

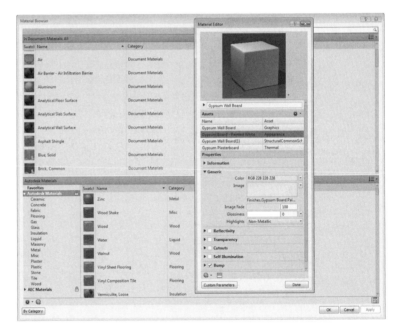

One common material will be paint (shown in Figure 10.42). Here, we have applied paint as the finish type (called Cool White Matte) to describe the finish type for Gypsum Wall Board, one of our most common building materials. As you can see on the Assets option, you have the ability to change some of the properties of the paint named Gypsum Board – Painted White. You can alter the reflectance (flat, eggshell, semigloss, gloss, and so on) and how the paint is applied to the wall (rolled, sprayed, and so on). Each of these will affect the reflectance of the paint in a different way.

Another material you should look at is glazing. Getting the proper glazing settings will determine how much daylight you are getting inside the space. Select the Appearance options, shown in Figure 10.43. There are a few critical settings for glazing:

Color   The color of the glazing will partially determine light transmittance. Set your glazing color to reflect the color you will have in your design. The software supplies several common glazing colors.

FIGURE 10.43
Glazing material

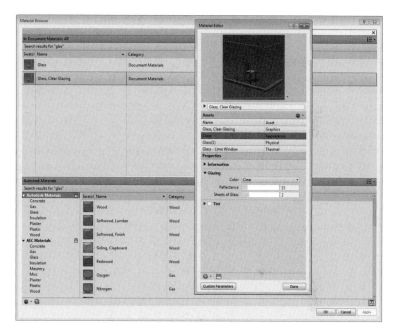

Reflectance   As with different colors, reflectance will also help determine how much light you will get inside a space. You will see that if you use the Replace feature at the top to select one of the preset glazing colors, it will also give you a default value for reflectance.

Sheets Of Glass   The number of sheets of glass will determine how the light will be refracted as it moves from outside the building to the inside. Typically, in a Revit window family, you model glass as a 1" (25 mm) single pane for ease of modeling. Modifying the number of panes in this location will allow you to keep your modeling simplified but still maintain a level of accuracy in the daylighting analysis.

Depending on the stage of design you are in, you might not know what your final material is, but you want to apply some defaults to the material types so you can perform some preliminary lighting analysis. When in doubt, here are some default reflectance values you can apply to the generic materials:

- Floors: 20% reflectance

- Walls: 50% reflectance

- Ceilings: 85% reflectance

EXPORTING TO 3DS MAX DESIGN

Once you have your materials defined and the model is ready to go, you need to define the view from which you want to export. To do this, select the camera tool from the View tab and create a perspective view of the area you want to analyze (Figure 10.44).

FIGURE 10.44
Define an interior camera view for exporting

Now you are ready to export this view to FBX. To do so, click the Application menu and select Export ➢ FBX. Once this is done, you can open 3ds Max Design and import the model.

Although this is a Revit book, we recognize that in today's design workflow not everything can happen within one application. Because of the general ease of performing daylighting in 3ds Max Design, you are going to finish the analysis in this other application. Before you begin in 3ds Max Design, there are a couple of things to note. First, you need to have a copy of 3ds Max Design, not 3ds Max. They are similar applications but the Design flavor of 3ds Max allows you to perform daylighting. Regular 3ds Max does not have this feature. Second, keep in mind that daylighting is science. The more accurate you are in following the steps, the more accurate your final results will be. These steps will be similar between 3ds Max Design 2009 and 3ds Max Design 2010. Here are the steps:

1. Open 3ds Max Design. From the Customize drop-down choose Units Setup. If you are in the United States set your units to American, as shown in Figure 10.45. This will report your analysis in footcandles. You'll need to specify this setting only once.

2. Click the Application menu, select Import ➢ FBX, and browse to your file. Select the file you exported and click OK. You'll get the dialog box shown in Figure 10.46. Here, you'll want to make sure the drop-down menu at the top is set to Autodesk Architectural (Revit). This dialog box also has a button at the bottom called Web Updates. From time to time, Autodesk updates the FBX importing routine that will help get a more accurate import. Periodically click this button to make sure your FBX import is current. Then click OK.

FIGURE 10.45
Changing the unit settings per your location

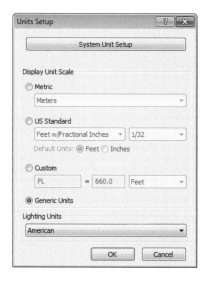

FIGURE 10.46
The FBX Import dialog box

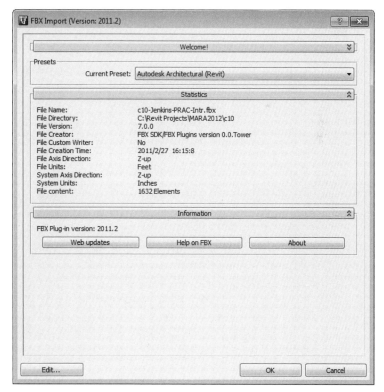

3. From this point, you'll have the imported Revit model in 3ds Max Design. It should look like the generic 3D view in the Revit interface. To get to the view you exported from, click the white text in the upper-left corner of your view window and choose Default 3D View (if you didn't rename the view prior to export) or the view name you exported from the Camera flyout. This should bring you back to the same view you created in Revit.

4. Now, we're going to step through some settings in the 3ds Max Design dialog boxes and drop-downs. You should notice the Lighting Analysis menu at the top of the screen (if you don't have this, you don't have the right flavor of 3ds Max). Click the Lighting Analysis menu and choose Lighting Analysis Assistant.

5. The Lighting Analysis Assistant has four tabs. By default, it opens on the General tab, shown to the left in Figure 10.47. This tab allows you to load some presets for daylighting analysis. Choose the Load Lighting Analysis Render Preset from this tab. You should also notice the lighting scale at the bottom of the dialog box. This will give you minimum and maximum color values for your daylighting simulation. Feel free to play with these values to achieve a desired graphic during this process.

FIGURE 10.47
Lighting Analysis
Assistant settings
on the General and
Materials tab

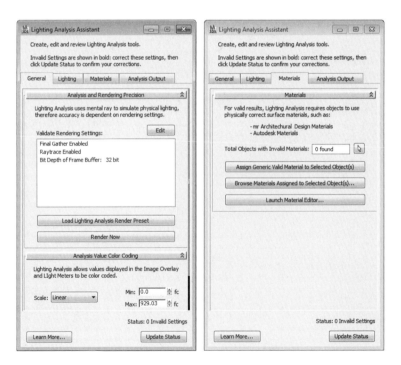

6. Next select the Materials tab, shown to the right in Figure 10.47. This tab will show you if you have any materials in the import that are invalid and will therefore not reflect light properly. If you have invalid materials, it's probably a good idea to go back to the Revit application and fix them. Doing so will ensure that they are valid in the daylighting

analysis, but if you alter them in 3ds Max Design, you'll need to alter them every time you perform another daylighting analysis. If you need to locate the materials that are invalid, you can select the Pick button and it will highlight all the invalid materials in the project. At this point, you can also choose to ignore them as they might not be visible within your view and therefore not necessary to correct.

7. Now let's jump back to the Lighting tab, shown to the left of Figure 10.48. On this tab, you're going to set the building location, time of day, and the rendering engine you want to use to perform the daylighting analysis. All of these settings will be created in other dialog boxes that are spawned from this dialog box. Don't worry — we'll step through them one at a time.

FIGURE 10.48
The Lighting tab in the Lighting Analysis Assistant

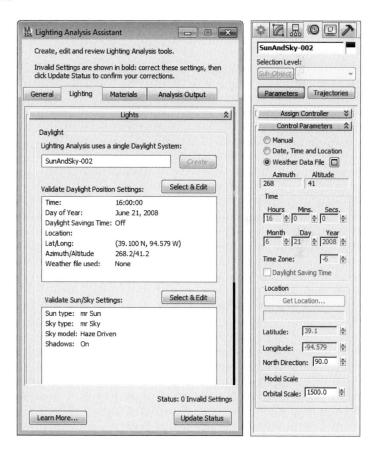

8. To begin, click the Select & Edit button at the top. This will activate the sidebar menu, as shown to the right in Figure 10.48, that allows you to modify the position of the sun. You're going to want to change the Orbital Scale value at the bottom of this menu to something like 1500. This doesn't affect any analysis, but it will move the visualization of the sun off the ground plane and up into the sky. The other thing you want to do is select the Weather Data File radio button. This will activate the setup button right next to this selection.

9. By clicking the Setup button from the General tab, you will open yet another dialog box called Configure Weather Data. Here you can set the building location and time of day. 3ds Max Design works off TMY2 weather data files created by the US Department of Energy. You'll need to navigate to their website

```
http://apps1.eere.energy.gov/buildings/energyplus/cfm/weather_data2.cfm/
region=4_north_and_central_america_wmo_region_4
```

and download an EPW file. This file contains the average weather for your given location over a 30-year interval. Once you've downloaded the EPW file, click the Load Weather Data button (shown in Figure 10.49) and browse to the file, select it, and click OK.

FIGURE 10.49

Loading the weather file in the Configure Weather Data dialog box

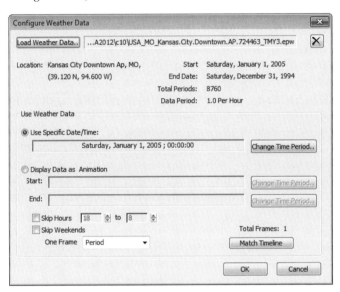

10. Click the Change Time Period button. This will pull up another dialog box (yes, you're now four deep) and give you a slider to change the date and time of your analysis (Figure 10.50). If you're performing an analysis for LEED EQ 8.1, you'll want to set it to June 21 at noon. You might notice that as you move the slider back and forth, the dates jump forward and backward over time. This happens by design. Over the 30-year span contained in the EPW file, it is displaying the specific day and year of the weather file that had weather that most closely reflected the average conditions over that 30-year span. Set your time and date and click OK. Click OK again to exit the Configure Weather Data dialog box.

FIGURE 10.50

Setting the date and time from the imported weather data

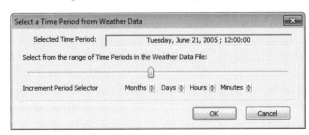

11. Still on the Lighting tab, click the Select & Edit button next to Validate Sun/Sky Settings. Doing so activates the sidebar menu. From this menu, find the mr Sky Parameters heading and set the Sky Model drop-down to Perez All Weather (Figure 10.51).

FIGURE 10.51
Choose Perez All Weather as a sky model.

12. Okay, you are nearly done with the settings. Choose the last tab, Analysis Output. You need to create a light meter in which to calculate the daylight (Figure 10.52). Click the Create A Light Meter button, and in a plan view of your model, drag two points to create a grid.

FIGURE 10.52
Click Create A Light Meter and define a plane in a plan view.

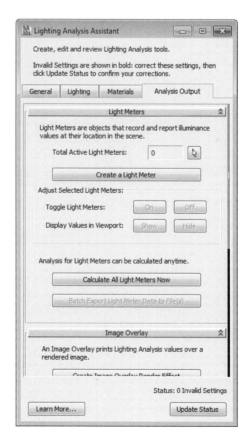

13. This will also activate the sidebar menu and give you the option to add node points to the light grid. If you're after your LEED analysis, you'll need to relocate the grid to 30" (75 cm) above the floor line and have meters every 2' (60 cm) in both directions. Your final grid will look like Figure 10.53. Once that is set, click OK to dismiss this dialog box.

FIGURE 10.53
Creating the light meter grid

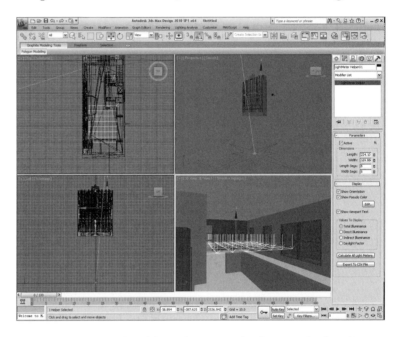

14. From the Rendering drop-down on the ribbon, choose Render Setup and select the Indirect Illumination tab. On this tab, you want to set Final Gather to 3 (Figure 10.54). Final Gather will calculate the number of times light will bounce within the space. A setting of 0 means no light bounces and will give an inaccurate reading. A setting of 7 will be highly accurate, but it will take considerably more processing power to create as the light bounces calculate exponentially. A setting of 3 optimizes the accuracy and speed for your output.

15. You're now ready to perform the analysis. On the Analysis Output tab of the Lighting Assistant, click the Calculate All Light Meters Now button. This will render the light meters to give you a final image, like Figure 10.55. You'll be able to get a footcandle reading for each of the light meters as well as a color gradation showing you light and dark spots within the view.

Once you've mastered the ability to perform these types of daylighting analyses, you'll find that it is fairly quick and easy to iterate several designs and images. With a few more steps, you can render the final scene with a daylighting grid overlay (Figure 10.56).

In each of these scenarios, it's important to vet your results. Don't take the values at their face values; review them to make sure they are accurate. So that you have a scale in which to value your results, Table 10.1 gives you some footcandle readings that you can use to figure out how much light is a proper amount based on the tasks you are performing within a space.

FIGURE 10.54

Set Final Gather to 3

FIGURE 10.55

The final analysis

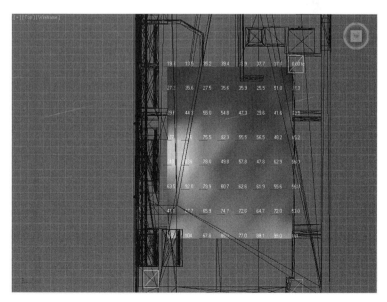

FIGURE 10.56
A rendered daylighting scene

TABLE 10.1: Footcandle readings

ACTIVITY	CATEGORY	LUX	FOOTCANDLES
Public spaces with dark surroundings	A	20-30-50	2-3-5
Simple orientation for short temporary visits	B	50-75-100	5-7.5-10
Working spaces where visual tasks are only occasionally performed	C	100-150-200	10-15-20
Performance of visual tasks of high contrast or large size	D	200-300-500	20-30-50
Performance of visual tasks of medium contrast or small size	E	500-750-1000	50-75-100
Performance of visual tasks of low contrast or very small size	F	1000-1500-2000	100-150-200
Performance of visual tasks of low contrast or very small size over a prolonged period	G	2000-3000-5000	200-300-500
Performance of prolonged and exacting visual tasks	H	5000-7500-10000	500-750-1000
Performance of special visual tasks of extremely low contrast	I	10000-15000-20000	1000-1500-2000

A–C for illuminances over a large area (such as lobby space)
D–F for localized tasks
G–I for extremely difficult visual tasks

The Bottom Line

Embrace sustainable design concepts. Understanding the concepts behind sustainable design is an important part of being able to perform analysis within the Revit model and a critical factor in today's design environment.

Master It What are four key methods for a holistic, sustainable design?

Leverage schedules. Using schedules helps you track many of your design elements throughout the whole design process. These schedules can also be used to validate programmatic information during conceptual design.

Master It Explain how to create a schedule from a conceptual mass that will show the programmatic areas for each floor level.

Use sunshading and solar paths. Understanding the effects of the sun on a building design is a critical way to create and form space. Revit has tools to help you identify how the sun will affect the design and where shade and shadow will fall inside and outside the building over the course of a year.

Master It How can you use Revit tools to produce still and animated solar studies from interior and exterior views to understand shading and the sun's effect on the building and space?

Prepare and export your model for energy analysis. Being able to predict a building's energy performance is a necessary part of designing sustainably. Although Revit doesn't have an energy modeling application built into it, it does have interoperability with many applications that have that functionality.

Master It Explain the steps you need to take to get a Revit model ready for energy analysis.

Analyze your project for daylighting. Not only can proper daylighting in a building save energy, it can make the inhabitants happier and healthier. Through analysis, you can now quantify the amount of light you're getting in any space and measure the footcandle readings before you begin building. This allows you to iterate the design-making modifications to maximize your daylight while balancing the amount of glazing against solar heat gain and mechanical needs.

Master It Understand how much daylight you need to perform certain tasks. How much daylighting is needed for the following?

◆ Working in an office

◆ Reading a book

◆ Working on a detailed model or reading very small text for an extended period of time

Chapter 11

Working with Phasing, Groups, and Design Options

Most projects will progress through various stages and phases. As a result, it's necessary to distinguish the element of time in your project: when something is created, if it is demolished, and what it will look like when the project is complete. In addition, design is about maintaining relationships between repetitive elements. Sometimes this repetitive element can be a single component in your project, such as a light or a piece of furniture. But it can also be an entire collection of elements, such as a typical room in a hotel or hospital.

Another fundamental aspect of design is the iteration of options. You have to be able to see many ideas simultaneously and in context with other ideas. The client and contractor need to see options and alternates. It's important that these options not be fully independent, separate files so that the results can be analyzed and compared.

This chapter focuses on these three concepts: time, repetition, and iteration of options. In Autodesk® Revit® software, they're addressed with phasing, groups, and design options.

In this chapter, you'll learn to:

- ◆ Use the Phasing tools to create, demolish, and propose a new design
- ◆ Understand and utilize groups
- ◆ Create and use design options

Using Phasing to Apply the Element of Time

Phasing is the software's method of allowing you to add the element of time to objects in your project. It's easy to think of an architectural design in terms of what something is, where something is, and how it will be assembled. Phasing adds the dimension of *when* something is, which is incredibly useful and powerful.

Phases are most useful for doing the kinds of tasks that require you to show when elements are being introduced into your design. But a few words of caution and clarification: We don't recommend using extensive phasing to simulate construction sequencing or 4D. It might seem like a great idea at first, but ultimately it'll break your model and lead to a lot of confusion across your project team.

The reasons for this are threefold. First, using phasing to illustrate construction sequencing will not allow you to use phasing for its intended use. So if you need to show stages of existing, demolition, new construction, and so on, you'll find yourself having to work around sequences of Week 1, Week 2, Week 3, and so on. You will have traded more functionality in one area for limited functionality in another area.

The second reason is that it will break connections between elements that are normally joined. For example, in Figure 11.1 two walls intersect that belong to the same phase. The fact that they are graphically and geometrically joined is the desired condition.

FIGURE 11.1
Wall joins in the same phase

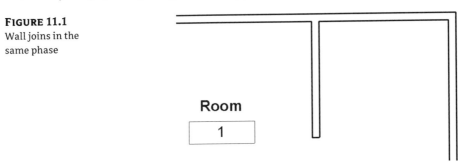

But when walls are not from the same phase, their join condition may not clean up as intended, as shown in Figure 11.2. This can create a lot of tedious cleanup that probably isn't the best use of your time.

FIGURE 11.2
Joins across different phases may not always clean up as intended.

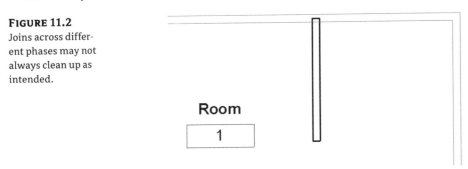

Finally, the best reason to not use phasing as a construction sequencing tool is that there's a better way that allows elements of various sequence properties to be scheduled, viewed, and even color-coded based on the sequence value that you define: project parameters.

By using project parameters, you're able to create and assign an instance parameter value to everything in your project that you'd want to assign a construction sequence, as shown in Figure 11.3.

Once you've created this instance parameter, you'll be able to create view filters and filter rules that override the default condition of an object based on your parameter, as shown in Figure 11.4. Each construction week value is being given its own rule.

Combined with visibility and graphic overrides, you're able to create a filter that modifies the graphics based on a parameter, as shown in Figure 11.5.

FIGURE 11.3
Creating a construction sequence instance parameter for project geometry

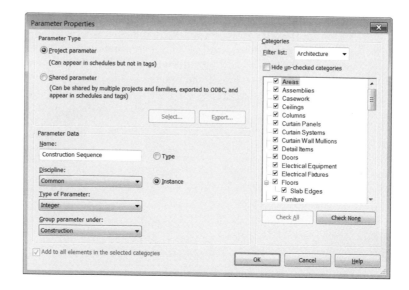

FIGURE 11.4
Applying filters by parameter

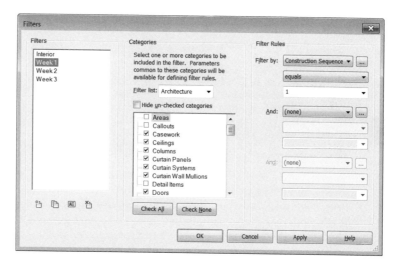

FIGURE 11.5
View filters and graphic overrides settings

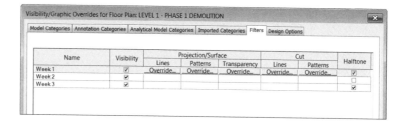

The result is being able to modify the graphics of a view to illustrate some metadata about the objects in a far more flexible and predictable way than mere phasing, as shown in Figure 11.6. The other benefit is that this technique is not limited to views of geometry. View filters can be applied to any view, including schedules, which will allow you to group and filter schedules based on your unique project parameter.

FIGURE 11.6
Using parameters and view filters to override graphics

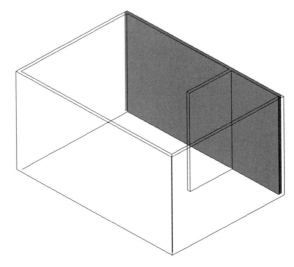

Now that you understand a better way to create sequencing in Revit using parameters and filters, we'll discuss how phasing is best used. To work along with the steps in the following section, download and open the file c11_Phases.rvt from this book's companion website at www.sybex.com/go/masteringrevit2013.

What Can Be Phased?

At a high level, only three types of elements can be associated with a phase in Revit: geometry, rooms, and views. Geometry is anything that you would use to model your design, like host components such as walls, floors, ceilings, and so on as well as family components such as doors, windows, furniture, lighting, and so on. When you place geometry in a view, the Phase Created property is assumed to be the phase assigned to that view. For example, if you create a view and set its phase to Existing, all elements you place in that view will automatically be assigned to the Existing Conditions phase. After an element is placed in the project, the phase can always be changed in the Properties palette, as shown in Figure 11.7.

Rooms are also given phase properties, but there is an important difference: The phase property of a room cannot be changed after placement, as shown in Figure 11.8. If you want to change the phase of a room, you'll need to delete and re-create the room in the desired phase. You'll also find it faster to press Ctrl+X to cut the rooms from one view and then press Ctrl+V to paste them into a view that has been set to the desired phase.

The phase of an element when initially placed is often confusing to a new user, but remember that it's quite simple: The phase of the view that you're placing the element into determines the element's phase, as shown in Figure 11.9. This is more critical for rooms than for building elements because the phase of a building element can be changed after placement. But there may be occasions when you're placing many elements that you intend to be in a particular phase, and you'll want to create a view with that phase as active. Then you can place the elements in that view and not worry about changing them later.

FIGURE 11.7
Changing the phase of geometry

FIGURE 11.8
The phase of a room may not be changed after placement.

FIGURE 11.9
Changing the phase of a view

Phase Settings

Let's get into the details of phase settings. Applying the notion of time to your project may seem complicated, but it is actually quite simple to implement. There are three basic aspects you need to understand about phasing:

◆ What are the major phases of your project?

◆ How will you use the phase property to filter a view?

◆ What is the graphic convention to convey an object's phase?

These aspects are expressed in the three tabs of the Phasing dialog box. On the Manage tab, click the Phasing button to open the Phasing dialog box, shown in Figure 11.10.

FIGURE 11.10
The Phasing dialog box

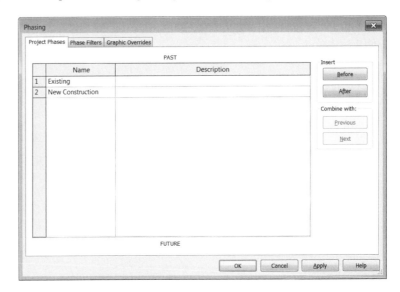

PROJECT PHASES

Assigning project phases is where you might get most confused. You might think that you need a phase for every different view that you'll be creating. And in the most common of phased projects, you'll have views to illustrate Existing, Demolition, and Proposed conditions. But since this dialog box shows only Existing and New Construction, new users will mistakenly create a new phase for Demolition.

If your project is a simple, three-phase project (existing conditions, demolition, new construction), a phase dedicated to demolition isn't necessary. Basically, the Project Phases tab is for determining when the geometry is being created (*not* demolished). When would you want to create more phases? When you need to *create* geometry in more than these two phases.

For example, think of a staged construction project that will happen in two new phases. In this scenario, you are designing with a start time for the building itself followed by another phase for interiors, allowing the owner to split funding for the project into two budgets. In phase one, the building core and shell are built. In the second phase, interior construction occurs. Your first phase is labeled "Shell and Core." Your other phase is labeled "Interiors." This phasing also gives a contractor who is familiar with Revit the ability to use the model to see what needs to be built and when.

In the Project Phases tab of the Phasing dialog box, create the two phases as we just described (Figure 11.11). Note that you can simply rename the New Construction phase **Shell and Core**. Click the Insert After button to create an additional project phase and then rename it **Interiors**. We'll use them in a sample exercise in a moment. When you're creating phases, you might notice there's no Delete button. You don't want to delete any geometry put on a phase that is no longer useful in a project. What you can do is merge two phases using either of the Combine With buttons on the right.

FIGURE 11.11
Creating additional project phases

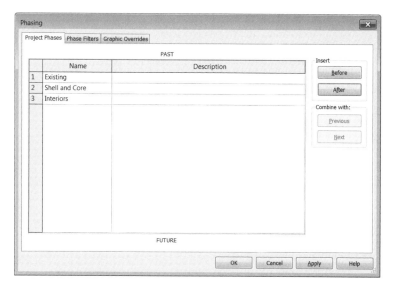

Once you've created these additional project phases, pick any project geometry and look at its instance parameters. You'll notice that it can be assigned to any one of these three phases, as shown in Figure 11.12.

FIGURE 11.12
Assigning available phases

PHASE FILTERS

The next tab in the Phasing dialog box is Phase Filters (Figure 11.13). Seven predefined phase filters are listed.

FIGURE 11.13
The Phase Filters tab, with seven predefined phases

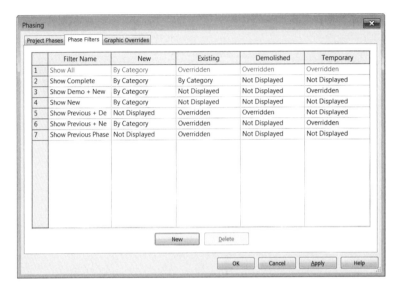

Don't be concerned if the filter names seem a bit cryptic at first. What's really important is the four graphic conditions that can be overridden: New, Existing, Demolished, and Temporary. Let's take a moment to explore how these graphic conditions are applied to a virtually unlimited number of user-defined project phases. Any object you place into a project has certain states relative to any particular phase. In other words, you might ask the following questions about a model element:

◆ Was it created in the current phase? That's *new*.

◆ Was it created in a previous phase? That's *existing*.

◆ Was it created in a previous phase and demolished in the current phase? That's *demolished*.

◆ Is the object created and demolished in the same phase? That's *temporary*.

As you can see, phase filters are relative settings. That is, the filters are relative to the phase property of the object and the phase of the view in which the object is displayed. Also realize that phase filters are applied only to views, not model elements.

Now let's explore the predefined ways a phase filter can be applied. Select any of the drop-downs, as shown in Figure 11.14. You'll notice that the phase filter can override the graphics in one of three ways:

◆ By Category: The object can be shown by its category settings or *not* overridden. It will be displayed in the project just as it does by default.

◆ Overridden: This means that you can define a graphic override for that object. We'll get into the graphic overrides in a moment.

◆ Not Displayed: The object is hidden in the view.

FIGURE 11.14
Setting a filter
override

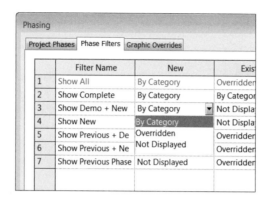

Once you understand how each of the phase filters displays objects, phases can begin to make sense. For example, the Show Complete phase filter shows New and Existing elements *By Category*. But Existing and Temporary elements are not displayed at all. Use this setting when you want to show the model in a finished condition. Another example is to use the Show New phase filter in a schedule such as a door schedule. The Show New filter will include only those doors that are assigned to the phase that is also assigned to the schedule. The schedule will not list any existing doors or doors that were demolished.

If there's any remaining confusion, it probably involves the naming convention of Show Previous + Demo. A better name might be Show Existing + Demolition, but *Existing* is a bit misleading because this setting is showing the previous phase, which is not necessarily existing elements. They might be Temporary elements that need to be demolished. Therefore, Show Previous makes more sense.

GRAPHIC OVERRIDES

The Graphic Overrides tab is the final tab in the Phasing dialog box (Figure 11.15). This dialog box relates back to the Overridden assignment of the previous tab.

FIGURE 11.15
The Graphic
Overrides tab

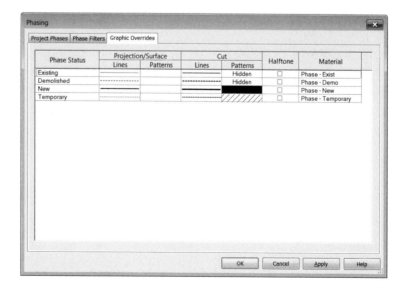

This tab allows you to override geometry in a few areas; the Lines and Patterns characteristics of Projection/Surface and Cut (which refers to the cut profile of objects cut). You also have the option to just halftone the element. Finally, you can assign a unique Material setting when rendering. Although this ability is helpful for rendering with phase information, it can also be useful for rendering everything to a matte material, something we discuss in Chapter 12, "Visualization." As it is, phasing can show you where you are (new construction) and where you're coming from (existing), but not where you're going (future).

Geometry Phase

Here's a simple exercise to illustrate each of the phases in a single view. First, open a new project using a default template. Next, draw four walls in parallel and then open a 3D view (Figure 11.16).

FIGURE 11.16
Four generic walls

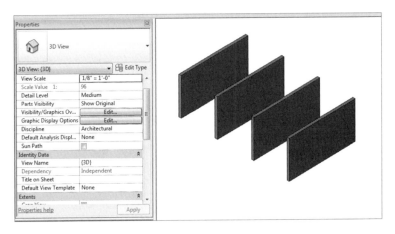

By default, all of these walls have been created in the New Construction phase because the phase of the view is New Construction. Now, selecting each of the walls from left to right, associate them with each of the following phase settings:

Wall 1: Phase Created: Existing / Phase Demolished: None

Wall 2: Phase Created: Existing / Phase Demolished: New Construction

Wall 3: Phase Created: New Construction / Phase Demolished: None

Wall 4: Phase Created: New Construction / Phase Demolished: New Construction

In Figure 11.17 you'll notice that the Existing (not Demolished) and the Proposed (not Demolished) look similar. Graphically, this might not be enough to demonstrate the different phases, so let's change the graphic properties of this wall so it's visually more distinct.

FIGURE 11.17
Default shaded
overrides for
phasing

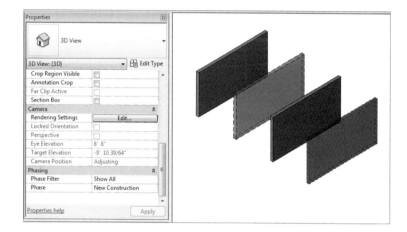

Go to the Manage tab and select Phases; then click the Graphic Overrides tab. Next, select the option to open the Material setting for the Phase-Exist material. This opens the Material Browser dialog box highlighting the Phase-Exist material (Figure 11.18).

FIGURE 11.18
The Material
Browser dialog box

If the Material Editor dialog box (Figure 11.19) did not also open, click the edit icon at the right end of the Phase-Exist row in the Material Browser dialog box.

FIGURE 11.19
The Material Editor dialog box

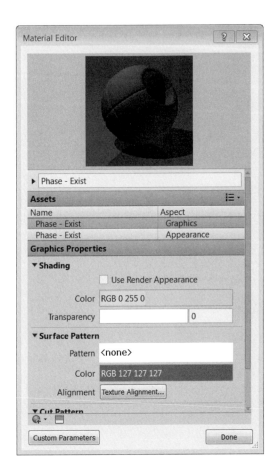

In the Material Editor dialog box, make sure the Graphics asset is selected because this is the setting you want to change. In the Shading settings, click the property next to Color and the Color dialog box will open. Assign a lime greenish color with the following RGB values: Red=0, Green=255, Blue=0 (Figure 11.20). Click OK to close the Color dialog box.

Click Done to close the Material Editor and click OK to close the Material Browser. When you finish changing these settings, you'll have the result shown in Figure 11.21, with each phase shown distinctively within the view.

Now you can *really* graphically tell the phases apart. Once you settle on a color and graphic scheme, we recommend making this particular setting part of your default project template. That way, new users would be able to distinguish the phase of an object far more clearly, and the standard will be consistent throughout your office.

View Phase

Now that we've talked about the phase properties of geometry, we'll cover the phase properties of views. Starting with the view from the previous example (the 3D view), examine the view properties in the Properties palette, provided there are no elements highlighted (Figure 11.22). Note that we have collapsed some of the property groups at the top to show the Phasing properties at the bottom of the list.

FIGURE 11.20
Overriding the color value

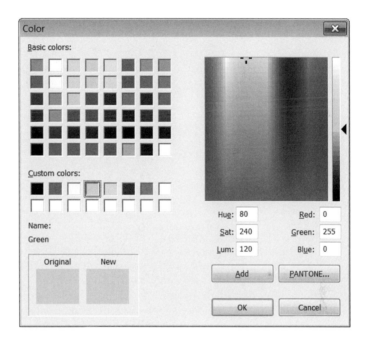

FIGURE 11.21
Finished shading values

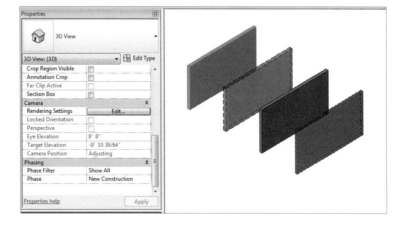

FIGURE 11.22
Phasing options for
a view

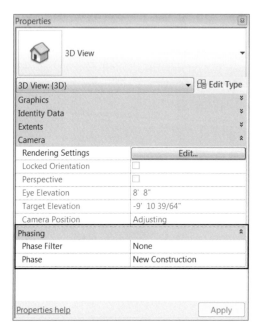

Remember that all the graphic overrides and filters for phasing are *relative* to the phase that is assigned to geometry or a view. By default, the New Construction phase is assigned to new views created in your project. This phase assignment can be changed at any time from the Properties palette. The phase property can also be assigned to a view template for easier management of this important parameter.

The next important step is to apply the most appropriate phase filter. To illustrate how a phase filter changes the way objects are displayed in a view, you will step through several filters in the following exercises.

First, let's start by changing the phase filter to Show All (Figure 11.23). Choosing these settings will show all the elements and override their graphics based on their construction phase and whether they're demolished. It also gives you a sense of all the elements as they exist in time.

FIGURE 11.23
Show All and New
Construction

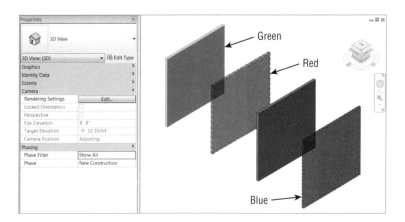

Although this is great for 3D views, where every phase has a distinct color, it's also useful for working in a plan, elevation, or section. To turn this graphic visibility on, return to the Level 1 floor plan and change the Graphic Display setting to Shaded or Consistent Colors. You'll be able to clearly distinguish between objects in different phases, as shown in Figure 11.24.

FIGURE 11.24
Shaded plan view of phased elements

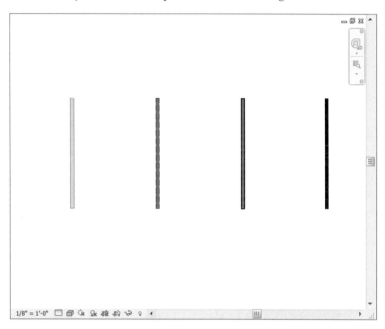

Now let's start moving through each of the phase filters. But here's an important note: Rather than sequentially moving through the various phase filters from top to bottom, let's move through them in a way that makes *sequential* sense.

Return to the 3D view and keep the phase filter set to Show All, but change the phase to Existing (Figure 11.25). This will show only the objects created in the Existing phase — and their graphics are not overridden. The two walls that were assigned to the New Construction phase are not shown in the view because Revit Architecture does not provide a way to see future construction beyond the phase assigned to the view.

FIGURE 11.25
Existing phase only

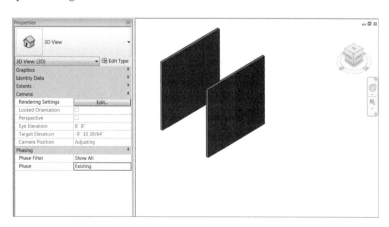

Set the phase of the view to New Construction and set the phase filter to Show Previous + Demo (Figure 11.26). This filter still shows only the existing walls (the walls from the previous phase). One of the walls is clearly being demolished. Keep in mind that the graphic overrides that are being applied are relative to what you'd be seeing through the lens of the New Construction phase.

FIGURE 11.26
Show Previous + Demo

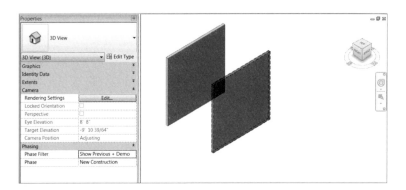

Now select Show Previous Phase as the phase filter, as shown in Figure 11.27. The demolished element is no longer shown.

FIGURE 11.27
Show Previous Phase

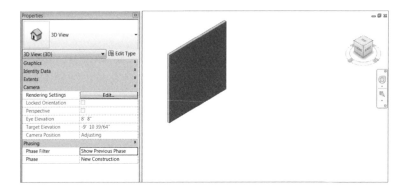

We'll move forward another moment in time and set the phase filter to Show Previous + New. This shows only the remaining elements (not any of the demolished content) from the present and previous view (Figure 11.28). It is not always necessary to click Apply in the Properties palette each time you want to apply the settings you've just changed. Dragging your mouse outside the palette has the same effect as clicking Apply.

This brings up another interesting point. Why not show the remaining existing elements as well as the proposed and temporary elements? Although you could also create a new phase filter, for this example, we'll change the settings of the Show Previous + New graphic phase filter (Figure 11.29). Choose the Manage tab and select Phases again. Choose the Phase Filters tab, and in the Show Previous + New row, go to the Temporary column and change the setting to Overridden.

Click OK to exit the dialog box. Figure 11.30 shows the result.

FIGURE 11.28
Show Previous +
New elements

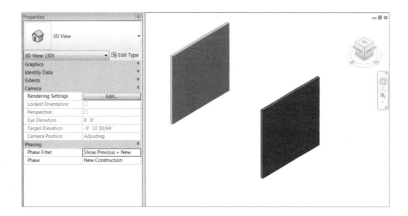

FIGURE 11.29
Changing the phase
filter settings

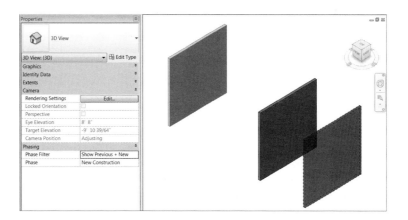

FIGURE 11.30
Existing to remain,
proposed, and tem-
porary elements
displayed

The next order of sequence will be to set the view to Show Demo + New, which will show demolished elements from the present phase as well as any new elements from the present phase (see Figure 11.31).

Moving forward in time, let's now show only the elements in the New Construction phase. Set the phase filter to Show New and only one wall will be displayed, as shown in Figure 11.32.

Now comes the final phase filter setting, Show Complete (see Figure 11.33). This shows only the existing elements that remain un-demolished from all previous phases up to the phase assigned to the view. Elements that are demolished in any phase are not displayed and neither existing nor new elements are overridden. This phase filter is most often used for camera views where a rendering may need to be generated of the finished conditions without any sort of graphic overrides.

FIGURE 11.31
Show Demo + New

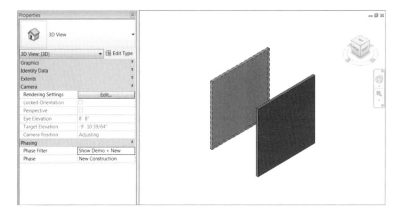

FIGURE 11.32
Showing only new elements

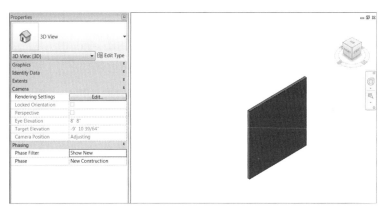

FIGURE 11.33
Showing finished conditions

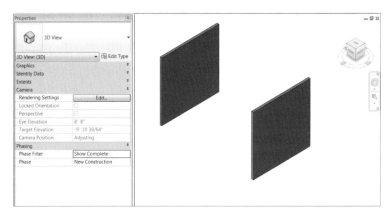

Creating and Using Groups

It's easy to think of groups as functionally similar to blocks in AutoCAD or cells in MicroStation, but groups can be much more. They are great at maintaining repetition within your project, but there are some major differences:

◆ Creating groups is quite easy. And whether it's a 2D or 3D group, the insertion point for the group is easily defined and modified. The same can't be said of simple 2D blocks in other applications.

◆ Updating groups is a breeze. It's easy and intuitive to modify a group after it's been created. Practically anyone on your team can do it, which means that design workflow will not bottleneck in your project team.

◆ Copying groups throughout your project is also a breeze. Groups can be copied across different levels, rotated, and even mirrored (although mirroring isn't such a good idea, but more on that later).

There are a few good practices that you'll want to keep in mind when using groups. But they're so straightforward that you'll wonder how you've ever worked without them.

Creating Groups

You can create two kinds of groups in Revit. One is just for geometry, and they're called *model groups*. The other is just for view-specific content like text, tags, dimensions, and so on, and they're called *detail groups*. You can create one kind of group or the other explicitly. But if you try to create a group with both model and detail elements, Revit is smart enough to create a separate detail group that's associated with the model group.

To demonstrate this, open a new project using the default template and start by drawing four walls, as shown in Figure 11.34. Add the dimensions shown in the figure as well.

FIGURE 11.34
Four walls and dimensions

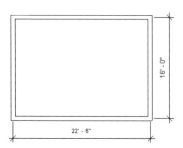

Select the walls and dimensions you just created and click the Create Group button from the contextual ribbon on the Create panel. Keep the default name Group 1 for both Model Group and Attached Detail Group (Figure 11.35).

Now select the group of walls and copy it to the side of your original group. You'll notice that only the model-based group is copied, which is fine for now (Figure 11.36).

Associating the detail group is simple. Select the group and then click the Attached Detail Groups button from the contextual ribbon and you'll see the dialog box shown in Figure 11.37. Select the check box for Group 1 from the list and click OK.

FIGURE 11.35
Creating the model
and attached detail
group

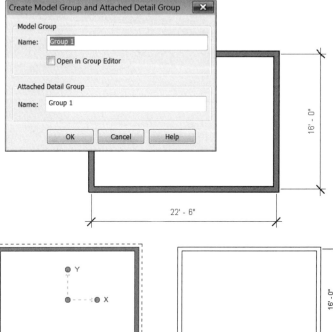

FIGURE 11.36
Copied group

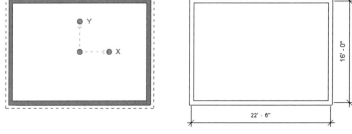

FIGURE 11.37
Attached Detail
Group Placement
dialog box

The results are fairly straightforward (Figure 11.38). Both groups are now identical with geometry and dimensions.

FIGURE 11.38
Identical groups

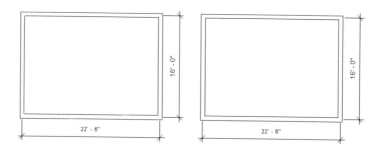

Modifying Groups

Now that you've created two identical groups, let's add a door to one of the walls that belong to the group, as shown in Figure 11.39. But don't add the door to the group — just place it in one of the walls as you would with any non-grouped wall.

FIGURE 11.39
Adding a door out-
side of Edit Group
mode

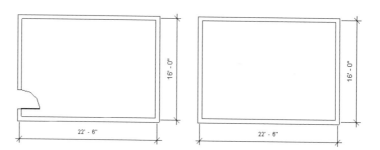

Now you can select the group to the left and click Edit Group from the contextual tab in the ribbon. You'll enter a special editing environment, as shown in Figure 11.40, and the background will appear a light yellow. This color is to alert you that you are in the Edit Group mode. Here you'll be able to add, remove, and attach other elements to your group.

Now add the door to the group by selecting the Add function from the Edit Group panel. You'll notice that you can't add the door numbers because this is a model group and tags are 2D components. Now finish the group by selecting the green check and you'll notice that both groups have a door in the same location (Figure 11.41).

The process is essentially the same for modifying groups: Enter Edit Group mode, make the changes and/or additions, and then finish the group.

FIGURE 11.40
Group Edit mode

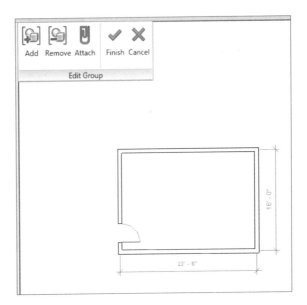

FIGURE 11.41
Finished group

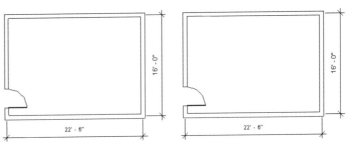

Creating New Groups

Sometimes the easiest way to make a new group is to copy and modify an old one. To do this, first duplicate the group. A quick way to do this is to right-click the name of the group you want to duplicate in the Project Browser, as shown in Figure 11.42.

FIGURE 11.42
Duplicating a group

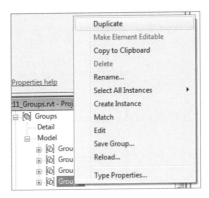

Back in the view window, select your group. Notice in the Type Selector that you can swap between groups in the same way you can swap between types within a family. Using this method, highlight the group you created at the beginning of this exercise and swap the new group you created by duplicating. Exchange Group 1 for Group 2.

Select the group and enter Group Edit mode for this second group, and edit it as shown in Figure 11.43; then finish the group.

FIGURE 11.43
Modifying the second group

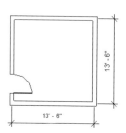
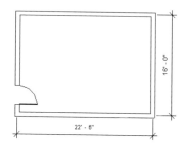

Groups have insertion points that need to be considered before you exchange one group for another. When you create a group, the insertion point is initially at the geometric center of all the elements in the group. The group's origin is also identified by x- and y-coordinates.

But keep in mind that as you edit the group, the insertion point doesn't move until you deliberately relocate it. This can be seen in Figure 11.44; editing the geometry for Group 2 retains the same insertion point that was active when the group was initially created. Even though we've modified the group, the insertion point remains where it was originally when the group was created.

FIGURE 11.44
Insertion points in different groups

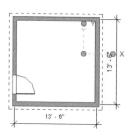
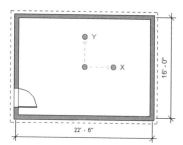

Moving the insertion point is an easy matter of dragging (and if necessary, rotating) the Insertion Point icon to a common location before swapping one group for another (Figure 11.45).

FIGURE 11.45
Relocating insertion points

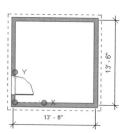
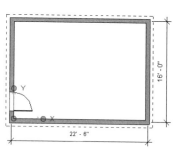

Once you've done this, swapping groups occurs at the same relative location. Figure 11.46 illustrates Group 1 being swapped for Group 2, and vice versa. But common insertion points are being maintained.

FIGURE 11.46
Exchanged groups

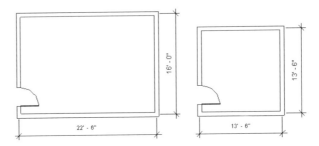

Excluding Elements within Groups

There will be occasions where everything in a group works great and it works throughout the project — except for that one particular case where a condition is slightly different. In the past, you had to create new groups for each slight exception, which might have been conceptually consistent but often led to an exponentially growing list of group variants. You were left with little ability to cohesively modify them as the project size (and number of groups) continued to grow.

This workflow is now deftly handled by excluding elements from groups. The rest of the groups are intact, and schedules are aware of excluded elements. Figure 11.47 shows an example. We've copied a group above another one of the same type. But in this condition, there's a column right in the middle of the door.

FIGURE 11.47
Group conflicts

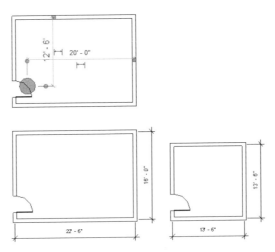

We don't want to destroy the integrity of the group and give up being able to quickly modify similar elements, but we also cannot advance the design with the column located where it is shown. To resolve this, first select the door within the group (by using the Tab key), right-click, and select Create Similar from the context menu to place a new door where you want it to go. This door will not be part of the group (you can't place elements as exceptions). In this case, the new door has been placed above the grouped door, and its swing direction has been flipped (Figure 11.48).

FIGURE 11.48

Adding a new door

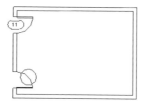

Now you can exclude the door that conflicts with the column as an exception to the rest of all the other groups. This process can be a bit confusing at first because you don't enter Group Edit mode to exclude members from groups. Simply hover over the group and tab through until the door is highlighted. Then select the door, as shown in Figure 11.49.

FIGURE 11.49

Selecting elements
in groups

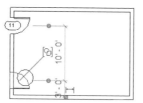

Once this is done, you'll notice an icon in the upper-left portion of the door (Figure 11.49). Clicking this icon will allow you to exclude the door as an exception to the group, and the wall will heal itself as if the door was never there. When you click the icon, it will appear with a red hash through it, notifying you that the element is now excluded from the group. Click in the white space of the view to deselect and the door will be excluded.

Selecting the group will reveal any hidden elements in the group that are excluded (Figure 11.50). Just tab through to select the hidden door to include the component back into the group.

FIGURE 11.50

Excluded elements
not shown

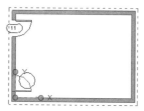

Saving and Loading Groups

Even though we consider Revit to be the only whole-building BIM application in the world (by integrating the building, content, documentation, and multiuser workflow into one database), there are times when you'll want to share the data across many files.

Just as you wouldn't want your family components locked up inside a project file, there are good reasons to keep commonly used groups outside your project. You might even want to keep them in a folder just as you do your custom content so you can use them again later on similar projects. You can do so by saving groups outside your projects.

Saving groups is a matter of right-clicking the group name in your Project Browser and selecting Save Group (Figure 11.51).

FIGURE 11.51
Saving groups

You'll then be prompted to save the group as an RVT file. You can open this file as you would any other RVT file if you'd like to modify it later and then reload the group into the project in order to update all the instances. To load an external group into a project, choose Load As Group from the Insert tab in the ribbon.

Be aware that when you load the group in a project, if the group name already exists, you'll be given a warning. You can overwrite the existing group (by selecting Yes) or load with the option to rename the group that's being loaded (by selecting No). Or you can cancel the operation altogether (Figure 11.52).

FIGURE 11.52
Loading modified groups

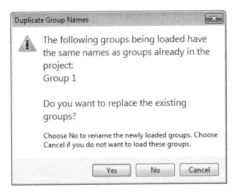

What's really great is that when you reload the group, Revit even remembers to exclude previously excluded elements from the group that's been modified in another session. Figure 11.53 shows that a desk and chair have been added to the group. The group has been reloaded, overwriting the original group, but the exclusion remains intact.

FIGURE 11.53
Retaining excluded
group elements

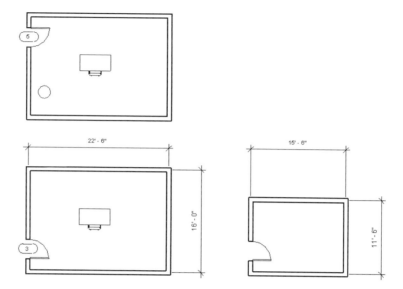

Creating Groups from Links

Because groups are also RVT files, they can be linked into the project environment as well. Although you can't edit a link in place (as with a group), there are some excellent reasons you might want to start a group as a link and then bind the link at a later time, which will convert it to a group. Groups and links can also exist within design options (more on design options later in this chapter). To follow this workflow, use these steps:

1. Select Link Revit from the Insert tab (Figure 11.54).

2. Browse to your group and click Open.

FIGURE 11.54
Adding groups as
links

After the link has been placed, you can copy it throughout your project as you would any other element in Revit. Keep in mind that all the functionality between groups and non-grouped elements will not behave the same as links and the rest of your project. For example, in Figure 11.55, the upper-right collection of walls and furniture is a link, not a group. As a result, walls are not cleaning up between links and groups in the same way they are between groups or other walls.

This graphic restriction may not be a concern during programming and predesign, when links allow for a lot of rapid flexibility. After you've resolved your design using links, you can bind them into the project environment by selecting the link in a view and clicking Bind Link from the contextual ribbon.

FIGURE 11.55
Walls don't join to
linked models

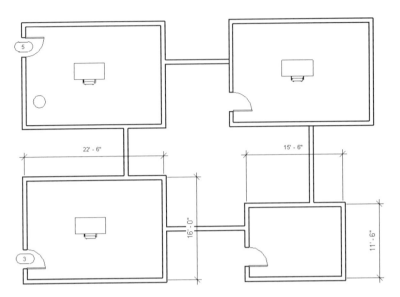

Rather than "explode" the link into separate and unrelated elements, Revit converts the link
to a group. Once this happens, the previous graphic issue is resolved as walls easily join across
groups, as shown in Figure 11.56.

FIGURE 11.56
Resolved wall
graphics

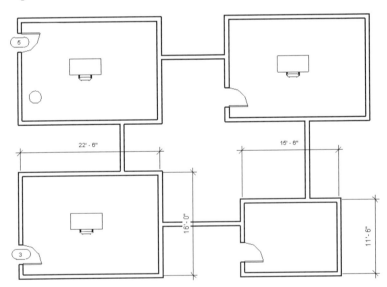

Best Practices for Groups

Groups are great for creating and maintaining design iteration within a single project. And
they're also great for maintaining consistency across multiple projects because groups can be

saved and loaded across multiple files. They can even be linked as separate RVT files and then converted to groups at a later time.

As with everything in Revit, there are some important exceptions that you will want to note. Nearly every time a problem crops up with groups, it's usually the result of ignoring one of the following best practices:

Don't put datum in your group.   Avoid putting datum objects (levels and grids) inside your group. First, you can't manage the extents of the datum objects unless you're in Group Edit mode, which can create conflicts elsewhere in your project. Of course, you will have the option to *not* include the datum objects when you bind your link. Again, doing so doesn't necessarily create a technical hurdle, but it can create a lot of confusion. We've seen situations where duplicate levels are deleted only to find out that those levels were hosting content in the project.

Don't nest groups.   In other words, avoid creating groups within other groups. Although nesting can save time in some situations when the design is preliminary and your team is trying to distribute content and design ideas quickly, you'll likely find a point of diminishing return as the design evolves. You can't get to all the features and functionality of Revit when you're in Group Edit mode. And if you're nested deep into groups and trying to modify project properties, you'll quickly get frustrated digging in, out, and across nested groups to go back and forth between your group and the project.

Group hosted elements and their hosts together.   You want to keep your hosted elements and hosts together. For example, try not to group doors and windows without their host walls. Technically, nothing keeps you from creating a group of windows without their host walls. If any of the windows in the group become unhosted and then deleted, this will delete the respective windows in related group instances – even if they are properly hosted. Another example is that elements such as plumbing fixtures that don't need to cut their host shouldn't be hosted. Instead, they should be face based (or assigned the option Moves With Nearby).

Don't use attached relationships in groups.   Avoid attached relationships within groups. In other words, give walls explicit heights in the Properties palette rather than attaching their tops and bottoms to levels or other hosts (like floors and roofs). If you manipulate the datum or attached host and the relationship creates inconsistent conditions, you'll see a warning asking you to fix the groups (Figure 11.57).

FIGURE 11.57
Avoid attaching
with groups.

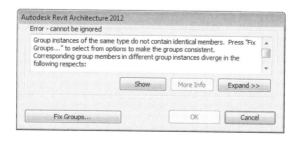

Fixing the group really doesn't fix the group. It actually explodes it or creates a new group that is no longer referenced to the first group (Figure 11.58).

FIGURE 11.58
Resolving attach-
ments warning

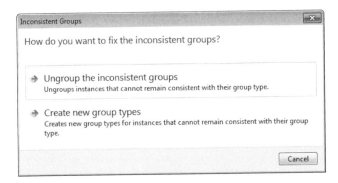

Don't mirror groups. Finally, and maybe most important, don't mirror groups. Instead, it's better to create left and right versions. Does mirroring work in concept? Yes. Does it work in the real world? Not really.

Think about it. You'd love to be able to mirror that precious prototype coffee shop, right? Well, Revit doesn't disallow mirroring of content as a parameter. Mirror the coffee shop and now the baristas are foaming milk on the right rather than the left. This might look great in a rendering, but it doesn't make sense for the company that manufactures espresso machines.

And now the display cases have power supplies on the wrong side. The cash register has keys on the wrong side. The desk in the manager's office now has drawers on the left and fil-ing cabinets on the right. And to make matters worse, the sink in the bathroom now has hot water coming from the wrong faucet. Again, it makes all the conceptual sense in the world to be able to mirror a building — and a group. But trying to make it work can cost a lot of time and money. And that's just a coffee shop. If you think it's a good idea to mirror a hospital room or a surgical theater or some other mission-critical building or civil construct, well...it could end badly. Or you will have to work very, very late.

If you'd like to download the file that has been created during the examples, you can find it in the Chapter 11 folder on the book's companion website (www.sybex.com/go/masteringre-vit2013); the file is called c11_Groups.rvt.

Making Design Options for Design Iteration

Revit provides a set of tools for developing multiple design iterations in the context of one project. You can use these tools to explore alternative designs without the need to save multiple inde-pendent versions of your model as you move in different directions. Using design options, you create, evaluate, and mock up a wide range of options in the context of one project file. You're free to investigate multiple roof configurations or different entry canopies, explore various furniture, office layouts, and stairs — quite literally anything that can be modeled. This functionality allows you to create views that show each option so the two designs can be compared.

Design options work in the following manner. First, you have a *main model*, which includes all the elements you've modeled that are fixed and not affected by the options you want to explore. The main model can be thought of as a backdrop or stage on which different options are displayed. Elements in the main model are always visible by default, whereas design options — such as different furnishings for the interior, or different canopies over an entrance — come and go, appearing and disappearing depending on what you're editing or viewing. Put another way, the main model includes everything else that's *not* in the design options.

You can make as many options as you need — there is no limit. You can create views for each option that show only that option displayed against the main model and thus be able to place these views on a sheet to compare your designs. You can then present them to a client, to the project architect, or to other stakeholders in the design process. Once you settle on a design option, you *accept* it as the primary design solution going forward by adding it back to the main model. Doing so deletes all elements in the design option set that you won't use going forward. That is, some elements become embedded in the architecture, whereas others disappear forever.

Creating Design Options

Let's start simple, establish the principle, and then add complexity later. Start a new project using the default architectural template file. Create four simple walls with a wall down the middle of the space, as shown in Figure 11.59.

FIGURE 11.59
Starting design options

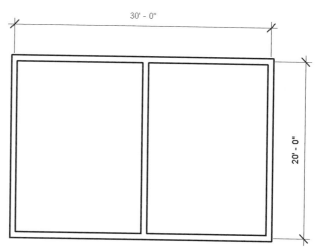

We're going to configure this simple space into a design option that divides the space vertically in one option and horizontally in the other:

1. From the Manage tab in the ribbon, locate the Design Options panel (Figure 11.60) and then click on the Design Options button. You can also access the Design Options tool from the status bar at the bottom of the application window.

FIGURE 11.60
Design Options panel

2. In the Design Options dialog box, click New in the Option Set area to create a new option set. This will automatically create one design option within the set.

3. Click New in the Option area of the dialog box to create another option, as shown in Figure 11.61. Click Close to dismiss the dialog box.

FIGURE 11.61
Creating an option set and two options

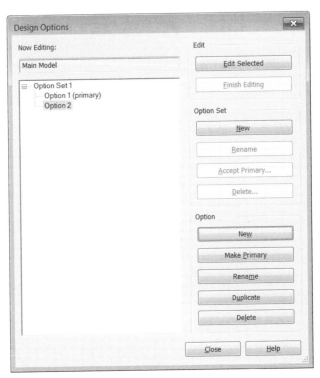

Now that you've started creating design options, everything in the project is now in the *main model*. Let's start adding elements to one of the two options.

4. Select the center vertical wall, which will immediately initiate the Modify | Walls contextual tab in the ribbon. With the wall segment selected, you can find the Add to Set button in either the Manage tab in the ribbon or the Design Options toolbar in the status bar (Figure 11.62).

FIGURE 11.62
Finding the Add To Set tool

5. In the Add To Design Option Set dialog box, add the wall to Option 1 but not Option 2, as shown in Figure 11.63.

FIGURE 11.63
Adding elements to
option sets

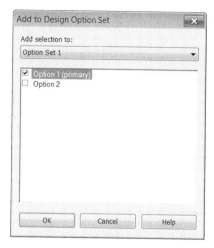

Note that when the elements are added to the option set, they immediately become un-selectable within the main model. This is because an option called Exclude Options in the Design Options toolbar is checked by default. The purpose of this option is to support a workflow in which design options are explicitly edited. Otherwise, it is assumed you are working exclusively on other parts of the building design. Of course, you can disable this option at any time by deselecting the check box in the status bar.

Editing Design Options

Selecting a design option to edit allows you enter a special mode called Edit Option mode. In this mode, you can add elements from outside the option set or create them from within the option set. The elements that are not inside this option set turn light gray, indicating that they are not editable.

Entering Edit Option mode is quite easy. From the drop-down list in the Design Options toolbar or from the Design Options panel in the Manage tab, select the option you wish to begin editing (Figure 11.64).

FIGURE 11.64
Accessing the Edit
Option mode

Once you have entered Edit Option mode, add one horizontal wall dividing the space, as shown in Figure 11.65. Note that anything else you add to the project while in Edit Option mode will be assigned to that design option. You can also modify or delete any elements in the selected option in this mode.

To exit the Edit Option mode, return to the Design Options drop-down list and select Main Model. Remember that only the primary option will appear by default; therefore, when you finish adding the horizontal wall to Option 2 and you return to Main Model, the horizontal wall will disappear and the vertical wall will reappear. In the next section, you'll learn how to control the visibility of design options.

FIGURE 11.65
Adding a wall in
Edit Option mode

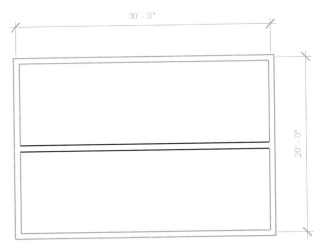

Viewing and Scheduling Design Options

You'll notice that whenever you switch between Option 1 and Option 2, the view automatically changes to show the option that you've selected. Initiating design options automatically creates a new tab in the Visibility/Graphic Overrides dialog box. By default, a design option's display shows as Automatic (Figure 11.66). This means that the primary design option (in this case, Option Set 1) will be shown in the view.

FIGURE 11.66
The Design Options
tab displays
Automatic

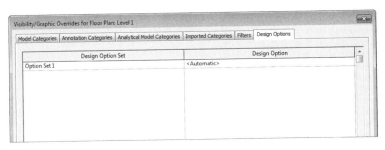

The Design Options tab is available for any view, even for schedules. Selecting the Visibility/ Graphic settings in the view properties of a schedule filters the schedule according to the desired design option.

If you want to specify or lock a view to a particular design option, open the Visibility/ Graphic Overrides dialog box and select the Design Options tab. From the drop-down list, change the setting from Automatic to one of the design options (Figure 11.67).

For working views, it's fine to leave the view properties set to Automatic so that the view switches to actively show the desired design option; however, using the Visibility/Graphic settings can be particularly useful for views that are being placed on sheets. To show multiple design options on one sheet, you'll need to duplicate any relevant views and use the Visibility/ Graphic settings to set a specific design option for each view.

FIGURE 11.67
Locking the view to
a design option

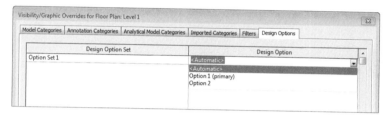

Removing Design Options and Option Sets

As your project grows and begins to resolve more detail, it may be necessary to delete an option set, accept the primary design option, or delete a single design option. While some of these options might yield similar outcomes, there are important differences. Remember that you can create an unlimited number of option sets and any number of individual options within each set. Maintaining too many design options may have adverse performance effects on your project file, so you should be conscious of the status of all design options. As always, each option set should be named appropriately so that your project team can understand the intended use of each study.

ACCEPTING THE PRIMARY DESIGN OPTION

The most common outcome of a design option study is to accept one option and delete all other options. The Design Option tools are built to support this workflow quite effectively.

To accept the primary design option, open the Design Options dialog box from the Manage tab or the status bar. Select the associated option set from the list and click the Accept Primary button, as shown in Figure 11.68.

When you accept the primary option in an option set, the geometry associated with the primary option is integrated into the main model. Any geometry on other options within the selected option set is deleted.

You will proceed through a series of warnings and confirmations before completing the process. If any views are specifically assigned to display the options being deleted, you will have the option to delete or retain such views (Figure 11.69). This is a good way to keep your project file clean and free from extraneous views related to the rapid iteration process of design options.

FIGURE 11.68
Accepting the primary design option

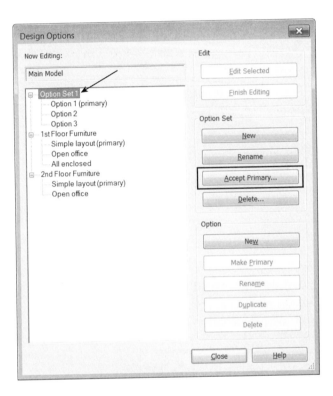

FIGURE 11.69
Delete or preserve views related to deleted design options.

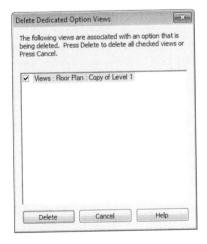

DELETING AN OPTION SET

Do not confuse the ability to completely delete an option set with the ability to accept the primary option and delete all other options within the set. If you delete an option set, *all* options within the set are deleted. This workflow is less common because you usually study options for some element of your design that will need to be included in one form or another. Sometimes you may just need to study a potential addition to the scope of your project and it doesn't get accepted. This is where it is useful to completely delete an option set.

To delete an option set, return to the Design Options dialog box and select the option set. Click the Delete button in the Option Set area as shown in Figure 11.70. As in the previous exercise, you will be prompted with a series of warnings and confirmations because of the content you are about to permanently delete from your project.

FIGURE 11.70
Deleting an option set

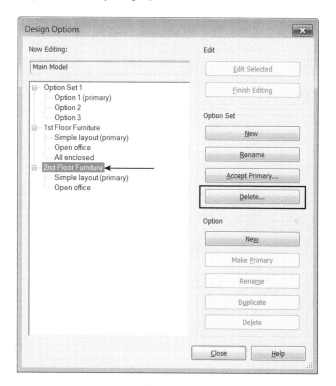

DELETING AN INDIVIDUAL OPTION

Another common workflow in the iteration of design is to delete just one of the options within an option set. This may occur for various reasons, but let's say you didn't want to continue exploring the option for all enclosed offices in the furniture layout for the first floor of your project. In Figure 11.71, we have the Design Options dialog box open and the All Enclosed option selected within the 1st Floor Furniture option set. From here, you would click the Delete button in the Option area as shown in the figure.

FIGURE 11.71
Deleting an option
within an option set

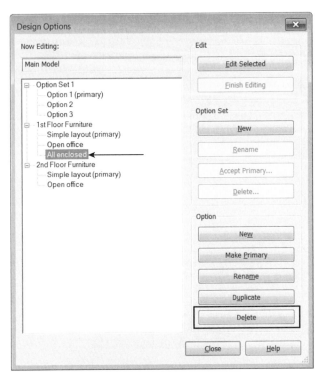

You cannot delete the primary option in an option set. Some other option must be assigned as the primary option before you can delete the original primary option. To make an option the primary option, open the Design Options dialog box, select an option, and click the Make Primary button.

PUTTING IT ALL TOGETHER

Now it's time to bring it all together — phasing, groups, and design options. Let's create a tenant finish package in two phases. The first phase will resolve construction on one side of the space, and then we'll turn to the other side of the space to complete the renovation. We'll also rely on groups for collections of components. Finally, we'll create a design option for the second space. Ultimately, you need to visualize the exercise in plan, perspective, and schedule.

Download the c11-Exercise.rvt file from this book's companion website to get started. Before you start this exercise, remember that this model will be the existing condition. So rather than create the existing walls and then change their phase, let's start by duplicating a view and changing the phase of that view so that the walls and other content are displayed as existing.

Duplicate Level 1 floor plan and name the duplicated view **LEVEL 1 - EXISTING**, as shown here.

Then click inside the view to activate the view's properties; make sure the phase is set to Existing.

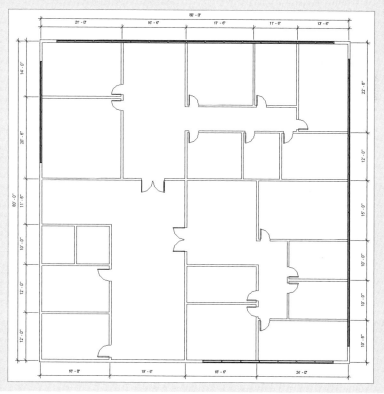

Existing Plan

Leave the phase filter set to Show All for now. Don't be concerned that the elevation tags have disappeared in the view. View tags are also phase aware, and they're in the New Construction phase. The overall space is 80 x 80 (24 m x 24 m). We've also added some exterior dimensions as a reference. The finished existing plan is shown here.

As you can see, the finished existing space is really two areas. In this scenario, the tenant in the lower-left space is expanding and will be taking over the upper space.

The idea is that we're going to demolish the space in stages. We don't want to upset the existing tenants to complete the phased work.

PHASE ONE: DEMOLITION

Some of the existing walls will remain. But you don't want to demolish them in this view. That's because the demolition should take place at the start of the New Construction phase. But there's going to be two construction phases (so there will also be two demolition phases). If you haven't created those two phases, do so now, as shown here.

Now duplicate the Level 1 floor plan again and rename the duplicated view as shown here. This will be the view that displays the demolished elements.

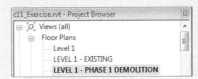

Go to that view and be sure to change the Phase to New Construction - Phase 1 and Phase Filter to Show Previous + Demo, as shown here.

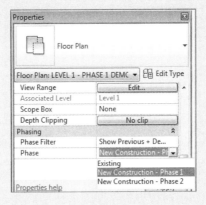

Demolish the walls as shown here. You don't have to demolish the doors if you first demolish the walls that host them.

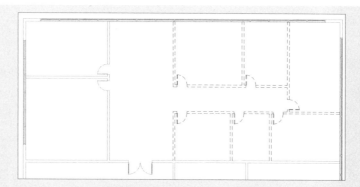

Next, you will add the new elements. First, replace a portion of the walls around the upper-left spaces with storefront glazing. Because the new storefront is proposed and the interior walls exist, this action will automatically demolish the openings. The illustration shown here is a perspective of the work so far. Recall that we've shaded the existing walls so that they'll stand out more from the proposed walls and that the demolished walls are in shown in red.

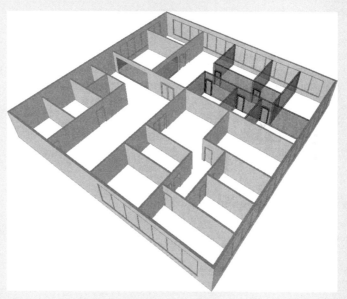

PHASE 1: PROPOSED

Duplicate Level 1 floor plan and rename the duplicated view **LEVEL 1 - PHASE 1 PROPOSED,** as shown here.

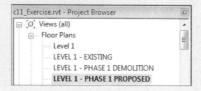

Make sure the Phase is set to New Construction - Phase 1 and Phase Filter is set to Show Previous + New, as shown here. This view will show only the existing elements that remain after demolition and the proposed content.

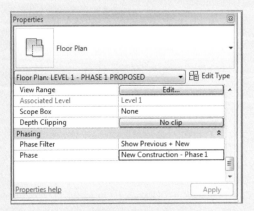

Now start adding furniture to the space. You'll add a reception area and other office furniture. Add desks, tables, shelving, and chairs.

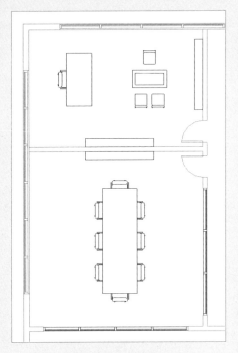

Start adding open office furniture. But group the assembly before you start copying through the office space.

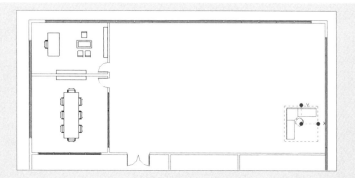

Here is the completed space in a plan view.

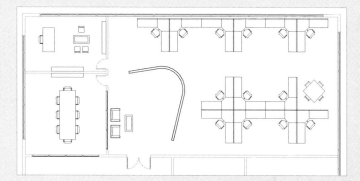

Shown next is the space in a perspective view. Note that the demolished walls are not being shown. To give some graphic clarity and allow you to see through the context of the existing walls, we've temporarily set the transparency value of the existing material (in the phase properties) to 50%.

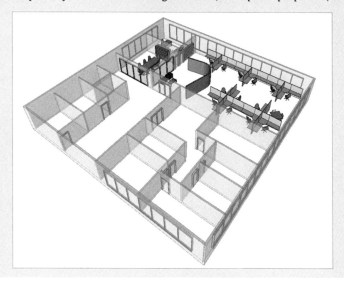

PHASE 2: DEMOLITION

Start Phase 2 by duplicating the plan view LEVEL 1 - PHASE 1 DEMOLITION. Then rename the view **LEVEL 1 - PHASE 2 DEMOLITION** and set the Phase to **New Construction - Phase 2** as shown here.

Now demolish the existing walls as shown here. Note that you'll have to split the long wall between Phase 1 Proposed and Phase 2 Proposed in order to allow only a portion of the wall to be demolished.

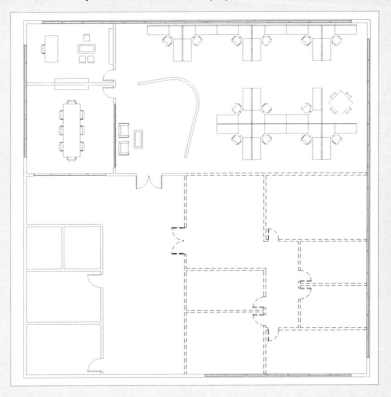

Shown next is a perspective view showing the proposed demolition for the second phase. Don't be confused by the proposed content from New Construction - Phase 1 showing as existing. This is correct because that content is now considered existing when seen through the lens of New Construction - Phase 2.

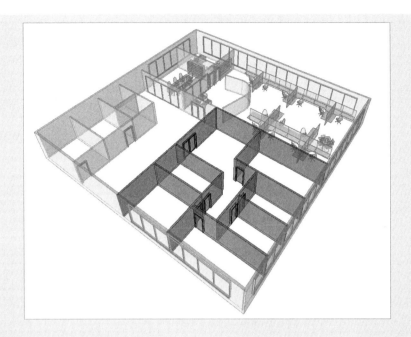

PHASE 2: PROPOSED

Now you'll duplicate the view again for the start of proposed work. Duplicate the plan view **LEVEL 1 - PHASE 1 PROPOSED** and rename it **LEVEL 1 - PHASE 2 PROPOSED**. Set the Phase to **New Construction - Phase 2** as shown here.

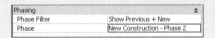

Start working in your new plan view, adding proposed elements as shown. Don't worry about getting the design right — just get the idea right. Here's the plan view.

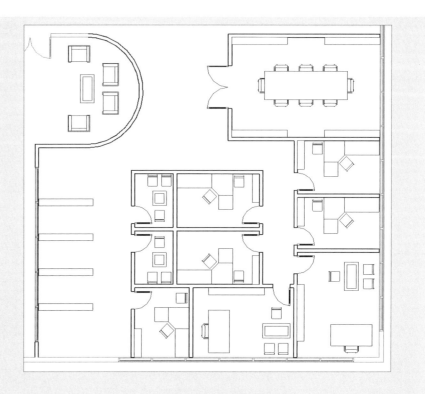

Just remember, adding elements in the view with the appropriate phase and phase filter settings are the easiest way to avoid confusion. Here's a perspective of the same view.

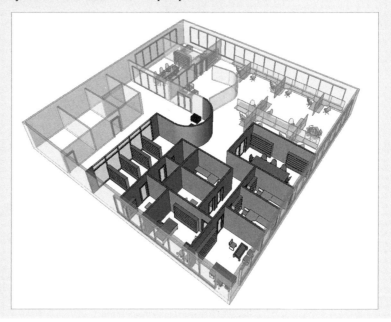

Now that you're finished with the demolition and proposed work in both phases, take a moment to set up a perspective view and then duplicate it three more times. Each of the views will show each phase sequence. Your Project Browser should look similar to this.

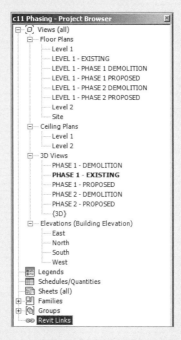

Except for the existing perspective view, here are all the tiled views thus far.

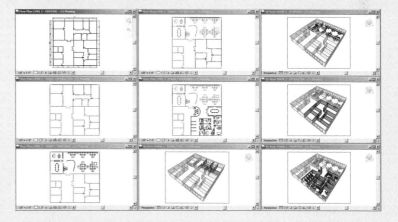

SCHEDULING

Now let's create a schedule for walls that will quantify demolition for each phase. As a sidenote, we believe it would be helpful to be able to create multicategory schedules that would allow both host and component categories to be scheduled at the same time — for example, you could schedule demolition for both walls and doors in the same demolition schedule. But this is not presently possible. So we'll create the schedules individually.

First, there's no phase filter to show only demolished elements. You'll need to create a Demo Only filter, as shown here in the first row.

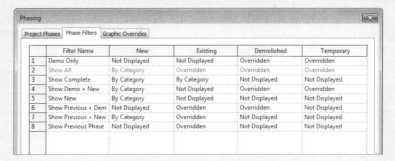

	Filter Name	New	Existing	Demolished	Temporary
1	Demo Only	Not Displayed	Not Displayed	Overridden	Overridden
2	Show All	By Category	Overridden	Overridden	Overridden
3	Show Complete	By Category	By Category	Not Displayed	Not Displayed
4	Show Demo + New	By Category	Not Displayed	Overridden	Overridden
5	Show New	By Category	Not Displayed	Not Displayed	Not Displayed
6	Show Previous + Dem	Not Displayed	Overridden	Overridden	Not Displayed
7	Show Previous + New	By Category	Overridden	Not Displayed	Not Displayed
8	Show Previous Phase	Not Displayed	Overridden	Not Displayed	Not Displayed

You can visually confirm what the filter will show by applying it to a working view.

Start by creating a schedule for walls that are being demolished by volume. You also need to estimate the cost of disposal for each phase. Create the schedule as shown here.

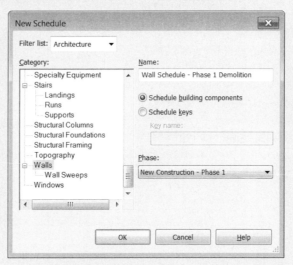

The following screenshot shows the schedule fields that you'll need to create. You'll be able to select only the Type and Volume fields from the Available Fields selection.

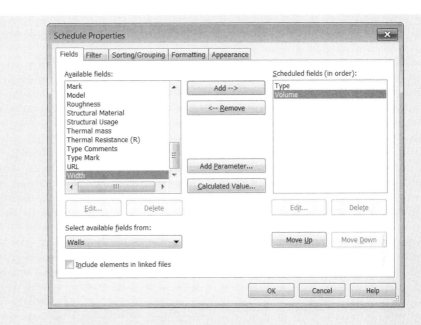

In addition to the default fields of Type and Volume, you'll also need to create a project parameter for the cost-per-unit volume (CF) per wall type. Click Add Parameter and fill out the Parameter Properties dialog box, as shown here. Choose Type because you want to be able to add one value per wall type, not per each instance. Click OK to close the Parameter Properties dialog box.

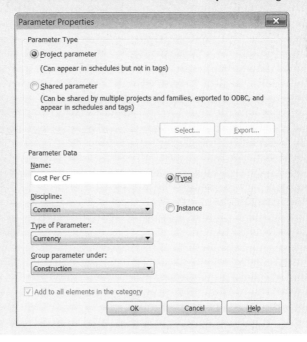

You'll need to add a calculated value in order to multiply the demolished walls' volume by the cost per units and get the total. Click the Calculated Value button in the Schedule Properties dialog box. We've divided the Volume value by 1 CF to keep the units consistent.

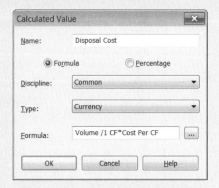

The next tab, Sorting/Grouping, should match the settings shown here.

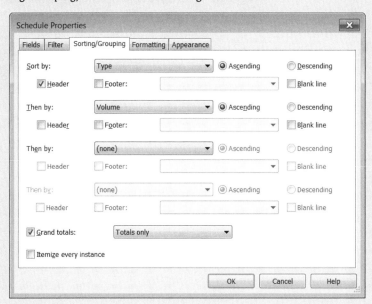

Choose the Formatting tab and select Disposal Cost. Be sure to check the Calculate Totals box.

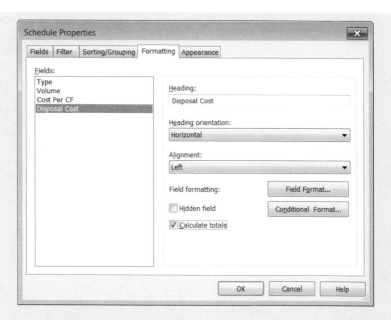

Now click the Field Format button for the Disposal Cost calculated value. In the Format dialog box, clear the Use Project Settings check box and change the unit symbol to $. You can also select the Use Digit Grouping setting as an option. Click OK.

When you're done, click OK to finish the schedule. In the Properties palette, make sure the Phase setting for the schedule is set to New Construction - Phase 1 and the Phase Filter is set to Demo Only. The schedule will appear displaying the following values. Your schedule may be slightly different because the amount of demolition will vary between our example and your exercise project.

For the Phase 2 demolition schedule, don't start over. Duplicate the previously created schedule and just change the phase in the Properties palette, as shown here.

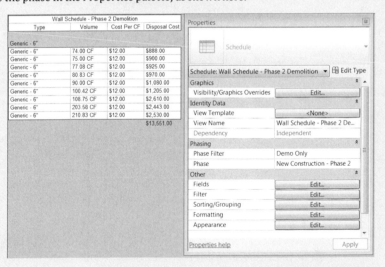

All that's left is to assemble the views on sheets. We'll need to use only two sheets. Each sheet will show a combined Phase 1 Demolition and Proposed view (plans, perspective, and schedules).

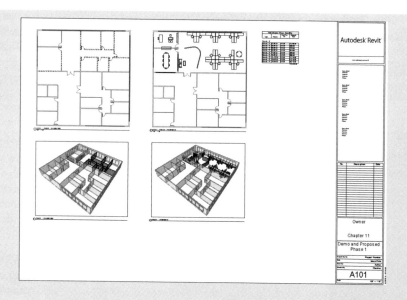

DESIGN OPTIONS

Everything looks great, but as to be expected, you need to show another option for Phase 2. This is easily done!

First, create a new design option set and two options, as shown here. Notice that we've renamed the set for clarity.

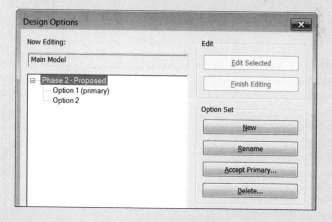

Here's a great tip. To isolate what you need to assign to Option 1, set the phase filter to Show New. This will turn off any existing conditions from the previous phase.

Now select everything in the view, return to the Manage tab, and click Add To Set. Deselect Option 2, as shown here, and click OK. This will add everything selected to the Option 1 (primary) design option. Then set the phase filter back to Show Previous + New.

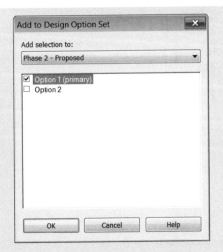

Now duplicate LEVEL 1 - PHASE 2 PROPOSED, and rename it **LEVEL 1 - PHASE 2 PROPOSED - OPTION 2**. This will be your working view for the second design option.

Next, open the Visibility/Graphic Overrides dialog box and select the Design Options tab to specify the second option. Click OK to close the dialog box.

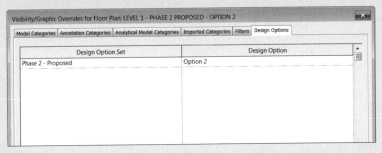

From the Design Options toolbar, select Option 2 in the drop-down list to make Option 2 active for editing and create another design iteration, as shown here.

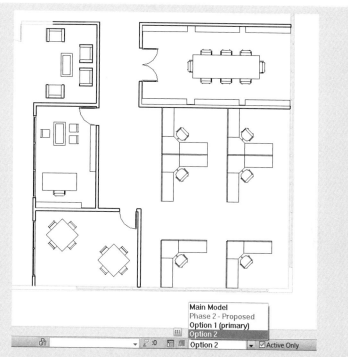

Place this design option on the sheet next to the Phase 2 demolition views, which are displaying the first option (primary) by default. You can also duplicate the perspective view of the first option; remember to change the Design Options setting in Visibility/Graphic Overrides to show Option 2:

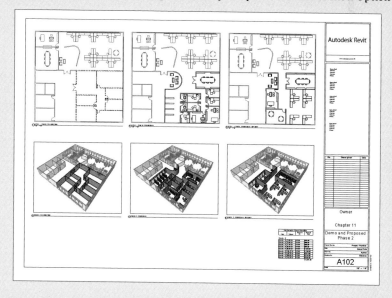

If you'd like to download the file used in this example, you can find it in the Chapter 11 folder at this book's website; the file is called c11_Exercise_COMPLETE.rvt.

The Bottom Line

Use the Phasing tools to create, demolish, and propose a new design. Time is such an important element to the design process and nearly impossible to capture with traditional CAD tools. Don't use phasing for construction sequencing (there's a better way). Embrace phasing for *communication*, not just *illustration*.

> **Master It** How can you use phasing to communicate your design across a series of key stages? What kind of project is best suited to phasing?

Use the Groups tool effectively. Groups are great for creating collections of both host and family component geometry. Just remember to apply best practices and you'll avoid a lot of common roadblocks. Individual model elements within groups will always appear properly in schedules, as you'd expect. And creating exceptions in groups allows you to make subtle changes without creating a new group.

> **Master It** Why shouldn't you mirror groups?

Create and use design options to manage big design ideas. Like groups, design options work great when you follow the rules. Design options are intended for design iteration that is bounded and well defined — not for putting multiple buildings in one project file. Remember that links, groups, and phasing can exist within design options. Always keep hosted elements with their host when using design options.

> **Master It** Suppose you have a multistory tower. How could you show multiple design options for the entire vertical exterior enclosure?

Chapter 12

Visualization

Visualization in Autodesk® Revit® Architecture software — or with any tool (even a pencil) — isn't an exact science. It still requires a patient, aesthetic eye. The most important thing you can do to successfully visualize your work starts with one thing: listen. That's right — it's your ears that make you a great artist! You need to be able to understand what your client is trying to accomplish because you're not really trying to visualize something — you're trying to communicate something *for someone else*. First learn to listen and you'll understand what your client needs to communicate. And you'll be far more successful!

In this chapter, you'll learn to:

- ◆ Create real-time and rendered analytic visualizations
- ◆ Render emotive photorealistic visualizations
- ◆ Render Sequence and Workflow

The Role of Visualization

We believe that anyone can use Revit to create compelling, emotive visualizations. What's really great is that your visualizations are based on the same coordinated design information you're using to document your project. But there are a few challenges:

- ◆ Creating emotive visualization is usually such a small part of your project's overall workflow that it's hard to spend the time necessary to hone your rendering skills. This is the reason that photorealistic renderings, both still and moving image, are often the realm of a specialist who deeply understands the techniques and workflow needed to create compelling imagery.

- ◆ The reality is that visualization is both art and science, but especially art. You'll never be able to just push a button and get a beautiful image. There's a world of difference between something that's photorealistic and something that's emotive and compelling. In other words, the button says Render, not Make Beautiful.

- ◆ Most important, visualization is about communication, something that many people forget to take into account. Don't ever create a rendering until you know what you're trying to accomplish. You must know your audience and understand what needs to be communicated (keeping in mind that the person requesting the rendering isn't always the intended audience). Otherwise, you'll likely spend hours doing something that is perfectly and exactly *wrong*.

We've learned this all the hard way. Imagine the disappointment after spending hours creating what we thought was an amazing rendering only to find that the client wanted something more gestural and sketchy. Or imagine our frustration after we created something unresolved and fuzzy only to find out that the client needed images that are polished and resolved, something more suitable for finished marketing materials. Rendering is about more than visualization. It's about communication. What you may need to communicate may be completely opposed to emotively well lit, photorealistic material and entourage.

You'll likely struggle with two important points about rendering in Revit, and unfortunately, there's very little that you can do about it:

♦ Although engineers often analyze in order to design, architects often visualize in order to design. But if your intent is to put all of this visual iteration into Revit just to render it, you'll probably get frustrated over all the chaff you're putting into a database that you want to keep light and flexible (particularly during early design). The reality is that Revit is most useful during early design to communicate analytic rather than photorealistic information.

♦ You'll never be able to render out of Revit more than you put into it. The level of detail required to create deeply emotive and detailed visualizations is not very likely the level of detail required to create accurate documentation. In fact, creating, changing, and resolving that level of detail may bring your project documentation to a grinding halt!

For example, the next time you're in your favorite coffee shop, take a moment and look at the espresso machine. Examine the detail of materials, hardware, and parts — the knobs, switches, and valves. Is this the level of detail that you want to have in your Revit project? Probably not! In fact, it's more likely that the documentation of a coffee shop simply requires a believable placeholder for an espresso machine; it needs to properly schedule and be only generally believable across all your project views.

But deeply emotive renderings often require specific detail and design resolution. In other words, not just "any" espresso machine will do! It needs to be a particular make, model, and manufacturer. Yet, if you're resolving this level of detail for visualization, it's likely that you're too deep into the weeds, spending valuable project time carefully modeling the valves on espresso machines.

So even though Revit has the ability to help you create great renderings, the level of detail required at the beginning of a project (when analytical relationships are still being resolved) is too much detail for schematic design. Even when the project is well resolved and established, the level of detail required for a highly finished and photorealistic visualization is far beyond what's required to complete your project documentation. So what is the point of this chapter?

Our focus is to get you somewhere in the middle. You need to understand how Revit works, but you also need to understand that although something may be technically feasible, it may not be practicable from a workflow standpoint. Overall, our goal is to help you focus on communication, not just visualization. So if you're happy with visualizing your project at its current level of development (not too far ahead and not overly detailed), you're going to have a lot of success rendering inside Revit.

Analytic Visualization

There are two key models of communication: analytic and photorealistic. Think for a moment about Google Maps: There's an option to view both Map and Satellite modes. Think of the Map mode as your analytic view and the Satellite mode as your photorealistic view. Both views are important, depending on what you're trying to communicate. If you're simply trying to understand directional information, the Map view is better. But if you're trying to show someone what something looks like with regard to trees and other real-world features, the Satellite view has obvious advantages.

It's also interesting to note that real-time information is easier to maintain in analytic views. For example, Google Maps has the option to show live traffic data. But this doesn't mean that they're showing actual cars moving on actual streets in photorealistic mode. Rather, they're color-coding the streets based on overall traffic patterns and movement.

The same is going to be true when you're visualizing your project in Revit. More often than not, you'll have the ability to show analytic information in real time. But showing photorealistic renderings of your project will require additional time (perhaps even days) in order to render your views.

Therefore, *analytic visualization* abstracts your model to communicate information that is not available by viewing the project literally. For example, massing studies are analytic representations of the building's overall form during the earliest design stages. Massing is useful to visualize geometric proportion and site context, and also for creating sun and shadow studies as well as preliminary energy analysis.

Even as you get into more of the project development and detail, materials may be a distraction whereas textures may not. Keeping your materials abstract and analytic allows you to help keep your focus on communicating the big ideas of your project. For example, does the spatial arrangement elegantly fulfill the design requirements? How is the vertical/horizontal stacking? We'll show you how to communicate these ideas in the following sections.

Monochromatic Views

Traditionally, architects built monochromatic, physical models that communicated the essence of the design without being too literal too soon. You can accomplish the same technique in Revit.

For example, take a look at the rendering in Figure 12.1, which has been created by rendering the view with all the default materials active.

FIGURE 12.1
Default material rendering

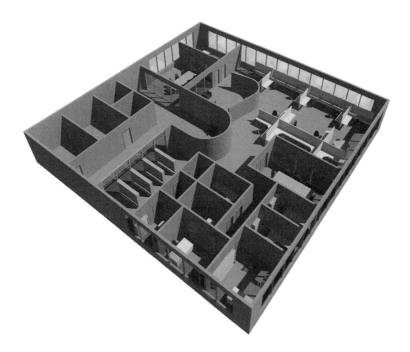

The challenge is that to get the materials correct, you'll have to commit a significant amount of time to selecting, testing, editing, and refining many material selections for an otherwise simple view that's quite early in the design stage. You don't have time for resolving all this specificity when doing so might result in something having the right material but in the wrong location.

Figure 12.2 shows the same view rendered analytically, with all the materials set to an abstract matte white setting.

FIGURE 12.2
Abstract rendering

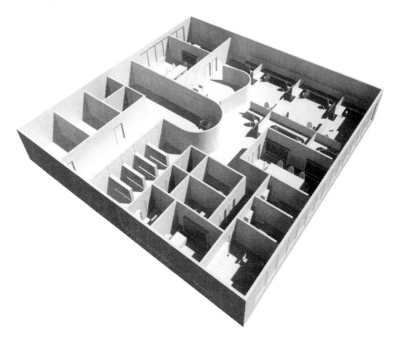

By selecting a matte material for everything in the view, you're able to focus on form-space and light-shadow relationships. Using the graphic overrides that are available with the Phasing tool can create a rendering like this quickly and easily. This technique is much faster than trying to select neutral materials for everything in your view (this same technique is also reviewed in Chapter 26, "Revit for Film and Stage"). Here are the steps to create a matte rendering using the material overrides in Phasing:

1. On the Manage tab, select the Phases button to open the Phasing settings dialog box. Select the Phase Filters tab (Figure 12.3).

FIGURE 12.3
Phasing settings

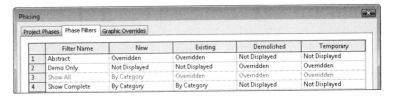

	Filter Name	New	Existing	Demolished	Temporary
1	Abstract	Overridden	Overridden	Not Displayed	Not Displayed
2	Demo Only	Not Displayed	Not Displayed	Overridden	Overridden
3	Show All	By Category	Overridden	Overridden	Overridden
4	Show Complete	By Category	By Category	Not Displayed	Not Displayed

2. Create a new phase filter called **Abstract** (as you can see in Figure 12.3, we've already created it for this exercise). Set the New and Existing material assignments to Overridden.

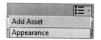

3. On the Graphic Overrides tab, create a new material. You'll do this by clicking inside the Material box. This will open the Material Browser. In this new dialog box, select the New Material button at the lower-left corner . Name the new material **Abstract** (Figure 12.4).

4. For the actual material assignment, select the Asset drop-down and choose Appearance. In the Asset Browser, type **Ivory** in the filter window at the top and choose Ceramic. Finally, pick 1in Square – Ivory from the Asset window by double-clicking it. This material will give the rendering a nice overall white finish without too much reflectivity.

FIGURE 12.4
Material
assignments

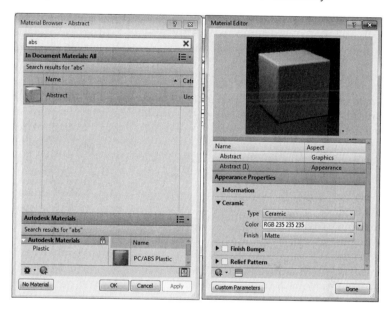

5. Now assign this material to your New and Existing phase objects by selecting this same material for those phases (Figure 12.5).

CERT OBJECTIVE

FIGURE 12.5
Assigning abstract
material

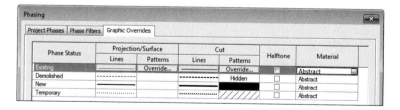

That's it! When you want to render a project view with this abstract material assignment, simply assign the phase filter and phase in the render view; you'll get an abstract, matte rendering as a result (Figure 12.6).

FIGURE 12.6
Phase and phase
filter in the view's
Properties palette

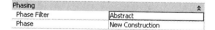

The previous example showed how to do an analytic rendering of a 3D view. But you can also see analytic information in a number of view types, not just in 3D but also in 2D views. For example, color-filled room and area plans illustrate information about your project's spaces. These plans are a representation of the space type.

Project Parameters

Viewing information about your project in a variety of ways is easy, and one way to do this is with view filters. In this section, first you'll create a view filter based on a project parameter, and then you'll create one to illustrate a user-defined project parameter. A filter can be used to alter the default display properties of elements on a per-view basis. As you can see from the Filters dialog box in Figure 12.7, you can apply up to three filters to a single filter type to override the graphic values of 2D and 3D content as well as spaces.

FIGURE 12.7
Filters dialog box

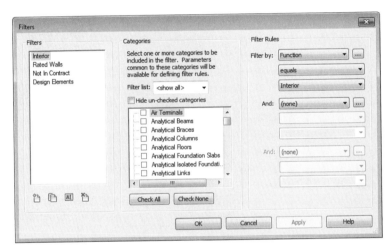

Figure 12.8 shows a simple example of how this works. In the view, there are walls that are two-hour rated. You'd be able to see this in a schedule, but how would you see it in a project view (2D or 3D)? You can easily show that with filters.

To apply a filter to your view and visualize the rated walls, follow these steps:

1. First, open the Filters tab in the Visibility/Graphic Overrides dialog box (type **VG** on the keyboard), shown in Figure 12.9. Click the Add button to begin the process of creating and applying a new filter.

2. Create a new filter called **Rated Walls**, as shown in Figure 12.10. In the Filter Rules group on the right side of the dialog box, select Fire Rating from the Filter By drop-down menu. Set the filter to Equals in the next drop-down, and from the third drop-down menu, make this setting 2. Make sure the filter is selected in the column on the left and click OK to add it to your Visibility/Graphics settings.

FIGURE 12.8
The default
view - unfiltered

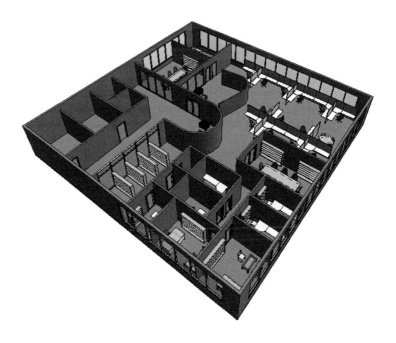

FIGURE 12.9
Selecting the Filters
tab

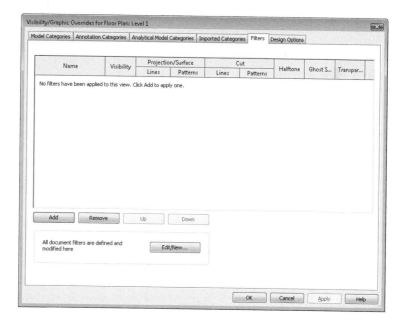

FIGURE 12.10

Creating the filter, category, and filter rules

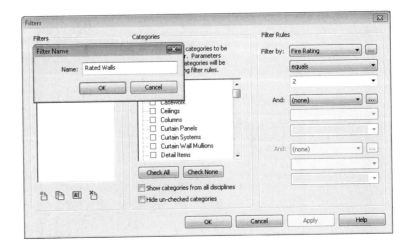

3. When you return to the Visibility/Graphic Overrides dialog box, you'll see that the filter is ready to be applied (Figure 12.11).

FIGURE 12.11

Our added filter

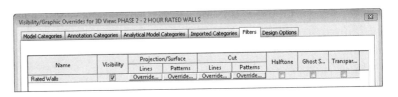

4. The next step will be to customize the Rated Walls filter so that items that fall into the filter category will have a specific graphic effect. Set the Projection/Surface override for Pattern to Red and Solid. Do this by selecting the Override button in that category to bring up the dialog box shown in Figure 12.12. You'll also want to choose the Overrides buttons under the Cut heading for both Lines and Patterns and set each of their colors to Red.

FIGURE 12.12

Graphic overrides

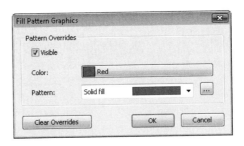

5. When you're finished, click OK to return to the view of the project. You'll see that the filter is overriding the project-defined graphics of the two-hour rated walls (Figure 12.13).

FIGURE 12.13
Applied filter in
Shaded view

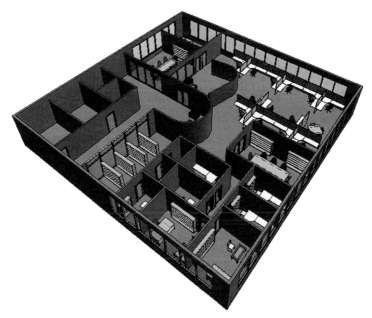

What's wonderful about this is that you're able to visually coordinate and verify your project schedules with project views that confirm what is being described in the schedules. This even works in Hidden Line view, as shown in Figure 12.14. Changing elements in the schedule or from the project environment will immediately update in all views of your project.

FIGURE 12.14
Applied filter in
Hidden Line view

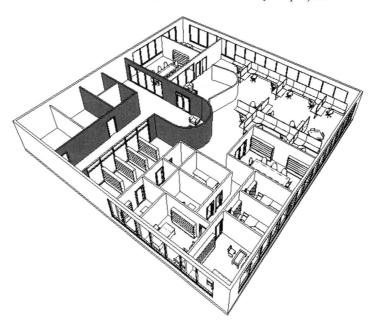

User-Defined Parameters

Now let's look at another example where a particular parameter is not in the default project environment. In this example, you need to show the space as functionally complete, but a lot of the content that is shown in the image isn't actually in the scope of work for your contract. To demonstrate this, you'll make two changes to the image.

First, this kind of parameter will have to be applied across many categories of elements — furniture, equipment, appliances, and so on. Second, it may apply to one element but not apply to another element in the very same category, name, and type. For example, under the Furniture category, the designer can be specifying the desks and cubicles but not the chairs. To do this, you'll want to make sure you're using an instance parameter (not a type parameter). Here are the steps:

1. Open a 3D view of the model and right-click it to rename the view. Call the new view **PHASE 2 – 2 HOUR RATED WALLS**. In the view, return to your Filters dialog by opening the Visibility/Graphic Overrides dialog box (VG) and create a new filter named **Not In Contract**.

2. Make sure you select numerous categories of elements that you want to be able to distinguish as Not In Contract. For this example, we chose Electrical Equipment, Electrical Fixtures, Furniture, and Furniture Systems, as shown in Figure 12.15. When you're done, select <More Parameters...> from the Filter Rules drop-down list.

FIGURE 12.15
Multicategory selection

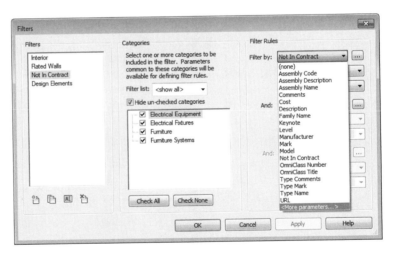

3. This will open the Project Parameters dialog box. You need to make a new parameter called Not In Contract. Select the Add button. This will take you to the Parameter Properties dialog box. Type in the name of the new parameter, **Not In Contract**. From the Type Of Parameters drop-down menu, choose Yes/No. Finally, select the same categories you selected in step 2, as shown in Figure 12.16. This user-defined project parameter will allow you to distinguish elements across a number of categories.

4. Apply your parameter to the filter. In this case, you're instructing Revit to override the graphics when the value of Not In Contract equals Yes in the Filter Rules settings (Figure 12.17).

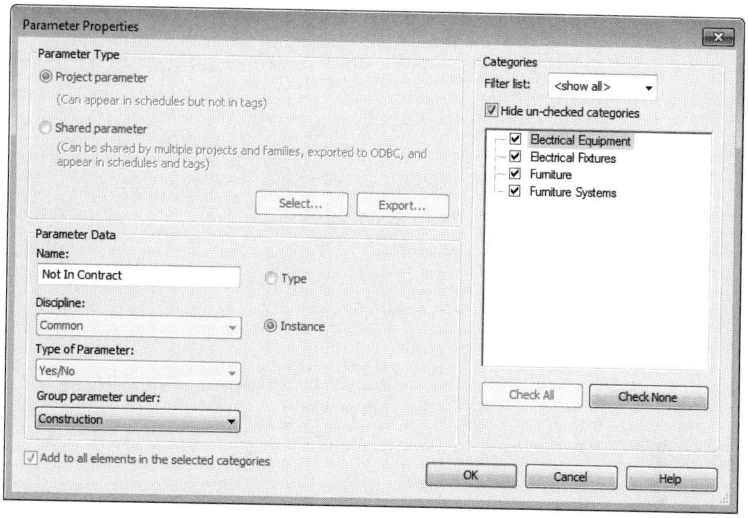

FIGURE 12.16
User-defined
instance
parameters

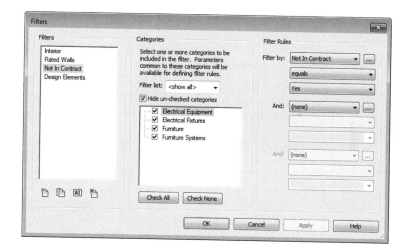

FIGURE 12.17
Filter parameters

5. Returning to the Filters tab in the Visibility/Graphic Overrides dialog box, you'll define how the graphics will be overridden. Once again, you're overriding the surface pattern with a solid color, this time yellow (Figure 12.18).

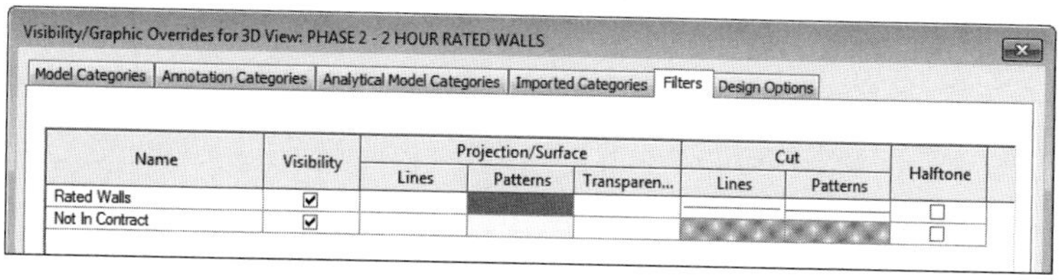

FIGURE 12.18
Graphic over-
rides for the Not In
Contract filter

6. Back in the 3D view, select some elements from the categories that you've just created a filter for. You'll notice that as you select the object in your file, the instance parameter for Not In Contract is available in the Properties palette. (Figure 12.19).

FIGURE 12.19
Instance
parameters

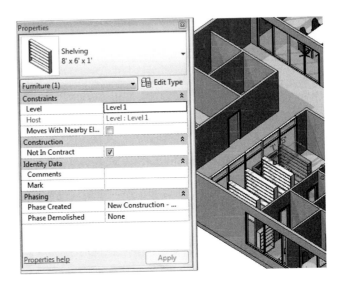

Select the check box. As you do, the solid color will be applied to the components, as shown in Figure 12.20, because the filter that you created now applies to the elements that you've selected, even in Hidden Line views!

FIGURE 12.20
Not In Contract
graphic override

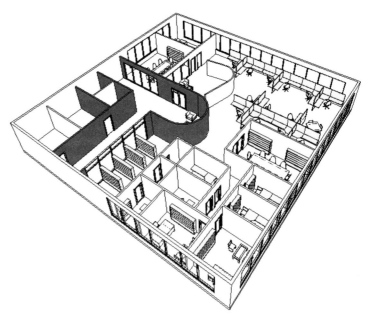

Identifying Design Elements

Finally, this process of using filters can be valuable for identifying "generic" host design elements as you move between design iteration and design resolution. Figure 12.21 shows a filter that has been applied to a view to highlight any walls, floors, ceilings, or roofs that have the term *Generic* used in their family name.

FIGURE 12.21
Identifying generic elements

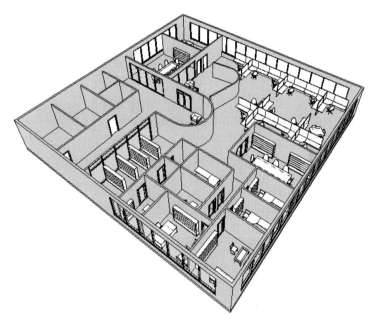

Typically in a design project, we work to replace generic elements with ones that have a more detailed label. Using a filter to identify those, you can quickly locate what needs more detail from within your project. The default template already uses the term *Generic* to describe basic design host elements, which makes them easy to filter, as shown in Figure 12.22.

FIGURE 12.22
Generic host element filter

Solar and Shadow Studies

For sun and shadow studies, you can use another analytic visual style that allows you to communicate natural lighting based on your project's location, orientation, and time of year. The sun's path can also be displayed (Figure 12.23), and you can edit the path of the sun both directly by dragging the sun or sun path within the view and indirectly through time-of-day settings.

FIGURE 12.23
Visual sun path

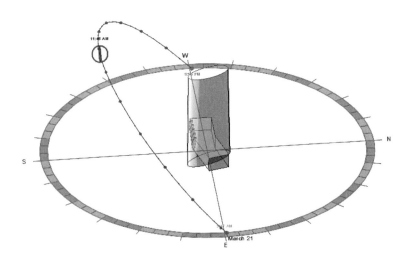

The sun path can be activated from the view control bar. You'll also notice the Sun Settings setting in the Sun Settings pop-up menu. This setting will allow you to give an exact location, time, and date for the sun. Opening the Sun Settings (Figure 12.24) allows you to more specifically select the settings for your particular view and solar study type.

FIGURE 12.24
Sun settings

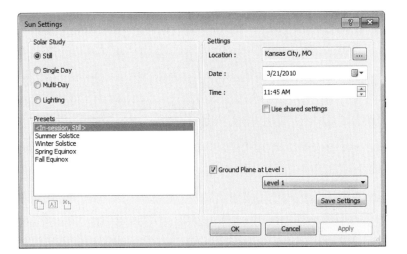

There are four types of solar studies that you can create in Revit:

- The Still setting allows you to create a study of a particular time, date, and location.

- Single Day allows you to create a study over an entire day at intervals of 15, 30, 45, and 60 minutes.

- Multi-Day allows you to create a sun study over a range of dates at intervals of an hour, a day, a week, and a month.

- A Lighting study is not related to a particular time, date, or place. It's more useful for adding graphic depth and texture with "sunlight" from an analytic top right or top left.

Single images are created using the Rendering dialog box. However, animations of single and multiday solar studies are created by clicking the Application menu and selecting Export ➤ Images And Animations ➤ Solar Study. This feature is covered in more detail in Chapter 10, "Conceptual Design and Sustainability."

For either single or multiday sun studies, you can set your project location through the Sun Settings dialog box. In the upper-right corner is the Location button shown as a square with three dots in it. Selecting this button will pull up the Location Weather And Site dialog box (Figure 12.25). Here you can select your project location from the map or via the Project Address drop-down menu. Select your city and click OK to close the dialog box. This will set the location of your project universally for this model, so if you are using the energy modeling tools or sun settings, or exporting the project for use in another application, this setting will locate the project on the globe for all those uses.

FIGURE 12.25
Locating the project

Regardless of whether you choose to use Still, Single Day, or Multi-Day, analytic visualization is incredibly useful for quickly communicating information about your project in a way that isn't literally associated with the actual real-world material assignments of your project elements. While photorealistic visualization would render wood as "wood," an analytic visualization could be used to identify which wood materials were sustainably harvested, recycled, or LEED certified. Analytic visualization is concerned about what something *means*, not just what it looks like. Because analytic visualizations can often be viewed in real time, your project information remains visually concurrent and up-to-date.

Photorealistic Visualization

When compared to analytic visualization, *photorealistic visualization* is more concerned with the emotive, experiential qualities of your space and content. Materials are carefully selected for accuracy and real-world simulation. But quite often, real-world isn't enough. Put another way, if analytic visualization is about what something *means*, photorealistic visualization is about how something *feels* or is experienced.

In many cases you'll find yourself tweaking materials and lighting in order to "theatrically" increase the nature of the space. Embellishing your project with non-project entourage is probably essential, and we'll cover important techniques to keep that content from cluttering up the views that are necessary for documentation. In addition, lighting is key, which means you'll have to contend with considerably longer rendering times. Let's look at some of the settings that impact the outcome of the renderings in Revit.

Visual Styles

In this section, we'll describe the various visual styles that are available in the View Control Bar with regard to rendering. Figure 12.26 shows the view control bar of an orthographic view and the View Control Bar of a perspective view. The major difference is that orthographic views are set to a scale.

FIGURE 12.26
2D and orthographic
View Control Bar and
perspective View
Control Bar

Note that 2D project views can't be rendered. But you can orient an orthographic view to a 2D orientation and render.

LEVEL OF DETAIL

The first option controls the level of detail in the view (Figure 12.27).

FIGURE 12.27
Level of detail

What is visible by default in a view is initially determined by the scale of the view, as shown by selecting Manage ➢ Additional Settings ➢ Detail Level. Figure 12.28 shows the default settings.

But this level of detail setting can be overridden after the view is created. This fact is important for two reasons. First, changing the scale after the view is created will not automatically reset the level of detail, and second, rendering a view with a more granular detail level will (generally speaking) take more time. Even though the results will not be visible to the naked eye, the calculations required to render what you won't be able to discern (because the objects are so small) will still be computed.

So it's very important that you render at the appropriate level of detail.

FIGURE 12.28
View scale-to-detail level

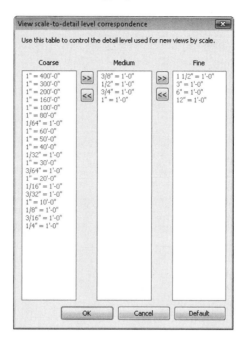

To illustrate this, look at the two perspectives in Figure 12.29. Although these two views look identical, one will rotate, refresh, and render faster than the other. This is because they're also set to different levels of detail.

FIGURE 12.29
Nonidentical views

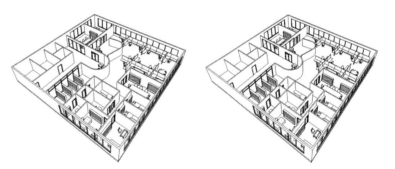

The reason for the difference in refresh rate at this scale is because the differences are barely a pixel in size. The view on the left is set to a Coarse level of detail. But the view on the right is set to a Fine level of detail. Although this different detail level doesn't have much of an effect on the content in either view, there is a critical difference.

The Executive Chair family has been modified so that the casters at the base of the chair display only at a Fine level of detail. The results are shown in Figure 12.30.

FIGURE 12.30
Detail level of chair

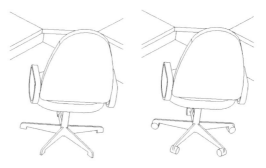

This difference may not have a large effect on a small project, yet it can have a significant effect on your project when you render (not to mention the additional time it will take when you export and print). So be sure that before you render a view, the level of detail is appropriately set. If you're far away from the building or your view is quite broad, a Coarse detail level is quite sufficient. But if you're zoomed in on a particular detail or part of the building (or just a single office or room), a Fine detail level might be more appropriate.

VISUAL STYLES AND GRAPHIC DISPLAY

The visual style of your view can be one of six settings (Figure 12.31).

FIGURE 12.31
Visual styles

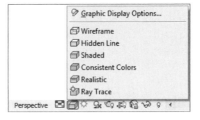

The Wireframe view (Figure 12.32) maintains only the edges of objects. Faces are hidden.

FIGURE 12.32
Wireframe view

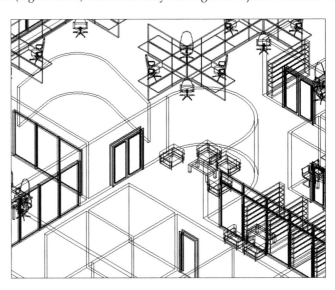

Hidden Line keeps both the edges and faces visible (Figure 12.33). This view style is used by default in 2D and 3D views.

FIGURE 12.33
Hidden Line view

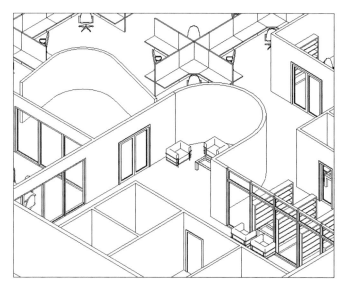

The Shaded view is updated in Revit 2013 and shows faces in their shaded value with accentuated edges (Figure 12.34). Note the change in color depending on an object's orientation. This effect is particularly pronounced on curved surfaces. In previous versions of Revit, this view was called Shaded With Edges.

FIGURE 12.34
Shaded view

Consistent Colors view removes the color variation based on an object's orientation to the viewer. Colors are strict interpolations of the shaded value (Figure 12.35) and, therefore, have a flatter yet more consistent appearance.

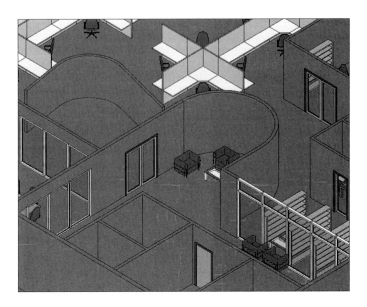

The Realistic setting provides real-time overlays of geometry with the material that will be used during a photorealistic rendering, as shown in Figure 12.36.

New to Revit 2013 is the Ray Trace view option (Figure 12.37). This view will perform a quick render of the project with the view window based on your current view settings. Based on your computer's processor, it will take a bit of time to render the view, but once rendered, the view remains interactive. As you modify elements, Revit will dynamically update the rendering. Note that this is a fairly processor-intensive view type, so if you're working in this view, make sure you close other applications that might consume RAM or processor resources so your view use is quick and fluid.

FIGURE 12.37
Ray Trace view

The Graphic Display Options dialog box allows you to control all of your views' graphic options (Figure 12.38). These are the model display (which we've just reviewed) and the shadows, lighting, photorealistic exposure, and background settings. This dialog box also allows you to save views as templates to quickly transfer the settings to other views. It's important to understand how these settings impact the visualization in your view. As we just stepped through the Model Display options, let's step through the options in this dialog box to round out your understanding of how you can modify the view to get the desired effect in your renderings and visualizations.

One view type in the Model Display options that's not accessible in the view control bar is Transparency. This slider at the top of the Graphic Display Options dialog box allows you to make all the elements within the view transparent to an equal degree. In previous versions of Revit, this was the Ghost Surfaces setting, but the percent of opacity/translucency was not modifiable. In Figure 12.39, the view has been set to 40 percent transparent.

FIGURE 12.38
Graphic Display
Options dialog box

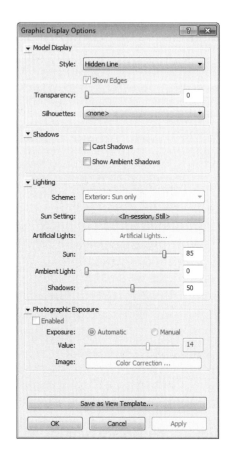

FIGURE 12.39
Perspective view
with transparency

The Silhouettes option allows you to override the edges of objects when the edges are defined by space (Figure 12.40). In Figure 12.41, the image on the left illustrates the view without silhouettes, and the image on the right shows the view with Wide Lines enabled.

FIGURE 12.40
Silhouettes style

FIGURE 12.41
No silhouettes
vs. Wide Lines
silhouettes

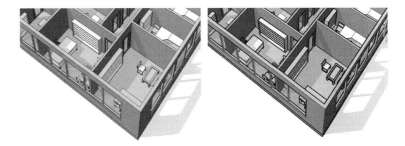

SHADOWS

The Shadows toggle is available in the Graphic Display Options dialog box, but there's also a toggle in the View Control Bar . Both will toggle shadows on and off based on the sun settings we discussed earlier in this chapter. The ability to turn shadows on in real time is a terrific feature that helps you add an improved sense of depth to your view (Figure 12.42).

FIGURE 12.42
Default shadows on

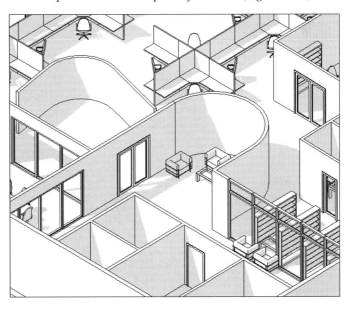

Keep a couple of things in mind when turning on shadows. First, it takes a bit longer for the screen to refresh when shadows are turned on. So you'll probably want to keep shadows off in your working views as you zoom in, zoom out, and rotate.

Second, the default settings could use adjusting. To do this, choose the Sun Setting button in the Graphic Display Options dialog box. You'll notice this button will report the current settings for the sun angle. Choosing this setting will take you to the familiar Sun Settings dialog box (Figure 12.43). Choose the Lighting radio button and select a sun angle from the top right. This will show a sun angle regardless of the building's orientation or location on the globe. Once those settings are made, click OK and notice the changes in the sun angle within the view.

FIGURE 12.43
Sun Settings
dialog box

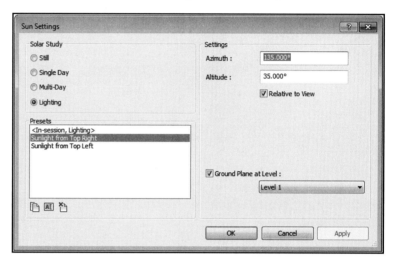

Back in the Graphic Display Options dialog box, you also have the ability to modify the sun's intensity, shadow intensity, and ambient lighting intensity with the sliders. Changing these can dramatically change the amount of shade or shadow that appears in your view (Figure 12.44).

FIGURE 12.44
Increased sun
intensity setting

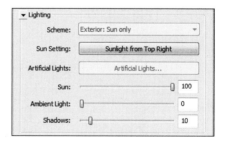

AMBIENT LIGHT AND SHADOWS

The ambient light and shadows, combined with other graphic options such as edge enhancements and real-time materials, allow you to create emotive, real-time views of your project that do not require renderings.

To activate ambient light and shadows, open the Graphic Display Options dialog box and select Show Ambient Shadows, as shown in Figure 12.45.

FIGURE 12.45
Ambient light and
shadows

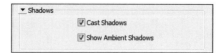

The results are noticeable, particularly around the intersections of objects. Shaded elements are embellished by highlights in the center of objects and deeper shading at the edges. The result is almost a watercolored effect that considerably softens the shaded view. The effect can be accentuated when combined with the option to enhance the silhouette of edges for even more real-time effects. Figure 12.46 demonstrates the differences in effect between shadows with and without ambient shadows turned on.

FIGURE 12.46
Activating ambient light and shadows: (a) without ambient shadows; (b) with ambient shadows

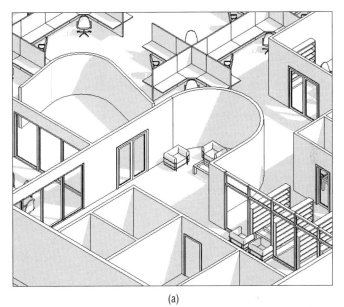

(a)

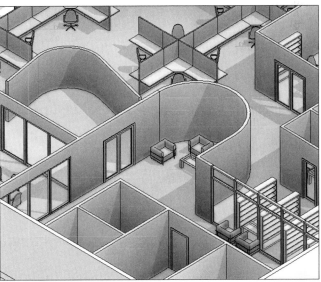

(b)

PHOTOGRAPHIC EXPOSURE

Photographic Exposure allows you to control the color range within the view (Figure 12.47). This option is available only when your model display is set to Realistic.

FIGURE 12.47
Photographic
Exposure settings

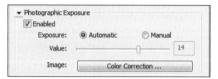

Without this setting enabled, the Realistic view types tend to be rather dark. This setting allows you to lighten the views and correct the highlights, shadow intensity, color saturation, and whitepoint to get the best possible image (Figure 12.48). Photographic Exposure also has an automatic setting that allows you to let Revit pick the best possible combination between those settings.

FIGURE 12.48
Manually
modifying the
Photographic
Exposure settings

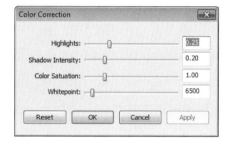

BACKGROUND

The final setting in the Graphic Display Options dialog box is the Background setting (Figure 12.49).

FIGURE 12.49
Background
settings

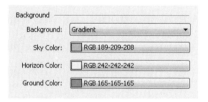

Selecting the Background option allows you to simulate a horizon without rendering. This is a great feature if you're presenting anything live within the model environment because it gives a visual plane for the building to sit on. Figure 12.50 shows the default settings on the building elevation.

FIGURE 12.50
Background
settings

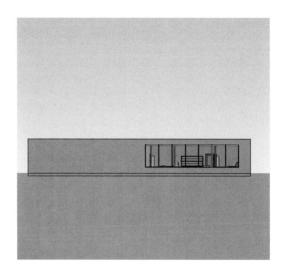

Section Box

Before we get into the rendering process, let's discuss the section box. By selecting the Section Box option from the Properties palette for the view, you create a rectilinear matrix around your project that may be pushed and pulled to isolate a portion of your project within the view (Figure 12.51).

FIGURE 12.51
Activating the sec-
tion box

In Figure 12.52, the section box has been pulled to isolate a portion of the project. This technique is helpful for isolating a smaller portion of a larger project. But a word of warning: Be careful toggling the section box off and on. The extents of the section box will reset and you'll have to pull them back into place. Very frustrating! If you want to see the whole project and the sectional view, it's best to use two separate views.

From the Properties palette for the view, select Edit Type. Upon opening the Type properties, you'll notice that there's a setting to determine the coarse poche material, which determines the color and fill of the poché (Figure 12.53).

The poché can be seen in all display types (Wireframe through Realistic), but it is only displayed in a view that is set to the Coarse level of detail. We recommend that you set the default color to black.

FIGURE 12.52
Pulling the section box to isolate a portion of the project

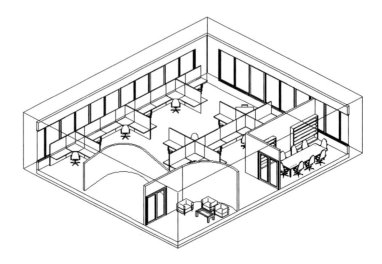

FIGURE 12.53
Poché settings

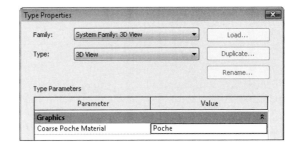

Here's why. As shown in Figure 12.54, the regions between host elements (like the walls and floors) are shown as discrete geometries. Yet it's often more desirable to show the poché as solid across these boundaries.

FIGURE 12.54
Regions between host elements are shown as discrete geometries

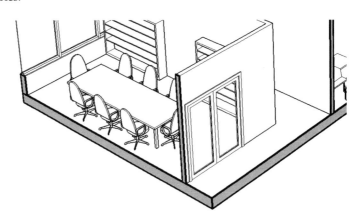

You can use the Join Geometry option to clean up the lines between elements. But this approach is time consuming and often leads to other problems in your file when a lot of things get "joined" just to create graphic impression.

One simple way to clean this up graphically is to select a poché color that is the same as the color of the lines between elements: black. Again, it's not the most desirable result, but it's fast, doesn't require manual joining of geometry, and reads well (Figure 12.55).

FIGURE 12.55
Solid poché black

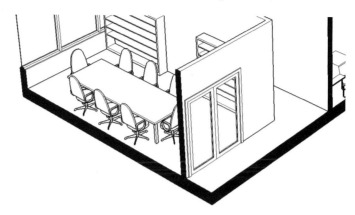

CERT
OBJECTIVE

Rendering Settings

You can access the Rendering dialog box by clicking the teapot icon on the View tab or at the base of the view in the view control bar . Figure 12.56 shows the Rendering dialog box.

FIGURE 12.56
Rendering
dialog box

An important setting in this dialog box is Resolution. It's easy to spend far too much time creating a rendered view because rendering times increase exponentially when the resolution doubles. Think of it this way: If you're rendering a view at 150 dots per inch (dpi) and then you render the same view at 300 dpi, the image is now four times larger, not twice as large ($1 \times 1 = 1$ and $2 \times 2 = 4$). If you were to render the view at 600 dpi, it would be 16 times larger ($4 \times 4 = 16$), and you could reasonably expect the 150 dpi image that rendered in a few minutes to take considerably longer at 600 dpi.

How large you need to render something depends on what you're going to use it for: screen or print. Don't expect a rendering the size of a $3'' \times 5''$ postcard to work for a $3' \times 5'$ banner.

So what resolution is big enough? Well, it's probably better to render things a bit larger, which will give you some flexibility if you need to increase the size of your image later.

Revit provides five present quality settings (Figure 12.57).

FIGURE 12.57
Quality settings

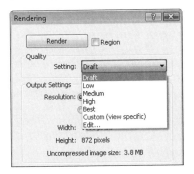

Figure 12.58 illustrates the range between the Draft settings and the Best setting. These settings will not only control the quality of the output but the time it takes to render. It's recommended to perform a quicker draft render to get a feel for your scene setup before doing a best quality render. This will keep you from losing a lot of time waiting for the rendering to complete in order to make adjustments.

FIGURE 12.58
(a) Draft setting;
(b) Best setting

(a)

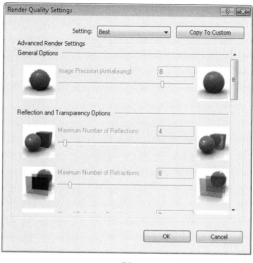

(b)

The Output Settings options (Figure 12.59) help you determine the level of resolution that your image can be saved at when rendered. The screen resolution is simply the resolution of the view on your monitor.

FIGURE 12.59
Output Settings
options

You should be much more interested in the printer settings because of the likelihood that you'll need to print your views. Again, the resolution is important, because you're printing for something that will be viewed at some distance (arm's length or a few feet away) with the naked eye. Rendering beyond what can reasonably be seen will add a lot of time to your renderings. While the default printer resolutions are shown in Figure 12.60, you can input other values by typing them in the dialog box.

Estimating your image resolution is easy. If the image is going to be viewed on a screen, 150 dpi is likely sufficient and even gives you some flexibility if the image has to be slightly larger. If you need to print the image, 300 dpi will work the majority of the time. Now take the longest dimension of your image (height or width) and multiply the dimension by the needed resolution. That's all you need to figure out your image pixel size.

Here's a test: Figure 12.61 was rendered at each default setting of the screen resolution. The image size was *only* 3″ × 2″ — too small to be very practical, but it was sufficient to chart render times rendering at 150 dpi and 300 dpi.

FIGURE 12.60
Printer settings

FIGURE 12.61
Rendered project

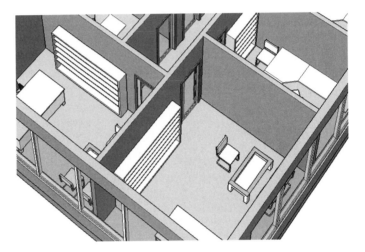

We kept the image small so the renderings could compute faster, left the lighting scheme to Exterior: Sun Only, and set the background color to solid white. As you can see in Figure 12.62, the time to complete each setting does not increase linearly. This fact is important to keep in mind as you change your quality settings and resolution, especially between High and Best, because there is a greater than six times increase in rendering time! Make sure the increase in time is worth the effort.

FIGURE 12.62
Quality render
times

	Total Rendering Time in Seconds	
	150dpi	**300dpi**
Draft	32	112
Low	42	121
Medium	99	309
High	423	1338
Best	2646	8318

Creating Your View

Creating and modifying your camera controls is almost as important as what you're creating. If you're not careful, you can easily unimpress the viewer by selecting the wrong view and aspect ratio of the camera and controls.

Perspective views communicate far more depth than orthographic views (Figure 12.63). Unless the view needs to be at dimensioned scales, we prefer to use perspective views of the project.

FIGURE 12.63
Orthographic vs.
perspective view

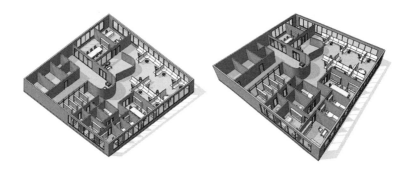

Locking Your View

Once you've created your view, you might want to consider locking it so it can't be accidentally rotated (Figure 12.64). Once your view is locked, you'll also be able to tag elements in it.

FIGURE 12.64
Lock view settings

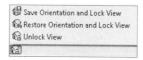

There are three options available from the Lock 3D View option. Save Orientation And Lock View keeps the current orientation and prohibits anyone from rotating the view. Once this option is selected, the Keynote command on the Annotations tab becomes available.

Selecting Restore Orientation And Lock View allows an unlocked view to be returned to its previously saved orientation and relocked. Any tags and keynotes that were previously placed in the view are restored.

Selecting Unlock View unlocks the view and allows you to orbit and navigate it. But keep in mind that when you unlock the view, any placed tags and keynotes disappear — and if you save the view from the unlocked and modified state, any tags and keynotes previously placed in the view are deleted.

Still Image Camera

When you create your camera view, the first point to select is your eye elevation, and the second point is the target elevation. Keep in mind that when you rotate your view, the rotation is centered on the target elevation (Figure 12.65).

Also, realize that there is effectively a boundary box, which defines the extents of your camera view. You can see this by going to another view, like a plan, and then selecting the camera from your Project Browser, as shown in Figure 12.66.

Once you can see your camera, you can select and move it around your project. Doing so allows you to move your camera closer and farther. You can also select the clipping planes of your camera and edit the front and back planes of your camera's view.

The aspect ratio of your camera is also important. For example, a television ratio of 4:3 seems far less expansive and dramatic than a 16:9 wide-screen ratio. Figure 12.67 illustrates this; the image on the left is 4:3 and the image on the right is 16:9. The result is that the view on the left seems too tight and constrained, whereas the view on the right is far more natural.

Size
Crop

Crop

To change the aspect ratio, select the view boundary and then select the Size Crop option on the Modify Camera tab. In the resulting dialog box, you can change the aspect proportionally or nonproportionally (Figure 12.68). Keep in mind that this setting doesn't zoom your camera forward and backward; it simply changes the relative height and width of the view.

FIGURE 12.65

Placing the camera

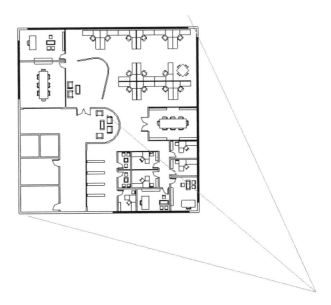

FIGURE 12.66

Selecting Show
Camera

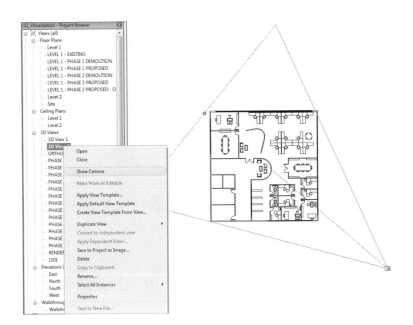

FIGURE 12.67
Aspect ratio

FIGURE 12.68
Crop Region Size
dialog box

To dolly your camera, simply activate the Navigation Wheel (Figure 12.69). You can quickly pull up the Navigation Wheel by selecting the lower icon in the dock menu on the right side of the screen. You'll be able to zoom, pan, and orbit as well as control other view features using the Navigation Wheel. Using this tool can take some getting use to because it will "follow" your mouse cursor across the screen. This is helpful because it will give you a dynamic menu to change and modify your view, but don't forget to turn it off before you start modifying geometry. Simply select the same button again and it will disappear until you need it again.

FIGURE 12.69
Navigation Wheel

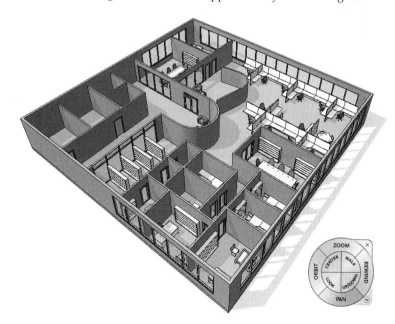

Animation Path

Creating an animation path is much like creating a series of cameras. To create a camera path, select the Walkthrough option from the View tab (Figure 12.70).

FIGURE 12.70
Creating the
walk-through

From your plan view, start placing a series of cameras by placing the camera location, and then the camera direction. Note that each time you pick a location these cameras will become the key frames in your animation. When you have placed the last camera, press the Esc key and your finished path will appear (Figure 12.71).

FIGURE 12.71
Finished camera
path

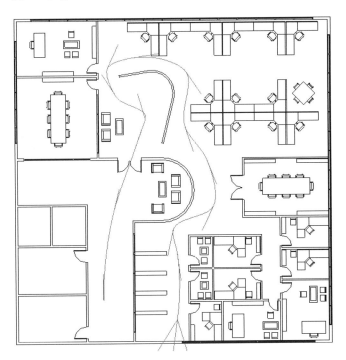

Right-clicking the path will allow you to go to the series of views that you just created (Figure 12.72).

FIGURE 12.72
Going to the camera
view

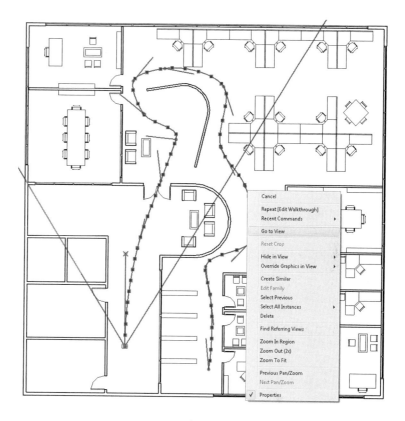

The walk-throughs are created in the Project Browser. Simply click the view as you would any other view to open the walk-through. Figure 12.73 shows the first view in the path that we've just created along with the Walkthrough view properties.

FIGURE 12.73
Walkthrough
properties

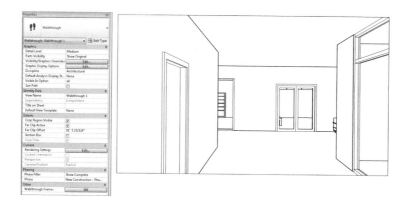

Let's modify the aspect ratio to 16:9. Select the view boundary and select Size Crop. By default, the view is 6″ × 4 1/2″. An 8″ × 4 1/2″ ratio is proportionally 16:9 (Figure 12.74). The view is now wider and less constrained.

FIGURE 12.74
Setting the aspect ratio

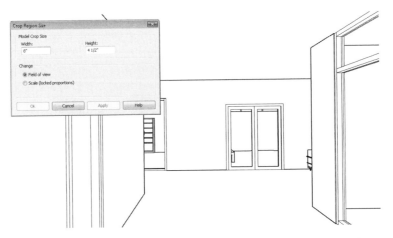

We're going to export a Hidden Line view for testing (especially before rendering), but we want to give the walk-through more depth. So change the Silhouettes option to Wide Lines in the Graphic Display Options dialog box we reviewed earlier in this chapter (Figure 12.75).

FIGURE 12.75
Setting the graphic display options

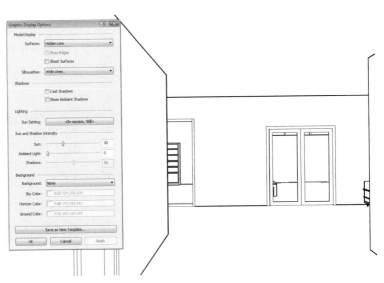

It's not desirable to simply walk with the camera facing the same direction that you're walking. So you're going to modify the camera directions. This will require that you open a couple of views, as shown in Figure 12.76. This way, you'll be able to see the results of your work in one view while working in another. Open the plan view of Level 1 where you created your walk-through and open the walk-through itself. Tile those views using WT on the keyboard. Make sure those are the only two views you have open; otherwise, you'll end up tiling several views you don't need.

FIGURE 12.76
Tiled camera and views

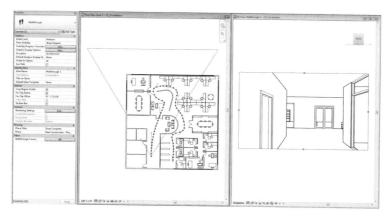

A couple of important points should be noted. First, you're showing the plan and the camera view at the same time. This allows you to see both the graphic and analytic camera, which is important for modifying views. As you can see, when you select the boundary of the view on the right, the camera path highlights in the view on the left.

Since the view is selected, you have the option of editing the crop size just as with any other camera. But you also have the option of editing the walk-through, as shown in Figure 12.77.

FIGURE 12.77
Edit Walkthrough option

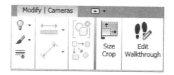

Click the Edit Walkthrough option, and you'll see the context toolbar, shown in Figure 12.78.

FIGURE 12.78
Key Frame Editor context toolbar

After you open the Key Frame Editor, the camera path now shows important controls (Figure 12.79).

The red dots along the path represent key frame locations (when you placed your camera, remember?), and the red dot directly in front of the camera will allow you to control the rotational direction. By default, all the cameras face ahead relative to their location on the path. But you can edit the default so that the camera can follow one direction but face another direction.

Since the default path is 300 frames in length, it would take a long time to go to each frame and edit what you see. It's better to jump ahead from key frame to key frame, editing fewer locations. When you do this, Revit will interpolate the frames between the key frames for you. As you jump ahead key frame to key frame, try to experiment rotating the camera to the left and right as well as glancing up and down. This can be done from the plan view on the left or from the camera view on the right.

Once you've edited your key frames, you can export the animation from the Export menu by clicking the Application Button and choosing Export ➤ Images And Animations ➤ Walkthrough.

FIGURE 12.79
Camera path and
controls

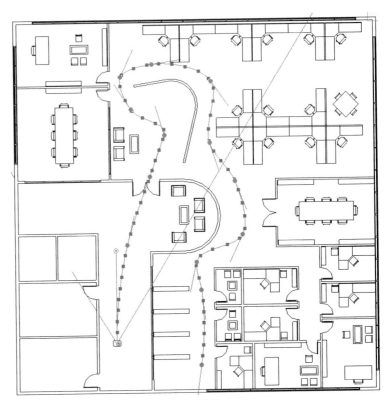

The options to export an AVI are the same as all of the options for rendering still images (Figure 12.80).

FIGURE 12.80
Graphic format
controls

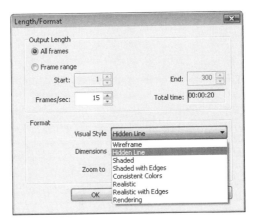

A 15 frames-per-second (fps) frame rate is minimal to keep the animation smooth. But if you increased the frame rate, the animation length would shorten and it would seem like you were running (rather than walking) through the scene. What can you do? Simply add more frames to your animation.

At the bottom of the camera properties, open the Walkthrough Frames dialog box (Figure 12.81). By increasing the total frames, you can also adjust the relative fps to maintain the desired speed.

FIGURE 12.81
Default frame count

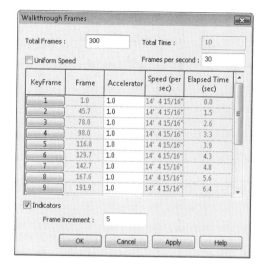

So, for example, if you wanted to increase the fps to 30 but maintain the same travel speed, you would also increase the Total Frames setting to 600 (see Figure 12.82). Simple!

FIGURE 12.82
Increasing the
frame count

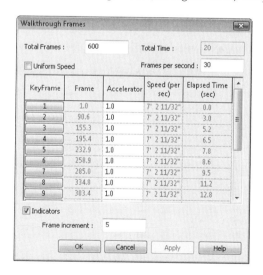

Finally, where a lot of people struggle is with the speed of their animation. Unless you're breaking up your animation into separate paths (which will be combined later into a single sequence), it's necessary to be able to speed up or slow down your camera's movement. In Revit, you can uncheck the Uniform Speed option to speed up or slow down the camera during a single animation study.

Although there's no exact rule for this, you can imagine the results. Think about how a plane seems to speed up relative to the ground as it approaches to land. In fact, it's slowing down. Yet your relative distance to the ground influences the perception of how fast you're moving. So even though you're slowing down, as you get closer to the ground, it seems as if you're moving faster. And when you're at 30,000 feet, it seems as if you are barely moving at all. Just imagine how the astronauts feel in space. Although it might seem as if they're barely moving at all and the Earth slowly spins below, in fact they're orbiting at over 17,000 miles per hour. Don't hit any space junk!

The same visual effect plays a part in your renderings. The farther you are from something, the faster your camera can move as you fly by and still seem smooth and fluid. But you will need to slow down considerably if you're walking through the building, where a comfortable pace is 6 to 8 feet a second.

We've exported the animation from this portion of the chapter. If you want to investigate the file or animation, you can download the c12_Visualization.rvt file or the c12_Visualization_Animation.avi from the Chapter 12 folder on this book's website at www.sybex.com/go/masteringrevit2013.

Rendering Sequence and Workflow

You'd be surprised, but many people actually render in the wrong sequence. The workflow for creating compelling renderings is not the same workflow you use to resolve your design process. If you try to do one like the other, the result is a lot of wasted time and frustration. Consider a reasonable design process to create a building that moves from intent to content:

1. Host components (walls, floors, stair, railings, and so on)

2. Family components (doors, windows, and so on)

3. Furniture, fixtures, and equipment

4. Assembly details and documentation

But if you're rendering in the order of the previous process, your results will be skewed. That's because to create photorealistic renderings, you're probably modifying your views in the following order:

1. Geometry (host and family components)

2. Materials (host and family components)

3. Cameras (setting up your views)

4. Lighting (lots of errors and rendering, adjusting, rendering, and so on)

5. Render (final renderings)

The challenge is that this is not the workflow for creating great renderings. If you're focused on the design process of *visualization*, the intent-to-content workflow is more along the lines of the following:

1. Geometry (host and family components)

2. Cameras (setting up your views)

3. Lighting (using matte materials)

4. Materials (host and family components)

Yes, this is as simple as it gets: cameras, and then lights, and then materials. But in Revit, lights don't usually show up until the building is well resolved because you're placing lights meant to be the lights in the building, not just for "rendering." So the design process is simply out of sequence with the visualization process.

Additionally, you need to evaluate the lighting neutrally, not with materials to distract you. As you're placing your content, a lot of stuff already has material assignments. You need to find a way to neutralize the material settings while you figure out lighting. The great thing is that you've already got all the parts to do this from earlier in the chapter. Now you just need to put it all together!

Geometry and Cameras

Geometry and cameras are the first step. You don't want to wait to see your project in perspective until after you've designed it. Unfortunately, you still can't design in perspective views in Revit, but ideally this will change. The point is that you need to be able to experience the space as you're designing, so go ahead and create perspective views of your project so that as you design, you can see the results in real time.

To demonstrate the rendering workflow, we're going to use the c12_Rendering Workflow. rvt project file located on the book's companion website. To get started, open the RENDER - CONFERENCE ROOM 3D view. As you can see in Figure 12.83, we've already adjusted the shadows and sunlight as well as applied silhouette edges to the view.

FIGURE 12.83
Viewing our project
in Hidden Line view

Right away, this isn't a bad view to have in your document set. The linework, subtle shadows, transparency of the glazing, and 16:9 aspect ratio help create a balanced view that doesn't require rendering. So don't be afraid to put these live views into your document set for quick reference.

Sunlight

Now let's render the view. Keep in mind that the rendered material applied to the Abstract phase override is solid white (which we set up earlier in this chapter), so you'll want to turn off the visibility of your curtain panels if you want to see through the glazing. Open the Rendering dialog box by clicking the teapot icon in the view control bar. Make the following settings in this dialog box, as shown as well in Figure 12.84:

◆ Quality: Medium

◆ Output Settings: Printer and set to 300 dpi

◆ Lighting: Exterior: Sun Only

◆ Background Style: Color, with color set to White

FIGURE 12.84
Rendering settings
for our view

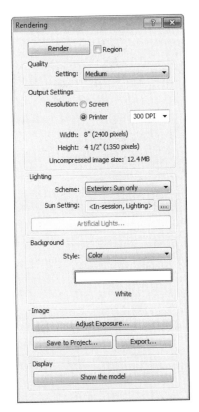

The reason we're using Printer as the Output setting is that 300 dpi is sufficient for the printing of this page. And an 8" wide image will suffice for the anticipated width of this book. Low quality is also sufficient based on our experience because it's not worth the extra jump in time to render much higher than this first pass.

Figure 12.85 shows the results of the rendering. The scene can be viewed beyond the immediate space of the conference room. Take particular note of the shadows and how the lighting drops off from the edge of a shadow.

Of course, this image is being rendered with the sun, which doesn't count for interior renderings; it's just a benchmark. But you can begin to see the level of detail and materiality, and the "look and feel" of the space. Now that you know what it looks like, you can turn off the sun and start placing some artificial lights.

Since you're rendering abstractly using a phase override, everything is going to be solid white. But if your "light" source is behind a solid lens, it's not going to render very well.

FIGURE 12.85
Sun Only rendering

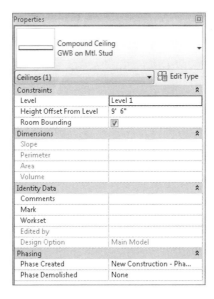

The best way we've found to handle this (until Revit allows for more analytic rendering) is to create an Object subcategory for the lens that surrounds the light source. Doing so allows you to control the visibility of the lens of the lighting fixture and allows the light to seemingly pass through the object. Unfortunately, this approach will not give the most realistic effect because many lighting effects result from light passing through translucent objects (like lenses or shades). But it's the best you'll be able to do for now to resolve lighting *before* you resolve materials.

Before you can add lighting, you need to add a ceiling to the spaces. To keep things generic, we've added the default compound ceiling to all the spaces (Figure 12.86). It's just a placeholder for your ceiling that will change later. But the important thing is that you don't get hung up centering ceiling tiles during your design process. Rooms will change dimensions, and all that time spent centering will go to waste.

FIGURE 12.86
Ceiling settings

Artificial Lighting

Now open the Level 1 Reflected Ceiling Plan view and load the family `Downlight - Recessed Can.rfa` from the default family files in Revit. You'll find the family in the default family folder under Lighting ➤ Architectural ➤ Interior. Place it in the ceiling and along the two walls, as shown in the reflected ceiling plan (Figure 12.87). The exact dimensions aren't important — just get the idea right.

FIGURE 12.87
Lights in ceiling

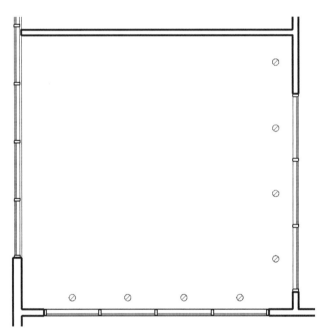

This light family doesn't have a lens, so you don't have to create an Object subcategory for the lens. But before you start to render these artificial lights, we need to explain the process and technique of using light groups.

CERT OBJECTIVE

Light Groups

There are times you'll want to isolate the lights that are being calculated and rendered in a particular view. You might want to test the lighting that will result from having certain lights on and others off, just as in a real space. Revit allows you to create light groups for this purpose. Doing so saves you a lot of time compared to turning individual lights off and on manually.

By default, whenever you place lights in your project, they're not placed in any group. They're "unassigned," just like the lights shown in Figure 12.88. This dialog box can be found by clicking the Render tool from the view control bar, and then selecting the Artificial Lights button from the Rendering dialog box. Here you can assign and create all kinds of lighting groups.

Besides the assignment for the light group, you also have the option of turning down the Dimming value. This option is great for giving your space a half-lit effect.

Now let's create two light groups for this space. Select the Artificial Lights button from the Rendering Settings dialog box. Then select New and create the two groups Conference Right and Conference Left, as shown in Figure 12.89. You're also working from a 3D axonometric view, which will allow you to see the ceiling plan from above. This ability will be helpful for selecting lights from above if necessary.

FIGURE 12.88
Light groups

FIGURE 12.89
Creating light groups

Now assign the lights to the groups. Just select the lights and then assign to the light group from the context drop-down menu in the Options bar, as shown in Figure 12.90. Then do the same thing for the lights along the other wall.

Now return to the interior perspective. Before you start to render the view, let's test the light groups by rendering only the lights in the right group. To do this, turn off the lights in the left group by simply clicking the check box for that group in the Artificial Lights dialog box. Figure 12.91 shows the results.

Let's complete the rendering of the space with the other light group turned on. Keep in mind that the more lights you have turned on in your view, the longer the calculations will take, and, therefore, the longer it'll take to render your view. Figure 12.92 shows the results of this second rendering. This figure also illustrates the ability to adjust the exposure in a completed rendering.

FIGURE 12.90
Assigning light groups

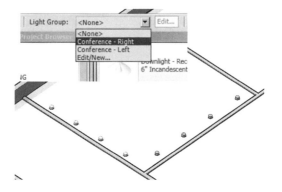

FIGURE 12.91
Rendering light groups

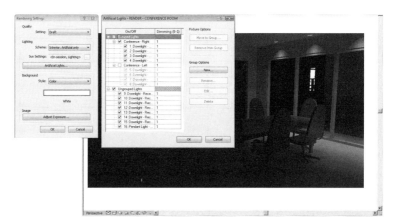

FIGURE 12.92
Rendering both light groups

By default, the image will have a sepia tone. You can remove the sepia tone by adjusting the White Point value.

Keep in mind that what you're looking for is how the lighting affects the space. Are the lights too close or too far apart? In Figure 12.93, we've added more lights to brighten the room. Add some additional lighting along the other two walls.

FIGURE 12.93
Adding more lights

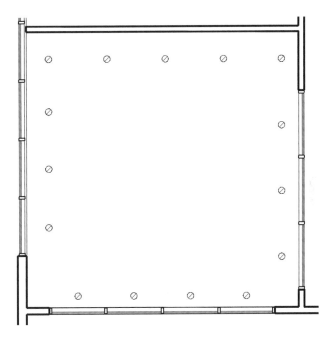

After rendering the space with all the lights, what's becoming apparent is that the lights aren't illuminating the conference table (Figure 12.94). You need to add a nice linear lighting source above the table in order to understand the effect that light will have on the space. Again, it's important that you do this without the distraction of materials.

FIGURE 12.94
Rendering without
center lights

Use the Revit family Pendant Light - Linear - 1 Lamp found in the family folder under Lighting ➤ Architectural ➤ Interior and place it over the conference table, as shown in Figure 12.95. A great technique is to use a 3D view that's oriented to the top and then set the view to Wireframe.

FIGURE 12.95
Placing the light in top-oriented 3D Wireframe view

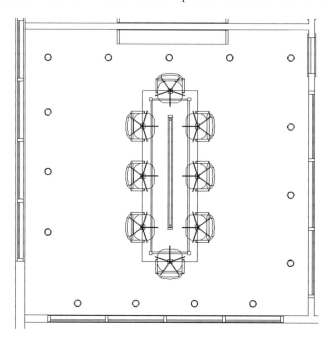

This approach allows you to place elements in the ceiling but also see their context and center the light properly with regard to the conference table and chairs. This time you'll have to put the lens in an Object subcategory. Figure 12.96 shows the light in 3D. The type properties of the light have also been adjusted to allow the light to hang down from the ceiling, as shown.

FIGURE 12.96
Conference table light

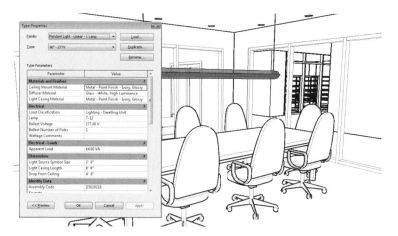

The light doesn't have a lens, but you'll make one and then assign it to a subcategory in order to test a rendering with the lens turned off and on. First, check the visibility settings of Lighting

Fixtures, and in the Visibility Graphics dialog box, notice that the Object subcategories are only Hidden Lines and Light Source. This will change in a moment when you add Lens to the list.

Select the linear light you placed over the conference table and open the family in the Family Editor. Open the Right elevation. Now, create an extrusion, as shown in Figure 12.97.

FIGURE 12.97
Extrusion sketch

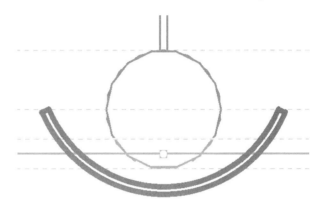

You'll be prompted to select a work plane. Select the work plane, Light Source Axis, shown in Figure 12.98.

FIGURE 12.98
Selecting a work plane

Don't forget to align and lock the finished extrusion to the reference planes in the front elevation, as shown Figure 12.99.

FIGURE 12.99
Align and lock

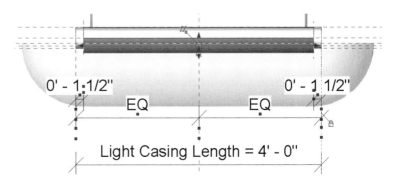

Also, it is important to note that there's a lens of sorts in the light fixture, which you can see in Figure 12.100. Delete this geometry from your light because you've already created a new lens.

FIGURE 12.100
Delete the original
lens geometry.

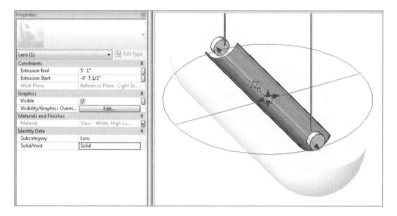

Now reload the light family into your project. At this point, if you were to render the view, you'll notice that light can't make it past the lens, as shown in Figure 12.101.

FIGURE 12.101
Rendering with a
lens

Eventually, the lens will have a translucent material that will allow the light to shine through. But for rendering matte images, you may not want the light blocked so severely. You'll control this by assigning a subcategory to the lens geometry that will allow you to turn off all the lenses in the view at one time, particularly if you use the same naming convention for all the lenses that you put in your lighting fixtures.

Now return to the light family and create a parameter to control the material of the lens. You'll also create and assign the lens to an Object subcategory. Let's step through how to do these things.

First, select Object Styles from the Modify tab. Then create the Object subcategory and name it Lens, as shown in Figure 12.102.

Close the dialog box and then select the lens. Now you can assign this geometry to the subcategory that you just created in the Properties palette (Figure 12.103).

FIGURE 12.102
Creating the
subcategory

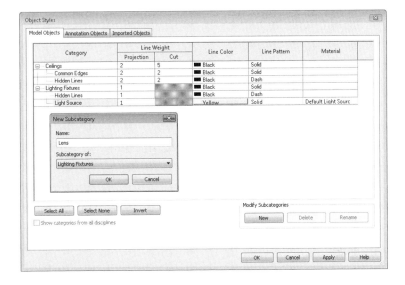

FIGURE 12.103
Assigning the
subcategory

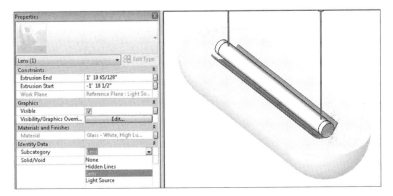

Now that you've created and assigned the subcategory, let's assign the material parameter. You already have the material parameter Diffuser Material from the geometry that you deleted. So just assign this to the new lens, as shown in Figure 12.104.

FIGURE 12.104
Creating and
assigning the mate-
rial parameter

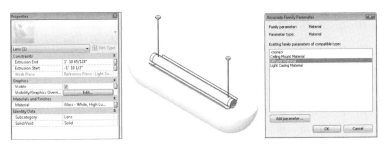

Don't worry about assigning an actual material for now. In practice, it'll only change in the project. So you'll wait to assign it in the project environment rather than in the Family Editor.

Reload the light into the project and open the Visibility Graphics dialog box for the view. There's a subcategory for the Lens part of the lighting fixture. Uncheck this value, as shown in Figure 12.105. The lens is turned off, which is perfect!

FIGURE 12.105

Deselecting the
Lens subcategory

Now re-render the view. The results will look like Figure 12.106. Note that the lens for the linear light isn't showing, but this is fine. You're after the lighting effect of the lighting fixture. The lens will come back on when you render with all the materials showing.

FIGURE 12.106

Rendered view

If you want your rendering to seem more complete than just a rendering of the building elements, you'll have to add entourage. But you don't want to clutter all your views with the kinds of things that you want to add that will not be part of your document set.

WORKING WITH ENTOURAGE

Worksets are great for controlling this part of your project. By creating a workset called Entourage, you'll be able to place your project content on a workset where all of its visibility can be quickly and easily controlled. But before creating and assigning elements to this workset, make sure the workset is turned off by default in other views.

This means that the entourage will not show up in existing or new views until you turn them on, otherwise, you'll have to turn this workset off in all present and future views. This will save you a lot of time as you add entourage to your project.

Materials

Now that you have determined the right lighting effects using matte materials, you can set the phase back to Show Complete. You'll also want to turn on the visibility for the curtain wall panels as well as the lens in the linear lighting fixture and render the view. Keep in mind that with all the new materials, transparency, and reflectivity, it will take quite a bit longer to re-render the view (Figure 12.107).

FIGURE 12.107
Rendering with material

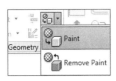

Once you render the view and you can start to see the transparency and reflectivity in the curtain panels, the rendering takes on a much more realistic effect. You can also see the materials in the table and chairs as well as the lens for the linear light above the conference table.

At the moment, all of the materials that are assigned to the walls in this view are based on the properties of the wall. And creating surface materials for every different wall would result in a very long list of wall types! A better method of assigning materials on a case-by-case basis is to use the Paint tool.

To assign materials to host elements, select the Paint tool on the Modify tab.

To add a unique material to a wall, hover over the wall and select the surface. To remove a unique material assignment, select the Remove Paint tool, hover over the wall, and select it. The paint material will be removed.

The Bottom Line

Create real-time and rendered analytic visualizations.   Analytic visualization is about communicating information about your project in a nonliteral way, and it's very important! It's not about showing real materials in the project but using filters to visualize important metadata.

Master It   During the renovation of a space, you want to reuse the doors rather than throw them away. How would you illustrate this?

Render emotive photorealistic visualizations.   Photorealistic visualization is also about communicating design ideas but in emotive ways that are much closer to how the space will be experienced, including real lighting, materials, and entourage. Just remember that the time it takes to calculate and render your views will change dramatically based on the quality and resolution of your views.

Master It   Would the rendering for a PowerPoint presentation differ from a rendering being printed for a marketing brochure?

Understand the importance of sequencing your visualization workflow.   The sequence of design — building, content, materials, and cameras — is not the same as the sequence for visualization (geometry/cameras, lighting, materials). Lighting is far more important than materials of actual objects. Get the lighting right and the materials will look great, but not the other way around.

Master It   How do you create a rendering environment that replaces the actual materials with matte materials in order to study the effects of lighting on your design?

Part 4

Extended Modeling Techniques

In Part 3 we covered a variety of topics that are primarily useful in — although not exclusive to — the earlier design phases of a project. As you continue to develop your designs, there will be an increased specificity to the elements required in the building information model. You will need to expand your knowledge of the fundamental components of a building model, including walls, floors, roofs, stairs, and railings. In addition, you will likely be required to understand and create your own families. This part will dig deep into rich, component-building skills necessary for mastering Autodesk® Revit® Architecture software.

Chapter 13

Walls and Curtain Walls

According to the American Institute of Architects (AIA) document *E202 BIM Protocol Exhibit* (the AIA's current contract document for BIM), there are five levels of model development ranging from 100 to 500. If you examine excerpts from the model content requirements describing each level of development (LOD) for the design professions — LOD 100, LOD 200, and LOD 300 — the evolution of modeling granularity becomes apparent. Although LOD 100 represents a conceptual level of information defined as "overall building massing," LOD 200 and LOD 300 are represented by "generalized systems or assemblies" and "specific assemblies," respectively. This chapter will help you create walls that comply with both LOD 200 and LOD 300.

Four different kinds of walls can be created: basic walls, stacked walls, curtain walls, and in-place walls. In this chapter, you'll explore the skills you'll need to create and customize walls to meet the needs of your design. You will also dive into the new and exciting realm of complex curtain wall and panel generation made possible with the conceptual massing tools in Autodesk® Revit® Architecture software.

In this chapter, you'll learn to:

- ◆ Use extended modeling techniques for basic walls
- ◆ Create stacked walls
- ◆ Create simple curtain walls
- ◆ Create complex curtain walls

Using Extended Modeling Techniques for Basic Walls

As you might already know, walls in the Revit environment are made from layers of materials that can represent generic placeholders for design layouts to complete assemblies representative of actual construction. These layers are assigned functions that allow them to react to similar layers in other walls as well as in floors and roofs. The function assignments within object assemblies give you a predictable graphic representation when you join these types of overlapping elements.

After you have become familiar with the basic modeling functions for walls, you'll probably need to create your own wall types to achieve more complex designs. As you also add more information into the source of your building model, you will be able to extract more useful results through intelligent tagging and schedules. In the following sections, we'll show you how to get the most out of your basic wall types.

Creating Basic Wall Types

Walls and curtain walls are Revit *system families*, which means they exist in a project but cannot be saved as individual families outside of the project file (RFA files). Other system families include floors, ceilings, roofs, stairs, railings, and mullions. There are only three ways to create or add new system families to your project:

◆ Duplicate a type from one that already exists and modify its properties

◆ Copy and paste them in as objects from one project to another

◆ Use the Transfer Project Standards tool

In Chapter 4, "Configuring Templates and Standards," we discussed different strategies for managing standard content through the use of templates. If you have a series of standard wall types you use on every project, you have the option of either storing them in your main project template using the *subtractive method* or storing them in separate container project folders in an *additive method*. If you need to make new, custom types that are not part of your template, you can create new wall types on the fly at any stage of a project by duplicating existing types, adding or removing wall layers, and adjusting the parameters to meet your requirements. Regardless of which method you employ to manage templates and standard system families, we will show you how to create and customize your own wall types in the following sections.

Within a project file, you can access and edit a wall type in one of two ways:

◆ In the Project Browser, scroll down to the Families category, locate any wall type, right-click it, and select Properties, or simply double-click the wall type name.

◆ Select a wall in the model or start the Wall command, open the Properties palette, and click Edit Type.

The Type Properties dialog box will appear (Figure 13.1). If you don't see the graphic preview to the left, click the Preview button at the bottom of the dialog box.

FIGURE 13.1
The Type Properties dialog box for a wall

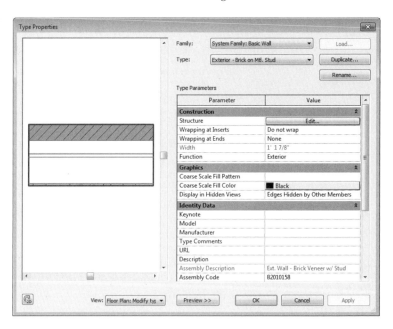

Project Gallery

This gallery is a collection of some of the work being produced by architects and designers in the trenches using Autodesk® Revit® software. The work shown here is all real work for real clients (or projects done by real students), and the work represents the full gamut of how these firms use Revit as a tool. Some are using Revit strictly for documentation and visualization, whereas others are pushing toward sustainability or construction. Firms range in size from just four people to a few hundred architects. Regardless of the size of your office or your IT department, you can produce truly elegant work using building information modeling (BIM).

University of Kansas

Brooklyn Film Forum Conceptual Project   The Brooklyn Film Forum helps artists create new works through the use of new and evolving technologies while also creating a place for a diverse group of artists to meet. Its goals are to create an environment to support the creation and dissemination of independent media that promotes democracy, community participation, cultural preservation, access, and lifelong learning to a diverse community of artists and audiences. The forum assists with commissions and residencies, production services, education and information programs, and the presentation and distribution of work.

Images in this section courtesy of Lauren Hickman, LEED AP, Master's in Architecture at the College of Architecture at the University of Kansas.
Source: http://sadp.ku.edu/

BROOKLYN FILM FORUM

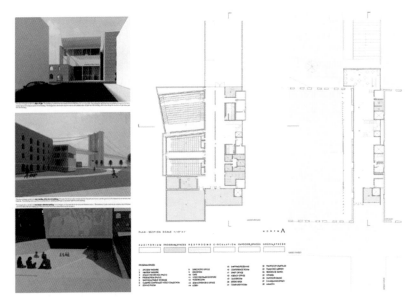

LakeFlato

Texas Home   A private ranch house and family retreat that is in addition to an existing residence located in North Texas. It consists of six independent structures nestled among a grove of oak trees. Each structure serves a specific function. A central "living room" acts as the public pavilion of the compound, while the two guest wings, two accessory buildings, and motor court complete the courtyard. Breaking up the program in this way allows the compound to be used comfortably for either large groups or just a family.

The structures, built of local indigenous materials such as western red cedar, stone, weathered steel pipe, and natural metal panels, find their formal inspiration from the modest vernacular ranch buildings, barns, and sheds. Covered walkways connect the six independent structures and frame a series of courtyards anchored by existing oak trees. These outdoor rooms capture the prevailing breezes and help cool the adjacent interior spaces. The project is defined by its modest scale, simple detailing, and seamless integration into the landscape.

Images in this section courtesy of LakeFlato.
Source: http://www.lakeflato.com

LAKE | FLATO

el dorado Architects

Richardson Memorial Hall Renovation   The Richardson Memorial Hall Renovation is a collaboration between el dorado Architects and FXFowle. The main goal of the conceptual study was to maximize the functional and operational performance of the building, which houses the Tulane School of Architecture. The project includes the renovation of the historical 1909 Richardsonian structure and the addition of an innovative four-story structure to the east. The design addresses a fundamental shift that has occurred in recent years in architectural education — toward more flexibility and connectivity. The renovated building will encourage more interaction between students, faculty, and administration, and between the school itself and the New Orleans community at large.

Images in this section courtesy of el dorado Architects and FXFowle.
Source: www.eldo.us

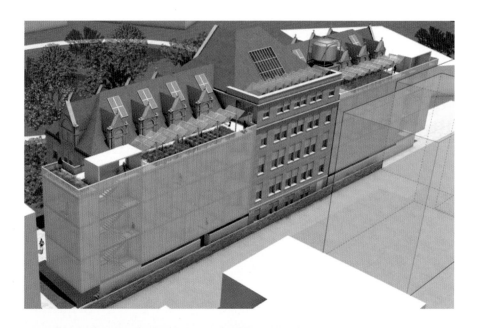

el dorado

FXFOWLE

Project Sauron

The Evil Lair Sometimes you're an evil genius trying to design your lair. If you're unfamiliar with recent trends in lair design, the use of BIM has become an important feature during design, into construction (clashing rockets with your cave entrance), and well into facilities management. Evil lairs don't run themselves and the hidden truth is it takes a lot of henchmen to keep a lair running like clockwork.

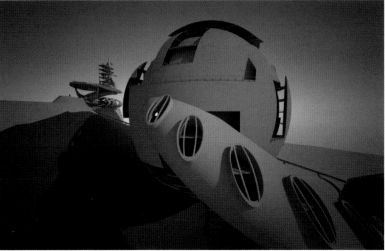

Images in this section courtesy of Project Sauron.
Source: https://twitter.com/#!/ProjectSauron

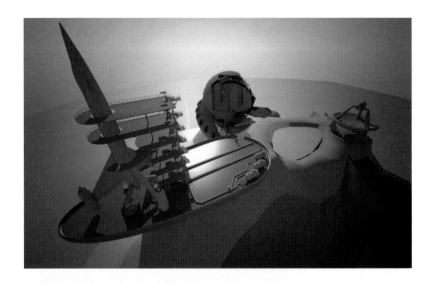

AECOM

University of Houston Hofheinz Pavilion   The University of Houston hired AECOM to develop designs for a proposed new 40,000-seat football stadium and the renovation of Hofheinz Pavilion. The pavilion, which will be home to the University of Houston Cougars men's and women's basketball teams and the women's volleyball team, includes two new practice courts and seats 8,593 spectators.

Ole Miss Stadium Expansion   Ole Miss University hired AECOM to assist in the phase I development of a new basketball arena and football stadium expansion. The proposed arena would be centrally located on campus and would seat approximately 10,500. The football stadium expansion would enclose the north end zone and would include suites, clubs, and additional seating. The initial scope for both projects included concept design, cost estimating, and fundraising materials.

Images in this section courtesy of AECOM.
Source: www.aecom.com

Open Studio

303 Accelerator   This project is capitalizing on significant shifts in the way office space is defined and is reinterpreting how to deliver a highly adaptable environment over the growth and often unknown change of an early startup company. Drawing momentum from a number of local upstart high-tech companies, this multitenant project will assemble some of the most advanced and yet-to-be-known companies into one building along with like-minded innovators in real estate and design to provide temporary, monthly, or long-term office space for companies of one looking to draw from others' energy or companies of ten who simply can't define their real estate needs from month to month.

Crossroads 404   The Crossroads office building is a 1980s multitenant, seven-story office building, recently acquired for repositioning in the San Diego office market. The building had three major issues limiting its competitiveness — image and finding the building from the highway, identification of primary entry, and most important, a precast and brick skin that was failing and spalling off the building. The solution was to reclad the entire building skin (excluding windows) with an updated look that would address each of the issues while maintaining current occupancy and minimal disruption to the existing tenants. The solution is a combination of a lightweight honeycomb-backed metal panel rain screen (light-colored field material) and a fiber-cement rainscreen to accent the entry and public spaces. The address of the building was simplified and branded as "404" with orange metal accents along the high portion of the highway façade and at the second level near the main entry.

open studio | architecture

HOK

Spa and Wellness Resort Set on the coast of Dubai, the project is a luxury spa and wellness resort. Among the resort facilities and in a privileged location in the site, the Breakwater Restaurant is an iconic 360-degree view lantern for fine dining. Based on the concept of a free-standing flower about to blossom and to allow for a dramatic transformation between day and night, the building is based on the arrangement of elliptical shapes and wrapped in organic "sails" that will shield the sun yet allow views out. The organic sails were modeled as NURBS surfaces in Rhino and then imported into Revit as hosts to highly customized curtain walls, where the mullions formed the structural framing and the horizontal shading panels.

Images in this section courtesy of HOK.
Source: http://hok.com

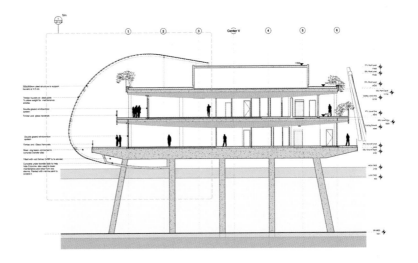

EDITING WALL STRUCTURE

The first aspect we will discuss is the editing of a wall type's structure. To access these settings, select Structure as the parameter to edit. This will open the Edit Assembly dialog box, shown in Figure 13.2. From here you can add or delete wall layers, define their materials, move layers in and out of the core boundaries, and assign functions to each layer. You can also add sweeps and reveals or modify the vertical constraints of the layers.

FIGURE 13.2
The Edit Assembly dialog box lets you define the construction layers of a wall type.

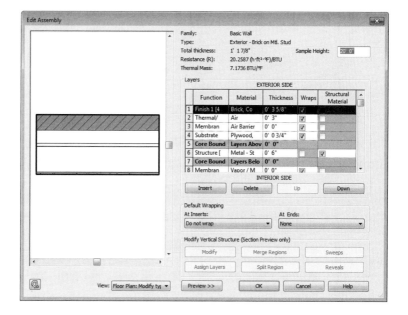

This dialog box is divided into four zones: the Preview window, the Layers table, the Default Wrapping option, and the Modify Vertical Structure options (which are active only when the preview is set to section display). The area above the Layers zone holds basic reporting about the wall type: its family name, sample height in the Preview window, thickness, and thermal properties.

Preview window   On the left side of the dialog box, you will see a graphic preview of the wall structure in plan or section. If you didn't activate it in the Type Properties dialog box, click the Preview button at the bottom of the dialog box. To switch from the default plan view to the section view or vice versa, click the drop-down list next to View to choose an alternate viewing option. In the preview, the core boundaries of the wall are shown with green lines. Note that in the section preview, each wall layer is highlighted in blue when you select a row in the Layers table. Also note that you can change the height of the wall shown in the section preview by modifying the Sample Height value in the upper-right part of the dialog box. You can use any mouse-based navigation method to adjust the preview as well as activate the SteeringWheels® feature by clicking the button at the bottom right of the dialog box.

Layers table   The Layers table is where you add, delete, move, and define layers of the wall structure. Each wall layer is represented as a separate row of information. Two of the rows are gray, representing the core boundaries of the wall (which will be discussed in greater detail later in this chapter in the section "Wall Core"). The table is divided into five columns:

Function This column provides six choices for wall layer functions that relate to the purpose of the material in the assembly. Each of these functions defines a priority that determines how it joins with other walls, floors, and roofs. Note that the numeric priority is more important to understand than the name of the function itself.

◆ Structure [1] defines the structural components of the wall that should support the rest of the wall layers. This function gives the highest priority to a wall layer and allows it to join with other structural layers by cutting through lower-priority layers.

◆ Substrate [2] defines continuous board materials such as plywood, particle, and gypsum board.

◆ Thermal/Air [3] defines the wall's thermal insulation layer and/or an air gap.

◆ The Membrane Layer is a zero-thickness material that usually represents vapor prevention.

◆ Finish 1 [4] specifies a finish layer to use if you have only one layer of finish.

◆ Finish 2 [5] specifies a secondary, weaker finish layer.

With the exception of the Membrane Layer, which has no priority assigned, all the other layers have a priority value from 1 to 5. These priorities determine how to clean up the intersections between various layers when two or more walls are joined. The principle is simply explained: Priority 1 is the highest and 5 is the lowest. A layer that has a priority of 1 will cut through any other layer with a lower priority (2, 3, 4, or 5). A layer with priority 2 will cut through layers with priority 3, 4, or 5, and so on. In Figure 13.3, layers with the same priority clean up when the two intersecting walls are joined. Notice the way the finish layers don't join on the right side of the vertical wall because one has a priority 4 and the other is priority 5.

FIGURE 13.3
Layers with the same priority clean up when joined.

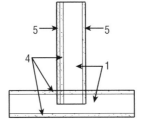

Material Associating a material to a wall layer provides graphic (color, cut/surface patterns, and render appearance), identifiable (mark, keynote, description, and so on), and physical characteristics (for analysis purposes) for each wall layer. Using material takeoffs, you can calculate quantities of individual materials used in wall assemblies throughout your project. Keynoting and material tagging functionality is also supported through wall layers and is discussed in greater detail in Chapter 19, "Annotating the Design."

A material definition also affects cleanup between layers of joined walls. If the priority of the layers is the same and the material is the same, the software cleans up the join between these two layers. If the priority of the layers is the same but the materials are different, the two layers are separated graphically with a thin line. In Figure 13.4 the structure layer of one of the joined walls was simply changed from Metal - Stud Layer to Metal - Stud Layer 2.

FIGURE 13.4
Two layers with the same priority but different materials. The separation between the two layers is indicated with a thin line.

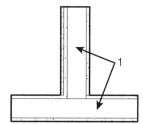

> **Thickness** This value represents the actual thickness of the material. Note that the membrane layer is the only layer that can have a thickness of zero.
>
> **Wraps** Wall layers rarely end with exposed edges at wall ends or wall openings, windows, or doors. This option allows a layer to wrap around other layers when an opening or wall end is encountered. Figure 13.5 illustrates the layer wrapping of the outer wall layer based on the closure plane defined in the window family. Layer wrapping will be covered in greater detail later in this chapter.

FIGURE 13.5
Layer wrapping is a result of a coordinated approach between wall layers and hosted families such as windows.

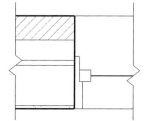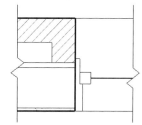

> **Structural Material** This value represents whether the material within the wall assembly is load bearing or structurally significant in any way. In the example here, you can see that the Structure [1] Functional material, Metal Studs, was given a check mark by default.

Default Wrapping Although you can specify whether each wall layer will wrap in the Layers table, you must also specify whether these options are activated at all in the wall type. To activate this option, you must decide whether the wrapping should occur at openings, wall ends, or both. For inserts, you can choose Do Not Wrap, Exterior, Interior, or Both. Similarly, for wall ends the options are None, Exterior, and Interior. The default wrapping parameters appear in both the Edit Assembly dialog box and the wall's Type Properties dialog box.

Modify Vertical Structure These settings are available only when you enable the section view in the Preview window. In this area of the Edit Assembly dialog box, you can add articulation to the wall type using any combination of cornices, reveals, trims, and panels. We will discuss these in the section "Adding Wall Articulation" later in this chapter.

In summary, editing a wall type's structure begins with adding or deleting wall layers. Each layer is assigned a priority, material, thickness, and wrapping option. To move layers up and down in the table or to add and remove layers, use the buttons at the bottom of the Layers table. Next we will cover some more complex aspects of wall structure in greater detail: *wall cores, function,* and *layer wrapping.*

WALL CORE

One of the unique functions of a basic wall is its ability to identify a core. The wall core is more than a layer of material; in fact, it can comprise several material layers. It defines the structural part of the wall and influences the behavior of the wall and how it interacts with other elements in the model. The core boundaries are references to which you can dimension or constrain sketch lines when you use the Pick Walls selection option for floors, ceilings, or roofs.

The example shown in Figure 13.6 illustrates a sample floor in Sketch mode where the outer core boundary of the wall was selected using the Pick Walls method. Note that the core boundaries of the wall are shown as dashed lines for clarity.

FIGURE 13.6
A wall's outer core boundary is used to define an edge of the floor.

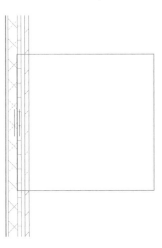

When floors generated with the Pick Walls method intersect the walls that were picked during Sketch mode, you will receive a prompt to automatically join the geometry and cut the overlapping volume out of the wall:

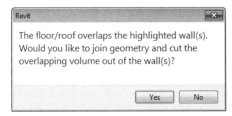

If you click Yes to this message and examine the intersection of the wall and floor in a section view, you will see the result of the joined elements (Figure 13.7). Note that you can get the joining prompt to appear again simply by selecting the floor, clicking the Edit Boundary button in the ribbon, and then clicking Finish Edit Mode (green check icon). If any portion of the selected floor and related walls still overlap but are not joined, the prompt will be displayed.

FIGURE 13.7
Section detail of joined wall and floor slab

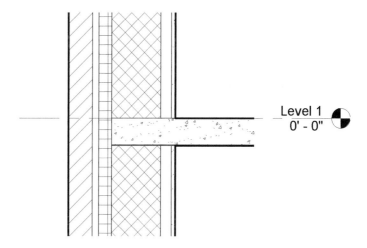

Level 1
0' - 0"

FUNCTION

The Function type property of walls is a simple list of values, but it can be used in very powerful ways. A wall's function can be used to filter schedules or as view filters — for example, if you wanted to hide interior walls for a series of drawings only showing core and shell (exterior) elements. The Function property also affects the default placement behavior when you create new walls. The behaviors associated with each function are as follows:

- Interior (Default height for new walls is set to the level above the active level.)
- Exterior (Default height is Unconnected: 20'-0" [8 m].)
- Foundation (Default height is determined as *Depth*, specified down from the active level.)
- Retaining (Default height is Unconnected: 6'-0" [2 m].)
- Soffit (Default height is Unconnected: 1'-0" [250 mm])
- Core shaft

The Function type property can also be used when exporting from Revit to CAD formats. You can export walls of different functions to specific layers assigned in the DWG Export Settings dialog box, shown in Figure 13.8.

LAYER WRAPPING

To create a layer wrapping solution for openings that reflect real-world conditions, you must define two settings. First, select the layer(s) of the wall structure you want to wrap and check the boxes in the Wraps column of the Edit Assembly dialog box. You must then specify the default wrapping behavior for the wall type. These default settings can be set in either the Edit Assembly or Type Properties dialog box, as shown in Figure 13.9.

FIGURE 13.8
Wall functions can
be assigned to dif-
ferent layers for
exported CAD files.

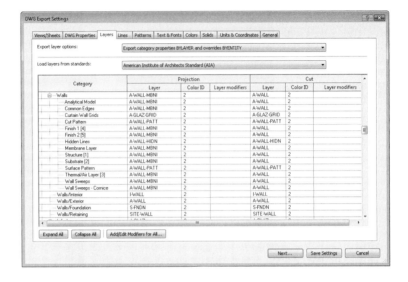

FIGURE 13.9
Default wrapping
options can be set
in Edit Assembly or
Type Properties.

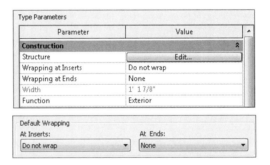

Specifying the layer wrap settings in the wall type alone may not be sufficient to generate the graphic results you desire. Another set of rules established in hosted families allows you to further customize how layers in a wall will wrap to inserted objects. The following exercise will illustrate this functionality.

Begin by opening the file c13-Wall-Wrapping.rvt from this book's website: www.sybex.com/go/masteringrevit2013. Activate the Level 1 floor plan, and you should see a wall with an inserted window as shown here.

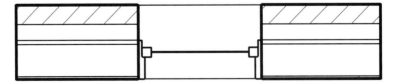

Next, you're going to follow the steps below to create the wall wrap:

1. To begin the exercise, select the wall, open the Properties palette, and click Edit Type. Notice that Wrapping At Inserts is set to Do Not Wrap and Wrapping At Ends is set to None.

2. Click OK to close the Type Properties dialog box.

3. Select the inserted window and click Edit Family on the Modify | Windows tab in the ribbon.

4. When the Window family opens, go to the Project Browser and activate the floor plan named Floor Line.

   You will notice that this window family has been slightly modified from the original Fixed window family in the Revit default library. Two reference planes have been added that allow the depth of the window frame and the wall wrapping to be customized.

5. Find the reference plane named Closure, select it, and open the Properties palette. Find the parameter named Wall Closure and make sure the option is checked, as shown in Figure 13.10.

FIGURE 13.10
Assign the Wall Closure parameter to a reference plane.

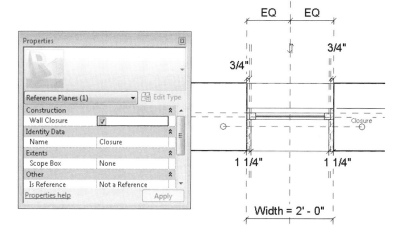

6. Create a dimension between the exterior face of the sample wall and the Closure reference plane. Note that you may need to use the Tab key to ensure that you have selected the wall reference and not the centerline of the wall or any other extraneous reference plane.

7. Click the Esc key or the Modify button to exit the dimension command and select the dimension you just created.

8. On the Options bar, find the Label drop-down list and choose <Add Parameter…>.

9. In the Parameter Properties dialog box, type **Exterior Wall Closure** in the Name field and click OK to close the dialog box.

10. Click Load Into Project from the Family Editor panel in the ribbon. Note that you may be prompted to select a project or family if you have more than the two sample files open. When prompted with the Family Already Exists dialog box, select Overwrite The Existing Version.

11. In the Level 1 floor plan of the example project, select the wall and click Edit Type from the Properties palette. From the Structure parameter, click Edit.

12. In the Edit Assembly dialog box, find row 1, which will have a function of Finish 1 [4], and the material Masonry - Brick. Make sure the Wraps option is checked.

13. Set the Wrapping At Inserts option to Exterior and click OK to close both dialog boxes.

You should now see the masonry layer wrapping into the opening in the wall created by the inserted window. You can now customize the depth at which the brick will wrap.

14. Select the window and click Edit Type from the Properties palette. Find the Exterior Wall Closure parameter and change the value to 0'-6 5/8".

15. Click OK to close the Type Properties dialog box. Notice how the depth of the wrapped masonry layer changes in the plan view.

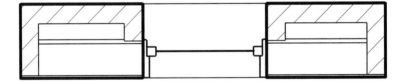

Adding Wall Articulation

If you need to develop more complex and articulated finishes expressed horizontally along the vertical surfaces of certain walls, you can customize wall types in a variety of ways to achieve just about any aesthetic effect. Reveals and sweeps can be added to a wall type, and you can edit the vertical extents of material layers. You can find a good example of this kind of wall in the default project template. The wall type Exterior - Brick and CMU on MTL. Stud (Figure 13.11) contains a variety of sweeps, reveals, and vertical modifications of material layers.

To access these settings, select any wall in your project and click Edit Type in the Properties palette. You can also find the wall type in the Project Browser; double-click it to open the Type Properties dialog box. Once it is open, make sure the preview pane is open and the view in the preview is set to Section. Within the Type Parameters options, click the Edit button in the Structure field to open the Edit Assembly dialog box and begin modifying the layers and vertical articulation of the wall type, as shown in Figure 13.12.

FIGURE 13.11
Sample wall with
added articulation

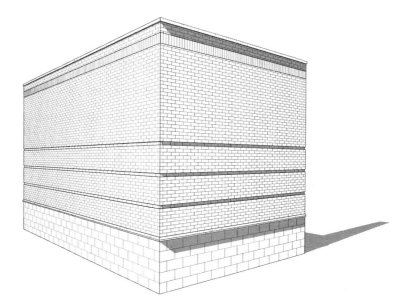

FIGURE 13.12
With the section
view active, tools
for modifying the
vertical structure
become active.

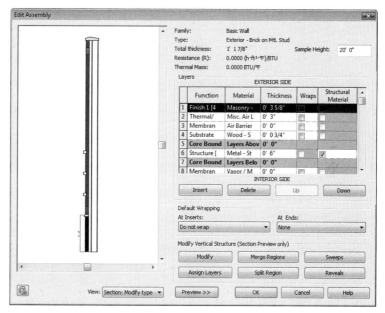

In the following sections, we'll examine how to create these types of articulation in your wall type. To begin the exercises, create a new project using the default.rte or DefaultMetric.rte template. Create a single wall segment using the type Exterior – Brick On Mtl. Stud. You will create a new wall type based on this wall throughout the following exercises.

ASSIGNING TWO DIFFERENT MATERIALS ON THE FINISH FACE OF A WALL

We will begin our series of exercises by creating a new wall type based on an existing layered wall structure. Select the wall segment you created using the type Exterior – Brick On Mtl. Stud and open the Type Properties dialog box. Click the Duplicate button and create a new wall type named **Mastering - Wall Exercise**.

Now let's assume that you need to create a partial region of the finish face where the material is different. For example, you might want to use a split-face concrete block at the base of the wall instead of brick:

1. With the Type Properties dialog box open, click the Edit button in the Structure field to open the Edit Assembly dialog box. Make sure the Preview Pane is open and the view is set to Section.

2. In the upper right of the Edit Assembly dialog box, change the Sample Height value to 6'-0" [2 m]. Use either the SteeringWheel button at the lower left of the dialog box or your mouse to zoom into the shorter segment of wall in the Preview Pane.

3. Click the Split Region button under Modify Vertical Structure and move your mouse pointer along the inside face of the brick layer to a point 4'-0" [1200 mm] above the bottom of the sample, as shown in Figure 13.13. Note that when you split the layer, the thickness value of the layer indicates it is variable.

FIGURE 13.13
Splitting the exterior finish into two materials

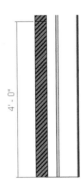
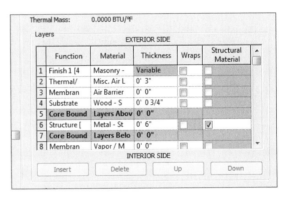

	Function	Material	Thickness	Wraps	Structural Material	
1	Finish 1 [4	Masonry -	Variable	☐	☐	
2	Thermal/	Misc. Air L	0' 3"	☐	☐	
3	Membran	Air Barrier	0' 0"	☐	☐	
4	Substrate	Wood - S	0' 0 3/4"	☐	☐	
5	Core Bound	Layers Abov	0' 0"			
6	Structure [	Metal - St	0' 6"	☐	☑	
7	Core Bound	Layers Belo	0' 0"			
8	Membran	Vapor / M	0' 0"	☐	☐	

Thermal Mass: 0.0000 BTU/°F

Layers

EXTERIOR SIDE

INTERIOR SIDE

Insert   Delete   Up   Down

4. Click the Insert button to add another row immediately below the first exterior layer. Change its function to Finish 1 and its material to Masonry. To open the Material dialog, select the material assignment under the Material column. Using the Graphics tab, set the cut pattern to Masonry – Concrete Block. Then click OK to close the Materials dialog box.

5. Click the Assign Layer button, select the new row you created in the previous step, and then click the lower portion of the split region in the section preview.

6. Click OK to close all open dialog boxes and save your project for additional exercises in this chapter.

After you assign a material row to a split layer, you'll notice that the thickness values of the two layers are linked but you can't change them in the table. To change the thickness of a split wall layer, click the Modify button and select one of the faces in the section preview. Edit the temporary dimensions to change the thickness of the layer.

You may also notice that once a layer is split and an additional layer is assigned to the split portion, the resulting portions can only be the same thickness. To create a similar result with a layer of varying thickness, you will need to create a stacked wall. We will discuss this later in "Creating Stacked Walls."

If you encounter a situation where you need to merge horizontal or vertical layers that already exist in a wall type, use the Merge Regions button and select a line in the section preview between two layers. Once the mouse pointer is over a line between two layers, an arrow indicating which layer will override the other appears, as shown in Figure 13.14.

FIGURE 13.14
(A) Merge vertical layers; (B) merge layers that were previously split.

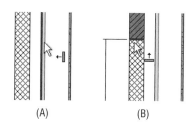

(A)   (B)

SWEEPS AND REVEALS

Many walls have horizontal articulations that are either attached to or embedded in the wall assembly. Cornices, soldier courses, and reveals are examples of elements that can be incorporated into wall types. To begin adding these, we will continue our previous exercise of creating a new wall type named Mastering - Wall Exercise. In the following exercise, you will add a bull-nose sweep to the wall:

1. Return to the wall's type properties and open the Edit Assembly dialog box.

2. Click the Sweeps button to open the Wall Sweeps dialog box. Click the Load Profile button and open the file `c13-Profile-Bullnose.rfa`, which can be downloaded from this book's companion website.

3. Click the Add button to insert a sweep row. Change the values in the row as follows:

   ♦ Profile: c13-Profile-Bullnose: $3\frac{5}{8}$" D × 2" H

   ♦ Material: Concrete - Precast Concrete

   ♦ Distance: 4'-0" [1.2 m]

   ♦ From: Base

   ♦ Side: Exterior

   ♦ Cuts Wall: Checked

   ♦ Cuttable: Checked

4. Click Apply and you should see the sweep appear just above the split region, as shown in Figure 13.15.

FIGURE 13.15

Bullnose sweep
added to wall
assembly

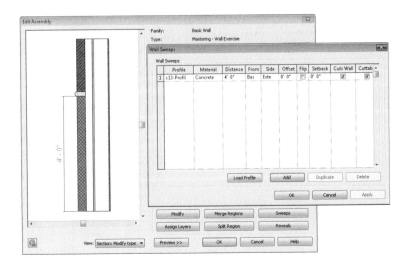

Notice that the loaded profile was created for predictable results when placed in a wall assembly. For your own wall, you may need to adjust the offset, flip, and setback values to achieve the desired results. Next, you'll add a different profile to the same assembly.

5. Click OK to close the Wall Sweeps dialog box. In the Edit Assembly dialog box, change the Sample Height value to 12'-0" so that the next sweep addition won't conflict with the one you just added. Adjust the section view as required to see the whole wall.

6. Click Sweeps to reopen the Wall Sweeps dialog box. Click Load Profile again and navigate to the default library. From the Profiles folder, select either Cornice-Precast.rfa or M_Cornice-Precast.rfa.

7. Click Add to create another new row and change the values in the row as follows:

   ◆ Profile: Cornice-Precast

   ◆ Material: Concrete – Precast Concrete

   ◆ Distance: 0'-0"

   ◆ From: Top

   ◆ Side: Exterior

   ◆ Offset: –0'-3 $\frac{5}{8}$" [–76 mm]

8. Notice that the order of the rows is automatically adjusted, based on the vertical relationship of the sweeps added to the wall. Click OK to close the Wall Sweeps dialog box.

   Notice that a negative value for Offset was specified to bring the cornice sweep into the exterior finish layer. Vertical adjustments can be made by assigning positive or negative values in the Distance column.

9. Click OK to close all open dialog boxes and save the project file for additional exercises in this chapter.

The process to create reveals is almost identical to that used to create sweeps. Simply click the Reveals button to open the Reveals dialog box. Experiment with adding your own reveals to the wall type you're creating throughout this chapter's exercises. We've added two reveals to the wall assembly (Figure 13.16) using the default Reveal-Brick Course profile family.

FIGURE 13.16
Reveals have been added to the compound wall assembly.

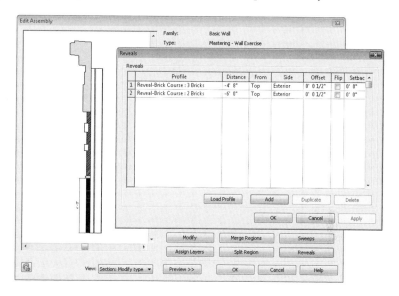

If you create two or more walls using your new compound wall type, you'll see how nicely the sweeps wrap around corners in a 3D or camera view, as shown in Figure 13.17.

FIGURE 13.17
Camera view of compound wall with reveals and sweeps

Modifying Wall Sweep Returns

In the previous exercises, you learned how to include sweeps and reveals in the assembly of a wall type; however, you can also apply a sweep to a wall if it's only needed in a limited location. For example, you might need to create a fancy wainscot molding in one special room. To accomplish this, go to the Architecture tab in the ribbon and click Wall and then Wall Sweep. Note that you can place a sweep on a wall vertically or horizontally by changing the placement option in the ribbon while the Wall Sweep tool is active. Select a wall sweep type from the Properties palette and pick the wall faces to which you'd like to apply the sweep. If necessary, the sweep can be adjusted vertically in an elevation or section view.

Although profile families can be used in them, a wall sweep is a system family that exists only in a Revit project. New sweep types can be created only by using the Transfer Project Standards tool or by duplicating existing types within your active project. And keep in mind that once wall sweeps are added to your project, they can be scheduled like any other project component.

Let's take a look at how to customize the returns of a wall sweep:

1. Select the sweep and it will display grips at each end. You can simply drag either end of the sweep as required.

2. To change the way the sweep returns or turns a corner, click the Modify Returns button in the Modify | Wall Sweeps contextual ribbon. Notice that there are some additional settings in the Options bar.

   You can change the angle of the return or return it to a straight cut, but for now leave the options as Return and Angle = 90°.

3. The mouse pointer changes to a knife symbol, and when you click somewhere on the end of the sweep, it creates a new segment that can be wrapped around the edge of a wall or opening.

4. After picking one of the ends of the sweep, press Esc or use the Modify tool to exit the command.

5. Select the sweep again and drag the control to adjust the length of the sweep return around the corner of the wall. Figure 13.18 shows how the return can be wrapped around the edge of a wall.

Modeling Techniques for Basic Walls

In the previous sections, we explored methods to create a variety of basic wall types. When you begin to use these types to assemble your building model, there are still more methods at your disposal to further customize how walls are applied. Let's take a look at techniques you can use for modeling basic walls. Note that some of these techniques can be used for stacked walls and curtain walls as well.

Extending Wall Layers

In many types of construction, you'll need layers of materials to extend within or beyond the constraints of the wall. Some common examples include the extension of sheathing and siding on an exterior wall or gypsum wallboard extending only slightly above the ceiling for interior partitions (Figure 13.19).

FIGURE 13.18
Modified wall sweep returns: (a) without the return; (b) with the return checked

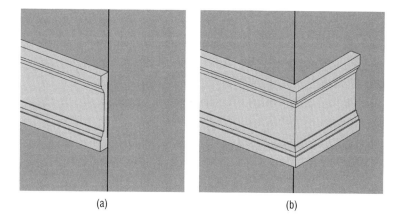

(a)   (b)

FIGURE 13.19
Examples of wall layers extending past or within the constraints of the wall

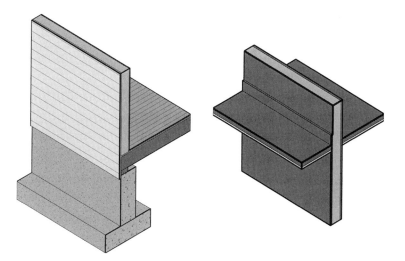

Enabling the extension of layers within a wall assembly requires you to unlock specific edges in the section preview of the Edit Assembly dialog box. Once layers have been unlocked, an instance parameter of the wall becomes active: either Base Extension Distance or Top Extension Distance (depending on which edges you unlocked). You can enter this value directly in the Properties palette or adjust it graphically in a section view by dragging the small blue triangle control at the edge of the unlocked layer. Let's go through an exercise to explore this functionality:

1. From the Architecture tab of the ribbon, select the Wall tool to create a new wall using any generic type. Select it and duplicate it by editing the type. Name the new type **Exterior Siding**.

2. Click Edit in the Structure field to open the Edit Assembly dialog box.

3. Add a new layer to the exterior of the wall, set its function to Finish (4), use the material Siding - Clapboard, and assign a thickness of $\frac{3}{4}$ " [18 mm].

4. Open the Preview Pane and switch to section view. Zoom into the bottom of the wall.

5. Select the Modify button and click the bottom edge of the exterior siding layer. Click the padlock icon to unlock the layer (Figure 13.20). Note that you can unlock as many layers as you like; however, the unlocked layers all need to be adjacent. For example, you cannot unlock wallboard layers on both sides of a framing layer.

FIGURE 13.20
Using the Modify button, click the padlock icon to unlock layers.

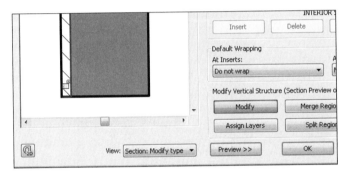

6. The siding layer is now unlocked. Click OK to close all open dialog boxes. Make sure the wall segment you created is still selected and the Properties palette is open. You'll see that the Base Extension Distance parameter is now enabled. Change the value to –10" [–250 mm] for this parameter and check the wall in 3D. You'll see that the siding layer is now extending 10" [250 mm] below the base of the wall, as shown in Figure 13.21.

7. If you switch to a section view and set Detail Level to Medium or Fine, select the wall and you will see small blue triangles at the edges of the layers that can be modified (Figure 13.22). You can drag the controls to the required offset or use the Align tool to set the unlocked edge to another reference object. If you Tab+select the edge, you can use the Move tool to set a precise distance as well.

Notice that there are also controls for layers that are locked. Editing the wall with a control of a locked layer changes the Base Offset or Top Offset value and will automatically adjust any Base Extension or Top Extension distances you previously established.

EDITING WALL JOINS

In another common design and construction scenario, you may need to specifically control how two or more walls behave when they intersect. There are a number of ways to customize these occurrences. Let's examine two scenarios where wall joins may need to be edited: phasing conditions and acute angled corners.

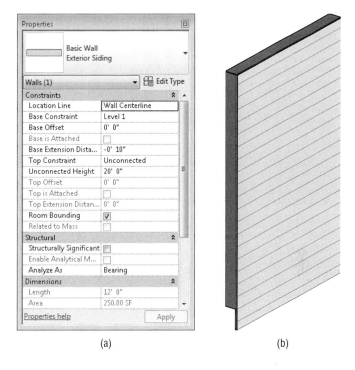

FIGURE 13.21
(a) Modifying the wall layer to have a base extension; (b) the resultant wall with an extended siding condition

(a)   (b)

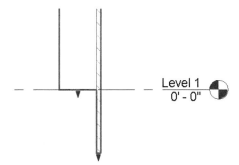

FIGURE 13.22
Unlocked layers can be modified in a section view by dragging or with the Align or Move tool.

When you create a model for a renovation of an existing building, you will likely create elements that are existing, demolished, and new. In the example shown in Figure 13.23, a new wall and a wall to be demolished are intersecting an existing wall. Notice that the walls are cleaning up with each other as they normally would if they were all in the same phase.

FIGURE 13.23
Wall joins will clean up by default regardless of phasing.

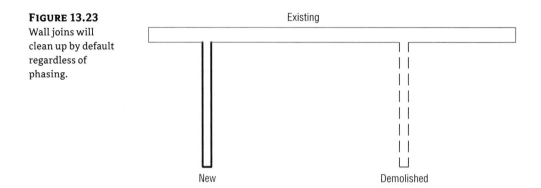

If you would like to change the graphic behavior of the new and demolished walls when they intersect the existing wall, follow these steps:

1. Select the new or demolished wall. Right-click the grip control at the end of the wall you'd like to modify and select Disallow Join. This will cause the walls to overlap, as shown in Figure 13.24.

FIGURE 13.24
Walls with disallowed joins will overlap.

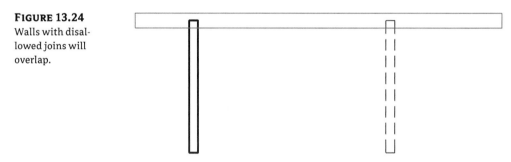

2. To complete the operation, you can use the Trim/Extend Single Element or Trim/Extend Multiple Elements tool, or simply drag the endpoints of the walls to create the most appropriate intersecting condition (Figure 13.25).

FIGURE 13.25
Use Trim/Extend or drag wall endpoints to complete the modification.

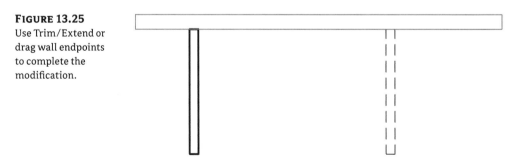

For walls that meet at an acute angle, you can use the Edit Wall Joins tool to control the resolution of the intersection:

1. From the Modify tab in the ribbon, locate the Geometry panel and select the Wall Joins tool.

2. Hover your mouse pointer over an intersection of two walls at an acute angle. You will see a box appear around conditions that can be modified with this tool (Figure 13.26).

FIGURE 13.26
Use the Wall Joins tool to modify intersecting wall conditions.

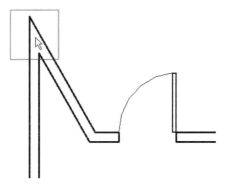

3. In the Options bar, you will see a number of choices to help you customize the joining condition between the walls related to the selection.

4. To cycle through the available options, choose one of the joining types (Butt, Miter, or Square Off), and then click the Previous or Next button. Some options are shown in Figure 13.27.

MODIFYING WALL PROFILES

CERT
OBJECTIVE

An important extended modeling technique for walls is the ability to customize the elevation profile of a wall segment. There are two ways you can accomplish this: by attaching the wall's top or base to another element or by editing the sketch profile of the wall. You can apply these methods to basic walls, stacked walls, and curtain walls.

To attach a wall to another element, select a wall segment and you will see the Attach Top/ Base button in the contextual Modify Tab. Once this command is activated, select either Top or Base, and then pick an object. Walls can be attached to roofs, ceilings, floors, reference planes, and even other walls. Figure 13.28 shows a stacked wall that has been attached to a curvilinear roof by extrusion.

FIGURE 13.27
Various corner conditions can be chosen with the Wall Joins tool: (a) butt; (b) miter

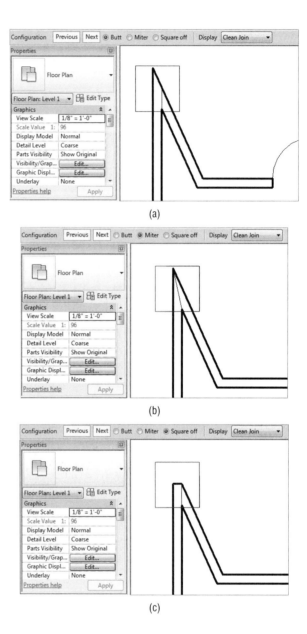

(a)

(b)

(c)

When you use the attach method, be mindful of how the software treats walls that are attached to other objects. After you use this method, the instance parameters Top Is Attached and Base Is Attached will show the status of the selected wall's attachment. These are read-only parameters and are for information only. Be aware that the top constraint and any other offset or height value will not display the actual height of the wall when it is attached to something. For example, if a wall whose base constraint is Level 1 and top constraint is Level 4 is attached to a floor slab on Level 2, the wall's top constraint will still be listed as Level 4 in the Properties palette. This anomaly does not affect other calculations such as wall length, area, and volume.

FIGURE 13.28
Stacked wall attached to an extruded roof

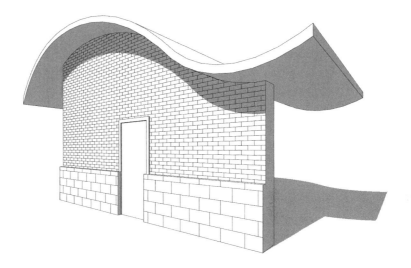

AUTOMATICALLY ATTACHING WALLS TO FLOORS

When you create a standard floor by sketching a boundary, the floor is hosted on a specific level. After you complete the boundary sketch and finish the editing mode, Revit offers you some help to attach walls to the floor. Any wall whose top constraint is the level on which the floor is hosted can be automatically attached to the bottom of the floor.

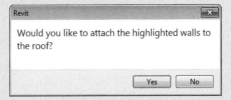

As a bonus, you can access this functionality at any time — not just when you create a floor. If you forgot to attach the walls to the floor when you first modeled the floor, simply select the floor and then click Edit Boundary. Click the Finish Edit Mode button and you should be prompted to attach walls to the floor.

The second method of modifying wall profiles is to edit the sketch profile of the wall. To do this, select a wall and click the Edit Profile button in the contextual Modify Tab. This will open a Sketch mode in which you can draw a new boundary for any edge of the wall shape, as shown in Figure 13.29. Click Finish Edit Mode to complete the operation.

FIGURE 13.29
The sketch elevation boundary for a stacked wall instance is edited.

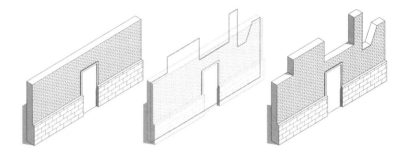

Creating Custom In-Place Walls

If you are working on traditional architecture, restoration of historic buildings, or free-form design, you may need to create walls that are irregular in shape. The Model In-Place tool, found in the Component drop-down list on the Architecture tab, lets you create any wall style independent of the constraints of the layer structure described in the previous sections of this chapter. Figure 13.30 shows an example of such a wall created with the solid geometry tools also found in the Family Editor.

FIGURE 13.30
Manually constructed wall used to create nonvertical surfaces

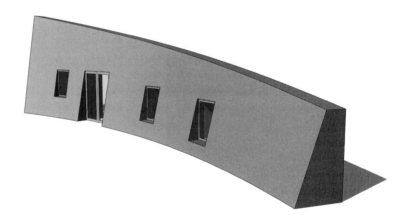

You can refer to Chapter 15, "Family Editor," to explore the various modeling techniques available in the Model In-Place mode. Remember that the selection of the family category is important to the behavior of the custom geometry. Select the Walls category to allow your custom elements to be scheduled with other walls and to place hosted elements such as doors and windows.

Creating Stacked Walls

Walls in a building — especially exterior walls — are often composed of several wall types made out of different material combinations and with different widths that stack one on top of another over the height of the façade. Because these walls usually sit on top of a foundation wall, you would likely want to establish an intelligent relationship among the different wall assemblies so the entire façade acts as one wall (for example, when the foundation wall moves and you expect walls on top of the foundation to also move). This is where stacked walls can help.

Stacked walls allow you to create a single wall entity composed of different wall types stacked on top of each other. Before you can create a stacked wall, some basic wall types need to be preloaded in your project. To help you understand how stacked walls work and how to modify one, follow these steps:

1. Open a new session and make sure at least three levels are defined (for this exercise, Site doesn't count as a level). If you don't have three levels, switch to an elevation view, add a few levels, and then go back to the Level 1 floor plan view.

2. From the Architecture tab on the ribbon, pick the Wall tool and select Stacked Wall: Exterior – Brick Over CMU w Metal Stud (you can find stacked wall types at the bottom of the list in the Type Selector). Draw a segment of wall in the Level 1 floor plan.

3. Select the wall segment. In the Properties palette, click the Edit Type button and then duplicate the wall type to create a new stacked wall called **Mastering Stacked Wall**.

4. Click the Edit button in the Structure field to open the Edit Assembly dialog box. Open the preview pane and set the view to Section. When you're editing the stacked wall type, you'll notice that the Edit Assembly dialog box (Figure 13.31) is slightly different from when you're working with a basic wall. Rather than editing individual layers, in this dialog box you are editing stacked wall types and their relationships to each other.

FIGURE 13.31
The Edit Assembly dialog box for stacked walls

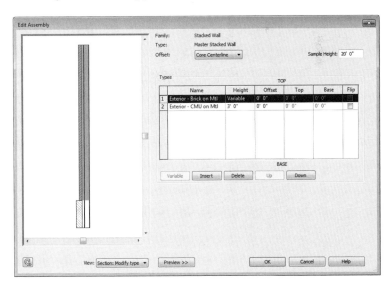

5. Click the Insert button to add a new wall to the stacked wall assembly. A new row appears in the list and allows you to define a new wall. Select the Generic - 12" [30 cm] wall type from the Name list and enter a Height of 10'-0" [3 m] (the width value is not important in this exercise).

6. At the top of the dialog box, find the Offset drop-down list and change the setting to Finish Face: Interior. This will align the interior faces of the stacked walls and allows you to use the Offset field in the Types table to adjust each stacked wall type in a predictable manner.

7. Select the row of the generic wall type by clicking the row's number label at the left side of the table. Click the Variable button to allow the wall to vary in height to adjust with varying level heights. Note that one row must have a variable height, but only one row in the assembly can be assigned as such. All others must have a specific height value.

8. Go back to the Level 1 floor plan and draw a new wall with the Mastering Stacked Wall type, setting its top constraint to Level 3 in the Options Bar.

9. Cut a section through the model and change the heights of Level 1 and Level 3 to see the effect this has on the wall (make sure the level of detail in the section is set to Medium so you can see the layers of the wall). You'll see that changing Level 2 does not change the bottom walls because they are of a fixed height; however, changing the height of Level 3 changes the height of the variable wall.

At any time, you can break down a stacked wall into its individual wall types. To do this, select a stacked wall, right-click, and select Break Up. Once a stacked wall is broken up, the walls become independent and there is no way to reassemble them back to a stacked wall. The base constraint and base offset of each subwall are the same as the stacked wall. For example, if the stacked wall was placed on Level 1, the base constraint for an upper subwall would still be Level 1, with the height difference accounted for in the wall's Base Offset parameter. This can be modified in the Properties palette if necessary.

The following are some important notes about stacked walls from the Revit user's guide (from the section "Vertically Stacked Wall Notes"):

◆ When you create a wall schedule, vertically stacked walls do not schedule, but their sub-walls do.

◆ When you edit the elevation profile of a stacked wall, you edit one main profile. If you break up the stacked wall, each subwall retains its edited profile.

◆ Subwalls can host sweeps; stacked walls cannot.

◆ Subwalls cannot be in different phases, worksets, or design options from that of the stacked wall.

◆ To place inserts such as doors and windows in a stacked wall, you may need to use the Pick Primary Host tool to switch between subwalls composing the stacked wall. For example, the door shown in Figure 13.32 is outside the upper wall because the main host of the door is the bottom subwall.

FIGURE 13.32
Inserts may not
host correctly in
vertically stacked
walls.

FIGURE 13.32
Inserts may not
host correctly in
vertically stacked
walls.

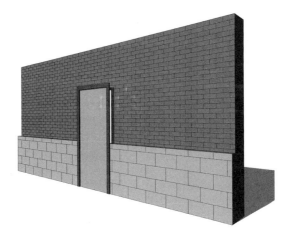

To place the door properly, select it and then click Pick Primary Host from the Modify |
Doors tab in the Host panel. Place your mouse pointer over the wall and select the upper
subwall (you may need to press the Tab key to select the correct component). The door
will then be properly hosted in the upper wall, as shown in Figure 13.33.

FIGURE 13.33
Use the Pick
Primary Host tool
to adjust inserts in
stacked walls.

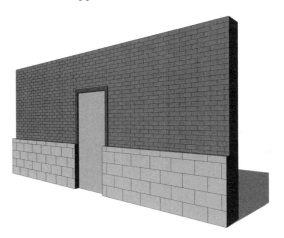

Creating Simple Curtain Walls

Curtain walls and curtain systems are unique wall types that allow you to embed divisions,
mullions, and panels directly into the wall. They have a distinct set of properties yet still share
many characteristics of basic walls. A *curtain system* has the same inherent properties as a curtain wall, but it is used when you need to apply a curtain wall to a face. Curtain systems are
usually nonrectangular in shape, such as the glazed dome shown in Figure 13.34.

FIGURE 13.34
Glazed dome cre-
ated with a curtain
system

A curtain wall is defined by the following elements and subcomponents:

The curtain wall   A curtain wall is drawn like a basic wall and is available in the Type Selector when the Wall tool is activated. It has top and bottom constraints, can be attached to roofs or reference planes, can have its elevation profile edited, and is scheduled as a wall type. When a curtain wall is selected in a model, the overall curtain wall definition is displayed as a dashed line with extensions at both ends of the segment.

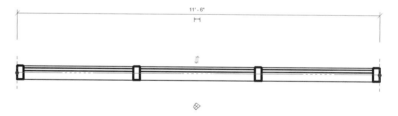

The dashed line of the overall curtain wall definition represents the location line of the wall. This is important if you are placing a curtain system on a face because the placement will be based on the location line. The location line of a curtain wall also determines the measurement of room area. Even if the Room Area Computation option is set at Wall Finish, a room's area will be measured to a curtain wall's location line.

So how do you adjust the location line of a curtain wall? This is accomplished by modifying the offsets in the mullions and panels you assign to a curtain wall or system. We'll cover this process in the section "Customizing Curtain Wall Types" later in this chapter.

Curtain grids   These are used to lay out a grid, defining the physical divisions of the curtain wall. You can lay out grids freely as a combination of horizontal and vertical segments, or they can be predefined in a curtain wall's type properties in regular spacing intervals. Figure 13.35 shows a freely designed layout of curtain grids and expressive curtain panels in between.

FIGURE 13.35
Curtain wall with regular orthogonal grids and expressive curtain panels

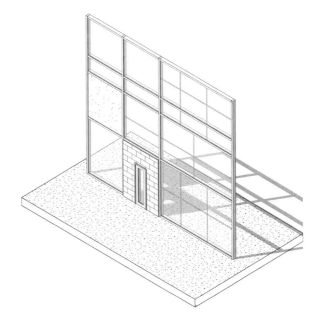

Mullions These represent the structural profiles on a glass façade and they follow the curtain grid geometry. Mullions can be vertical or horizontal and can be customized to any shape based on a mullion profile family. Offsets specified in a mullion's type properties affect how the mullion is placed relative to the curtain wall's location line.

Curtain panels These fill in the space between the curtain grids. Offsets in a curtain panel's type properties determine how the panel is placed relative to the curtain wall's location line. Curtain panels are always one of the following:

Empty panels No panel is placed between the grids.

Glazed panels These can be made out of different types of glass that can have any color or transparency.

Solid panels Panels can be created with custom geometry in the Family Editor and can include anything from doors and spandrels to shadow boxes and solar fins.

Wall types as infill When you have a panel selected, you can also choose a basic wall type from the Type Selector to fill the space between the curtain grids. All wall types in the project will be available for your selection. An example of this application would be interior office partitions in which the lower portion is a standard wall and glass panels fill the upper portion.

Designing a Curtain Wall

Let's go through a quick exercise to become familiar with the creation of a simple curtain wall. To create a curtain wall, you can either model a standard wall and then change its type to

Curtain Wall or select a curtain wall type from the Type Selector when the Wall tool is active. Here are the steps:

1. From the Architecture tab in the ribbon, select the Wall tool. From the Type Selector (in the Properties palette) select Curtain Wall 1.

2. In the Level 1 floor plan, draw a single curtain wall. Go to a 3D view to see the result.

The basic curtain wall definition has no predefined grids or mullions. The wall segment you see is just one big system panel that you will need to divide. Note that if you create a curved segment for a curtain wall, the panels are always straight segments. Thus, if you try to make a curved segment with Curtain Wall 1, there will be only one straight panel segment between the endpoints of the curve until you start to divide it up with curtain grids.

3. Divide the wall into panels using the Curtain Grid tool from the Architecture tab. Position your mouse pointer over the edges of the wall to get a preview of where the grid will be placed (select a vertical edge to place a horizontal grid or select a horizontal edge to place a vertical grid).

There are some snapping options when you are placing curtain grids that will help you divide the panels and subsequent divisions at midpoints and thirds. Watch the status bar for snapping prompts because there are no graphic indicators of the snapped positions other than the mouse pointer pausing. Place grids on the wall segment so that you get something like the wall shown in Figure 13.36.

FIGURE 13.36
Curtain wall with
a few manually
applied grids

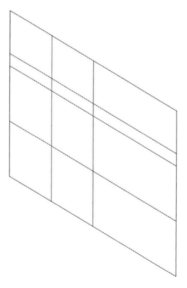

4. From the Architecture tab, select the Mullion tool. Notice that you can select from a variety of mullion types in the Type Selector; however, the default choice is adequate for this exercise. At the right end of the ribbon, you will see the Placement panel with three options for placing mullions: Grid Line, Grid Line Segment, and All Grid Lines. You can

place mullions on the curtain wall using any of these methods. Give each a try to see how they work.

MODIFYING PANELS AND MULLIONS

Next you'll replace panels in the wall you just created. As we explained earlier, panels are sub-components of the overall curtain wall, so you may need to press the Tab key to select a panel and view its properties. Special selection tools for curtain walls are available in the right-click context menu when you highlight a mullion or a panel. In the following exercise, you will replace the narrow band of glazing panels with solid panels:

1. In a 3D view, select one of the glazing panels in the narrow horizontal band (press the Tab key to select it if necessary).

2. Right-click and choose Select Panels ➢ Along Horizontal Grid, as shown in Figure 13.37.

3. With all the glazing panels selected along the horizontal grid, go to the Type Selector and find the type named Solid under the family system panel (note that the Glazing panel type is in the same family as the Solid panel).

FIGURE 13.37
Select multiple curtain panels along a grid with commands in the context menu.

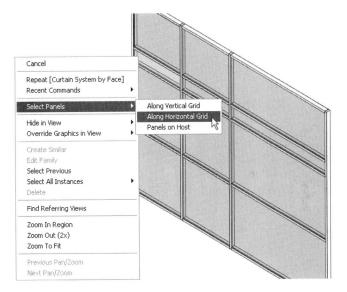

CUSTOMIZING CURTAIN GRID SEGMENTS

Finally, you will practice the techniques to add or remove segments of curtain grids to refine our curtain wall design. One important fact to remember when working with curtain grids is that they are always *implied* across the extents of the curtain wall. When we say they are implied, we mean they are not necessarily expressed on all panel segments. To further elaborate, you will add a curtain grid to the midpoint of the right, center panel and delete the division between the two panels to the left of the added grid, as shown in Figure 13.38.

FIGURE 13.38
Individual grid lines
are added or deleted
to further custom-
ize the design.

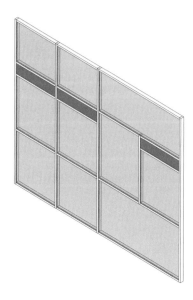

Follow these steps:

1. Begin by activating the Curtain Grid tool from the Architecture tab. In the Placement panel at the right end of the ribbon, click the One Segment button. Hover your mouse pointer over the bottom edge of the right-center panel, snapping to the midpoint of the panel (Figure 13.39).

FIGURE 13.39
A single segment is
added to the center
panel of the curtain
wall.

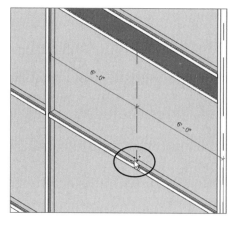

2. The second step is tricky. You *do not* continue creating another division in the short panel above the center panel. Instead, press the Esc key or click the Modify tool to exit the Curtain Grid command. Select the vertical grid line you created in step 1 (you may need to press the Tab key until you see the dashed line indicating the curtain grid). Notice that the grid extends the entire height of the wall (Figure 13.40).

FIGURE 13.40
Select the curtain grid in order to add or remove individual segments along it.

3. With the curtain grid selected, click the Add/Remove Segments button in the Modify | Curtain Grids panel of the Modify tab. Pick the segment of the curtain grid that passes through the short panel. Press the Esc key and you should see that the short panel is also split in half.

4. Activate the Mullion tool and place mullions on the division between the two center panels, as shown in Figure 13.41.

FIGURE 13.41
Mullions are applied to the segment added in the center panels.

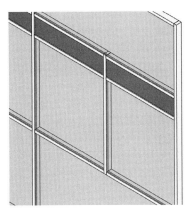

5. Press the Esc key or click Modify. Select and delete the horizontal mullion between the two left panels (this step is optional).

6. Similar to the process of adding grid segments, select the horizontal curtain grid below the narrow band and click the Add/Remove Segments button in the ribbon. Click the segment in the left-center panel. If you did not delete the mullion in step 5, a warning will appear prompting you to delete the mullion segment. The result should look like the wall shown in Figure 13.42.

FIGURE 13.42
A segment was removed from the left panel to complete the customized design.

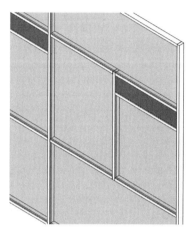

PLACING DOORS IN CURTAIN WALLS

In the final exercise of this topic, you will swap one of the curtain panels for a door panel. Door families for curtain walls can be found in the Doors folder of the Revit default library, but they behave differently than regular doors. The height and width of the curtain wall door is driven by the curtain grids — not the type properties of the door. Follow these steps:

1. From the Insert tab on the ribbon, locate the Load From Library panel and click the Load Family button. Navigate to the Doors folder of the Revit default library and load the Curtain Wall Dbl Glass.rfa family.

2. Zoom into the bottom-middle panel in your curtain wall. Delete the mullion under this segment as shown in Figure 13.43. (You don't want to have a tripping hazard at your door!) Remember, you may have to press the Tab key to select the mullion.

FIGURE 13.43
Delete the mullion below the panel where the door will be placed.

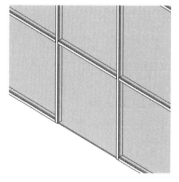

3. Select the bottom-middle panel and go to the Type Selector. Find the `Curtain Wall Dbl Glass.rfa` family and select it from the list so the results look like the wall in Figure 13.44. The door swing can be adjusted in plan as with any other door.

FIGURE 13.44
System glazing panel has been swapped for a double door panel family.

PLACING CORNER MULLIONS

Revit includes special mullions to be used at the corners of two curtain walls. These mullion types are unique in that only one is needed to connect two wall segments. In the default project template, you will find four corner mullion types, as shown in Figure 13.45: (a) V Corner Mullion, (b) Quad Corner Mullion, (c) L Corner Mullion, and (d) Trapezoid Corner Mullion.

FIGURE 13.45
Available curtain wall corner mullions

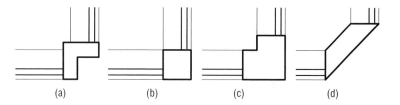

(a)   (b)   (c)   (d)

Corner mullions cannot be customized beyond the shapes included in the Revit project template; however, you can modify the material assigned to the mullions as well as the offset and depth dimensions in the type properties. When you use corner mullions between two segments of curtain wall, they will automatically adjust to the angle between the segments, as shown in Figure 13.46.

FIGURE 13.46
Corner mullions adapt to angles between curtain wall segments.

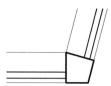

Before you place a corner mullion, make sure the endpoints of the two curtain wall segments are cleanly connected. You can drag the endpoint controls of the walls or use the Trim/Extend To Corner tool. To place a corner mullion, simply use the Mullion tool and select one of the corner edges of either one of the wall segments. If you have already placed a regular mullion at the end of a curtain wall segment, select the mullions along the vertical edge, and then use the Type Selector to choose a corner mullion type. Remember you can use the context menu (right-click and select Mullions ➤ On Gridline) to make the selection easy.

Customizing Curtain Wall Types

In the previous exercises, you learned the fundamental techniques of building a simple but custom curtain wall design. To reap some additional productivity from the curtain wall tool, you can predefine almost all the properties necessary to generate a complete curtain wall assembly simply by placing the wall in your project. In the following sections, we will examine one of the curtain wall types included with the default project template.

Begin a new project with the `Default.rte` or `MetricDefault.rte` template and create a wall segment 30′ [9 m] long using the type Curtain Wall: Storefront. Switch to a 3D view and you will see that the wall already has vertical and horizontal divisions along with mullions placed on the divisions. In the example shown in Figure 13.47, we have placed an additional curtain grid and swapped one of the panels for a door type.

FIGURE 13.47
Sample curtain wall
storefront type

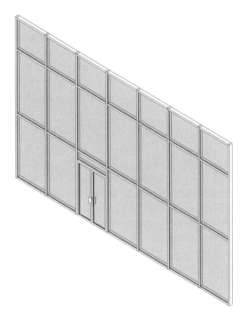

Select the sample of storefront wall you had previously created and click the Edit Type button in the Properties palette. The settings that drive the generation of this type of wall are relatively easy to understand. Let's review some important options related to these properties:

Automatically Embed When this option is enabled, any instance of this curtain wall type will embed itself inside other wall segments. This is useful for modeling extended areas of ribbon or strip glazing (Figure 13.48) instead of using a window family.

FIGURE 13.48
The Automatically Embed option allows curtain walls to be placed inside basic walls.

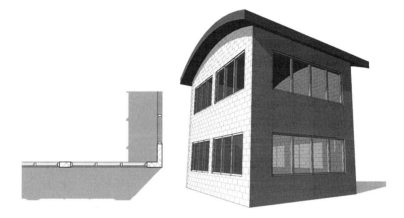

Join Condition This option defines the behavior of the mullion joins. It can be one of the following:

- Not Defined (join conditions can be overridden as necessary)
- Vertical Grid Continuous
- Horizontal Grid Continuous
- Border And Vertical Grid Continuous
- Border And Horizontal Grid Continuous

Display In Hidden Views This option is new to Revit Architecture 2013 and allows you to control the graphic display of individual components over several views. The options for this can be one of the following:

- Edges Hidden By Other Members (the default)
- Edges Hidden By Element Itself
- All Edges
- None

Grid Pattern: Layout   There are four options to define how the vertical and horizontal grids will be arranged in your curtain wall:

Fixed Distance   The most common setting, which allows you to specify spacing between gridlines. Leftover panel segments must be accounted for in the overall length of the wall.

Fixed Number   Divides the wall segment into equally spaced panels. When you select this option, the Spacing parameter becomes disabled. In its place, a new integer parameter named Number will appear in the instance properties.

Maximum Spacing   Indicates the maximum spacing distance. Curtain panels will be equally divided over the length of the wall segment, not to exceed the Spacing value.

Minimum Spacing   Indicates the minimum spacing distance. Curtain panels will be equally divided over the length of the wall segment, no smaller than the Spacing value.

Mullions   This option allows you to specify the mullions that will be automatically applied to the curtain wall. Corner mullions can be applied to either Border 1 or Border 2 for the vertical mullions, but use them carefully — their resolution at corners will depend on how you construct your wall segments.

Modifying Pinned Panels and Mullions

You may have already noticed that when a panel or mullion is selected from a predefined curtain wall type, they appear with a pushpin icon. This indicates that these elements are part of a system and cannot be changed without additional action.

To change or delete a predefined panel or mullion in a curtain wall instance, select the element and click the pushpin icon. The icon will change to a pushpin with a red *X* next to it. At this point, you can change the element using the Type Selector or delete it (only mullions can be deleted). Be careful when you attempt to unpin elements from a curtain wall as you cannot re-pin back to the predefined system. Within the active Revit session, you may be able to return to an unpinned curtain wall element and still find the unpinned icon. This allows you to fix any accidental unpinning, but once your project is closed and reopened, you can no longer re-associate the unpinned elements.

Creating Custom Curtain Panels

A curtain panel does not have to be confined to a simple extrusion of glass or solid material. You can create any kind of panel family to satisfy your design requirements. When creating a new panel, be sure to select the `Curtain Wall Panel.rft` or `Metric Curtain Wall Panel .rft` family template file. The width and height of the panel are not explicitly specified in the family; instead, the outermost reference planes will adapt to the divisions in the curtain wall into which the panel is embedded. If required, you can adjust the panel geometry to offset within or beyond the reference plane boundaries in the family. This is useful for creating butt-glazed curtain wall assemblies.

COMPLEX CURTAIN WALL APPLICATIONS

Although covering several specific examples in detail is outside the scope of this chapter, we will offer some real-world examples of creating your own custom curtain panels. Refer to Chapter 15 for guidance on creating your own families. These examples are included in a sample file named c13-Curtain-Wall-Custom.rvt on this book's companion website (www.sybex.com/go/masteringrevit2013).

Spider Fittings and Sunshades   Generic models can be nested in a curtain panel family. In the example shown here, two instances of the spider component are placed on one edge of the panel. Visibility parameters are assigned to the two spider fittings that enable either the top or bottom spider to be displayed as needed. The spider fittings were downloaded from RevitCity.com and the sunshade is a Kawneer model 1600 SunShade – Planar, downloaded from Autodesk Seek (http://seek.autodesk.com).

Spandrel and Shadowbox   Often in glazing applications, the spacing of horizontal members will consist of a pattern including a narrow band or spandrel to mask the floor and ceiling sandwich. Revit software does not currently have the ability to define two spacing values, but you can create the spandrel or shadowbox in a single panel family. In the example shown here, the spandrel height is a type property of the custom panel family. Standard mullions are applied to the wall.

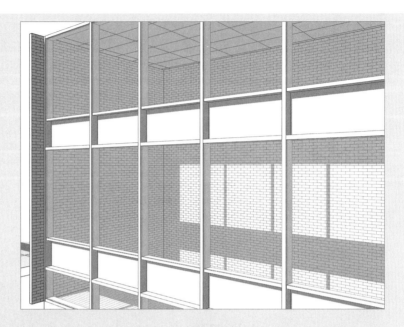

Louvers   Our last example shows how metal louvers can be embedded in a curtain panel family. The image shown here is a panel developed with a nested generic model. The louver fins are arranged in a parametric array within the generic model, and then the generic model is placed in the panel. The edges of the louver array are constrained to the reference planes in the panel. This parametric louver curtain panel was downloaded from RevitCity.com.

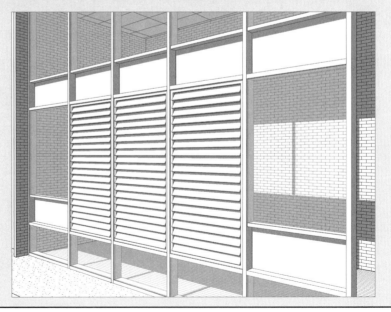

Creating Complex Curtain Walls

Often at the early stages of design, as an architect or designer, you need to be able to model curtain wall systems that indicate design intent. These systems need to be flexible and robust enough to allow us to explore design iteration, but they also need to be useful enough downstream as your project moves from concept to design development and then on to fabrication.

In Revit Architecture you can build conceptual curtain walls utilizing Revit conceptual massing tools. There are two potential workflows, and it's important to understand the differences. You can model your curtain wall system directly within the project environment from massing forms, or you can build it as a family within a conceptual design environment.

Project environment   You can build your forms directly within your project environment using the in-place massing tools. When concept curtain walls are constructed through the In-Place Mass tool, the conceptual design environment does not have 3D reference planes and 3D levels.

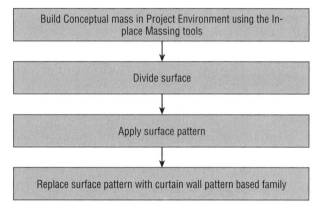

Conceptual design environment (CDE)   You create your concept curtain wall designs in the Revit conceptual design environment (CDE), which is a type of family editor. These forms reside outside the project environment. You can then reference these massing families into a project environment, allowing you to explore contextual relationships with the building form.

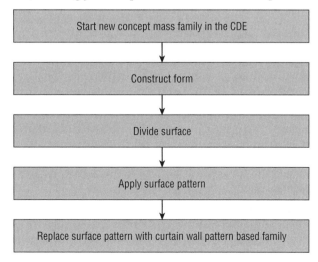

You start by designing your conceptual form that will represent the shape and form of the surface of the curtain wall. You are then able to subdivide the surface of this form using a grid system, referred to as a UV grid. As surfaces are not always planar (flat), a UVW coordinate system is used to plot location across the surface. This grid system automatically adjusts following the natural contours of a nonplanar surface or form. The UV grid is then used as a guide for patterning the surface. You can investigate how you might panelize the surface to make it constructible by applying a geometric pattern to it. This pattern provides a basic graphic representation of how the panel may look. These graphic patterns can then be replaced with parametric components that automatically conform to the divided surface.

Dividing the Surface

Let's take a look at the basic tools that will allow you to divide the surface of a conceptual form:

1. Start by opening c13-Square-Panel.rfa from this book's companion website. This file represents a simple conceptual shape for a curtain wall design (Figure 13.49).

FIGURE 13.49
Conceptual shape to be used as a basis for a complex curtain wall design

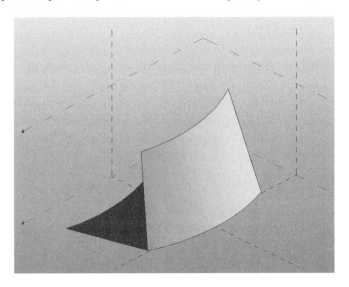

2. Select the form and then click Divide Surface on the Modify | Form tab in the ribbon. This will divide the surface of the form and you will see horizontal and vertical grids displayed. This is the *UV grid*.

   Note that you can control the display of the UV grid when it is selected (Figure 13.50). To modify the display, click the U Grid or V Grid button in the UV Grids And Intersects panel on the Modify | Divided Surface tab of the ribbon.

3. Make sure the UV grids are both displayed and the surface is selected. Notice how the Options bar provides a number of settings for you to modify the divided surface. You can control the U grid and V grid by a number or with a specific distance. If you select the Number option, you can enter a number of divisions that will distribute evenly across the surface.

FIGURE 13.50
A surface of the conceptual form has been divided and the UV grid is displayed.

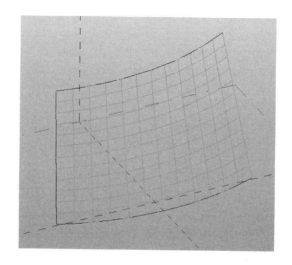

4. Select Distance, which will allow you to enter a specific absolute distance between grids across the divided surface. Under the Distance setting, there is a drop-down menu that also allows you to specify a Maximum Distance or a Minimum Distance value; these are similar to the constraints described earlier in this chapter for basic curtain walls. Make sure the surface is divided by number, with a U grid of 10 and a V grid of 10.

5. With the UV grid selected, you will see a 3D control (x-, y-, and z-axis arrows), and an icon appears in the center of the surface. Click the icon to enable the Configure UV Grid Layout command. The display will change (Figure 13.51) and you can now apply specific settings to control the UV grid even further. You have the ability to alter the rotation of the grid, the UV grid belt, and justification of the UV grids at the surface borders. These grid configuration parameters can also be found and modified in the Properties palette.

FIGURE 13.51
The UV grid can be configured by clicking the icon at the center of the surface.

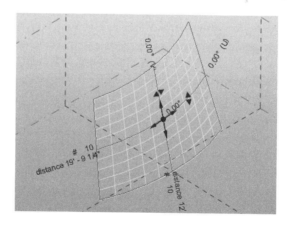

6. In the Properties palette, set the U Grid Rotation value to 45 degrees and the V Grid Rotation value to 45 degrees; then click Apply. Notice how the modified values are updated in the 3D view with the Configure UV Grid Layout command activated.

In the Configure UV Grid Layout mode (Figure 13.52), you will see a number of controls — all of which relate to parameters you can also access in the Properties palette. The arrow cross in the middle of the grid is the *grid justification* marker. You can drag it to any side, corner,
or center of the grid, which will adjust the value of the Justification property of both U and V grids.

FIGURE 13.52
The UV grid can be modified directly or via the values in the Properties palette.

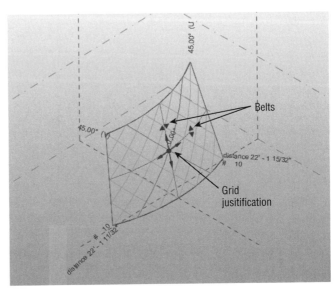

The *belts* represent the lines along the surface from which the distance between grids is measured. The distance is measured by chords, not curve lengths, and can be seen in the Properties palette as the Belt Measurement parameter for both U and V grids.

Dividing the Surface with Intersects

As you have seen in the previous exercise, the Divide Surface tool allows you to divide the surface of a form using the natural UVW grid of the surface. However, if you want to divide the surface with a customized grid pattern, you divide it by intersecting geometry. By using the Intersect feature, you can divide the surface based on the following:

♦ Intersecting levels, reference planes, and even lines drawn on a reference plane

♦ A mixture of U or V grids and intersects

Let's take a look at an example based on our previous file, which will demonstrate how you can use a series of defined reference planes to divide a surface:

1. Start by opening the file c13-Square-Panel-Intersects.rfa from this book's companion website.

   Notice that a series of reference lines have been drawn in the X plane; you will use these reference lines to divide the surface of the form.

2. Select the surface and choose Divide Surface from the ribbon. Click the U Grid tool on the ribbon to disable the display of the U grids.

3. With the surface still selected, click the Intersects button on the ribbon. Select all the reference planes in the X plane and then click the Finish icon in the Intersects panel on the ribbon. This will divide the surface based on where the reference planes intersect the surface of the form. Note that you could also choose Intersects ➤ Intersects List to choose named references such as levels or named reference planes instead of picking them in the model view.

4. Go to the Project Browser and open the 3D view named 3D Surface to review the results (Figure 13.53).

FIGURE 13.53
The surface is divided by intersecting planes and lines.

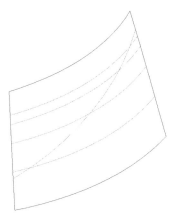

Applying Patterns

Surface patterns allow you to quickly preview in a graphical manner how a panel will work across the surface of the form. Because you are not working with complex geometry at this stage, the editing and adjustment to the design concept is quick. Revit provides a number of predefined patterns that are available from the Properties palette, and they can be applied to your divided surface. You will now apply a surface pattern to a form:

1. Start by opening c13-Square-Panel-Pattern.rfa from this book's companion website.

2. With the UV grid on the form selected, you will notice in the Type Selector that the default empty pattern named _No Pattern is applied to the surface. Open the Type Selector and you will see that you can apply one of a number of predefined patterns to the surface. Click the Rectangle Checkerboard Pattern type to apply it to your surface (Figure 13.54).

3. Experiment with the various predefined patterns and adjust the UV grid as required to play with the proportions of the patterns.

At any time, you can display both the underlying surface divisions along with the pattern display. With the grid selected, click the Surface button in the Surface Representation panel on the Modify | Divided Surface tab. This display should give you a better understanding of the relationship between the pattern definition and the spacing of the surface divisions.

FIGURE 13.54
Surface with
Rectangle
Checkerboard
Pattern applied

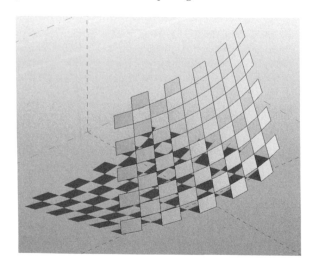

Editing the Pattern Surface

There will be situations where you will want to edit and control the border conditions for pattern surfaces. Patterned surfaces may have border tiles that intersect the edge of a surface, and they may not end up as complete tiles. You can control the border tile conditions by setting them to Partial, Overhanging, or Empty in the Border Tile instance property of the patterned surface. You will now modify a conceptual curtain wall to examine how the different border conditions affect the surface:

1. Start by opening `c13-Square-Panel-Border.rfa` from this book's companion website.

2. Select the surface, and in the Properties palette, locate the Border Tile parameter under Constraints. Set the value to Empty and click Apply or drag the mouse out of the Properties palette. Notice that the tiles at the borders are no longer visible, as shown in Figure 13.55.

FIGURE 13.55
Border parameter
set to Empty

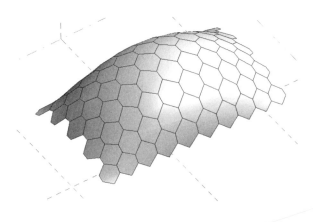

3. Next change the Border Tile parameter to Overhanging and click Apply. The border tiles will now show in their entirety, extending beyond the edge of the surface.

Surface Representation

When editing a surface in the conceptual design environment, you have the option to choose how surface elements will be displayed. A number of options are available to you, allowing you to customize how you show or hide the various elements that make up a divided surface in a view. If you select either the U or V Grid icon, this will enable or disable the UV grid in the view. The Surface icon allows you to display the original surface, nodes, or grid lines. The Pattern icon allows you to hide or display the pattern lines or pattern fill applied to the surface. The Component icon allows you to hide or display the pattern component applied to the surface. If you decide to make any changes to the display using the Surface Representation tools, these changes will not carry through into the project environment. To globally show or hide surface elements, you will have to alter this from the Visibility/Graphic Overrides dialog box.

In the Surface Representation panel, you will also notice a small arrow in the bottom-right corner. Clicking this arrow will open the Surface Presentation dialog box, where you will find additional display options for the surface, patterns, and components. You also have the ability to display nodes and override the surface material of the form. Let's practice controlling the surface representation of your form:

1. Start by opening c13-Square-Panel-SurfaceRep.rfa from this book's companion website.

2. With the surface selected, go to the Surface Representation panel in the ribbon and click the arrow in the bottom-left corner to open the Surface Representation dialog box (Figure 13.56).

FIGURE 13.56
Use the Surface Representation dialog box to further customize the display of your form.

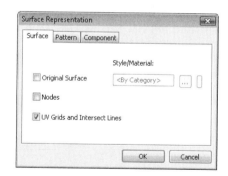

3. On the Surface tab, enable Nodes if is not already enabled; this will display a node at each intersection of the UV grid, as shown in Figure 13.57.

Adding Definition

So far, you have created a surface, subdivided it, and applied a graphical representation to the form. You can now begin to add actual component geometry similar to mullions and panels. Note that although the underlying graphic pattern will remain, the component geometry will take precedence. To begin this process, you will create special curtain panel families using the Curtain Panel Pattern Based.rft or M_Curtain Panel Pattern Based.rft family template. This type of panel family can be applied to the divided surface to populate it with architectural components, adding realistic definition to your conceptual curtain wall surface.

FIGURE 13.57
Nodes are displayed at the intersection of the U grids and V grids.

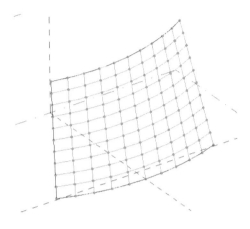

BUILDING A PATTERN-BASED PANEL FAMILY

In the following exercise, you will build a simple rectangular panel and apply it to your divided surface:

1. Click the Application menu, choose New ➤ Family, and select the Curtain Panel Pattern Based.rft family template.

   Figure 13.58 shows the pattern-based curtain wall family template, which consists of a grid, a series of reference lines, and adaptive points. The grid is used to lay out the pattern of the panel. The adaptive points and reference lines act as a rig, defining the layout of the panel. You can construct solid and planar geometry within and around the reference lines to form the panel.

FIGURE 13.58
The rig in the pattern-based curtain panel family

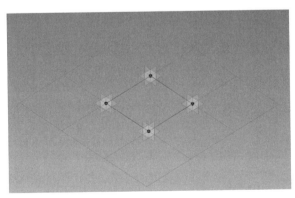

When a panel is applied to a divided surface, the points in the panel adapt to the UV grid and the panel will then flex accordingly. As a general rule, the grid pattern in your curtain panel family should match the pattern on the divided surface to which it is applied. For example, if you have applied a hexagonal pattern to your divided surface, make sure the curtain panel family is also using a hexagonal pattern.

2. You now need to decide what pattern you will use for the component. To change the pattern, select the grid, go to the Type Selector, and change the pattern to Rhomboid. Notice how the adaptive points and reference lines update to reflect the change. Review the various patterns that are available to you. Revert back to the Rectangular pattern.

Modeling a pattern-based curtain panel is similar to how you would sketch and construct a form within the conceptual design environment. You use points, lines, and reference lines to construct geometry.

CHANGING PATTERNS WITH GEOMETRY

It is important to understand that if you decide to switch your curtain panel grid pattern after creating solid forms, the geometry will not automatically adapt to the new pattern you choose. The geometry will be left orphaned and you will need to delete any geometry and remodel, based on the new pattern.

---

3. Select one of the adaptive points and drag it. These points will not move horizontally, only vertically. As you move the point, the reference lines attached to the point will alter the shape. Therefore, as you build geometry on the defined reference lines and an adaptive point is moved or adjusted, the reference lines are altered and the geometry constructed along the reference lines updates to reflect the change.

4. To reset the adaptive points back to the grid, select the grid and you will notice a Reset Points To Grid button in the Options bar. Click the button to reset the points.

5. Select the four reference lines and click the Create Form ➢ Solid Form button in the ribbon. You will see two icons appear in the middle of the model view (Figure 13.59), giving you the option to create an extruded form or a flat planar surface. Select the icon for the planar surface.

6. Next we will flex the geometry to test its consistency. Select one of the adaptive points and move it vertically. Observe how the geometry flexes, as shown in Figure 13.60, and then reset the points to grid.

7. Switch to the Architecture tab in the ribbon, and from the Draw panel, select the Point Element tool. Place a point on one of the reference planes, as shown in Figure 13.61. This point becomes a hosted point; observe how its symbol is smaller than the symbol for the adaptive points. Select the point, and from the Properties palette, change the value of the Show Reference Planes parameter to Always. This will make it easier to build geometry using the hosted point in later steps.

FIGURE 13.59
Geometry options
are presented when
you are using the
Create Form tool.

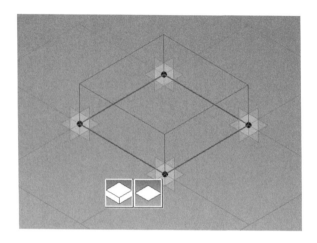

FIGURE 13.60
The panel form
will flex when the
points are dragged
vertically.

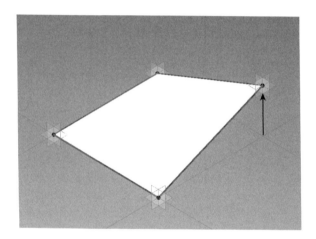

FIGURE 13.61
A reference point is
placed on one of the
reference lines.

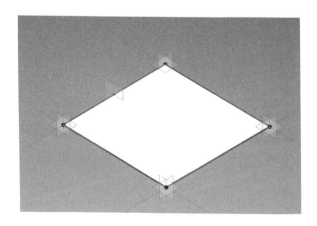

8. From the Architecture tab and the Work Plane panel, click the Set button (Set Work Plane tool) and pick the work plane of the hosted point.

9. Draw a circle with a radius of 6 inches [150 mm] on the work plane of the hosted point, as shown in Figure 13.62. It can be a little tricky drawing the circle onto the active work plane of the hosted point. Therefore, use the Show Work Plane tool to display the active work plane for the point. This will make the process of sketching the circle easier.

FIGURE 13.62
Draw a circle on the vertical work plane of the hosted point.

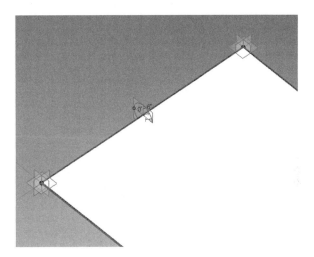

10. Select the circle and the four default reference planes, and then choose Create Form ➢ Solid Form. This will sweep the circle profile along the four reference planes, as shown in Figure 13.63.

FIGURE 13.63
Creating a form from a circle and four reference lines

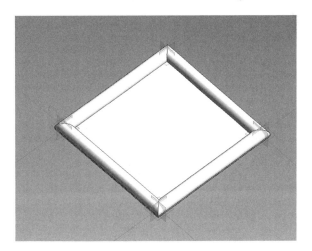

When building your curtain panels, consider how you will assign geometry to appropriate subcategories. This will ensure that you have full control over the elements from a visual and graphical point of view. For details on assigning geometry to subcategories, refer to Chapter 15.

11. Save the family as **Square-CWPanel.rfa**.

APPLYING COMPONENTS TO A DIVIDED SURFACE

Now that you have created a pattern-based curtain panel family, you'll need to load this family into your conceptual mass family and apply it to the divided surface, replacing the graphical pattern with the actual component.

1. Download and open the file c13-Square-CWSystem.rfa from this book's companion website.

2. Load the family file Square-CWPanel.rfa you created in the previous exercise into this file by clicking Load Family on the Insert tab of the ribbon, or switch to that file and click the Load Into Projects button.

3. In the conceptual mass file, select the pattern and divided surface. In the Properties palette, click the Type Selector, and scroll down the list until you find the name of your pattern-based curtain panel family. Note that your new panel family will be listed under the pattern within which it was designed. The component will now be applied to the patterned surface, as shown in Figure 13.64. Note that the more complex the surface and component, the longer it will take to load.

FIGURE 13.64
The pattern-based curtain panel component is applied to a surface in a conceptual mass family.

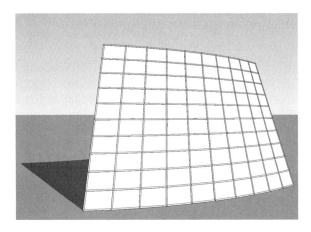

CREATING A PYRAMID CURTAIN WALL PATTERN-BASED FAMILY

Now that you have mastered the technique of constructing a simple planar curtain panel, let's take a look at how to create a pyramid type panel. You will add a type parameter to your pyramid curtain panel so that you can vary the apex of the panel:

1. Start a new family using the Curtain Panel Pattern Based.rft family template.

2. Place a reference point, ensuring that it snaps to the middle of one of the reference lines included within the template. Place another reference point on the reference line opposite to the one you previously placed, as shown in Figure 13.65.

FIGURE 13.65
Hosted points are
placed at the mid-
point of two refer-
ence lines.

FIGURE 13.65
Hosted points are
placed at the mid-
point of two refer-
ence lines.

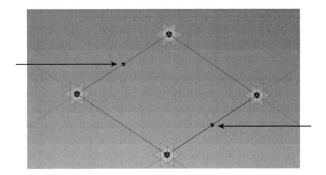

3. From the Architecture tab in the ribbon, click the Reference tool and ensure that 3D Snapping is activated in the Options bar. Draw a reference line between the two newly placed hosted reference points, as shown in Figure 13.66.

FIGURE 13.66
A reference line is
drawn between two
hosted points.

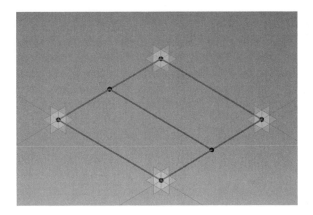

4. Place another reference point, so that it becomes hosted, at the midpoint of the previously created reference line (Figure 13.67). Select this reference point, and from the Properties palette, make sure that Show Reference Planes is set to Always.

5. From the Architecture tab, choose the Set Work Plane tool and select the work plane of the hosted point at the middle of the previously drawn line. Activate the Reference Line tool and uncheck the 3D Snapping option. Draw a reference line vertically in the Z plane from the hosted point. Ensure that the start point of the reference line is locked to the hosted point. You may need to drag the end of the reference line, nearest to the point, in the Z direction before dragging it back to the hosted pointed. This will ensure that the lock symbol will appear.

6. Select the vertical reference line to display the temporary dimension, and turn this into a permanent dimension by clicking the dimension icon.

FIGURE 13.67
Place a hosted point at the midpoint of the reference line.

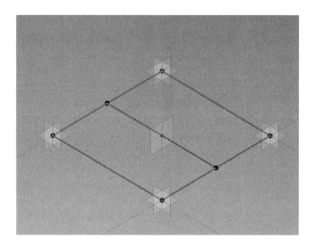

7. Select this dimension and then choose <Add New Parameter…> from the Label pull-down in the Options bar. Assigning this dimension to a parameter will allow you to alter the apex of the pyramid panel as needed. In the Parameter Properties dialog box, name the parameter **Apex_Height**. Click OK to close all open dialog boxes.

8. Add a series of reference lines using the 3D Snapping option from the apex to the four points on the base of the pyramid, as shown in Figure 13.68.

FIGURE 13.68
Reference lines are created from the corners to the apex.

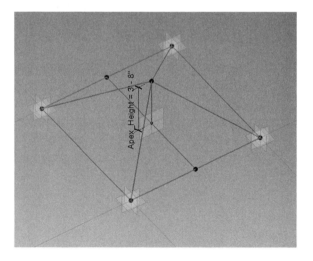

9. You will now create faces on each slope to complete the pyramid shape. To do this, select one reference line from the base and two reference lines on the sloping edges (use the Ctrl key to add lines to your selection), and click the Create Form button. Select the planar triangular face rather than the extrusion (Figure 13.69).

FIGURE 13.69
Select three reference planes, and then use Create Form to generate each face of the pyramid.

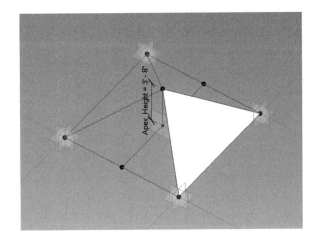

10. Repeat step 9 for the three remaining faces until you have a completed pyramid, as shown in Figure 13.70.

FIGURE 13.70
All four sides of the pyramid have been created.

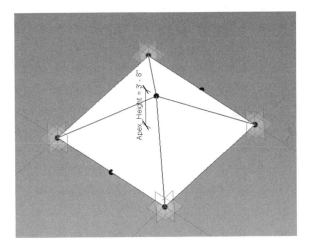

11. It is important that you flex the pyramid to check that you can control the height of the apex. Open the Type Properties dialog box and you will see the parameter named Apex_Height. Change the value a few times and click Apply after each change. The pyramid panel should change in height. Save your file as **Pyramid-Panel.rfa**.

12. Open the file c13-Pyramid-Project.rfa from this book's companion website. Load your Pyramid-Panel.rfa family into the c13-Pyramid-Project.rfa. Select the surface, go to the Type Selector, and choose Pyramid-Panel. Your pyramid shape curtain panel will now be populated across the divided surface, as shown in Figure 13.71.

FIGURE 13.71
The pyramid panel
is populated across
the entire surface.

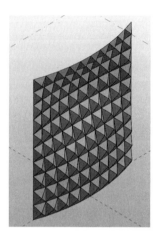

Creating Custom Patterns

Although Revit includes a variety of patterns you can use for conceptual curtain walls, at present there is no way to create your own pattern-based curtain panel template. The current patterns shipped with the software are hardwired, so there is no way to modify them either; however, with a bit of creative thinking, you can utilize the provided templates to construct panels that will conform to a custom pattern concept. When you consider building a custom panel, it is important to take into account how it will repeat vertically and horizontally. You will need to break it down into its smallest module. If you think about a repeating architectural pattern such as a masonry wall, its individual component can be broken down into the brick that forms that pattern, which is in essence a rectangle. An example of a hexagon-shaped panel, constructed within a rectangular pattern, is shown in Figure 13.72.

FIGURE 13.72
A hexagonal panel is
constructed within
a standard rectan-
gular pattern.

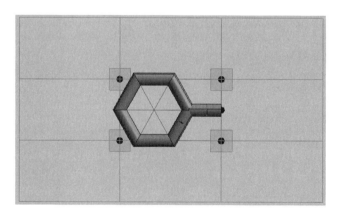

Once you have decided on the design for your panel, look at how the panel could be modularized. To do this, consider laying out the pattern utilizing graph paper. This will certainly help you better understand the layout before attempting to construct the panel using an appropriate template. In Figure 13.73, you will see the hexagonal panel applied across a divided surface.

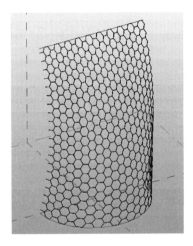

Limiting the Size of Pattern-Based Families

When designing complex curtain wall systems, the goal is to limit the variety of panels. The more variety you have, the higher the cost because you have to create a greater number of unique panels. When you divide a surface, the panel sizes can vary quite dramatically. While you do not actually have the ability to limit panel sizes, you can start to reduce the size and variety of panels by nesting curtain panels inside other panels. In the following exercise, you will learn how to nest panels to limit size variation:

1. Start by creating a simple pattern-based curtain panel family (use either `Curtain Panel Pattern Based.rft` or `M_Curtain Panel Pattern Based.rft`). Make sure the grid is set to the Rectangular type.

2. Select the four reference lines and use the Create Form tool to generate a planar surface.

3. Similar to the previous exercise, place a hosted point on one of the edges of the surface, and then draw a circle with a 6″ [150 mm] radius on the point's work plane. Use Create Form to generate a swept profile on two edges to represent a mullion, as shown in Figure 13.74. Save this panel as `Limit-Panel-1.rfa`.

4. Start another new pattern-based curtain panel family, again using the Rectangular grid pattern. Select the four reference planes and use Create Form to generate a planar surface rather than an extrusion.

5. Select the planar surface and click the Divide Surface tool from the ribbon. You will divide this surface and set the UV grid by number, setting U Grid to 2 and V Grid to 2, as shown in Figure 13.75.

FIGURE 13.74
A panel with a swept profile is created to be nested into another panel family.

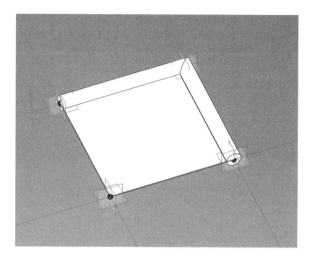

FIGURE 13.75
Create another pattern-based family and divide the surface into a 2 x 2 grid.

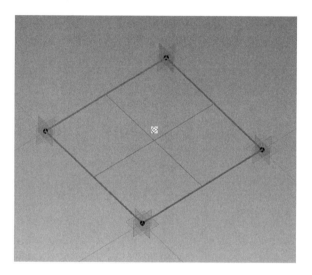

6. Load the Limit-Panel-1 family into the divided surface panel.

7. Select the divided surface and apply your panel to the divided surface by choosing Limit-Panel-1 from the Type Selector. This will nest the panel into the subdivisions of the divided surface (Figure 13.76). Save this panel as **Limit-Panel-2.rfa**.

You can now apply this nested panel into any divided surface. Download and open the file c13-Limit-Panel-Project.rfa from this book's companion website.

8. In the c13-Limit-Panel-Project.rfa file, select the pattern and divided surface. From the Type Selector, select the name Limit-Panel-2. Note that your new panel family will be listed under the pattern within which it was designed. It will take a few seconds for the software to replace the pattern with the real geometry of the panel. But observe that by nesting the panel inside other panels, you have been able to limit the size and variety of the panels (Figure 13.77).

FIGURE 13.76
The simple panel is nested into the divided surface of the host panel.

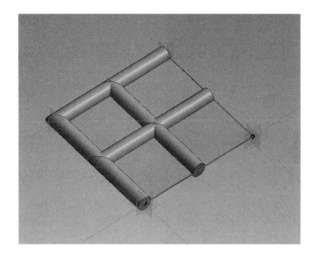

FIGURE 13.77
The host panel containing the nested panel is populated on a divided surface.

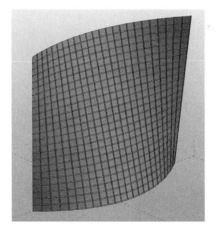

Using the Adaptive Component Family

So far the examples look at using the UV grid to nest in curtain wall pattern–based families; however, there will be situations where you may want to manually place a panel, specifically at border conditions where you may need to construct custom panels. To do this, use the Adaptive Component functionality that is available to you in the pattern-based curtain panel. This functionality is designed to handle cases where components need to flexibly adapt to many unique, related conditions. This new functionality also addresses the problems of creating and placing pattern component panels (triangular, pentagonal, hexagonal, and so on) on nonrectangular and irregularly spaced grids. In the following exercise, you will create an adaptive panel and manually place it along the border of a divided surface:

1. Create a simple pattern-based curtain panel family (Curtain Panel Pattern Based.rft or M_Curtain Panel Pattern Based.rft) and use the rectangular grid pattern. Select each of the four adaptive points and notice that each point has a number from 1 to 4.

2. Select one of the points; from the Properties palette, change the Show Placement Number parameter to Always.

3. Select all the reference planes in the family and choose Create Form; select the Planar Surface option. Save this panel as **My Adaptive Panel.rfa**.

4. Download and open the file c13-StitchSurface-Project.rfa from this book's companion website.

5. Load the panel you previously created into c13-StitchSurface-Project.rfa.

   Notice that in c13-StitchSurface-Project.rfa the UV grid has been enabled as well as the nodes at the intersections of the UV grid (Figure 13.78). You will use these nodes to snap your panel.

FIGURE 13.78
Sample surface with nodes displayed

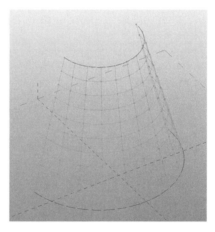

6. Locate the Families category in your Project Browser and expand the Curtain Panel tree. You will find the My Adaptive Panel type in this list. Drag it into the 3D view window.

7. With the panel attached at your mouse pointer, place the pointer onto one of the nodes on the subdivided surface to place the first point. Place the remaining points onto the corresponding nodes, as shown in Figure 13.79. Observe how the panel will adapt based on its placement in the surface division.

FIGURE 13.79
Placing an adaptive
panel into a divided
surface

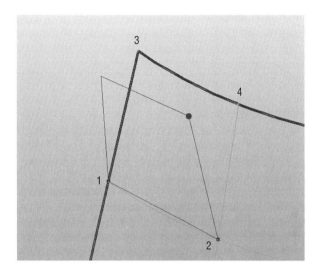

Scheduling Pattern-Based Panels

Now that you have completed the design of your pattern-based curtain wall families, you may want to use Revit scheduling capabilities to assess the quantity and area of panels in your conceptual curtain wall system. This can be useful for calculating approximate costs at the early stages of design. You can schedule panels that have been applied to an in-place mass directly in the project environment; however, it is not possible to schedule panels in the conceptual design environment. You will first have to load your concept mass into a project, where you will then be able to schedule the panels. In this example, you will open a sample file, load it into a project, and then create a schedule, which will list all the panels that make up your conceptual curtain wall:

1. Download and open the file `c13-Square-Panel-Schedule.rfa` from this book's companion website.

2. Start a new project using either `default.rte` or `MetricDefault.rte`; then load the file `c13-Square-Panel-Schedule.rfa` into your new project.

3. From the Massing & Site tab in the ribbon, click the Place Mass button and select c13-Square-Panel-Schedule from the Type Selector. Make sure that the Place On Workplane icon is selected in the Placement panel and place the massing component in the Level 1 floor plan.

4. Open the Default 3D view to view your model (Figure 13.80).

5. From the View tab in the ribbon, click Schedules and then click Schedules/Quantities. This will open the New Schedule dialog box. Select Curtain Panels from the Category list and click OK.

6. You will now define the fields that will be included within your panel schedule. Choose Family in the left column and click the Add button to add this field to your schedule. Next add Area and then Count.

FIGURE 13.80
A conceptual curtain wall is loaded into a project and placed using Place Mass.

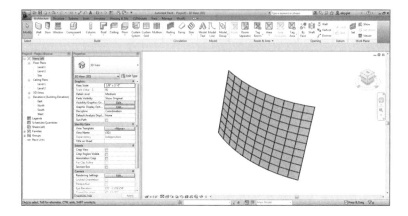

7. Click the Sorting/Grouping tab and check the options for Grand Totals and Itemize Every Instance.

8. Click the Formatting tab and select the Area field. Make sure the Calculate Totals option is selected. Do the same for Count.

9. Click OK and your schedule will be created. If you scroll down to the bottom of the schedule, the total area and the number of custom panels in your conceptual curtain wall will be listed.

THANKS TO DAVID LIGHT

A portion of this chapter was written with the help of David Light. David Light is the Revit Specialist for HOK London, focusing on Revit and BIM as well as helping to drive forward the firm's global buildingSMART principles. David was first introduced to Revit software at version 4.5 just after the Autodesk acquisition and has had an unhealthy passion for the technology ever since. Before joining HOK, David worked for the UK's Autodesk Premier Solutions Center providing coaching, training, and consultancy in Revit Architecture and Revit Structure. David has developed a reputation as one of the leading UK experts in Revit and is a popular speaker and blogger on all things Revit and BIM. David writes for the blog http://autodesk-revit.blogspot.com.

The Bottom Line

Use extended modeling techniques for basic walls. Walls in Revit are made from layers of materials that can represent generic placeholders for design layouts to complete assemblies representative of actual construction.

Master It   How can you customize the profile of a wall?

Create stacked walls.   Exterior walls are usually composed of several combinations of materials with varying thicknesses. These various wall types can be combined into a single entity called a stacked wall.

Master It   How do you create a stacked wall?

Create simple curtain walls.   A curtain wall is an assembly of parts including curtain grids, panels, and mullions. They can be created in predefined types with regular horizontal and vertical spacing along with specific panel and mullion types.

Master It   How do you add a door to a curtain wall?

Create complex curtain walls.   The Revit conceptual massing environment can be used to create complex curtain wall configurations. Pattern-based panel families can be loaded into the massing environment and populated on a divided surface. These populated surfaces can then be loaded and placed in a project model for documentation and scheduling.

Master It   How do you create a complex divided surface?

Chapter 14

Floors, Ceilings, and Roofs

Floors, ceilings, and roofs, which may seem like simple building components, can sometimes prove to be difficult to model and detail in your project designs. In previous chapters, you read about using conceptual design tools to create masses that help drive building elements. In this chapter, we expand on the development of these sketch-based objects.

In this chapter, you'll learn to:

- ◆ Understand floor modeling methods

- ◆ Model various floor finishes

- ◆ Create ceilings

- ◆ Understand roof modeling methods

- ◆ Work with advanced shape editing for floors and roofs

Understanding Floor Modeling Methods

Floors are likely to be one of the first sketch-based elements you will encounter in Autodesk® Revit® Architecture software. Many families in the default libraries are floor hosted, so you must first have a floor before you'll be able to place such components. Consequently, these components will be deleted if the floor that hosts them is deleted. You can find a more detailed discussion on creating families in Chapter 15, "Family Editor," but for now let's review the fundamental types of floors that can exist in a Revit project: a floor, a structural floor, a floor by face, and a pad.

Floor

The traditional floor object is a sketch-based element that comprises any number of material layers as defined by the user. The top of the floor object is its reference with respect to the level on which it was created. As such, changes to a floor's structure will affect its depth down and away from the level. You can start modeling floors with generic types, which are similar to generic walls containing a single layer, and then change the generic floors to more specific assemblies later in the development of your project. You can use floors in a variety of ways to meet the needs of a specific phase of design. In early phases, for example, you can create a floor type to represent the combined floor, structure, plenum, and ceiling assemblies of a building. Commonly referred to as the *sandwich*, a sample is shown in Figure 14.1.

During intermediate phases of design, you can model ceilings so the floor types can include only the floor and a structural layer, as shown in Figure 14.2. Columns may be created, but more precise horizontal structural framing may not be modeled yet. The layer within the floor type represents an assumption of the maximum depth of structural framing.

FIGURE 14.1
A single floor type
may be used to show
the entire floor/ceil-
ing sandwich in early
design.

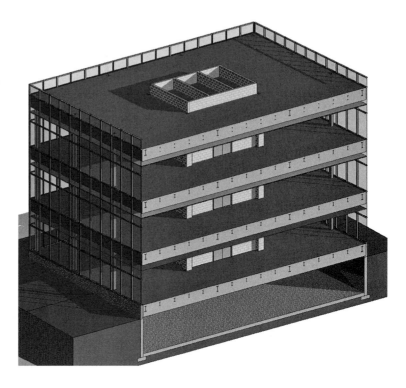

FIGURE 14.2
This floor assembly
includes an assump-
tion for the depth of
structural framing.

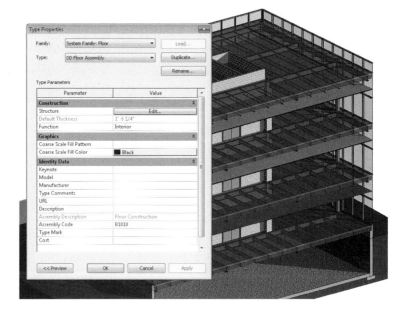

In later phases approaching and including construction, floors should be modeled as close to actual conditions as possible. You should accommodate detailed finish conditions for floors as well as coordination with a resolved structural system. Accurate modeling of these conditions will help support consistent quantity takeoffs and interference detection. Figure 14.3 illustrates an example of a more accurate floor slab.

FIGURE 14.3
Floor assemblies for construction should be accurate and separate from structural framing.

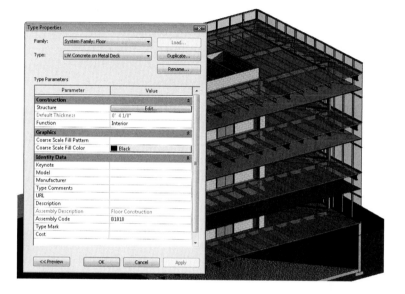

These floor assembly types are offered as suggestions for the sake of increased productivity. As such, they should be used with care, especially when performing quantity takeoffs for estimating. For example, the *area* of a floor will be the only accurate value to be extracted from a floor sandwich model in early design, not a volumetric material takeoff. For more information on the use of models by others, we recommend referring to the AIA document *E202 BIM Protocol Exhibit*, which lists authorized uses of a model at various levels of development. You can download a sample of this document for free from www.aiacontractdocuments.org/bim.

COLLABORATION AND THE OWNERSHIP OF FLOORS

Whether or not you are working under an integrated project delivery (IPD) contract, the so-called ownership of floors should be carefully considered for the collaboration process between an architect and a structural engineer. Floors can be one of the most contentious elements of a building design because they can be simultaneously construed as architecture and structure.

The model element author (MEA) for floors should be discussed and clearly defined for each phase in your project BIM execution plan. Remember that element ownership can pass between the architect and the structural engineer when it is appropriate for a given phase. For example, the architect may choose to be the MEA for floors in schematic design but pass ownership to the structural engineer in design development and construction documentation.

With a basic understanding of floors as elements of the building system, let's look at some properties of floors that allow expanded uses in the Revit model. These properties and floor types can help expand your use of floor systems to create better documentation.

Structural Floor

The structural floor is similar to a traditional floor but has structural functionality, such as the ability to indicate span direction and to contain structural profiles. For example, you can specify a composite metal deck profile, which will display in sections and details generated within your project. You can create a structural floor by selecting the floor element and clicking the instance property called Structural (Figure 14.4). Note that because Structural is an instance property, any floor type can become a structural floor.

FIGURE 14.4
Structural parameter in a floor's instance properties.

Once the Structural parameter check box has been selected for a floor, you can edit its type properties to add a structural decking layer. Let's create a new structural floor so you can explore how this is done:

1. Open the file c14-Floors-Start.rvt from the book's companion website (www.sybex.com/go/masteringrevit2013), and activate the Level 3 floor plan.

2. Go to the Architecture tab in the Ribbon, and from the Build panel, select Floor ➤ Structural Floor.

3. In the Draw panel of the Modify | Create Floor Boundary tab, make sure your options are set to Boundary Lines with the Pick Walls tool, as shown in Figure 14.5.

FIGURE 14.5
Use Pick Walls mode to draw boundary lines.

4. In the Options bar, specify an offset of 0'-3" [75 mm]. This setting will place the floor boundary just within the inner face of the curtain wall mullions because the location line of the curtain wall is at the center of the mullions that are 5" deep.

5. Begin picking the exterior curtain walls by selecting one of the north-south-oriented walls first. Note that the first wall you pick will determine the span direction of the

structural floor. You can change this at any time by picking the Span Direction tool from the Draw panel and then selecting one of the boundary lines in the floor sketch. Pick the remaining exterior walls to complete the floor boundary.

Properties

6. Once you have finished defining the boundary lines of the floor, open the Properties palette by pressing Ctrl+1, typing **PP**, or clicking the Properties icon at the left end of the ribbon.

7. Click Edit Type in the Properties palette. Select Generic - 12" as the active type and click Duplicate. Name the new type **Structural Slab**.

8. In the Edit Type dialog box, click the Edit button in the Structure row to open the Edit Assembly dialog box.

9. In the Edit Assembly dialog box, find the layer of the assembly that represents the generic floor you duplicated. This should be row 2. Change the material of this layer to Concrete – Cast-in-Place Concrete and change the thickness to 0'-6".

10. Select row 3 and click the Insert button. There should now be four layers. Select the new row 3 and set its function to Structural Deck [1]. Note the new Structural Deck properties that appear below the layers, as shown in Figure 14.6.

FIGURE 14.6
Setting a layer's function to Structural Deck exposes additional options.

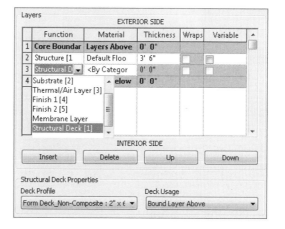

11. The value for the Deck Profile should default to Form Deck_Non-Composite: 2' x 6", but this depends on whether you have a structural deck profile loaded into your project.

If you don't have a structural deck profile loaded, finish the floor, select the Insert tab of the ribbon, and click Load Family. In your default Autodesk content library, find the `Profiles` folder and open the `Metal Deck` subfolder. Pick an appropriate deck profile and click Open to load it. Select the Structural Slab floor and click Edit Type in the Properties palette to continue the exercise.

12. Activate Wall Section 1 and you should see the completed slab at Level 3. Notice that you do not see the details of the structural decking when Detail Level is set to Coarse. If you activate the callout at Level 3 (Detail At Level 3), you will see the structural decking because the callout's detail level is set to Medium. This difference is illustrated in Figure 14.7.

FIGURE 14.7
Structural floor as represented in coarse detail level (left) and Medium detail level (right).

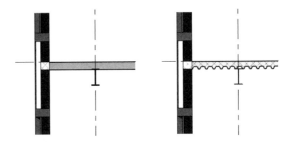

Floor by Face

This floor modeling method is used when you have generated an in-place mass or loaded a mass family. After you assign mass floors to a mass, you can use the floor by face method to assign and manage updates to floors, as shown in Figure 14.8. This type of face-based modeling is discussed in greater detail in Chapter 9, "Advanced Modeling and Massing."

FIGURE 14.8
The Floor By Face tool can be used to manage slabs in more complex building designs.

Pad

A pad is technically not a floor but has properties similar to a floor. What differentiates a pad is its ability to cut into a toposurface and define the lowest limits of a building's basement or cellar. If desired, the pad can be configured to represent a slab on grade, as shown in Figure 14.9. The Pad tool can be found on the Model Site panel of the Massing & Site tab. If you don't see this tab, don't forget to turn it on by clicking the Application button and choosing Options ➢ User Interface.

FIGURE 14.9
A pad can be config-
ured as a slab on grade
for a basement.

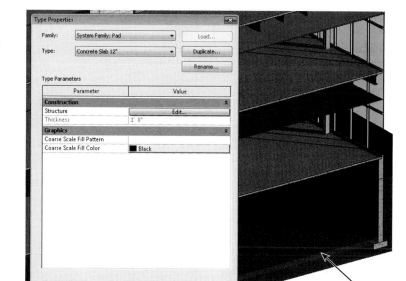

Slab Edge

Slab Edge is a tool that allows you to create thickened portions of slabs typically located at the boundaries of floors. A slab edge type is composed of a profile family and a material assignment. It is important that the material assignment of the slab edge match that of the floor to which you will apply the slab edge in order to ensure proper joining of geometry. Let's explore the application of a slab edge to a floor at grade:

1. Open the file c14-Design-Floor.rvt from the book's companion website and activate the 3D view named Floors Only.

2. Click the Architecture tab in the ribbon and select Floor ➤ Slab Edge from the Build panel. Note that this tool is also available from the Structure tab.

3. If necessary, orbit the 3D view so that you can see the bottom of the lowest floor slab. Pick all four, bottom edges of the floor slab at the level named Ground.

4. Activate the view Section 1 and you will see the slab edge applied to and joined with the floor, as shown in Figure 14.10. Remember that the material in the slab edge type must match the material in the floor type properties for the geometry to join properly.

Creating a Custom Floor Edge

You can apply a great deal of flexibility to a floor assembly in early design. As we described earlier, you can create a floor for early design phases that accommodates the floor, structure, plenum, and ceiling in a single floor type. You can also apply a customized edge to this type of assembly for more creative soffit conditions at exterior walls, as shown in Figure 14.11.

FIGURE 14.10
Thickened slab edge applied to the bottom of a floor.

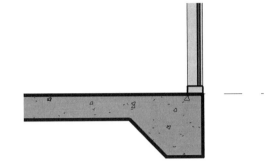

FIGURE 14.11
Customized edge applied to a floor assembly in early design

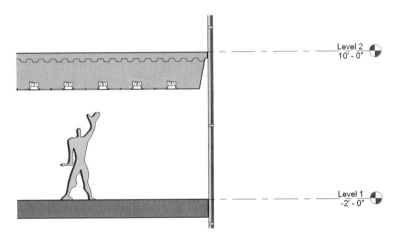

Level 2
10' - 0"

Level 1
-2' - 0"

Let's run through a short exercise so you can practice this skill:

1. Open the file c14-Design-Floor.rvt from the book's companion website and activate the view Section 1.

2. Select the floor at Level 1 and open the Properties palette. Change the type to Design Floor Sandwich.

3. Begin a new in-place component by going to the Architecture tab and selecting Component ➤ Model In-Place from the Build panel.

4. Set the Family Category to Floors and specify the name as **Floor Edge-L1**.
   Notice that you are now in Family Editing mode, and the ribbon will have different tabs and panels.

5. Click the Create tab and select Void Forms ➤ Void Sweep from the Forms panel.

6. Click the Pick Path tool from the Sweep panel and choose all four top edges at the perimeter of the floor at Level 1. You can activate the 3D view Floors Only to complete the picking of all four edges, as shown in Figure 14.12.

7. Click the Finish Edit Mode icon in the Mode panel when all four edges of the floor have been picked.

FIGURE 14.12
Pick edges of the void
sweep in a 3D view.

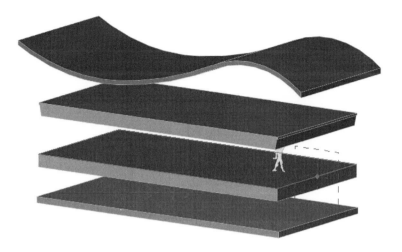

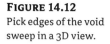

FIGURE 14.12
Pick edges of the void
sweep in a 3D view.

8. Open the Properties palette if it isn't already visible.

Note that you might need to reactivate the Select Profile mode if the Properties palette lists only Family: Floors. To do this, click the Modify | Sweep tab in the ribbon and click Select Profile in the Sweep panel.

9. In the Profile parameter, select SD Sandwich Edge : 36″ w 6″ Slab from the drop-down list, as shown in Figure 14.13.

FIGURE 14.13
Select a loaded profile
family for the void
sweep.

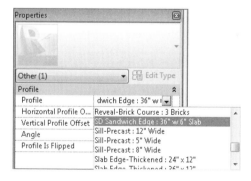

Note that the SD Sandwich Edge profile has been preloaded for the convenience of this exercise. If you would like to explore how this profile was created, expand the Families tree in the Project Browser and find Profiles ➤ SD Sandwich Edge. Right-click it and choose Edit from the context menu.

10. You may need to adjust the orientation of the profile so that it faces in toward the floor, as shown in Figure 14.14. To do so, make sure the profile is selected and click the Flip button in the Options bar.

FIGURE 14.14
Make sure the sweep
profile is facing toward
the floor.

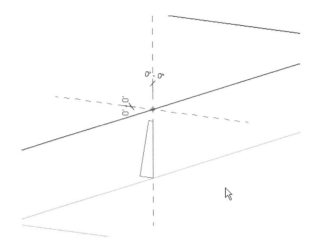

11. Select the Modify | Sweep tab in the ribbon and click the Finish Edit Mode icon from the Mode panel.

12. Select the Modify | Void Sweep tab in the ribbon and select Cut ➢ Cut Geometry in the Geometry panel. Pick the void sweep and then the floor at Level 1.

13. Click Finish Model in the In-Place Editor panel at the right end of the ribbon.
    Activate the Section 1 view, and you should see that the floor sandwich assembly at Level 1 has been customized in a similar way to the floor at Level 2 (Figure 14.15). You can experiment with adding embellishing detail components as shown in the section.

FIGURE 14.15
The edge of the floor
sandwich assembly
for Level 1 has been
customized.

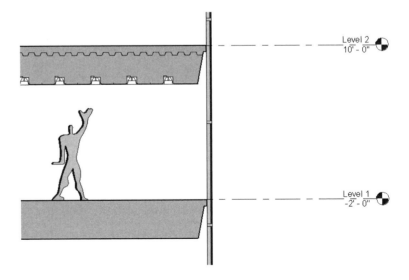

Sketching for Floors, Ceilings, and Roofs

Because floors, ceilings, and roofs are sketch-based objects, the method you use when creating the boundary lines is critical to the behavior of the element to those around it. The recommended method is to use the Pick Walls option, as shown previously in Figure 14.5.

By selecting the walls to generate the sketch for the roof, you are creating an intelligent relationship between the walls and the roof. If the design of your building later changes and the wall position is modified, the roof will follow that change and adjust to the new wall position without any intervention from you (Figure 14.16).

FIGURE 14.16
Using the Pick method:
(A) original roof; (B)
the entrance wall
position has changed,
and the roof updates
automatically; (C) the
angle of the wall to the
right of the entrance
has changed, and the
roof changes to a new
shape.

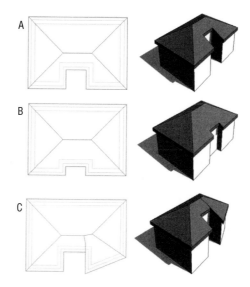

Also notice in Figure 14.16 that the illustrated roof was generated with overhangs beyond the exterior faces of the walls. You can specify an overhang or offset value for a floor, ceiling, or roof in the Options bar *before* picking walls to define the sketch.

If your building design is using curtain walls, be careful with the location lines of these walls. The location line of a curtain wall is defined relative to the offsets specified in the mullion and panel families that make up the curtain wall type. As discussed in Chapter 13, "Walls and Curtain Walls," you have many options when defining the relative location line of your curtain wall types. Refer to the exercise in the section "Structural Floor" earlier in this chapter for an example of picking curtain walls with an offset based on a centered location line.

Modeling Floor Finishes

You can apply floor finishes in a variety of ways. Most methods are based on the thickness of the finish material. For example, a thin finish such as carpet might be applied with the Split Face and Paint tools, whereas a thicker finish such as mortar-set stone tile might be a separate floor type.

Split Face for Thin Finishes

One of the easiest ways to divide a floor surface for thin finishes is to use the Split Face and Paint tools. This method will require a floor to be modeled and an appropriate material defined with at least a surface pattern. Note that you can schedule finishes applied with the Paint tool only through Material Takeoff schedules. Let's explore this method with a quick exercise.

1. Open the file c14-Design-Floor.rvt from the book's companion website and activate the Level 1 floor plan. You will see an area of the floor that is bounded by a wall and two reference planes.

2. Click the Modify tab in the ribbon, activate the Split Face tool from the upper-right corner of the Geometry panel, and pick the floor in the Level 1 floor plan 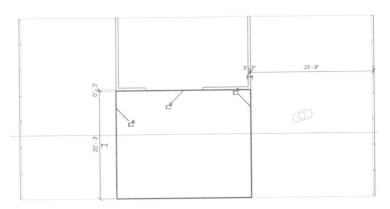.

3. Draw a rectangle in front of the three interior walls, as shown in Figure 14.17.

FIGURE 14.17
Sketch a rectangular boundary with the Split Face tool.

Note that you can constrain — or lock — the sketch lines to the interior walls, reference planes, and floor edge. You may do so in this exercise, but constraints should be used sparingly in larger projects to avoid slower model performance and updating calculation time.

Also notice that you generated a complete rectangular sketch instead of only three bounding lines. You do not need to draw the boundary line at the edge of the floor; however, if you don't include that line and the floor shape is modified in the future, the split face may be deleted because it is no longer a closed-loop sketch.

4. Click the Finish Edit Mode icon in the Mode panel.

5. Return to the Modify tab in the ribbon and activate the Paint tool in the Geometry panel, just below the Split Face tool.

6. In the Material Browser, type **carpet** in the filter search at the top. This will minimize your choices, allowing you to select Carpet Textile from the remaining list (Figure 14.18). Click Done when you've finished.

7. In the Level 1 floor plan, click near the edge of the split face you created earlier to assign the material. The result should look like the sample shown in Figure 14.19.

FIGURE 14.18
Choosing the Carpet
Textile material.

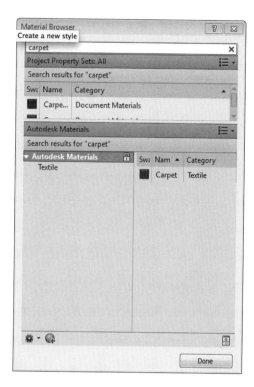

FIGURE 14.19
Completed application
of carpet tile material
to a split face on a floor.

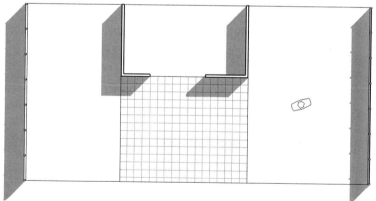

Modeling Thick Finishes

Thicker finish materials such as tile, stone pavers, or terrazzo can be applied as unique floor types and modeled where required. For large areas of finish such as a public atrium or airport terminal, you can assign these materials within the layers of a floor assembly. When you need to add smaller areas of thick floor finishes, there are two scenarios you may encounter: with a depressed floor and without.

In areas such as bathrooms, a thick-set tile floor may require the structural slab to be depressed in order to accommodate the thickness of the finish material. In the example illustrated in Figure 14.20, the main floor object has been cut with an opening at the inside face of the walls. Another floor has been modeled with a negative offset value to accommodate the thickness of the tile material, and the tile has been placed as a unique floor element.

FIGURE 14.20
The thick tile finish and depressed slab are modeled as separate elements.

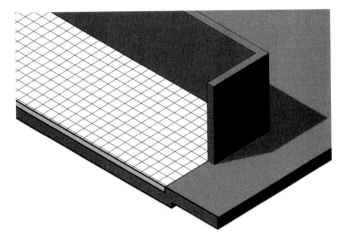

If you don't need a finish but just a slab depression, you can create it with an in-place void extrusion. Select the Architecture tab on the ribbon and click Component ➤ Model In-Place. Choose the Floors category and create a void extrusion where you need a slab depression. Remember to use the Cut Geometry tool to cut the void from the floor before finishing the family. As an alternative, you can create a floor-based generic family that contains a parametric void extrusion. You can download the file c14-Slab-Depression.rfa as an example of this type of family from the book's companion website.

Finally, if the structural requirements allow a thick finish to be applied to a floor without dropping the structural slab, a finish floor element can be modeled directly in place within the structural slab. As shown in Figure 14.21, the tile floor has been graphically embedded in the structural floor using the Join Geometry tool. To do this, click the Modify tab on the ribbon and click Join Geometry. Be sure to pick the finish floor *before* the structural floor or you will get an error.

FIGURE 14.21
The thick tile finish floor has been joined with the structural floor.

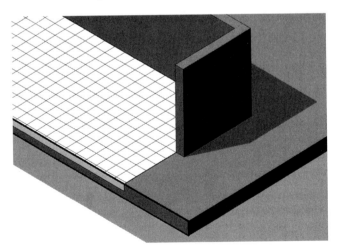

Creating Ceilings

CERT OBJECTIVE

Ceilings are system families composed of sketch-based elements that also serve as hosts for components such as light fixtures. Like other host elements such as floors and roofs, if a ceiling is deleted, hosted elements on that ceiling are also deleted. Ceilings are classified as either Basic Ceiling or Compound Ceiling. The Basic Ceiling family does not have a layered assembly and is represented in a section as a single line; however, it does have a material parameter that can display surface patterns in reflected ceiling plans and 3D views. The Compound Ceiling family allows you to define a layered assembly of materials that are visible when displayed in a section view. As with floors, you can change ceiling types by selecting a ceiling in your project and choosing another type from the Type Selector in the Properties palette or with the Match Type Properties tool.

Both the Basic Ceiling and Compound Ceiling types can serve as a host to hosted family components. Ceilings also serve as bounding elements for the volumetric calculation of rooms. This is critical when using environmental analysis programs such as Green Building Studio® or Autodesk® Ecotect® Analysis. For more information about analysis for sustainable design, see Chapter 10, "Conceptual Design and Sustainability."

You can create a ceiling in one of two ways: automatically or by sketching a boundary. When you select the ceiling tool from the Architecture tab of the ribbon, you can switch between the Automatic Ceiling and Sketch Ceiling modes at the right end of the ribbon.

In Automatic Ceiling mode, the software will try to determine the boundaries of a ceiling sketch when you place your cursor inside an enclosed space. If an enclosed space cannot be determined, your cursor will still indicate a circle/slash and you must switch to Sketch Ceiling mode. In this mode, you can use the Pick Walls method as discussed earlier in this chapter to create intelligent relationships with the bounding walls of the ceiling.

Ceilings are best modeled in ceiling plans even though they can be created in a floor plan. When you place a ceiling, its elevation will be based on the level of the current plan with an offset from that level. With the Properties palette open, the Height Offset From Level value can be modified as you create ceilings.

ROOM BOUNDING PERFORMANCE

Floors, ceilings, and roofs all have the ability to be room bounding elements. This parameter can be found in the instance properties of each object. If you are not using volume calculations for rooms or you don't intend to use the model for environmental analysis, you might consider turning off the Room Bounding parameter in horizontal objects. In larger Revit projects, unnecessary applications of the Room Bounding parameter may lead to reduced model performance.

Understanding Roof Modeling Methods

In today's construction environment, roofs come in a great number of shapes and sizes. They can be as simple as a pitched shed roof or can involve complex double-curved surfaces or intersecting vaults. Once you understand the fundamental concepts, tools, and logic pertaining to roofs, you will be able to design almost any roof shape.

Roofs are similar to floors and ceilings because they are sketch-based elements and can be defined in generic types or with specific material assemblies. You can also change a roof element from one type to another in the same manner you can a floor or ceiling. A fundamental difference between floors and roofs is that a roof's thickness is generated *above* its referencing level, not below. You can also easily create slopes in roofs by defining slopes in the roof's sketch lines. In general, roofs can be constructed in four different ways: by footprint, by extrusion, by face, or modeled in-place. The following sections provide a closer look at these approaches and reviews their application in real-world scenarios.

Footprint Roofs

Use the roof by footprint method to create any standard roof that more or less follows the shape of the footprint of the building and is a simple combination of roof pitches (Figure 14.22).

FIGURE 14.22
A simple roof created using the roof by footprint method.

These roofs are based on a sketched shape that you define in plan view at the soffit level and that can be edited at any time during the development of a project from plan and axon 3D views. The shape can be drawn as a simple loop of lines, using the Line tool, or can be created using the Pick Walls method that also should result in a closed loop of lines.

To guide you through the creation of a roof by footprint and explain some of the main principles and tools, here is a brief exercise demonstrating the steps:

1. In a new project, open a Level 1 plan view and create a building footprint similar to Figure 14.23. Make sure the height of the walls is set to Unconnected: 0'-0" [6000 mm].

FIGURE 14.23
Sample building outline to be sketched on Level 1.

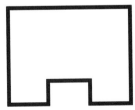

2. Activate the Level 2 plan; then select the Architecture tab in the ribbon and click Roof ➢ Roof By Footprint.

3. From the Draw panel in the Modify | Create Roof Footprint tab, select the Pick Walls tool (this should be the default).

4. When you've chosen to create a roof by footprint, the Options bar displays the following settings (change the Offset value to 1'-0" [300 mm]).

To define whether you want a sloped or flat roof, use the Defines Slope check box in the Options bar. The Overhang parameter allows you to define the value of the roof overhang beyond the wall. When the Extend To Wall Core option is checked, the overhang is measured from the wall core. If the option is deselected, the overhang is measured from the exterior face of the wall.

5. After defining these settings, place your cursor over one of the walls (don't click), and using the Tab key, select all connected walls. Your display should look like Figure 14.24.

FIGURE 14.24

Roof sketch lines are automatically drawn after Tab+selecting the bounding walls, and they are offset from the walls by the value of the overhang as defined in the Options bar.

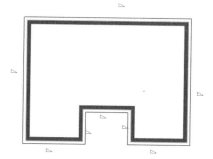

6. Select the two north-south walls within the alcove, open the Properties palette, and uncheck the Defines Roof Slope parameter, as shown in Figure 14.25.

FIGURE 14.25

Uncheck the Defines Roof Slope parameter for two of the roof's boundary lines.

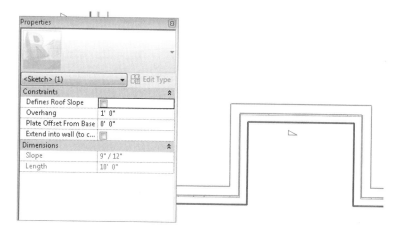

7. Click the Finish Edit Mode icon in the Mode panel of the ribbon. If you are prompted with the question, "Would you like to attach the highlighted walls to the roof?" click the Yes button. Activate a 3D view, and your roof should like the image in Figure 14.22 shown earlier.

If the shape of the roof doesn't correspond to your expectations, you can select the roof and select Edit Footprint from the Mode panel in the Modify | Roofs tab to return to Sketch mode, where you can edit lines, sketch new lines, pick new walls, or modify the slope.

To change the slope definition or angle of individual portions of the roof while editing a roof's footprint, select the sketch line of the roof portion for which you wish to change the slope and toggle (check) the Defines Slope button in the Options bar, toggle the Defines Roof Slope parameter in the Properties palette, or right-click and choose Toggle Slope Defining. If you mistakenly made all roof sides with slope but wanted to make a flat roof, you can Tab+select all sketch lines that form the roof shape and clear the Defines Slope box in the Options bar.

Roof slope can be measured in different ways: It can be set as an angle or percentage rise. All slope measuring options can be found in the Manage tab by selecting Project Units in the Project Settings panel and then selecting Slope to open the Format dialog box (see Figure 14.26). If the current slope value is not in units you wish to have (suppose it displays percentage but you want it to display an angle), change the slope units in the Format dialog box — you will not be able to do that while editing the roof slope. Setting it here means specifying the way you measure slopes for the entire project.

FIGURE 14.26
Format dialog box for slopes.

Here are some of the important instance properties you should be aware of and need to set properly; all are found in the Properties palette shown in Figure 14.27.

Base Level   As in other Revit elements, this is the level at which the roof is placed. The roof moves with this level if the level changes height.

Room Bounding   When this is checked, the roof geometry has an effect on calculating room area and volume.

Related To Mass   This property is active only if a roof has been created with the roof by face method (Conceptual Mass tools).

Base Offset From Level   This option lowers or elevates the base of the roof relative to the base level.

FIGURE 14.27
Roof instance
properties.

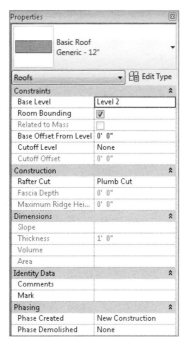

Cutoff Level   Many roof shapes require a combination of several roofs on top of each other — for this you need to cut off the top of a lower roof to accommodate the creation of the next roof in the sequence. Figure 14.28 shows an excellent example of this technique.

FIGURE 14.28
The cutoff level applied
to the main roof and
a secondary roof built
on top of the main roof
using the cutoff level as
a base.

Cutoff Offset   When the Cutoff tool is applied, the Cutoff Offset value also becomes active and allows you to set the cutoff distance from the level indicated in the Cutoff Level parameter.

Rafter Cut   This defines the eave shape. You can select from Plumb Cut, Two Plumb Cut, or Two Plumb Square. When Two Plumb Square is selected, the Fascia Depth parameter is activated, and you can set the value for the depth.

Rafter or Truss   With rafter, the offset of the base is measured from the inside of the wall. If you choose truss, the plate offset from the base is measured from the outside of the wall. Figure 14.29 illustrates the difference between the rafter and truss settings.

FIGURE 14.29
Rafter setting (left) and truss setting (right) for roofs.

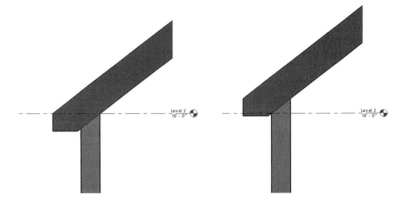

Roof by Extrusion

The roof by extrusion method is best applied for roof shapes that are generated by extrusion of a profile, such as sawtooth roofs, barrel vaults, and waveform roofs. Like the roof by footprint method, it is based on a sketch; however, the sketch that defines the shape of the roof is drawn in elevation or section view (not in plan view) and is then extruded along the plan of the building (see Figure 14.30).

FIGURE 14.30
An extruded spline-shaped roof.

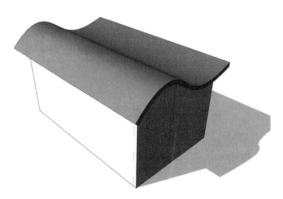

Roofs by extrusion do not have an option to follow the building footprint, but that is often needed to accommodate the requirements of the design. To accomplish this, you can use the Vertical Opening tool to trim the edges of an extruded roof relative to the building outline.

Let's briefly review the concept behind the Vertical Opening tool: You create a roof by extrusion by defining a profile in elevation or 3D that is then extruded above the building. The extrusion is usually based on a work plane that is not perpendicular to the building footprint, as shown in Figure 14.31. If the shape of the building is nonrectangular in footprint or the shape of the roof you want to create is not to be rectangular, this tool will let you carve geometry from the roof to match the footprint of the building or get any plan shape you need using a plan sketch.

FIGURE 14.31
Extruded roof created at an angle to the building geometry.

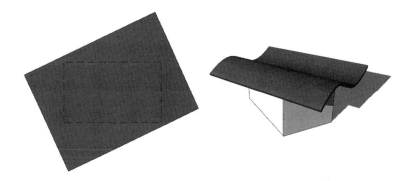

With sketch-based design, any closed loop of lines creates a positive shape, every loop inside it is negative, the next one inside that negative one will be positive, and so on. In Figure 14.32, a roof by extrusion was drawn at an angle to the underlying walls, but the final roof shape should be limited to a small offset from the walls. To clip the roof to the shape of the building footprint, the Vertical Opening tool was used to draw, in plan view of the roof, a negative shape that will remove the portions of the roof that extend beyond the walls.

FIGURE 14.32
The Vertical Opening tool with two sketch loops trims the roof to the inner loop.

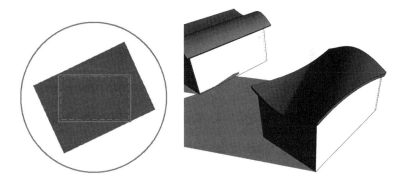

Roof In-Place

The roof in-place technique accommodates roof shapes that cannot be achieved with either of the previously mentioned methods. It is the usual way to model historic roof shapes or challenging roof geometries such as those illustrated in Figure 14.33. The figure shows a barrel roof with half dome (Extrusion + 1/2 Revolve), a dome roof (Revolve only or Revolve + Extrusion), and a traditional Russian onion dome (Revolve only).

FIGURE 14.33
Examples of modeled
in-place roofs.

To create an in-place roof, select the Architecture tab in the ribbon and click Component ➤ Model In-Place from the Build panel. Select Roofs from the Family Category list and click OK. While you remain in the In-Place Family editing mode, you can create any roof shape using solids and voids of extrusions, blends, revolves, sweeps, and swept blends (Figure 14.34). More advanced editing techniques are discussed later in this chapter, in the section "Advanced Shape Editing for Floors and Roofs."

FIGURE 14.34
Organic-shaped roof
created using the
Swept Blend modeling
technique.

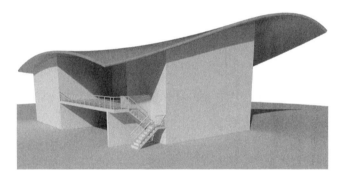

Roof By Face

The Roof By Face tool is to be used when you have created an in-place mass or loaded a mass family. These types of roofs are typically more integrated with the overall building geometry than the examples we've shown for in-place roofs. You can find more detailed information about using face-based methods in Chapter 9.

Sloped Glazing

In Chapter 13, you learned that a curtain wall is just another wall type made out of panels and mullions organized in a grid system. Similarly, sloped glazing is just another type of a roof that has glass as material and mullions for divisions. Using sloped glazing, you can make roof lights and shed lights and use them to design simple framing structures.

To create sloped glazing, make a simple pitched roof, select it, and use the Properties palette to change the type to Sloped Glazing. Once you have done that, activate a 3D view and use the

Curtain Grid tool from the Build panel of the Architecture tab on the ribbon to start applying horizontal or vertical grids that define the panel sizes; then you can apply mullions using the Mullion tool in the Build panel. Figure 14.35 illustrates an example of a standard gable roof that has been converted to sloped glazing.

FIGURE 14.35
Sloped glazing is created by switching a standard roof to the Sloped Glazing type and assigning grids and mullions.

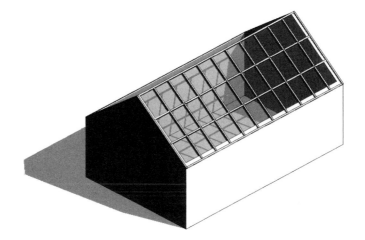

Slope Arrows

If your design calls for a sloped roof with an unusual footprint that does not easily lend itself to utilizing the Defines Slope property of boundary lines, slope arrows can be added within the sketch of the roof. First create the sketch lines to define the shape of a roof, but don't check Defines Slop in the Options bar. Instead, choose the Slope Arrow tool from the Draw panel. Draw the slope arrow in the direction you want your roof to pitch. Select the arrow, and in the Properties palette, you can set any of the parameters as shown in Figure 14.36. The Specify parameter can be set to either Height At Tail or Slope. If you choose Height At Tail, be sure to specify the Height Offset At Head parameter as the end result of the desired slope.

FIGURE 14.36
Defining the properties of a slope arrow added to an irregular footprint roof sketch.

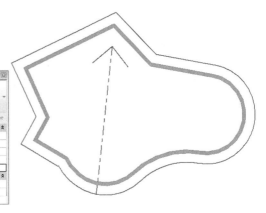

CREATING A DORMER STEP-BY-STEP

Roofs with dormers generally cause grief for architects, so we'll guide you through the creation of one:

1. Create the base of a building, set up three levels, and create a roof by footprint with Defines Slope checked for all sides.

2. Approximately in the position indicated in the following illustration, on Level 2, create the four walls of a dormer. Set their height to a value that makes them extend above the roof. (For easier verification, create a cross section through the dormer to check the height of the dormer walls, and if necessary, modify their height in the element properties so that they extend above the roof.)

3. Using the Roof By Footprint tool, create a pitched roof on top of the dormer walls.

4. If you switch to a side elevation view, you will notice that the dormer roof probably does not extend to meet the main roof, so you will need to use the Join/Unjoin Roof tool, located in the Modify tab in the Edit Geometry panel, to join the main roof and the dormer. Select the Join/Unjoin Roof tool, select the main roof as the target, and then select the edge of the dormer roof to extend.

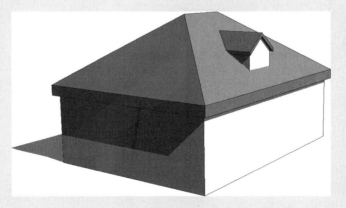

5. From the Opening panel on the Architecture tab, select Dormer. Now pick first the main roof, and then the dormer roof, and then select the sides of the walls that define the dormer. Select the inside faces of the walls. Unlike with most sketches, you will not need to provide a closed loop of lines in this case. Finish the dormer opening.

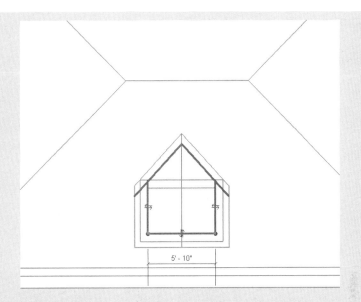

6. The last thing to do is to go back to the section view you previously created and edit the elevation profile of the side walls to make sure they don't extend below or above the roofs. Note that you should not use the Top/Base Attach tool; instead, select the wall and use the Edit Profile tool available in the Mode panel of the Modify | Walls tab to edit its elevation profile and manually resketch the edge lines of the walls to get the triangular elevation profile as shown.

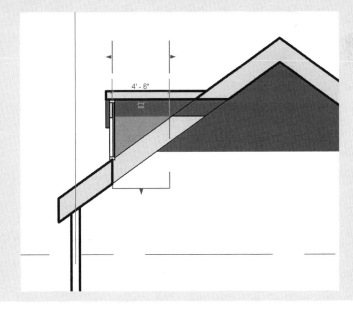

The correct dormer opening as shown cuts the roof in two directions.

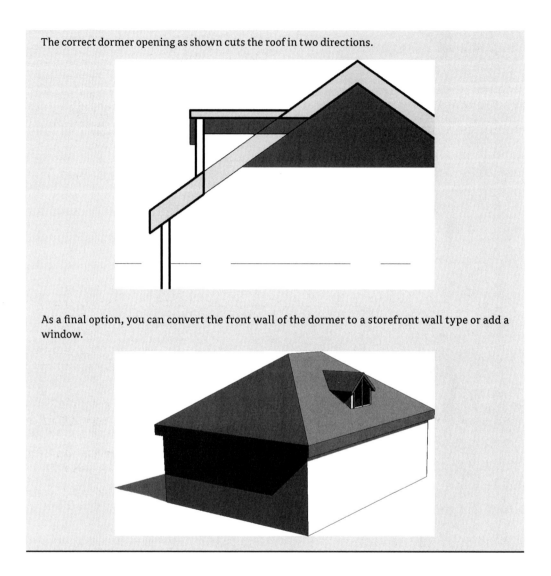

As a final option, you can convert the front wall of the dormer to a storefront wall type or add a window.

Advanced Shape Editing for Floors and Roofs

No flat roof is ever really flat! Revit tools allow for tapered insulation over a flat roof and similar conditions to give the roof a small pitch. A rich set of shape-editing tools for roofs and floors help create and modify such conditions quickly and accurately. These powerful tools are modifiers that are applicable to roofs and floors and will allow you to model concrete slabs with multiple slopes for sidewalks or roof assemblies with tapered insulation (see Figure 14.37).

FIGURE 14.37
Roof with sloped drain-
age layer.

The set of tools available for editing floor and roof shapes appears in the ribbon when a flat floor or roof is selected.

Let's take a look at what each tool is designed to do:

Modify Sub Elements   This tool allows you to directly edit element geometry by selecting and modifying points and edges. If you don't create any additional points or split lines before activating this tool, the object's outer edges and corners will be available for editing.

Add Point   This tool allows you to add points on the top face of a roof or floor. Points can be added on edges or surfaces and can be modified after placement using the Modify Sub Elements tool.

Add Split Line   This tool allows you to sketch directly on the top face of the element, which adds vertices so that hips and valleys can be created when the elevations of the lines are modified using the Modify Sub Elements tool.

Pick Supports   This tool allows you to pick linear beams and walls in order to create new split edges and set the slope and/or elevation of the floor or roof automatically.

Once a floor or roof has been modified using any of these tools, the Reset Shape button will become active. You can use this tool to remove all modifications you applied to the selected floor or roof.

Creating a Roof with a Sloped Topping

Let's do an exercise that shows you how to make a roof with a sloped topping like the one shown in Figure 14.38 (shown in plan view).

FIGURE 14.38
A roof plan showing
a roof divided in seg-
ments, with drainage
points

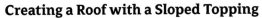
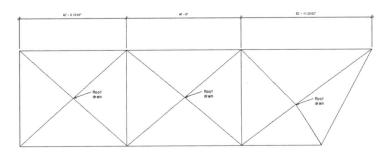

Follow these steps:

1. Open c14-Roof-Edit.rvt from the book's companion website.

2. Select the roof that has already been prepared for you.

3. Activate the Add Split Line tool (note that the color of the rest of the model grays out while the roof lines are dashed green).

4. Sketch two ridge lines to divide the roof into three areas that will be independently drained. The ridge lines will be drawn in blue.

5. Using the same tool, draw diagonal lines within those areas to create the valleys. Make sure you zoom in closely when drawing the diagonal lines, and be sure that you are snapping in the exact same dividing points. (If you notice that the split lines are not snapped to the correct points, select the Modify Sub Elements tool, pick the incorrect lines, delete them, and try again.)

   You have split the roof surface into many regions, but they are still all at the same height and pitch. You should have a roof that looks like Figure 14.39. Press the Esc key or click the Modify button to stop the editing mode.

FIGURE 14.39
Using the Add Split Line tool, you can create ridges and valleys.

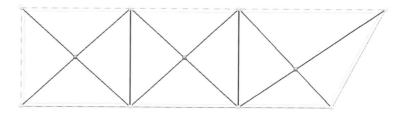

6. Switch to a 3D view.

7. To add a slope, you need to edit the height of the drainage points or the heights of the edges and ridges created by the split lines. For this exercise, you will raise the elevation of the boundary edges and ridges. Activate the Modify Sub Elements tool and select an edge of the roof (dashed green line). New controls that allow you to edit the text will appear, and you can either move the arrows up and down or type in a value for the height. Type in **1′ 0″** [30 cm].

8. Repeat step 7 for all boundary edges and the two north-south split lines forming the ridges between the drainage areas.

9. Make a section through the roof — if possible, somewhere through one of the drainage points. Open the section; change Detail Level to Fine to see all layers. The entire roof structure is now sloped toward the drainage point.

Applying a Variable Thickness to a Roof Layer

What if you wanted the insulation to be tapered but not the structure? For that, the layers of the roofs can now have variable thickness. Let's see how to apply a variable thickness to a layer of the roof assembly.

1. Select the roof, open the Properties palette, and select Edit Type to view the roof's Type Properties. Click Edit in the Structure row to edit the layers of the roof assembly.

2. Activate the preview. You will notice that in the roof-structure preview, you do not see any slopes. That is correct and will not change. This preview is just a schematic preview of the structure and does not show the exact sloping. Look for the Variable column under Layers, as shown in Figure 14.40. This allows layers of the roof to vary in thickness when slopes are present. Check the Variable option for the insulation material.

FIGURE 14.40

Specify variable layers of material in the Edit Assembly dialog box.

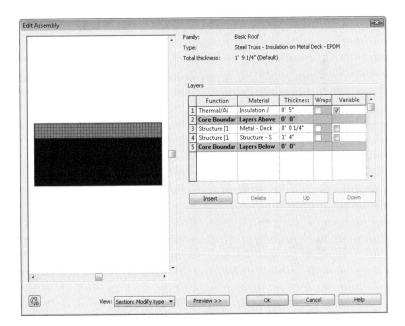

3. Go back to the section view and observe the changes in the roof assembly. As you can see, only the insulation is tapered, while the structure remains flat.

Note that you will only be able to modify an adjustable layer of a floor or roof with a negative value to the next nonadjustable layer of the assembly. In the earlier exercise, for example, if you modified the drainage points by more than –0'-5" [–13 cm], an error would be generated, and the edits to the roof would be removed. You must think about the design requirements of your roof or floor assembly when planning how to model adjustable layers. An alternative approach to the previous exercise might have been to increase the thickness of the insulation layer in the roof assembly to that required at the high pitch points. The drainage points could then be lowered relative to the boundary edges and ridge lines.

The Bottom Line

Understand floor modeling methods. Floors make up one of the most fundamental, sketch-based system families used in a Revit model. You can customize them to accommodate a variety of assumptions at various stages of design.

Master It How can you create a structural floor with integrated metal decking?

Model various floor finishes. Thick and thin floor finishes can be created to support tagging, scheduling, and quantity takeoffs.

Master It How would you represent a thin finish material in your project such as carpet?

Create ceilings. Ceilings are sketch-based system families that can host objects such as light fixtures and HVAC diffusers.

Master It What's the best way to model a ceiling within a space?

Understand roof modeling methods. Roofs can be modeled as simple single-pitch shed roofs or complex extrusions of sinuous curves.

Master It What is the best way to create a single vault roof?

Work with advanced shape editing for floors and roofs. A small but powerful toolset is available for extended editing of floor and roof objects. These tools allow you to create warped floor slabs and tapered layers of roof assemblies.

Master It How do you create a drainage point in a flat roof slab?

Chapter 15

Family Editor

If you're not designing or documenting a building, you're probably designing or placing the stuff that goes inside it: structural members, doors, furniture, lighting, equipment, and more. If you think about it, this effort is a significant part of the design process. If the surrounding walls, floor, and roof or ceiling contain the space, it might be said that the content describes the function and utility of a space. In other words, content provides context. In many respects, it gives the space meaning. The rhythm of placement, orientation, and elevation of content can turn a mundane space into an elegant and memorable one.

In Autodesk® Revit® Architecture software, the Family Editor is where you'll model all the content that isn't built as part of the project. If you're familiar with other 3D modeling applications, the good news is that it will be easy to get started. But the *really* great news is that if you've never modeled in 3D, learning to create 3D content for the first time is a very satisfying process.

The key isn't just being able to model; you can model in 3D in lots of applications. The Family Editor offers the ability to make content that will flex appropriately as your design changes; you can iterate your design without starting over. Sometimes you'll need to change the height, width, or length. Other times you'll need to modify the material, and in some cases you'll need to nest geometry into another family in order to create assembled options on the fly.

Creating content in Revit often involves assigning parameters. At first, parameters might seem new and frightening. But parameters are just values that you assign to what you're making so that you can quickly and easily change it, and there's no programming involved. This workflow is much superior to the ones you've probably used to model in 3D in other applications, where changing a model often means storing and then manually recalling endless earlier versions.

So relax, and prepare yourself for getting excited about design. Once you get your mind around creating parametric content in the Family Editor, you'll probably realize you can do anything in Revit.

In this chapter, you'll learn to:

◆ Understand the Family Editor

◆ Choose the right family template

◆ Create and test parameters

◆ Know why formulas are important

Understanding the Family Editor

Plenty of generic 3D modeling applications allow you to create content that will be used in designing your buildings, and modeling in 3D is certainly a big part of the Family Editor. But the key to the Family Editor isn't that you're modeling *anything* but that you're modeling *something*. Something specific. The thing that you're trying to design is meant to be a particular thing and behave in a particular way.

So when you're modeling in the Family Editor, you're not just trying to model *how* and *what* something is, you're also trying to predict how it might change. Anticipating change is key to creating great, flexible content that is able to quickly and easily reflect your design changes.

For example, take a simple table. If you were to model this table in a program like SketchUp, what you'd have when you're done is exactly what you've modeled. But think about the design process and how something might need to change: height, length, width, or material. In the real world, each of these parameters is critical. Suppose you have only three options for each of these values — this results in 81 permutations! Who has time to manually create each of these options? But this is what you'd have to do if you were using a generic modeler rather than Revit, where these options are driven by rules. By using parameters to define dimensions, materials, nested elements, and more, creating additional options can be done on the fly.

As you probably know, your design is going to change. Being able to anticipate change will help you understand not only how best to approach Revit but also how to keep from becoming a frustrated designer, faced with what seem to be the unpredictable whims and demands of your clients, consultants, and contractors.

Putting the Family Editor in Context

We'll start by putting the Family Editor in context. Without oversimplifying or complicating matters, think about how you'd organize a design problem: constraints, building, content, documentation, and workflow. Interestingly enough, this approach parallels the way Revit views the design process: data, host families, component families, views, and worksharing.

Data Before you start designing in 3D, you're going to need some context! What are the likely levels in elevation or key structural locations in the plan? Data helps give context to almost all the building and project components. Without data (at least levels), there is almost no context to start designing your project. Fortunately, the default Revit template has two levels, and the default view is Level 1.

Keep in mind that everything Family Editor needs to be created with regard to its relationship in the project. Even if it's not relating to geometry, it's relating to the data in the project: a grid or level. Knowing how your family component will respond to data in the project environment is critical.

Host families In Revit, the main building elements are called host or system families. Host and system families are all geometry, but it's geometry that's built within the project environment, not in the Family Editor (although some host families may contain component families). Walls, floors, roofs, and ceilings are the most common host families.

After data, families often have to be hosted by system families (or at least need to maintain a particular relationship). You need to know whether your family will have to maintain some relationship to system families in your project.

Component families   Component families are created outside the project environment. They're loaded into the project and then distributed as needed. When you change the type properties of a component family, you're changing the properties of all components of the same type. But when you change the instance properties of a family component, you're changing only the instances that you've selected.

Views   Your model includes schedules, 2D views (plans, elevations, and sections), 3D views (orthographic and perspective), and even drafting views for drawing whatever you like and then associating it with the model.

Many views have scale- and detail-level properties. The detail level is particularly important to consider when creating a family component because you often don't need to show every facet and detail in every view and scale. Fortunately, this view scale-to detail level relationship is automatically defined in Revit. So once you place your family component in Revit, it will automatically hide or reveal detail based on the scale of a view in your project (Figure 15.1).

FIGURE 15.1
Default view scale detail

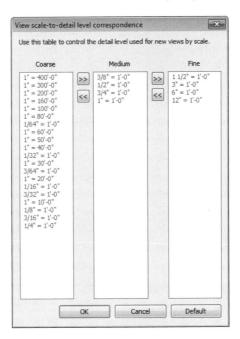

Worksharing   Worksharing allows all your team members to access the Revit project at the same time in a flexible, nonlinear manner. One moment you're moving a wall, the next moment you're adding a door, and the next you're adding a tag or changing the look of the schedule. Revit is able to handle this kind of nonlinear and unpredictable change quickly and easily.

Choosing the Right Family Template and Category

Now that you have a better understanding of where your component families sit in relation to your overall project, we'll discuss some specifics. If you attempt to create a new family

(Application menu ➤ New ➤ Family), you'll notice that there are a lot of different templates (Figure 15.2).

FIGURE 15.2
Template categories

Selecting the right template is important because it determines a lot of the family's behavior. In some cases, you can change the category of the template that you've selected from one to another. For example, as shown in Figure 15.3, a Generic Models family template is capable of being turned into another template. This is helpful if you need to schedule a family in a different category than the one you initially selected. But in many cases, categories cannot be switched, and nonhosted or non – face-based components cannot be changed to hosted or face-based (and vice versa). That's why you need to choose the category carefully.

FIGURE 15.3
Switching between
family categories

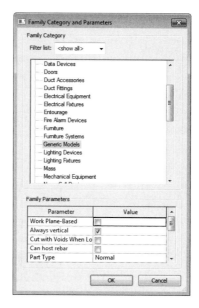

Some categories are hardwired for specific behavior, and if you change from that category to another, you can't go back. For example, if you start a family in one of the baluster templates, you can switch to another template. But after having done so, you cannot switch back to a baluster family. Knowing what you want to create before you begin helps you minimize the amount of switching you need to do later in the process.

SCHEDULING

Remember as you start a new component that the category you select ultimately controls how the family component will schedule. If you're trying to determine which template to select, it is helpful to ask yourself or your team members how the family should schedule. Figure 15.4 shows some of the many schedule categories that are available in Revit.

FIGURE 15.4
New Schedule
dialog box

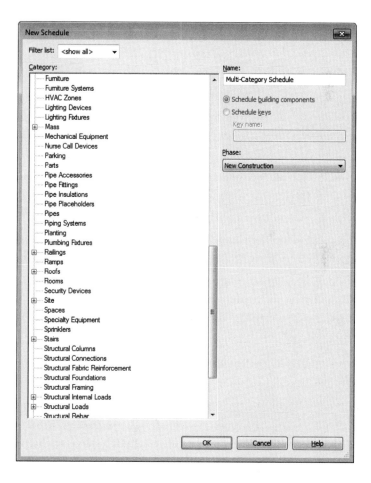

PROJECTION AND CUT VALUES

Another important characteristic of the family category is that it will control whether a family will "cut" when intersecting a view plane (plan, section, elevation, and so on). For example, convention dictates that when furniture encounters a cut plane, you should show a projected view.

Revit respects this convention by cutting some categories while not cutting others. You can figure out which categories cut or don't cut by going to the Manage tab and clicking Object Styles. The Object Styles dialog box is shown in Figure 15.5.

FIGURE 15.5

Cut properties via Object Styles

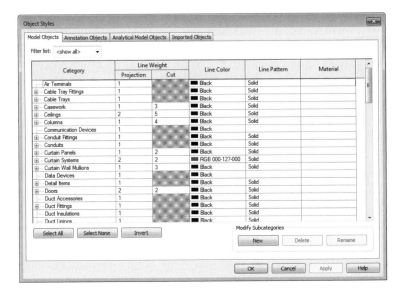

As you can see, categories such as Casework, Ceilings, and Columns cut, whereas categories such as Communication Devices, Conduit Fittings, and Conduits do not.

Another important characteristic of the object properties is the default line weights given to objects when they're placed in a project. These line weights affect both projection and cut values. Just remember that it's probably best not to manipulate the Line Weights dialog box (Figure 15.6) unless you know what you're doing. If you intend to increase or decrease the line weight of a category of objects, use the object properties rather than the Line Weights dialog box.

ASSIGNING PARAMETERS

As you start to get into the parameter that can control a family's geometry, material, or other value, keep in mind that it's not always necessary to create components as fully parametric. This is especially true of the first pass. The location and spacing of content is often more important than whether the family can flex geometrically.

Nonparametric families often occur when the component being modeled is specific and highly unique. It may have parameters that control materials or a few other values, but not much more. At this point, little more than selecting the right category and insertion point is necessary. It's often far more efficient to maintain design relationships by modifying the component in the Family Editor and then reloading it into the project — at least until more is known about the design. When more is known, you can open the family and embed more parameters.

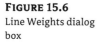

FIGURE 15.6
Line Weights dialog
box

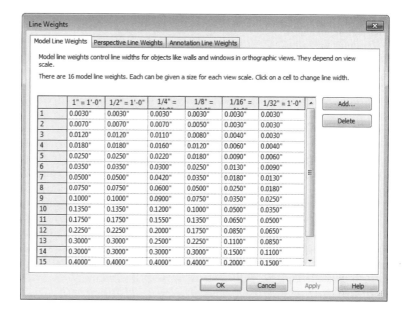

Creating a Family Component

Now that we've discussed some of the basic definitions and rules of the Family Editor,
we'll talk about the hierarchy of creating a family component. As previously discussed, not all
families are created in the Family Editor. Host families, for example, such as walls,
floors, and ceilings, are created directly in the project environment. It's possible to create
component families in the project environment, but it's important, in most cases, to avoid
doing so.

Creating what Revit calls in-place families is often a dead-end process that robs you of hours
of otherwise productive time for a number of reasons. First, an in-place family should be used
only in cases where the object that you're making is not likely to be moved, rotated, or copied.
Any attempt to move, rotate, or copy an in-place family can often have unintended consequences that are difficult to pinpoint. For example, if you model an in-place family and then
create copies in your project, they may all initially look the same, but in fact you're copying new
instances. So modifying one of the instances is going to leave the others untouched, which can
be frustrating if you've copied the instances thinking that later changes would ripple through
the project.

Second, each copied instance will schedule independently from the other instances as separate line items. This is often not desirable because you may want to group like elements together
in a schedule.

Finally, there's no way to convert an in-place family into a component family. In some cases,
you can copy and paste sketch lines or other 2D elements between the project and family environments. But if you try to copy and paste geometry from the project environment to the Family
Editor, you'll get the warning shown in Figure 15.7. The only way to proceed is to start again in
the Family Editor.

FIGURE 15.7
It's not possible to
copy content from
your project to the
Family Editor.

The bottom line is that if you're going to use more than a single, highly unique instance in a project or across projects, it's probably best to create the component in the Family Editor, not as an in-place family.

So you need to consider the following criteria before you create a family component, particularly since some of the criteria can't easily be changed (if at all). You'll probably have to start over if you choose poorly. We've also tried to order the criteria for creating a family component from most to least restrictive. Most restrictive means you may have to start over. Least restrictive means you may get away with changing a parameter or value after you've already started the family.

Hosted vs. Nonhosted

The first and most important question you need to ask yourself as you select your template is whether the family is meant to be hosted or nonhosted. If you make the wrong decision here, you'll have to start over to switch between these types.

First, keep in mind that hosted objects are meant to cut their host or create an opening or depression. Obviously a window needs to cut the wall that it will go into. Or a fire extinguisher case will often need to create a recess in the wall in which it will be placed. Second, if the component is to be hosted and you're certain that it needs to create an opening in its host, it can cut only one host. For example, a window that is wall-hosted may not be hosted by a roof or ceiling.

Want to see a bad example of this? Open the Tub-Rectangular-3D family component that comes with Revit in the Family Editor (Figure 15.8).

FIGURE 15.8
Wall-hosted plumb-
ing fixtures

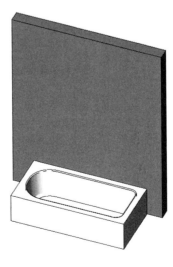

What's wrong with this picture? Well, first, not all tubs need walls, so you'll have to make another family that has no host in order to place the tub where there is no wall. This seems a bit redundant because one tub will do.

Second, if you delete a host, all the nested elements are deleted as well. This makes some sense when you delete a wall that contains a window. But it will certainly lead to a lot of frustration if you delete a wall that contains bathroom fixtures!

But what if you want the tub to move with the wall? There's a better way. Simply place the element and select the Moves With Nearby Elements option (Figure 15.9). When the host moves, the component will move as well.

FIGURE 15.9
Moves With Nearby
Elements option

We can't stress this enough: Stay away from creating hosted relationships between objects that do not require hosting (that do not cut or otherwise modify the host). This discussion brings up an interesting point. Rather than use hosted elements, why not make elements face-based? There are some advantages:

◆ You don't have to decide on a particular host. Any surface will do: Wall, Ceiling, Top Of Casework, anything that has a face. This is great if the lighting component you're creating needs to cut into a wall, floor, and ceiling!

◆ A face-based element can cut the face of geometry in both the project and family editing environment. So the light fixture that cuts a wall in a project can cut the face of a piece of casework in the Family Editor.

◆ Deleting the host will not delete the component. Is this always desirable? Well, maybe yes and maybe no. But what's important is that you have the option if the component is face-based. You won't have the option if the component is hosted.

Finally, one last point with regard to hosting and face-based elements: Why not simply model the elements, share the parameters, and then nest? This approach often gives the most flexibility.

Family Category

After you've decided whether you're going hosted or nonhosted, you must choose the correct family category. As mentioned earlier in the chapter, this step is also critical. The reason you need to select the category carefully is because some categories can be switched after the fact, but that is not always the case. This is particularly true when the component has behavior that is specific or unique.

For example, lighting fixtures contain elements that allow the light to render once placed in the project environment. Balusters are another example of elements that have specific behaviors built in.

Insertion Point

Now that you've defined the hosting and family category, the rest is pretty flexible. If you choose poorly, you'll probably be able to recover most if not all of your work if something needs to change. But some considerations should come before others, which is why we believe that the insertion point is the next most critical criterion on your list for family creation.

The insertion point determines the location about which the family will geometrically flex — not just in plan view but also in elevation. The reference level in the Family Editor directly corresponds to the datum level in your project. Keep in mind that not only does this relate to the visibility of your component in a view, it also relates to how the component will schedule. This is important for a couple of reasons. First, when the family expands or contracts geometrically, the insertion point will remain relatively fixed.

But second (and often more important), the insertion point is the point of reference when two family components are exchanged. This is critical if the "design" family that you've used as a placeholder is being swapped out for something more specific at a later date. If the insertion points are not concurrent, the location of the new family will not agree with the location of the old one.

For example, in the default Desk.rfa file in the following example, the insertion point is located at the center of the object (Figure 15.10). This means the desk will flex about this point. But this is not desirable if the desk, table, or furniture object that you are about to swap out for this example has a different insertion point or if the family needs to flex from a different location.

FIGURE 15.10
Default Desk.rfa family component

Keep in mind that changing the insertion point is easy. As you would expect, you don't move the geometry to the insertion point. Rather, you simply select two reference planes and then make sure the Defines Origin option is selected. Based on our experience, we recommend that the insertion point for this particular family would best be located at the face of the desk, as shown in Figure 15.11. This would allow the desk to flex with respect to the seating so that if the desk is larger or smaller, you won't have to spend time relocating all the chairs.

Reference Points, Planes, and Lines

If you're confident that what you're about to model in the Family Editor will need to flex (have a modifiable length, angle, location, and so on) from within the rules of the family, then it's important that you start modeling the geometry by first creating the rules that will allow the geometry to move.

With few exceptions, you don't want to give parameters to the geometry itself. Instead, you'll want to create the necessary reference planes, lines, and points first. Then associate the parameters to these references and whenever possible test the parameters to make sure the references are flexing properly. Once you're confident the references are flexing, you can build the geometry in context to the references, again testing to make certain that when the references flex, the geometry is flexing as well.

FIGURE 15.11
Redefining the
insertion point

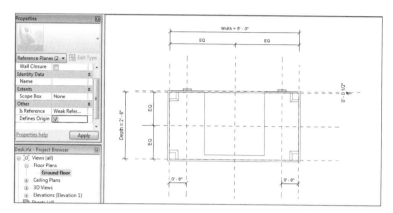

Which reference you use is based on how you want the geometry to flex:

Reference points   These have three planes that can be set to host sketch lines or geometry. You can also use a series of points to control a line or even a spline. Other objects, such as reference lines or other geometric surfaces, can also host reference points. You can select reference points from the ribbon panel shown in Figure 15.12.

FIGURE 15.12
Reference points in
the Draw dialog box

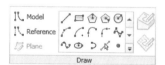

However, reference points are available only in the categories of certain families: Mass, Adaptive Mass, and Curtain Panel Pattern Based.

Reference planes   These define a single plane that can be set to host sketch lines or geometry. They're best for controlling linear geometric relationships. Reference planes don't have endpoints. This is important because you don't want to use reference planes for controlling angular or directional relationships.

The linear relationships of length, width, and height are perfectly well suited for controlling the geometric parameters of the default `Desk.rfa` family component. All of the geometric options are parallel to one another (Figure 15.13).

FIGURE 15.13
Reference planes
controlling the
parameters of the
default Desk.rfa
family

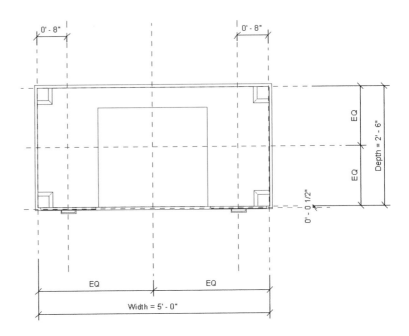

Reference lines   By definition these have endpoints and are great for controlling angular and directional relationships. They can have four points of reference, two along the length of the line (which are perpendicular to each other) and one at each end that is perpendicular to the line.

You can also create curved reference lines, but they have only planes that may be used for hosting at each end. There are no references along the curved line (Figure 15.14).

FIGURE 15.14
Straight and curved
reference lines

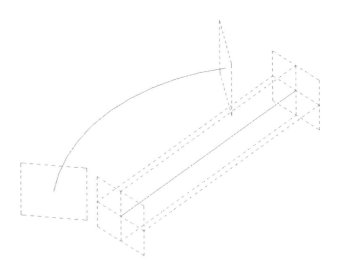

The great thing about reference lines is that because they contain endpoints, they're able to manage angular relationships.

PARAMETERIZING REFERENCE LINES

Here's a simple tutorial for parameterizing reference lines. Don't even try this with reference planes. It would fail to work — because by definition, planes don't have endpoints. So when you try to parameterize an angular value between two reference planes, they tend to lose their angular origin. Fortunately, lines have endpoints, so controlling them from an endpoint is far more predictable.

First, open a Generic Model template and draw a series of connected reference lines. If you are deliberate and make them all the same length and angle, it'll save some time. Here's what you should have when you're finished.

Now take a moment and add length and angle dimensions to each of the lines. Parameterize all the length parameters together, and then do the same for the angles. If you've drawn your reference lines carefully (all the same length and angle), you'll be able to parameterize them by selecting the dimensions all at once. If they're different, you'll need to select the lengths (and angles) one at a time and associate them with the appropriate parameters. When you're finished, your family should look like this:

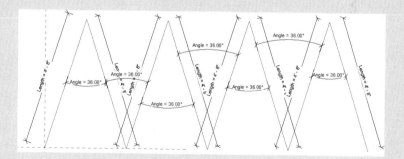

Now comes the interesting part: Create a single swept form by picking each of the reference lines together. After you've finished your sweep, you'll realize that when you flex the angular and length parameters, the sweep will remain associated with the reference lines. The following image shows you some of the iterations you can produce with the same family by changing the parameters.

With this technique, you can imagine that modeling accordion panels shouldn't be a problem. You can show the panels as open or closed, driving the individual segment lengths from an overall length that is divided among the individual segments.

Visibility Settings

The time it takes for Revit to generate or regenerate a view depends on how much stuff in the view needs to be displayed. One of the great things about Revit is that it automatically assigns the level of detail based on the scale of the view.

When you're building smaller parts of a larger component (or if the elements are not visible in certain orientations), you should assign those elements to reveal themselves only at a certain level of detail (or certain orientations). Doing so keeps Revit from having to manage more information than necessary and helps you keep your views uncluttered. Here's a rule of thumb: Once the separate lines that represent something print as a single, merged line, there's little point in having that element display in that view or at that scale. Although this was an entirely intuitive realization when drawing with a pencil (don't draw over the same line twice), unfortunately computers have allowed us to draw beyond a point of diminishing returns.

To see how to fix it, open the default Desk.rfa family, which is fairly well built, but if you look closely, you'll notice that orientation and detail level are not being fully specified. All of the drawer faces and hardware are showing up at every view in every section or elevation.

STARTING WITH EXISTING CONTENT

Let's face it — we've all downloaded Revit families from a number of widely available online sources to get a first design pass at a piece of content. Autodesk Seek, Revit City, and the AUGI forums are all great places to start. But when you download a family component, take a moment to make sure that the detail level and orientation of detail are appropriate.

In this Desk.rfa family, everything is showing up in every level of detail. This isn't necessarily a big deal with just a few objects. But multiply this by all the other elements that will make up your plans, reflected ceiling plans, elevations, and sections and you'll notice that your views don't refresh, rotate, print, and export as fast as you'd expect. When this happens, one of the first things you look for is an object in a view that is being shown at a level of detail that is far too high. In some cases the object prints as only a small, black dot. But when you zoom in, you'll notice that it's full of detail.

Controlling the detail parametrically is done through the Family Element Visibility Settings dialog box (Figure 15.15).

FIGURE 15.15
Family Element
Visibility Settings
dialog box

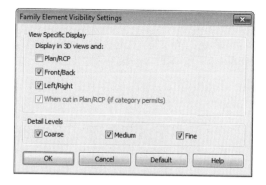

Notice that the box for the Plan/RCP option is unchecked. This is appropriate for the desk because little more than the surface of the top of the desk needs to show up in plan. The legs, the hardware, and even the faces of the drawers don't need to show up in plan.

But what about the elevations? By turning off the Thin Lines option from the Graphics panel of the View Tab, you can see that all the geometry is showing up at every level of detail in a view that's set for 1/8″ = 1′-0″ [1:100] (Figure 15.16).

FIGURE 15.16
Lines beginning to
merge

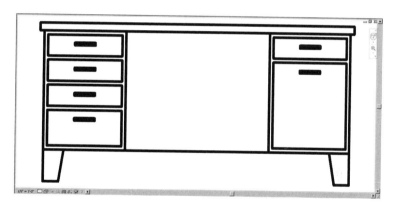

In these cases, Zoom To Sheet Size is your friend. Figure 15.17 shows the same desk in elevation when that option is active. It's obvious that you'd never need that level of detail at that scale.

FIGURE 15.17
Zoom To Sheet Size

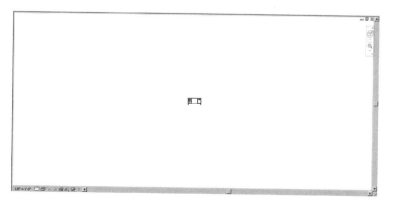

It should be apparent that there's far more detail than necessary for this view, and the solution is simple. Set the drawer faces to show up at a Medium detail level or finer, and set the hardware to show up only at a Fine detail level. Do this to all your content, and performance should noticeably increase (Figure 15.18).

FIGURE 15.18
Adjusting the detail level

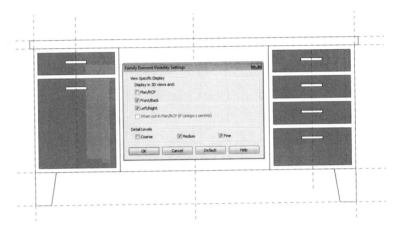

Materials

Materials are crucial to a family. But what is possibly more important is the Shading setting and the Transparency value of the material because they communicate much about the intent of your design in the early stages (Figure 15.19).

FIGURE 15.19
Shading and Transparency settings in the Materials Editor dialog

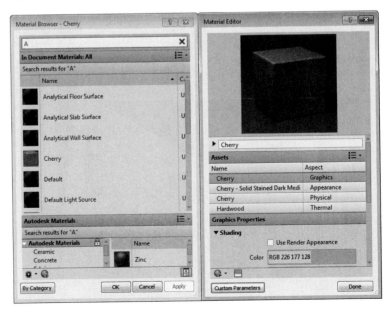

In addition, material options are often not easily created in Revit. Yes, a family can have a material parameter. But expressing many different parameters for visualization purposes is probably left to the visualization specialist who understands the subtleties of creating an emotive image, not just a rendering — and it's unlikely they'll be using Revit to iterate or emotively visualize your design.

Beyond visualization, however, materials in Revit are used for a host of other things. Graphic representation in construction documents and material takeoffs are two examples. If the materials in your families are something you will need to schedule or view graphically, it's a good idea to define them.

Multiple materials can be assigned to a family. They are assigned based on model solids, so if you have multiple solids (sweeps, extrusions, etc.), each individual one can be given an individual material.

You have two options to define a material within a family, both being handled in the solid's object properties shown in the Properties pallet. By default, the material is set to <By Category>. Select this option and you can change the material to any material shown in the Material dialog box. Or make a new one. This is a great use for the family if you know the material is not going to change. If you know that your casework is not going to be anything but blonde maple, go ahead and set the material within the family. Your other option is to use the tiny little button on the right of the Material field in the Properties pallet to define a new parameter. In this case, you can call the material something like "casework material as a property". If you were to use this same parameter for all your casework families, once it's placed in the model, you can change that material via the Material dialog box and it will update all your casework families (using that parameter name) at once.

Dimensions

As mentioned earlier, dimensions are useful for controlling the geometry parameters of your families. It's best to keep the dimensions outside of Sketch mode. Let's use the desk as an example. In plan view, you can see all the reference planes and dimensions (Figure 15.20).

FIGURE 15.20
Parameterized
dimensions

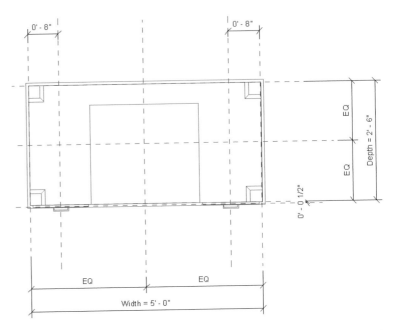

Now select the main body of the desk and select the Edit Extrusion option. What you'll find are dimensions from the underside of the desktop to the outer reference planes (Figure 15.21).

FIGURE 15.21
Dimensions inside
Sketch mode

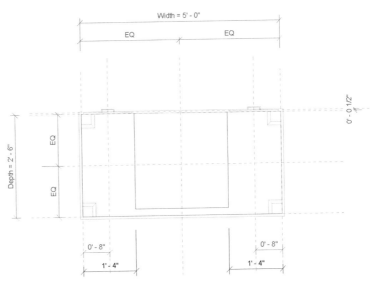

These dimensions are only visible while in the Sketch mode of the desktop. This is fine in the sense that they'll work. But as a best practice, don't put parameterized dimensions inside Sketch mode. When you complete the sketch, the dimensions will be hidden. Then when you're trying to troubleshoot or modify parameters, you won't be able to easily find the corresponding values in the model view.

Object Styles and Subcategories

Revit has predefined a number of hardwired family categories. These categories can't be modified or added. As mentioned earlier, they define how elements display, schedule, export, and so on. But within the default object categories, you can create subcategories for model, annotation, and imported objects (Figure 15.22).

FIGURE 15.22
Object Styles dialog box

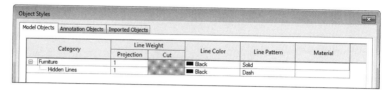

Although you can use subcategories to control the visibility of some part of the whole component, keep in mind that the detail level and visibility settings already manage visibility. The subcategories are most important when you're exporting your project because each category and subcategory is permitted its own CAD layer (Figure 15.23).

FIGURE 15.23
Export options for categories and subcategories

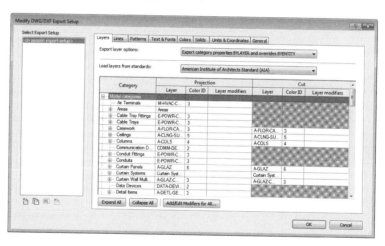

So if your project is being exported to CAD in such a way that you'll need to associate objects with granular layer settings, creating and assigning subcategories to elements is necessary. It's best not to rely on subcategories to manage visibility.

Type and Instance Parameters

CERT
OBJECTIVE

Many users new to Revit start to panic when they have to select between a type and an instance parameter for the first time. Don't panic. Keep in mind that you can change these two items after you set them initially. Whenever you reload the family into the project environment, the previous settings will be overwritten.

The key difference between the two is that modifying a type parameter always modifies all the other components at the same time. Think of a type as a set of identical elements. Change one item in the set and all the other items of that type in the model change to match. Door sizes are a good example of this. Doors come in standard sizes: 32", 34", 36" [80 cm, 85 cm, 90 cm]. On the other hand, an instance parameter modifies only the components that you have selected. A good use of an instance parameter would be the fire rating on a door. Not every 36" [90 cm] door will be fire rated, so you'll need to identify which ones individually. Figure 15.24 shows the parameters of the default Desk.rfa family.

FIGURE 15.24

Parameters of the Desk.rfa family

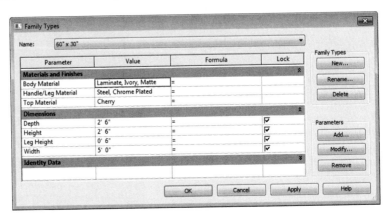

You can tell all these parameters are type parameters because any time you have an instance parameter, the text (default) appears after the parameter value. In this case, it's likely important that the dimensions are type parameters. You don't want users to create random or arbitrary Depth, Height, and Width values.

On the other hand, each new option can create a lot of new types. By default, loading a family into your project will also load all the types. If you want to create the potential for many types but be selective about which types are loaded, you can use a type catalog to load only specific types.

USE NESTING AND PATTERNS FOR QUICK TURNAROUND

Geometry from one family can be loaded into another family. This process is called *nesting*, and it allows you to create a single element that will be used many times in one or more families. This is much more desirable than creating an element and then grouping and copying it around the same family. Become accustomed to using nesting whenever possible because it'll save you a lot of time when your design changes.

First, it's much easier to change and control the location of a nested family. The nested family can also have references and parameters that can control it when nested.

But more important, the nested family can be controlled by a "Family Type" parameter, which will allow you to select the desired nested families as another parameter in the family. This feature is incredibly powerful for creating design iteration within families that are in your projects.

Second, as soon as you have a reasonable representation of your family, get it in the project. Don't be afraid to start simple and update it later. Users sometimes obsess about the details and hesitate to load the family into the project until it's "perfect." This tendency can hold up a project. So get the idea in the project first and make it ideal later. Just take care about the insertion point so that when you modify it (or exchange it with something more detailed), its relative location will remain the same.

Finally, look for opportunities to use model patterns in lieu of geometry. Doing so is important in the project environment, but it's also important (and often overlooked) in the Family Editor. Model patterns graphically regenerate far faster than small geometric parts and pieces.

Using Advanced Modeling Techniques

Creating complex geometry isn't always as easy as opening the Family Editor and starting to model the shape that you think you're trying to create. Sometimes you need to model one form in order to create another form. And sometimes you need to model a complex, parameterized form in order to parameterize the actual shape that you're trying to create. So that you understand these advanced techniques, we'll first cover the available geometry types that can be created in Revit.

There are five discrete geometry types in the Family Editor: extrusions, blends, revolves, sweeps, and swept blends. Both solid and void forms can be modeled from these shapes.

Which one you select is important, but our advice is to use the simplest form that will express what you're trying to model, keeping in mind how the geometry is likely to change.

In other words, an extrusion, blend, sweep, or swept blend can be used to create initially similar forms. It's impossible to tell them apart (Figure 15.25). But once these forms change, you'll understand that they can iterate into very different shapes (Figure 15.26).

FIGURE 15.25
Initially similar
forms

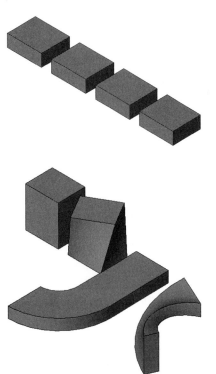

FIGURE 15.26
Upper left to lower
right: extrusion,
blend, sweep, and
swept blend

Creating Solid and Void Relationships

One of the great things in Revit is that the relationship between solid geometry and cutting void is nonlinear. Solids that are joined together may still maintain independent relationships. They're not locked together after they're joined.

Additionally, not all voids must cut all solids. The void may selectively cut one solid but not another solid, even though the two solids are joined together. For example, in Figure 15.27 we've joined the solids from the previous image and overlapped them with a single void. Notice how the void is cutting all of the joined solids. Figure 15.28 shows the results of finishing the sketch.

FIGURE 15.27
Single extruded void overlapping all joined solids

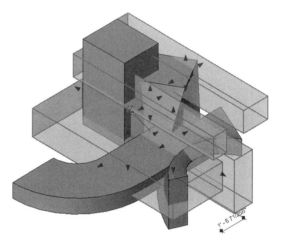

FIGURE 15.28
All joined solids cut

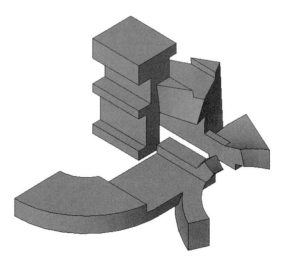

This is often not desirable because now you'll have to go back and "uncut" three of the four joined solids. So in many cases you'd rather model a void that only selectively cuts. The trick here is not to model the void as a void. If you do, then by default it will cut all the solids that came before it. Rather, model the geometry as a solid (Figure 15.29).

FIGURE 15.29
Initially modeling
the desired void as
a solid

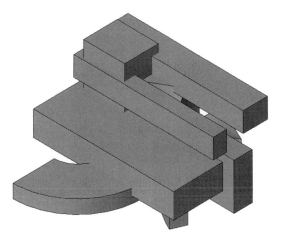

Now you can convert the solid to a void from the Properties dialog box, as shown in Figure 15.30.

FIGURE 15.30
Converting a solid
to a void

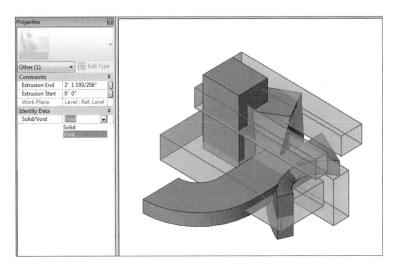

Figure 15.31 shows the result. The void doesn't cut any of the solids. This result is desirable when you want to complete the void and still see it because by default, once a void cuts a solid, it becomes invisible, which makes it rather hard to find. This technique still shows the void for editing.

FIGURE 15.31
Noncutting voids
remain visible

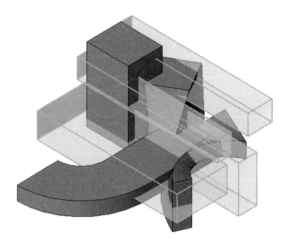

Now you can selectively cut only what you want to cut (Figure 15.32).

FIGURE 15.32
Selectively cutting
forms

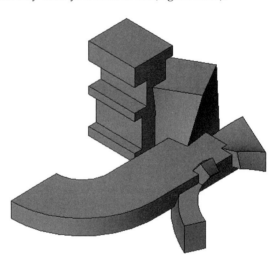

To review this file, you can download it from the Chapter 15 folder at the book's website (www.sybex.com/go/masteringrevit2013); it's called Solid Void.rfa.

Carving Geometry

If you're really 3D savvy, creating complex geometry often involves creating what you need with complex modeling tools in order to reach some final result. The process in Revit is often different and has some wonderful benefits as well.

Think of a sculptural process as being additive or subtractive. Creating sculpture as an additive process means that you're casting the desired shape. Creating sculpture as a subtractive process means starting with more stuff than you need and then carving away until you have the final result.

Many complex geometry applications create complex forms as an additive process. In other words, you create a form and then manipulate that result with other tools — pushing, pulling, and twisting until you've morphed the final shape.

Think of Revit as more of a hybrid process that relies heavily on a subtractive approach that carves away what you don't need. Although this may seem a bit counterintuitive at first (because in many 3D modeling tools, cutting geometry is a linear process that doesn't lend itself well to parametric editing), in Revit the void is a live thing that can be quickly and easily modified.

For example, you may not believe that the form shown in Figure 15.33 has been created in Revit. If you're trying to create this form using an additive process, it's quite complicated. But if you create it using a subtractive approach, then it's quite easy, and the results can be surprisingly elegant.

FIGURE 15.33
Sculptural forms

Furthermore, the form consists of only three (copied) extrusions and a single void. But it's easily done with just a few steps.

COMPLEX FORMS MADE SIMPLE

Creating that sculptural form in Figure 15.33 is not hard. Don't believe us? Follow these steps:

1. Create the extrusion sketch shown here in a Front/Back elevation. In this case, the overall height is 6′ [2 m]. The width is 0′ − 4″ [10 cm].

2. When you finish the sketch, set the overall length to 9′ − 0″ [3 m]. This is the resulting shape.

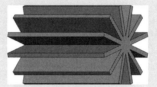

3. Go to your Left/Right elevation and use Copy/Rotate to move the form 90 degrees so that the copy is vertical. You'll also have to select the Disjoin option.

4. Go to the Top/Bottom view and use Copy/Rotate to move the original form 90 degrees so that the copy is facing left/right.

5. Use the Join Geometry tool and join all three forms together. When you're done, the form should look like this:

Now it gets really interesting! We'll show you how to cut multiple solids from a single void after you initially modeled the void as a solid. Here's the sketch of the solid revolve in the Front elevation.

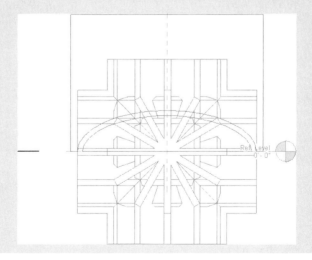

6. When you finish the form, you want to make certain that none of the geometry from the star form is showing outside the revolve that you've created, as shown here.

7. Change the solid revolve into a void. The void won't cut! This is what you want: the ability to model solids and voids with the flexibility to cut the void when you're ready, not before.

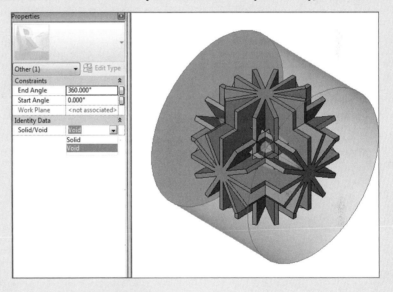

Here's a tip for cutting a lot of geometry with a void without having to select elements one by one. First, select the void and select Cut To Clipboard (or press Ctrl+X). This will remove the void! Don't worry.

8. Select Paste ➢ Aligned To Same Place. Another, much-less-known option is to press Ctrl+V for paste. But when the form starts to hover, select 0, and then press Enter. This will paste the element at 0,0,0, the origin of the original element.

As a result, you should begin to understand that complex form-making in Revit is quite often a subtractive process — you create more geometry than necessary and then use a void to carve away what you don't need.

There are some great examples of creating sculptural forms in Chapter 26, "Outside the Box — Film and Stage." Carving geometry is a technique that set designer Bryan Sutton (profiled in that chapter) uses extensively. If you want to explore this file further, just look in the Chapter 15 folder on the book's website for the file c15 Egg Sculpture.rvt.

Using Geometry to Drive Geometry

As discussed previously, reference planes, points, and lines are most often used to drive geometric form. If you've been using Revit for any length of time, you've been creating parametric content. But there will be some cases where these three options alone are just not enough. This is particularly difficult with linear or tubular forms, as shown in Figure 15.34.

FIGURE 15.34
Chair with tubular structure

To learn how to drive geometry with geometry, follow these steps:

1. Open a Furniture template, and add reference planes to control the height of the seat back and the seat. Figure 15.35 shows the reference planes and other locked dimensions.

2. Now you'll model the "negative space" that would define the centerlines of the tubular structure with a solid extrusion. Make the overall form 20" [6 m] wide. Once you finish the line of the inner sketch, simply offset about 1" [3 cm] or so (Figure 15.36).

FIGURE 15.35
Parameterized
reference plane

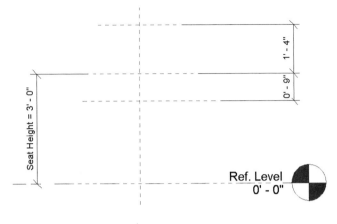

FIGURE 15.36
Extrusion sketch in
elevation

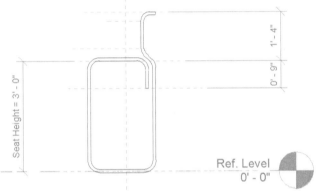

Figure 15.37 shows the finished form. Now you have to start adding the voids that will shape the back of the seat and backrest.

FIGURE 15.37
Finished extrusion

3. Create the two individual voids in the Front/Back elevation orientation (Figure 15.38).

FIGURE 15.38
Voids that cut the
seat back and seat
rest

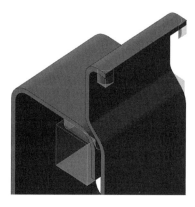

When you're done, you've completed a path that represents the path of the structural tubing (Figure 15.39).

FIGURE 15.39
Complete path

4. Select the Solid Sweep tool and pick the edges that make up the centerline of the structural tubing. Then sketch the profile that you want to follow along this path (Figure 15.40).

CREATING SEPARATE PATHS FOR COMPLEX SWEEPS

You may find that you're unable to create the edge-based sweep with one continuous path because of the complex curves that happen at the back of the seat and seat rest. Simply create multiple paths where a singular path would break the sketch.

When you finish the path-based sweeps, you'll have the result shown in Figure 15.41.

5. Model the extrusions for the leather seat and seat back. We've also added some additional reference lines to control the vertical location of the leather seat rest (Figure 15.42).

FIGURE 15.40
Picking edge-based
sweeps

FIGURE 15.41
Edge-based sweeps
with extrusion
hidden

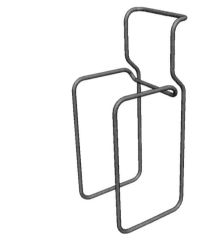

FIGURE 15.42
Additional refer-
ence planes

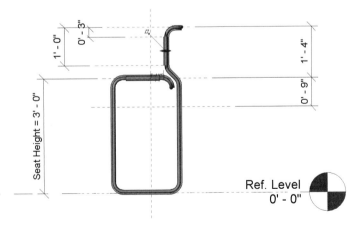

6. Now the tubular geometry is being controlled by the extrusion. But of course you don't want to see the extrusion in the project environment. This is easily fixed. Just select the extrusion, and in the Properties dialog box, deselect the Visible option under Graphics (Figure 15.43).

FIGURE 15.43
Deselect the Visible option to hide the extrusion in the project environment.

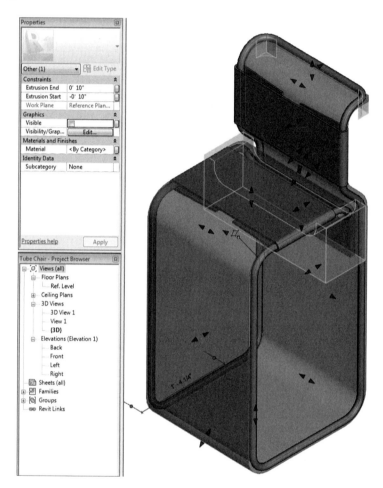

Once loaded into the project, the extrusion will be hidden, and because of the parameters that drive the extrusion, you can create new types (Figure 15.44). And assigning the seat back and tubing appropriate materials will further enhance the family.

If you want to explore this file further, just look in the Chapter 15 folder on the book's website for the file c15 Tube Chairs.rvt.

FIGURE 15.44
Final form in
the project
environment

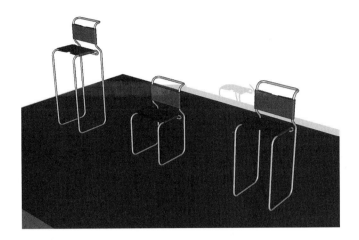

Building a Shelf Using Formulas and Type Catalogs

The real challenge in modeling in 3D is being able to predict and elegantly maintain change and iteration. Once you're able to do this, you really start to work effectively.

To get to this point, you need to understand nesting, family types, formulas, and type catalogs, and in the following sections, we'll walk you through an exercise that includes these techniques. Specifically, you'll build a simple shelf. A shelf is something we're all familiar with, and designing a shelf that elegantly changes with your design is a wonderful thing. Once you learn these techniques, you can apply them to many other concepts in Revit when you're creating elegant content.

The shelf family you will create in the following exercises will contain many brackets, so the brackets will be nested. Which bracket is used will depend on Family Type parameters. Then, the number of brackets will be controlled by formulas that add brackets as the shelf increases in length. Finally, you'll use type catalogs to select only the desired permutations.

Figure 15.45 shows some possibilities for the final shelf.

FIGURE 15.45
Finished shelf
examples

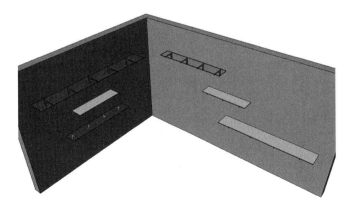

Modeling the Brackets

You'll start by building one of the two brackets:

1. Open a Generic Model template. Starting in the Left elevation view, create a reference plane to the left of the Center Front/Back reference plane to control the support depth.

2. Add a dimension from the Center Front/Back Reference plane (which is also the insertion point) to your new reference plane.

3. Parameterize the Length value as a type parameter, calling it **Support Depth**. When you're done, what you have should look like Figure 15.46.

FIGURE 15.46
Parameterized
reference planes

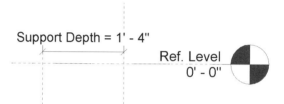

4. Sketch the extrusion shown in Figure 15.47. You won't need to lock any of the sketch lines. Their proximity to the reference planes will cause them to flex. We'll also change the overall thickness of the bracket to 1/4" [6 mm], being careful to distribute half the bracket thickness to either side of the Center Left/Right reference plane.

FIGURE 15.47
Sketch and
Properties settings

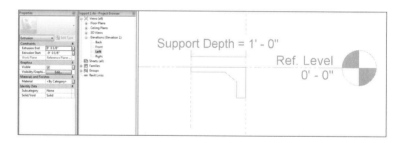

5. Save the bracket as **Support 1.rfa**. It should look like Figure 15.48.

As a general principle, if you have to model an iteration that is similar to an existing example, don't start from scratch. Instead, open the existing example and modify it.

6. Click Save As, and call this new family **Support 2.rfa**.

7. Go back to the Left elevation and edit the previous extrusion. Offset the sketch lines 1/4" [6 mm], as shown in Figure 15.49. Generally speaking, try offsetting sketch lines to create openings rather than adding voids. The results are flexible and faster to model.

FIGURE 15.48
Completed bracket

FIGURE 15.49
Offset and copy the
sketch lines.

8. When you finish the sketch, your new bracket should look like Figure 15.50. Now save the family, and you're ready to nest these two brackets in your shelf family.

FIGURE 15.50
Support 2.rfa

Nesting the Brackets

To nest these two brackets in your shelf family, follow these steps:

1. Open a Furniture template (this is a shelf, after all) and go ahead and nest both brackets into this template. Don't place them — just load them for later.

2. Close the bracket families, leaving only the Furniture family open. Save this new family, calling it **Parametric Shelf.rfa**.

3. Let's start in a plan view. As a rule, try to create all your reference planes and associated parameters in as few views as possible. This will save you time later.

4. Create the additional reference planes, dimensions, and type parameters as shown in Figure 15.51. For reference, we've put a temporary circle at the default insertion point. Also note that when the shelf flexes, it will distribute evenly to either side of the Center Left/Right reference plane because of the EQ dimension below the Shelf Width length parameter (Figure 15.51).

FIGURE 15.51
Parameterized reference planes

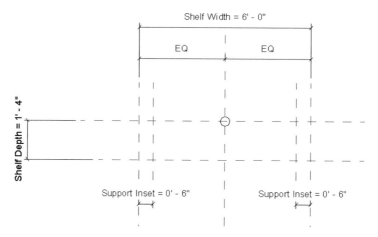

5. Now let's model the shelf geometry from this same view. Again, there's no need to lock any sketch lines to the reference planes. Also, note the constraints in Figure 15.52. Extrusion Start is 0" and Extrusion End is negative 1/2". This means that the shelf is 1/2" thick. As a result, the top of the shelf will initially be aligned with the level it's placed on in the Revit project.

FIGURE 15.52
Extrusion sketch for shelf

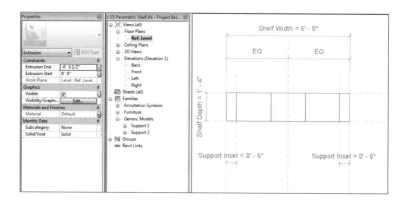

6. Return to your plan view and place the Support 1 bracket. Then go to the Right elevation and move the bracket into place, as shown in Figure 15.53, so that it's under the shelf. Just place one bracket. The rest will come later! Also, you don't need to apply Align/Lock to the bracket.

FIGURE 15.53
Support one bracket under the shelf.

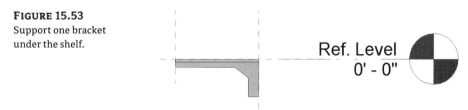

7. Now associate the Bracket parameter with the parameter that controls the depth of the shelf. Select the bracket and then select Edit Type to bring up the Type Properties dialog box shown in Figure 15.54. Note that the Support Depth value isn't associated with anything.

FIGURE 15.54
Nesting the support depth

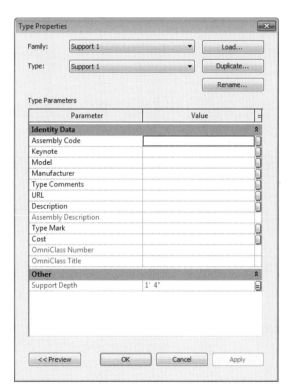

8. Click the square button to the far right of the Support Depth parameter. This will bring up another dialog box. Select the Shelf Depth parameter, as shown in Figure 15.55.

FIGURE 15.55
Parameterized
reference planes

Now when the Shelf Depth length changes, the bracket will grow to match.

Assigning Family Type Parameters

Now that you've nested the brackets and tested the parameters, you'll continue by adding
Family Type parameters, which will allow you to select between the nested bracket families:

**CERT
OBJECTIVE**

1. Select the bracket and look toward the top of the view. There's a value called Label. Pull
   down the menu and select Add Parameter, which will open the dialog box shown in
   Figure 15.56. In the Name field, enter **Support Type**.

FIGURE 15.56
Parameterized
family type

2. Now you can select between the different bracket types in the Family Types dialog box. Set the Bracket Support value to Support 2. It's already associated because both brackets are of the same Generic Model category (Figure 15.57).

FIGURE 15.57
Family type
Support 2.rfa

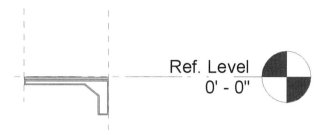

3. While you're in this view, select the Edit Type option, associating the Support Depth value of Support 2 with the Shelf Depth of this family (just as you did a moment ago for Support 1).

Creating Parametric Arrays

Now that you've associated Family Type parameters to the brackets, you'll continue by creating a parametric array to control the number of brackets on a case-by-case basis once the family is loaded into the project environment:

1. Return to the Front elevation. Select the bracket; then select the Array command, and make an array with the settings shown in Figure 15.58. Put the second bracket on the right side of the Center Left/Right reference plane.

FIGURE 15.58
Creating the array

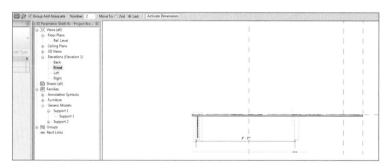

2. Now you're going to parameterize the array. Select either of the brackets and you'll notice they're now in groups. Select the line that extends above the shelf and extends to either side of the groups. When you select this line, you'll be given an option to parameterize the grouped array (Figure 15.59).

FIGURE 15.59

You can parameterize the grouped array.

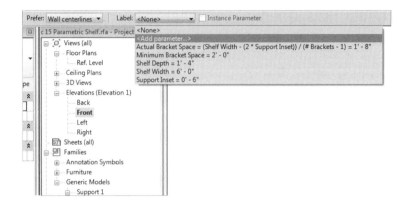

3. Select <Add Parameter...>, and complete the dialog box as shown in Figure 15.60. By default, the array has two brackets, which is fine for now. You'll parameterize this later.

FIGURE 15.60

Parameterizing the number of brackets

4. Go back to the Front elevation and align/lock the brackets to the reference plane that is associated with the support inset. If you'll remember, we modeled the bracket on the Center Left/Right reference plane in its family. This reference plane is now a reference that you can use when the family is nested. As a result, you'll be able to use this reference when aligning and locking to the reference plane in the shelf project (Figure 15.61).

After you've aligned and locked both brackets, their locations should flex when you change the Shelf Width parameter. Test this now. As a best practice, it's a good idea to test the parameters after every few steps.

FIGURE 15.61
Be sure to lock the shelf bracket when aligning.

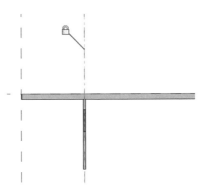

Using Formulas

Next let's create a formula that adds brackets as the length of the shelf increases. We'll show how to do this simply at first, and then we'll add some complexity:

1. Open the Family Types dialog box. Rather than specify the number of brackets (# Brackets), add a formula to the right of this value under the Formula column:

   (Shelf Width / 3′ [1 m]) + 1

   The reason you add 1 to the end of the line is that if for some reason the width of the shelf is less than the specified width between brackets (3′ [1 m] in this example), then the number of brackets might result in one and that will cause the family to fail, since you have to have at least two elements in an array. But you're not permitted to have an array of less than two. A value of 1 would cause the formula to fail. Besides, a shelf with one bracket tends to be a bit unstable. By specifying the first and last location of the array, you guarantee a bracket at each end of the shelf.

   Now that you've got down the basics, let's make the array more sophisticated.

2. Remove both the Support Inset values from the overall Shelf Width value:

   (Shelf Width − [2 * Support Inset]) / 3′ [1 m] + 1

   This is better. However, this formula also will lock the relative spacing between the brackets to 3′ [1 m]. If you want to keep the value flexible, you'll create a Length parameter that allows you to reiterate the bracket spacing.

3. Open the Family Types dialog box, and in the Parameters options, select Add; then input the values shown in Figure 15.62.

4. Click OK, and close the dialog (Figure 15.63).

FIGURE 15.62
Creating the
Minimum Bracket
Space parameter

FIGURE 15.63
Completed dialog
box

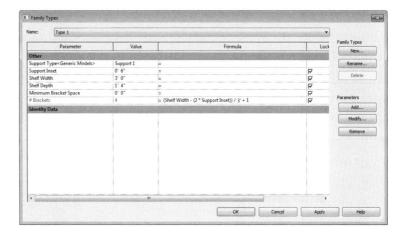

5. Reopen the Family Types dialog box, and use the parameter you've just created in place of the fixed 3′ [1 m] value. Give the Minimum Bracket Space parameter a value (otherwise, when you apply the formula it won't work). In this case, give the Minimum Bracket Space a value of 3′ [1 m].

6. Substitute Minimum Bracket Space + 1 for 3′ [1 m] + 1 as the text in the formula. Remember that spelling and case are important, so copy and paste will help (Figure 15.64).

7. Flex the family and experiment with different Bracket Spacing, Shelf Width, and Support Inset values.

It's not possible (or desirable) to set the actual or real bracket spacing. But it may be helpful to know this value as real-time feedback. So next you'll create the formula that will report this value.

FIGURE 15.64

Completed formula

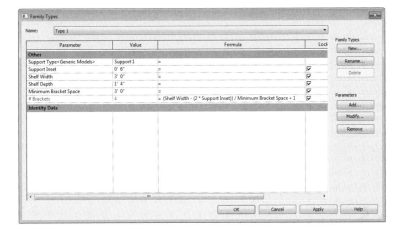

8. Open the Family Types dialog box, and click Add to create a new Length parameter called Actual Bracket Space, using the settings shown in Figure 15.65.

FIGURE 15.65

Creating the Actual Bracket Space parameter

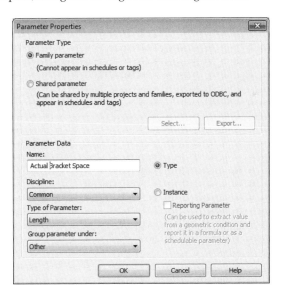

9. Then add the following to the Actual Bracket Space formula field:

(Shelf Width − [2 × Support Inset]) / (# Brackets − 1)

This will report the real value of the bracket spacing, not just the minimum specified (Figure 15.66).

FIGURE 15.66
Creating the Actual
Bracket Space
parameter

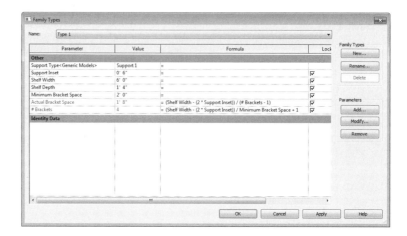

Associating Materials

Now let's associate the material of the shelf with a parameter to control the material:

1. Select the shelf and then click the button to the right of the Material row (Figure 15.67).

FIGURE 15.67
Selecting Material
properties

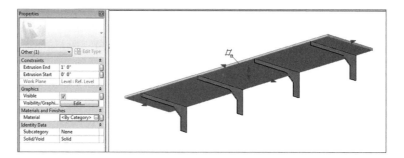

2. Click the Add Parameter button in the Associate Family Parameter dialog box (Figure 15.68).

3. Add the Material parameter, as shown in Figure 15.69. In this case we've named the parameter **Shelf Material**.

FIGURE 15.68
Associate Family
Parameter dialog
box

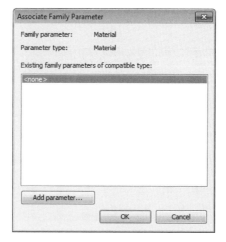

FIGURE 15.69
Adding the Material
parameter to the
shelf

Now you can open the Family Types dialog box and see that the material of the shelf geometry has been parameterized to associate with a material (Figure 15.70). Once this family is loaded into the project environment, you can change the material of a shelf as a type. You'll also be able to specify the bracket as well as the spacing of the bracket.

Figure 15.70
Material parameter
in the Family Types
dialog box

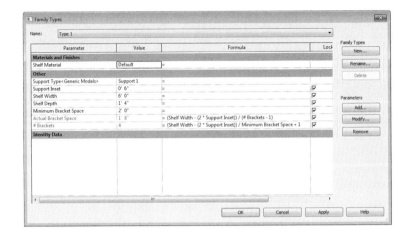

Creating and Editing Type Catalogs

Let's consider all the possible permutations of this shelf. Imagine the following:

◆ Two Materials (Wood and Glass)

◆ Two Support Types (Support 1 and Support 2)

◆ Two Support Inset Lengths (3″ and 6″ [8 cm and 16 cm])

◆ Three Shelf Widths (2′, 4′, 6′ [60 cm, 1.2 m, 1.8 m])

◆ Three Shelf Depths (8″, 12″, 16″ [20 cm, 30 cm, 40 cm])

How many type permutations might exist?

Easy! $2 \times 2 \times 2 \times 3 \times 3 = 72$ types

That's a lot of types to build and load into a project, especially if you only want to use just a few of the types in your project. You have a couple of options:

◆ Some of the type parameters may work as instance parameters. That can reduce the number of types significantly. For example, if the material parameters became instance parameters, you could reduce the number of types by half. But still, that's far too many types.

◆ You can create a type catalog. Using this approach, you can store all the types in a text file that allows you to be selective about which iterations are loaded into the project. So instead of dozens and dozens of different types, you can just load the ones that you want. This will keep your file much lighter. Also, if you need to create additional types, it's a simple matter of adding the values to the type catalog.

Type catalogs can be intimidating at first because small errors will cause either the type catalog or the corresponding family to fail, so just go slow and test frequently. You don't want to test the catalog at the end of your process and be faced with untangling spaghetti.

We'll start simple. First, keep in mind that the type catalog needs to be in the same location as the family that it references, and it should have the same name. So in this case the family is called `Parametric Shelf.rfa`, so the type catalog will be called `Parametric Shelf.txt`. In addition, spelling counts, and parameter names are case sensitive as well, just as when you're working in the Family Editor.

Parameter values can be expressed as length, area, volume, angle, force, linear force, and "other." For this example, you'll be using length (for lengths) and other (for Family Types). You'll use decimals when appropriate. Although you could create this catalog in Excel and export it as a comma-delimited text file, we'll walk you through creating the type catalog as a text file (which is a little bit harder, but we'll explain a lot in the process):

1. Create a text document in the same location as your Parametric Shelf family. Do so by right-clicking your Desktop and selecting New ➤ Text Document from the context menu (Figure 15.71).

FIGURE 15.71
Creating a text document

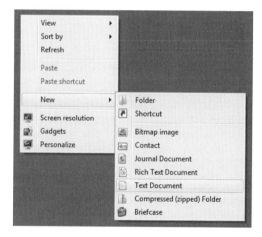

2. Rename the file to match your shelf family, and then open it in Notepad (Figure 15.72).

FIGURE 15.72
Opening the type catalog

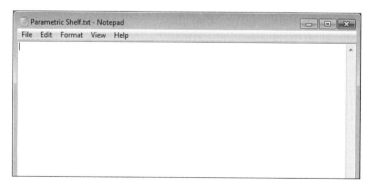

3. Begin by adding the type names that match the family types. You've already created one type (Figure 15.73). Don't worry about matching all the values — you can change them in the type catalog. Just get the names correct for now.

FIGURE 15.73

Family types to be matched

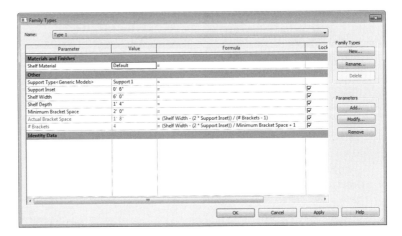

4. Let's start simple and test by specifying only the shelf material in the type catalog. Be sure to place a comma at the beginning of the header line (by default this is the type name). Also note that there is no comma at the end of the header line.

,Shelf Material##other##

Type 1, Wood

Type 2, Glass

5. After you save the text file and family, you should test the type catalog. Open a new project, and start to load the family into this empty project file. You should get the type catalog shown in Figure 15.74. If you don't see this extra dialog box, make sure to check the filenames of your family and text files. They have to be identical.

6. Now let's start to add the other header values and types in the type catalog. Be sure to save and test frequently:
   ```
   ,Shelf Material##other##,Shelf Width##length##feet,Shelf Depth##length##feet,
   Support Inset##length##feet,Minimum Bracket Space##length##feet,Support ~CA
   Type##other##
   Type 1,Wood,4,1,0.5,2,Support 1
   Type 2,Glass,6,1,0.5,2,Support 1
   ```

Figure 15.74 shows the result when you attempt to load the family into the project.

FIGURE 15.74
Completed type
catalog

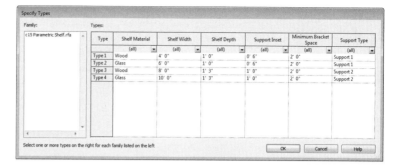

Now that you've created the type catalog in a text editor, you'll want to consider editing (or even creating) it in Excel. The important thing is that you'll need to import and export the catalog in a specific way:

1. Be sure you import the type catalog file as comma delimited. Open Excel and then select File ➤ Open. Browse to your text file and open it. Select Delimited in the first dialog box and you'll see your type catalog as shown in Figure 15.75.

FIGURE 15.75
Type catalog
opened in Excel

2. Select Comma as the delimiter in the second dialog box (Figure 15.76).

FIGURE 15.76
Select Comma as
the delimiter.

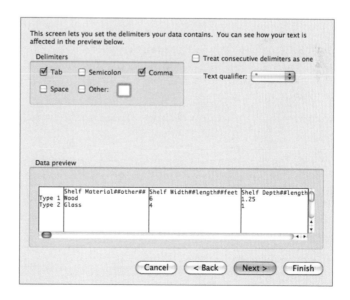

3. Now that you have your open catalog, you can fit the columns to the proper width and begin to add additional types. We've also added two additional types in this example (Figure 15.77).

FIGURE 15.77

Adding new types

4. It's important to save the file with the appropriate settings. Select File ➢ Save As and select Comma Separated Values (.csv), and you can save yourself an extra step by changing the file suffix to .txt. You may want to save the file under a different filename so you don't overwrite your original file until you've tested it (Figure 15.78).

FIGURE 15.78

Saving the type catalog from Excel

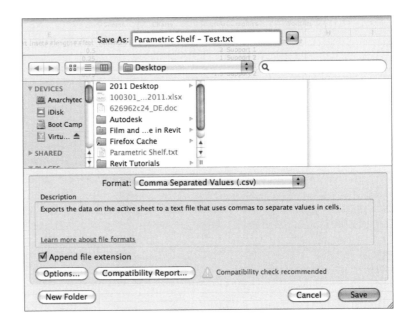

5. Finally, be sure to test all the types in your type catalog in an empty project. You can do so by attempting to load all the types. You'll be given a warning if one of the types cannot be loaded.

From left to right, Figure 15.79 shows Type 1 through Type 4, respectively. If you want to download the shelf family and type catalog, look in the Chapter 15 folder on the book's website for the files c15 Parametric Shelf.rfa and c15 Parametric Shelf.txt.

FIGURE 15.79
Completed family
types

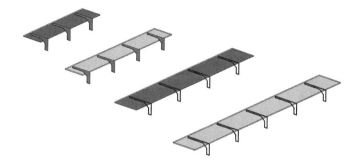

The Bottom Line

Understand the Family Editor.   Before you start modeling a piece of content in the Family Editor, take a moment to think about how you expect that piece of content to "behave" in your project. Don't be afraid to model a first pass quickly. But also be thinking ahead with regard to how it might change. The Family Editor isn't just an environment to model geometry; it also determines how the content that you create will behave in the project environment.

   Master It   Choosing the right template is critical. You can convert from one family template to another, but this is not always the case. Why would you want to choose a door template rather than a Generic Model template?

Choose the right family template.   Some categories and parameters are more important than others. If you choose poorly, there's no backing up. You may simply have to start over and create the family correctly.

   Master It   Why are you concerned whether a family component should be hosted or not? What would happen if you selected a hosted template and then decided it should be non-hosted (or vice versa)?

Create and test parameters.   Reference planes, points, and lines are the "bones" of your component. Parameterize the bones, and the geometry will follow along. Be sure to test the parameter and reference relationships before you start assigning geometry.

   Master It   Why build, parameterize, and test the references first? Why not just model the geometry?

Know why formulas are important.   Sometimes parametric behavior will depend on the parameters that directly control it, but often these parameters will be expressed as a relationship to something else.

   Master It   Why are formulas so important? Why not just create the parameters you need and then modify them as needed in the project environment?

Chapter 16

Stairs and Railings

Creating stairs and railings in Autodesk® Revit® Architecture software can be challenging. Iterating and resolving your design idea is very much like working in a spreadsheet, and designing in a spreadsheet without some graphical feedback can be frustrating. In addition, stairs and railings are often sculptural as well as functional, and there's just so much sculpture you can design with the out-of-the-box functionality.

An entire book can be written about mastering stairs and railings, considering the breadth of functionality in these tools and the unlimited number of design configurations they can be used to create. Instead of walking through a few examples of creating stairs and railings, this chapter will give you foundational knowledge about the rules, parts, and key functionality of these tools so that you can use them in the most effective way possible for your own designs. We will also give you some ideas to tackle tougher design challenges by thinking *outside the box*.

In this chapter, you'll learn to:

♦ Understand the key components of stairs and railings

♦ Design railings with default tools and those outside the box

♦ Understand the different stair tools and apply them to custom designs

♦ Implement best practices

How to Approach Stairs and Railings

Designing and iterating complex stairs and railings in any software application can be difficult. You will need to deeply understand the rules and constraints of the application; in effect, learning the *language* of the application. To communicate fluently in that language, you need to be able to think fluently. You almost have to be able to think beyond the individual words and begin to arrange whole ideas.

Regardless of how well you know how to use a particular application, you have to contend with imagination and creation of elegant and complex design issues. Sometimes stairs and railings are straightforward and functional (for example, a steel or concrete egress stair) and there's not much room for creative thinking. But in many cases, stairs and railings are conceived as feature elements within a space. They'll be touched and experienced up close. They may be extraordinarily complex and spatial — almost an inhabited sculpture (Figure 16.1).

Image courtesy of Dougal McKinley

When these two worlds collide — amazing design idea meets perceived software functional limitation — frustration may be the result for an entire design team. This frustration is especially sharp when you look back at the kinds of designs that were imagined and realized with simple paper and pencil, yet would challenge almost any 3D modeling software (Figure 16.2). Computers were supposed to make this easier, right? Fortunately, you have a few options.

FIGURE 16.2
Complex feature
stairs

For example, you can use a generic modeling application such as SketchUp, Bonzai, Maya, Rhino, or Autodesk® 3ds Max® software to model your stair and railing designs. Of course, stair and railing creation will require greater fluency compared with modeling other, more rectilinear objects. But there's a drawback. Even though you'll eventually come to understand the rules for creating and manipulating geometry in a generic modeling application, what still remains difficult is the design idea and managing design iteration. Although many of the generic applications on the market give you the *tools* to design complex forms, they seldom give you the *rules* to manage the iteration of your design.

In Revit Architecture, the situation is often reversed: You'll frequently have the rules to iterate and manage your design, but the geometry creation tools can be limiting at times. In other words, Revit Architecture is purpose-built for designing building elements and relating them to the rules of commonly constructed relationships (doors associate with walls, furniture associates with floors, and so on). The software is biased toward relationships specific to designing a building and maintaining those relationships as the design changes. To make things a bit more complicated, there's a specific language for creating stairs and railings in Revit Architecture. For example, Figure 16.3 illustrates the Edit Baluster Placement dialog box for a baluster condition.

FIGURE 16.3

Edit Baluster Placement dialog box

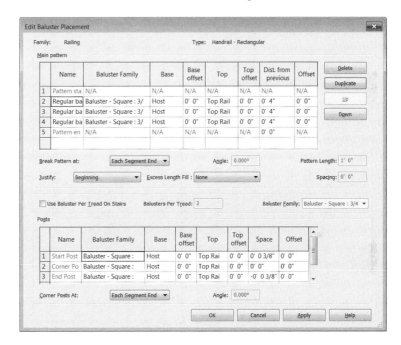

From a design iteration standpoint, it's important that your building elements understand their relationships to other elements. These elements also need to view, schedule, and maintain change appropriately in a parametric model. To accomplish this, you can use the stair and railing functionality within Revit Architecture in some interesting and innovative ways.

A good approach has always been to try to find a solution that is both technically correct and aligned with the extensibility of the BIM data. We have two simple approaches to determining when to use a solution that is aligned with the intended use of the software and when to think out of the box:

◆ If your design is best defined as *common* (regular-shaped, repeated elements), then you'll likely be able to use the stair tools out of the box (think egress stair).

◆ If your design is more sculptural (organic, free-form), you'll likely be working outside the constraints of the default stair tools. This is because there are just too many exceptions and limitations to make using the default stair tools worthwhile.

The possibility of your design not fitting within the confines of the stair tools doesn't mean that you can't maintain a proper balance of component relationships when using other tools like the Family Editor. Remember that the Family Editor lets you maintain many relationships in a project by editing single elements and then reloading to maintain efficiency in design iteration.

Revit Architecture 2013 includes a new tool for creating stairs called Stair By Component. Because this is a fundamental departure from the Stairs tool in previous versions of the software, the older method remains as Stair By Sketch (Figure 16.4). Throughout this chapter, we will do our best to explain the differences between the two tools because they handle stairs in slightly different ways. Eventually, the Stair By Sketch tool will likely be removed, but in the meantime, you can create stairs using either tool.

FIGURE 16.4
The new Stair By
Component tool

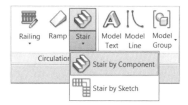

Throughout this chapter, we will describe methods to create stairs and railings *outside the box*. Can these types of designs be accomplished with the new tools *inside the box*? We're just not sure yet. These methods (workarounds) have been developed over many years working with the original tools. It will take time to experiment with the new tools and let them mature within the software.

Here's a summary of the workarounds (outside the box) you'll find in this chapter:

◆ Using railing balusters for tread supports

◆ Creating custom rails and transitions with exported geometry

◆ Using railings for other scenarios where repeated components and swept paths are needed

Whatever your approach, your solution should maintain a balance of *efficient predictability*. Design efforts are often distributed across people and teams; your approach should not be so unique that someone else would have trouble understanding how to modify your design when it changes (and it will). And with that, let's move on to describing some essential parts of stairs and railings.

Key Components of Stairs and Railings

Details of what each of the instance and type parameters do and how they affect your railing and stair design have been covered in other books and various user forums. The following sections are about the parts of the functionality that are important to being able to create interesting stairs and railings.

Stairs and railings are system families, so they exist only within the project environment. As you should already know, these types of families can be shared between projects only by copying and pasting, using the Transfer Project Standards tool, or including them in your project templates. There are several component family templates that serve as subsets of stair and railing system families, such as profiles, posts, and panels.

The Basic Rules of Stairs

Before you start to create any stairs in a project, you should become familiar with the basic rules related to these special elements in Revit Architecture. We will discuss the actual geometric components later, but first let's review the parameters that drive the geometry. When you launch the Stair tool, it is assumed that you want a stair to be generated between two levels. If you start the tool from a floor plan view, the base level will be the level associated with the floor plan view and the top will be the next level above. Keep in mind that this may be a level that is not the next major level above; it could be a minor level such as a mezzanine. Always check the instance parameters in the Properties palette when you are creating a new stair. You can also assign top and base level offsets in the instance parameters the same way you can for walls.

Using the overall height determined by the base and top levels, the stair object will be equally divided into risers. The maximum riser height is defined in the type properties of every stair type. The overall height of the desired stair will be equally divided into risers not exceeding the defined maximum riser height. Tread depth is specified in the stair's type properties as well, but that may be overridden if you manually lay out the treads in Sketch mode.

In addition to the simple rule of overall height/riser height, some public agencies require a stair calculation to be employed for dimensional compliance. This type of calculation can be enabled from the stair's type properties as well. Click the Edit button in the Calculation Rules parameter and specify the criteria in the Stair Calculator dialog box (Figure 16.5).

Whether you use Stair By Component or Stair By Sketch, the stairs you create will be associated with a base level and top level. You can also assign offset distances to the base and top levels. Because the stairs remain associated with these datum objects, if the datum objects are adjusted or the offsets are redefined, the stairs will automatically adjust within the calculated rules. This means that if the height reduces, the riser count will remain but each riser will be shorter. In other words, the footprint or plan of the stair will remain unchanged. If the height of a stair run increases and an automatic adjustment would violate the maximum riser height, you will receive a warning that the actual number of risers is different from the desired number of risers. In other words, the footprint of the stair is not changed automatically. It is up to you to edit the stair to add more risers where you feel they are appropriate.

Components of Stairs

Whether you use the Stair By Sketch or Stair By Component tool, the basic elements of a stair are similar. The main part of the stairs — the risers and treads — is called the *run* in Revit Architecture. The structural elements are known as *stringers* in the Stair By Sketch tool, and they are called *supports* in the Stair By Component tool. Finally, *landings* are addressed as unique elements in the Stair By Component tool. In the Stair By Component tool, each of these three basic elements (run, support, landing) is defined with its own unique type properties. When you use Stair By Sketch, they are all defined in the properties of each stair type.

FIGURE 16.5
The Stair Calculator
dialog box

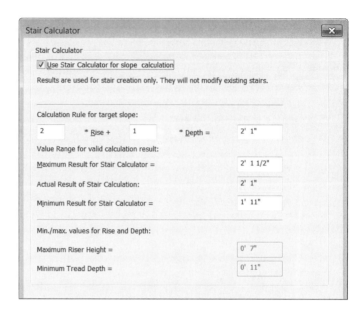

Run The critical parts of a run are the construction, material definitions, and tread and riser settings. There are two system families for runs in the default project template: Monolithic Run and Non-Monolithic Run. Monolithic runs are used for cast-in-place and precast concrete stairs, whereas non-monolithic runs are for wood, metal, and various other stair types.

Support The supports for an assembled stair usually take one of two forms. In Revit Architecture, these are referred to as *carriage* (open) or *stringer* (closed), as shown in Figure 16.6. Note that Carriage and Stringer are system families you can find in the Project Browser under Families in the Stairs category. After you select either the Carriage or Stringer option in the stair type properties, you can select one of the respective support types. For example, the Right Support property may be Carriage (open) and the Right Support Type value would be Carriage – 2″ Width. Note that you cannot select a custom stringer or carriage profile when you use the Stair By Sketch tool.

FIGURE 16.6
Stair support
options

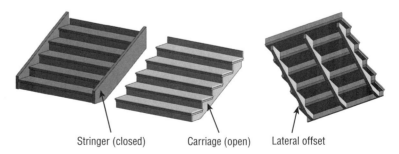

Stringer (closed)   Carriage (open)   Lateral offset

Landing   Landings are the transitional elements between runs. As such, one of the main settings in the type properties for a landing is Same As Run. With this setting enabled, you are left with only the identity data and the material property for monolithic landings. If the Same As Run setting is disabled, you can treat the landing as another tread with the same opportunities to apply a thickness and a nosing profile.

Components of Railings

The critical parts of a railing are the profiles, different kinds of balusters, and the nested types within each railing family. In the 2013 version of the software, additional functionality is available to help integrate different railing parts into a more cohesive system. Keep in mind that these features are brand new; therefore, they may have a tendency to behave inconsistently until the tools mature. In Figure 16.7, a common railing is shown to illustrate the fundamental parts of a railing type. Note that some of the terminology has changed from previous versions of Revit Architecture.

FIGURE 16.7
The integrated parts of a railing type

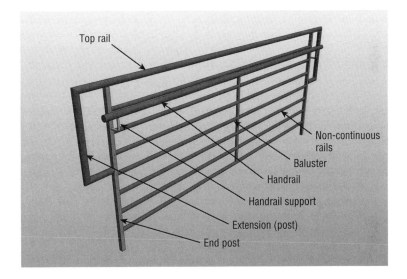

Let's examine some of these railing components in greater depth:

Profiles   The profile is the most basic component used to model a railing. All the rails, posts, and balusters are generated from profile families. You can have as many profiles per railing as you like, but you can't have more than one shape in a profile family (RFA) file. In each profile family, the shape needs to be a closed loop — no gaps or overlapping lines allowed. Furthermore, all the railing profiles will be swept parallel to their host objects. In Figure 16.8, the top rail and all the intermediate rails are simple circular profiles swept along the path of the railing.

FIGURE 16.8
Multiple profiles
per railing

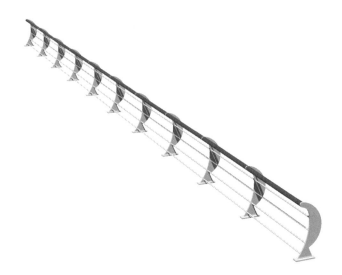

Balusters   There are three kinds of baluster family templates you can use to customize a railing type:

◆ *Baluster posts* have built-in instance parameters to control the height of the baluster so that it can adjust automatically when used within a railing type in a project (Figure 16.9). The posts are used at the start, end, and transitions of railings.

FIGURE 16.9
Baluster post
template

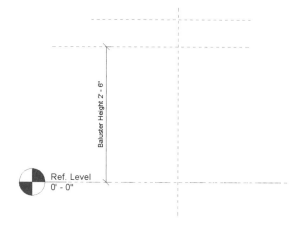

◆ *Balusters* are the main, repeated vertical structure of most railing designs. They have instance parameters as well that control the vertical length and the angle of the top and bottom of the baluster (Figure 16.10). When you create your own custom baluster families, you must constrain the geometry to these reference planes so the baluster will adapt to the settings in the railing type.

FIGURE 16.10
Baluster template

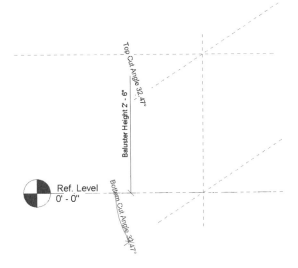

◆ *Baluster panels* have controls much like the baluster, but there are additional reference planes to control the overall width of a desired panel (Figure 16.11).

FIGURE 16.11
Baluster panel
template

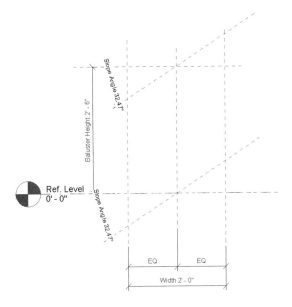

Top rail New to the 2013 version of the software, the top rail is now a separate component of a railing type. That is to say, it will not appear in the Edit Rails dialog box anymore. Instead, you will find the Top Rail settings in the type properties of the railing and they consist only of a height and a type. The top rail is now a nested system family that you can find in the Project Browser under Families ➢ Railings ➢ Top Rail Type. Find these types in the Project Browser and double-click Circular – 1 1/2″ (Circular – 40 mm). You will find more detailed settings to control this subset of railing functionality (Figure 16.12). Let's take a look at some of the properties of a top rail:

FIGURE 16.12
Top rail type
properties

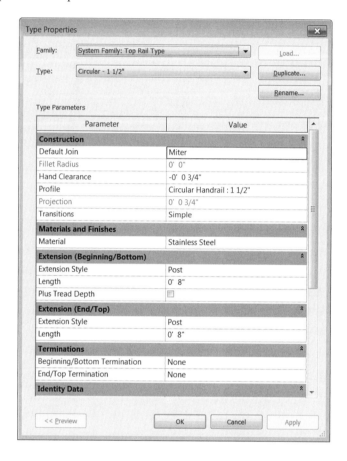

Construction   The first category of properties in a top rail defines the basic construction of the rail. Here you will select a profile and specify other behavior such as default join condition, transitions, and hand clearance.

Terminations   Another new railing option in this software version is a termination. This is a family component that can be used at the end of a rail or rail extension. There is only one termination family loaded in the default project template, but you can create your own family using the Termination.rft family template.

Extensions   When you need a rail to extend beyond its main sketch definition of the railing, an extension can be specified as part of the rail type. In previous versions of the software, this used to be accomplished with a customized post. Now the extension is an integrated part of the rail, which is a little more logical. Note that in the settings for Extension (Beginning/Bottom), you can select an option called Plus Tread Depth. This is to accommodate common building codes that require a stair handrail to be extended the length of one tread plus some standard distance. Extension Style is a setting that gives you three predefined designs for the rail extension: Wall, Floor, or Post (Figure 16.13).

Remember, you can customize a rail's extension by pressing the Tab key to select the rail. You then click Edit Rail in the contextual tab in the ribbon, and then click Edit Path.

FIGURE 16.13
Options for rail extension styles

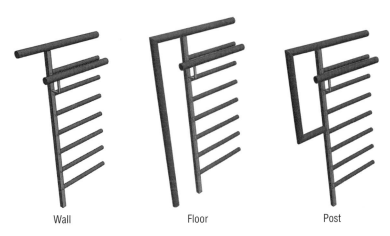

Wall   Floor   Post

Handrail The handrail is another system family that is nested within a railing family, and its properties are almost identical to those of the top rail family. The one exception is that handrails can use support families. From the Project Browser, navigate to Families ➤ Railings ➤ Handrail Type and then double-click Circular – 1 1/2" (or Pipe – Wall Mount in the metric project template) to open the Type Properties dialog box for a handrail (Figure 16.14).

FIGURE 16.14
Type properties for handrail supports

Supports	⌃
Family	Support - Metal - Simple
Layout	Align With Posts
Spacing	4' 0"
Justification	Begin
Number	3

Beyond selecting a support family, you will notice there are settings for Layout that include Align With Posts, Fixed Number, Fixed Distance, Maximum Spacing, and Minimum Spacing. These are the main controls that will enable or disable the other settings for Supports, including Spacing, Justification, and Number. Click OK to close this dialog box.

Rail structure (non-continuous) Let's return to the type properties of the main railing family. In the Project Browser, navigate to Families ➤ Railings ➤ Railing and double-click Guardrail – Pipe (900 mm pipe using the metric project template). In the Rail Structure (Non-Continuous) parameter, click the Edit button to open the Edit Rails dialog box (Figure 16.15). In this interface, you can insert rails defined by profile families as well as set their relative height, horizontal offset distance, and material. Note that these rails are considered non-continuous because they will be intersected by any balusters you define in the Baluster Placement settings.

FIGURE 16.15
The Edit Rails
(Non-Continuous)
dialog box

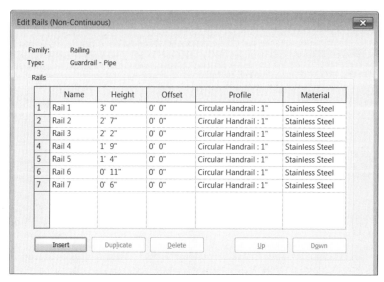

Baluster placement When you return to the type properties of the railing, locate the Baluster Placement parameter and click the Edit button to open the Edit Baluster Placement dialog box (Figure 16.16). As you can see, there are options for the main pattern and the posts and an option for how the balusters will be used on stairs.

The Main Pattern section of the dialog box is where you would assemble all your baluster types and then space and host them accordingly. You can also decide how you want the pattern to repeat (or not repeat) itself at the ends of sketched line segments. The Posts section is used to specify which baluster is used at start, corner, and end conditions (and the frequency of corner posts). Click OK to close both open dialog boxes.

That's a high-level overview of the properties of railings and what they're used for. We've covered the primary features necessary to create great railings using both in- and out-of-the-box techniques.

FIGURE 16.16
Edit Baluster
Placement dialog
box for the
Guardrail – Pipe
family

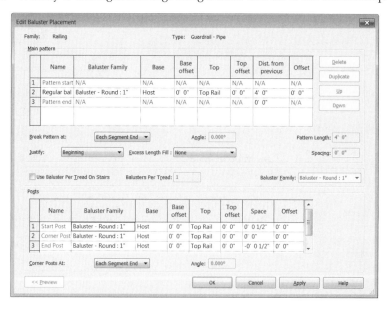

Using the Tab Key with Stairs and Railings

With the new changes to stairs and railings in this version of the software, you will need to be even more comfortable with your use of the Tab key when selecting objects. Railings now consist of nested families for top rails and handrails. Stairs are divided into runs, landings, and supports. When you first select a railing or stair, you will be selecting the parent type. You could then click Edit Type in the Properties palette to change the child types; however, there are some unique instance properties and editing capabilities exposed when you use the Tab key to directly select one of the nested elements.

For stairs, one of the important features of a run is whether it begins or ends with a riser. This property is critical in determining how a stair interacts with an adjacent floor slab. In previous versions of the software, these properties were found in the type properties of the stair. Now they are instance properties of the run. The only way you can access these properties is by hovering your mouse pointer over a stair and then pressing the Tab key once to select the run. The instance properties of the run will then be shown in the Properties palette. You can also access the run width in the same manner.

For railings, you can use the Tab key to access editing functions of top rails and handrails. If you hover the mouse pointer over a top rail and then press the Tab key once to select the rail, you will find an Edit Rail button in the contextual ribbon. Activating this tool allows you to customize the path of the continuous rails to build or customize extensions.

Look for a video explaining the procedure to edit rail paths on our YouTube channel at www.youtube .com/user/masteringrevit. Just remember that changes you make to the path of a rail instance are not propagated to other rails of the same type. If you have a custom rail extension condition that needs to be replicated throughout your project, we recommend creating a custom baluster post family. It will be easier to edit and reload one family than to revisit every railing instance throughout the project if the design of the rail is changed.

Creating Railings

We consider in-the-box techniques to mean using the functionality in interesting and useful ways and leveraging intended functionality. But keep in mind that the metadata may or may not remain associated with the category of element that you're creating. For example, you can use the Railing tool to create railings, but you can also use it to distribute repetitive elements along a path that may not be railings at all — something we'll discuss later in this chapter. As a result, your schedules need to be watched carefully so that certain elements are properly counted and unwanted elements are ignored.

Understanding the Railing Tool

Railings can be created anywhere in a project. They can be placed on stairs, ramps, floors, and roofs, but they are not hosted elements. The railing does not need to be dependent on a host object to exist. From the Architecture tab in the ribbon, you will find the Railing tool in the Circulation panel. Click the Railing flyout and you will see Sketch Path and Place On Host. You would use the Sketch Path tool to create a railing on a flat surface such as a slab edge. When the Place On Host tool is activated, you must select a stair or a ramp. Notice in the contextual ribbon that you have the option to specify whether the railing will be oriented above the tread or the stringer (Figure 16.17) — although this can be modified after the railing has been placed.

FIGURE 16.17
Set options for tread or stringer placement of railings.

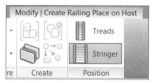

Let's explain the placement of a railing on a stair a little further. When you use the Place On Host method, the railing path is automatically assigned to the edge of the stair that represents the outside face of the tread and the inside face of the stringer (if one is defined). The railing orientation is simply flipped to either side of this path — toward the tread or toward the stringer. In the Properties palette, you will find a parameter named Tread/Stringer Offset that is set to -0' -1" [-25 mm] by default. Most rail and baluster families are developed about a center axis; therefore, the Tread/Stringer Offset value pushes the railing to one side or the other of the railing's path. To modify this orientation after a railing has been placed, select a railing and either click the flip arrow that appears in the view window or right-click and select Flip Orientation from the context menu. Note that the Tread/Stringer Offset value will remain the same no matter which way the railing is oriented.

When you use the Place On Host option of the Railing tool, be aware that you will not be able to click on stairs that already have railings. You will not be prompted with a warning or an error — you simply can't select the host object. If you do find a stair or ramp on which you would like to place a railing, also be aware that one railing type will be applied to both sides of the host object. If you want a different railing for the outside of a circulation element, you can use the Place On Host tool and change one of the rails with the Type Selector later. If you are using the Stair or Ramp tool, you can choose the option to automatically place railings when the stair or ramp is created. When either of these tools is activated, you will find the Railing button in the contextual tab in the ribbon (Figure 16.18).

FIGURE 16.18

Integrated railings can be defined in the Stair or Ramp contextual ribbon.

Click the Railing button in the contextual ribbon and the Railing dialog box will appear (Figure 16.19). From the drop-down list, you can choose any railing type defined in the project or choose Default or None. For stairs only, you can define the placement of the railing to be along the treads or the stringers.

FIGURE 16.19

Choose a railing to be placed with a stair or ramp.

For all other manual railing configurations, you will likely use the Sketch Path tool. This tool functions in much the same way as other sketch-based elements in Revit Architecture; however, you must be aware of the unique settings in the Options bar. Let's examine this tool with a quick exercise:

1. Create a new project using the default project template. From the Architecture tab in the ribbon, locate the Circulation panel and select Railing ➢ Sketch Path. In the Type Selector, choose Handrail – Pipe (or 900mm Pipe in the default metric project).

2. Draw three line segments in a U-shaped configuration. The lengths don't really matter — just make sure each segment is connected to the other.

3. From the contextual ribbon, select the Preview setting in the Options panel. Activate the Default 3D view and you will see the railing as it will appear when the sketch is finished.

4. Press the Esc key or click Modify in the ribbon. Select the middle sketch segment, and in the Options bar, change the Slope setting from By Host to Sloped. Select the last segment, and in the Options bar, change the Height Correction to Custom and set the value to 4′ -0″ [1200 mm].

5. Click the green check mark in the ribbon to finish the sketch and you will notice that the slope setting automatically adjusted the middle rail according to the height of the last sketch segment.

You might notice that the balusters are extending all the way down to Level 1. That's because the Base parameter for the balusters in the railing type properties is usually set to Host. In the absence of a host object such as a stair in the previous example, the host is the level. To adjust the railing to accommodate this scenario, you would have to set the Base parameter relative to one of the other rail elements and use a negative offset distance.

Where would you need to use these sketch segment options for railings? You can use them to customize a railing that has been placed on a host. For example, you may need to continue a railing from a stair run onto a flat landing. Let's try this out in an exercise:

1. Download and open the file c16-Railing-Tool.rvt from this book's companion website at www.sybex.com/go/masteringrevit2013.

2. There is a sample stair from Level 1 up to Level 2 and a railing has already been placed on the stair. Activate the Level 2 floor plan. Select the railing along the outer edge of the stair and click Edit Path in the contextual ribbon.

3. In the Draw panel of the contextual ribbon, select the straight line segment and draw a line from the end of the existing railing sketch as shown in Figure 16.20. Include a short segment extending in the direction of the existing sketch line, and then draw the next segment to the perpendicular edge of the floor landing.

FIGURE 16.20
Draw two new sketch lines to extend the railing path.

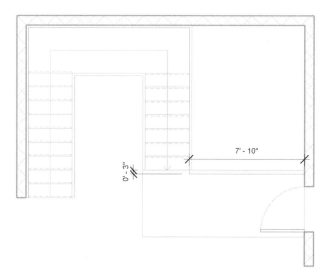

4. Select each new sketch segment you drew in step 3, and from the Options bar, set the Slope option to Flat. Now, this step may not be necessary because the railing sketch should be aware that the floor below is flat, but this is the best way to ensure consistent results with manually sketched railing paths.

5. Click the green check mark in the contextual ribbon to finish the sketch and activate the Default 3D view to observe your results (Figure 16.21).

FIGURE 16.21
The existing railing has been extended onto the landing.

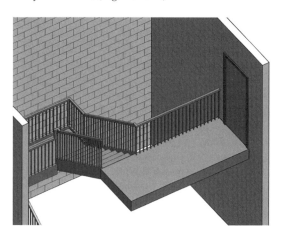

Railings outside the Box

What we mean by creating railings *outside the box* is that you can use other tools and family types to create railing-like geometry. Usually this occurs when the railing is a small, unique, or highly repetitive element.

Generally speaking, maintaining order in Revit Architecture projects is often about managing repetitive relationships. These repetitive elements may be managed by creating family components, groups, and even separate project files. For railings, there is an obvious choice: Create the railing in a project, then create a group of the finished railing, and then copy that group throughout your project.

Despite this seemingly obvious workflow, it's often faster to manage and update hundreds of component families than it is to update hundreds of groups. The railing may also be prefabricated and installed on site as a single component, perhaps filed under the category of Specialty Equipment. If you decide to use the category of Specialty Equipment, keep in mind that the category won't cut in sections; you'll always see a projected elevation. So, choose a category (like Generic Model) if you need to see the family cut in a section view.

What kind of highly repetitive railing conditions are we referring to? Sports stadiums, theaters, hotel balconies (Figure 16.22), apartment buildings, and so on all have railing conditions that are highly repetitive. Railings modeled as a singular component in the Family Editor are perfect for these kinds of situations, where only a few family components can cover hundreds of conditions.

FIGURE 16.22
Repeated railings
on a hotel

CUSTOM HANDRAIL JOINS

Custom handrail joins are known to frustrate many Revit Architecture users. If the Railing tool cannot create a condition that meets your needs, you can create a custom transition or join in the Family Editor and then nest the custom family into a baluster family to be included with your railing type. Providing a detailed exercise on this workflow would be too lengthy to cover within this chapter and would represent only one unique condition; therefore, we will provide an overview of the steps required to implement this solution.

1. Model the basic railing parts.   Create as much of the railing as possible with the Railing tool. You will need some geometry as a reference for creating a custom join condition, so you will need some basic context to be exported from a project and used in the Family Editor. For custom joins in particular, you will probably need to model a separate railing path for each run to eliminate the default transition between runs, as shown in Figure 16.23.

FIGURE 16.23
Separate railing paths are modeled for each run.

2. Create a 3D section box for export.   From any 3D view, enable the Section Box in the Properties palette and adjust the boundaries of the box to just the area of the transition (Figure 16.24). This will allow you to use the rail transition as a reference without the burden of a large amount of superfluous geometry.

3. Export to CAD.   Using the 3D view with the section box, export the view to a DWG model file. You can find this command in the Application menu under Export ➤ CAD Formats ➤ DWG. In the DWG Export dialog box (Figure 16.25), make sure the Export drop-down is set to Current View/Sheet Only. You may also find better results if you customize the export setup (click the ellipsis button at the top of the dialog box), and in the Solids tab, choose ACIS Solids instead of Polymesh.

4. Import the DWG model into the Family Editor.   From here, it is your choice to either create a new baluster post family or customize an existing one. In the Family Editor, select Insert ➤ Import CAD and then select the DWG file you previously exported. You will likely need to adjust the location of the imported reference geometry, so use the Move tool in the elevation and plan views to achieve the desired alignment.

FIGURE 16.24
Use a 3D section box to limit the geometry for export.

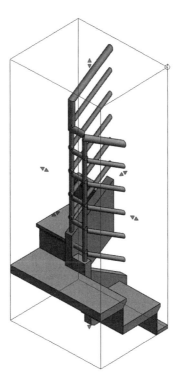

FIGURE 16.25
Exporting the railing context

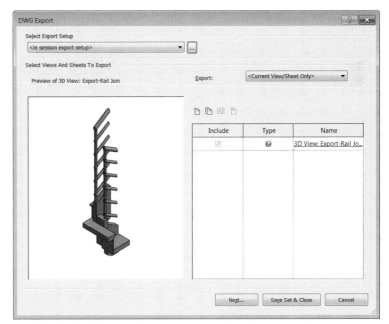

5. Create reference planes and model the custom join.   After you import the reference CAD model, create some reference planes to establish the datum for the custom rail geometry (Figure 16.26). It is particularly useful to model each unique slope as its own sweep and then use Join Geometry to combine the two sweeps (Figure 16.27). When you've finished modeling the custom join condition, delete the DWG reference model and clean up any imported object styles. A quick way to do this is with the Purge Unused tool found in the Manage tab. When you launch this tool, you will not find any listing of imported object styles; however, if you click OK, it will indeed purge the unused styles from the deleted CAD file.

FIGURE 16.26
Use reference planes in context with the imported railing geometry.

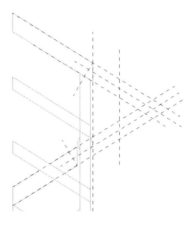

FIGURE 16.27
Modeled handrail join in context with railing export

6. Add the custom baluster to the railing type.   Save the custom baluster post file and load it into your project file. Remember that you should have a separate railing for each stair run and this custom baluster will need to be added to only one railing type; therefore, you will need to create a duplicate railing type. Select the lower railing on the stair run and click Edit Type in the Properties palette. Click Duplicate to create a copy of the original rail type. In our example, we created a type called Handrail – Pipe – Custom Join. In the railing type properties, click the Edit button for Baluster Placement. In the Edit Baluster Placement dialog box, find the list of Posts and change the End Post to the custom baluster family you loaded (Figure 16.28).

FIGURE 16.28
Edit the end post to include the custom join baluster family.

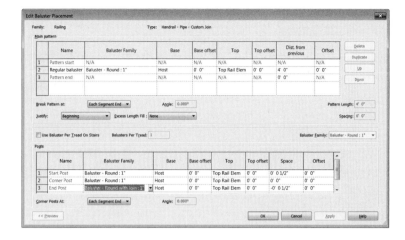

7. Adjust the custom join for final fit. Through a system of careful measurements (as well as a bit of trial and error), you'll want to elevate, rotate, and finally nudge the custom join geometry in the baluster family until it's in the correct position with regard to the upper and lower handrail runs in the project (keeping in mind that the lower run is a separate sketch). Just remember to reload the baluster family into the stair project to make sure that your adjustments are correct.

After a few moments, you'll end up with a custom connection, as shown in Figure 16.29. The great thing about this technique is that it works with multistory stair conditions. You can download the completed project in the `Chapter 16` folder at the book's website; the file is named `Custom Handrail Join Project.rvt`.

FIGURE 16.29
Completed handrail join

CURTAIN WALL OR GLASS RAILINGS

The most challenging of railings often require exceptions to the rules and the ability to manually locate balusters or panels that are not part of the routine railing definition. If you tried to define each of these exceptions as a different railing type, your project would be overflowing with railing types. The best solution for these types of railings is to diverge from the Railing tool and use the Curtain Wall tool.

By using the Curtain Wall tool, you'll be able to create railings by modeling the balusters and panels inside the Curtain Panel family template (Figure 16.30). Another nice feature about this technique is that the railing can be used as a room bounding element because it is actually a wall. That makes this perfect for mezzanine conditions that require area calculations — certainly more efficient than creating redundant room separation lines!

FIGURE 16.30
Curtain panel as a railing

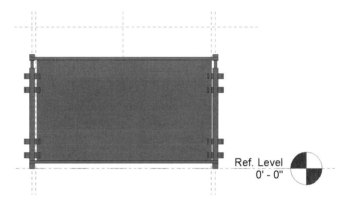

Start by creating a single panel using the Curtain Panel template. The family may contain not only the panel for the railing, but also the balusters. Once you load this panel into your project, you can create curtain walls with predefined panel widths (Figure 16.31).

FIGURE 16.31
Curtain panel railing with custom baluster locations

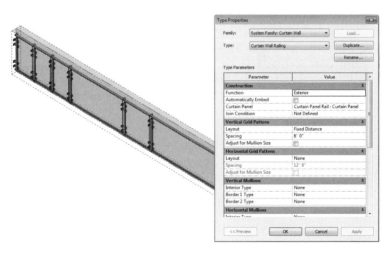

Since curtain panels allow you to unpin predefined grids (as well as create other grid locations), you'll be able to quickly and easily make exceptions to the rules that you previously defined (Figure 16.32) and create several unique baluster locations specific to the installation.

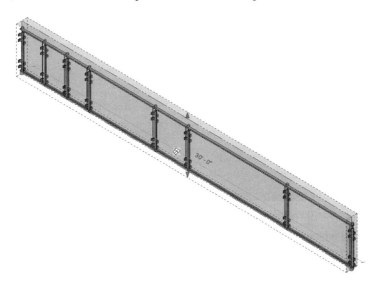

FIGURE 16.32
Adjusted baluster locations

When you're creating railings as curtain walls, be sure to filter your schedules accordingly to prevent these "railings" from being included in your curtain wall schedules. If you want to download this example project, it's in the Chapter 16 folder on the book's companion website and is named Curtain Wall Railing.rvt.

These outside-the-box techniques should give you some great ideas for making custom railings faster and more interesting than you could ever have imagined.

Using the Railing Tool for Other Objects

Currently, Revit Architecture doesn't have a specific tool to allow components to be quickly and easily distributed along a user-defined path. In some cases you could use line-based families, but these don't work in curved conditions. You could also experiment with adaptive components in the conceptual massing environment, but that could be too complicated for a simple, repeating element. In the meantime, we think you should consider using the Railing tool to distribute elements along paths for a variety of uses besides just for railings.

When using railing functionality outside of a railing to distribute elements along paths, keep in mind these three rules:

◆ You'll likely want to nest your family into a baluster family template (rather than creating it directly as a baluster). This is because the existing parameters within the baluster family can cause your geometry to fly apart if it needs to move up and down as a single element.

◆ Don't expect your nested element to schedule or tag. If you need the elements to schedule or tag individually, you probably want to place them individually (or use another technique, like a line-based family).

◆ Don't share parameters of nested families in an attempt to schedule. Your element won't schedule properly — it'll break.

In some cases, you'll want the railing family to have associated profiles, like the shading device in Figure 16.33. The railing profiles are used to create the shading fins and the balusters are the support elements.

FIGURE 16.33
Railing as shading device

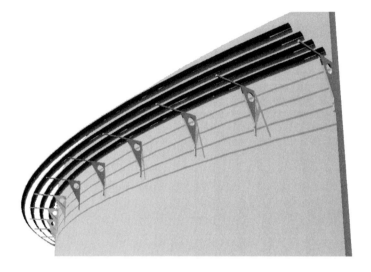

Using railings to quickly and evenly distribute components along a path is great during design and allows for quick iteration. Outdoor elements like lampposts are particularly appropriate for distributed placement (Figure 16.34). In this example, a lamppost has been nested into a baluster family.

FIGURE 16.34
Lamppost nested into a baluster family

Once this lamppost has been nested in the baluster family, you'll be able to create a custom "railing" with the lamp designated as the "baluster." This will allow you to quickly and easily distribute lampposts along a sketch at specific intervals that can be modified as a parameter. So, for example, if the lamppost was originally distributed on 60' [18 m] centers, you could very quickly redefine it to occur on 40' [12 m] intervals (Figure 16.35).

FIGURE 16.35
Lampposts distributed along a path as a baluster family

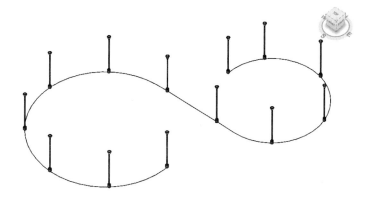

You can use this for any repetitive elements that must be placed on center and evenly distributed along a path. Other uses might include pipe bollards and outdoor planting.

Even a design pass at light rail tracks (including railcars) can be distributed along paths (Figure 16.36). In this case, the rail sleepers are balusters and profiles are used to create the rails and the rail bed. The monorails are easy too. The vertical supports and railcars are balusters, and the suspended track is the rail profile. This file can be downloaded from the Chapter 16 folder on the book's companion website. Look for the Monorail and Railway Railing.rvt file.

FIGURE 16.36
Transportation components as railings

CAREFULLY IDENTIFY CUSTOMIZED MODEL ELEMENTS

In this chapter we will make a few suggestions to use tools designed to create one type of element to generate other types of model elements. We highly recommend you take care in identifying such elements so that they may be clearly understood by other people who might use your model. If not clearly identified, these elements could cause trouble in BIM uses such as 3D coordination, quantity surveying, estimating, and where specification databases are connected to the design model. Here are some suggestions for identification:

◆ Using the Assembly Code property to assign an appropriate system description

◆ Providing a unique and clearly recognizable Type Name value

◆ Providing a clear description in the Type Comments field

Whatever method you choose to identify these types of customized elements, be sure to indicate the method in your project's execution plan. Whether it is a BIM execution plan, project execution plan, or other similar document, this type of communication and collaboration is essential to the reduction of errors and rework.

Creating Stairs

Various common configurations of stairs can be created using the tools provided in Revit Architecture. With the improvements in the 2013 release, some designs that used to require an outside-the-box (workaround) approach are now possible. Examples include three-run stairs (when the stair run turns back onto itself, creating an overlapping condition) and stringers with custom profiles.

Despite the improvements to the stair tools, there's still no way to anticipate every unique and sculptural design condition. In these cases, we'll show you techniques that aren't exactly using the stair tools as intended, but the results will geometrically resemble stairs (and their railings).

Understanding the Stair Tools

As we've already mentioned, there are now two different tools for creating stairs in a project environment — Stair By Component and Stair By Sketch. Each of these tools uses the core stair parts (runs, supports, landings) in slightly different ways. When you choose the Stair By Sketch tool, you are using 2D sketch lines that represent boundaries and risers. While you have access to a Run function in Sketch mode, it is merely automating the generation of the 2D sketch. You do not have direct access to manipulate the 3D geometry of the stair when you use Stair By Sketch. In addition, the entire stair element is bound to the rules and settings in the stair type — you cannot customize individual parts.

If you choose to use the Stair By Component tool, you have the ability to customize runs and landings within the overall stair element. You also have the unique ability to edit the stair in a 3D view. That is to say, the stair remains visible as a complete model when you edit the stair (Figure 16.37) compared to a Stair By Sketch that collapses down to the 2D layout lines when edited.

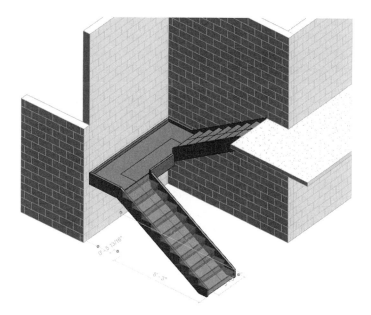

There are now additional subcategories of the Stairs object style that allow you to further customize the appearance of stairs and their related elements (Figure 16.38). One of the new subcategories is Riser Lines — providing an additional dashed line parallel to the edge of the riser that indicates the nosing length. You can customize the appearance of these elements in Object Styles from the Manage tab in the ribbon. You can also adjust the visibility of the stair elements for any view in the Visibility/Graphic Overrides dialog box and optionally save the settings to view templates.

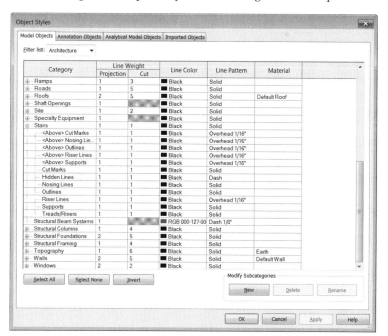

The fundamental concept behind this new stair tool is that the major components of a stair (run, landing, support) are nested system families that can be independently customized. While both stair tools are being maintained in the software, understanding the difference between all the families and types will be difficult.

Let's take a look at the Project Browser under Families ➢ Stairs. The family called Stair is the parent system family for the Stair By Sketch tool. If you expand Stair, you will see the stair types that will be available to you if you launch the Stair By Sketch tool.

For the Stair By Component tool, there are three new system families that function as the parent families. The following families are the top-level families into which other families are nested:

♦ Assembled Stair

♦ Cast-in-Place Stair

♦ Precast Stair

Under each of these families is where you define a type to be used in your projects. For example, under the Cast-in-Place Stair family, you will find the Monolithic Stair type, which uses nested families for the run, landing, and support. To better understand this nesting, let's look at the family hierarchy of the Monolithic Stair type in a simple list:

♦ Family: Cast-in-Place Stair

   ♦ Type: Monolithic Stair

      ♦ Run Type: 3/4" Nosing

      ♦ Landing Type: 7" Thickness

      ♦ Support Type: None

In the Project Browser, you will find listings for the following nested families under the Stairs categories:

♦ Carriage

♦ Monolithic Landing

♦ Monolithic Run

♦ Non-Monolithic Landing

♦ Non-Monolithic Run

♦ Stair Cut Mark

♦ Stringer

INSTANCE PROPERTIES OF STAIR COMPONENTS

We have discussed the hierarchy of nested families and types for component stairs, but there are even more parameters available as instance properties of runs, landings, and supports. When you use the Stair By Sketch tool, the Width parameter is available as a simple instance parameter, accessible in the Properties palette when you are sketching the stair or afterward when a stair is selected. When the Stair By Component tool is activated, you can set the width of a run only after it has been created. If you Tab+select the run within a stair assembly, you can access the Actual Run Width property and change it.

The Begin With Riser and End With Riser properties are critical to integrating a stair with adjacent floor slabs. In the Stair By Sketch tool, these parameters are available only in the Type Properties dialog box, which means that you would need to create a new stair type if either of these conditions needed to be customized. For component stairs, these properties can be found in the instance properties of each run. You will need to Tab+select a run within a stair instance to enable or disable these parameters, but it is ultimately more flexible to use throughout your project.

Another important group of instance properties is assigned to the stair supports. If you Tab+select a support for any component stair, you will see parameters including Lower End Cut and Upper End Cut in the Properties palette. These can be assigned to Vertical Cut, Horizontal Cut, or Perpendicular — options that are not available with the Stair By Sketch tool.

USING COMPONENT STAIRS IN ASSEMBLIES

Note that stairs created with the component method cannot be added to assemblies. Use the Stair By Sketch method if you intend to document a stair with the Assembly functionality. See Chapter 21, "The Construction Phase," for more information about assemblies.

Components for Customizing Stairs

A key concept in making the best use of Revit Architecture is to not get hung up in how elements and tools are named or labeled. For example, we previously described how to use the Railing tool to create a shading device — which is obviously not a railing. This same concept applies to stairs — don't overlook the nosing profile family as a device for creating interesting shapes that complete the tread because the shape of the nosing is not limited to traditional nosing profiles. Any shape that needs to extend beyond the face of the tread is fair game to model with the nosing profile family. Just remember that you're limited to a single profile per tread and stair run (Figure 16.39). You'll also want to pay particular attention to the insertion point of the nosing profile, because the intersection of the reference planes coincides with the top of the tread and the face of the riser.

FIGURE 16.39
Custom nosing profile

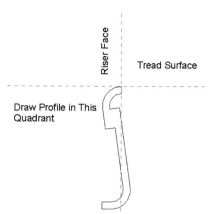

Figure 16.40 shows an example from a real stair that was designed to have each tread fabricated from a single plate of steel and then rolled to form the face of the riser above it. Here, each of these treads can be welded behind the lip of the tread above it. It's a fairly elegant idea that can be accomplished by using a custom nosing profile to create the appearance of a continuous tread. Look closely and you can see where the actual tread ends and where the nosing profile begins. Final linework can be adjusted or hidden (if necessary) when you're creating the details.

FIGURE 16.40
Continuous tread and nosing profile

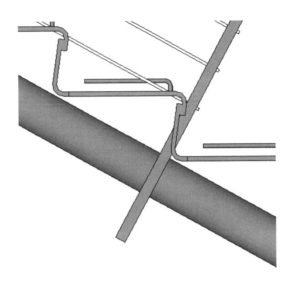

Make sure that if you're using a custom profile to represent both the nosing and the riser, you set Riser Type to None in the stair type properties. If you don't, the profile won't be assigned correctly; it will overlap with the default riser. Figure 16.41 shows these stairs in their final form using our custom profile. If you'd like to investigate this stair further, it's in the Chapter 16 folder on the book's companion website and is called Henrys Stepp.rvt.

FIGURE 16.41
Example of a cus-tomized stair and railing

UNDERSTANDING THE STRINGER

Stringers in Revit Architecture are good for creating a number of standard wooden or steel conditions. What's important is that in the Stair By Sketch tool, the default stringers can be only rectilinear in shape and may be positioned to either side of the stair (left and right) or the middle. If you want a custom shape (left, right, middle, or otherwise), use the Railing tool (Figure 16.42) for sketched stairs. The stair will host this railing containing the custom stringer profile (or just the custom profile, with no handrail). For component stairs, you can use a custom profile family within the support type properties.

Notice in Figure 16.42 that the last profile is not part of the traditional portion of the railing. Instead, this profile is used to indicate a custom stringer profile (Figure 16.43). But it has been assigned to the railing to maintain a particular relationship to the stairs.

FIGURE 16.42

Use the Railing tool to create a custom stringer profile.

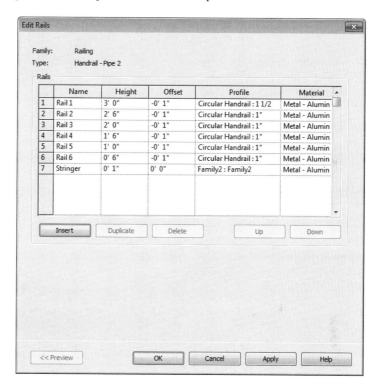

FIGURE 16.43

Railing profile

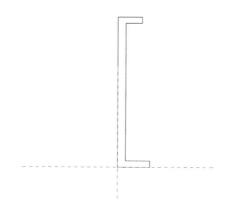

In Figure 16.44, we've isolated the railing from the stairs to illustrate the finished railing: the handrail, two glazed and continuous panels, and the custom stringer.

FIGURE 16.44
Completed railing profile

This railing with a custom stringer profile is perfect for a multitude of stair conditions, straight or curved or even a combination (Figure 16.45). This technique finishes off the stair nicely and exposes the structure in interesting ways.

FIGURE 16.45
Finished stairs

Although the stringer usually occurs to the left or right of the treads, this is certainly not always the case. In some situations you'll want to create a middle stringer using a custom profile. Just remember that this will be a railing that will be hosted by the stair and may not even contain a handrail, just the profile for the stringer (Figure 16.46). In this case, the railing is still being hosted by the stairs; however, there isn't any railing geometry above the tread.

FIGURE 16.46
Custom middle
stringer profile

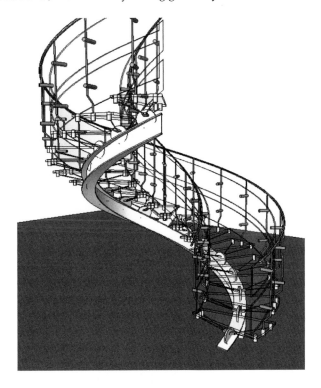

For component stairs, you can use the same custom profile, but instead of using a railing family, it can be assigned to a support type. To accomplish this, you must first create a duplicate support type in the Family Browser. Navigate to Families ➤ Stairs ➤ Stringer and right-click Stringer – 2 Width (Stringer – 50 mm Width if you're using a metric template), and then select Duplicate from the context menu. Double-click the duplicated type to open the Type Properties dialog box (Figure 16.47). Rename the type, and then select the custom profile family in the Section Profile parameter. Use the remaining controls to further customize the position of the custom stringer profile.

This workflow applies to a carriage support as well. Repeat the previous steps, but look for those support types under Families ➤ Stairs ➤ Carriage. As a final note about custom support profiles, you must ensure that the proper usage property is specified in the profile family. When you are in the Family Editor, click the Family Category And Parameters button in the ribbon and make sure the Profile Usage parameter is set to Stair Support (Figure 16.48).

FIGURE 16.47
Create a custom
support type.

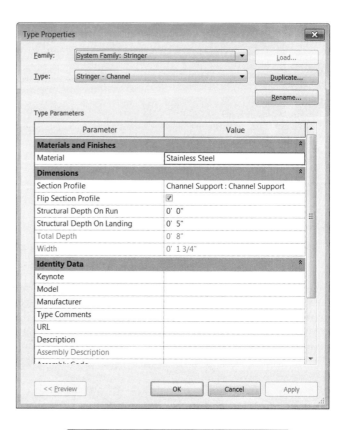

FIGURE 16.48
Setting the Profile
Usage parameter for
a custom support
profile

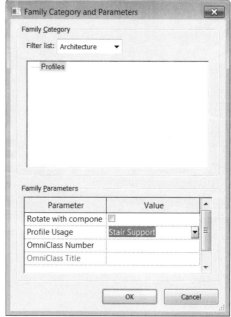

USING BALUSTERS AS TREAD SUPPORTS

Common tread shapes can be pretty boring, so let's move on to custom tread conditions. In situations where you need to be a bit more inventive, you're going to create a custom baluster. This technique can either create a custom support element for the default treads or it can indicate the actual tread.

But instead of the baluster being vertical, it's going to be horizontal. This horizontal baluster will be used in conjunction with the default tread. This baluster may even completely envelop the tread.

First, we need to discuss a few rules for creating a customized tread support for the default tread (Figure 16.49):

FIGURE 16.49
Baluster as tread support

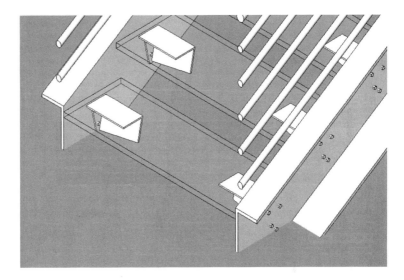

◆ Not every baluster needs a railing. If your baluster support isn't going to be a part of the "real" railing, just create another "railing" that is hosted by the stairs. Sketching another path for your custom railing that only contains the tread support baluster can accomplish this in a few steps. Another technique is to copy an existing railing, then paste it to the exact same location and change the type to your custom supporting baluster.

◆ The baluster family template needs to be used for the component that will act as the tread support. Otherwise, it can't be associated to the railing.

◆ If you have a complex support element, it may be helpful to model the desired support element as a generic family. When you're finished, nest this generic element into the baluster family. You may want to do this because the baluster templates have hardwired reference planes and parameters (which is fine if you're making a baluster that needs to geometrically flex). But in this case, we've found that these reference planes and parameters may cause your baluster to fail when you load it in the project as a result of these parameters flexing. By modeling the geometry elsewhere and nesting it, you avoid this hassle because it moves as a single component.

◆ Designating the level of detail is crucial. Assigning Coarse, Medium, or Fine levels of detail leads to much faster graphics regeneration, view panning, and model rotation. So if you're nesting one component into another family, the detail that you're assigning at the deepest level will be respected through nesting (Figure 16.50).

FIGURE 16.50
Single component that will be used as a tread support

Once the component is complete, you can nest it into a baluster template, as shown in Figure 16.51. If necessary, it's also possible to assign parameters to the dimensions in the nested configuration.

FIGURE 16.51
The generic model nested into a baluster family

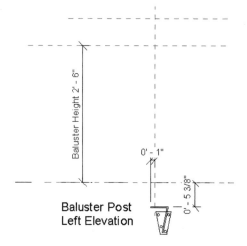

The completed stairs are shown in two different configurations in Figure 16.52. Many configurations are possible once you correctly define a single stair type. If you'd like to investigate this stair further, it's in the `Chapter 16` folder on the book's companion website, and the file is called `Angled_Support_Stair.rvt`.

FIGURE 16.52
Completed stairs
with angled tread
supports

Note that a custom baluster support might be modeled to contain the real balusters that are intended to support railings. This can simplify and shorten modeling time. In the example shown in Figure 16.53, the baluster support geometry also contains the railing elements on both the right and left sides. If you'd like to investigate this stair further, it's in the Chapter 16 folder on the book's companion website; the file is called Support Tread.rvt.

FIGURE 16.53
Complex balus-
ter support with
balusters

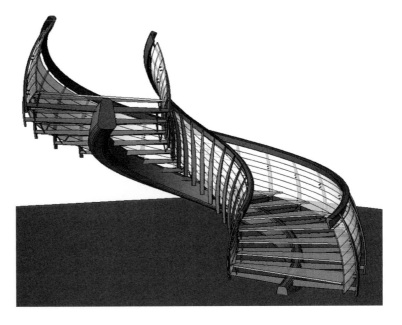

The previous support baluster can be brought together with a custom profile for the center stringer, handrails, and glazed panels (Figure 16.54). You can download this example from the `Chapter 16` folder on the book's companion website; the file is called `Center Baluster Support.rvt`.

FIGURE 16.54
Complex tread support as a baluster

Once you've begun to experiment with creating balusters as tread supports for stairs, you'll notice you have options for making more complete and finished conditions.

Start and end posts are useful and can help complete the structure of your custom railing and baluster system, particularly if you want to properly anchor and connect your custom stair and railing. The example in Figure 16.55 uses only start and end posts to anchor the custom railings and stair structure. It builds on the previous example of using a baluster as a support element for a tread.

FIGURE 16.55
Baluster as a support element

To finish this stair, you need to create start and end posts that anchor the stair. As with the previous handrail join exercise, you'll want to model the bulk of the custom stair with the custom railing. Then you'll export the stair parts for importing into the baluster template (or the generic model template that will be nested into the baluster template).

Figure 16.56 shows the results after the start and end posts are modeled.

FIGURE 16.56
Finished start and
end posts with a
connection

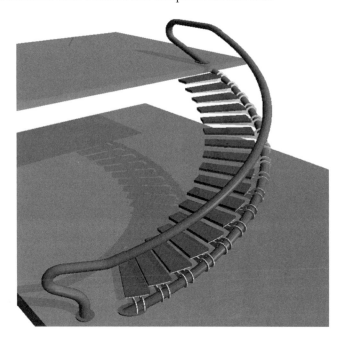

When it all comes together, the results can be elegant and interesting. All of this is available through the default Stairs tool. You can download this stair from the `Chapter 16` folder on the book's companion website; it's called `Tube Stair.rvt`.

Now let's go one step further. There's no reason that the baluster support element needs to exactly conform to the shape of the tread. And there's no reason that the support element can't contain the actual baluster that is intended to support the handrail.

Take a look at the support element in Figure 16.57. Not only does it contain the support element, but the support element has been modeled to exceed the shape of the tread that will be modeled by the Stairs tool.

FIGURE 16.57
Support and
baluster as a generic
model

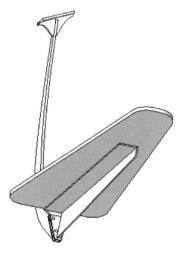

Keep in mind that we've modeled the support element as a generic model and then nested it into a baluster post template (Figure 16.58). Again, this keeps the baluster together so it's not affected by the built-in reference planes and parameters.

FIGURE 16.58
Baluster and sup-
port nested into
a baluster post
template

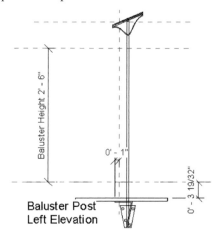

Baluster Post
Left Elevation

Once this custom baluster post is loaded into the project, simply associate it with the stair and its railings. Remember to select the One Baluster Per Tread option. When finished, the default tread is simply an inlay to the more complete tread support (Figure 16.59). In more complex conditions, it may be desirable to envelop the entire tread with the support geometry. Doing so will allow you to create complex tread shapes that are not dependent on the default tread and use the functionality of the stair and railing objects to properly locate, rotate, and elevate each of your custom treads. If you want to examine this stair further, check out the file `Curved Tread Support.rvt` in the `Chapter 16` folder on the book's companion website.

FIGURE 16.59
Finished stair with
integrated baluster
and support

Figure 16.60 shows an example using this technique. The tread support elements have been modeled using blends in order to sweep under the metal plate while changing direction from vertical to angle. This will accommodate the angled pipe rail that will support the stair.

FIGURE 16.60
The top and under-side of a tread support

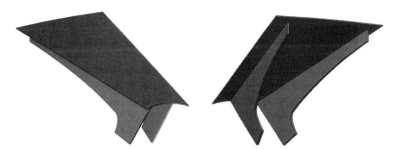

Treads come together in a particularly interesting stair and railing configuration. There is obviously a more conventional outer railing for this stair. But the inner railing doesn't have any elements that occur at hand height. The entire inner railing exists to support the baluster sup-ports (that in turn support the default treads). The end post is being used to anchor the entire structure through the second level. You can find this example, Highlights.rvt, in the Chapter 16 folder of the book's companion website. Figure 16.61 shows the finished stair. Note that the large structural element is actually a baluster that's been designated as the end post.

FIGURE 16.61
Completed stair with large end post

Stairs outside the Box

As we approach outside-the-box techniques, the goal is to create elegant stairs, knowing that the metadata may not correspond to the geometry. This is usually the only option to complete a design within BIM where there's no in-the-box technique and without the need to resort to strictly 2D representation. Because the metadata — the information part of BIM — isn't being coordinated properly, you'll want to take particular care with regard to tagging and scheduling.

A solid spiral wall to be used as a railing or a support element can easily be created in the Family Editor and then associated with the stair as a start post. Of course, this geometry could also be created as an in-place element. But then you'd lose the advantage of being able to quickly and easily relocate the stair in your project (or create a multistory condition).

In Figure 16.62, you can see the default tread with a baluster being used as a support element. What's interesting about this configuration is that rather than being configured as a circular stair, the path is made of two concentric arcs.

FIGURE 16.62
Baluster used as a
support element

Rather than create this as an in-place family under the stair, the swept blend was modeled as a baluster post in order to associate it with the beginning of the custom baluster. To make sure the path is correct, the path of the custom railing that's associated to the support baluster is copied (Figure 16.63).

Now you can use this path as you create each of the blended sweeps (creating only one swept blend per path). In this case the blends are being modeled so that there's a 3" [75 mm] gap between the undersides of the default treads. The final swept blend is shown in Figure 16.64.

FIGURE 16.63
Copied path of the custom railing

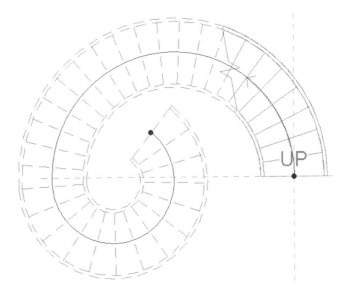

FIGURE 16.64
Finished swept blend

Figure 16.65 shows what you get when it all comes together. The swept blend has been created in a baluster template. This baluster is then loaded into the project environment and associated with the railing that contains the overall support baluster. This is also useful if you have to

create walls that need to follow either side of a stair. If the condition exists only once, you may opt to create this as an in-place component.

FIGURE 16.65
Finished stair
condition

But if it occurs more than once or might be rotated and relocated (as well as occur on many levels), we recommend that you create this as part of the stair and railing definition. Then it will be easier to maintain relationships throughout the project. To investigate this stair, download the Concentric Stair.rvt file from the Chapter 16 folder on the book's companion website.

Now let's put it all together. When it comes to feature stairs, few stairs are as immediately recognizable as the glass stairs and walkways that have been designed for Apple by Bohlin Cywinski Jackson (Figure 16.66). Although these stairs seem incredibly challenging, there's very little about the feature stair at Apple's Fifth Avenue retail store that *can't* be modeled out of the box!

Even though the stairs are very sculptural, there are quite a few repetitive relationships that are easily identified and defined. Of course, what doesn't strictly conform to the rules of the Stairs tool will have to be modeled elsewhere. First, let's model the treads and landing. We're assuming some dimensions since we don't have the actual drawings or measurements to work from: 2" [50 mm] thick, 6'-0" [2 m] wide, and a 4'-0" [1.2 m] interior radius (Figure 16.67).

FIGURE 16.66
Feature stair at the
Apple Store in New
York
Image courtesy of Dougal
McKinley

FIGURE 16.67
Finished tread
configuration

A small support pin is used to support the treads. One pin per tread supports the inner portion of the tread, but two pins per tread support the outer portion (so right away we'll have to create two separate handrail types for the stair). Figure 16.68 shows the pin family.

FIGURE 16.68
Support pin as a
baluster

With this in mind, we're able to place the pin as a baluster after modeling it as a generic model and then nesting it into a baluster family template (not a baluster post), which will allow it to conform to the elevation of the landing. Since the pin is so small, it is only assigned to the Fine level of detail so it doesn't show up unless the Detail Level property of a view is set to Fine.

As just mentioned, two handrail types are needed because they will host different baluster definitions. The inner handrail has one pin support per tread, whereas the outer handrail has two pin supports per tread (Figure 16.69).

FIGURE 16.69
One and two pins
per tread with
handrails

As for the start and end posts, two families are needed: one for the start configuration and another for the end. They include the horizontal extension beyond the end of the railing sketch. Once you've added these posts, the stair really starts to come together (Figure 16.70).

FIGURE 16.70
Treads, support balusters, and railings

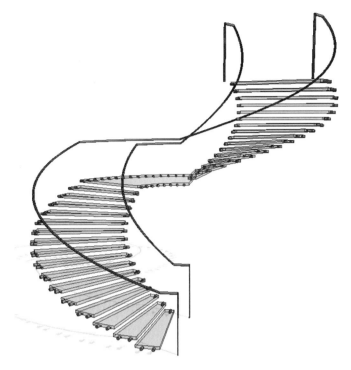

This concludes the portion of the stair that can be modeled out of the box. Export this 3D context for the remainder of the stair, which will be modeled as a generic family and then nested into a baluster post and assigned as a start post. There's a third railing in this stair (which contains no railing profile). This "invisible" railing is hosted by the stair and creates the remaining elements, as shown in Figure 16.71.

FIGURE 16.71
Glazed panels with connections

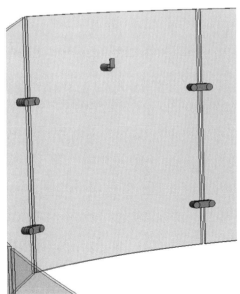

Two swept blends form the upper and lower glazed and curved panels, and a regular sweep forms the panels at the landing. At the same time, a single extrusion forms the center, glazed cylinder. When all this geometry is modeled, a single void (in plan) is extruded vertically and creates all the discrete panel separations at one time.

The panel supports and the actual balusters that will support the railing are modeled elsewhere and then nested into this family. This approach will allow the object to be quickly updated from a single location. Keep in mind that the handrails in the project will be used to host the baluster "pins" (one or two per tread); the handrail supports will be nested into this family. Each panel has a single baluster element (Figure 16.72).

FIGURE 16.72
Final geometry
before nesting into
baluster family

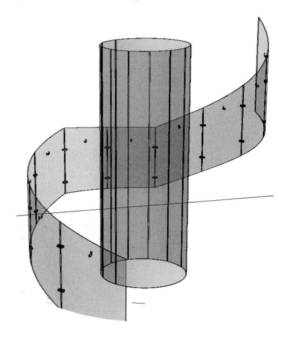

Now you're ready to associate this baluster post with a center railing (which contains no handrail). A couple of details are shown in Figure 16.73.

FIGURE 16.73
Completed stair and
details

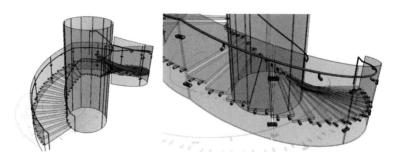

Figure 16.74 shows the finished stair. Yes, there's a lot more to the stair than this: the platform, elevator, landing, and so on. At the end of the day, there's nothing to keep you from modeling the entire stair in the Family Editor and then placing it in the project as a generic model. In some cases, this is exactly the kind of modeling control that complex and sculptural stairs need. Are they stairs? No, they're probably more like inhabitable sculpture. And trying to design sculpture in a spreadsheet is harder than just modeling what you want in the Family Editor. But what about "parameters," you ask? Well, sometimes defining the parameters takes more time than making the change manually in one place and then reloading the results into your project. If you're interested in downloading this stair, it's in the `Chapter 16` folder of the book's companion website; the file is called `Apple Stair.rvt`.

FIGURE 16.74
Completed stair, panels, and core

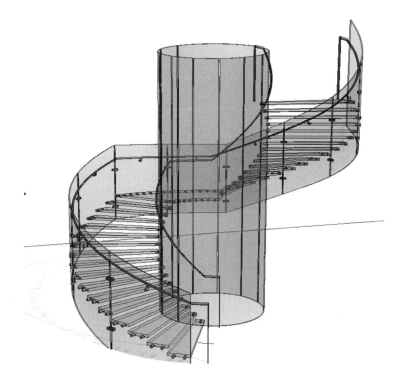

Annotating Stairs

A new annotation is available for treads. From the Annotate tab in the Tag panel, you will find the Tread Number tool. When this tool is activated, you can place a string of labels on any component stair. Note that the tread number annotation can be placed at the sides, the middle, or the quarter points along the run width (Figure 16.75).

FIGURE 16.75
The Tread Number
annotation counts
individual treads or
risers.

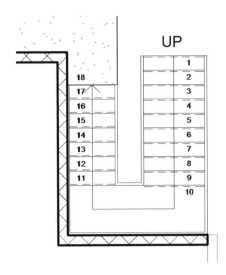

To customize the tread number annotation, select a tread number instance you have already placed in a view and you will find additional parameters in the Properties palette, such as number size, orientation, and display rules (Figure 16.76). You can also change the start number in the Options bar.

FIGURE 16.76
Customize the
tread number in the
Properties palette.

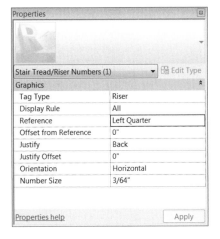

The arrow and label for stairs is now controlled independently of the stair type for component stairs. If you created a stair with the Stair By Component tool, you will notice that the arrow and label can be selected separately. When they're selected, you can change the type of annotation in the Type Selector and you have additional parameters in the Properties palette (Figure 16.77).

FIGURE 16.77
Settings for
the Stair Path
annotation

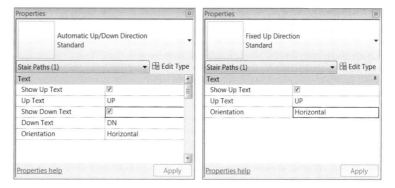

Because the stair path annotation for component stairs is a separate element, it can simply be deleted when you don't need it in a view. To replace the annotation, go to the Annotate tab in the ribbon, and from the Symbol panel, click the Stair Path button and pick a stair to apply the annotation.

Finally, the cut mark that displays with stairs in a plan view can be slightly customized. The settings for cut marks are stored in yet another system family that is nested within the component stair type properties. In the Project Browser, navigate to Families ➤ Stairs ➤ Stair Cut Mark to find the types available in the default project template. Double-click any of these types to observe the properties for customizing the cut mark (Figure 16.78). To assign a Cut Mark Type value, open the Type Properties dialog box for a component stair type and look for the Graphics heading.

FIGURE 16.78
Parameters for
the Stair Cut Mark
family

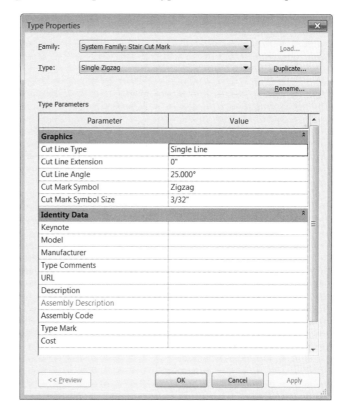

Real World Scenario

IMPORTANT BEST PRACTICES

Here are some best practices to consider with regard to creating complex stairs and railings:

♦ Don't forget to nest your family components whenever possible and appropriate. This will keep the components together when associated with some other template that contains hardwired parameters and reference planes. It will also save you time during design changes and iteration.

♦ Don't struggle with creating the stairs in this chapter. If you get stuck, you can download the sample stairs from this chapter's files and use them for a starting point when creating your custom stair. Just remember, it's usually easier to build and test a custom stair or railing in a sample project first. Then copy and paste or use Transfer Project Standards to get the custom stair or railing from the test project to your actual project. Download sample files for this document at the book's website. You'll probably want to copy your custom stairs and railings in an easy-to-access project that contains several finished examples (since they can't be kept as family components).

♦ The level of detail and visibility is crucial if you care about graphic refresh times and printing. As you model the components of your custom stairs and railings, assign appropriate orientation and level of detail (Coarse, Medium, or Fine). You'll notice a difference when you pan and rotate your model.

♦ Take care to filter schedules. Using a curtain wall as a railing may have certain advantages, but you also want to make sure your curtain wall schedules are filtered to exclude these types of elements.

Overall, be careful when reaching into your bag of tips and tricks! You need to weigh the cost of implementing a new process against the cost of doing what's familiar. Make sure that you're maintaining a balance between *predictability* and *efficiency*. There are frequently two extremes that you need to avoid:

♦ *High predictability; low efficiency.* In other words, most people will grasp the solution that you intend to implement; they'll fully understand the technology and technique. But they'll also quickly realize that managing design changes and iteration will be highly manual and time-consuming. And the rest of the team will doubt your leadership and understanding of the technology and processes.

♦ *High efficiency; low predictability.* In other words, the solution will be very efficient to manage the design, but only you or a few team members will understand what you've created. Everyone else on the team will resist making any changes to your creation out of fear that they'll break it.

So, what's important with creating interesting and innovative stairs and railings is that you manage to strike a balance between these two extremes. Just remember these four simple characteristics:

Beneficial　Not just to you, but to the project team.

Efficient　Implementation and changes that are fast and predictable.

Elegant　Understood by the team and by any new team members.

Repetitive　Can be used on many projects.

If you can't remember these guidelines, the handy acronym of BEER should help. When you are not sure which solution is the best one to follow, your team will tend to gravitate to whatever allows them to have a beer at the end of the day.

In other words, whatever allows them to decompress, reenergize, and come back to work the next day refreshed, focused, and enthusiastic will ultimately win out. And keep in mind that this principle isn't just important to stairs and railings or Revit or BIM; it's important to having an interesting life.

The Bottom Line

Understand the key components of stairs and railings.   Having a complete understanding of the components of stairs is important. You don't want to set about breaking the rules until you understand how best (and when) those rules can be broken.

>   **Master It**   What are the essential parts of stairs?

Design beautiful custom stairs with the default toolset.   Designing in a spreadsheet is hard. Step back and consider what you're trying to accomplish. If you look at the components that make up stairs, you'll see some interesting opportunities.

>   **Master It**   How would you create a continuous tread that wasn't monolithic? What would you do if you wanted to create a custom stringer? Are balusters always vertical and used to support handrails? What if your particular stair just can't be modeled in the Stairs tool?

Create elegant exceptions to the Stair and Railing tools.   From model patterns to geometric intricacy, there's a lot that can be created with the Railing tool. When this doesn't work, look to the Curtain Wall tool for "railings" that can contain space and allow "balusters" to be conveniently unlocked.

>   **Master It**   Why would you not use a railing to manage repetitive relationships? What if you need to accurately distribute geometry along a path?

Implement best practices.   There are specific best practices when creating custom stairs and railings. Pay attention to nesting geometry, maintaining the right level of detail, and filtering schedules so the metadata ends up in the right place.

>   **Master It**   Is it possible to create solutions that are too efficient? What's the big deal with detail levels? And finally, what's the most important thing to remember before creating an elegant workaround?

Part 5

Documentation

Up to now, we've discussed how to create an Autodesk® Revit® Architecture model and use BIM to derive interesting forms, create parametric content, and perform analysis on your design. Part 5 focuses on how to document those designs in the construction document phase and ultimately present those drawings to project stakeholders.

- ◆ **Chapter 17: Detailing Your Design**
- ◆ **Chapter 18: Documenting Your Design**
- ◆ **Chapter 19: Annotating Your Design**
- ◆ **Chapter 20: Presenting Your Design**

Detailing Your Design

As you've seen so far, you can show information in Autodesk® Revit® Architecture software in a variety of ways, including 3D perspectives, axons, and perpendicular views, be they plans or sections. In each of these cases, the geometry is typically modeled based on a design intent, meaning that your goal isn't to model everything but enough to demonstrate what the building is going to look like. To this end, it becomes necessary to embellish parts of the model or specific views with detailed information to help clarify what you've drawn. These take the shape of 2D detail elements in Revit that you will use to augment views and add extra information.

In this chapter, you'll learn to:

◆ Create details

◆ Add detail components to families

◆ Learn efficient detailing

Creating Details

Even when creating details, Revit has a variety of parametric tools to allow you to leverage working in a BIM model. You can use these tools to create strictly 2D geometry or to augment details you are trying to create from 3D plans, sections, or callouts. To become truly efficient at using Revit to create the drawings necessary to both design and document your project, it's important to become acquainted with these tools — you will find yourself using them over and over again throughout your process.

All of these view-based tools are located on the Detail panel of the Annotate tab (Figure 17.1). This small but very potent toolbox is what you will need to familiarize yourself with in order to create a majority of the 2D line work and components that will become the details in your project. To better demonstrate how these tools are used, let's step through each of them.

FIGURE 17.1
The Detail panel of the Annotate tab

Detail Line

The Detail Line tool (Figure 17.2) is the first tool located on the Detail panel of the Annotate tab. This tool is the closest thing you'll find to CAD drafting. It allows you to create view-specific line work using different line weights, tools for drawing different line shapes, and many of the same manipulation commands you would find in a CAD program.

FIGURE 17.2

The Detail Line tool

Detail lines are view specific — they will only ever appear in the view in which they're drawn. They also have an arrangement to their placement, meaning that you can layer them underneath or on top of other objects. This is especially important when you begin using regions, detail lines, and model content to create your details.

Using the Detail Line tool is fairly easy. Selecting the tool will change your ribbon tab to look like Figure 17.3. This new tab will have several panels that allow you to add and manipulate line work.

FIGURE 17.3

The Detail Line toolset

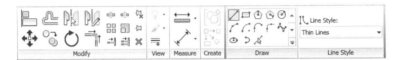

There are three major panels on this new tab: Modify, Draw, and Line Style. Because of their use sequence (selecting the linetype, creating the shape, and modifying the line), we'll talk about them in order from right to left.

Line Style This panel includes a drop-down menu that allows you to choose a line style and line weight in which to produce the line work in this view. The drop-down (Figure 17.4) has all the default Revit line styles as well as any custom ones you might have made for your project or to accommodate office standards. The active line will be the one displayed in the drop-down window before it's expanded.

FIGURE 17.4

The Line Style drop-down menu

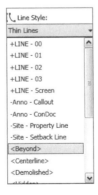

New line styles can be added at any time in the project, and many offices find it necessary to add custom line styles beyond the thin, medium, and wide ones available in Revit out of the box. To add more styles or to just see the complete list, choose Additional Settings from the Manage tab and select Line Styles (Figure 17.5).

FIGURE 17.5
Modifying the line
styles

This opens the Line Styles dialog box. When you expand the Lines node at the top, Revit reports a full list of the line styles available in the model (Figure 17.6). Keep in mind that the listed line weight is relative to the scale of the view and scales automatically.

FIGURE 17.6
The Line Styles dia-
log box

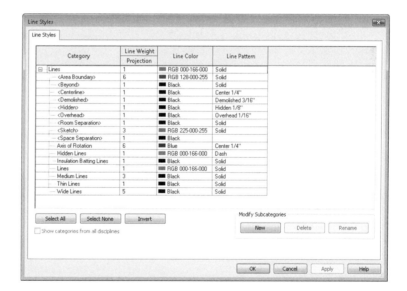

Draw The Draw panel (Figure 17.7) contains a number of shapes that are quickly available to draw within your view. The tools allow you to create lines, boxes, circles, splines, ellipses, and arcs. The last tool in the bottom row is the Pick tool. This tool allows you to select a line or portion of a model element (say an edge) and add a line over the top of it.

FIGURE 17.7
The Draw panel

Modify The Modify panel (Figure 17.8) allows you to modify any of the line work already placed within the view. This panel contains several tools you can use to modify lines. Tool icon size is based on frequency of use; the larger icons are the tools you will tend to use most. The larger tools, from left to right, are Align, Offset, Mirror (axis), Mirror (line), Move, Copy, Rotate, and Trim.

FIGURE 17.8
The Modify panel

Regions

The next tool on the Detail panel of the Annotate tab is the Region tool (Figure 17.9). *Regions* are areas of any shape or size that you can fill with a pattern. This pattern (much like a hatch in Autodesk® AutoCAD® software) will dynamically resize with the region boundary. Regions layer just as detail lines do and can be placed on top of or behind line work and model objects. Regions also have an opacity and can be completely opaque (covering what they are placed on) or transparent (letting the elements show through).

FIGURE 17.9
The Region tool

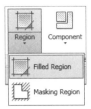

There are two types of regions: filled regions and masking regions. *Filled regions* allow you to choose from a variety of hatch patterns to fill the region. These are commonly used in details to show things like rigid insulation, concrete, plywood, and other material types. *Masking regions*, on the other hand, come in only one flavor. They are white boxes that can have (or not have) discernable borders to them. Masking regions are typically used to "hide" or *mask* certain content from a view that you don't want shown or printed.

When selecting the Region tool, you will be taken directly into Sketch mode, and you'll have a series of tools similar to those for drawing detail lines. The Draw panel allows you to create any number of shapes with all the associated tools to move, copy, or offset the line work.

When creating either kind of region, it's important to note that you cannot complete Sketch mode unless the region is a closed loop. This means that there needs to be a continuous, closed line that creates one single shape. Multiple shapes are not supported when making regions. If you need more than one shape, you'll have to create more than one region.

Another aspect of regions is the line work that borders a region. When beginning the Region tool, you'll be able to choose the line style you want to use for the border of the region from the Line Style drop-down (similar to creating detail lines). You can change line styles for any of the segments of the region and even make them all different if needed.

One especially useful segment line style is the <Invisible> line. When drawn in Sketch mode, this appears as a gray line, but once the sketch is completed, it becomes an invisible line, allowing you to create boxes or other region shapes without discernable borders. When used with a masking region, it can create a completely invisible box that allows you to hide elements that are unwanted in a particular view. Figure 17.10 shows the same masking region in two instances, one selected and the other not selected. You can see how the masking region visually disappears, covering the filled region.

FIGURE 17.10

A masking region selected and not selected

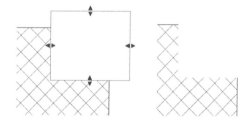

Filled regions have slightly more options because, unlike with a masking region, you can control a filled region's pattern. When selecting the Filled Region tool, you'll still need to create a boundary for the region to fill. Now, however, you can also select a region type from the Properties palette (Figure 17.11). Region types are another type of Revit family. A region type created in one view can be used in any other view, and modifying the properties of a region in one view changes it in all the other views.

FIGURE 17.11

Selecting a filled region type from the Type Selector within the Properties palette

You'll notice that many of your region names in Figure 17.11 show material types. You'll typically end up using several common material types, so it's a good idea to get these regions into your office template.

STANDARDIZING REGION NAMES

Having some sort of standard applied to your region names can help you organize the Filled Region drop-down in a logical way that is easy for the project team to understand. You'll notice in Figure 17.11 that we've organized the region names around a two-number MasterSpec division prefix. Because MasterSpec is tied to the keynoting system as well, project teams tend to be familiar with the naming convention. This approach also keeps similar material types together rather than all of the materials being sorted alphabetically. Take Concrete and Precast Concrete as an example. You can see in Figure 17.11 that those material types are very close together in the drop-down list based on their prefix.

The filled regions also have additional properties. By highlighting any placed region, you can go to its type properties (Figure 17.12). These properties allow you to control the fill type, opacity, line weight, and color of the region.

FIGURE 17.12
Type properties for
a filled region

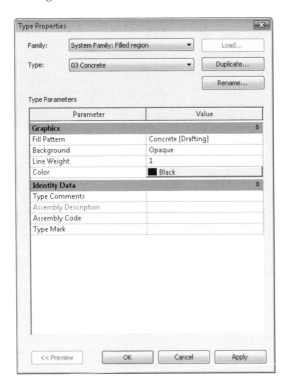

FILLED REGION TYPES

Beyond the ability to control opacity (transparent or opaque), two other filled region types are available. These types — model and drafting — create region patterns with different properties and will scale in different ways. You can create both of these regions by opening the Filled Region properties and clicking Duplicate.

Drafting Regions

A drafting region (Figure 17.13) is a region type typically used for patterns. Some examples of a drafting region hatch might be diagonal lines in an area plan or crosshatched lines to show the difference between two departments.

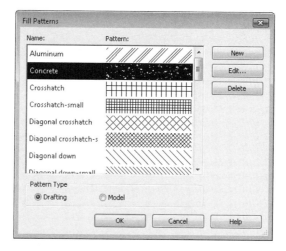

Drafting regions are created by specifying a distance between two or more lines relative to the printed sheet. In the example of diagonal lines, you might adjust the properties so the lines are 1/4″ apart. This means that regardless of the view scale, the diagonal lines will always be 1/4″ apart on the printed sheet. As you scale the view up or down, the lines will appear closer or farther apart, with the sheet view always remaining consistent.

Model Regions

The model regions (Figure 17.14) is the other type of filled region you can create. Model regions keep a consistent spacing relative to the model, not the view. You might use a model region to show ceiling tiles or brick courses or to show a 4″ grid in a bathroom tile pattern. Model regions behave as if they've been "applied" to the surface and will rotate and move with the surface. So in the example of a 4″ bathroom tile, you would create a 4″ perpendicular crosshatch model pattern. As you change the scale of the view into which this region is inserted, the lines within the region will always be 4″ apart while appearing closer together or farther apart on the printed sheet.

FIGURE 17.14
Filled Region model patterns

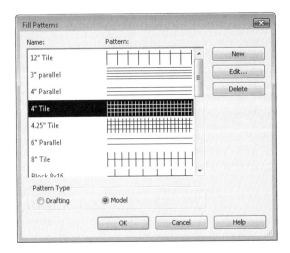

CREATING A NEW FILLED REGION TYPE

To create a new filled region type, begin by duplicating an existing region and modifying its properties. To create a new type, follow these steps:

1. Select the Filled Region tool and click the Edit Type button in the Properties palette.

2. Click Duplicate in the Type Properties dialog box.

3. Name your new region type and click the button in the Fill Pattern field.

4. Make sure you have the proper type of filled region (model or drafting) selected at the bottom of the Fill Patterns dialog box; click the New button.

5. In the New Pattern dialog box (Figure 17.15), you'll have two additional options for creating a pattern. To create a simple pattern, choose the Simple option. This lets you create a pattern based on regular line spacing that is parallel or perpendicular to the other lines in the pattern. Selecting Drafting or Model in the Fill Patterns dialog box orients the spacing to the sheet view or the model accordingly.

   For more complex pattern types, you can choose the Custom option (Figure 17.16). Here, you can name the pattern and import one from an external PAT (pattern) file such as an ACAD (AutoCAD database) pattern file. Make sure that when you import the pattern, you scale it exactly how you'd like it to appear. Once it is imported, you cannot rescale the pattern and you will be forced to re-create it.

6. With the pattern type imported or set, click OK. The last variable to set for a pattern type is Orientation In Host Layers. This drop-down menu allows you to select from three options for the orientation of the pattern within the region (Figure 17.17).

FIGURE 17.15
New Pattern dialog
box

FIGURE 17.16
Importing custom
patterns

FIGURE 17.17
Orientation In Host
Layers options

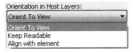

Orient To View This option will keep any directionality associated with the pattern relative to the view. If the view is rotated, the pattern will be rotated as well. This is also the default selection.

Keep Readable This option will rotate the directionality of the pattern relative to the bottom or right side of the sheet on which the view is placed. It will act much like annotation text does and automatically align itself to the nearest readable side.

Align With Element This option is specifically useful if you want the orientation of the pattern aligned with the region boundaries. A classic example of this is in rigid insulation. Rigid insulation is typically shown as a perpendicular crosshatched pattern oriented to the slope of the roof. By defining this pattern within the material type for Rigid Insulation, we're able to have the slope of the insulation pattern follow the slope of the roof (Figure 17.18).

FIGURE 17.18
Aligning the pattern with the element

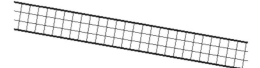

Note that this orientation type doesn't allow you to rotate a filled region — it only associates directionality with model elements.

7. When you're finished, click OK until you exit all the dialog boxes. The same region patterns that you've created for a filled region can also be associated with material surfaces or cuts using the Settings ➢ Materials dialog box.

Components

The Component drop-down menu allows you to insert a wide array of component types into your model. These are 2D detail components, or collections of detail components in the case of a repeating detail. Detail components are schedulable, taggable, keynotable 2D families that allow an additional level of standardization within your model. Some examples of 2D detail components are blocking in section, steel shapes, metal studs in plan or section — just about any replicated 2D element that comes in a standardized shape.

DETAIL COMPONENTS

Detail components are 2D families that can be made into parametric content. In other words, a full range of shapes can be available in a single detail component. Because they are families, they can also be stored in your office library and shared easily across projects.

To add a detail component to your drawing, select Detail Component (Figure 17.19) from the Component drop-down list located on the Annotate tab and use the Type Selector to choose from ones that are already inserted into the model. If you don't see a detail component you want to insert in the Type Selector, click the Load Families button on the Modify | Place Detail Component tool located on the Annotate tab under Detail and insert one from the default library or your office library.

FIGURE 17.19
The Detail
Component tool

Adding Detail Components and Embellishing the View

Making a detail component is much like creating a 2D family. Let's step through making a simple 2D detail component.

From the book's companion website (www.sybex.com/go/masteringrevit2012), download the JenkinsMusicBldg.rvt file and open the view Exterior Detl, Typ. You'll create some detail components and regions to get started with a typical window detail. The first thing you'll want to do is use the Callout tool to create a new detail of the windowsill. Create a new callout and name it **Exterior WindowSill, Typ**. The starting view will look like Figure 17.20.

FIGURE 17.20
The windowsill
detail before
embellishment

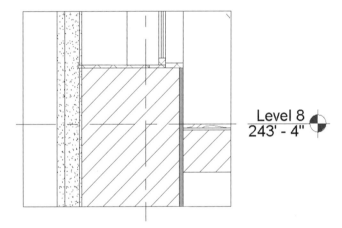

Then follow these steps:

1. You'll notice that you have some detail elements that can't exist in real-life construction. For example, you'd never run the Sheetrock back behind the floor slab, and there's no room for flashing or blocking below the window. You'll need to modify this view to rectify these conditions. Let's start with the floor slab and fix the Sheetrock. To do this, we'll cover a portion of this area with a filled region. Select the Filled Region button from the Annotate tab.

2. Set the line style to invisible and create a box bounding the floor slab (Figure 17.21). You'll notice that three of the boundary lines are on cut planes: the top and bottom edges of the box. Select these edges and use the Line Style drop-down to change the line weight to Medium.

FIGURE 17.21
Modifying the boundary of the filled region

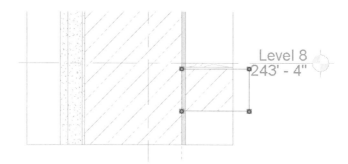

3. Click the Edit Type button in the Properties palette to open the Type Properties dialog box. Because there is no defined region type that is identical to existing materials, you'll need to make one. Click Duplicate, name the new region type **00 Existing**, and click OK.

4. Set Fill Pattern to Drafting and choose ANSI31. Then modify the following settings:
   Background: Opaque
   Line Weight: 1
   Color: Black
   Click OK when you're done.

5. Now that the region is defined, click the green check mark to complete the sketch. Your finished filled region will look like Figure 17.22.

FIGURE 17.22
Modifying the boundary of the filled region

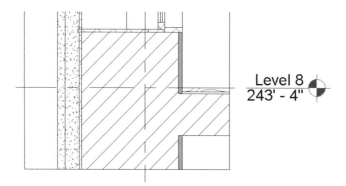

6. Say you know that as part of the windowsill condition, you have a 1″ gap between the bottom of the windowsill and the existing masonry opening. This isn't reflected in the window detail currently because the window family was created to cut a square opening just big enough for the window. For this detail, you need to create a masking region under the windowsill so you can add some other components like blocking. Choose the Masking Region tool from the Region flyout on the Annotate tab.

7. With Line Style set to Thin Lines, create a box 1″ deep under the windowsill (Figure 17.23).

FIGURE 17.23
Adding a masking region

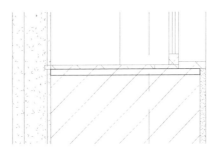

8. With the box created, click the green check mark to complete the sketch. The finished sill will look like Figure 17.24.

FIGURE 17.24
The completed sketch

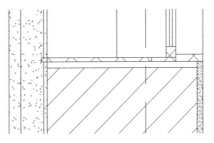

The next step is to add some detail components for blocking and trim. Click the Application menu, choose New ➤ Family, and choose `Detail Component.rft`. When creating detail components, as with any other family, you start with two reference planes crossing in the center of the family. This crossing point is the default insertion point of the family. The first family, Blocking, is straightforward:

1. Start by selecting the Masking Region tool on the Home tab and drawing a box with the lower-left corner at the origin. The box should be 1" high and 3 1/2" wide. You're using the Masking Region instead of the Lines tool so you can have a clean, white box that you will be able to use to layer over other elements you might not want to see.

2. On the Home tab, click the Lines tool and draw a line across the box denoting blocking. The family should look like Figure 17.25.

FIGURE 17.25
Creating a blocking detail component

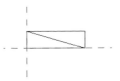

3. With the drawing finished, click the Application menu, select Save As ➤ Family, and name the family **06 Blocking**. Place it in a folder with the Jenkins model.

4. With the family named, click the Load Into Project button to add the family to the Jenkins model.

5. On the Annotate tab, click the Detail Component button. The component you inserted will be the one that will become the default component, and you will be able to see the name 06 Blocking in the Type Selector. Insert a piece of blocking at the left, right, and center of the sill (Figure 17.26).

FIGURE 17.26
Inserting and placing the blocking

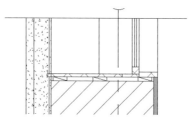

6. With the blocking inserted, you want to make one more detail component for the baseboard. Create a detail component, using the same steps as earlier, measuring 1/2" wide by 6" high and called **06 Baseboard**. The reason you want to create these elements as families and not just as filled regions is so that later in the detailing process, you can annotate them using the Revit keynote tool (explained in Chapter 19, "Annotating Your Design"). Families will have a lot more functionality and versatility later down the line for faster documentation. With the baseboard added, the detail looks like Figure 17.27.

FIGURE 17.27
The sill detail with base

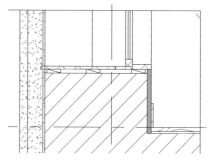

7. Not all of the detailing will be able to be completed using components. Sometimes it is easier and more effective to simply use line work to create the necessary features in a detail. For these purposes, you want to create some flashing at the windowsill. To do this, you're going to use the Detail Line tool. Choose the tool and choose Medium Lines from the Line Style drop-down menu.

8. Using the Detail Line tool, draw in some flashing for the windowsill (Figure 17.28).

FIGURE 17.28
Adding flashing using detail lines

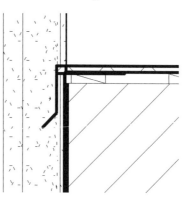

Arranging Elements in the View

So far you have created all of the content in order and have not had to change the arrangement of any of the elements. However, knowing how to change arrangement is an important part of detailing so you don't have to draw it all in exact sequence. Arrangement allows you to change the position of an element, such as a line or a detail component, relative to another element. Much like layers in Photoshop or arrangement in PowerPoint, Revit allows you to place some elements visually in front or behind others. You'll see the Arrange panel on the far right once an element or group of elements is selected and the Modify menu appears (Figure 17.29).

FIGURE 17.29
The Arrange panel

From here, you can choose among four options of arrangement:

Bring To Front   This brings the selected objects all the way to the front of the stack. In Figure 17.30, you have two detail lines on top of a masking region, which is also on top of a filled region. Select the detail lines and choose Bring To Front, and the lines are now on top of all the other elements.

FIGURE 17.30
Bring To Front

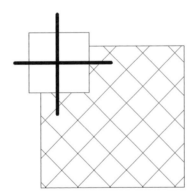

Bring Forward   This option brings the selected elements one step closer to the front in a given sequence. In Figure 17.31, we've selected the masking region and chose Bring Forward, and now it appears on top of one of the detail lines. Note that each of the detail lines is its own layer within this stack.

FIGURE 17.31
Bring Forward

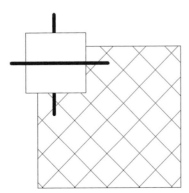

Send To Back   This option does the exact opposite of the Bring To Front tool and will send an object all the way to the back of the stack. In Figure 17.32, we've chosen the masking region again and sent it to the back.

FIGURE 17.32
Send To Back

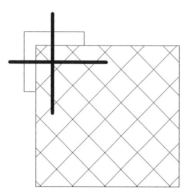

Send Backwards   The fourth option, Send Backwards, will step the selected elements one step backward in the stack. In Figure 17.33, we've chosen the horizontal detail line and sent it backward; it now appears behind the filled region.

FIGURE 17.33
Send Backwards

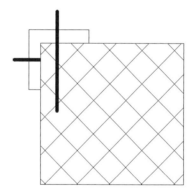

REPEATING DETAIL COMPONENT

Repeating elements are common in architectural projects. Masonry, metal decking, and wall studs are some common elements that repeat at a regular interval in architectural projects. The Revit tool to help create and manage these types of elements is called the Repeating Detail Component and it's located in the Component flyout on the Annotate tab (Figure 17.34).

FIGURE 17.34
Choosing Repeating
Detail Component

This tool lets you place a detail component in a linear configuration where the detail component repeats at a set interval. This allows you to draw a "line" that then becomes your repeating component. The default Revit repeating detail is common brick repeating in sections (Figure 17.35). Creating elements like this not only lets you later tag and keynote the materials but also gives you some easy flexibility over arraying these elements manually.

FIGURE 17.35

A brick repeating detail

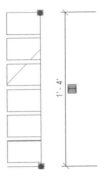

Before you create a repeating detail component, we'll cover the properties behind one so you can get a better idea of how they work. Selecting the Brick component and choosing Edit Type gives you the Type Properties dialog box shown in Figure 17.36.

FIGURE 17.36

Type Properties dialog box for a repeating detail

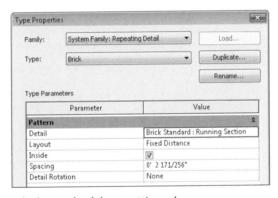

Here's a brief description of what each of these settings does:

Detail This setting allows you to select the detail component to be repeated.

Layout This option offers four different modes:

Fixed Distance This is the absolute spacing between components; for example, a strictly defined center-to-center measurement.

Fixed Number This mode sets the number of times a component repeats itself in the space between the start and endpoint (the length of the path).

Fill Available Space Regardless of the value you choose for Spacing, the detail component is repeated on the path using its actual width as the Spacing value.

Maximum Spacing The detail component is repeated using the set spacing, and the number of repeated components is set so that only complete components are drawn. Revit creates as many copies of the component as will fit on the path.

Inside   This option adjusts the start point and endpoint of the detail components that make up the repeating detail.

Spacing   This option is active only when Fixed Distance or Maximum Spacing is selected as the method of repetition. It represents the distance at which you want the repeating detail component to repeat. It doesn't have to be the actual width of the detail component.

USING REVIT TO PERFORM MATH

In the example of the brick, you have a distance of 2 171/256″. Since brick repeats every three bricks in 8″, you don't have to know the exact distance between each brick. Revit is formula driven, so you can enter **8″ ÷ 3** into this field and it will calculate the distance for you.

Detail Rotation   This option allows you to rotate the detail component in the repeating detail.

With these settings in mind, you need to create a custom repeating detail for the sill detail you've been working on. The exterior of the building is terracotta brick and will have visible joint work every 8″. Follow these steps:

1. Begin by selecting a new Detail Component family. Click the Application menu, select New ➤ Family, and choose `Detail Component.rft` from the list.

2. Create a masonry joint 6″ long and 3/8″ high with a strike on one of the short ends (Figure 17.37) using a filled region. Save the family as **04 Grout** and load it into the project.

FIGURE 17.37
The grout detail
component

3. Now, back in the project, choose the Repeating Detail Component tool. Choose Edit Type from the Properties palette and Duplicate from the Type Properties menu. Name the new type **04 Terracotta Grout** and click OK.

4. You need to change the properties of this new type to reflect the detail component you just created and its spacing. Change the following fields:

   Detail: Set this to **Brick Standard : 4 Grout**, the family you just created.

   Spacing: Set this value to **8″**.

   You can leave the rest of the fields alone. Click OK when you're finished. The type properties will look like Figure 17.38.

FIGURE 17.38
The repeating
detail's type
properties

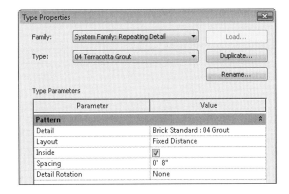

FIGURE 17.38
The repeating
detail's type
properties

5. Since you're still in the Repeating Detail command, you can simply begin drawing a "line" with the repeating detail. Starting at the base of the view, draw a line all the way up the left edge, placing the new joint over the terracotta exterior.

6. You can further finesse the appearance by placing one of the joints directly below the windowsill. This will appear placed on top of the flashing you drew earlier, so select the flashing detail line and choose Bring To Front. The completed detail will look like Figure 17.39.

FIGURE 17.39
The finished win-
dowsill detail

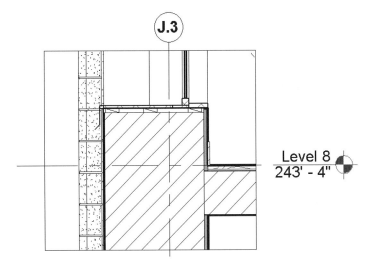

Although this detail still needs annotations before you could think about placing it onto a sheet, you can begin to see how you have used the 3D geometry of the model and were able to quickly add some embellishment to it to create a working project detail. For now, save this detail. You'll return to it later in the chapter.

Insulation

The best way to think of the Insulation tool is as a premade repeating detail. You'll find this tool on the Detail panel of the Annotate tab (Figure 17.40).

FIGURE 17.40
The Insulation tool

Selecting this tool allows you to draw a line of batt insulation, much like a repeating detail. Figure 17.41 shows a typical line of insulation.

FIGURE 17.41
The insulation in
the model

When selecting the Insulation tool, you can modify the width of the inserted insulation from the Options bar (Figure 17.42). The insulation is inserted using the centerline of the line of batt, and you can shorten, lengthen, or modify the width either before or after inserting it into your view.

FIGURE 17.42
Modifying the insu-
lation width in the
Options bar

Detail Groups

Detail groups are similar to blocks in AutoCAD and are a quick alternative to creating detail component families. They are collections of 2D graphics and can contain detail lines, detail components, or any collection of 2D elements. While you will probably want to use a detail component to create something like blocking, if you plan to have the same blocking and flashing conditions in multiple locations, you can then group those conditions and be able to quickly replicate them in other details. As with blocks in AutoCAD, manipulating one of the detail groups will change all of them consistently.

There are two ways to make a detail group. Probably the more common is to create the detail elements you'd like to group and then select all of them. In the contextual Modify tab that shows up, click the Create button (Figure 17.43). When you're prompted for a group name, name the group something distinguishable rather than accepting the default name Revit wants to give it (Group 1, Group 2, and so on).

FIGURE 17.43
Selecting elements
and then creating a group using
the Create Group
button

The other way to create a detail group is by clicking the Create Group button in the Detail Group flyout on the Annotate tab (Figure 17.44). You will then be prompted for the type of group (Model or Detail) and a group name before you can select any elements for the group.

FIGURE 17.44
Click the Create
Group button on
the Annotate tab,
and then select the
elements.

When selecting the elements, you'll be taken into Edit Group mode. Your view will have a yellow transparency overlaid on top of it, and elements within the view will appear gray. To add elements to the group, click Edit Group ➤ Add (Figure 17.45). Here you can also remove unwanted elements from your group. When you're finished, simply click the finish green check mark.

FIGURE 17.45
The Edit Group
panel

You can place any group you've already made using the Place Detail Group button from the Detail panel of the Annotate tab (Figure 17.46). Groups insert like families, and you can choose the group you'd like to insert from the Type Selector on the Properties palette.

FIGURE 17.46
Inserting a detail
group

Linework

Although not part of the Annotate tab, the Linework tool is an important feature in creating good line weights for your details. Revit does a lot to help manage your views and line weights automatically, but it doesn't cover all the requirements all the time. Sometimes the default Revit lines are heavier or thinner than you'd desire for your details. This is where the Linework tool comes in handy; it allows you to modify existing lines in a view-specific context.

To use the Linework tool, choose the Linework button from the View panel on the Modify tab. This will add the familiar Line Styles Type Selector panel on the right of the tab and allow you to select a line style from the list. Simply choose the style you want a particular line to look like and select that line in the view. The lines you pick can be almost anything; cut lines of model elements, families, components, whatever. Selecting the line or boundary of an element will change the line style from whatever it was to whatever you have chosen from the Type Selector. Figure 17.47 shows a before and after of your sill detail with the line work touched up.

FIGURE 17.47
Before and after the
Linework tool

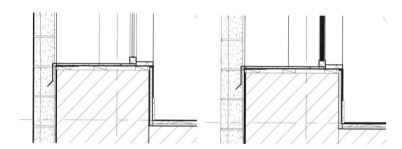

You can also choose to remove lines using this tool. By selecting the <Invisible> linetype, you can make some line work disappear. This is a good alternative to having to cover unwanted line work with a masking region. If you press and release the Tab key as you hover over one line, it highlights the entire chain of lines for selection!

DETAIL COMPONENTS AND PROJECT TEMPLATES

If you find you are inserting the same detail components over and over again, load them into your project templates and make them readily available when you begin any new project.

Adding Detail Components to Families

Earlier in this chapter, you investigated how to embellish a view by adding detail components, detail lines, and other elements. By doing so, you not only made the detail you were working with more complete, but you also added content to the model that could be reused in other details. Combining these principles, you can extend this theory to family creation where you can modify 3D families to include elements from 2D details.

Since you have the ability to change the level of view detail from Coarse to Medium to Fine within your project, you can use these settings in connection with detail components to modify families and add even more versatility to them. For example, embedding detail components into families will help eliminate repetition by adding components to typical conditions.

Building these types of families is not complicated, but it does require a bit of knowledge about how a family is created and assembled and a bit of planning around the building design and detailing. In this chapter's example, you have found that the window you detailed earlier in this chapter is a typical window and a typical condition in many other parts of the building. Since this window type will show up in all the sections throughout the project, you'll now add some of the common features from the detail components directly to the family so you don't have to draw and redraw them every time this window appears.

Adding Details to a Window Family

Because you already created the sill condition in the window detail, it will be an easy reference when working on the family. Start by opening the Jenkins model you downloaded earlier in this chapter and locating the Callout Of Exterior Detl, Typ view you have been working on. This view (Figure 17.48) shows a windowsill condition with some flashing and blocking.

FIGURE 17.48
The windowsill detail

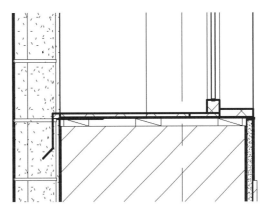

Then follow these steps:

1. Begin by selecting a window. Then right-click and select Edit Family from the context menu. The detail you are working from is a section condition and there's no section described in this family. To add one, from the View tab choose the Section tool and cut a section through the plan of the window facing the same direction as your project detail.

2. Since you are adding elements to this section, assume you've decided to add some additional information about the window itself. During the course of the design, you've chosen a window manufacturer and gone to its website to download sill, head, and jamb conditions, and you want to create another detail component from this file. Click the Application menu and select New ➤ Family ➤ Detail `Component.rft`.

3. From the Insert tab, choose Import CAD and navigate to the `ASCMDDH3a.dwg` file you downloaded from the manufacturer's website (or in this case, from the book's companion website). Before you import the file, you need to make some adjustments to this dialog box. Change the following fields:

   Colors: Black and White

   Layers: Specify

   Import Units: Inches

   This will import the CAD file at the right scale and allow you to choose the layers you want to import. When your dialog box matches Figure 17.49, click Open.

FIGURE 17.49
Importing a CAD
detail

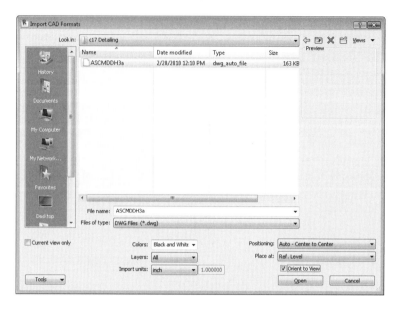

4. Before the CAD detail completes its import, you get to choose which layers you'd like to import. When the Select Layers/Levels To Import/Link dialog box appears, uncheck the following layers (Figure 17.50), and then click OK:

Pel_Defpoints

Pel_Hatch

Pel_TXT

FIGURE 17.50
Selecting layers to
import

The imported CAD file will look like Figure 17.51. You'll need to perform a bit of cleanup before you can make this into a usable detail component.

FIGURE 17.51
The imported CAD
file

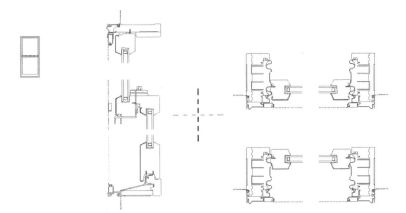

5. Highlight the imported CAD file, and from the Modify tab choose Full Explode (Figure 17.52). This will break the CAD file down into individual components and allow you to not only edit some of the level of detail but also remove elements you don't need.

FIGURE 17.52
Exploding the CAD
file

6. From this point, you can delete all of the other CAD information except for the sill condition. That bit can also be cleaned up and much of the detail removed. Many times downloaded CAD files have more detail in them than will show well graphically in detail drawings, so cleaning out some of the extra line work will benefit visibility later when you print. The cleaned detail should look like Figure 17.53.

FIGURE 17.53
The final sill detail

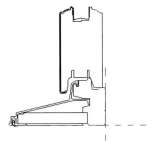

7. While the remaining line work is what you want to use in your detail component, you don't want to use the CAD lines that you've imported. You need to convert those line styles to Revit line styles so you don't clutter the project file with extraneous linetypes. In your windowsill detail, select all the line work. Once the lines are selected, choose the

Line Styles drop-down menu from the Modify tab. For this detail, you want to change all the line styles to Detail Items, so select that from the drop-down list (Figure 17.54).

FIGURE 17.54
Changing the line styles

8. Before you can finish this detail, there is one more element that needs to be added. If the detail was inserted as it is right now, any model elements would appear through the line work, and you want this detail to layer over the top of any other information. To do this, you need to add a masking region around the detail. Choose the Masking Region tool from the Annotate tab, and using the Pick tool, pick the border of the sill detail to form a closed loop and create the masking region shown in Figure 17.55. And as mentioned previously, pressing and releasing the Tab key as you hover over one line highlights the entire chain of lines for selection.

FIGURE 17.55
Making the masking region

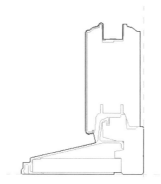

9. With the addition of the masking region, you're ready to save the detail and load it into the project. Save the detail to the project's family location and name it **08 WindowSill**. When this is done, click the Load Into Project button and load the detail into the Double Hung window family (Figure 17.56).

FIGURE 17.56
Loading the detail
into the window
family

With the final missing detail component created, you can begin adding the other elements
to this detail. You want to create some of the common conditions that appeared in the earlier
detail: the blocking, flashing, and masking region:

1. In the Section 1 view of the window detail, click the Component button. Start by placing
   the windowsill you just created. Place it over the modeled window so it creates an extension of the existing condition (Figure 17.57).

FIGURE 17.57
Adding the
windowsill detail to
the window family

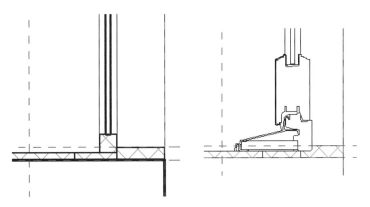

2. Next, similar to how you added additional detail earlier in the project, you will want
   to embellish this new addition to the detail. Start with the masking region. Select the
   Masking Region tool from the Annotate tab. Revit will ask you to select a work plane
   on which to draw your masking region. From the Name list, choose Reference Plane:
   Center, which is the reference plane that cuts the window in half in plan (Figure
   17.58).

FIGURE 17.58
Select a reference
plane for the mask-
ing region.

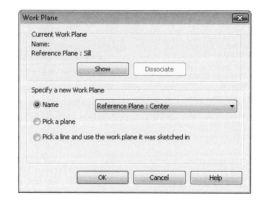

3. Create the masking region the same as before: 1" tall and the width of the wall (Figure 17.59). Be sure to constrain the vertical dimension to 1" and lock the other edges to the reference plane (top) and wall edges (left and right). This will allow the masking region to resize with the wall should they be different sizes when the window family is imported into the model.

FIGURE 17.59
Drawing the mask-
ing region

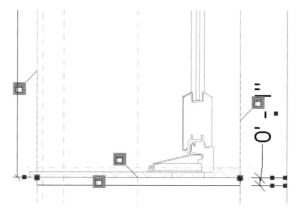

4. On top of the masking region, you will want to add the blocking. Choose the Detail Component button from the Annotate tab, and then choose Load Family from the Modify context menu. Browse to the 06 Blocking family you created earlier and load it into the project. Place the blocking in the same locations you placed it earlier. It should look like Figure 17.60 when finished.

FIGURE 17.60
Placing the 06
Blocking detail
component

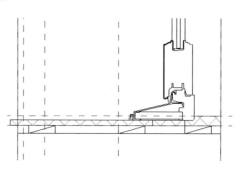

Symbolic Line

5. As a last item to create, you will need to add the flashing to the detail. In a family, there are no detail lines but instead symbolic lines.

6. Symbolic lines are used to show 2D projections or cuts for 3D families. They are commonly used to create any of the 2D line work in a family you will need because not everything in the families is modeled. One of the most familiar uses of symbolic lines is the plan projection of the door swing. In this detail, use the symbolic line Frame/Mullion [Cut] (Figure 17.61) to create the necessary flashing.

FIGURE 17.61
Adding symbolic lines

7. The finished flashing will look like Figure 17.62. At this point, you're done adding information to the detail, and you can move on to modifying some of the elements you've inserted to add some additional flexibility to the family.

FIGURE 17.62
Finishing the flashing

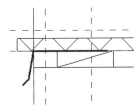

 Real World Scenario

DOORS AND SYMBOLIC LINES

In the architecture industry, doors are typically modeled in a closed position but shown as open and with a door swing direction in plan view. To get this dual representation, in the Family Editor turn off the visibility of the door panel (extruded solid form) in the plan view and draw the 90-degree open door panel and its swing using symbolic lines.

Symbolic lines can be controlled using the same visibility settings available for detail components and the solid model elements in the family. You can use the same logic and draw the dashed lines that represent the door opening direction in elevations.

At this point you could insert the window family back into the project and have it look identical to the detail you created earlier. While it will have the desired look you want, when the detail is drawn at 1/2″ = 1′-0″ scale (as it is in the project), these additional elements will make the detail look muddled when you show this window at larger scales. So that you can use this same family regardless of scale, you want to modify the Visibility settings.

Visibility Settings

The Visibility Settings tool, found on the Modify tab, allows you to control when elements appear in families based on several variables. Visibility settings are controlled by the Coarse, Medium, and Fine settings for the detail level within a view. These settings are completely independent of any of the family type parameters.

Depending on whether the element for which you want to control the Visibility settings is a drafting or model element, you'll have different options to control the visibility. For a model element, you can see from the Family Element Visibility Settings dialog box (Figure 17.63) that allow you to determine the visibility for any of the following views:

Plan/RCP

Front/Back

Left/Right

When cut in Plan/RCP

All of the detail levels (Coarse, Medium, Fine)

FIGURE 17.63
The Family Element Visibility Settings dialog box for model elements

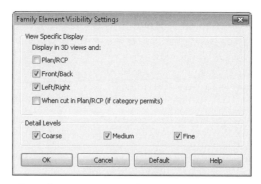

For drafting elements, the number of options is more limited. Since these elements appear in only one view, you have the choice to control the detail level and whether the elements selected are visible when the family is cut in section (Figure 17.64).

FIGURE 17.64
The Family Element Visibility Settings dialog box for drafting elements

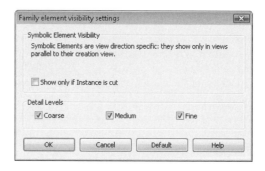

For the detail you have been working on, all of the elements you will want to manipulate are 2D. Select the inserted blocking, sill detail, and masking region, and click the Visibility Settings button. Uncheck the boxes for Coarse and Medium detail level. You also want to select Show Only If Instance Is Cut. The Family Element Visibility Settings dialog box should look like Figure 17.65.

FIGURE 17.65
Selecting "Show only if Instance is Cut" from the Family Element Visibility Settings

With this complete, click OK. The modifications to this family are now finished, and you can load it back into the model and test the changes you've made. Click the Load Into Project button.

First, delete the blocking, masking region, and flashing you added earlier in the chapter. Now, you can quickly cycle through the levels of detail to see how the new family's visibility changes with the detail level. Figure 17.66 shows the windowsill in Coarse detail. Note that part of your existing conditions for the building show the existing walls in a gray fill. Figure 17.67 shows the wall condition in a Medium detail level. Here you do not yet see the details you've added, but the gray fill is replaced by the masonry hatch. Finally, in Figure 17.68, at a Fine level of detail, you can see the elements you added to the family appear in the view. Because you have this window installed in multiple locations within the model, the same views will be present anytime you cut the model in section.

FIGURE 17.66
The window detail at Coarse

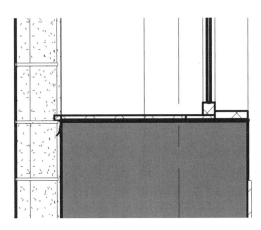

FIGURE 17.67
The window detail
at Medium

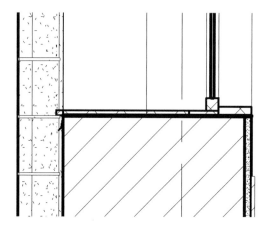

FIGURE 17.68
The window detail
at Fine

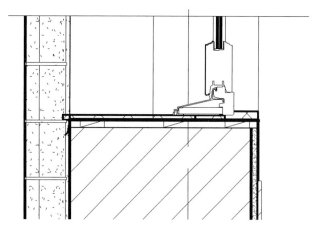

Learning Efficient Detailing

As you get more practice creating details in Revit, you'll find certain workflows support more flexibility and speed. Here are some tips to keep in mind when creating your details:

- If your modeling is reasonably detailed to begin with, the detailing will go much faster because you will need to add fewer components. However, you must strike a balance and not make an overly detailed model because that would negatively impact performance. When wondering what to model or what to make into a detail component, ask yourself the following questions:

    - Will I see or use this in other views in the project?

    - Will it affect other aspects of the project (like material takeoffs)?

    - How large is it? (Our office tends to use 2D detailing for details 1½" and smaller.)

- Remember to import only CAD files that you have already cleaned up. Only bring in what you need to reduce your overhead and keep file performance optimal.

- There is no limit to how much information you can place in a detail component. If you will be seeing similar conditions throughout the model, put in as much as you can.

- You can use detail components at every scale within the model, so it is a great way to draw the information only once.

- If the lines describing geometry merge when printed into a single graphic element, there's little point in showing that geometry at that scale. You might consider making the model simpler.

Real World Scenario

FIXING AN OOPS

The first time the detail shown here was loaded into the model, it didn't look as we expected it to look. Part of creating families is knowing how to fix them when they don't quite turn out the way you expect. In the case of this window family, the first time it was loaded into the project, it looked like this.

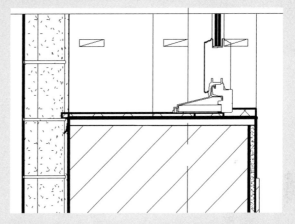

Clearly, it is not possible or desirable to install blocking at the location at which this blocking is shown. In this case, the problem occurred because the blocking family wasn't locked to a reference plane and when the window changed heights to accommodate all the family types, it left the blocking floating in space.

The fix for this condition is to open the window family again and use the Align tool to lock the top of each piece of blocking to the reference plane (shown here). When the family is reinserted into the model, it appears correctly.

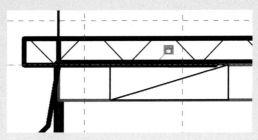

The Bottom Line

Create details. Details in Revit are a combination of 2D elements layered on top of 3D model elements or sometimes just stacked on top of each other. Creating good, easy-to-read details typically requires some embellishment of the 3D model.

> **Master It** What are the three primary categories of detail elements and how are they used?

Add detail components to families. You can make creating details in Revit easier by adding some of the detail elements directly to the family. In this way, when you cut sections, make callouts, or enlarge plan conditions, your "smart" details can begin to construct themselves.

> **Master It** Because you don't always want elements to appear in every scale of view, how can you both add detail elements to your families and still limit the amount of information that is shown in any given view?

Learn efficient detailing. As you master detailing in Revit, you'll begin to learn tips and tricks to make your process of creating details more efficient.

> **Master It** To help you assess how much effort you should be putting into your details, what are three questions you should be asking yourself before starting any detail?

Chapter 18

Documenting Your Design

While the industry continues to move toward a 3D building information model as a construction deliverable, today we still need to produce 2D documents for a construction set or design reviews. Using the integrated documentation tools in Autodesk® Revit® Architecture software, you can create these sets with more accuracy and dependability than in the past. In this chapter, you will take the elements you have previously modeled and detailed and begin to create the documentation for your design.

In this chapter, you'll learn to:

◆ Document plans

◆ Create schedules and legends

◆ Use details from other files

◆ Lay out sheets

Documenting Plans

In this chapter, we'll introduce a scenario that will mimic what might happen on a real project in a preliminary design phase. We are going to assume that you'll be using the c18-Sample-Building.rvt model from the book's companion website: www.sybex.com/go/masteringrevit2013.

Here's the story: You have recently completed some preliminary design work in advance of your upcoming client meeting. You will need to lay out the plans, elevations, and perspectives on some presentation sheets for the meeting, but you will also have to include some building metrics, such as area plans and schedules of overall spaces. You have also been thinking through some of the details and would like to show a few of those as well. Secretly, you had some details developed for a similar project that never made it off the ground, so you plan to borrow some of those details and bring them into this one. With this scenario in mind, you must create some area plans, schedules, and legends. You need to import your design ideas, some of which were done in another Revit project and some of which were created in CAD. Finally, you must create a presentation sheet and lay out all these views so that you can print them before your meeting.

In the following sections, you'll start with the area plans. For the purposes of program verification, you have decided you need to establish the building areas for the existing building so the client can get some preliminary pricing back from the contractor. Before you create your area plans, we'll discuss some of the various ways Revit can calculate areas.

Room Areas

The simplest way to calculate areas is to use the room objects. Room tags can report room name, department, area, and any of the other properties of a room. These properties can also be scheduled and tabulated to report the total area. With rooms, however, the areas that they report are limited to how those spaces are defined. With the c18-Sample-Building model open, choose the Architecture tab, and then the flyout menu on the Room & Area panel. Click Area And Volume Computations, which opens the Area And Volume Computations dialog box. You will see the options for room area computation in the project. The choices are as follows:

- At Wall Finish
- At Wall Center
- At Wall Core Layer
- At Wall Core Center

Because each setting is global for the project, a level of consistency is ensured for room calculations; however, the global nature of the settings makes it difficult to use the room objects for gross area calculations. Room calculations can give you an accurate net area — or *carpet area* — that refers to the area between the finished wall surfaces considered as occupied space. This value can also be reported in the room tag or schedule by selecting the first choice, At Wall Finish, from the Area And Volume Computations dialog box. Select this option and click OK.

Let's see how this is reflected on the floor plans. Open the Level 2 floor plan. In this plan, we have already established the rooms and added room tags; however, the tags do not show the room areas. To modify this setting, follow these steps:

1. Select any of the room tags, and from the Properties palette, choose Edit Type.

2. In the Type Properties dialog box, choose the Show Area check box. Click OK to exit the dialog box.

Now you should see the areas reflected in the room tags, as shown in Figure 18.1. This is because the Show Area setting was created as a Yes/No parameter assigned to the visibility property of the area label within the room tag family. If you want to explore this functionality further, you can open the tag family. Select the room tag and click Edit Family in the Modify | Room Tags contextual tab in the ribbon.

FIGURE 18.1
Room area reflected
in the room tag

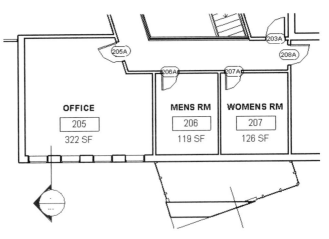

If you select any one of these room tags, you can also see the area that it is calculating (Figure 18.2). When adding rooms, you are not limited to only rooms that are bound on all sides with walls. If you note the lounge and lobby spaces in Figure 18.2, there isn't a wall dividing the two rooms, yet they are shown as being independent of each other. Using room separation lines, which can be found under the Room flyout on the Room & Area panel of the Architecture tab, you can create room boundaries without being limited to adding walls.

FIGURE 18.2
The room object shows what area is being calculated.

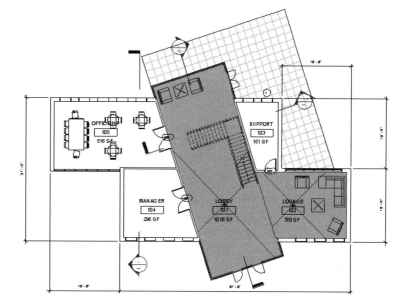

Since area calculation using rooms doesn't usually include wall thicknesses, let's look at another way to calculate areas, using area plans.

Area Plans

Area plans are views of the model used to calculate defined two-dimensional spaces within the model according to prescribed calculation standards but with the added ability to customize the area boundaries. The software allows you to create as many area calculation schemes as you need to depict the design. Area boundaries can exist only in area plans and can either be manually placed or automatically associated with walls. If they are automatically placed, the areas within them will be calculated based on the BOMA standard.

BOMA AREA

BOMA stands for the Building Owners and Managers Association. Widely used in the United States by architects, developers, and facility managers alike, it was created to help standardize office building development and spatial needs. BOMA uses its own set of standards for calculating areas that have some nuances relating to exactly where the area boundaries between spaces fall, depending on the Area Type property. You can find more information on BOMA standards at www.boma.org.

The default project template includes two predefined area schemes: Gross and Rentable. To add to the list of available area schemes, click the Area And Volume Computations button located on the Architecture tab and under the Room & Area flyout.

When the Area And Volume Computations dialog box opens, choose the Area Schemes tab (Figure 18.3). Here you can add as many new area schemes as your design requires. For each area scheme, you can create associated plans, schedules, and area boundary layouts; however, be careful not to add too many superfluous area schemes on larger projects because doing so is known to degrade performance and increase file size.

FIGURE 18.3
The Area Schemes tab in the Area And Volume Computations dialog box

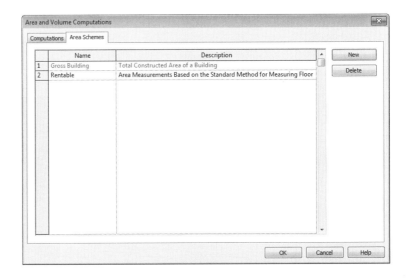

Create a new area scheme by clicking the New button. By default this will be a rentable type plan based on BOMA calculation rules. You will see a new area scheme in the list. Click in the Name field of the new row and rename the scheme **Usable Area** (Figure 18.4). Click OK to close the Area And Volume Computations dialog box.

FIGURE 18.4
A new area scheme

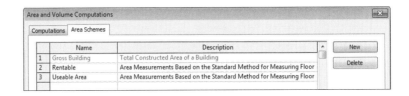

CREATING AN AREA PLAN

To continue the exercise, you need to create area plans for your presentation. You can create an area plan from two locations: One is located on the Room & Area panel of the Architecture tab. The other is located on the Create panel of the View tab. Follow these steps:

1. From the Architecture tab in the ribbon, find the Room & Area panel, click Area, and then Area Plan. You are prompted with the New Area Plan dialog box, shown in Figure 18.5.

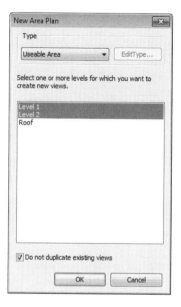

2. From the Type drop-down, choose Usable Area. Select Level 1 and Level 2.

3. Click OK. You are prompted with the option to automatically generate area boundaries for exterior walls. Because you selected more than one level, you will receive a prompt for each level for which a plan is being generated.

   This creates new area plans for you under a new node in the Project Browser: Area Plans (Usable Area).

4. In the Project Browser, select both Level 1 and Level 2 under Area Plans (Usable Area). Right-click and select Apply View Template from the context menu.

5. In the Apply View Template dialog box, choose Area Plan from the list of view templates, click OK to apply the template, and close the dialog box. Alternatively, you can assign the View Template called Area Plan to the views (located under the Identity Data of the views properties).

   View references, furniture, and floor patterns are turned off based on the settings you defined in the view template (Figure 18.6). For more detailed information on using view templates, refer to Chapter 4, "Configuring Templates and Standards."

   When looking at the area plan on your screen, you'll notice a thick purple line running around the inside face of the exterior wall. This is the area boundary line. *Note that we have changed the default properties of the Area Boundary line type in the figures within this project for clarity.* The software has attempted to calculate your plan area based on some predefined rules. For the most part, it does a reasonable job of figuring out what the boundaries are, but from time to time those lines need some adjusting. You will learn over time whether this automation works based on the complexity of the perimeter walls in your designs. If they are complex and not clearly closed, the results of the automated boundary placement may be undesirable.

In the Project Browser, find the node Area Plans (Gross Building) and open either of the plans. Notice the difference in the application of the area boundaries to the exterior walls. The area boundaries are applied to the outside faces of the exterior walls. In the Usable Area plans (Figure 18.6), the boundaries are assigned to the inside faces of the exterior walls — also adapting to window elements.

To complete this part of the exercise, you will place additional area boundaries to subdivide the interior space into different spaces.

6. Activate the Level 1 area plan for Usable Area. From the Architecture tab, select the Room & Area panel; click Area, and then click Area Boundary Line.

   Note that the default drawing method is set to Pick, and in the Options bar, the Apply Area Rules setting is checked. Remember that this setting determines whether the location of the boundary will be affected by the Area Type property of the areas placed on either side of the boundary.

7. Pick on the interior walls indicated in Figure 18.7.

8. Activate the Level 2 area plan for Usable Area, and using the same method, add area boundaries to the interior walls indicated in Figure 18.8. You will need to use the Trim tool to adjust the line for the wall at the end of the corridor.

FIGURE 18.6
Area boundaries have been automatically assigned to the exterior walls.

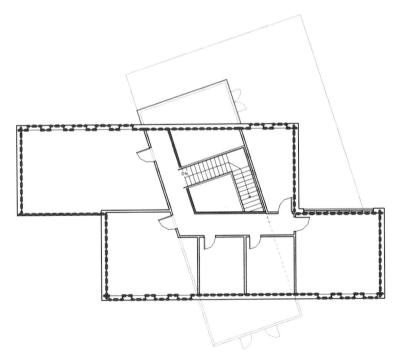

FIGURE 18.7
Place additional area boundaries on Level 1 as shown here.

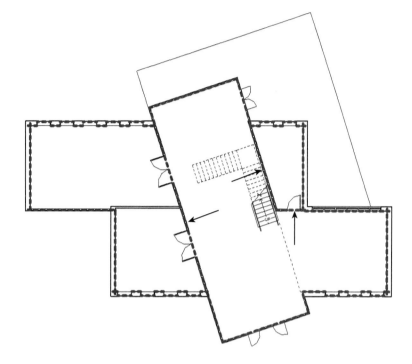

FIGURE 18.8
Place additional area boundaries on Level 2 as shown here.

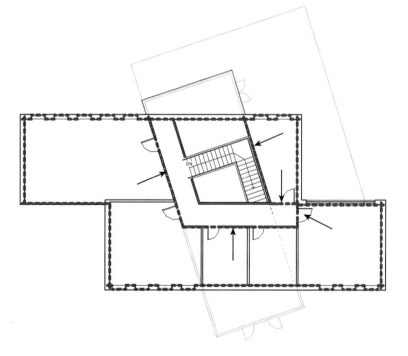

ADDING AN AREA

Like room elements, areas need a closed boundary in order to be placed, and they have properties to which you can add attributes that are "taggable." You can have any number of areas visible in an area plan, but unlike rooms, areas can be seen and tagged only in area plans. In this section's exercise, you will place areas within the boundaries you created in the previous exercise:

1. Back in the Area flyout on the Architecture tab, choose the Area tool.

   The Area tool places an area in a manner similar to placing a room, and it gives you a bound area with a large X in it (Figure 18.9). It also reports the area of the space bound by the purple area lines. In Figure 18.9, the area is reported as part of the tag.

FIGURE 18.9
The placed area element

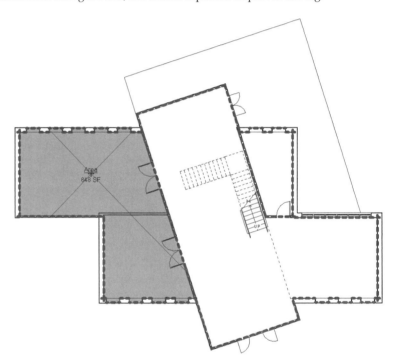

2. Place areas in each of the zones defined by the area boundary lines in Level 1. Change the names of the areas to **OFFICES**, **LOBBY**, and **SERVICES**, as shown in Figure 18.10.

3. Select the OFFICES area, and in the Properties palette, change the Area Type property to **Office Area**. Select the SERVICES area and change its Area Type property to **Store Area**.

   Notice how some of the area boundaries change to different wall faces as the Area Type property is modified. This behavior is based on the BOMA area measurement standards and is dependent on either allowing Revit to automatically assign area boundaries or using the Apply Area Rules option when you are placing the boundaries yourself.

FIGURE 18.10
Rename the areas
placed on Level 1.

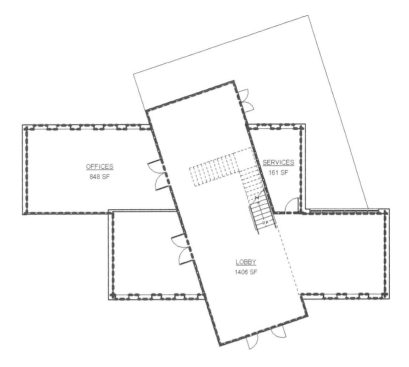

Rooms are not visible in the area plans, based on the settings in the view templates we provided in the sample project. If you do not turn off the visibility of rooms in area plans, you may mistakenly select a room object instead of an area. Always be sure to check the Type Selector to verify that you have selected an area or a room.

DELETING AREAS

As you complete this exercise, you may have accidentally placed an area outside the boundaries of the design, or you may have placed two areas within the same space. First, realize that you must delete the area, not just the area tag, to remove the area element; however, the area actually remains in your project. You are prompted with a warning as shown here:

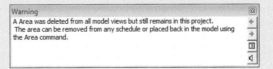

To completely remove an area from your project, you must remove it from an area schedule. The Area and Level properties of deleted areas are shown in a schedule as Not Placed. You can pick these rows in a schedule and choose Delete from the Rows panel of the ribbon.

---

4. Activate the Level 2 area plan for Usable Area and place areas in the zones defined by the area boundaries.

5. Rename the areas **OFFICES**, **CIRCULATION**, and **SERVICES**, as shown in Figure 18.11.

FIGURE 18.11
Rename the areas
placed on Level 2.

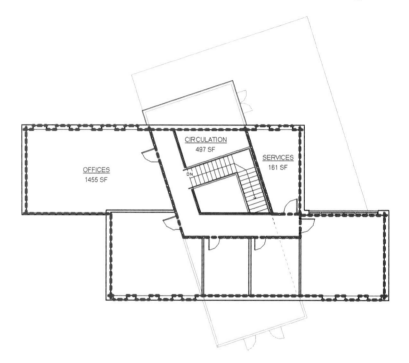

6. Select the OFFICES area and change the Area Type property to **Office Area**. Select the CIRCULATION area and change Area Type to **Major Vertical Penetration**.

MODIFYING AREA PLANS

Areas, like rooms, can be modified at any time during the design process. They can be modified dynamically if the area lines are locked to a wall or other element that has been moved as part of the design, or they can be modified manually.

If you delete an area line, you'll get the warning message shown in Figure 18.12. This message tells you that you have removed one or more of the boundary lines for an area and the software can no longer calculate the area as closed.

If you are in the midst of modifying a space, finish your modifications and replace any area lines that you've deleted or removed as part of the design change. Once the area is whole, it will recalculate the space.

In this section, you've created an area plan that will give you a graphic representation of the space you've defined with area lines. But what if you want to show this same information in a spreadsheet format? All you need to do is set up a view type in the model that allows you to look at the same information in a different format. For this, you can use a schedule.

FIGURE 18.12
Modifying an area
boundary generates
a warning.

CREATING COMPLEX AREA PLANS

In some cases, as when designing for specific clients like the General Services Administration (GSA), you might have to create and maintain a series of area plans for each floor. At times, larger clients have the need for more robust area plans detailing spaces for gross area, rentable, and individual department areas. All these additional calculations can slow file performance, depending on the complexity of the building. One way around this is to make a separate project file for the area plans, and then link the building project to this secondary file. By linking the building model to a file with area plans, you can improve model performance by not adding that overhead to your project file. You can also quickly create or print area or department plans without interfering with the workflow of the rest of the team.

Creating Schedules and Legends

CERT
OBJECTIVE

Schedules are lists of elements and element properties within the model. They itemize building objects such as walls, doors, and windows as well as calculate quantities, areas, and volumes. They also list document elements such as the number of sheets, keynotes, and so on. Schedules are yet another live way to view a Revit model. Once created, they are constantly kept up-to-date with any changes that occur to the model itself.

Legends are a way to graphically display building components, elements, or annotations used in your model. Legends can be created for displaying information such as door types, wall types, key plans, or general notes. Legends are unique in their behavior as a view because they are the one view that can be placed on multiple sheets. Building components in legends are not included in schedule quantities.

Schedules

In a project workflow, creating schedules of objects, areas, or quantities is usually one of the most laborious tasks for architects. When this process is performed manually, it can take a very long time and typically results in errors, requiring much checking and rechecking of the information. All the elements have information about their properties defined within the model. You also have the option to add additional information or categories to any existing element. For example, doors have properties such as size, material, fire rating, cost, and so on. All of this information can be scheduled and quantified. Because the schedule is linked to the element within the model, making changes to the schedule itself makes changes to the element in the model, and vice versa.

The Revit environment has several types of schedules, all of which can be accessed from the Create panel of the View tab. You can also create schedules by right-clicking the Schedules/Quantities node in the Project Browser. You can create five primary types of schedules:

Schedule/Quantities This is the most commonly used schedule type. This schedule allows you to list and quantify all element category types. You would use this type to create tabular views for doors, walls, windows, areas, rooms, and so on.

Material Takeoff This type of schedule can list all the materials and subcomponents of any Revit family category. You can use a material takeoff to schedule any material that is placed in a component or assembly. For example, you might want to know the volume of concrete within the model. Regardless of whether the concrete is in a wall, floor, or column, you can configure the schedule to report the total amount of that material in the project.

Sheet List This schedule allows you to create a list of all the sheets in the project. In addition to the number and name of the sheet, you can include the current revision number, date, and revision description.

Note Block This schedule lists the notes that are applied to elements and assemblies in your project. You can also use a note block to list the annotation symbols (centerlines, north arrows) used in a project.

View List This schedule shows a list of all the views in the Project Browser and their properties. A view list is useful for managing your project because the schedule is a bidirectional view, which allows you to edit many view properties such as name, scale, and phase.

Each of these schedule types gives you the ability to select related element properties that you can mix and match to track elements within the model. When you create a new schedule, you must first select a category of objects to itemize (Figure 18.13). You can also filter the schedule based on the various disciplines by selecting the Filter List drop-down at the upper left.

FIGURE 18.13
Creating a new schedule

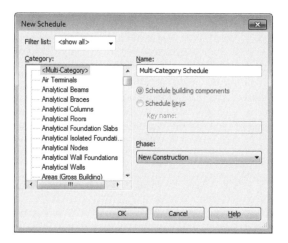

While the most common schedules are based on a single object category, you can also create some schedules that span categories. The first option in the dialog box in Figure 18.13 is the <Multi-Category> schedule. You might want to schedule all the casework and furniture in a project simultaneously, or all the windows and doors if they are being ordered from the same manufacturer. A Multi-Category schedule allows you to combine a number of different categories into one schedule. One of the limits of this schedule type is that you cannot schedule host elements (walls, floors, ceilings, and so on), only their materials and family components. For the following example we'll select <Multi-Category> schedule as the category.

KEY SCHEDULES

As long as you don't need a multicategory schedule, there is a special kind of schedule that gives you the ability to populate a list of values before placing any actual objects in your model as well as manage these values from one location. Known as a *schedule key*, it can be selected when you first create a schedule. A common example of the use of a schedule key is to manage room finishes. In this use case, you create a schedule key named Room Finish Type. You add the parameters Floor Finish, Base Finish, Wall Finish, and Ceiling Finish to the schedule. In the schedule, use the New Row button to create room finish types. For example, you could create types for Executive Office, Standard Office, Service Corridor, and Rest Room.

The parameter Room Finish Type will then appear in the element properties of every room object. The parameters that are assigned to a schedule key can be edited only in the key schedule — not in the room properties. This might seem inconvenient; however, you can manage large numbers of objects with common parameters. For example, if the floor finish for all the rooms in your project that were assigned as an Executive Office type needed to change from carpet to ceramic tile, you would simply change the schedule key and all instances of that room type would update.

After you select the <Multi-Category> category, you are presented with the Schedule Properties dialog box. This is the main interface by which you set and later modify any of the organizational or appearance characteristics of your schedules. The dialog box consists of five tabs: Fields, Filter, Sorting/Grouping, Formatting, and Appearance. Let's step through each of these tabs and examine how they affect the form and function of the schedule:

CERT OBJECTIVE

Fields The Fields tab (Figure 18.14) lets you select the data that will appear in your schedule. The list of available fields on the left will vary based on the category you choose to schedule. If you've assigned any project parameters to those categories, they will be available here as well. Also notice the option Include Elements In Linked Files at the lower-left corner. Enabling this option will allow you to schedule across multiple files, and it can be a great tool for larger projects. The order of the fields you add to the Scheduled Fields list at the right side (top to bottom) determines the order of columns in your schedule from left to right.

FIGURE 18.14
The Fields tab

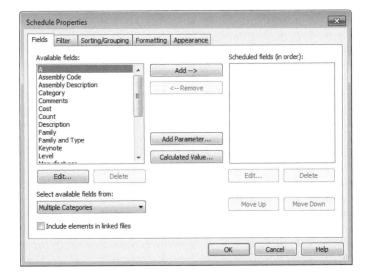

Filter   On the Filter tab (Figure 18.15), you can filter out the data you don't want to show in your schedule. Filters work like common database functions. For example, you can filter out all the sheets in a set whose names don't begin with the letter *A*. Or you can filter a material list so that it shows only items containing Concrete. Filters only operate on certain schedule fields. For instance, you can't apply a filter to the Family And Type field.

FIGURE 18.15
The Filter tab

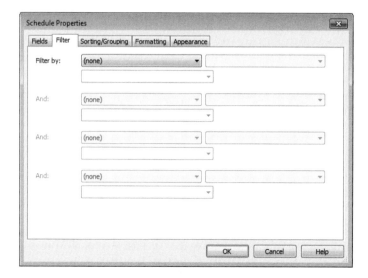

Sorting/Grouping   The Sorting/Grouping tab (Figure 18.16) lets you control the order in which information is displayed and which elements control that order. For instance, if you are creating a sheet index, you can choose to sort by sheet number or sheet name, depending on how you'd like the information displayed. You can also decide whether you want to show every instance of an item or only a summary of object types by using the Itemize Every Instance check box at the bottom.

You can also determine how to summarize the reported information in your schedule. By checking the Footer options at any grouping or the Grand Totals option, you have the ability to show a title, count, totals, or all three. You must designate one or more fields to calculate totals in the Formatting tab to display results in grouping footers or the grand totals row.

Formatting   The Formatting tab (Figure 18.17) controls the display for each field and whether the field is visible on the schedule. It also controls other elements of the field, such as justification, display name, and orientation of the header. This tab also allows you to use the Calculate Totals check box for use with the footer or Grand Totals options in the Sorting/Grouping tab. Note that you may also need to use the Calculate Totals option for certain numerical fields if you intend to deselect the Itemize Every Instance option in the Sorting/Grouping tab. For example, if you include the Area property of walls and choose not to itemize every instance, the area appears as a blank field in the schedule unless you check the Calculate Totals option.

FIGURE 18.16
The Sorting/
Grouping tab

FIGURE 18.17
The Formatting
tab allows you to
change unit formats
and specify fields in
which you need to
calculate totals.

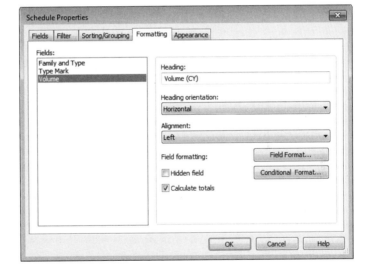

The Hidden Field option is also an important feature to help you customize your schedules. You can use this option when you need to include a field just for filtering or sorting but you don't want to see it in the schedule, such as a custom sorting parameter for drawing sheets. You can also select it when you want to use a field as the header of a group of elements in a schedule. For example, you may include the Family and Type fields, but you only want the family listed as a grouping header because you don't need to show the family name repeatedly in every row of your schedule.

Appearance   The Appearance tab (Figure 18.18) controls the graphical aspects of the schedule, such as font size and style of text for each of the columns and headers in the schedule. It also allows you to turn the schedule grid lines on and off and modify the line thickness for the grid and boundary lines. For revision schedules, you can also specify whether the schedule reads from top to bottom or from bottom to top.

FIGURE 18.18

The Appearance tab

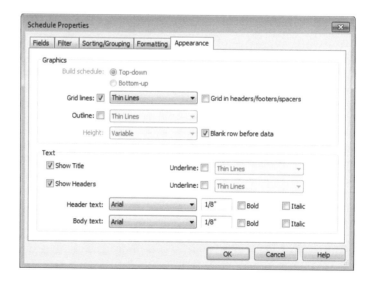

Once you've established the fields and look of your schedule, clicking OK gives you a preliminary layout. The schedule's layout can be modified at any time during the project, but this gives you a basis from which to begin. To modify the schedule at any time, you can access any tab of the Schedule Properties dialog box from the five corresponding buttons in the Properties palette when the schedule view is active.

Schedules have their own special tab on the ribbon that is active when you are viewing a schedule outside of a sheet. This tab (Figure 18.19) allows you to select the properties, add and delete rows where the type of schedule allows, and show or hide columns within the schedule.

FIGURE 18.19

The Schedule tab in the ribbon

Another key feature of this tab is the Highlight In Model button. This button allows you to select any element in the schedule and locate that element within the model. Let's say you want to locate a particular door from your door schedule. Select the respective row in the schedule and click the Highlight In Model button; you will see a different view with that door highlighted. This technique can be a useful way to locate elements in the model, especially for larger models.

Now that you have an idea of the elements that compose a schedule, let's explore the work-flow with two exercises. You will first create a simple wall schedule within the `c18-Sample-Building.rvt` project file and then create a Usable Area schedule based on the areas you defined earlier in this chapter.

MAKING A WALL SCHEDULE

In this exercise, you will create a schedule of building elements that is filtered to report only certain types of walls and is simplified to show only a summary of each unique wall type within the project. Make sure you have the `c18-Sample-Building.rvt` file open, and then follow these steps:

1. From the View tab in the ribbon, locate the Create tab, click Schedules, and then click Schedules/Quantities. The New Schedule dialog box opens.

2. Choose Walls from the Category list and click OK.

3. In the Fields tab, choose the following wall properties from the Available Fields list and add them to the Scheduled Fields list (in order):

   ◆ Function

   ◆ Family

   ◆ Type

   ◆ Area

4. Switch to the Sorting/Grouping tab, set the first Sort By field to Family, and check the Header and Blank Line options. Leave the Itemize Every Instance option checked for now.

5. Click OK to close the dialog box and observe the amount of data that is available for this schedule. Let's refine the schedule even further.

6. In the Properties palette, scroll down to find the Edit buttons related to the five tabs in the Schedule Properties dialog box. Click the button next to Filter. Set the first filter drop-down to Function equals Exterior.

7. Switch to the Formatting tab and select the Function field from the list. Check the Hidden Field option and click OK to view the result in your schedule.

   Note that now only the exterior walls are being listed. Walls with any other function property are not being itemized. Although the Function field is not shown, it must be included in the Scheduled Fields list to be used as a filter.

8. From the Properties palette, click the Edit button related to the Sorting/Grouping tab. Uncheck the Itemize Every Instance option and check the Grand Totals option. From the Grand Totals drop-down list, choose Totals Only.

9. Switch to the Formatting tab and select the Family field from the list. Check the Hidden Field option. Next, select the Area field, check the Calculate Totals option, and set the alignment to Right.

10. Click OK to close the dialog box and observe the final modifications to your wall schedule (Figure 18.20).

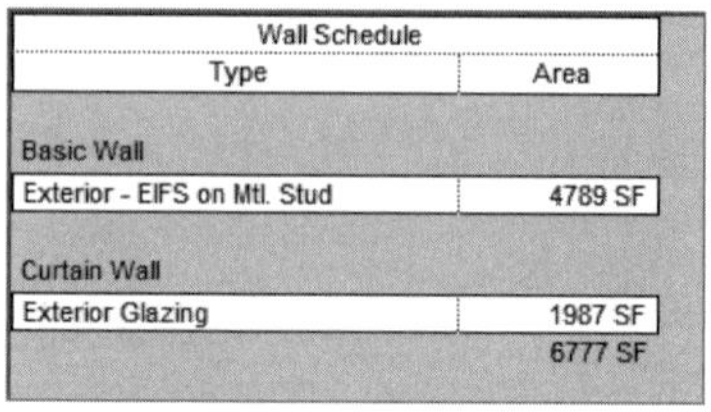

Wall Schedule	
Type	Area
Basic Wall	
Exterior - EIFS on Mtl. Stud	4789 SF
Curtain Wall	
Exterior Glazing	1987 SF
	6777 SF

FIGURE 18.20 The finished wall schedule displays a summary of elements.

In this simple wall schedule exercise, you saw that a large amount of model data can be succinctly itemized and displayed using a combination of parameters within the elements. Only the exterior wall types were itemized, and the total area for each type was reported, including a grand total of all types.

MAKING AN AREA SCHEDULE

In our next exercise, you will create an area schedule specifically for the Usable Area scheme you established earlier in this chapter. The process is similar to that of creating a wall schedule.

To create the schedule, follow these steps:

1. From the View tab in the ribbon, select Schedules and then Schedule/Quantities. From the Categories list, select the Area (Usable Area) schedule type and click OK.
2. On the Fields tab, notice that the available fields in an area table are much more limited than they were in the Walls table in the previous exercise. For this schedule, you need only four fields: Level, Name, Area Type, and Area. Choose those from the Fields list on the left, and using the Add button, move them to the right.

   Remember that the order of the fields in this list will determine the order of the columns in your final schedule. Use the Move Up and Move Down buttons as needed to order the list correctly.
3. Next, choose the Sorting/Grouping tab. From the first pull-down, choose to sort by level and check the Header and Footer boxes with the Totals Only option. Check the Itemize Every Instance option at the bottom. Also, select the Grand Totals option, and from the associated pull-down, choose Title And Totals.
4. In this schedule, you want to make the areas read as they would in a spreadsheet — right justified and totaled. Choose the Formatting tab and select Area from the list on the left. Change the justification to Right and check the Calculate Totals box. Select the Level field and check the Hidden Field box.
5. Click OK to close the dialog box and observe your results (Figure 18.21). The areas placed on each level should be listed under a header and the total area should be calculated at the bottom of each grouped level. Finally, the sum of all areas is displayed as a grand total at the bottom of the schedule.

FIGURE 18.21
The final schedule
is an organized list
of areas according
to their level.

Area Schedule (Usable Area)		
Name	Area Type	Area
Level 1		
LOBBY	Building Common Area	1406 SF
SERVICES	Store Area	187 SF
OFFICES	Office Area	848 SF
		2441 SF
Level 2		
OFFICES	Office Area	1444 SF
CIRCULATION	Major Vertical Penetration	513 SF
SERVICES	Building Common Area	156 SF
		2113 SF
Grand total		4554 SF

ADDING SCHEDULES TO YOUR TEMPLATES

On a typical project, you will find that you will use the same schedules time and time again. Spend the time to make them consistent with your office's graphic standards, and add them to your office template. That way, you won't have to make them over and over again. As you add content to your model, the schedules will automatically populate, in effect filling themselves out.

You will find yourself making the same schedules for each and every project. Take the ones you find the most universal and make them a part of your default template. As you add content to the model, these will start to auto populate.

If you have a schedule in another project and you want to add it to your project, there's no need to re-create it. Open both projects in the same instance of Revit. Go to the sheet on which the schedule you want to copy appears. If it's not on a sheet, you'll need to place it on one. Then simply highlight it and copy it (press Ctrl+C) to the Clipboard. In your destination project, go to any sheet and press Ctrl+V to paste it. Once the paste is finished, the schedule should be there with all the formatting from the previous project but with all the information from your current model.

CREATING A SHEET LIST

Using a sheet list schedule, you can create a tabular view of sheets in your project — even including drawings provided by consultants. This type of schedule allows you to create placeholders for sheets that are not yet created or will not be a part of your discipline's drawing set.

In the sample workflow, you have created area plans for the Usable Area scheme. Eventually, you may want to create another area scheme based on departmental spaces. You haven't created them yet, but you want to create your sheet list, including the area plans that you will create later. To do so, follow these steps:

1. Select the Sheet List tool from the Schedules flyout in the View tab.

2. The Sheet List Properties dialog box opens to the Fields tab. On this tab, select two fields from the categories on the left and move them to the column on the right. Select the Sheet Number and Sheet Name categories.

3. On the Sorting/Grouping tab, choose to sort by sheet number and make sure the Itemize Every Instance check box is checked. Click OK to close the dialog box.

4. To begin adding sheets to the sheet list, click the New button in the Rows panel. This will give you a row with the next sequential number based on the last number you entered. Change the sheet number in the new row to P101 and click the New button again. The next new row should be P102. Change the names of P101 and P102 to **LEVEL 1 AREA PLAN** and **LEVEL 2 AREA PLAN**, respectively.

You can continue populating the schedule in this way, adding any sheet names you need or plan to have in the presentation package. Next, you will begin to create a sheet directly from a row in the sheet list.

5. Start by selecting the New Sheet button from the ribbon. This will give you a dialog box similar to Figure 18.22.

FIGURE 18.22
Converting a place-holder into a sheet

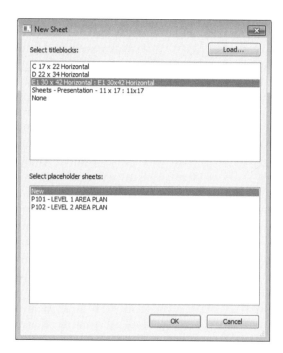

6. Select the type of sheet border you'd like to use from the list at the top. Choose the C size sheet border for this exercise.

7. Select P101 - LEVEL 1 AREA PLAN from the list of placeholder sheets and click OK.

This will create a sheet from the line item in the schedule using the same name and sheet number. The new sheet will appear under the Sheet node in the Project Browser with the correct number and name. You will begin to add views to this sheet later in this chapter.

Legends

Legends are unique views because they are the only view type you can place on more than one sheet. They can become great tools for things like general notes, key plans, or any other view type that you will want to have consistent across several sheets. It's also important to note that anything you place inside a legend view — doors, walls, windows, and so on — will not appear or be counted in any schedules. Legend elements live outside of any quantities present in the model.

The Legend tool is located on the Create panel in the View tab. There are two types of legends you can create from this menu: a *legend*, which is a graphic display, or a *keynote legend*, which is a text-based schedule. Both legend types can be placed on multiple sheets, but for this exercise, you'll focus on the legend. The keynote legend will be handled in more detail in Chapter 19, "Annotating Your Design."

As part of the sample workflow, you may want to present some of the wall types as part of your presentation package to demonstrate the Sound Transmission Class (STC) of the walls and the overall wall assembly. Since these wall types will be appearing on all the sheets where you are using them in plan, you'll make them using a legend.

To make a legend, choose the Legend button from the View tab under the Legends flyout. Creating a new legend is much like creating a new drafting view. You'll be presented with a New Legend View dialog box (Figure 18.23), where you can name the legend and set the scale. For this legend, name it **WALL LEGEND** and choose 1″ = 1′-0″ [1:10] for the scale.

FIGURE 18.23

Creating a legend

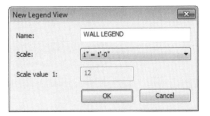

The legend you've created will look like a blank view. At this point, it's up to you to add content. The simplest type of legend would be adding notes such as plan or demolition notes that would appear in each of your floor plans. You could do this simply by using the Text tool and adding text within this legend view; however, in this example you want to add more than just text.

To add wall types or any other family to the legend view, expand the Families tree in the Project Browser and navigate to the Wall family. Expand this node and then expand the Basic Wall node. Select the Interior – 4 7/8″ Partition (1-Hr) wall type and drag it into the view.

With the family inserted into the view, it will appear as a 3′ [1000 mm] long plan wall. Change your view's detail level from Coarse to Medium or Fine so you can see the detail within the wall. With that done, highlight the inserted wall and look at the Modify | Legend Components settings in the Options bar (Figure 18.24).

FIGURE 18.24
Select a legend com-
ponent to access its
properties in the
Options bar.

This menu will be consistent for any of the family types you insert. The menu consists of three sections:

Family   This drop-down menu allows you to select different family types and operates just like the Type Selector does for other elements within the model.

View   The View option lets you change the type of view from plan to section.

Host Length   This option changes the overall length (or in the case of sections, height) of the element selected.

Let's make some minor adjustments to the wall. Let's change View to Section and change Host Length to 1'-6" [500 mm].

The wall now looks like a sectional element. By adding some simple text, you can embellish the wall type to better explain the elements you're viewing (Figure 18.25).

FIGURE 18.25
Add other annota-
tion to embellish
the wall type
section.

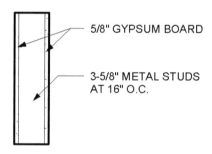

Continue the exercise by adding the Exterior — EIFS on Metal Stud wall type to the legend along with some additional text notes.

Using Details from Other Files

It is not uncommon to have details in your Revit model that were originally created in a CAD program. Sometimes these are details taken from a manufacturer's website, and sometimes they can be details drawn in other projects or from an office library, and you simply want to reuse them in your project rather than re-create them. Regardless of where they have originated, Revit has the ability to work with 2D detail elements and import or link them into the model for use in your project.

The software allows you to both link and insert CAD files into your model to be used in your documentation. You can find both of these functions on the Insert tab. There are several file types you can both insert and link into a Revit project: DWG, DXF, DGN, SAT, and SKP. There are benefits and drawbacks to using either a linking workflow or an imported one. In the following sections, we'll step through the differences between the two and discuss when and why you should use either of these methods.

Linking vs. Importing

You will want to get CAD data into your Revit model at a variety of stages in the project process. Sometimes it could be the building site you've received from your civil consultant; sometimes it's manufacturer details you need for documentation. In each case, the CAD files can be temporarily imported or linked or can permanently become part of the documentation. In addition, the size of these CAD files can vary greatly. Knowing when to import and when to link can help save you from dealing with a lot of frustration later in your project by keeping the file sizes low and the model easy to manage.

LINKING

The Link CAD tool is on the Insert tab on the Link panel. This panel also controls all the other types of linking you might want to do for external files such as DWF markups or decals (images).

Link CAD

We recommend you use linking when you have files that will be updated throughout the design process. This can be a 3D site drawing that you'll be receiving regularly from your civil engineer or 2D CAD details you'll receive from another drafter on your project who isn't familiar with a Revit workflow. By linking the files, you'll ensure that as those external files get updated, the information in the Revit model will reflect those changes. Linking creates a live connection between the model and the external files — much like an Xref in Autodesk® AutoCAD® software.

Linked files are also easy to remove from your project, leaving no trace of imported line styles, layers, or hatch patterns. This makes linking an efficient option for temporary study files as well. Linked CAD files behave in a unique way in the Revit environment because they will always appear in your project, even if the source file can't be found or it no longer exists. If a linked file cannot be found, you'll receive an error message like the one shown in Figure 18.26. The linked data will still display in your Revit project, but the data that will be displayed will only be the last known version.

FIGURE 18.26
Unresolved
References dialog
box

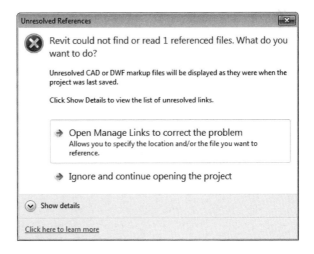

Import
CAD

IMPORTING

The Import CAD tool is on the Import panel of the Insert tab. The Import panel contains additional tools to import files from other sources. From here, you can import views and images from other Revit files and manage those imports through another dialog box.

Use the Import CAD function when you want to embed files within your model. This might be valuable when you want to insert 2D or 3D geometry to trace over and you don't want to link the file. Or if you have completed details done in CAD and you want to make them a permanent part of your model, you can do so through an import.

When importing CAD data, the data will insert as a single object — like a family — in the model. You can manage layers by turning them on and off in the Visibility/Graphic Overrides dialog box, but you'll be unable to edit any of the geometry without exploding the CAD file. If you want to explode the file, you can highlight it and choose Full Explode or Partial Explode from the menu; however, we don't recommend this. Think of a Revit project as a database full of objects. An inserted CAD file is a single object in the database. An exploded CAD file can be thousands of objects. Each time you explode a CAD file, you're adding overhead to your model that you might not be able to remove later. Good file management will help you keep your files small and able to react quickly.

 ## Real World Scenario

TIPS ON IMPORTING CAD DETAILS

At times in the project, your workflow will necessitate using 2D information from a past project, a manufacturer's library, or another resource in your current Revit project. To optimize the performance of your imported CAD files within your model, we recommend that you take some steps to prepare the CAD file before import. Here are some general tips to help your import process:

♦ If the file you'd like to import contains hatches or annotations, delete them before importing and use filled regions and the Revit Text or Keynote tool for annotations. This will help keep your graphics consistent (in the case of hatch) and allow you to edit the verbiage and location of any notes.

♦ Import only one detail at a time so you can take better advantage of the software's ability to manage sheet referencing. If you have a series of details organized in a single CAD file that you want to use in documenting your project, isolate each detail, save it as a separate file, and then import.

♦ Make sure you import the CAD details using the proper line weights, colors, and styles. Check your CAD file before importing into your Revit project to make sure it is consistent with your office's standards.

♦ If the imported geometry is something you really want or need to edit, it's better for your model and overall file size to import the CAD file into a detail component (if it's 2D) and explode it and edit it in the Family Editor. This way, when you import it into your project file, it is still a single object rather than thousands.

♦ Revit software doesn't allow line segments shorter than 1/32″. Although this is seemingly a very small line, many manufacturer details have small segment lines in them. When CAD details are exploded, those short lines will be deleted and can leave your line work looking incomplete.

For more complete coverage on the process of importing or linking CAD data, please refer to Chapter 8, "Interoperability: Working Multiplatform."

Reusing Details from Other Revit Projects

We've discussed that you sometimes want to reuse details or geometry from projects done in CAD. But what happens when you want to reuse details from projects completed in the Revit environment? Thankfully, there are a couple of simple ways to take your Revit details and drawings with you from one project to the next.

SAVING A SINGLE DETAIL

Everyone is familiar with the problem of having a detail very similar to the one you need to create in a previous Revit project. Now the question is, How do you get it into your project? In the case of a single, 2D detail, it can be quick work to get the file from one project to the next:

1. First, open the file with the detail you'd like to collect and activate the view in which this detail appears. Select all the geometry and annotation within the drafting view and create a group using the Create Group button on the Modify | Multi-Select contextual tab.

2. The group will by default be created as a detail group (since all your geometry is only 2D). Give the group a name, making sure the name is unique enough not to overlap with any view names in your current project or the project you're going to import into.

3. With the detail grouped and named, expand the Groups node in the Project Browser. Now, expand the Detail Group node and find the detail you just created. Right-click the detail and choose Save Group from the context menu.

4. As part of the Save As process, you'll get the Save Group dialog box (Figure 18.27). This will allow you to create a separate RVT file for your group — basically a stand-alone project file. Save the group in a location where you'll be able to find it again and close your project file. There's no need to name the group because the new file will name itself the same as the group name.

   We have created a sample file using this method for use in the remainder of this exercise. Make sure you download the file `c18-Jamb-Detail.rvt` from the book's companion website.

5. Open the `c18-Sample-Building.rvt` project file saved from the previous exercises in this chapter.

6. From the View tab, click Drafting View to create a new view and name it **JAMB DETAIL**. The scale does not matter because it will inherit the scale of the imported detail.

7. From the Insert tab of the ribbon, choose Insert From File and then Insert 2D Elements From File.

8. In the Open dialog box, navigate to and select the c18-Jamb-Detail.rvt file. You will then see the Insert 2D Elements dialog box, which is shown in Figure 18.28. Highlight Drafting View: JAMB DTL from the list box and select the Transfer View Scale check box. Click OK to close the dialog box and begin the import.

9. Click anywhere in the drafting view to place the imported elements, and then click the Finish button in the ribbon to complete the command.

FIGURE 18.27
The Save Group dialog box

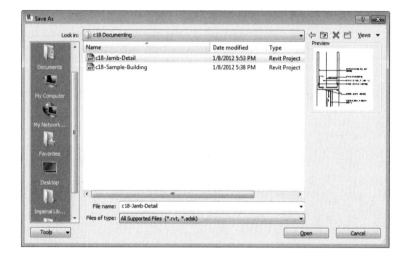

FIGURE 18.28
Choose the detail group from the Insert 2D Elements dialog box.

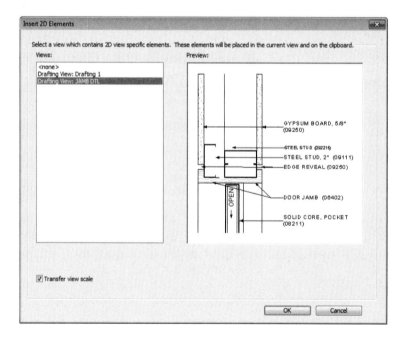

SAVING MULTIPLE DETAILS

As you create more and more details in Revit projects, you will inevitably want to save some of them to an office library or some sort of localized resource so you can quickly locate the good ones again. Revit allows you to selectively save multiple views from a single project into a separate, stand-alone file. This workflow will work for both 2D and 3D content.

A quick way to get any view isolated to an external file is to right-click the view in the Project Browser and choose Save To New File from the context menu. It might take the software a few moments to compile the view content, but you will be presented with a dialog box asking you to locate the new file. Once the view is exported, it functions like any other RVT file. You can open these new views directly and edit or manipulate any of the content or elements within the file. You'll also see a streamlined version of the Project Browser having only the nodes that relate to the content you've exported.

Another way to export multiple views is to click the Application menu and choose Save As ➤ Library. This command allows you to save multiple views into a single RVT file that acts as a library for those views. Here are the steps:

1. Start by opening the file with the views you want to save. Click the Application menu and select Save As ➤ Library ➤ View.

2. This will give you the Save Views dialog box (Figure 18.29). It will show a list of view names on the left and a preview window on the right side. Click the check box for each of the views you want to save into a separate file. Once you have all your view names established, click OK.

FIGURE 18.29
Exporting multiple views to a separate file

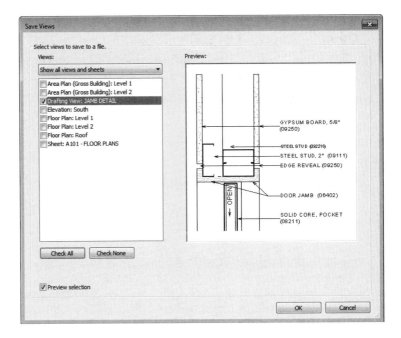

The software might take a few moments to export the views depending on how many you've chosen and how large the overall file size is. Once the process is completed, you'll have a separate file to import those views back into Revit projects. This import process is just as simple as exporting. Here's how to import the views:

1. Open the project into which you'd like to import the views. From the Insert tab on the ribbon, choose Insert From File and then Insert Views From File.

2. The new dialog box will look very similar to the Save Views dialog box. You will have a list of the views you can import from the column on the left and a preview of those views on the right. Check the box for the views you want to import and click OK (Figure 18.30).

FIGURE 18.30
Importing multiple views into a project

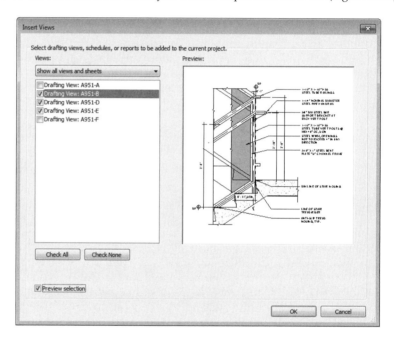

You can also import entire sheets of details using this method. If sheets exist in the file you have selected with the Insert Views From File command, they are listed as options to insert. When sheets are inserted, the details placed on each sheet are automatically imported into the project as well.

Laying Out Sheets

Throughout this chapter, you have created and imported several different kinds of views, from area plans and schedules to legends and details. Eventually you will need to lay those out onto sheets so they can be printed or exported as PDF or DWF and sent to others for review.

Creating sheets is easy. As you've already seen, you can create sheets through a sheet list schedule. You can also create sheets by right-clicking the Sheet node in the Project Browser and selecting New Sheet from the context menu. Regardless of which method you use to create them, in the following sections we'll walk through laying out these views on sheets and show you how to manipulate each view further once it's placed on a sheet.

Adding the Area Plan

In the following exercise, you will continue to use the c18-Sample-Building.rvt file saved from previous exercises in this chapter:

1. Open the P101 – LEVEL 1 AREA PLAN sheet in the view window by double-clicking it in the Project Browser. Now, let's add your first view — the Usable Area plan for Level 1. To do this, simply drag and drop it from the Project Browser and onto the sheet. The view will show at the proper scale and with a view title already established. You can then drag the view across the sheet to place it where you'd like to have it, which in this case is centered at the top of the sheet.

   After placing the view, however, you'll notice that the purple area lines are still visible. If you print the sheet at this point, the software will print those lines as thick, black lines that border your floor plate. This may be undesirable, so you need to do some view management to turn those lines off. One way you can do this is by activating the area plan from the Project Browser and working within the view itself. Since you have the view already established on a sheet, there's no reason to go back to the original view when you can work on it directly through the sheet.

2. Right-click the view on the sheet and choose Activate View from the context menu.

Activating a view is like working in model space through paper space in CAD. You're working on the actual view but you're doing so while it is placed on the sheet. This gives you the benefit of seeing how changes to the view will affect the layout of the view on the sheet. At times, it could be undesirable to enlarge the crop window for the view to show more information on the sheet. Doing so will take up valuable sheet real estate and should be balanced by the amount of space the other views on this sheet need. Working through the sheet allows you to see how this all works live on it so you can make any adjustments on the fly. You'll also notice that once the view is activated, all the surrounding materials (the sheet and any other views) turn gray. This is to alert you to the fact that you're working in the view and are not active on the sheet.

In this view, however, you want to make some modifications to the visibility and turn off the area boundaries so they are not visible when you print. To do this, open the Visibility/Graphic Overrides dialog box by pressing VG on your keyboard or navigating to the command via the context menu.

In the Visibility/Graphic Overrides dialog box, pan down in the Model tab (activated by default) and choose the Lines node. Uncheck the box for <Area Boundaries> and click OK. The boundary lines should disappear from the view.

Now you're ready to get out of the activation mode and add some additional views to the sheet. To do this, right-click anywhere within the view and choose Deactivate View from the context menu.

DEACTIVATE ACTIVE VIEWS

Keep the following in mind: Once you activate a view and complete your edits, you must deactivate it. As you can see on the sheet, activated views gray out the surrounding sheet context. If you were to print at this point, the sheet would print as gray with only the activated view showing in black.

With the view on the sheet, you will want to make some other adjustments to help clean the sheet layout up a bit. One thing you will want to do is modify the view title's location and length. To do this, click the view itself and the view title will activate, showing in purple. This might sound a bit counterintuitive, but selecting the view title itself will allow you to relocate the view and title around on the sheet.

With the view title active, you'll notice the blue grip at the end of the title line. By grabbing the grip, you can shorten the view title. You can now also grab the view title itself by clicking and holding the left mouse button down and drag the title closer to the view itself (Figure 18.31).

FIGURE 18.31
Move the view title by selecting it directly, not by selecting the viewport.

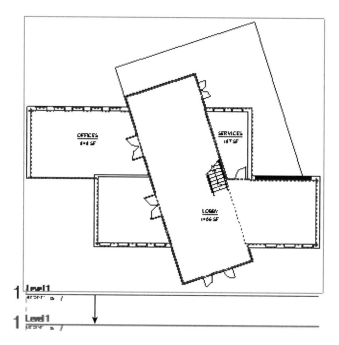

Using Guide Grids

If you have multiple plans, elevations, or sections that need to be placed at the same location on a series of sheets, the Guide Grid command can help you manage this. Guide grids are nonprinting grids that can be associated with sheets. The grids allow you to snap or align elements such as reference planes, other grids, or crop regions to specific locations relative to the sheet border.

You can create as many unique guide grids as required in a Revit project. First, activate the P101 sheet to establish your first guide grid. Complete the following exercise before placing the next area plan on a new sheet:

1. From the View tab in the ribbon, select Guide Grid from the Sheet Composition panel. Name the new grid **C-Sheet Area Plans**.

2. When you see the grid appear on the sheet, select it and look at the Properties palette. Change the spacing to 3" [75 mm].

3. Select the outer boundary of the guide grid and activate the Move command (press MV on the keyboard). Snap to one of the grid intersections within the guide and then move it to the upper-left intersection of the inner sheet border.

Where you place the guide grid and the spacing of the grid itself will depend on exactly how you plan to use it. In our example, we only need to identify a single common point to which we will align our area plans. The location of the boundary of the grid is not important; the boundary cannot be snapped to.

4. Access the view properties of the sheet and scroll down to find the Guide Grid property. Make sure it is set to C-Sheet Area Plans.

5. Select the area plan already placed on sheet P101 and activate the Move command. Snap to the intersection of the two reference planes visible in the plan and then to a nearby intersection on the guide grid.

Note that some traditional modifying methods do not work with guide grids. For example, you cannot use the Align command.

6. If you haven't already done so, create a new sheet using the P102 - LEVEL 2 AREA PLAN placeholder. In the Properties palette, make sure the guide grid is specified and note that it is now in exactly the same location as on the previous sheet.

7. Drag the Level 2 Usable Area plan onto the sheet and then use the Move command to adjust the location of the plan to the same location as on the previous sheet (Figure 18.32).

FIGURE 18.32
Use Guide Grids to help align views among a series of sheets.

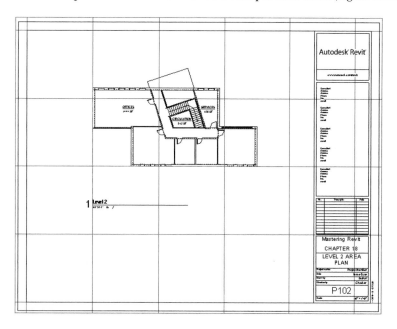

If you haven't noticed already, model views of the same scale will always snap to each other without any special grids. What you might not realize is that this also works between views of different types as long as they are of the same scale. For example, you can drag an elevation from the Project Browser onto sheet P102 and see how it snaps in relation to the plan. Sections can also be aligned with elevations and with plans. Even 3D views can be aligned with each other.

Adding the Schedule

With the largest view, the area plan, on the sheet, you can use the bottom portion of the sheet to lay out your other views. For the second view, let's add the area schedule you created. To do this, drag and drop it from the Project Browser in much the same way you added the area plan. The inserted view will look like Figure 18.33. You'll notice some differences in how this view looks from the way a schedule looks when it's not on a sheet. Specifically, you can now see the header text and the fonts you chose in the schedule properties. You'll also be able to see the grid lines and their associated line weights from the Appearance tab of the schedule properties.

FIGURE 18.33
A schedule placed on a sheet

Area Schedule (Usable Area)		
Name	Area Type	Area
Level 1		
LOBBY	Building Common Area	1406 SF
SERVICES	Store Area	187 SF
OFFICES	Office Area	848 SF
		2441 SF
Level 2		
OFFICES	Office Area	1444 SF
CIRCULATION	Major Vertical Penetration	513 SF
SERVICES	Building Common Area	156 SF
		2113 SF
Grand total		4554 SF

With the schedule on the sheet, it looks a bit tight. You have the ability to redefine the column spacing so you can make any visual adjustments to the schedule while it is on the sheet to help it read better. These adjustments do not change the actual schedule — just its appearance on the sheet.

To do this, highlight the schedule by selecting it. The schedule will turn blue, and you'll have a few new grips to help you make adjustments (Figure 18.34). The blue inverted triangles will allow you to modify the column widths. Grab them and drag them left or right to change the column sizing.

FIGURE 18.34
A schedule can be manipulated when it is placed on a sheet.

Area Schedule (Usable Area)		
Name	Area Type	Area
Level 1		
LOBBY	Building Common Area	1406 SF
SERVICES	Store Area	187 SF
OFFICES	Office Area	848 SF
		2441 SF
Level 2		
OFFICES	Office Area	1444 SF
CIRCULATION	Major Vertical Penetration	513 SF
SERVICES	Building Common Area	156 SF
		2113 SF
Grand total		4554 SF

You'll also notice a blue cut symbol . This cut symbol lets you break the schedule into multiple vertical columns on the same sheet. This tool can be especially handy if you have a long schedule like a room schedule or door schedule and it has too many rows to fit vertically on your sheet. Selecting this tool will break the schedule in half (and you can break it into half again and again) so that you can take advantage of the horizontal real estate. If you choose to separate your schedule in this fashion, it will still retain all the necessary information and all the portions will continue to automatically fill themselves out dynamically as a single schedule would. You also have the opportunity to change the overall height of the schedule once it is broken up by grabbing the grips at the bottom of the schedule and dragging up and down (Figure 18.35). Doing so will draw or push rows from the adjacent schedule portion so that all of your information is continuous.

FIGURE 18.35
Changing the schedule height

Area Schedule (Usable Area)		
Name	Area Type	Area
Level 1		
LOBBY	Building Common Area	1406 SF
SERVICES	Store Area	187 SF
OFFICES	Office Area	848 SF
		2441 SF

Area Schedule (Usable Area)		
Name	Area Type	Area
Level 2		
OFFICES	Office Area	1444 SF
CIRCULATION	Major Vertical Penetration	513 SF
SERVICES	Building Common Area	156 SF
		2113 SF
Grand total		4554 SF

GETTING THE VIEWS TO LOOK THE WAY YOU WANT

On a typical project, there will be multiple views shown in the same way. These can be plans, elevations, or sections, but you will find yourself laying out crop boundaries, scale, visibility graphics, and many other settings for each of these views. Rather than creating them all manually, use view templates, which are a great way to apply settings to a view or to transfer settings between views.

The simplest way to do this is to get one of your views (say a plan) set up visually just the way you want it. Once you do that, right-click the view in the Project Browser and choose Save As View Template. You can then right-click all your remaining plans in the Project Browser and choose Apply View Template from the context menu and they will all take on the settings of your previous view.

In addition, you can go back and change these settings manually at any time by selecting the Manage tab and then View Templates from the Settings flyout menu.

For more information on view templates, please refer to Chapter 4, "Configuring Templates and Standards."

Finishing the Sheet

Now that you have those two views on the sheet, it is a simple matter to add the remaining views. To add the wall legend you created, you will drag and drop it from the Project Browser in much the same way you did with the other two views.

In this case, the wall legend came onto the sheet needing little modification. Following this same workflow, you can also add a drafting view from the imported detail to the sheet, completing P102 (Figure 18.36).

FIGURE 18.36
The finished sheet

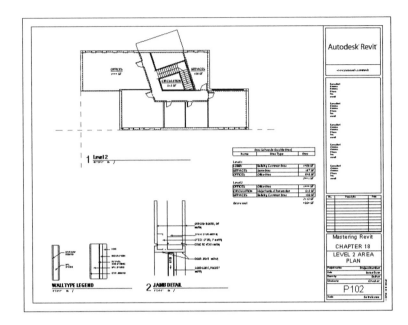

The Bottom Line

Document plans. With Floor plans you can create visual graphics that help to define how a space is laid out. However, Revit provides other tools such as area plans to help you describe space.

> **Master It** List the four types of area plans that you can create and note the two that Revit creates automatically.

Create schedules and legends. Schedules are another view type; they allow you to show information about the model in a nongraphic format. Schedules can also be used to dynamically report quantities of elements inside the model.

> **Master It** Understand how to create schedules and report additional information about the elements in the model. How would you create a simple casework schedule showing quantities of types?

Use details from other files. In many project workflows, you will need to incorporate details from other projects. Reusing these details can aid in the speed and efficiency of project documentation.

> **Master It** There are several ways to reuse details from other projects. Name one and list the steps to perform the tasks necessary to quickly move a detail from one project to another.

Lay out sheets. Eventually in a project it will become necessary to create sheets that will become the documentation set. Knowing how to create a good sheet set provides you with another venue to communicate with contractors, clients, and other team members.

Master It To properly create a sheet set, you need to understand the dynamics of adding views to a sheet. In the Revit environment, there is only one way to add views to a sheet. What is it?

Chapter 19

Annotating Your Design

No set of documents is complete without the annotations to describe the drawings. Even when you are using a digital, parametric model, you will still need to provide annotated documents. It is necessary to add dimensions, tags, text, and notes to the drawings to properly communicate with owners, contractors, and the rest of the design team.

In this chapter, you'll learn to:

◆ Annotate with text and keynotes

◆ Use tags

◆ Add dimensions

◆ Set project and shared parameters

Annotating with Text and Keynotes

Notes are a critical part of communicating design and construction intent to owners and builders. No drawing set is complete without descriptions of materials and the work (Figure 19.1).

FIGURE 19.1
An annotated detail

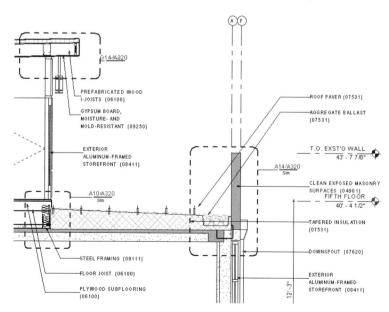

There are two ways for you to note your drawings in Autodesk® Revit® Architecture software. Both are located on the Annotate tab and highlighted in Figure 19.2. One of these methods is the Text command (shown on the left), and the other is the Keynote command (shown on the right).

FIGURE 19.2

Text and keynotes

The Text object consists of a resizable field into which you can enter text with optional features including leaders, bullets, or numbers. Text can be used for annotations, sheet notes (such as general notes), or legends; they can be used generally anywhere you need to add a description or a note. Keynotes are predefined text fields that are linked to elements and materials through a data file. Keynotes can be scheduled and standardized across the project but can't be directly edited within the application. Both keynotes and text have specific uses across the project. Let's look at both.

Using Text

Text is quick and easy to add to any view (including 3D views), and like other drafting elements, it is view specific. Text added to one view will not appear in any other location within the model, nor will the actual type that you insert into the text box hold any sort of parametric values.

You can access the Text tool from the Text panel on the Annotate tab (shown earlier in Figure 19.2). To begin adding text, select the Text tool and first observe the settings in the contextual ribbon. You can specify an option for a leader, the position of the leader, and the justification of the text. It is easier to set these options before you place a text object, but they can always be adjusted later.

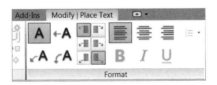

After you have selected the most appropriate settings in the ribbon, go to a place in a view where you'd like to place the text object. You will have the opportunity to use one of two methods to create the text object. If you click once, the position you clicked will be the origin of the text object and the text will not have a defined width. Using this method, you may need to use the Enter key to fit the text to your needs. This method may cause some difficulty in the future if you need to resize the text box or if you change the scale of the view.

The other option is to hold down the left mouse button while you click to place the origin of the text. Then drag the mouse pointer to specify the boundary of the text object. Don't worry about the vertical extents of the boundary; you just need to set the width of the text box. Using this option gives you greater flexibility if you need to resize the text box or if the scale of your view changes, because the word wrapping will be handled automatically. With the Text command active, you'll be presented with the standard mouse pointer crosshair, but it will have a small *A* in the lower corner to let you know you are adding text and not other elements.

Once you place a text object in a view, you can write much as you do in applications like Microsoft Word. Once you are done typing, click outside the text box. Your finished text box will look like Figure 19.3.

FIGURE 19.3

A highlighted text box

REMOVE EXISTING WOOD
WINDOWS. STORE ON SITE.
CLEAN EXISTING MASONRY
OPENING. SAND PATCH
MORTAR AS NEEDED USING
TYPE-N MORTAR AND COLOR
APPROVED BY ARCHITECT.
REPLACE EXISTING WOOD
SILLS WITH CAST STONE.
PROFILE TO MATCH.

You'll also notice that once you're finished with your initial text, you have a few tools available:

Grips The round grips on either side of the text box allow you to resize the box.

Move There is a move icon that appears in the upper-left corner of the text box. In addition, hovering your mouse anywhere within the highlighted text will also display a move cursor. You can click and drag from within the box or click the move icon on the upper-left corner to relocate it. When you're moving text with the move icon (or the Move command), the text *and* leader will relocate together. When you're moving text by dragging, the leader end will remain pinned while you relocate the text box. These methods let you move either the text or the text and the leader, depending on your need.

Rotate The upper-right corner shows a rotate icon. Clicking this icon allows you to rotate the text box as you would any object in a project. Remember that text will always position itself to be read left to right if it is horizontal or bottom to top if it is vertical in a view.

A text family behaves like other families because it maintains a parametric relationship throughout the project. Making changes to a text family type in one location (changing font, font size, color, and so on) changes all the instances of that family throughout the model. To modify a text family, select a block of text or choose the Text tool. This opens the Type Selector, shown in Figure 19.4.

FIGURE 19.4

Type Selector for text

Here, the controls are rather limited and deal primarily with instance parameters for an individual text object (alignment, location, and so on), which you can also set on the ribbon. The Type Selector also allows you to select a different text type or edit the properties of the currently selected type. Click the Edit Type button to open the text family's type properties. Figure 19.5 shows the properties for $\frac{3}{32}$" [3 mm] Arial text.

FIGURE 19.5
Type Properties
dialog box

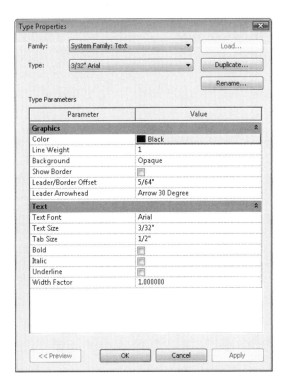

In this dialog box, you have more control over the style of the text. Here you can modify typical text properties, such as font, size, and width factor. You can also add formatting to the text, such as bold, italic, and underline.

When any text object is selected in a view, additional tools become available on the ribbon. The Format panel is divided into four sections that allow you to modify the instance of the text you've placed. Figure 19.6 shows the Format panel when the overall text object is selected and when you activate the text within the object. Let's look at this panel in some more detail to better understand the toolset:

CERT OBJECTIVE

Leaders The leftmost section of this panel (A) allows you to designate the type and style of leader you want to add to your text box. When you activate the Text tool, the upper-left A is selected by default (as in Figure 19.6), which designates that no leader is currently added. The other choices all will add a leader to the text. Reading from left to right, the options are no leader, a single-segment leader, a double-segment leader, and an arced leader. Leaders can be added at any time when you're placing or editing text and can also be removed at any time. Remember that when you're removing leaders, they will disappear in the order in which they were added.

FIGURE 19.6

The Format panel in the contextual ribbon when placing text (a); selecting a text object (b); and editing text within the object (c)

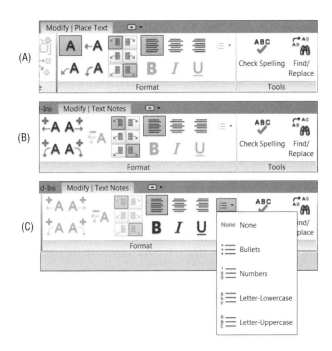

Leader location The second portion of this panel (B) dictates leader location. Leaders can be added to the left or to the right and at the top, center, or bottom of the text box. The top example in Figure 19.7 shows the default with a left leader springing from the upper left of the text; leaders that spring from the right side typically come from the end of the text box (at the bottom). A double-segment leader springing from the left and right will look like the bottom example in Figure 19.7.

FIGURE 19.7

Text with a leader

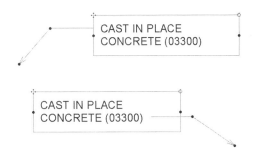

Format The third portion of the Format panel (C) controls the format of the text. These features — justification, bold, italicized, and underline — can also be added to the type properties of the text family by clicking Edit Type in the Properties palette; however, you can add them to individual text within a text object by using the contextual ribbon.

Bullets The rightmost portion of the Format panel allows you to add a bulleted or numbered list to the text box. By default, this style of formatting is not added, but by selecting the text box or the text within the box, you can add bullets, numbers, or letters to the text.

Using Keynotes

Keynotes are annotations that use a parameter to connect specific elements or materials in the model to descriptive information stored in an external .txt file. You can control the formatting of the keynote's font style, size, and justification in the same manner you can format standard text, but keynotes behave more like a tag family. Formatting changes must be made in the keynote's family (RFA) file and reloaded into the project.

Inserting a keynote allows you to choose a value from the .txt file and apply it to a material or element. Because keynotes act as families, they can also be scheduled where standard text cannot. Before we discuss how to add different keynote types, we'll discuss the different ways a keynote can be displayed.

Without official corroboration from Autodesk, it appears that the keynoting functionality was designed to support the American Institute of Architects (AIA) proposal of the ConDoc system, in which a short numeric reference (usually based on MasterFormat® by the Construction Specifications Institute) followed by a two-letter suffix is used to label elements in a drawing. The keynote then references a list or legend that is located on the same sheet as the note and has a longer definition of the note. For example, a keynote on a detail might read 033000.AA, with a leader pointing to an element in the drawing. The associated list on the side of the sheet would read CAST IN PLACE CONCRETE. Figure 19.8 shows an example of a keynote legend.

FIGURE 19.8

A keynote legend

KEYNOTE LEGEND	
03300.AO	CIP CONC FLOOR SLAB (03300)
04810.BF	STONE CLADDING (04810)
05120.AC	STEEL BEAM (05120)
05310.AH	COMPOSITE FLOOR DECK (05310)
05500.BB	STEEL COLUMN (05500)
05500.BU	STEEL ANGLE (05500)
06105.AB	WOOD FURRING (06105)
06105.AC	PLYWOOD (06105)
06105.AD	1X IPE WOOD SUNSCREEN (06105)
07210.AB	RIGID INSULATION (07210)

Despite the intended use of a keynote, you are not restricted to using only the numeric code. You can also display the full, written description directly within the detail or view without the numeric reference key. Figure 19.9 shows an example of keynotes that display the full description instead of the key.

There is no wrong way to use keynotes, and Revit Architecture supports both methods of using them for annotation. Regardless of the method you use, keynotes will adhere to the same process for use. Once an element is tagged with a keynote, it will retain that keynote in all other views in the model. If an element has been tagged with a keynote in one view and is then annotated in another view, it will automatically display the same keynote value. This can become a very powerful tool you can use to add consistency throughout the project for annotated elements.

FIGURE 19.9
Keynotes displaying full text descriptions

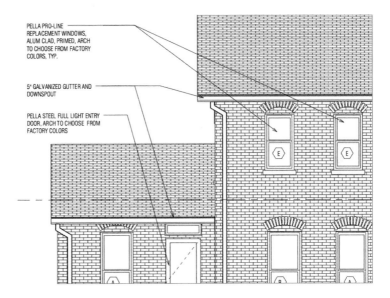

PELLA PRO-LINE REPLACEMENT WINDOWS, ALUM CLAD, PRIMED, ARCH TO CHOOSE FROM FACTORY COLORS, TYP.

5" GALVANIZED GUTTER AND DOWNSPOUT

PELLA STEEL FULL LIGHT ENTRY DOOR, ARCH TO CHOOSE FROM FACTORY COLORS

The Keynote command is located on the Annotate tab in the ribbon. When you select the Keynote tool, you have three options:

Element   Use Element keynotes to annotate elements and assemblies within the model, such as walls, doors, floors, or other family instances. This type of note is typically used if you want to annotate an entire assembly (such as a wall). Moving the Element keynote leader arrow off the object will change the value of the note based on the element to which it points. The keynote value for a family type can be preset within the family. We'll go into how to do that later in this chapter.

Material   Using the Material keynote type will allow you to annotate specific materials within any elements. You can add notes for materials like concrete, gypsum board, rigid insulation, metal studs, and so on. Moving the Material keynote leader arrow from one material to another will change the value of the note based on the material to which it points. Material keynotes can also be predefined as part of your project template. Material keynotes can be used in conjunction with Element keynotes.

If you want to predefine keynotes on project materials, go to the Manage tab and select Materials. The Material Browser and Material Editor dialog boxes will appear. In the Material Browser dialog box, select the material you would like to edit. If the Material Editor is not open, double-click on any material in the Material Browser. In the Material Editor dialog box, click the arrow next to the material name as shown in Figure 19.10.

Figure 19.10
Editing the identity
data for a material

User User keynotes are different from Element and Material keynotes because they are view specific and cannot be predefined. Although they are still tied to the same .txt file and will update in the same manner as other keynotes, they are not associated with any model objects. User keynotes are meant to be used for all the instances when you don't have a modeled element or material but you still need to define a note. Some examples of things you wouldn't necessarily model might be sealant, backer rod, or flashing.

User keynotes are used primarily in drafting views. To use any keynote, a given view must have at least one model element or component visible within it. In the case of a drafting view, you will need to insert a 2D component (such as wood blocking or a steel stud) because keynotes cannot be used to note linework. Because User keynotes are not locked to specific model geometry, once they are inserted, they can easily be copied or moved around within the view and pointed to any element. In this way, if you have sealant or flashing shown as linework, you can add a User keynote to the view and then adjust the note leader and the note value to call out the sealant properly. You can change the value of a user keynote at any time simply by double-clicking the note value; this modification will not affect any other notes within the project.

You can use all of these note types in conjunction with one another. Using an Element note to add a keynote to a wall doesn't mean you cannot also use a Material note to call out the individual materials in the wall assembly.

KEYNOTE BEHAVIOR AND EDITING

A core concept of the Keynote tool is how the notes react within the model. Assigning a keynote to an object lets you associate a text or numeric value with a family's keynote type parameter. This value is consistent for every instance of that element within the model or project. For example, all walls have a type parameter called Keynote that lets you set the keynote value. If you keynote a wall anywhere within the model, the keynote value in the type parameter will reflect that note. Consequently, any other wall of that type will be prepopulated with that keynote value. Changes to this keynote value will dynamically update the type parameter value and update any keynotes placed within the model tagged to this wall.

All keynotes within a project are tied to an external .txt file. This .txt file is the only location where the value of the keynotes can be edited. This file can be modified at any point to add or remove notes, and the edits can happen while the project is actively open. Figure 19.11 shows a sample of the file.

FIGURE 19.11
The keynote .txt file

```
Division 03        Concrete
030000   Concrete Division 03
033000.AA          C.I.P. CONCRETE (033000) 030000
033000.AG          LIGHTWEIGHT CONCERETE FILL (033000)      030000
034100.AA          PRECAST STRUCTURAL CONCRETE (034100) 030000
034500.AB          PRECAST ARCHITECTURAL CONCRETE (034500)      030000
034900.AA          GLASS-FIBER-REINFORCED CONCRETE (034900)      030000
Division 04        Masonry
040000   Masonry Division 04
042000.AM          CMU (042000)      040000
042000.BE          FACE BRICK (042000)        040000
042300.AB          HOLLOW GLASS BLOCK (042300)      040000
044300.AB          STONE MASONRY (044300)        040000
Division 07        Insulation
070000   Insulation and Sealants      Division 07
071326.AQ          BOARD INSULATION (071326)        070000
071800.AF          SHEET FLASHING (071820) 070000
072100.AD          CONCEALED BUILDING INSULATION (072100) 070000
074213.AA          METAL WALL PANEL ASSEMBLY (074213)      070000
076100.AA          SHEET METAL ROOFING (076100)      070000
Division 08        Doors and Windows
080000   Doors and Windows        Division 08
084413.AV          INSULATED SPANDREL PANEL (084413)      080000
085200.BG          MULLION (085200) 080000
```

This external file is designed to keep the annotations consistent by storing them in one repository. Every time you add or change a note value and reload the .txt file back into the Revit model, all of the keynotes dynamically update.

You can edit this .txt file or add one to the project at any time. You can have multiple keynote files for various projects, but you can have only one .txt file associated with a project at a time. You cannot assign multiple keynote files to one project model.

MANAGING KEYNOTES

A great way to ensure consistent use of notes throughout multiple projects is to create a master keynote file for each of your various project types. This master note list can be linked to elements and materials within your project template so that you can immediately begin inserting common notes into any project. Since this master list will likely be quite long, project teams can make a copy of the list and place it in their project directory. They can then safely delete the notes they won't be using over the course of the project, giving them fewer options to hunt through when they need to add a keynote.

A single keynote file also gives project management a level of control over the consistency of the notes that you won't be able to get if you use regular text. Spelling accidents or mislabeling can happen in a project when you use regular text objects. For example, it's easy to overlook a note that reads CIP CONCRETE on one detail and CAST-IN-PLACE CONCRETE in another. By placing all the notes into one file, the project manager or project architect has better control over how the note reads, thus ensuring consistency throughout all the sheets and details.

Because the keynote list is a separate .txt file, if you are transferring files to other offices or clients, you may need to include the .txt file along with the RVT file. If you don't send the .txt file, others will be able to see all of your keynotes but they won't be able to change or edit any of them.

THE KEYNOTE FILE

Three default keynote text files are available at the library locations. In Windows 7, they are found at `C:\ProgramData\Autodesk\RVT 2013\Libraries` (you may need to change the options in Windows Explorer to display hidden folders). Another way to find these files is to start a new project using the default template and go to the Annotate tab. Click the Tag panel drop-down and select Keynoting Settings. In the Keynote Settings dialog box, click the Browse button and you will be taken to the default library location.

These three keynote files are called `RevitKeynotesImperial.txt`, `RevitKeynotesImperial_2004.txt`, and `RevitKeynotesMetric.txt`. You can edit any of these files in Notepad or Excel and follow the format already established within the file. Let's look at the format of this file so you can understand how to customize the keynotes.

The first few rows of the file (Figure 19.12) designate the grouping of the notes. In this example, they consist of a label (Division 03) followed by a tab and then a description (Concrete).

FIGURE 19.12

The keynote .txt file header

```
Division 03  Concrete
030000  Concrete    Division 03
033000.AA  C.I.P. CONCRETE (033000) 030000
```

Directly below this header is a secondary, or minor, grouping. This secondary grouping follows the same format as the primary group and provides better control over how the keynotes are displayed within Revit. This line follows the same format as the first: Label (033000), then a tab, then a description (Concrete), then another tab, then a reference to the parent code (Division 03). This last entry must match the label in the line above. This designates the second line as a subset to the first line. You can add as many or as few subgroups as you'd like. In our case, we have subcategories for each division, but that's not necessary.

Below the grouping are the contents of that group. These lines are articulated in the following format:

Label [tab] Description (note body) [tab] Grouping

In the example shown in Figure 19.12, this reads as follows (where the [tab] is an actual tab, not the text):

033000.AA [tab] C.I.P. CONCRETE (033000) [tab] 033000

To get an idea of how this will all look once loaded into Revit, Figure 19.13 shows you the Keynotes dialog box with Division 03 expanded.

FIGURE 19.13
The Keynotes dialog box

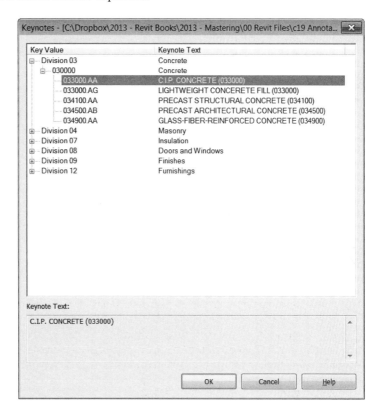

Using the keynote file approach lets you add, remove, or edit notes and groups of notes. This might seem frustrating to have to open and load a separate .txt file every time you want to add or remove notes from the keynote list. However, remember that this also maintains consistency and a level of control over the master list that isn't available with simple text objects. Although it might be slow at stages to get all the project notes into the .txt file, it also means that the time you'll spend checking and verifying the notes is dramatically reduced.

If you find that editing keynotes in an external .txt file that is segregated from the project environment does not suit your needs, tools are available online to help you manage keynotes using a graphical interface. Revolution Design has created a tool called Keynote Manager (`www.keynotemanager.revolutiondesign.biz`) that will manage your keynote list, create headings and subheadings, and format the .txt file in a way that Revit Architecture can read it. Tools like this are great for speeding up the editing process for keynotes and maintaining proper formatting of the .txt file.

Keynote Settings

Now that the keynote .txt file is established and you've begun populating it with annotations, you need to link it to your project. Loading this file into the project is simple and needs to happen only once. Additionally, loading this keynote file is a project setting, not a user setting. Once the file is linked, all team members will have access to the keynotes.

To access the keynote settings and load the keynote text file, choose the flyout at the bottom of the Tag panel on the Annotate tab (Figure 19.14) and select Keynoting Settings.

FIGURE 19.14
Accessing the
Keynoting Settings

This command will open the Keynoting Settings dialog box (Figure 19.15). Here, you can define the project's keynote file as well as adjust some other settings. To load the keynote file, click the Browse button and navigate to the .txt file you've created.

FIGURE 19.15
Keynoting Settings
dialog box

The following are some of the other variables you can set in the Keynoting Settings dialog box:

Path Type Path Type defines how Revit Architecture looks for your text file using one of three methods:

> **Absolute** The Absolute option follows the UNC naming conventions and navigates across your network or workstation for a specified location.
>
> **Relative** This option locates the text file relative to your RVT project file. If you move the RVT file and the text file and maintain the same folder structure, the keynote file will be found and automatically loaded.
>
> **At Library Locations** This option lets you put the text file in the default library location defined in the File Locations tab of the Options dialog box (Application ➤ Options).

Numbering Method Numbering Method defines how the keynotes are numbered:

> **By Keynote** This option allows you to number keynotes as they come from the associated text file.
>
> **By Sheet** With this option enabled, the keynotes are numbered sequentially on a per-sheet basis.

LOADING OR RELOADING KEYNOTES

Once the keynote .txt file is loaded into Revit Architecture, it is available for the team to use. As we've mentioned, changes can be made to this file on the fly while the project is open and active. Although this is true, if changes are made to the keynote file while the project is open, the keynote file will need to be reloaded into the project for the changes to be visible to other team members. There are two ways to do this:

◆ Open the Keynoting Settings dialog box and click the Reload button. Once this is done, you'll need to use Synchronize With Central (if the project is workshared) and your team members will also need to use SWC to gain access to the changes.

◆ Close and reopen your project file.

ADDING KEYNOTES

Download the project file JenkinsMusicBldg.rvt and the keynote file Standard_textnotes .txt from the folder for Chapter 19 on this book's companion website at www.sybex.com/go/masteringrevit2013. Make sure you place them in the same folder on your computer because the path setting for the keynote file is set to Relative in the RVT file. Open the RVT project file to begin the exercise.

To add keynotes to an element in a project model, choose one of the three keynote types from the Annotate tab; then in your view, select the object you want to annotate and insert a keynote. The sequence for inserting keynotes is arrowhead, leader segment, and then keynote. Similar to placing a tag, the keynote command (even the User keynote) requires an object to be selected to start the insertion sequence. If the object doesn't have a note already defined, you'll be prompted to pick a note from the Keynotes dialog box. Figure 19.16 shows a sample of this list.

FIGURE 19.16
Choosing a keynote
to insert

Let's explore this functionality with a quick exercise in which you will annotate a detail with keynotes. Follow these steps:

1. From the Project Browser, expand the Sections (Building Section) heading and activate the view named Window Sill Detail.

2. Go to the Annotate tab in the ribbon and select Keynote ➤ Element Keynote.

3. Select the window in the view and then place the leader and keynote. You will see that the keynote code has already been populated because the keynote has already been defined in the type properties for the window family.

4. Select the wall assembly and place another keynote. This time, the Keynotes dialog box will appear because no keynote was defined in the wall's type properties. Select the keynote labeled 042000.BE and then close the dialog box.

5. Go back to the Annotate tab in the ribbon and select Keynote ➤ Material Keynote.

6. Select the thin material at the right side of the wall below the window. Again, the Keynotes dialog box will appear because a keynote value was not defined in that material's identity data. Select the keynote labeled 092900.AA and then close the dialog box. The results will look like the image in Figure 19.17.

FIGURE 19.17
A section detail
with keynotes
applied

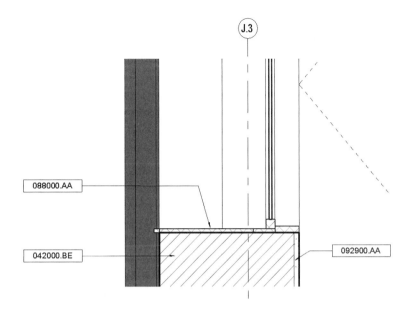

KEYNOTE LEGENDS

Depending on your choice of keynote and your workflow, you might want to create a legend on each sheet for your notes. You might want only the keynotes that are shown on a given sheet to appear in the legend. Or you might want to have one legend that will show all keynotes used throughout the project.

These legends usually reside on the side of a sheet near the title block information and can take one of two forms. The first type is all-inclusive and shows every note within the project. This style has the benefit of consistency between sheets in the set. The same note will always be in the same location in the list; however, this type of list can become quite long for larger projects. The other type of keynote list includes only the notes that show up on a particular sheet. This has the advantage of supplying a list of notes customized for each sheet without extraneous information. Creating either list manually has traditionally been challenging. One of the benefits of Revit Architecture is the ability to completely automate either list type, thus removing much of the chance for error in the process. Let's review how to create both types of lists.

Creating a keynote legend is simple: Choose the Legend button on the View tab and select Keynote Legend from the drop-down list (Figure 19.18). Once you launch the command, name the keynote legend, and then click OK.

FIGURE 19.18
The Keynote Legend
button

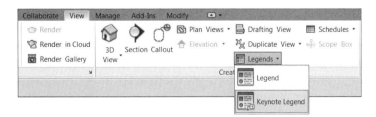

You'll be presented with what looks like a typical schedule dialog box, called Keynote Legend Properties. There are only two fields available in a keynote legend, and by default, they are both loaded into the Scheduled Fields side of the Fields tab (Figure 19.19). Those fields are as follows:

Key Value   This field contains the numeric value of the keynote.

Keynote Text   This field contains the text description for the keynote.

FIGURE 19.19
The Fields tab of the keynote legend

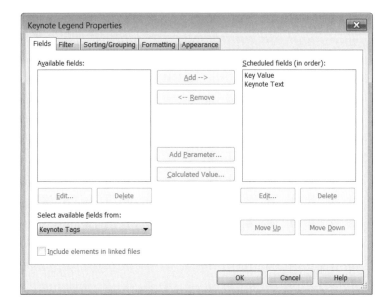

A keynote legend works like any other schedule as far as formatting and appearance go. By default, the sorting and grouping are already established because the key value is used to sort. The one special item of note is located on the Filter tab. At the bottom of this tab is a feature unique to this type of schedule: a Filter By Sheet check box (Figure 19.20). Selecting this box gives you the ability to filter the list specifically for each sheet set; leaving the box deselected will supply a full list of the keynotes over the entire project.

Like any other type of legend, a keynote legend can be placed on sheets again and again within the project. You're not limited to only one instance of the legend on a sheet as you are with other view types. Additionally, if you choose the keynote legend that filters by sheet, it will dynamically modify the note list based on individual sheet contents. As views are added or removed from a sheet or notes are added to the project, the keynote legend updates accordingly.

Keynote legends are considered to be another type of legend view and will appear under the Legends node of the Project Browser.

FIGURE 19.20

The Filter By Sheet option on the Filter tab in the Keynote Legend Properties dialog box

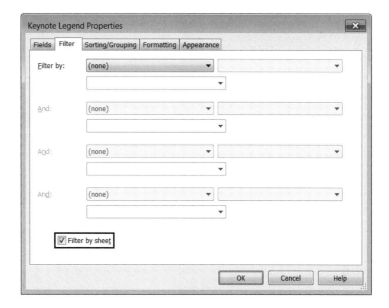

A Schedule for Keynotes

Creating a schedule for keynotes is a great way to find single-use notes and typos in a project. If you are working on a project team, there's always a chance that someone could be inserting an incorrect keynote into the project. Scheduling the notes is an efficient approach to managing the annotation process and gives you the tools to verify consistency. Scheduling keynotes allows you to do three things:

◆ List all the notes within a project and verify their spelling and accuracy.

◆ Find odd or one-off instances. Sometimes this can mean the note was accidentally placed in lieu of another note.

◆ Make sure all the keynotes in the project are represented in the specifications.

The Keynote Family

Revit Architecture comes with a default keynote family that allows you to produce both keynotes and text notes using the default keynote .txt file. The family name is `Keynote Tag.rfa`. This family has four types that let you change note styles within the project. You can see the four note styles in Figure 19.21.

Here are the four default styles:

◆ Keynote Number

◆ Keynote Number – Boxed – Large

◆ Keynote Number – Boxed – Small

◆ Keynote Text

Each of these notes pulls information from the text file we discussed earlier in this chapter and reports it at the end of the leader. To change your keynotes between any of these options, select the keynotes and select a different type in the Type Selector.

FIGURE 19.21
Keynote styles
available in the
default tag

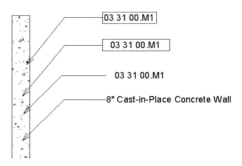

Annotating with Tags

Tags are text labels for elements such as doors, walls, windows, rooms, and several other objects that architects typically need to reference in a set of drawings. These tags typically refer to other schedules or information in other portions of the drawing set and are unique to the views in which they are inserted. In Revit Architecture, tags are intelligent, bidirectional graphics that report information stored in an object's properties. You can enter a value directly into the family properties or into the tag itself.

Once you've tagged an element and entered a value in the tag, the tagged model element will retain that value until you remove it. The value lives with the model elements in a project; it is not a property of the tag. That means you can delete or remove tags without fear of losing the data entered into the tag. It also means that once an element is tagged with information in one view, the same or similar elements will report the same information in any other view in which they are tagged without the necessity of entering the information twice. To explain this a bit better, take the example of a door tag.

You've placed a door tag in a view. The tag initially had ? as a value, meaning that the door number was blank. You've entered a door number of **3-1**. In another view, you can now tag the same door and have it automatically display a value of 3-1. You can also delete any, or even all, of the door tags for that door and have new tags you place also report the door number of 3-1.

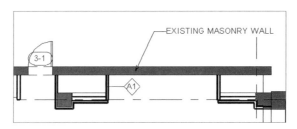

Keep in mind that you can also tag elements that are in linked models. While you cannot edit the properties of these elements (e.g., you cannot change the wall type or door number), you can add tags to any of the linked elements as if the same elements were part of your project file.

Tags are versatile elements for annotating your designs. A tag can display a door number, but it can just as easily display any other properties of the door, such as fire rating, cost, or material type.

Inserting Tags

Tags can be automatically inserted when a model element, such as a door or room, is placed within the project (by checking the Tag On Placement option in the Options bar), or they can be inserted later. The options to place a tag are all located on the Tag panel of the Annotate tab (Figure 19.22).

FIGURE 19.22
Tag tools in the
Annotate tab

When you're adding tags, it's not necessary to find or choose the right tag — Revit Architecture will do that for you. Tag types are specific to the elements to which they are being tagged. For example, you use a door tag to tag a door, but you can't use a door tag to tag a wall or other element within the project. Figure 19.23 shows you some of the tags that are available; there is a tag for each type of object. You can customize each of the tag family types so you can graphically differentiate your door tags from wall tags, room tags, area tags, and so on.

FIGURE 19.23
Listing of various
tag families

When inserting a tag, you'll have several placement options available in the Options Bar, as shown in Figure 19.24:

FIGURE 19.24
The Options bar
when placing a tag

Orientation   The first option allows you to orientate the tag horizontally or vertically. Tags, like text, will always read from either the bottom or right side of the sheet or view.

The Tags button   Clicking this button opens the Tags dialog box, where you can load various tags.

Leader   The final three options relate to the tag leader. You can select the Leader check box on (or off) to have a leader show (or not show). While attached leaders are the default for tags, the Leader drop-down can be changed from Attached End to Free End if you don't want to associate the end of the leader with the element you've selected. Using the Free End option allows the leader to float free of the object. The final option of this set for leaders is the default leader length. By default, the value is set to 1/2. When you're placing tags like wall tags that have leaders perpendicular to the wall they are tagging, it is a good idea to set a default length with which you are comfortable. You can adjust the tag location after inserting them, but sometimes it's easier to set a good default value in leader length.

Using the Tag Tools

CERT
OBJECTIVE

On the Annotate tab, you'll find there are several tools you can use to insert tags. Take a look back at Figure 19.22 to see these tools. Each has a different purpose and can be used in conjunction with other tools or separately to help document your project. Let's take a look at each one:

Tag By Category   The Tag By Category button is possibly one of the most frequently used Tag commands. As we mentioned before, several tags are available, allowing you to tag a host of elements in the model. Click the Tag By Category button when you want to tag one element at a time, regardless of its category.

Using this tag command will allow you to select a door, a window, a wall — whatever single element you want to apply a tag to in the model. As you hover over elements, the tag type that corresponds to that element will be shown. Should the element you are trying to tag not have the associated tag loaded in the project, you will be prompted to load it (Figure 19.25).

FIGURE 19.25
Loading a tag for
a specific element
type

Tag All   The Tag All command will do exactly that — tag all the untagged elements of a selected category within a given view. For example, you can tag all the doors. Or you can tag all doors, walls, and rooms — or any combination of any list of elements. When you select the Tag All command, the Tag All Not Tagged dialog box will appear (Figure 19.26). This dialog box displays a list of the elements in the view for which you have already loaded tags. Here, you can specify which elements can get tagged, what tag will be used, and if that tag will have a leader assigned to it. Use the Ctrl key on your keyboard to select more than one element from the list. When you've selected the categories you would like tagged, click OK.

FIGURE 19.26

Tag All Not Tagged dialog box

Tagging all the elements within a view can be a wondrous time-saver — but only if you're OK with the software choosing the location for each of the tags. For example, the tags will be placed in the middle of the rooms. For most spaces, that will work just fine. For other tag types, such as walls or doors, you might have to adjust tag locations to make sure everything reads properly.

Room Tag and Area Tag   These two tag types work in much the same way. They will tag the room elements or area elements, depending on the type of view in which you happen to be. In other words, room tags will work only in plans and elevations, whereas area tags can be placed only in area plans. To tag rooms or areas, simply select the tag type you want and select the room or area object. When you place rooms or areas initially, the tag option is selected by default.

Material Tag   The Material tag is used to annotate specific materials within a model element, similar to the material keynote. The main difference from the keynote is that the tag does not use an external .txt file to read additional information about the tagged element. The default material tag will display the Material Description value (Figure 19.27, left) as opposed to the Keynote value. You can always customize the material tag to display other values such as the Mark, as shown in Figure 19.27 (right).

FIGURE 19.27

Two options for tagging materials

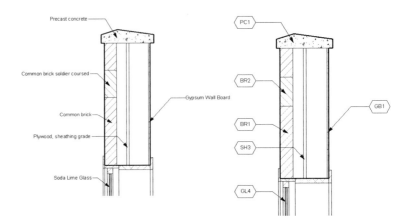

Multi-Category Tag   The Multi-Category tag allows you to use the same tag style in a project to tag elements of different categories. This tag type can be useful in a number of ways. Let's say you want to tag several elements in a floor plan and call out their manufacturer and unit cost. Historically, you would have to create a few different tag families to tag furniture, casework, lighting, and so on. Now a single tag type can do this for you. Let's step through making a Multi-Category tag.

From the book's web page, download the `JenkinsMusicBldg.rvt` file for Chapter 19 or continue with the file from the previous section. Then follow these steps:

1. Open one of the floor plans. In our example, we've chosen Level 3.

2. Click the Application menu and choose New ➤ Family. This will take you to the default family templates. Open the `Annotations` folder and choose `Multi-Category Tag.rft`.

3. In the Family Editor, go to the Create tab and select the Label tool. Click near the intersection of the reference planes in the view to place a label.

4. Once the label is placed in the view, the Edit Label dialog box opens (Figure 19.28). Here you'll see a list of the parameters that are common across multiple family types — Assembly Code, Cost, Family Name, and Model, among others. Select Manufacturer and Cost from the list and click the icon with the green arrow to add them to the Label Parameters list. Select the Break option in the Manufacturer row as shown in Figure 19.28. Click OK to close the dialog box.

5. Save the family as `MfrCost.rfa` and then click the Load Into Project button in the ribbon.

6. Back in the project file, select an element in the Level 3 floor plan. In our example, we've already chosen the dining room table, but you can choose another element, like a chair or another piece of furniture. When the tag is placed, you will see the familiar question mark, indicating that this element has no predefined value for either

Manufacturer or Cost. Place the tag and double-click the question mark. You may need to press the Esc key or click Modify in the ribbon first.

FIGURE 19.28
Adding parameters to a label

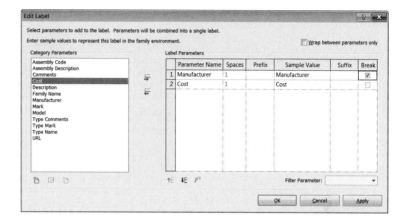

7. The Change Parameter Values dialog box (Figure 19.29) opens. This dialog box is used only when a tag has multiple parameters assigned to a single label. Otherwise, you would usually be able to type a value directly into a tag. Enter values for both Manufacturer and Cost, and then click OK.

FIGURE 19.29
Changing the parameter values

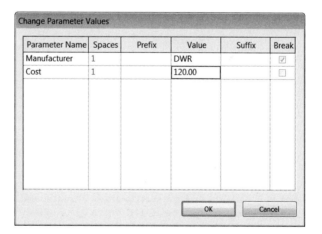

8. As you hover your mouse over other elements in this view, you'll notice the same behavior as with other tags. Elements that have predefined values will show the tag filled in while elements without values will have question marks. Add a few more tags, and you can begin to see some of the versatility of the Multi-Category tag.

Adding Dimensions

Dimensions are used to convey the distance or angle between elements or parts of elements. In Revit Architecture, a dimension is a bidirectional annotation, which means that you can edit the distance directly within the dimension string to move elements a specific distance apart and the dimension updates automatically as the distance between elements changes. Dimensions are annotations, making them view-specific elements that appear only in the view in which they're drawn. The Dimension tools are located on the Annotate tab.

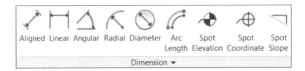

Like all annotations in Revit Architecture, dimensions will automatically adjust to the scale of the view. If you change the view scale, the dimensions automatically resize. By default, a linear string of dimensions only dimensions parallel entities. Nonparallel elements by their very nature have a dynamic dimensional relationship. Dimensions in Revit Architecture always read from the bottom or from the right, following standard architectural sheet layout conventions.

To place a dimension, choose any Dimension tool and begin selecting multiple entities. You can keep selecting multiple entities in any sequence, creating a dimension string across your view. Click anywhere in an open area of the view to finish selecting entities and place the dimension string.

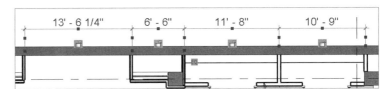

When any dimension tool is active, you will see two settings available in the Options bar that are specifically related to walls. The first drop-down allows you to specify the default method for dimensioning wall geometry. You can choose from wall centerlines, wall faces, center of core, or faces of core. This setting merely establishes the defaults — what will be selected when you first click on a wall with the dimension tool. If you need to select a different part of a wall, hover the mouse cursor over a wall segment and then press the Tab key to cycle through the available options. Each part of the wall segment geometry will highlight at the mouse pointer as you continue to repeatedly press the Tab key.

The second option allows you to pick either individual references (default) or entire walls. When the Entire Walls option is selected, click the Options button to modify the Auto Dimension settings, shown in Figure 19.30. In this example, we have chosen to dimension opening widths as well as intersecting walls. The dimension string shown was placed with a single click on the exterior wall!

FIGURE 19.30
Using the Auto
Dimension option

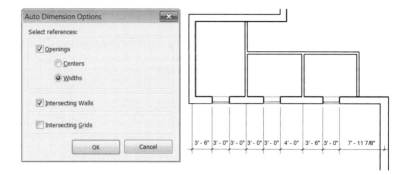

CERT OBJECTIVE

Once a dimension string is placed, you have several options to customize the string, the dimension values, and the witness lines. In Figure 19.31, you can see a typical aligned dimension string that has been selected after placement. Let's take a look at each of the available controls:

FIGURE 19.31
Controls for
dimensions

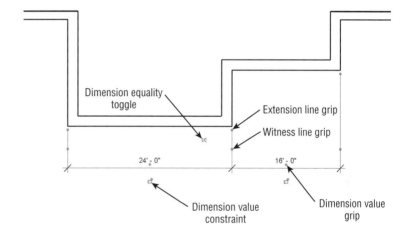

Dimension value grip To adjust the position of any of the dimension values, especially for shorter dimension strings where the value might overlap the witness lines, click and drag the dimension value grip to relocate the text. The leader settings associated with dimension values are found in the dimension type properties. If you need to reset the position of the dimension value, right-click on the dimension string and select Reset Dimension Text Position from the context menu.

Extension line grip The predefined distance that separates the dimensioned object from the beginning of the extension line is specified in the dimension type properties as Witness Line Gap To Element; however, you may need to manually adjust the extension line in some circumstances. Click and drag the extension line grip and you will also notice that the grip will snap into place near the predefined distance if you need to return the extension line to its original gap distance.

Witness line grip   The grip on each extension line that is closer to the dimension string is the witness line grip. This control allows you to move the witness line to a different entity. Click and drag this control to another object in the project and the dimension string will automatically update.

Dimension Value Constraint   The *lock* symbol allows you to preserve a dimension value so that it cannot be changed unless the constraint is removed. This functionality can be used to preserve dimension values for minimum widths of corridors, floor-to-floor heights, and other special features of your designs. As powerful as this feature is, you should use it only when absolutely necessary, because an overconstrained model can create problems you may have difficulty unraveling. Remember, *with great power comes great responsibility*.

Dimension equality toggle   Another powerful control included with dimensions is the ability to set all the values of a selected dimension string to be equal. And because the dimension is a bidirectional annotation, the model elements associated with the dimensions will be spaced equally as well.

USING DIMENSION EQUALITY

When you choose to use the dimension equality toggle, there are a few unique options to customize how the values are displayed. In the type properties of a dimension style, you can specify the default text displayed as well as a formula and how the witness lines are displayed (Figure 19.32).

FIGURE 19.32
Equality settings in the dimension style type properties

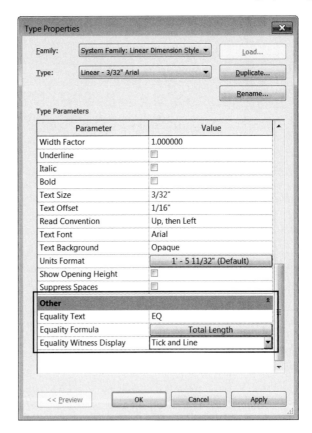

When you click the Equality Formula button, you can specify a customized string of values to best express the intention of the equality. In the example shown in Figure 19.33, the parameters Number Of Segments, Length Of Segment, and Total Length are selected with suffix symbols to display the complete result in the dimension string, as shown to the right in the figure.

FIGURE 19.33
Using a customized
equality formula

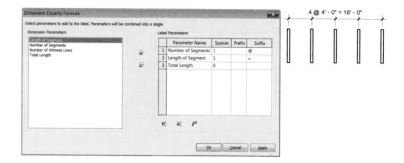

For any dimension string instance, you can choose from one of three options to display equality. From the Properties palette, the options are Value, Equality Text, and Equality Formula (Figure 19.34).

FIGURE 19.34
Changing the
EQ value on an
instance basis

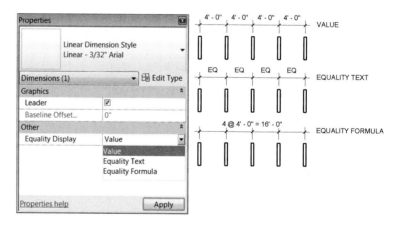

CUSTOMIZING DIMENSION TEXT

One of the main benefits of dimensions in Revit Architecture is that they cannot be overridden to display a different length or angle other than what is actually being measured. This may come as a shock if you have used Autodesk® AutoCAD® software in your past experience, but this restriction is necessary to maintain the integrity of the building information model.

Even though you cannot override the value of the dimension, you have the ability to either append some text to a dimension value or override the length or angle with a text string. To access these settings, select any dimension string and click one of the dimension values to open the Dimension Text dialog box. In the example shown in Figure 19.35, the text HOLD has been added to appear below the dimension string, indicating that the dimension is to be maintained during construction.

FIGURE 19.35

Custom text
appended to a
dimension value

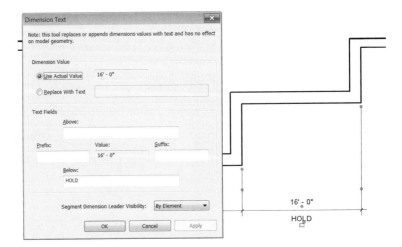

You'll notice the option Replace With Text at the top of the Dimension Text dialog box. While you might think you can override the dimension value with a string representing another length or angle value, a warning will prevent you from entering any numeric values.

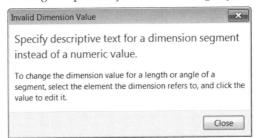

The Replace With Text option can be used to indicate various conditions for the purpose of construction tolerances. For example, you may have a series of similar conditions where new construction abuts existing conditions and you simply want the dimension to display VARIES, as shown in Figure 19.36.

FIGURE 19.36

Custom text replac-
ing a dimension
value

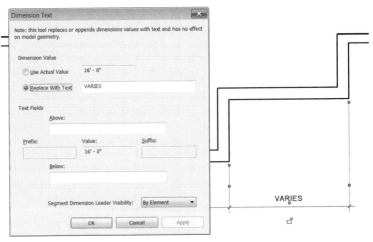

USING DIMENSIONS TO MODIFY GEOMETRY

We have trained hundreds of new Revit Architecture users through the years, and one of the most misunderstood concepts is how to use dimensions to modify model geometry. We just discussed the method for customizing dimension text, but users often will use this same method to make a change to model elements. This results in frustration when all you get is the Dimension Text dialog box.

To develop a clearer understanding of this concept, remember that a simple dimension string is a measurement between two objects. If you select the dimension, the software does not know which object you are intending to move. Instead, pick the model element first and then select an associated dimension to change its value, and the element will be moved.

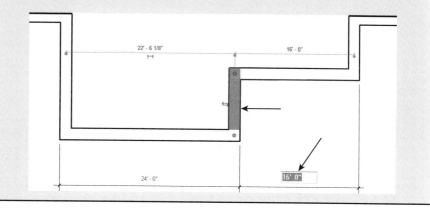

EDITING DIMENSION STRINGS

Edit
Witness Lines

As you continue to annotate your project with dimensions, you will likely need to edit dimension strings to combine, split, or add new witness lines. Most of these editing functions can be done with the Edit Witness Lines command. You will find this command in the contextual ribbon when you select a dimension string in a view.

Let's walk through each of these dimension-editing scenarios with some exercises. Download and open the file c19_Dimensions.rvt from this book's companion website at www.sybex.com/go/masteringrevit2013. Then follow these steps:

1. Activate the Level 1 floor plan and zoom in to the lower-left portion of the layout. You will see that some dimensions have already been placed and you will need to edit them (Figure 19.37).

2. Select the lower dimension string (indicated as A in the view) and then click on the Edit Witness Lines command in the contextual ribbon.

3. Click on the next vertical wall segment to the right of the layout and then the corner point. You may need to press the Tab key to place the dimension on the outer face of the wall and to snap to the angled corner.

FIGURE 19.37

Sample project with dimension strings

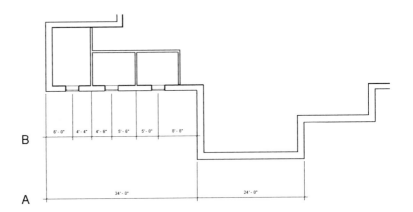

4. To complete this editing command, click in an open area of the view. Do not press the Esc key or you will lose the edits you just made. The results should look like Figure 19.38.

FIGURE 19.38

Adding witness lines to a dimension string

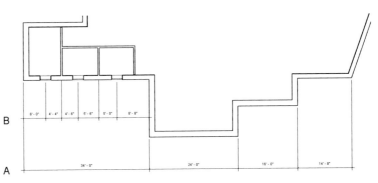

5. Now select the upper dimension string labeled as B in the view and once again activate the Edit Witness Lines command.

6. Click on each of the intersecting interior partitions to remove them from the dimension string. Click in an open area of the view to complete the command and the results should look like Figure 19.39.

A new feature that has been added to the software this year is the ability to delete any inner segment of a dimension string. In previous versions, to accomplish this type of modification, you would have had to remove several other witness lines beyond the segment you wanted to remove and then re-create them as a separate string. Now, you can hover your mouse pointer over one segment in a dimension string and press the Tab key once. An individual segment will highlight; select this segment and then press the Delete key. Try this with the outer dimension segment from the previous exercise (Figure 19.40).

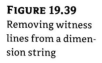

FIGURE 19.39
Removing witness lines from a dimension string

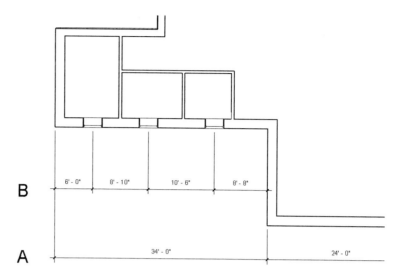

FIGURE 19.40
Delete an inner dimension string segment.

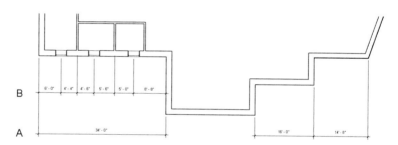

Annotating with Project and Shared Parameters

Every element in a project has a list of parameters that has been assigned to it by default. Some of these parameters, such as Assembly Code and Mark, are common parameters that are assigned to almost all object types. Others, such as Length, Height, and Volume, are unique to specific element types. Despite the plethora of default parameters, you may need to add custom parameters to elements. These custom parameters, like the default ones, can be tagged and scheduled.

Depending on how you'd like to use a custom parameter, you can add them to your elements in a few ways:

◆ If all you want to do is schedule the new parameter, you have a couple of options:

    ◆ Add the parameter directly within the schedule itself. This will add a new parameter to your element family. Adding a parameter using this method adds it only to the element family in the schedule. For example, say you want to schedule the sound transmission class (STC) of a wall. You could add this property directly within the wall schedule and the new parameter would be available only to objects in the Walls category.

♦ Add the parameter to the project. Using this method, you can still schedule the new parameter, but you will have the option to add it to multiple categories. So, if you want to add a parameter for Unit Cost, you can add that to both your door and window categories at the same time.

♦ If you want to be able to both schedule *and* tag your parameter, you will need to create a *shared parameter*. This parameter is created as part of a separate file that is shared between the tag family, the model family, and the project. An example of this kind of tag might be for door security hardware. You can create a parameter that is assigned to a door family as well as a door tag that will allow you to designate whether or not a door has a card reader to gain entrance to a room.

In the following sections, we will discuss how to create both of these parameter types as well as the pros and cons of each.

Creating Project Parameters

You can create custom project parameters at any time in the project cycle. Depending on how you create the parameters, you can assign them to one or more element categories within the model. You can also assign them to elements that have already been created or to element categories for elements that you have yet to create.

The following steps will allow you to make a custom parameter that will be schedulable but not taggable. For this example, pretend you are working on an existing building and reworking a space. Much of what is onsite will need to be demolished, but you would like to reuse all the elements that are salvageable. As you are documenting the existing conditions, you will want to schedule the elements you'd like to keep. To do this, you'll make a parameter called Reuse. Continue with the project file from the previous exercise (c19_Dimensions.rvt):

1. To add a new project parameter, go to the Manage tab in the ribbon and click the Project Parameters button. This will display the Project Parameters dialog box (Figure 19.41).

FIGURE 19.41
The Project Parameters dialog box

2. Click the Add button to open the Parameter Properties dialog box. Here you will be asked to define a list of properties for the new parameter. Let's step through what these selections will be (Figure 19.42 shows a view of the completed dialog box):

FIGURE 19.42
Setting the parameter properties

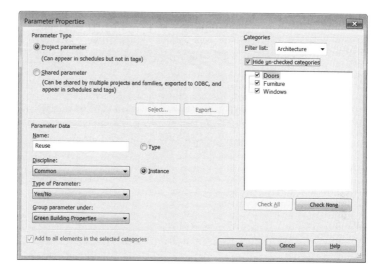

◆ Parameter Type = Project Parameter. Choosing between project and shared parameter is the first choice you'll need to make. We'll get to shared parameters later, so for now, leave it at the default of Project Parameter.

◆ Name = Reuse. This is used for describing the parameter as well as referencing it in schedules and the Properties palette.

◆ Discipline = Common. The Discipline drop-down menu will give you three choices: Common, Structural, and Electrical.

◆ Type Of Parameter = Yes/No. This setting dictates the format or behavior of the parameter. As you can see in Figure 19.43, there are a variety of parameter types. It's important to understand some of these options and, more specifically, their differences. If you start creating formulas with your parameters, you'll quickly understand how imperative it is to use the proper type. For instance, you cannot multiply Angle × Volume. Text cannot be added to a formula. Integers do not have decimal values. Many of these values are easy to understand if you apply a bit of logic.

FIGURE 19.43
Listing of available parameter types

◆ Type or Instance = Instance. This setting controls the uniqueness of the parameter itself. Both parameter types can be mixed within a given family. In this example, use an instance parameter because you want to designate whether something is reusable on an element-by-element basis. See Chapter 2, "Principles: UI and Project Organization," for more information on type and instance parameters.

◆ Group Parameter Under = Green Building Properties. This setting is an organization tool. When you open your element properties, depending on how many parameters you add, you can develop quite a long list. This tool allows you to group new parameters into any given category.

◆ Categories = Doors, Furniture, and Windows. This is where you define all the category types you'll associate with the new parameter. Category selections are flexible. If you decide you need to change categories after you create your parameter, you can easily come back to the Project Parameters tool and modify your selection.

3. Once you're finished, click OK. This will take you back to the Parameter Properties dialog box, where you can choose to add another parameter or, in our case, just click OK to exit completely.

Back in the model, you can now select a door (because it is one of the categories you chose) and see that you have added a Reuse parameter to it in the form of a check box (Figure 19.44).

FIGURE 19.44
The Reuse parameter in the family

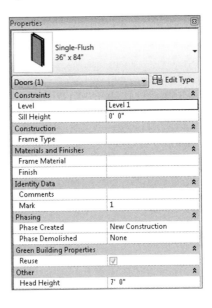

Now that you've created a custom parameter in the project, it's even easier to create one while in a schedule. You can create a custom parameter while creating a schedule or after the fact by modifying one. To create a parameter in a schedule, click the Add Parameter button in the Schedule Properties dialog box (Figure 19.45). Doing so opens the same dialog box that you see when you click the Project Parameter button, with the exception that the Categories selections will be grayed out because you can create parameters in schedules only for the element being scheduled.

FIGURE 19.45
Adding a parameter
while in a schedule

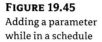

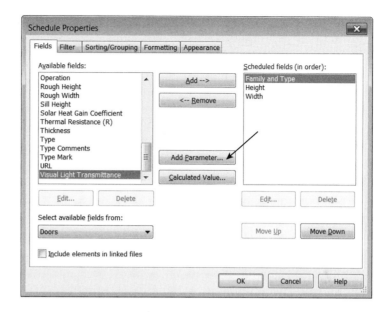

FIGURE 19.45
Adding a parameter
while in a schedule

Creating Shared Parameters

When you want to schedule *and* tag a custom parameter, you will need to use shared parameters. Earlier in this chapter, you learned that customized project parameters are useful for
scheduling the STC rating on a wall. You can also use them to, for example, schedule which
doors have security systems as part of the door hardware set, or to specify which equipment in
a lab will require special gases (oxygen, argon, and so forth). None of these parameters exist by
default in any families, but they are all values that you might want to tag or schedule, depending on the type of project you are working on.

These parameters do not exist in any of the tags either, so in order to tag these parameters,
you need to create them in both the tag and the element families.

Don't worry — it's not as complicated as it all sounds, but you will need to follow some steps
fairly closely. Once you have added a shared parameter to your project, you cannot modify it. If
you want to change it, you'll need to delete it and add the parameter again. So, it behooves you
to make your choices thoughtfully.

Let's look at the workflow behind creating a shared parameter. You'll do this by creating a
custom wall parameter called STC so you can tag the sound transmission class of the wall types.
To get started, navigate to the book's companion website and download the `JenkinsMusicBldg.
rvt` file in the folder for Chapter 19.

CREATING THE SHARED PARAMETER

The first thing you need to do is create a new, shared parameter file. This file translates the values of the shared parameter between the tag, family, and project. Follow these steps:

1. To create a shared parameter, go to the Manage tab in the ribbon and click the Shared
   Parameters tool. Doing so opens the Edit Shared Parameters dialog box (Figure 19.46).

FIGURE 19.46
Creating the shared
parameter

2. Click the Create button to open the Save As dialog box. Name your shared parameter file. For our example, we've named it STC; however, if you plan to make more than one shared parameter, you might want to name it something more universal. All of the shared parameters for a given project will ultimately live in the same file. Give the file a name and location that will make sense to the project team. Then click Save.

3. Now that you've saved the .txt file, you'll return to the Edit Shared Parameters window, where you'll assign this parameter to a group by selecting New under the Groups option (this keeps like elements grouped together). This group is a hierarchical collection. So, for the wall's STC, you will want to create a group called Wall Properties (Figure 19.47). This grouping allows you to easily sort different parameters within project categories. Once you name the group, click OK.

FIGURE 19.47
Creating a shared
parameter group

4. Once you have a group, you'll see that the Parameters buttons are now active. Click the New button and name the parameter **STC**. Leave the Discipline setting at Common. For Type Of Parameter, choose Integer. Since STC ratings are whole numbers, you can use the Integer type and eliminate any decimal places you'd have if you used Number as the type (Figure 19.48). Once you've entered the settings, click OK.

FIGURE 19.48
Naming the param-
eter and setting the
type

5. You should see the new STC parameter in the Edit Shared Parameters dialog box. Click OK to exit this dialog box.

You've now created a shared parameter. The next step is to assign it to a category.

ASSIGNING THE SHARED PARAMETER TO A CATEGORY

The shared parameter is now defined, but you don't have it associated with any categories yet. To do so, follow these steps:

1. From the Manage tab in the ribbon, click the Project Parameters button to open the Project Parameters dialog box. You want to add a new parameter, so click Add.

2. The Parameter Properties dialog box opens. This time, select the Shared Parameter radio button, and then click Select. In the Shared Parameters dialog box, select the STC parameter you just created, and then click OK. You'll see that many of the fields are now grayed out in the Parameter Properties dialog box. This is because you have already specified this information in the shared parameter. In the Categories list, select Walls (Figure 19.49).

FIGURE 19.49
Assigning the
shared parameter to
a category

3. Click OK to exit the dialog box. You'll see the new shared parameter (STC) below your previous project parameter (Reuse) in the Project Parameters dialog box (Figure 19.50).

FIGURE 19.50
The shared parameter is now part of the project.

4. Now that the STC parameter is part of the project, you can begin assigning values to it. Open the Level 3 floor plan and select one of the walls. By scrolling down in the Properties palette, you'll notice that the STC parameter is now at the bottom (Figure 19.51). Enter a value of **45** and click Apply or simply move your mouse out of the palette.

FIGURE 19.51
Giving the new parameter a value in the project

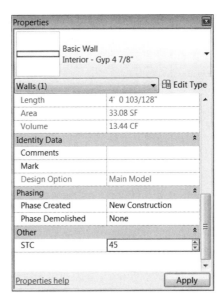

TAGGING THE SHARED PARAMETER

So far, you've created a shared parameter and added it to the Walls category in a project. These are all features you could have leveraged with a project parameter. The benefit of using a shared parameter is being able to tag it. The final step in this process is creating a tag to display the STC parameter in the wall.

1. The first thing you'll need is a new tag. Since you're tagging a wall, and there isn't a default wall tag type, you'll need to make a generic tag and apply it to a wall condition. From the Application menu, select New ➤ Family. In the New Family – Select Template File dialog box, open the Annotations folder, select `Generic Tag.rfa`, and click OK.

2. Next, you'll assign the correct category to the tag. By default, a generic tag is just that: generic. You want it to report information from the Walls category, so in the Properties panel in the Create tab, click the Family Category And Parameters button.

3. With the Family Category And Parameters dialog box open, choose Wall Tags from the list (Figure 19.52), and click OK.

FIGURE 19.52
Selecting the Wall Tags category

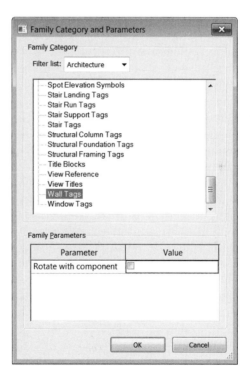

4. With the proper category selected, you need to add a label for your tag. From the Create tab in the ribbon, select the Label tool on the Text panel, and then click just above the intersection of the two reference planes in the view.

5. In the Edit Label dialog box, select Type Mark from the list of category parameters and add it to the Label Parameters list to the right (Figure 19.53). This will call out the wall type and help you associate the proper wall with the STC rating. Click OK to close the dialog box and zoom in closer to the label you just placed. Delete the red text note in the tag family template before continuing.

FIGURE 19.53
Adding the Type Mark parameter

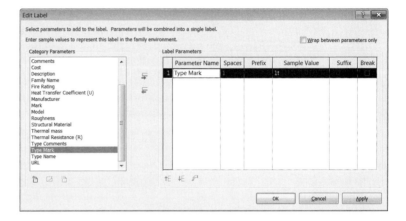

6. With the Type Mark parameter placed, let's add the STC parameter. Activate the Label tool again, and then click just below the intersection of reference planes in the view. In the Edit Label dialog box, click the Add Parameter button at the bottom of the Category Parameters list ⬚. This opens the Parameter Properties dialog box (Figure 19.54). Click Select to open the Edit Shared Parameters dialog box. Select STC and click OK, and then click OK again.

FIGURE 19.54
Choosing the shared parameter

7. You'll now see the STC parameter in the Category Parameters list. Select it and add it to the right side of the dialog box (Figure 19.55). Click OK to close the dialog box.

FIGURE 19.55
Adding the STC parameter to the label

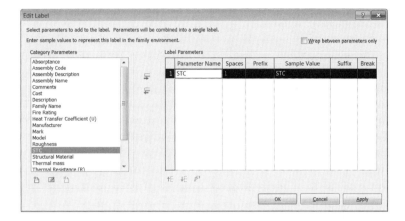

8. With all the labels added, you can brush up the tag with a bit of linework to help differentiate the tag from the rest of the drawing. For our example, we've created a simple, divided box, shown in Figure 19.56. Once this is done, save the family as Wall-STC.rfa and then load it into the project by clicking the Load Into Project button.

FIGURE 19.56
The customized wall tag

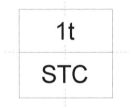

9. Back in the project, you're ready to tag the wall. Choose Tag By Category from the Annotate tab, and select the wall to which you have already given a value of 45 for the STC. You'll see the wall type and STC rating populate within the tag (Figure 19.57).

Once you've stepped through this workflow a few times, it will quickly become familiar and you'll be able to add custom parameters to projects and tag them without a second thought. One thing to keep in mind while you're doing all this, however, is that once you have added a shared parameter to your project, you will not be able to change any of the properties of the parameter itself. If you set the parameter type to Integer but you really wanted Number, you'll need to delete the parameter and start over. Also, when working with a team, remember that shared parameters work much like keynotes with their external .txt files. If you are sharing the project file with the idea that it will be edited by another team, be sure to include the shared parameter file.

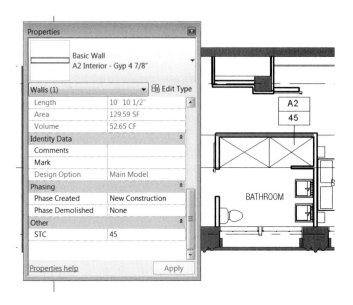

FIGURE 19.57
The shared parameter now shows up in the tag within the project.

The Bottom Line

Annotate with text and keynotes. Although a picture is worth a thousand words, you will still need notes to make drawings understandable and be able to call out key elements in each view. Understand how to create and modify text and keynotes for a complete set of documents.

Master It To properly utilize the keynoting feature, you'll need to understand what each of the three keynote types do and how they're used. List each and explain how they can be used in a project.

Use tags. Tags are text labels for elements such as doors, walls, windows, rooms, and several other objects that architects typically need to reference in a set of drawings. These tags typically refer back to other schedules or information in other portions of the drawing set and are unique to the view in which they are inserted.

Master It Inserting tags quickly can be a good way to make documentation time more efficient. How can you quickly tag a number of elements in the model at the same time?

Add dimensions. Dimensioning is a critical part of the project documentation, allowing you to communicate the distance elements are from one another.

Master It Adding dimensions is a necessary part in any project. However, in a project workflow you will typically want to change the location of a dimension's witness line without having to re-create the entire dimension. How do you move a witness line without remaking the entire dimension?

Set project and shared parameters. Revit Architecture lets users add as many custom parameters to an element as are needed to document the project. These parameters can be both tagged and scheduled, depending on how they are made.

Master It You need to add a custom parameter for your project to track the percentage of recycled content in materials. What's the best way to go about doing this?

Chapter 20

Presenting Your Design

Although Autodesk® Revit® Architecture software is most often used to create parametric content for documentation, it is often necessary to show designs to clients and other project stakeholders to get buy-in. Revit has tools that can be used to embellish views or create new graphics to help present the design.

In this chapter, you'll learn to:

◆ Add color fill legends

◆ Use 3D model views in your presentation

◆ Work with viewport types

Adding Color Fill Legends

There are many times in the design process when you will need to go beyond simple documentation and portray the spaces in a building in a different way. For example, you may need to communicate design intent, spatial adjacencies and allocations, or materiality. Since Revit knows what these things are in your model, you can use its parametric capabilities to do more than just documentation and show these other types of spatial parameters.

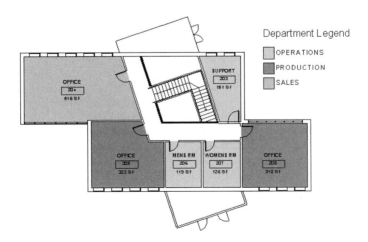

The Revit tool for creating these types of views is called the Color Fill Legend. You can use this tool to color areas and rooms in plans, sections, and elevations. It allows you to assign different colors to just about any of the room or area properties within the view. Here are just a few examples of the types of views you can create:

◆ Floor plans showing departments

◆ Floor plans showing spaces based on area value. An example might be rooms smaller than 500 square feet [50 sq m] as one color, rooms that are between 500 and 1,000 square feet [50 sq m to 100 sq m] as another color, and rooms bigger than 1,000 square feet [100 sq m] as a third color.

◆ Building sections showing different departments in different colors

◆ Plans, sections, or elevations portraying room finish types

There is an almost endless list of the types of color fills you can create to help communicate a wide variety of project-specific details. The Color Fill Legend tool is located on the Color Fill panel of the Annotate tab (Figure 20.1).

FIGURE 20.1
The Color Fill
Legend tool

To better demonstrate some of the uses of the Color Fill Legend tool, let's step through making a simple color fill plan showing room types.

Making a Color Fill Legend for Rooms

In many projects, it becomes necessary to display plans with some additional information about the spaces. Typically during the design phases, clients need to see how different departments are located adjacent to one another. Even in a simple residential design, it can be helpful to see how public spaces such as kitchens and living areas are located relative to the more private spaces of bedrooms and bathrooms.

In the sample building project used in Chapter 18, "Documenting Your Design," say you want to visually show the various space types in the floor plans. You want to graphically demonstrate which spaces have been assigned to various departments defined in the building's program of requirements. To get started, open the c20-Sample-Building.rvt model that's on the book's companion web page, www.sybex.com/go/masteringrevit2013. Then follow these steps:

1. Open the Level 1 – Color Fill floor plan in the c20-Sample-Building.rvt file and click the Legend button in the Color Fill panel of the Annotate tab. This will activate the Color Fill Legend tool and ask you to place a legend somewhere in the active view. Once the legend is placed, you can then define and customize its characteristics. Place the legend to the right of the plan.

2. After the legend is placed, you'll be presented with a dialog box similar to the one in Figure 20.2. This dialog box will prompt you to choose from a list of space types available in the current view and color schemes that have already been established within the model. From the Color Scheme drop-down, select Name and click OK.

FIGURE 20.2
Choose Space Type
and Color Scheme
after placing the
legend in a view.

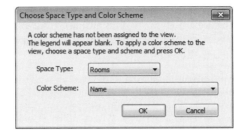

If you have already created a color scheme that you want to use in this view, it would be a simple matter of selecting it from this list and clicking OK, and the legend and view would be complete. The default project template contains a few simple color schemes from which you can choose when you place a legend. You started with a basic one that automatically assigns a color for each unique room name in the project; however, this type of presentation is not usually that useful.

In the subsequent steps of the exercise, you will create different color schemes to further explore more complex methods of presentation.

Edit
Scheme

3. After the legend is placed, you can then alter its properties or choose a different color scheme. Select the legend, and in the Modify | Color Fill Legends context menu, click the Edit Scheme button. This opens the aptly named Edit Color Scheme dialog box (Figure 20.3). This dialog box allows you add, rename, or delete color schemes on the left side and define the graphic properties and attributes of these schemes on the right.

FIGURE 20.3
The Edit Color
Scheme dialog box

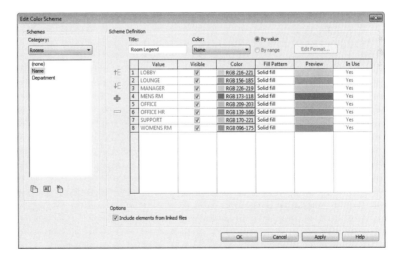

Notice a drop-down labeled Color at the top of the Scheme Definition area. This is the property by which the color scheme is being defined. It is currently assigned to color the plan according to room name. Each unique room name in the project is automatically generating its own color for the legend.

4. From the list of schemes at the left, choose Department. Notice that the Color drop-down now indicates the Department parameter, but there are no values defined in the list to the right. This is because text has not been added to the Department parameter for any of the rooms in the project.

For any parameter available to be used in a color fill legend, you can either enter the value in the Properties palette or predefine values in the color scheme. In the following steps, you will predefine values for the departments and then assign them to the rooms later.

5. At the left side of the table under Scheme Definition, click the green plus sign to add values to the color scheme for Department. Create four new values as follows:

- ◆ MANAGEMENT
- ◆ OPERATIONS
- ◆ PRODUCTION
- ◆ SALES

For now, you can use the automatic color and pattern assignments as is.

6. Click OK to close the dialog box. You will notice in the floor plan that the legend now shows the title "Department Legend" and it displays No Colors Defined. Even though you defined some department values, they will not show on the legend until you assign values to the rooms placed in the project.

7. Select one of the rooms at the left of the plan and look in the Properties palette. Find the Department property and click in the value field to access a drop-down list (Figure 20.4). Notice that the values available in the list are the values you added to the color scheme in step 5.

FIGURE 20.4
Assign values to room properties based on data assigned to a color scheme.

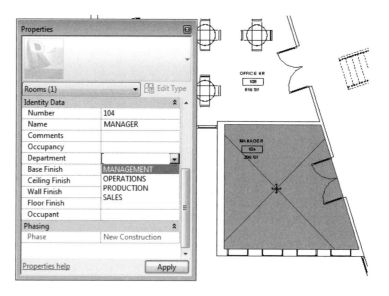

Assign the two rooms at the left side of the plan to the MANAGEMENT department, assign the LOUNGE space to the SALES department, and assign the SUPPORT space to the OPERATIONS department. Notice that as you make these assignments, the color fill legend will update and the space will fill with the matching color.

ASSIGNING COLOR FILLS WITHOUT A LEGEND

In the previous exercise, you generated color fills on a plan by adding a legend and then customizing the color scheme through the legend. You don't have to place a legend in order to color a plan with a color scheme. In the Properties palette for a view, you can find the Color Scheme property. Click the button in the value row to open the Edit Color Scheme dialog box and choose a color scheme to be assigned to the view. The plan will display the respective colors even without a legend shown on the view. You can always add a legend later by using the Legend tool in the Color Fill panel of the Annotate tab in the ribbon.

Customizing a Color Fill Legend

Although the software automatically assigns colors to each value in a color scheme definition, you'll likely want to change the colors or even the fill patterns to suit your presentation needs. In this section you will customize the color scheme and the legend created in the previous exercises. Because many firms typically have standards for presentation color schemes, it's a good idea to add your customized schemes to your office template.

In the following exercise you will create a copy of the department-based color scheme to use black line patterns instead of color fills. Download and open the file c20-Sample-Building-Part2.rvt from the book's companion web page. Then follow these steps:

1. Return to the Level 1 – Color Fill floor plan you used for the exercise in the previous section. Select the legend and click Edit Scheme in the ribbon to open the Edit Color Scheme dialog box.

Edit
Scheme

2. Select Department from the list on the left side and click the Duplicate icon at the bottom of the list. Name the duplicate scheme **Department (Black)**.

3. You can change any of the assigned colors by selecting any of the buttons in the Color column. Doing so opens a dialog box like the one in Figure 20.5 and allows you to select colors based on RGB values or PANTONE colors. Change the colors for each of the departments to black (R:0, G:0, B:0) and then click OK.

   Once you have defined the colors, take note of a couple of other features in the Edit Color Scheme dialog box. The first is the Options area under the Scheme Definition field. There is a single check box that allows you to pull values from linked projects. If you are working on a large building that is split into multiple files, this is a good way to tie all that information together into a single graphic presentation.

4. The other option you have is the ability to exclude various scheme definition values for a color scheme. Notice the Visible column next to the Value column in the scheme definition, as shown in Figure 20.6. Uncheck the box in the Visible column next to the value for OPERATIONS.

FIGURE 20.5
Click the button in
the Color column
to select a different
color.

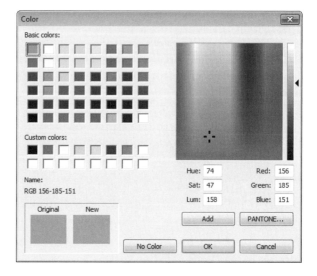

FIGURE 20.6
Use the Visible
option to exclude
values from the
legend.

Note that this setting will exclude the selected value wherever this color scheme is applied to a view. In this example, we might assume that the client does not need to see spaces that belong to the Operations department in color — just the remaining departmental spaces.

5. Next, click in each of the fields under the Pattern column to change the fill pattern to a variety of line-based patterns, as shown in Figure 20.7.

FIGURE 20.7
The pattern for
each value can be
customized.

Color	Fill Pattern	Preview
Black	Crosshatch	
Black	Diagonal crosshatch	
Black	Diagonal down-small	
Black	Diagonal up-small	

6. After clicking OK, you'll notice that the color fills have dynamically changed to reflect the modifications you made in your color scheme properties, as shown in Figure 20.8.

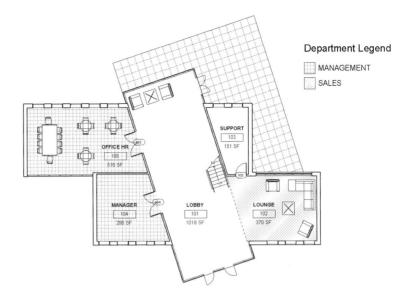

7. Open the Level 2 – Color Fill floor plan and place a color fill legend to the right side of the plan. Choose the Department (Black) color scheme and click OK.

   Notice that the pattern fills are automatically placed according to the department assignments. Also notice that spaces assigned to the Operations department are not colored, nor does the department name appear in the legend because the Visible setting was turned off in step 4.

You have created a color fill legend and placed it within a view, and you've seen a number of the settings and properties of the legend. Those settings reflect how the color fill legend will look and react to the plan or view in which it's placed, but there are other settings you can modify as well. The legend key itself has several properties that control fonts and swatch sizes. Select the legend and click the Edit Type button in the Properties palette to explore some of the other properties you can modify.

Figure 20.9 shows the type properties for a color fill legend. Notice that in this dialog box, you can change the font size and type as well as the size of the color swatches that appear in the legend.

An important type property for color fill legends is Values Displayed. The two options for this property are By View and All, and the default setting for color fill legends is By View. You might have noticed that none of the spaces on Level 1 are assigned to the Production department, and so that value does not appear in the legend placed on Level 1.

Try creating a duplicate color legend type named All Values and change the Values Displayed property to All. Notice that this legend type shows all department names, regardless of the department assignments on each level. This setting does not override the Visible options you specify in the color scheme settings; therefore, the Operations department will still not display when you use the Department (Black) color scheme.

FIGURE 20.9
Edit the visual and functional characteristics of a color fill legend in the Type Properties dialog box.

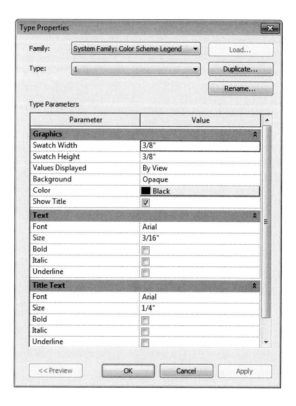

In summary, you can combine any color scheme with any color legend type — the two are not dependent on each other.

DON'T FORGET YOUR STANDARDS

It can take several tries between creating color fill plans, printing them to get the colors just right, and making adjustments. When you have one that works for you, take the time to do a couple of extra steps so you don't have to re-create this work in the future.

First, if it is a type of project that you'll be doing again and again, add the legend to your project template. This is as easy as placing the legend on a view and the view on a sheet (similar to a schedule) and copying it to the Clipboard. Open your project template and paste it onto a sheet, and your settings, colors, and naming conventions will be quickly transferred and saved for future use.

Using Numerical Ranges for Color Schemes

In the previous exercises, you explored how to utilize color schemes to create presentation material based on specific object properties. You can also create color schemes that display ranges of numerical values. In the following exercise, you will continue with the file c20-Sample-Building-Part2.rvt. With the Room color fill legend defined, you have seen an example of how to create color fill legends. A variety of other legend types are available, and some of these types allow you to define your own parameters when creating the legend itself. Let's step through this process again using a different legend type so you can see how you can define your own parameters in a color fill legend.

The next color scheme you will create is based on areas. Whereas the Department color scheme was defined by rooms that were already placed on plans, the area scheme is defined by numerical ranges you will need to define within the color scheme properties. Follow these steps:

1. Duplicate the Level 1 floor plan and name it **Level 1 – Area Range**. Place a color fill legend on the plan to the right of the building. You can choose any color scheme for now. Select the legend and click Edit Scheme in the contextual tab of the ribbon.

2. Create a copy of the Name color scheme, using the Duplicate icon at the bottom of the list. Name the new scheme **Area Range**.

3. From the Color drop-down list, choose Area (Figure 20.10). Click OK to the warning about preserving colors. You'll notice that all the room names and colors will disappear; they are replaced with values representing each unique room area.

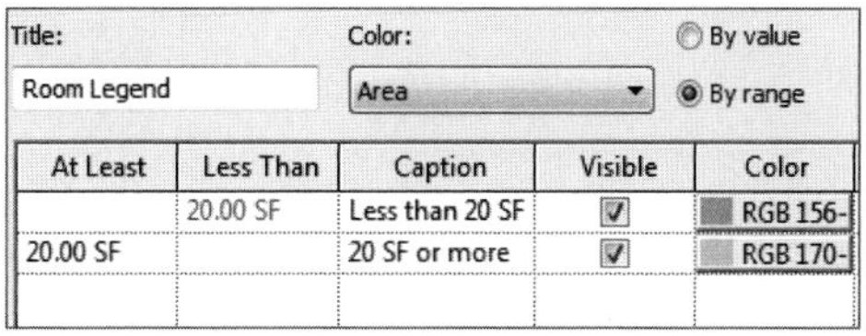

FIGURE 20.10
Select By Range to change the scheme definition.

Title:		Color:		○ By value	
Room Legend		Area	▼	● By range	

At Least	Less Than	Caption	Visible	Color
	20.00 SF	Less than 20 SF	☑	RGB 156-
20.00 SF		20 SF or more	☑	RGB 170-

This type of schedule — like a schedule of room names — is probably not that useful as a presentation method. Instead, let's create a series of colored area ranges to easily identify which spaces are within each range.

4. Next to the Color drop-down in the Scheme Definition field, select the By Range option. The static area values in the list below are now split into two columns labeled At Least and Less Than (Figure 20.10).

5. Click the green plus button two times so that you have four rows in the list of value ranges.

6. Starting from the bottom row, change the values to **800**, **500**, and **200**, as shown in Figure 20.11.

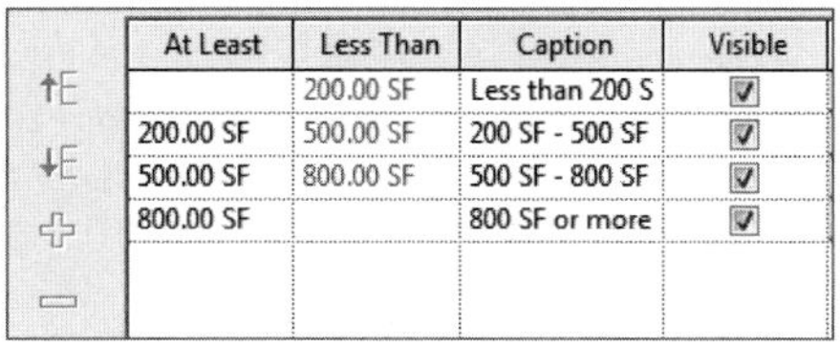

FIGURE 20.11
Modifying the values in the Scheme Definition field

At Least	Less Than	Caption	Visible
	200.00 SF	Less than 200 S	☑
200.00 SF	500.00 SF	200 SF - 500 SF	☑
500.00 SF	800.00 SF	500 SF - 800 SF	☑
800.00 SF		800 SF or more	☑

You can also try changing some of the colors assigned to each of the value ranges to make the presentation more meaningful or simply easier to read.

7. Click OK to update the color fill scheme and view the results in the plan (Figure 20.12). You'll notice that the rooms have colors defined based on their sizes rather than their names.

FIGURE 20.12
The finished floor
plan with color fills
by area range

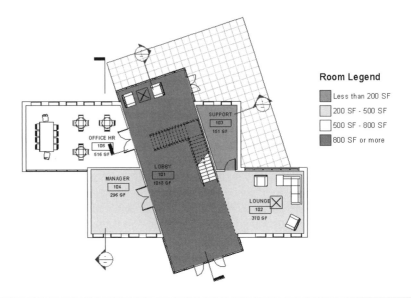

PROGRAM VERIFICATION WITH COLOR FILLS

Another, more advanced presentation technique can be achieved with color fills, and that is using value ranges for verification of your project's program of requirements. We showed you how to create a color fill scheme to illustrate ranges of spatial area; however, the results can be made even more useful for effective decision making.

The Area property of rooms will always display the actual value of the enclosed space. To compare the actual or designed area with the required area, a user-defined parameter must be created and populated. There are other applications that can accomplish this integration with Revit, including Trelligence Affinity (www.trelligence.com) and dRofus (www.drofus.no); however, the ability of an external application to feed the required program areas into the Revit model is irrelevant. The key is to compare the required area with the designed area and feed the difference into another user-defined room parameter. This can be accomplished using the Revit application programming interface.

Once the difference in area is captured in a room parameter, a color scheme can be established to color the ranges in the difference. For example, if the designed area is divided by the required area, you will get a percentage that can be included in a color scheme range. Color the higher percentages (positive and negative) with a noticeably visible color and the lower percentages with a more subtle color. If the range of acceptable differences is between 95 percent and 105 percent of the required area, then that range can be assigned no color and no pattern, as shown here.

Title: Department Legend | Color: Area Delta Percent | By value / By range | Edit Format... 12%

At Least	Less Than	Caption	Visible	Color	Fill Pattern	Preview	In Use
	75.0000%	Less than 75	☑	RGB 255-	Solid fill		No
75.0000%	95.0000%	75% - 95%	☑	RGB 255-	Solid fill		No
95.0000%	105.0000%	95% - 105%	☑		(none)		No
105.0000%	125.0000%	105% - 125	☑	Yellow	Solid fill		No
125.0000%		125% or mo	☑	Red	Solid fill		No

Presenting with 3D Views

In addition to using 2D views such as plans, sections, and elevations to convey your design intent, you can present the 3D model in a variety of ways. In Chapter 12, "Visualization," we discussed the methods for creating analytic and photorealistic visualizations; the following sections will help you to establish a new repertoire of presentation techniques for design and construction documents.

Orienting to Other Views

A quick and easy way to create more useful 3D views is by utilizing the Orient To View command. This command, which is somewhat hidden within the ViewCube®, allows you to create a 3D view that mimics the settings of a 2D view.

In the following exercise, you will continue to use the c20-Sample-Building.rvt file. You will first adjust the view range settings for the floor plans and then create a 3D view for each level. Finally, you will assemble the views on a sheet to complete the presentation.

1. Select Level 1 from the Project Browser and go to the Properties palette to examine the view properties. Click the Edit button in the View Range property.

2. In the View Range dialog box (Figure 20.13), change the Top value under Primary Range to **Level Above** and set the corresponding offset value to –1'-8" [–500 mm]. Repeat this step for Level 2.

FIGURE 20.13
Adjust the Top values for the plan's view range.

Note that although you are changing the top of the view range of the floor plans, you will not see any difference in their graphic display.

3. Right-click on the Default 3D view in the Project Browser and create two duplicates. Rename the duplicate views **Box-Level 1** and **Box-Level 2**.

4. Activate the view Box-Level 1 and right-click on the ViewCube. Select Orient To View ➢ Floor Plans ➢ Floor Plan: Level 1, as shown in Figure 20.14.

The view will be set to a plan orientation, but more important, a section box has been enabled that matches the extents of the Level 1 plan view. Try orbiting the view to see the results (Figure 20.15).

FIGURE 20.14
Orient a 3D view to
any other 2D view.

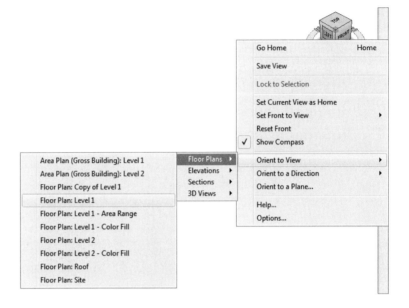

FIGURE 20.15
A 3D view after
being oriented to a
plan view

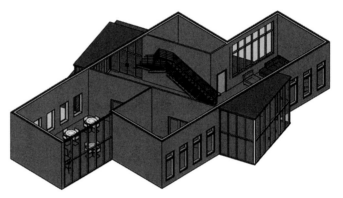

5. Right-click on the ViewCube and select Orient To A Direction ➤ Southwest Isometric.

6. Repeat steps 4 and 5 for Level 2.

7. Create a new sheet using the C size title block and drag the Box-Level 1 and Box-Level 2 views onto the sheet.

   Place the Box-Level 2 view directly above the Box-Level 1 view and you'll notice that the views will align vertically. You can align model views of various types on sheets as long as they are the same scale. This does not work for drafting views or perspective views.

We showed you how to create 3D representations of each level within your design using the Orient To View command. There is also a free Revit plug-in to automate this process; it was developed specifically for construction coordination by DPR Construction. The plug-in can be downloaded from http://modelslicer.dpr.com.

Annotating 3D Views

Be sure to lock a 3D orthographic view before adding text and tags as you would in a 2D view. This functionality is quite simple to implement. In the example shown in Figure 20.16, a section box was first applied to a 3D view.

FIGURE 20.16
Annotation can be applied to a 3D view with locked orientation.

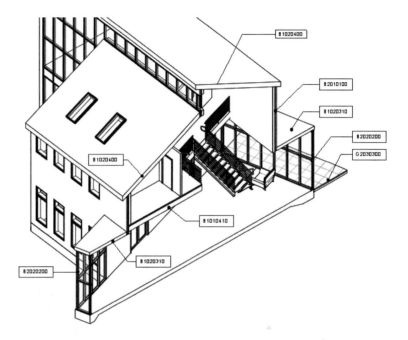

In any orthographic 3D view, you will find the Lock/Unlock 3D View button in the view shortcut bar as shown in Figure 20.17. Once you lock the view, you can begin to add tags, text, and dimensions in some circumstances, but you cannot change the orientation of the view unless it is unlocked.

FIGURE 20.17
The 3D view can be locked from the view control bar.

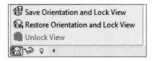

Once you have added annotation to a view, you may need to rotate the view. Return to the locked view tool and click Unlock View. You are now free to orbit the 3D view; however, the annotation you placed temporarily disappears. There are two ways to reset the orientation. If you wish to return the view to the originally saved orientation, click Restore Orientation And Lock View. The annotation will reappear.

If you decide to keep the new orientation, you can click Save Orientation And Lock View, but you will receive a warning about losing all of the previously stored annotations (Figure 20.18). If you click OK, you will need to replace all the annotations in the newly locked view.

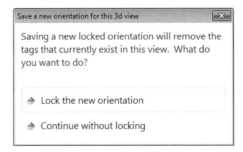

Editing Viewport Types

In the previous exercises, you might have noticed that the 3D views placed on the sheet displayed the default view title; however, we don't need the titles in this example. Options and properties related to the display of views on sheets are stored as *viewport* types. Although the name conjures up memories of Model Space and Paper Space in Autodesk® AutoCAD® software, it is actually quite different. The viewport does not determine the scale or anything else about the view itself; rather, it simply sets the parameters for how a view sits on a sheet.

Let's examine how to customize viewport types by completing an exercise that continues from the previous example of placing 3D views on a sheet:

1. Using the sheet with the two stacked 3D plan views, select one of the views and click Edit Type in the Properties palette. The Type Properties dialog box appears (Figure 20.19).

FIGURE 20.19
The type properties
of a viewport

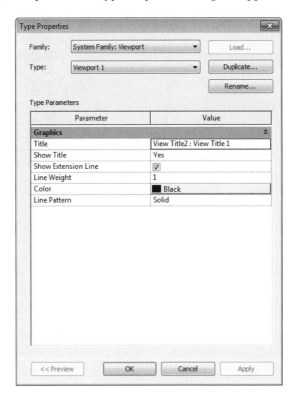

You'll notice that there are only a few properties in a viewport type, most of which are related to the extension line in the title.

2. Click the Duplicate button to create a new viewport type named **No Title**.

First, notice that you can change the View Title family selection in the first drop-down. However, in this exercise you will not need a view title.

3. Click the Show Title drop-down and select No.

An important option for the Show Title setting is When Multiple Viewports, which will display the titles only when multiple views are placed on a sheet. The view title is not displayed if only one view is placed on a sheet, as in an overall floor plan.

4. Click OK to close the Type Properties dialog box and you'll see that the viewport you had selected is already changed to the new type. Select the other viewport and switch it to No Title in the Type Selector.

When you have completed the exercise, you can also add some detail lines to the sheet to further embellish the descriptive presentation, as shown in Figure 20.20. Although you cannot snap to the geometry within the viewports, you can use the arrow keys to nudge the lines into alignment as required.

FIGURE 20.20
Customized view-
ports placed on a
sheet

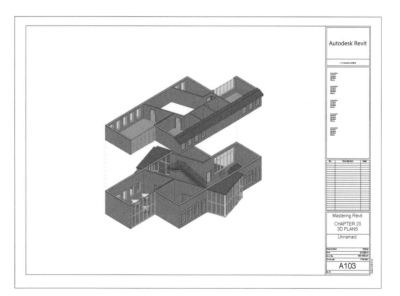

The Bottom Line

Add color fill legends. Color fills are a great way to illustrate data that otherwise might appear only in a schedule, such as department assignment, designed areas, and room finishes.

Master It There are a variety of ways to graphically display information using color fills. It can initially take a bit of time to get things organized, but once you create them, the legends can easily be transferred between views and projects. Describe how to add a color fill legend, once created, to your project template.

Use 3D model views in your presentation. Revit provides a variety of ways to help you visualize your designs — both while designing and during presentation. Understanding where these features are located and how and when to use them can help expedite the presentation process, depending on the look and feel you want to create with your images.

Master It Describe the process for creating an exploded 3D view of each level within your project.

Work with viewport types. Viewport types are simple to manage, but they are powerful when applied to the views you place on sheets. You can customize the view titles for any use case, from design presentations to construction documents.

Master It Describe the process for adding a new viewport type to your project.

Part 6

Construction and Beyond

In the previous chapters, we focused on the architect's role in design and construction using Autodesk® Revit® Architecture software. As the software continues to expand beyond being a tool for documentation, we want to touch on several other uses beyond the traditional scope of the designer. In the chapters in Part 6, we discuss how Revit can be used to augment design and documentation after construction documents are complete.

For this part of the book, we worked with leading industry experts in these individual fields. Thanks to all the contributors for their excellent looks into BIM.

Chapter 21

The Construction Phase

In this chapter, we will explore the use of Autodesk® Revit® Architecture software in the construction phase by design teams and builders. For design teams, the use of Revit Architecture usually entails markups, sketches, and revision management; however, a builder may approach BIM tools in unique ways. Many different BIM programs are available for builders to use in preconstruction and construction phase tasks, so we will not pretend that Revit Architecture is used by the majority of them.

In this chapter, you'll learn to:

- Add revisions to your project
- Use digital markups
- Model for construction

Adding Revisions to Your Project

Revisions allow designers and builders to track changes made to a set of construction documents during the construction phase of a project. Because the construction documents usually consist of numerous sheets, this methodology allows everyone on the team to track and identify which changes were made and when they were made during construction. The purpose is not only to ensure correct construction but also to create *as-built* documentation recording how the building was actually created to be delivered to building owners upon occupancy.

In a typical drawing set, revisions will look like Figure 21.1 when they are created and issued as part of the drawing set. Revision clouds themselves are created within views that are placed on the sheets. The revision tag is also placed within the view, but once the view is then placed on a sheet, the revision will appear in the sheet properties and on any revision schedule on the sheet itself.

To create a revision cloud in your project, select the Annotate tab and choose Revision Cloud from the Detail panel. This places you in a revisions cloud drawing mode, similar to Sketch mode, and allows you to bubble the revised detail or drawing. When you're finished, click the green check mark to complete the sketch and your annotation is done.

FIGURE 21.1
A typical revision

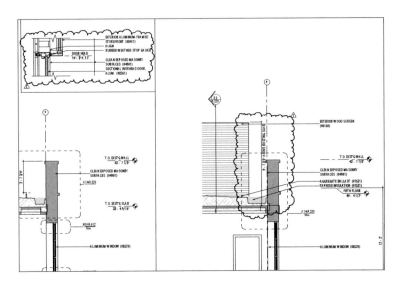

Typically in a project process, you'll have several rounds of revisions to a document set. Revit Architecture provides controls for this and gives you the ability to name and date the various revisions in your project to better track them. The Sheet Issues/Revisions tool is located in two places in Revit. You can find it on either the View tab as the Revisions button or on the Manage tab under Additional Settings (Figure 21.2).

FIGURE 21.2
Opening the Sheet Issues/Revisions dialog box

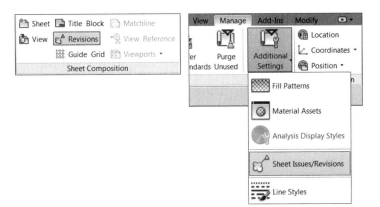

Either of these tools will open the Sheet Issues/Revisions dialog box (Figure 21.3). Here you can add, merge, issue, and define the visibility of revisions.

FIGURE 21.3
The Sheet Issues/
Revisions dialog
box

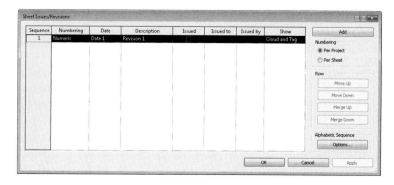

FIGURE 21.3
The Sheet Issues/
Revisions dialog
box

Let's review the major components of this dialog box beginning with the Revisions table:

Revision table   The Sheet Issues/Revisions dialog box starts with one default revision already in place, even though you may not have made a revision yet. This is only to give you a place to start—no revision will appear in your title blocks until you add revision clouds to your views. Each revision has a fixed number of parameters that you can enter. As you can see in Figure 21.3, the parameters include Numbering, Date, Description, and an Issued check box in addition to Issued To and Issued By columns and options for showing clouds and tags.

Numbering (table column)   The Numbering option allows you to number each revision numerically, alphabetically, or not at all. If you choose an alphabetic sequence, the sequence is defined in the Alphabetic Sequence options. Click the Options button in the lower-right portion of the dialog box to set your sequence and remove letters you don't want to use. For instance, some firms don't use the letters *I* and *O* because they are often confused with the numbers *1* and *0*. Figure 21.4 shows a sample of the dialog box. By default, an entire alphabet appears here. The None option allows you to add project milestones — unnumbered entries that appear in revision tables—to sheets without having to add revision clouds.

FIGURE 21.4
Sequence options
allow you to use any
order of letters or
numbers.

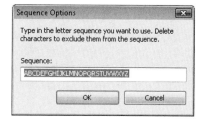

Issued   To issue a revision, click the check box in the Issued column. Doing so locks the revision clouds placed on sheets or in views associated with that revision, preventing them from being moved, deleted, or otherwise edited. The parameter values in the dialog box become inactive. This is to guarantee that the clouds and data do not change downstream once you issue a set of drawings.

REVISIONS IN A LIVE MODEL

During the construction process, the project model may still be changing. When you issue a revision, keep this in mind: While the clouds can become fixed in the project, the model will not be static. As you continue to make revisions to the model, it will always be up-to-date. So if you need to maintain an archive of all project phases or each revision, be sure to export the sheets either as DWF or PDF files as a snapshot of the sheets at time of issuance.

Show   This table column controls the visibility of revision clouds and revision tags that have been issued. As issues occur, you may want to hide just the clouds or just the tags from previous revisions. For example, if you've issued one revision and then add revisions to a later issue and want to clean up your drawing, you can choose to show the issued revision as the tag only—typically a small triangle with the revision number inside it—or not show anything at all by using the None option.

The Add button   This function is used to create a new revision. The new revision will automatically be placed in sequential order and only the sequence number will be automatically updated. You'll need to add your own description and date.

Numbering   You can choose to number revisions by sheet or by project. This is a global setting for the whole project, but one can be swapped for the other at any point. Which method you choose mainly depends on how your firm chooses to track revisions. The By Sheet setting allows you to have as many revisions as you want within the drawing set, but on each sheet, the list of revisions will remain sequential. For example, an issue named "Issued for Design Development" may be revision number 4 on one sheet and number 7 on another. Using the By Project setting will order your revision clouds based on the sequence established in the Sheet Issues/Revisions dialog box. In other words, all revisions with the same issue date would have the same revision number regardless of how many revisions appear on any given sheet. This approach might give you a greater degree of consistency throughout your document set but may limit you to the number of overall revisions you can use in the project. Either numbering method can be configured in advance and added to your project template.

Placing Revision Clouds

To place a revision, open a view in which changes to the project have occurred and use the Revision Cloud tool found in the Detail panel on the Annotate tab. Start drawing bubbles in a clockwise direction around the area you are calling out as a revision. Lines are automatically created that make a *cloud* (or series of arcs), as shown in Figure 21.5. When you're finished creating the cloud, click the Finish Sketch button at the right side of the ribbon.

By default, each new revision cloud will be assigned to the last revision in the Sheet Issues/Revisions dialog box. If you need to change the revision to which a cloud is assigned, select the cloud and use the Properties palette to change it (Figure 21.6).

FIGURE 21.5
Adding a revision
cloud to a view

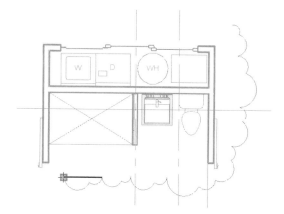

FIGURE 21.6
The revision cloud's
issue assignment
can be changed
in the Properties
palette.

As soon as you have placed a revision cloud on a sheet, any revision schedules placed in your title block will update to include the revision number, description, and the date you assigned in the Sheet Issues/Revisions dialog box earlier (Figure 21.7).

Like other objects, the graphics for revision clouds are controlled from the Object Styles dialog box, which can be launched from the Manage tab in the ribbon. Settings for revisions are located on the Annotation Objects tab. The default setting for the line thickness is 1. We recommend that you change this to something like 7 in your project template to give it the pop you will typically see in revisions.

FIGURE 21.7
The updated title block with the revision information

Enter address here		Project No. 05129

Schematic Design

G Date **07/20/05**

Revision	Description	Date Issued
1	Revision 1	5.01.2010

F

Tagging a Revision Cloud

Revision clouds can be tagged like many other elements. Similar to other tags, revision tags are intelligent and designed to report the revision number or letter that has been assigned to the revision cloud. To place a revision tag, use the Tag By Category tool in the Tag panel on the Annotate tab.

If a tag for revisions is not in your template, you will be warned that no such tag exists in your project. To continue, simply load a revision tag. The default tag is named Revision Tag. rfa and is located in the Annotations folder of the family library within a standard installation.

Once you have a tag loaded, you are ready to tag revision clouds. Hover the cursor over a revision cloud and click to place the tag. You will see a preview of the tag prior to placing it (Figure 21.8). Once the tag is placed, you can drag it around the cloud to reposition it and turn on and off the leader. With or without a leader, the revision tag will stay associated with the cloud.

FIGURE 21.8
Tagging a revision cloud

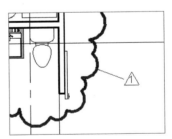

DISABLING THE LEADER

You can choose to use a leader line between the tag and the cloud, depending on your preference or your office standards. In many cases, the tag just needs to be near the cloud and a leader is not necessary. Disable the leader by selecting the tag and clearing the Leader option in the Options bar.

BIM and Supplemental Drawings

The process of making supplemental drawings (SDs)—also known as sketches (SKs)—entails making a change to an existing drawing and then issuing that change as a separate package during the construction process. Sometimes this can be a single 8 1/2″ x 11″ [A4] or 11″ × 17″ [A3] sheet where the new detail is then pasted over the old one in the document set. From a workflow perspective, this can be a little disruptive for a couple of reasons:

- ◆ Placing a view into a smaller sheet to issue the individual view can lead to other problems. Because there is only one instance of the view, it requires you to take views off your Construction Document sheet to place the view in a new sheet. The problem is the new sheet/detail is meant to replace a portion of your original document set, so your set is now out of sequence. You will need to remove the view from the sheet it was issued on temporarily (and remember to put it back) or duplicate the view and hope that you do not need to make last-minute additional changes.

- ◆ A supplemental drawing, once issued, is like a snapshot in time. It becomes a numbered change made to the drawing set at a given date. Because the model and all the views in the model always reflect the most current state of the project, making separate SD sheets and views within Revit will show any additional changes made to that view.

As a best practice, some architects leave all the revisions directly on the sheets where they were originally issued. The sheets can be printed to PDFs, and the PDFs (with the revision clouds) are imported into Adobe Illustrator or a similar application (where they can be properly scaled and cropped to the view or detail being revised and then placed on a template to be issued for the revision). This process not only creates a historic record of the revision, it also allows you to avoid issuing the full sheet while keeping your model up-to-date.

Using Digital Markups

Autodesk ® Design Review offers an efficient way to view and mark up 2D digital documents and 3D models. This workflow is different from revisions and is geared more toward informal design review rather than the management of sheet issues. For example, if your drawings must be reviewed for quality control and overall comments by a senior designer who might not be familiar with Revit Architecture, this tool can streamline the process. The senior designer, consultant, or any other third party can make comments and review changes directly in the digital file and return them to the Revit Architecture user who needs to modify the original model.

Using Design Review, you can view files in DWF or DWFx format. If you export sheets from Revit Architecture to DWFx and the markups are linked back into Revit Architecture, the markups will be automatically placed on the corresponding sheet. So there is no need on your part for any sort of alignment or placement of the revisions.

Design Review is a free tool that you can download from the Autodesk website: `www`
`.autodesk.com/designreview`.

Once it's installed, you can open any DWFx or DWF file produced by any Autodesk or other CAD/BIM software packages.

Publishing to Design Review

There are two ways to share your model using Design Review: as 2D drawings or a 3D model. If you publish to 3D, you create a single 3D representation of your model. Publishing to 2D can create either a single view or a whole collection of interconnected views and sheets packaged as one file. You can even combine 2D views and a 3D model in one DWFx file.

DWFx EXPORTS

You can export to DWFx from any view, except a schedule, in Revit Architecture. To export your views or sheets, select the Application menu and choose Export ➤ DWF/DWFx. The DWF Export Settings dialog box (Figure 21.9) will open. Here you can choose views/sheets to export in addition to specifying how the results will be published.

FIGURE 21.9
The DWF Export Settings dialog box

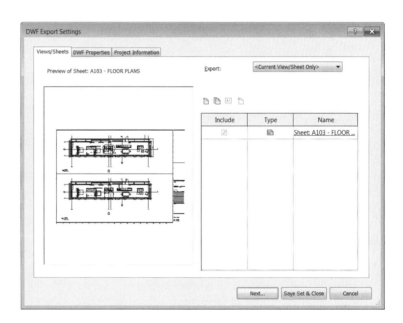

In the following exercise, you will open a Revit file and create a DWFx file for review:

1. Open the c21-JenkinsMusicBldg.rvt model, which can be downloaded from this book's website, www.sybex.com/go/masteringrevit2013.

2. Click the Application menu and select Export ➤ DWF/DWFx to open the dialog box shown in Figure 21.9.

3. Click the New Set icon at the top of the list of views and name the set **MASTERING SHEETS**.

Once you create the set, you will see a new drop-down appear in the dialog box; you can use it to control which views are displayed in the view list (Figure 21.10).

FIGURE 21.10

The Show In List drop-down is available only with a view set.

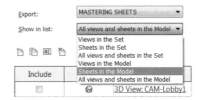

4. From the Show In List drop-down, select Sheets In The Model, and then select sheets A101 through A105. These five sheets will be added to the set to be published.

You can sort the list of views by any of the columns by clicking a column header. Try this by clicking the Name header.

5. To check the export size, select the DWF Properties tab and click the Print Setup button. In the resulting dialog box, you can set explicit sizes for your export. Click the option Use Sheet Size to automatically detect sheet sizes based on the title blocks you are using in the project.

6. Click Next and specify the name of the file and a location in which to save it. Make sure you check the box to combine all sheets into a single DWFx file (see Figure 21.11).

FIGURE 21.11

Manual file naming is available when you combine views for publishing.

7. Open the published DWFx file in Autodesk Design Review. Choose the Markup & Measure tab, and then add a few comments and markups on the A102 sheet.

Using the shapes and the draw tools on this tab, you can add clouds, arrows, and text to insert your comments or changes into the drawings. Once all your changes are created, save the file and it will retain all your changes. Figure 21.12 shows an example of a markup. While this is shown in black and white, markups can be done in a variety of colors and line weights to give them extra visibility on the page.

FIGURE 21.12

A marked-up DWF file

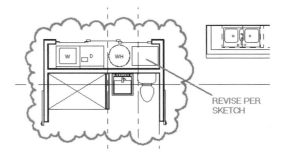

Importing a Design Review Markup

Once you've added markups to the DWFx file, save the file and close Design Review. You can then link the marked-up DWFx file back into the RVT project file. Continue to use the sample file from the previous exercise. You can also download the file JenkinsMusicBldg-MarkedUp.dwfx from this book's companion website at www.sybex.com/go/masteringrevit2013. This file already contains some markups to use in the following exercise. Follow these steps to import the marked-up file into the project file:

DWF
Markup

1. On the Insert tab, choose DWF Markup and then find and select the DWFx file you saved in the previous exercise.

When a DWFx file is selected, only the markups will be shown, not the entire DWFx file. If there are no markups in the file, nothing will be visible in Revit Architecture.

2. In the next dialog box (Figure 21.13), you will see the views in the DWFx file that contain markups and the sheets in the Revit project to which they will coordinate. In this example, there is one sheet with markups.

FIGURE 21.13
Sheets with associated markups are shown

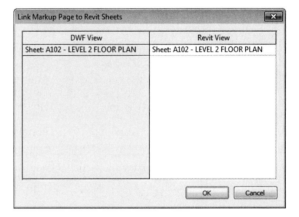

Link Markup Page to Revit Sheets

DWF View	Revit View
Sheet: A102 - LEVEL 2 FLOOR PLAN	Sheet: A102 - LEVEL 2 FLOOR PLAN

OK   Cancel

3. Open sheet A102 from the Project Browser and you will see the markup as an overlay in the same location it was created in Design Review.

Note that markups can be linked only to sheets. If you export a view and mark it up, it will not show up in Revit. Always work from sheets when using Design Review for markup transfer.

You cannot move or delete linked DWF markups—they appear with a pin if selected; however, you can do a number of things to graphically indicate that you've reviewed a markup:

Change its graphic appearance. Let's say you have 20 redline markups on your sheet. You need to keep track of which ones you've picked up. One way to do this is to graphically override each markup as you make the requested modifications. Select the markup, right-click, choose View ➤ By Element, and click Override Graphics. Choose a color to indicate "done." Yellow works well because it suggests a highlight marker.

Hide it. This approach is similar to the graphic override, but you hide the markup altogether. Select the markup, right-click, and choose Hide In View ➤ Element.

Remove it. You can remove markups by choosing Manage Links from the Manage tab. In the Manage Links dialog box, select the DWF Markups tab, select the markup, and click the Remove button. This removes all markups associated with the link.

Another way you can interact with a linked DWF file is by modifying the status or appending comments to each markup. These features can be accessed in the Properties palette when you select a markup.

4. In the A102 sheet view, select one of the markups you created and go to the Properties palette.

5. Change the Status drop-down to Done and then click the Edit button in the Notes field. In the Edit Text dialog box, enter some text related to the completion of the design modification requested in the markup.

6. Click the Apply button at the bottom of the Properties palette.

7. Open the Manage Links dialog box again and select the DWF Markups tab.

8. Select the row containing the DWFx file you linked in the previous steps and then click the Save Markups button. There is no alert or notification that the save process has completed, so just wait a few seconds.

9. Click OK to close the Manage Links dialog box.

10. Open the DWFx file again in Design Review and you will see that the status of the markups has been updated. The comments you added to them can be seen in the History area of the Markup Properties palette.

Using the DWFx file format along with the integrated tools within Revit Architecture, you have closed a communication and coordination loop that has traditionally been difficult to improve. This workflow also benefits larger project teams because you don't have to manage a central pile of drawing markups that need to be shared or distributed among several teammates. All the staff working on a project will have access to the same linked DWF markups.

Modeling for Construction

Now that we have reviewed some basic functionality a design team might use in the construction phase, let's take a look at how a builder (contractor, subcontractor, or construction manager) might use Revit Architecture in the industry today.

Revit Architecture is often referred to as a design application; however, contractors are using the software more frequently as both a model authoring and project analysis tool. Although builders use BIM tools to obtain different results than design professionals obtain, many of the processes and functions are the same; they are merely applied in unique ways.

In *Mastering Autodesk Revit Architecture 2011* (Wiley, 2010), we wrote about a technique to manually model each individual layer of a wall assembly to better understand the construction of the wall. This technique also supported more enhanced phasing and even construction sequencing simulation using software such as Autodesk® Navisworks®. The drawback to this approach was the complexity in managing far more building elements, and it was usually used by only the builder.

New functionality was introduced in Revit Architecture 2012 that supported a more interactive and flexible approach to construction modeling. The first addition was the ability to create *parts*, which are individual subsets of more complex layered elements such as walls and floors. The other addition allowed you to generate *assemblies*, which are segregated subsets of the project model with their own associated views, annotation, and sheets.

Although the following sections are under the main section heading "Modeling for Construction," these new tools are more about adaptive reuse of the model, which is hopefully a step in the right direction. The potential to minimize data loss between the design and construction stakeholders of a project can start to change how we approach collaboration and delivery of our buildings.

Creating Parts

Parts are designed to aid the user in subdividing larger model elements into smaller components for construction planning. Each part maintains a persistent relationship with the elements from which it was derived, and it can be subdivided into smaller parts if necessary. Parts can be generated from walls, floors, ceilings, and roofs, as long as they are of consistent thickness. They also have their own properties, such as volume, area, and height; as such, they can be scheduled independently of their original elements.

While it is likely this tool will also be used by designers to customize architectural elements, we will discuss only the workflow intended for the builder. In this section, we will show you the basic workflow for creating and dividing parts. We encourage you to explore this new tool further and to provide feedback to Autodesk on your findings. Follow these steps:

1. Open the file c21-Parts.rvt, which you can download from this book's website.

2. Activate the Default 3D view if it isn't already open. Notice that each of the wall, floor, ceiling, and roof elements in this sample model is composed of one object. A section box has been activated in this view that is exposing the layers within each assembly.

3. Select the floor at Level 2. On the Create panel in the contextual tab of the ribbon, click the Create Parts button.

What you may not immediately notice is that the original object has been visually replaced in the current view by the parts representing each layer of the floor assembly. It is still in the project model—it has not been deleted.

There is a new view property named Parts Visibility whose default value is Show Parts. This means that if parts have been created for any object, they will be displayed instead of the original. This property can also be set to Show Original or Show Both.

4. In the Project Browser, right-click on the Default 3D view and choose Duplicate View and then Duplicate. Rename the copy of the view **Original Model**.

5. Activate the view named Original Model. From the Properties palette, find the Parts Visibility parameter and change it to Show Original.

6. In the Project Browser, rename the {3D} view to **Parts Model**.

7. Activate the Parts Model view and repeat the process of creating parts for the wall, the ceilings, and the roof in the sample model.

In the previous exercise, you created an alternative way to view your model that begins to explore constructability. Without additional modification, you can start to interact with these individual components by examining their properties or even hiding them or overriding their graphic display.

MODIFYING PARTS

In addition to creating parts from original model elements, you can divide these parts into smaller ones. You can even change the phasing properties at the part level and use grips to modify the extents of the parts. Let's begin with an exercise to divide some parts using planes and sketched lines:

1. Go back to the Parts Model view and select the top part of the roof at the Roof level. This will be the layer representing insulation.

2. From the Part panel in the contextual ribbon, click Divide Parts. You will enter a sketch mode where you can either select intersecting datum or draw your own dividing lines.

3. Click the Intersecting References button in the contextual ribbon. You are presented with the Intersecting Named References dialog box (Figure 21.14). From the Filter drop-down, select All and notice that you can choose from levels, grids, and named reference planes. If a reference plane has not been named, it will not appear in this list.

FIGURE 21.14
You can use datum as one way to divide parts.

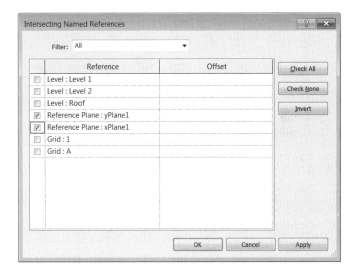

4. Check the boxes for the two reference planes named xPlane1 and yPlane1. Click OK to close the dialog box.

5. Click the green check in the contextual ribbon to finish the edit mode.

After you complete the process for dividing the part, you will notice that the part has now become four separate pieces. To experiment with how the parts maintain their relationship to the original object as well as the intersecting reference planes, go to the Level 1 floor plan and move the reference planes around, but try to keep them within the boundary of the sample floor. When you return to the 3D view, you will see that the divisions stay synchronized with the reference planes.

6. Activate the ceiling plan for Level 1. In the Properties palette for the view, change Parts Visibility to Show Parts. Select the Gypsum Wall Board part on the bottom of the ceiling below the Level 2 floor.

You can make sure you have the correct part selected by examining the Properties palette. The category filter at the top should display Parts (1) and the Material parameter should indicate Gypsum Wall Board - Ceiling.

7. Click the Divide Parts button in the contextual ribbon, and then click the Edit Sketch button to activate the sketching mode. Draw a diagonal line across the part from left to right, as shown in Figure 21.15.

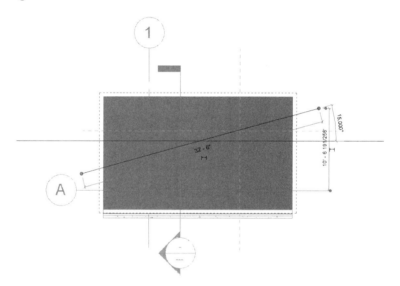

FIGURE 21.15
Sketch a line to divide a part.

If you need to sketch lines to divide parts, the lines do not have to be in closed loops, but they must intersect the boundaries of the part. Keep in mind that if the original element is edited so that its boundaries extend beyond any sketched part divisions, the part divisions will be deleted.

8. Click the green check mark in the contextual ribbon to finish the sketch, and then click it again to finish the part dividing mode.

9. Activate the Parts Model view and orbit the model so you can select the inside face of the wall. Select the part of the wall that would represent the gypsum wall board at the interior face of Level 2.

10. From the Properties palette, find the parameter named Show Shape Handles and check the box. You will see triangular shape handles on all four sides of the part, as shown in Figure 21.16. Drag the top shape handle down to indicate that the gypsum wall board is not to be installed to the full height of the wall assembly.

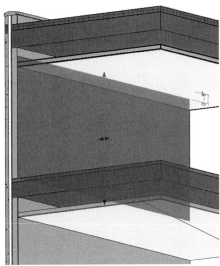

There are several other ways you can interact with parts in your project model. Select any of the parts and observe the Properties palette. You will see that you can override each part's material, phase created, and phase demolished (Figure 21.17).

FIGURE 21.17
Some part properties can be overridden.

Original Category	Walls
Original Family	Basic Wall
Original Type	Exterior - Brick and CMU on MTL....
Material By Original	☑
Material	Gypsum Wall Board
Construction	Finish
Phasing	☆
Phase Created	New Construction
Phase Demolished	None
Phase Created By Original	☑
Phase Demolished By Original	☑

DIVIDING PARTS WITH A GAP

In the previous exercise, you learned how to divide parts using datum objects and simple sketches. You also have the ability to divide parts with a defined gap as well as with a custom profile. Let's explore these options with another exercise:

1. Continue to work with the sample file `c21-Parts.rvt` from the previous exercise. Activate the Parts Model view and orbit the model to view the exterior face of the wall.

2. Select the main part of the exterior wall face that has the material assignment Concrete, Precast. Click the Divide Parts tool in the contextual ribbon.

3. In the Properties palette, set the Divider Gap parameter to 1" [25 mm].

4. Click the Intersecting References tool in the ribbon, set the filter to All, and then select Level 2, Reference Plane: yPlane1 and Grid: 1. Click OK to close the dialog box.

5. Click the green check in the ribbon to finish the dividing parts mode and the panel will be divided with a continuous gap as shown in Figure 21.18.

FIGURE 21.18
Parts divided with a
continuous gap

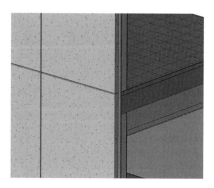

In addition to simple gaps, parts can be divided with a custom profile. A new family template called `Division Profile.rft` is now available in the default family template library. This profile family is similar to other profiles except that the completed sketch in the family does not need to be a closed loop. That said, the sketch must extend completely between the two reference planes associated with the Width parameter in the template.

A number of division profiles are loaded in the default architectural project template. You can find these in the Project Browser under Families ➤ Division Profiles. To examine how any of these are created, right-click Tapered Notch and select Edit from the context menu.

Let's explore how you can edit an existing division and apply a custom profile to the gap. Follow these steps:

1. Continue to work with the project file `c21-Parts.rvt` from the previous exercise. Activate the Parts Model view and orbit the model to view the exterior face of the wall.

2. Select any one of the divided parts of the main precast concrete portion of the wall. Once a part has been divided, you won't need to select all the parts to edit the division, just one. From the contextual ribbon, click Edit Division.

3. In the Properties palette, change the Split Profile Type parameter to Angled Step: Angled Step. Once you select a profile type, additional parameters are available in the Properties palette. Set the Edge Match parameter to Complementary (Figure 21.19).

FIGURE 21.19
Assigning a division
profile to a part

4. Click the green check mark in the ribbon to finish the division edits and you will see that the updated profiles are applied to all edges of the divided parts (Figure 21.20).

FIGURE 21.20
Parts divided with a division profile

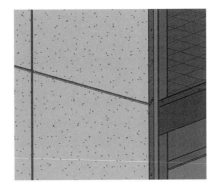

5. To explore different functionality with division profiles, repeat steps 2 through 4, but select the profile Notch and set the Edge Match parameter to Mirrored. Observe the change in behavior using a different matching property.

When you apply a custom profile to a division of parts, the profile is applied to all divisions. If you need to assign different profiles to different divisions, each of those unique divisions must be applied separately. Let's try this approach by continuing the exercise.

6. In the Parts Model view, select any of the precast concrete parts you generated earlier in this exercise. Click Edit Division in the contextual ribbon.

7. Click the Intersecting References button in the ribbon, and in the Intersecting Named References dialog box, set the Filter drop-down to All, and then deselect Reference Plane: yPlane1.

8. Click OK to close the dialog box, and then click the green check mark in the ribbon to finish editing the division.

9. While pressing the Ctrl key, select the two larger precast concrete panels to the right side of the wall. Click the Divide Parts button in the ribbon.

10. Click the Intersecting References button in the ribbon, set the Filter drop-down to All, and then select Reference Plane: yPlane1. Click OK to close the dialog box.

11. In the Properties palette, set the Divider Gap parameter to 0' 1" [25 mm]. Click the green check mark in the ribbon to finish editing the division.

You will now see that the custom profile was maintained for the other part divisions, but the rightmost vertical division has only a simple gap.

MERGING PARTS

Parts can be merged to form larger, more contiguous geometry; however, the parts to be merged must have the same material and the same creation and demolition phases, and the merged geometry must consist of a single connected component. Parts with gaps assigned to the divisions will not be merged.

To merge parts, press the Ctrl key while selecting multiple parts. In the contextual ribbon, click Merge Parts. Once parts have been merged, you can always edit them in the future. To edit merged parts, select the part and then click Edit Merged from the contextual ribbon.

Excluding Parts

Parts can also be excluded from a model to support more detailed construction conditions. To exclude a part, select the part and click Exclude Parts from the contextual ribbon. Excluded parts will not appear in any schedules; however, they are easily restored. To restore an excluded part, hover over the area with your mouse pointer where the part was excluded. You will be able to select the excluded part, but it will be indicated with a special icon. Click the icon on the excluded part or click Restore Parts in the contextual ribbon.

BE AWARE OF THE PARTS CATEGORY

Because parts are considered a separate category of elements in Revit Architecture, you should pay careful attention to how they might affect your views and view templates. Take a look at the visibility and graphic overrides for any view and you'll see that Parts is listed as an object category. This means that once you create parts for a model element—whether the original object was a floor, ceiling, wall, or roof—the parts are all treated as a singular type of object. For example, if you have surface patterns for floors hidden in a view and you create parts for a floor, the surface pattern will appear again unless you have hidden surface patterns for the Parts category as well.

Scheduling Parts

Another valuable aspect of using parts is the ability to schedule them—essentially a cleaner way to generate material takeoffs. You can create a parts schedule in the same manner you would for other object categories. Go to the View tab, click Schedules ➤ Schedule/Quantities, and choose the Parts category.

Select the Fields tab of the Schedule Properties dialog box, and you will notice the potential of the available fields (Figure 21.21). With a part schedule, you can report the original category of the object along with the part material and the usual geometric information.

FIGURE 21.21
A part schedule has access to some unique fields for reporting.

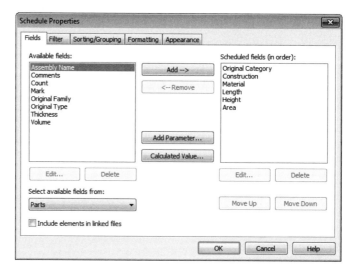

There is also a field named Construction that indicates whether the part was derived from a Core layer or a Finish layer. This field can then be used as a filter and/or sorting criterion in your schedule. An example illustrating the results of a part schedule is shown in Figure 21.22.

FIGURE 21.22
An example of a completed part schedule

Construction	Material	Length	Height	Area
Part Schedule				
Ceilings				
Core	Metal - Stud Layer			157 SF
Finish	Gypsum Wall Board			157 SF
Floors				
Core	Wood - Sheathing - plywood			165 SF
Finish	Carpet (1)			9 SF
Finish	Carpet (1)			34 SF
Finish	Carpet (1)			97 SF
Finish	Carpet (1)			25 SF
Core	Structure - Wood Joist/Rafter Layer			85 SF
Core	Structure - Wood Joist/Rafter Layer			80 SF
Roofs				
Finish	Roofing - EPDM Membrane			158 SF
Finish	Insulation / Thermal Barriers - Rigid insulation			158 SF
Core	Metal - Deck			158 SF
Core	Structure - Steel Bar Joist Layer			158 SF

Creating Assemblies

An assembly is a new way to organize related elements within your Revit project. The feature is designed to help users track and schedule a collection of elements as a single entity. In the case of precast concrete, for example, a column made of multiple families including reinforcing bars, mounting hardware, and corbels can be collected into a single assembly.

As you identify objects to be included in an assembly, you can also choose from a variety of views in which to document the element in isolation from the rest of the project model. A collection of assembly views can be thought of as shop drawings. Let's take a look at the workflow for creating an assembly.

In the following exercise, you can use any sample model to illustrate the process of creating assemblies:

1. In any view of your project, select a few model elements. Try to pick a few that are relatively close to each other.

2. From the Create panel in the contextual ribbon, click Create Assembly. You will be prompted to name the new assembly (Figure 21.23).

FIGURE 21.23
Create a name for the new assembly.

If you selected objects of different categories such as a wall and a ceiling, you have the opportunity to select which category the assembly will inherit. Choosing one category or the other does not seem to have an effect on the functionality beyond the organization that is exposed to the user.

When you create a new assembly, Revit automatically determines if another identical assembly exists in your model. If one exists, the new assembly inherits the name of the identical assembly. In a somewhat similar situation, if you were to create copies of an assembly throughout your project, the matching assemblies would function in a similar way to how groups function. The fundamental difference between assemblies and groups is in the propagation of changes. If you have identical assemblies in a project and you change one of them, Revit changes the name of the modified assembly and treats it as unique.

Creating Assembly Views

After you have created an assembly, you can create a series of views that are dedicated to that assembly. In other words, you will see only the elements included in the assembly within these views. In addition to plans, sections, and 3D views, you can generate parts lists and quantity takeoffs for an assembly.

To generate assembly views, select an assembly in any view and click Create Views from the Assembly panel in the contextual ribbon. You are prompted with a dialog box in which you choose the views assigned to the assembly (Figure 21.24).

FIGURE 21.24
Select views to be created with the assembly.

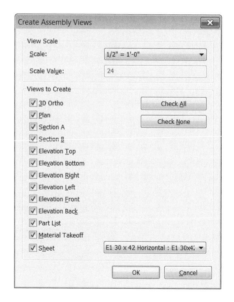

After you click the OK button, you will find the assembly views at the bottom of the Project Browser. Under the Assembly grouping, you will find each assembly listed with all of the associated views (Figure 21.25).

FIGURE 21.25
Assembly views are found at the bottom of the Project Browser.

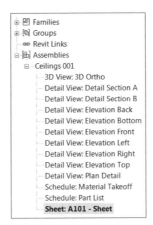

Although sections are automatically placed for the included elements, the individual views are not placed on the assembly sheet. To do this, activate the sheet within an assembly and then drag and drop the views onto the sheet. Note that assembly views can be used on nonassembly sheets and regular views can be placed on an assembly sheet. An example of views compiled into an assembly sheet is shown in Figure 21.26.

FIGURE 21.26
An example of a simple assembly sheet

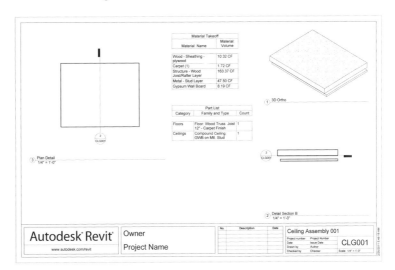

The Bottom Line

Add revisions to your project. You need the ability to track changes in your design after sheets have been issued. Adding revisions to a drawing is an inevitable part of your workflow.

Master It   Add to your project revisions that automatically get tracked on your sheet.

Use digital markups.   DWFs provide a lightweight means to digitally transfer and mark up multiple sheets in a document set.

Master It   Explain the workflow using DWF markups.

Model for construction.   Parts and assemblies allow a design model to be used in more detailed ways for the construction process.

Master It   Describe the method for breaking down a design-based model assembly into its individual components.

Chapter 22

Using Laser Scans in Revit

LiDAR, or laser scanning, is an emerging technology used to quickly locate geographic information and extrapolate that into a means that is insertable into an Autodesk® Revit® Architecture model. This type of scan is used to cut down the time of a traditional survey while collecting more data about the site or building. In this chapter, you'll learn to:

◆ Understand LiDAR

◆ Understand common uses of LiDAR

◆ Plan for a LiDAR survey

◆ Use the scan in a project

Understanding LiDAR

ABOUT THE CONTRIBUTING AUTHORS: TONY DiMARTINO AND ADAM HORN

Tony DiMartino is a project designer and BIM coordinator at HNTB Architecture. He has been a key contributor to the Revit implementation and standards at HNTB as well as with partner firms during project-based BIM design and coordination. He is also a board member for the Kansas City Revit Users Group.

Adam Horn is a technologist in the Incubation Center at HNTB and is currently performing R&D on data acquisition methods. He is a registered professional land surveyor with more than 12 years of experience in land surveying and data acquisition. Adam is a forward-thinking thought leader who maintains a cutting edge outlook on the AEC industry in order to identify and develop new technologies that will improve current best practices.

There are many forms of 3D reality data capture that can be used to collect existing conditions of the built or natural world. Light Detection and Ranging, or LiDAR, is a noncontact method of reality data capture that uses light amplification by stimulated emission of radiation (basically a laser) to emit a self-generated laser pulse and collect the returned light in order to measure the distance, intensity, and location values of any surface it touches. The laser return is stored as an x, y, z location point. LiDAR sensors have the ability to collect these range points at a very rapid rate, which increases with every new piece of hardware released to the market. Current hardware has the ability to collect up to 1,000,000 points per second, and this will likely be surpassed with the next generation of scanners.

LiDAR is a line of sight technology, meaning that it does not have the ability to penetrate through solid objects such as ceilings or walls. This is an important point to understand when performing a laser scan. A good rule of thumb is that if you can see it with the naked eye then the scanner will be able to capture it.

LiDAR as a technology has been around for several decades. However, it has only been in the last decade that it has become more accepted and widely used as a means of data collection. What was once reserved solely for the high-tech industry and early adopters that were willing to spend a lot of money to offer these services has now become more widely available. Due to the recent reduction in hardware costs and advances in software, LiDAR is now more accessible to projects than ever. For under $50,000, you can own and operate a top-of-the-line laser scanner. If one is really ambitious and has an aptitude for software development, one could own and operate a structured light scanner for under $100.

Hardware

Not all LiDAR scanners are created equal, and it is important to keep in mind the project requirements to apply the right scanner to the project. A successful project relies on deploying the correct technology, and using the wrong scanner will put the project at risk of not meeting scope, schedules, and budgets. Following are some basic rules of thumb for using or procuring LiDAR for a project.

First, it's important to understand the scanner itself. There are two types of scanners: a Time of Flight scanner and a Phase Shift scanner.

The Time of Flight scanner measures the time it takes for the emitted laser pulse to be returned to the scanner. The properties this type of scanner has that differentiate it are as follows:

- Slower collection rate; 50,000 points per second

- Longer range of up to 1,000' or 300 meters

- Lower resolution

- Smaller data file sizes

The Time of Flight scanner type is most effective for exterior applications, such as, for instance, site collection, exterior building conditions, and especially for tall buildings.

The other scanner type is called a Phase Shift scanner. This scanner measures the phase shift of the emitted laser compared to the light it receives when the pulse is bounced back to the scanner from the target. This type of scanner has the following properties:

- Fast collection rate; 1,000,000 points per second

- Shorter range of 65' or 20 meters

- Higher resolution

- Larger data file sizes

- Most effective in short range applications such as interior spaces and confined spaces

- Can require more setups (or scan points) due to the range limitations

Benefits of LiDAR

So now that you have a better understanding of LiDAR as a technology, we can begin to discuss the benefits of using LiDAR and how to deploy it on your project. The benefits are simple to understand, but they cannot be overstated. The first benefit is the level of detail that can be achieved with a scanner. A significant amount of detail can be collected with a LiDAR scan. There is a trade-off to this benefit, however, in the direct correlation between the level of detail, or resolution achieved, and the time that it takes to collect the data. Most scanners have the ability to change the scan resolution in the field. If the project focus is an interior space with a high level of detail, then it may be desirable to set the scanner to a higher resolution — similar to what you would do with a digital camera. If the project is of a broader scale, say to locate the exterior footprint of a building, then a lower resolution will suffice, allowing you to expedite the scan time.

To add additional configuration to the time-versus-detail equation, a Phase Shift scanner, set at its highest resolution, will still likely be faster than a Time of Flight scanner set at a lower resolution. The trade-off is that the Phase-based scanner will require more setups to collect the area due to the limited range. We will discuss this in more detail later in this chapter.

Another benefit of LiDAR is data collection speed. Although almost unfair, it is still necessary to compare LiDAR to traditional survey methodology on the basis of the speed of data collection. A scanner can collect data thousands of times faster than traditional survey equipment and can provide a true-to-scale, three-dimensional representation of the existing conditions of the project area. It is true that if all the project requires is four corners of a building or room, then a scanner is like using a sledgehammer for fine woodworking. However, if you are trying to understand a cluttered pipe gallery inside a pump room, then LiDAR is by far the better tool. It should never be said that LiDAR is a silver bullet and that it should be used on every job. We have personally been involved with projects that either utilized the wrong type of scanner or were not good candidates for LiDAR, and they resulted in negative outcomes.

As with most projects, safety is of paramount importance. This is one aspect of LiDAR that can be easily overlooked. LiDAR gives you the ability to measure objects without having to physically touch them, such as things that are out of reach, in a hazardous area, or in a confined space. In certain conditions or spaces, LiDAR can add a level of safety that is otherwise nonexistent. For example, with LiDAR you can measure electrical equipment that is not safe to touch, or you can collect information above a drop ceiling, or in other confined areas. You can also collect information in busy and congested areas without needing to enter those areas — areas such as, for example, a building that is under construction or a building that might be structurally failing and is not safe to enter.

It is true that, when used correctly, LiDAR scanners are very accurate and can collect information to within millimeters of their actual position. It is not because LiDAR is more accurate than other reality data-capture technologies, but rather that you have the ability to collect the entire spatially accurate environment. It really becomes about the ability to accurately locate things that were typically not located with high accuracy in the past, like window and door openings, mechanical fixtures, and external building detail. Again, it is not the overall accuracy that is valuable. Even if you did locate the things like architectural detailing with a traditional survey, it was typically not spatially correct to the rest of the building. Now imagine that you could have all of the internal and external building openings located and shown together in the same model, then throw in the architectural detailing and the building facades. That would be a very complete and accurate picture of the existing conditions of a building, and that is exactly what you get with LiDAR.

There are two forms of accuracy when talking about LiDAR: relative and absolute. Relative accuracy refers to the position of each x, y, z point in space and its location to all other x, y, z points in that same space. Absolute accuracy is concerned with the real-world position of the x, y, z points. It is important to be aware of the absolute accuracy of the point cloud if you are trying to position something on a site that has to be specifically located. In most architectural applications, relative accuracy is of more interest than absolute accuracy.

Understanding Common Uses

Imagine combining the clarity of a digital camera with the accuracy of a survey measurement device. Actually, you don't have to imagine this because this is essentially what a laser scanner provides. When you combine these two things, you have a representation of the existing world that will give you the ability to visualize things that have not been possible in the past. The following is a series of figures demonstrating some of the common uses for LiDAR scans:

Figure 22.1 shows the scan in section with a beam in elevation and a section drawn over it. One of the most common uses for LiDAR scans is creating as-built conditions of existing facilities. In this image, you can also see the black and white scan data in the background represented as a granular series of points.

FIGURE 22.1
Creating as-built drawings

The next obvious step past the 2D documentation is the creation of 3D model elements. In Figure 22.2 you can see the inside of a wastewater plant and all of the complex piping that runs through it. This isn't a photograph — it's actually the image from a scan. This image was overlaid into Revit to create the piping layout next to it. Imagine the amount of time it would take to measure and verify all this information in the field. With the LiDAR scan, it's all right there in 3D.

FIGURE 22.2
A LiDAR image and the 3D model derived from it

Another common use of LiDAR in the modeling environment is to verify existing conditions that you might already have modeled. What has changed or what was omitted from the model or construction? By overlaying the model with the scan, you can visually compare the two models (Figure 22.3).

FIGURE 22.3
Comparing existing
conditions to model
elements

LiDAR will also show you variation to a very fine degree within the scan data. In one example project, we had a building with significant floor deflection. By scanning the floor, we were able to tell that over a couple hundred feet we had almost 3 inches of variation over the floor system. That can be shown in the scan as a heat map (Figure 22.4).

FIGURE 22.4
LiDAR shown as a
heat map for floor
deflection

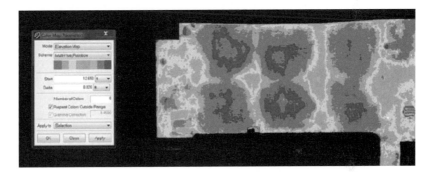

LiDAR modeling doesn't have to be done inside of a building. In Figure 22.5, this site was created and modeled from the LiDAR scan. You can also see the array of scanners that sit on the tripods out in the site.

FIGURE 22.5
Site modeling using
LiDAR

Finally, the obvious architectural use would be high-resolution scans of existing buildings to capture a full gambit of space with all the details it entails. Figure 22.6 shows a section of the main building from the site in the previous image. The yellow elements represent the scanners and scan points. You can see the level of detail in the scan by visualizing the hand railings and even masonry joints.

FIGURE 22.6
Creating as-built models

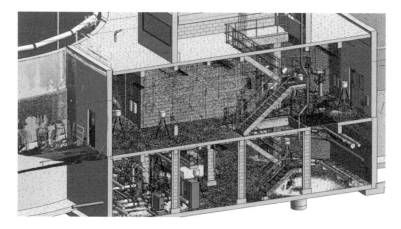

Planning for a LiDAR Survey

When considering LiDAR for a project, there are many things to think about to ensure a successful collection of point data. First and foremost, it is critical to remember that not all projects are good candidates for laser scanning. There are many reasons for this: schedule, scope, and budget, to name a few. If your project has a compressed schedule that prohibits the need for detailed data collection, then it might not be a good candidate. If the project requires only rough dimensions of the building to show an envelope and not the level of detail you see in the scans, then it is not necessary to scan the entire building. Or if you are looking for intricate architectural detail, which cannot be collected with LiDAR, then it is probably not a good candidate either.

However, in our current economic climate, it is more important than ever to create and offer differentiating technology or services to stay relevant within the profession. Even if your project budget is lean, you may be able to justify LiDAR because of the richness of the dataset. In other words, it may cost a little more money up front to collect the existing data, but it may provide immense value by allowing you to identify potential design problems at the early stages of a project that you would have not found otherwise. For example, you might not think to scan an existing building that was being demolished down to the structural elements. If you did, you would be mostly concerned with locating those structural elements, but when you scan the building, you find that the floor is severely deflected, which can cause design changes in the location of wall openings.

A similar scenario may be true if your project has a tight schedule. Again, it may cost the project some time on the front end to collect LiDAR data, but imagine the benefits of having a high-fidelity dataset from which to make design decisions. A classic example is the time saved on a project when it is determined in the design phase rather than in the construction phase that there are problems. The time and money that it will take the contractor to resolve these problems while constructing the project is no doubt greater than if it had been identified and resolved during the design phase.

Once you have determined that you will use LiDAR in your project, it is time to begin planning for implementation. This is likely the most important process in the entire LiDAR collection and delivery process because there are so many variables involved. If planning is done poorly, the project scope, schedule, and budget will no doubt suffer as a direct result. Even if your company does not perform the LiDAR collection, you should still have an understanding of the scan planning process so that you are able to communicate the project requirements to the service provider. In the next section, we'll discuss the basics of preparing for a scan.

Exterior or Interior

Knowing if you need an exterior or interior scan is important because it will largely determine the type of scanner that should be used. If your project is exterior in scope and/or requires you to collect information that is more than 80' away from the scanner, you will want to use/hire a Time of Flight scanner. If your project is an interior space that is limited to shorter lines of sight, you will want to use a Phase Shift scanner because of the high-speed data collection capabilities at short range.

SCANNER INTEROPERABILITY

There is no rule that says that you can't use a Time of Flight scanner in an interior environment or a Phase-based scanner in an exterior setting. However, the scanners are somewhat purpose-built for optimal operation within the environments that suit them. The recommendation is to use the right scanner for the right project to achieve the highest ROI.

Level of Detail

This is typically the most difficult question to answer and even more difficult to convey to the service provider who is performing the scanning and the owner who is receiving the deliverables. This is also one of the largest cost drivers for a LiDAR project, and if misunderstood or specified incorrectly, there is a risk that the scan won't meet your needs.

There are really two levels of detail in LiDAR project delivery:

Point cloud level of detail   This will affect the amount of field collection time. A higher level of detail = more field time = higher cost.

Level of detail of the derivatives   That is, what is the smallest scale of things you'll want in the scan? This will affect the amount of office processing and modeling time and typically refers to the lowest level of modeling detail. An example would be specifying scanning all pipes greater than or equal to 6″ (150 mm) diameter. Again, a higher level of detail = more modeling time = higher cost.

You must have a good grasp on your project needs when planning for LiDAR collection and modeling so that you can convey the project requirements. Unclear direction to a service provider can cause enormous blows to schedule and budget. For example, if you call a LiDAR service provider and say, "I need to have LiDAR collected on my project and I need it delivered as a 3D as-built model," that can mean many different things. You need to take the time to clearly specify the project requirements so that the provider doesn't spend two months modeling an entire building when you needed only the door and window openings.

Imagery

Some scanners have built-in digital cameras that take panoramic photos and stitch them together. The colors from the photos can then be draped onto the point clouds to give them a "true-color" appearance. Some scanners do not have a built-in camera and will deliver a point cloud in black and white pixels. This requires the service provider to collect the imagery manually and post-process it in order to drape it to the point cloud if color is desired. Figure 22.7 shows the possible difference with the same image. The image on the left is a color scan, while the image on the right is devoid of color. Depending on what you need to get out of the scan, one will be better than the other.

FIGURE 22.7
A color and non-color LiDAR scan

Schedule

When trying to set your scanning schedule, the trick is to manage your LiDAR delivery expectations with the level of detail that is required. In other words, if the delivery is simply a geo-referenced point cloud, that can be delivered shortly after field collection. If the delivery calls for a 3D model of the entire building, including the architectural, structural, mechanical, electrical, and plumbing components, it is going to take a while longer to create.

Unfortunately, there is no magic number for a schedule because all project requirements are different and all service providers are different. The best recommendation is to try to work with people in whom you have confidence.

Once you have answered these questions, it is a good time to plan out the scanner locations on the site to ensure proper coverage. This is also a good tool for estimating field time and cost. The best way to do this is to use existing maps or drawings that are available to plot out circles that represent the scanner locations. For example, if it is an interior scan, you can use an existing floor plan to plot out the circles. You will most likely be using a Phase-based scanner with an effective range of 60' (18 m). You can scale and plot 60' (18 m) diameter circles on the floor plan to look at the coverage. Once you have covered the area on paper, you will know how many scan setups you will need. From there it becomes simple math to get a rough estimate of the necessary field time, as in the following example:

25 scan setups (or circles) × 20 minutes per setup (Phase-based scanner) = 8 hours (approximately).

Using the Scan in a Project

Once your LiDAR scan is complete, you will have a point cloud to use. This point cloud is literally just that — millions of small points geo-located in a three-dimensional field. Now comes the part where you need to understand how to use this point cloud. There are many application programming interface (API) add-ons available for the import and use of point cloud data in Revit; however, it is possible to import point clouds directly into Revit. Point cloud importing became available with the release of Revit Architecture 2012, and you are allowed to import several raw formats of point cloud data: FLS, FWS, LAS, PTG, PTS, PTX, XYB, and XYZ. If you're having a scan performed on your building, you'll want to ensure that the point cloud you receive from the scanner will be one of those file types.

POINT CLOUD SIZE

Point clouds are made up of millions of points in a three-dimensional field. Because each point not only contains x, y, and z data but can also contain RGB color values (in the case of a color scan), point cloud files can be very large. They can be so large, in fact, that a single scan point can be 4 or 5 GB of space, making the entire scan require up to hundreds of gigabytes of storage. Holding one or more of these scans can eclipse your office's network capabilities. Be careful not to overload your network with scan data.

Once you receive the files from the scanner, the next step is to load them into your Revit model. This can be done by navigating to the Insert tab and choosing the Point Cloud button from the Link panel. Choosing this button will open the Link Point Cloud dialog box (Figure 22.8). You'll have the same options for positioning the point cloud that you do when linking in other Revit files — namely to link via center to center, origin to origin, or shared coordinates. Regardless of the method you choose, make sure you remember it. Your LiDAR scan will consist of a file for every scan point — which can be hundreds. You'll want to link them each in the same way so they all colocate properly.

FIGURE 22.8
Importing the point cloud data

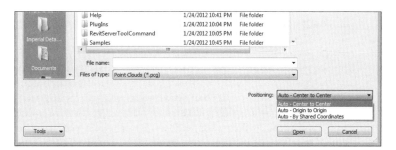

The first time you load one of these files into Revit, Revit will convert your scan file to a PCG file type. This will create a new file on your system, taking up more drive space. This processing time will take a while based on your processor speed, so be patient. It only has to happen once, but it will be once for every scan point you import.

LiDAR submittals will come as a separate file for each scanner setup. These files can be combined with third-party programs, but due to the size that each file can reach, it may not be the best workflow to combine many of them into one. Looking at groupings as functional regions of the building (e.g., building entry, exterior site, second floor foyer) is a good way to combine them. This way, you can unlink them from the project if it gets to be too much for your computer to process.

One recommendation for ease of use within the model is to import the point cloud data files into a separate Revit file and then import the new file into your main model. This will keep the main model from being weighed down by all the point cloud files. Another option would be to place the linked file in its own workset to simplify turning the inserted point clouds on or off. No one would want to manually turn on or off a hundred linked files!

We're going to walk through one way of handling point cloud data. The process described here is one we have found to be the most effective for multiple point cloud inserts. In this workflow, you have an existing building model and you're trying to verify the existing conditions with the scan data. Here are the steps:

1. Start a blank file using the standard Revit template. If you need to subdivide your model, now would be a good time to create a series of worksets that would allow you to group your point clouds in a logical way.

2. Convert the point cloud files to a PCG format by using the Insert Point Cloud tool. This process can be very tedious, so be patient (Figure 22.9). The default files will automatically convert when you import them into Revit for the first time. It is also possible to batch-convert these files with a third-party utility.

FIGURE 22.9
Converting the
point cloud files

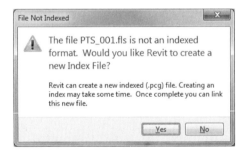

3. After each file is converted, you will have to repeat the import process for the new PCG file created. Make sure to save your file at reasonable intervals.

4. If a building model has already been started (in a separate file), it is recommended that you now align the first point cloud you've inserted by linking this point cloud Revit file into your building model Revit file. The best way to align the point cloud and building model is to find a good location and cut a section. Ideally this will occur at a wall, floor, or other piece of static geometry that is shared between your model and the point cloud.

   If visibility within your view is problematic, you can limit the view range or apply a scope box. This will allow you to limit the number of points within the view to get a decent reading; otherwise, too many points can get unclear and overwhelming (Figure 22.10).

FIGURE 22.10
Use a scope box
to limit the point
cloud

If you are having trouble navigating a small sliver of a 3D view, try selecting the section box and opening a floor plan or elevation to adjust the extents. This method of adjusting the section box in a different view other than the 3D view allows for less lag time and better control of the cut location.

5. After you import the first PCG file, a new option is available in the Link Point Cloud dialog box. When you go to insert the second or *n*th point cloud, the Positioning drop-down menu will give you the option to place the rest of your files from the origin to the last-placed point cloud (Figure 22.11). This will allow the point clouds to insert relative to one another. If you choose to split the point cloud Revit model into multiple Revit files, keep the last PCG imported to use in the other files for the "last origin placed."

FIGURE 22.11
Using the new
Positioning option
in the Link Point
Cloud dialog box

6. Place groups of imported PCG files on worksets. If you imported these into a separate file, don't worry — you can still access this information from the main model through visibility graphics. Keeping the point clouds separate will allow you to have a cleaner list of worksets in the main model.

   The worksets can also be helpful if you need to split up the point cloud Revit file into multiple files due to size. If you choose to split the Revit file into multiple point cloud files, it is wise to keep the original file to copy from, as explained in step 5.

7. Now open your main building model. Create a separate workset for the point cloud using the Point Cloud tab in the Worksharing dialog box. A good workflow is to leave the Visible In All Views check box unchecked. This will ensure that new views won't be created with your point cloud automatically turned on.

8. While in your building model, create a new 3D view and rename it giving it a label that indicates that the point cloud data is turned on within the view. Next, open the Visibility/

Graphic Overrides dialog box and select the Revit Links tab. Create a custom display setting for your linked point cloud file. Select the Worksets tab and turn on/off portions of the linked file by workset. This method is again to manage the amount of information you will be working with visually at one time. Click OK to close all the dialog boxes.

If you chose to place groups of PCGs in separate Revit models, you can place all those links on the same workset within the main model and turn them on and off by link. It is still recommended that the workset be set to Not Visible In All Views using this method.

9. After visibility graphics have been set up, go to your new 3D view and start to use the section box to cut a thin strip of the building, making the point cloud file easier to read. Figure 22.12 shows a thin strip of a point cloud linked into an existing building file.

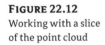

FIGURE 22.12
Working with a slice
of the point cloud

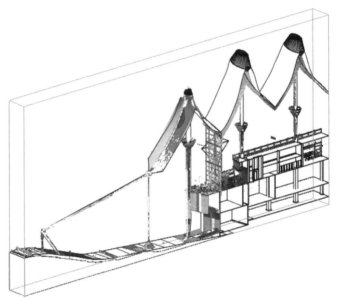

Source: Denver International Airport South Terminal Redevelopment Program, Preliminary
Design Concept, 2012

From here you can start to see areas of the model that need adjustments and move about the elements without too much resistance. While this was based on modeling and verifying an existing building, this same workflow would work for a building addition or any other scan scenario.

When to Use LiDAR Information

There are instances when a point cloud survey can be of use beyond simple wall alignment. In Figure 22.13, the tent structure needed to be more accurately modeled to give a more realistic picture of the existing conditions. The green lines show the current model and the point cloud is the almost solid-looking element.

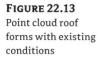

FIGURE 22.13
Point cloud roof
forms with existing
conditions

Source: Denver International Airport South Terminal Redevelopment Program, Preliminary Design
Concept, 2012

Point cloud data can also be used for verification of existing information. In Figure 22.14, the point cloud data is represented by the obvious pixels. The Revit file and the base survey are also colocated to signify any differences in the model that would need adjusting.

FIGURE 22.14
Defining settings
for imported DWG/
DXF line weights

Source: Denver International Airport South Terminal Redevelopment
Program, Preliminary Design Concept, 2012

The point cloud data from a LiDAR scan is not only used for determining the location of walls and roads. It is also used for renderings and animations of an existing area. Having a point cloud available to decide when and where to show a particular walk-through and building possible design iterations into it could result in a cost savings with fewer site visits. Programs are also available to view and stitch the photos from the scanner along with a way to jump from one scanner to the next to see different scanned areas.

Source: Denver International Airport South Terminal Redevelopment Program, Preliminary Design Concept, 2012

Another important aspect of point cloud data is the accuracy of the data. A floor in Revit is always a completely flat surface, whereas a floor scanned in an existing building has many imperfections and could even be slightly off axis or contain low and high spots.

The Bottom Line

Plan for a LiDAR survey.   You'll need to understand the differences between the types of scanners and how they're best used between indoor and outdoor scan conditions.

Master It   For your project, select the right LiDAR scan equipment and estimate the number of survey points.

Create a BIM from the point cloud.   Once you've completed the LiDAR scan, you'll have a point cloud of the building. The next step is to get that point cloud into BIM.

Master It   Describe the steps needed to go from a LiDAR scan to a BIM model of an existing building.

Know the limits of LiDAR.   LiDAR creates a series of points within a file and many files create a scan set. These can range into the tens or hundreds of gigabytes in file size. Understanding how to store and use this information is critical to maintaining stability in your Revit files.

Master It   Describe the limits to LiDAR modeling in Revit.

Chapter 23

Revit in the Classroom

Building information modeling presents an amazing learning opportunity for today's students by allowing them to quickly visualize a complete design concept in various ways.

Initially, students tend to focus on the *modeling* component of Autodesk® Revit® Architecture software, seeing it as little more than a SketchUp alternative. But perhaps more important and relevant is the *information* element; Revit is a database that can display information both graphically and nongraphically. This allows students to convey complex design ideas using multiple techniques that clearly communicate the intent.

These building information models are located in the real world, and they have access to local climate data. This presents a wonderful opportunity to compare different design options and study the effects of various environmental factors. This itself is an additional learning opportunity; the student must research to understand the data more thoroughly. This investigation helps to better inform each iteration of the design. While the software does present the information in an easily digestible format, the question of what to do next is still one for the student to answer.

In this chapter, you'll:

◆ Learn why BIM and Revit are core to the educational design process at Virginia Tech

◆ Understand how students use sustainability tools in Revit during their design process

◆ Understand how Virginia Tech leverages the use of Revit to maintain relationships with local design firms

◆ Use Autodesk Project® Vasari for real-time feedback and apply that to your design solution

◆ Learn how to clearly communicate design ideas and intent

Virginia Tech

The College of Architecture and Urban Studies at Virginia Tech was founded in 1964 and is among the largest of its type in the nation. It is composed of four schools: the School of Architecture + Design, the Myers-Lawson School of Construction, the School of Public and International Affairs, and the School of Visual Arts.

Washington-Alexandria Architecture Center

The Washington-Alexandria Architecture Center (WAAC) has been functioning as the urban extension of the Virginia Tech College of Architecture and Urban Studies, School of Architecture + Design in the Washington metropolitan area since 1980 (Figure 23.1).

FIGURE 23.1
VT WAAC

Since 1985, the WAAC has also served to house a consortium of architectural schools engaging the following universities:

Bauhaus-University of Weimar, Weimar, Germany

California Polytechnic State University, San Luis Obispo, California

Mississippi State, Starkville, Mississippi

Louisiana State University, Baton Rouge, Louisiana

Oxford Brookes University, Oxford, United Kingdom

Tallinn Art University, Tallinn, Estonia

Technion, Haifa, Israel

Texas A&M University, College Station, Texas

Universidad del Desarollo, Santiago, Chile

University of Bahrain, Isa Town, Kingdom of Bahrain

University of Mendoza, Mendoza, Argentina

Universidad San Francisco de Quito, Quito, Ecuador

Universidad Nacional Autónoma de México (UNAM), Mexico City, Mexico

Yokohama National University, Yokohama, Japan

The WAAC seeks to explore and expand design pedagogies and design processes related to the urban environment. It is ideally situated to utilize the resources of the national and international design, development, and planning community in the Washington-Baltimore metropolitan area. Visiting lecturers and adjunct faculty enrich the curriculum of the WAAC, and the WAAC participates in many collaborative efforts with metropolitan entities, such as the Smithsonian Institution and the National Building Museum.

Academics and Real-World Experience

The WAAC enrolls students in their fourth, fifth, and graduate years of study and grants degrees in the M.Arch.1 program for students with a five-year professional degree and the M.Arch.2 program for students with a four-year bachelor of science degree in architecture. M.Arch.3 students (students with initially a nonarchitectural baccalaureate degree) can attend the WAAC during their thesis level of study after they complete their first two years at the main campus in Blacksburg, Virginia. The WAAC also offers a master of science degree in landscape architecture as a three-year MLA program for individuals with a baccalaureate degree in other disciplines. Qualified candidates can earn a PhD in architecture and design research with a concentration in architectural representation and education.

All schools participating in the consortium share the common goal of providing their respective students with an academic environment that uses the metropolitan area as an educational laboratory in which to pursue studies of architecture, landscape architecture, urban design, and planning. Each member school provides three to fifteen students and one faculty member for an academic year, thereby establishing a diverse student body, varied faculty perspectives, and a broad educational program for those choosing to study at the consortium. All students remain enrolled in their individual schools, and courses are designed to provide appropriate academic credit for member institutions. All students must be upper-year undergraduates or at the master's level to participate as consortium residents.

The many architectural firms in the area also provide opportunities for employment and office experience to students of the WAAC, and class schedules are arranged to facilitate up to 20 hours of professional work weekly as well as to facilitate graduation into the professions via the Intern Development Program.

BIM and the Design Process

Building information modeling, in the form of Autodesk Revit, was first offered at the WAAC in the fall semester of 2006. It was a response to the wide adoption of BIM by local architectural firms in conjunction with a vision that it would serve as a powerful design tool. It is installed on all WAAC computers and students are also encouraged to download it for free via the Autodesk

Student Community. Classes are held once a week in the evening hours, which also allows area professionals to enroll. This helps to secure the bond between the school and the local architectural community.

Initially, one beginner course was offered each semester. The class was very well received; a lottery process was required to decide who was able to take the class. There was clearly a need for additional resources, so a second Revit class was introduced. This presented an opportunity for both beginner and advanced courses. The beginner course teaches the overall BIM concepts and fundamentals. The advanced course emphasizes parametric design and understanding the software as an engine of change.

ABOUT THE CONTRIBUTING AUTHOR: JOHN SCHIPPERS

John Schippers is the BIM -implementation manager at the Grunley Construction Company in Rockville, Maryland. Prior to this, he was the BIM manager at RTKL Associates Inc. in Washington, DC. He holds a master's degree in architecture from Virginia Tech and a bachelor's degree in architecture from University at Buffalo. In his spare time, he enjoys spending time with his family, tinkering with software, learning music theory, and playing table tennis.

Studio Integration

At the WAAC, students focus most of their energy on the design studio project. It made perfect sense, then, to incorporate Revit as a tool to inform and support the design studio process. Students are strongly encouraged to model their current studio project in Revit and work through the entire semester with it. As a result, there is much more attention given to using the software as a device to complement other digital and analog tools. In addition, they are heavily invested and work hard to integrate the building information model into their final presentation.

Site Analysis

The course begins with a concentration on the site and massing tools. During the beginning of the semester, students are tasked with finding a site for their design project and understanding the context. Revit supports this process; topography, site elements, and surrounding buildings are created as an initial exercise to familiarize the students with the massing and topography tools. For more complex landscape, 3D topography files from Autodesk® AutoCAD® software are linked to the Revit model and are used to generate the topography surface. Site diagrams are created to familiarize the student with basic orientation and site placement (Figure 23.2).

Vasari

Site analysis is fueled by taking the model through various sustainability studies using Autodesk Project Vasari, a conceptual modeling tool that integrates sustainability analyses. Since Vasari reads and writes RVT files, it's very simple for students to model and analyze in Vasari and later develop the design in Revit. Vasari introduces the students to three types of analyses: solar radiation, Autodesk® Ecotect® Analysis for wind tunnels, and conceptual energy analysis. All three are used.

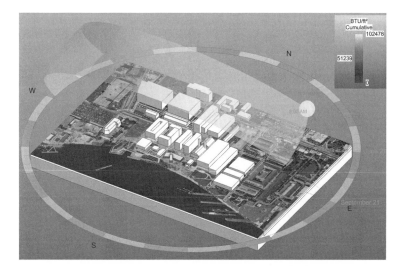

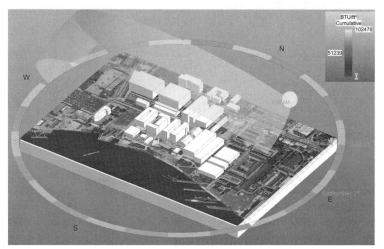

The solar radiation tool graphically displays the impact of the sun on any mass surface. Since most students are just beginning to formulate a design concept, the first exercise is to test some basic shapes on their site. This allows them to begin identifying design opportunities: A simple rectangle might reveal a pattern for photovoltaic panel placement or a simple rotation or twist might prove to be more effective at self-shading (Figure 23.3). These studies are then presented as simple diagrams, clearly indicating preliminary design decisions.

FIGURE 23.3
Vasari
solar radiation
studies

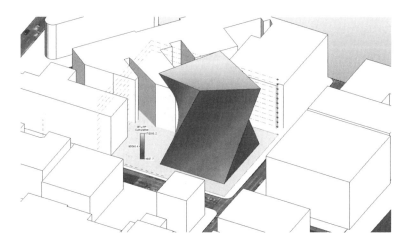

The Ecotect wind tunnel feature is another tool to help the student understand the climate of the site. It graphically illustrates wind travel patterns and gives a better understanding of the frequency and direction of the prevailing winds (Figure 23.4). As a result, students can better plan for passive cooling strategies and understand the importance of building placement. Wind data can be displayed graphically on a 2D plane or in 3D via flow lines (Figure 23.5).

FIGURE 23.4
Visualizing wind
direction and
frequency

The conceptual energy analysis tool also encourages a more sustainable design process because it presents a myriad of data that can be analyzed and studied further. Once the student defines the zone layout and basic glazing percentage of the building, the tool runs the analysis on Autodesk servers, leaving the host computer free to continue modeling. In a couple of minutes, a PDF is presented that gives a number of useful graphs such as fuel costs, electricity costs, heating loads, cooling loads, and annual carbon emissions (Figure 23.6). With this data, students can begin making more informed design decisions.

FIGURE 23.5
Vasari 3D wind studies with flow lines

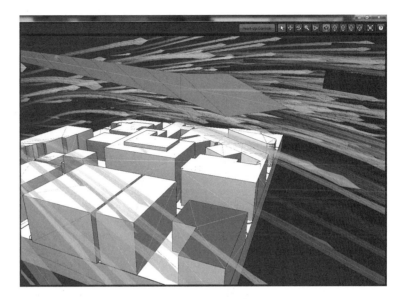

Design options become critical at this point because the Vasari data is most useful for comparative studies. It's not uncommon for students to propose 10 to 15 solutions and perform studies on each to compare the pros and cons. This comparison workflow might reveal patterns and encourages the student to further research implications of specific changes.

Conceptual Becomes Architectural

At this point, about halfway through the semester, the transition begins from conceptual to real: linking geometric forms to architectural elements. Mass objects can be used to generate architectural components such as walls, floors, and roofs. This workflow is ideal because the architectural elements are in sync with the mass; if the mass changes, the architectural elements can also be updated to match. Because of this relationship, the process does not have to be linear. A student may begin to transition to architectural elements but at any time can go back to the mass form to run additional energy studies. If the design changes, it's a simple click of a button to sync the architectural elements to the mass geometry.

Students are also encouraged to use the building information model for other purposes, for example, as an underlay to sketch on top of or to extract dimensions to build a physical model. The ability to visualize the design on screen before building it as a model has saved the students much time and money in mistakes, working out issues virtually rather than physically. Many also take advantage of the school's laser cutter, using the model to generate laser-cut components to assemble.

FIGURE 23.6
Conceptual energy
analysis

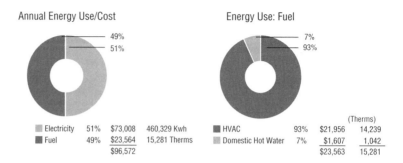

Annual Energy Use/Cost

■ Electricity	51%	$73,008	460,329 Kwh
■ Fuel	49%	$23,564	15,281 Therms
		$96,572	

Energy Use: Fuel

			(Therms)
■ HVAC	93%	$21,956	14,239
■ Domestic Hot Water	7%	$1,607	1,042
		$23,563	15,281

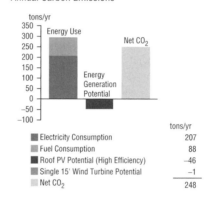

Annual Carbon Emissions

	tons/yr
■ Electricity Consumption	207
■ Fuel Consumption	88
■ Roof PV Potential (High Efficiency)	−46
■ Single 15' Wind Turbine Potential	−1
■ Net CO_2	248

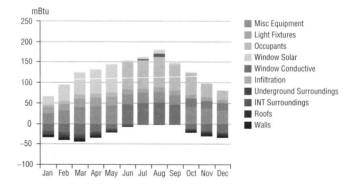

Monthly Cooling Load

■ Misc Equipment
■ Light Fixtures
■ Occupants
■ Window Solar
■ Window Conductive
■ Infiltration
■ Underground Surroundings
■ INT Surroundings
■ Roofs
■ Walls

Parametric Modeling

Parametric modeling is introduced in the beginner class, but it is explored more heavily in the
advanced session. Students are expected to model their studio project with special emphasis
on the parametric relationships of forms and objects. Parameter-driven forms allow students to

quickly study multiple options and make changes very quickly while maintaining the key relationships of their design.

The Curtain Panel By Pattern tool becomes very important, providing a means to rationalize complex surfaces. This gets the student thinking about how a complex form might get built and how best to model it to achieve that result (Figure 23.7).

FIGURE 23.7
Divided surface

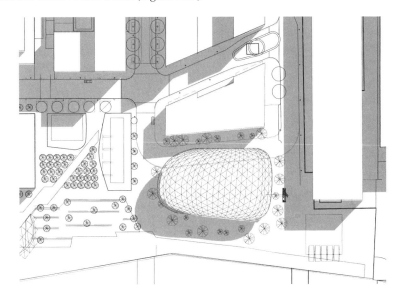

Presentation Techniques

Successfully modeling a project and using BIM as an effective design tool is very important, but that might be severely mitigated if the student is unable to clearly illustrate their design intent. Autodesk is rapidly improving the presentation tools in Revit; many effects that required Photoshop or Illustrator in the past can now be accomplished directly in Revit (Figure 23.8).

FIGURE 23.8
Revit section

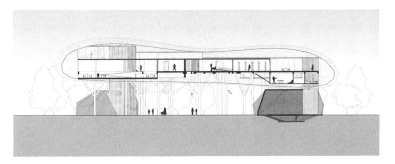

One of the biggest advantages of working with BIM is the ability to show nongraphical information in a graphical format. View filters become key to accomplishing this; it's very simple to distinguish between structural and nonstructural walls by highlighting the bearing walls with a color. This kind of graphical override not only allows students to better communicate their design intent, it also updates dynamically. In the past, this would be done in a postproduction software package like Adobe Illustrator. This process was time consuming and very linear; the drawing had to be imported and drawn over. If something changed, the file would need to be imported again and the graphics would need to be modified manually. Today, all of these presentation diagrams are kept in Revit and updated in real time (Figure 23.9).

FIGURE 23.9
Plan with filter applied

Throughout the semester, new rendering techniques are introduced. Out-of-the-box Revit rendering, via mental ray®, is sufficient for many purposes, but there are some instances where the student may either want to simplify the geometry or utilize advanced options. 3d Studio Max is presented to give the students these additional features. Revit can export to the FBX file format, which will maintain all materials assignments, lights, render appearances, and sky settings. One of the most popular techniques is one known as an ambient/occlusion base rendering, or dirtmap. This technique overrides all material settings and gives the appearance of a museum board model (Figure 23.10). It's extremely simple to apply and produces quickly rendered images. Revit recently introduced this functionality as well in the form of ambient shadows as a feature in the Graphic Display Options dialog box (Figure 23.11).

FIGURE 23.10
Dirtmap rendering
from 3ds Max

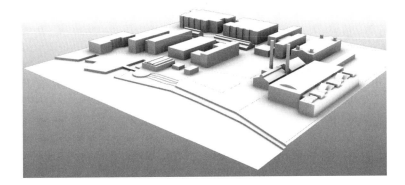

FIGURE 23.11
Revit hidden line
view with ambient
shadows

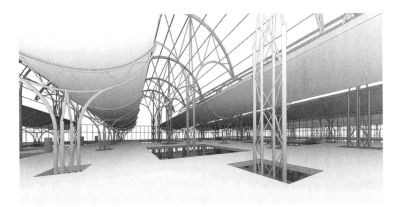

End of Semester Party

At the end of each semester, every student is required to pin up a final board showcasing their Revit project to celebrate the end-of-semester party. This is an informal event. Students are not required to speak about their work; it should speak for itself. All students and faculty are invited to celebrate, and local design firms are also requested to join. This has proven to be a great networking event, connecting students to potential employers. Local design professionals peruse the work and discuss it with students. BIM experience in an architect intern is highly sought after, so many professionals come to the party looking to establish relationships with potential future employees. Many students take positions with local firms and quickly take a leadership role with the Revit implementation. Over the years, there have been a few who got "stuck" with firms still using AutoCAD. When I run into them at school, it's always the same story: "I'd much rather be using Revit."

Student Showcase

Here you will find some examples of student work. Each of these students used BIM in a different way to support and inform their design. This augmented process proved to be a very valuable learning experience for each student.

Jonathan Brockett

In this student proposal for a center for musical studies on the Washington, DC, waterfront, the school itself and the park space with performance halls took on two very different characters. The school floats above as a cloud while the performance halls and park rest in the public ground floor. From this park a visitor can see the show created by the large-scale music visualizer that is part of the belly of the cloud school. It was challenging to try to develop this abstract idea into a more believable architectural project. Revit made for a much faster workflow when moving from these basic concepts and ideas, allowing me to see a more fleshed-out and readable project sooner (Figure 23.12).

FIGURE 23.12
Night rendering

The changeability and malleability of Revit made it possible to easily connect and alter parts of the project while maintaining the clarity and accuracy of the drawings. Having the ability to translate imported masses into Revit models and drawings certainly opened up a whole range of possibilities, giving depth and dimension to thin geometry. When dealing with the structure specifically, it was very intuitive in Revit to develop the musical forest of columns I saw underneath the belly of the school. All of this freed me to further my concept and create strong, believable images to make it understandable to others.

Once I developed and realized my project in Revit, it was easiest for me to export to 3ds Max for renders because I am comfortable using it. The model that comes out of Revit is extremely detailed and would take much longer to make in a typical modeling program. Plus, you would have to make the drawings separate when not using Revit. In short, the import and export functions of Revit serve to make it even more usable and malleable, especially for users new to it (Figure 23.13).

FIGURE 23.13
Interior rendering

Byron Knowlson

With this 70-unit multifamily housing project, Revit proved to be a vastly more efficient way of modeling and drafting than other programs. Within the overall form of the building, there are eight different unit variations. Revit allowed for each unit variation to be built in its own file and then linked in to the main building file. The various units could then be stacked, rotated, and mirrored to create the overall composition of the building (Figure 23.14).

With each of the units linked, changes to individual unit styles could be made in the base files, and then each instance of the unit in the main file would update in real time. This allowed for different building elevations and street perspectives to be viewed quickly, without the need to edit every unit separately. If a bedroom projection was extended, it was easy to see how that one change would affect the whole of the façade, where every one of those projections would extend simultaneously. This method of working allowed for faster decision making because a change could be analyzed in plan, section, elevation, and perspective simultaneously, ensuring that the design decision was working equally in all parts of the project.

In addition, all of the unit types were built using the same assembly of parts, arranged in varying ways and quantities, creating units ranging from 600 to 1,200 square feet. Again, if these components are linked and if, for instance, a bath core was changed, it would update in every unit where that style of bath core was present.

For this type of large-scale multifamily project, the nesting of components within units, units within the building, and the building within the site provides a way to edit any element in the building as well as multiple methods of ensuring that each of those decisions stayed true to the design intent (Figure 23.15).

FIGURE 23.14
Stacked
axonometric

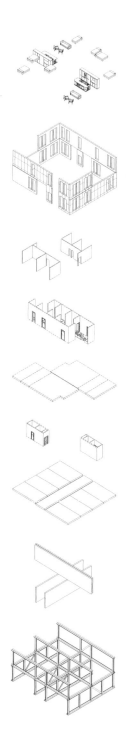

FIGURE 23.15
Interior rendering

FIGURE 23.15
Interior rendering

Scott Archer

In the design of a fashion design center, it becomes evident that the skin (or clothes) of the building is just as important as the fashions housed within. During my fourth year of architecture design education, I was tasked with a studio project focusing on the design of a building to house the teaching, making, showing, and selling of fashions within a constricted urban site and surrounding environment. Because of site restrictions and applicable building codes, the building's skin had a profound and tangible impact on the quality of spaces inside. Through parametric modeling in Autodesk Revit, I was able to digitally test, precisely refine, and accurately represent the design of the skin as a part of the entire building (Figure 23.16).

The skin system design is composed of a series of glass and screened panels set at 45 degrees to one another, creating a zigzag motif in plan. Comprising several configurations, the building's panels each operate in a different way and are placed according the programmatic requirements of the interior spaces. The panel configurations consisted of folding, pivoting, sliding, separated, stationary, and structural. Often when complex or operable building elements are designed, they have to be modeled multiple times in order to see all the operations of the elements. However, through the parametric modeling of Revit, I was able to efficiently model the entire skin by modeling one module of the skin system and adding an instance parameter to repeat it over the perimeter of the space enclosed. I was also able to include instance parameters to independently open and close the glass and screen elements of each component in various ways according to the panel type. For example, the pivoting panels swing from a common hinge point, while the sliding panels slide parallel to the window framing, and the folding panels collapse onto each other, completely opening and stacking at one side. Parametric modeling of the skin components of my design greatly increased the efficiency of the modeling, analysis, and refinement processes.

FIGURE 23.16
Panel
configurations

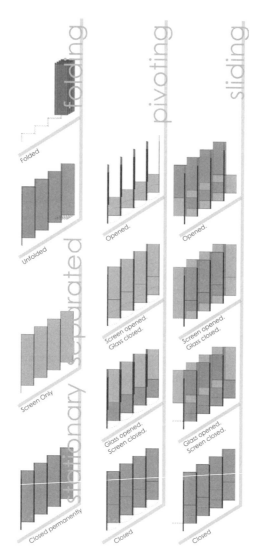

In addition to the parametric control of the panels Revit allowed, the representation of the operability was also much more legible in plan. Within the family design, hidden lines could be included for when the panels are in the open position to show the closed state and vice versa. Filters also allowed easy color coding of the various types of panels (folding, pivoting, sliding) to clearly show where specific panel functions were to be placed throughout the building. The well-developed connection between the three-dimensional modeled object and the two-dimensional representation is extremely significant and important in the use of Revit in the architectural design process. This project's design was completed more efficiently and was much more developed than what would have been possible without the parametric modeling and representation techniques that Revit provides (Figure 23.17).

FIGURE 23.17
Plan views

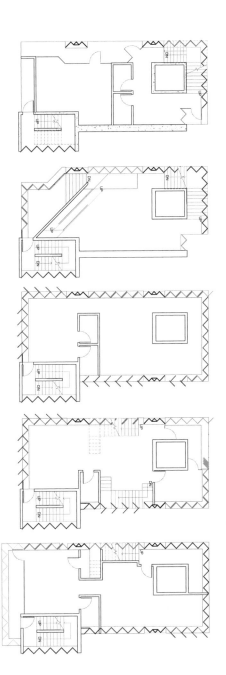

Wei Yao

My project was a green building design in the urban environment. The site was a typical townhouse lot in Washington, DC (Figure 23.18).

FIGURE 23.18
Solar radiation
studies

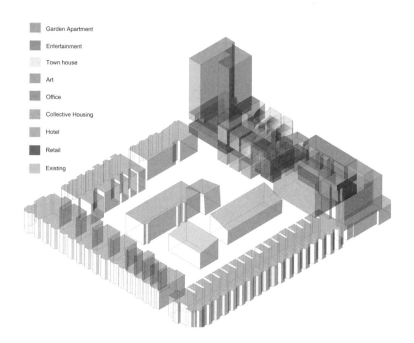

Garden Apartment

Entertainment

Town house

Art

Office

Collective Housing

Hotel

Retail

Existing

One of the major goals of the project was to use the architectural design to achieve energy savings. Revit allowed me to create a precisely built 3D model, which was very helpful for the design research. The solar radiation plug-in allowed me to take full advantage of the solar energy for all seasons. It provided a solid design basis to identify the spaces that needed shading design in summertime. By researching and testing the massing and components of the building, I was able to show how a natural ventilation system, air flowing inside and through the building, is clearly organized.

The Revit massing tool proved to be the ideal method for diagramming the different functions of the building and clearly communicating the layout (Figure 23.19).

Jose DaSilva

This studio project is a library design in Old Town Alexandria, Virginia, located near the Potomac River. The Vasari solar radiation and energy analysis tools were valuable at the start, helping me orient the building. The ability to show real-time shadows aided with the orientation of the canopy and roof design to achieve the protection the library required and the desired aesthetics.

Using Revit from conceptual to final design has helped me develop my studio project and provided greater efficiency. By defining parametric relationships for the structural elements, I had the flexibility to change the column sizes and trusses to any size I needed to fit the scale of the project and structural requirements. Also, updating elevations and floor plans is much easier using Revit, allowing more time to develop other parts of the project (Figure 23.20).

FIGURE 23.19
Massing studies

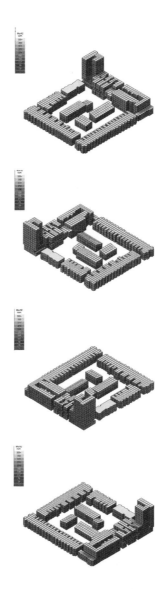

FIGURE 23.20
Overall building

The Bottom Line

Use Vasari early. Vasari makes it very easy to locate your building in the world and generate a quick context model. Even if you don't know the exact orientation and location, get it as close as possible during early design iteration.

Master It How would you create various design options in real-world context?

Utilize design options. Don't be afraid to model many different configurations and run them through different analyses. Every exercise is a learning experience and you may discover a pattern or an opportunity to exploit on your specific site.

Master It How would you create different options as massing studies within the same file?

Leveraging Vasari files in Revit Opening a Vasari file in Revit is perfectly fine because it's in the RVT file format, but you might notice that you don't have many components loaded; this is because the file was generated in Vasari. This may be a problem, especially if you'd like to use a custom template with all of your content preloaded.

Master It How would you open a Vasari file so you could take care of the full suite of design tools available in Revit?

Chapter 24

Essential Hardware

While Autodesk® Revit® Architecture software is a fantastic design tool on its own, there's a great ecosystem of hardware that is a wonderful complement. When most people think of hardware for Revit, they're referring to the computer that's directly in front of them. But it's much more. How you initiate a design process can be as intuitive as sketching. How you interface with the model can be much more elegant than "drawing" with a mouse. As the design develops, navigating the Revit model can be much more graceful than commands triggered with a keyboard.

In this chapter, you'll learn to:

◆ Make use of the iPad to quickly capture design ideas for use in Revit

◆ Utilize Wacom tablets to improve productivity during design and design review

◆ Employ 3Dconnextion motion controllers to intuitively navigate Revit

iPad

Architects have long sketched in order to capture design ideas. And since the iPad (Figure 24.1) was introduced, a number of sketching and drawing applications have developed that allow designers to quickly and easily capture design ideas in a digital format.

Capturing Images

Initially the iPad didn't have a camera, which meant that you needed to import a photo or other background from another source if you wanted some context for your design. But now the iPad features a 5-megapixel camera for both still images and video. While a 5-megapixel camera is pretty light by professional digital photography standards, it's more than sufficient for taking quick site photos and then using those images as backgrounds for early rapid iteration.

As for taking photos, I'd strongly recommend using a good panoramic photo tool. This allows you to exceed the boundaries of a single image. Microsoft's Photosynth (www.photosynth.net) is a really terrific tool and it's free! For example, Figure 24.2 shows a single photograph taken from the iPad. Not too bad — but lacks a lot of context.

FIGURE 24.1
The Apple iPad

FIGURE 24.2
A single photo from
the iPad

On the other hand, Figure 24.3 illustrates what's possible with a panoramic photo tool like Photosynth. This image provides context that exceeds the boundaries of a single 5-megapixel image.

FIGURE 24.3
A panoramic
image taken with
Photosynth

But if you still need to import background images from other sources like a web page or email, it's a simple matter of saving the image to your Photo app, and there are two good options. The first option is to browse to the image (web page, email, and so forth) and then press and hold your finger on it. This will reveal a menu that will allow you to save the image to your Photo app (Figure 24.4).

FIGURE 24.4
Saving an image from a web page

But what if you need to capture an entire web page on the iPad? There's a less-known but really helpful method of taking a screen capture from an iPad. To do this, simultaneously press and hold the power and home button and then release them. The screen will flash white for a second, indicating that a screen capture has occurred. The resulting image will be stored in your Photo app.

Digital Sketching

Once you've got your background and other images in the iPad, you're ready to use them as context for capturing quick design ideas. The best design app for sketching I've found so far is Autodesk® SketchBook® Pro for iPad ($4.99 on the App store). There is a free version called SketchBook Express by Autodesk that will give you a good taste of SketchBook Pro if you're hesitant to buy the full version.

The learning curve is very shallow while the tool set is very complete. There's a full suite of brush types that will allow you to sketch freehand (Figure 24.5) as well as the ability to create multiple layers that will allow you to sketch multiple design ideas using the same background image.

SketchBook Pro allows you to import photos and other images from a number of sources, including your Photo library and Dropbox folder, or you can directly use the iPad Camera tool. Once you're done sketching, you want to get the image off the iPad so you can share it with the others. There are a number of good options for sharing your sketch such as sending it to your Dropbox folder, or via email. You can even post it to Twitter.

FIGURE 24.5
Freehand sketching
on the iPad

Once the images are free from the iPad, you can use the resulting sketches on their own or import them into Revit as 2D context (such as plans and elevations). Now you and your design team can quickly and easily start massing and modeling in context with your design sketches. This process is covered in more detail in Chapter 2, "Principles: UI and Project Organization."

Stylus vs. Finger

Even though the iPad was designed to be used without a stylus, it's pretty difficult to get the right touch and feel when you're sketching without one. For one thing, your fingers really get in the way of seeing what you're sketching. So I use a stylus for taking notes. And having bought a few, I think there's some good options (as well as some not-so-good ones).

There are different capacitive tip types, and if you're not careful you'll select a stylus that will give you very poor results. One stylus tip type is not very dense — it's almost foam-like. Another type is dense and rubberized. Both will flex based on the amount of pressure you put on the tip and offer varying levels of sensitivity and accuracy.

The foam-type stylus pens are usually cheaper (less than $10). But the problem with a more foam-like tip is that you'll have to push harder in order for it to register a stroke. As a result, you won't be able to use lighter sketch strokes. But worse, the foam tip deforms over time and accuracy is reduced. Then you'll have to buy another stylus.

In my experience, the rubberized tips are a bit more expensive, but they last longer, don't deform, and are more sensitive. The Bamboo Stylus by Wacom is more expensive compared to a stylus that has a foam-like tip. But it works great with the iPad and comes in a nice selection of colors (Figure 24.6).

FIGURE 24.6
Wacom Bamboo
stylus for the iPad

Wacom Tablet

Designing with a mouse in one hand while inputting commands with a keyboard with the other hand is a pretty common approach since the advent of CAD, and the process hasn't evolved much with Revit. But it didn't used to be that way. Hand drafting allowed you to move your whole arm for broad strokes, use your wrist for more careful lines, and then apply only your fingertips for the finest of work. Zooming in and out meant standing back from your work or moving nearer for closer inspection. So it shouldn't be any surprise when someone develops a painful wrist condition. It's hardly natural to keep your wrist practically immobilized to carefully control mouse movements for hours at a time.

The Wacom tablet series is a great return to first practices. All of them use a stylus rather than a mouse as input devices. Furthermore, they offer levels of sensitivity far beyond what's available on the iPad. But these devices aren't necessarily competing with your iPad. They're really competing with your keyboard and monitor.

I think the best option is a Cintiq series because it allows you to work directly on the screen. There are three models ranging in diagonal screen sizes of 12", 22", and 24", shown from left to right in Figure 24.7.

FIGURE 24.7
The Wacom Cintiq

Digital Modeling

I've used the older Cintiq DTU-2231 extensively with Revit, and the bottom line is *I'll never go back*. Coupled with the wonderful handwriting recognition in Windows (it's far better than OS X), there's practically no reason to use a keyboard and mouse with Revit. All the familiar right-click contextual menus are available from the pressure-sensitive pen that prompts you when you can write text (Figure 24.8).

FIGURE 24.8
Contextual hand-
writing in Revit

Initially, using a touch screen felt slower after years of rapid picks and clicks, and it can seem a bit foreign to be reaching across the screen to access commands that seem more distant than a quick flick of the mouse or a keyboard shortcut. But this is a temporary condition.

Soon a natural rhythm sets in that feels far more efficient and elegant than going back and forth between picking something with a mouse, using the keyboard to type some text, and going back to the mouse. Working directly on the screen eliminates this annoying back and forth.

A Few Best Practices

One of the really great features in Revit 2013 is the ability to double-click a family component to edit the family. This is made even more elegant with a touch screen and a quick double-click of the pen. But the really nice thing about editing a family or entire project from a touch screen is the ability to focus in a way that's not possible staring head up at your monitor.

With a touch screen, it feels far more focused and free of distraction. You can also sit closer to a touch screen because there's no keyboard between you what you see. I've found the most natural position is much like you would approach sketching on a large sheet of paper. The paper is resting flat (or nearly flat) on your desk and one wrist is resting on the paper as you sketch — but in this case your wrist is resting on the touch screen. And this also means your peripheral vision is clear of the typical clutter that comes with looking up at a monitor.

This leads to another point. Since I'm right-handed, reaching across to the left side of the screen to change views and modify parameters isn't very ergonomic. This may seem a bit strange, but I suggest you rearrange the Project Browser and Properties palette so they're on the right side of the screen (Figure 24.9). It really works better this way!

FIGURE 24.9
Preferred screen
layout for the Cintiq

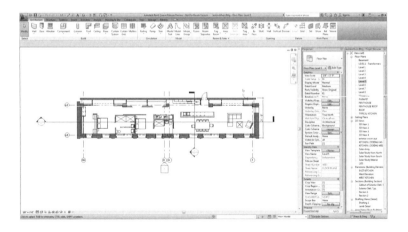

So what's the catch? Well, there are two and I wouldn't consider them significant in any way.

First, keyboard shortcuts aren't really an option without a physical keyboard. But I've found this really isn't an issue most of the time because I'm using shortcuts that are available from a right-click of the stylus (especially the Create Similar command). What I really miss is the ability to pan, zoom, and rotate as a keyboard and mouse combination. But I think there's a better way, which I'll cover in the next section.

Second, handwriting recognition struggles with writing dimensions (unless you want to tap on the keyboard option rather than use the handwriting tool) in feet and inches. So rather than write 8'-6", you'll want to use the decimal form of 8.5. That's about it. Whether you're working on a large floor plan or creating highly refined details, it's far more enjoyable when working directly on a touch screen.

3Dconnexion

Navigating the model in a conventional method in Revit means you're jumping between the mouse and the keyboard in order to pan, zoom, and rotate using both hands. But what if you wanted to navigate with just one hand? Well, that's where 3Dconnexion fills the void with its really terrific selection of 3D motion controllers. From left to right is the SpacePilot Pro, the SpaceExplorer, and SpaceNavigator (Figure 24.10).

FIGURE 24.10
3D mice by
3Dconnexion

After the drivers are installed, there's an addition icon at the bottom of the Revit Navigational Bar that looks like the SpacePilot. All the 3D mice have buttons for shortcut keys that can be mapped to a wide range of commands. This icon allows you to customize any of the buttons and other default settings (Figure 24.11) of the 3D mouse.

FIGURE 24.11
Shortcut access
from the Navigation
Bar

Zooming, panning, and rotating are completely intuitive with 3Dconnexion's 3D mice. After testing a number of models, I really like the SpaceExplorer for home use. But I expect power users will be more interested in the SpacePilot Pro. In addition to having some really great features for Revit, it allows you to map other application shortcuts, including email, calendar events, and more for quick access.

For portability there are two models of SpaceNavigator. The one for notebooks is a bit lighter, which helps with portability (as well as being slightly more expensive) compared to the regular SpaceNavigator. But because it is slightly heavier than the portable version, I find that the regular SpaceNavigator stays put on the desk as a result.

A Few Best Practices

This is where it all comes together. I mentioned in the previous section that navigating the Revit model with a touch screen alone could be challenging because there's no mouse-keyboard navigational control. Yet the 3D mice really excel in this area. As a result, they're a wonderful complement to using a touch screen. Once again, you'll find that a conventional mouse and keyboard become pretty unnecessary as far as Revit is concerned with this kind of setup.

All the 3D mice have shortcut buttons, but the SpaceNavigator has only two buttons. If you travel a lot, you might think you'll miss all the other buttons. But I don't think that's the case. There are only two really essential buttons you'll want to map for use with Revit: Zoom To Fit and Esc.

Zoom To Fit allows you to quickly see everything in your view and is really helpful with orienting you in the model after you've been zoomed in and you're panning around a floor plan for a while.

The other essential key that I map to the 3D mouse button is the Esc key. This allows you to easily stop a certain command without having to use the right-click function on the stylus.

Over the past year, I've found the ultimate setup for using Revit is a Cintiq touch screen and 3Dconnexion navigator mouse (Figure 24.12). My laptop sits just off to the side, running everything (usually with the lid closed). All the design just happens right in front of me. And the weirdest part is that I've found I really enjoy handwriting!

FIGURE 24.12
Cintiq touch screen and 3Dconnexion navigator mouse makes a great Revit setup.

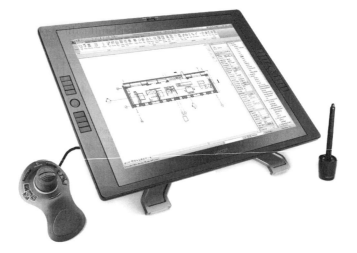

The Bottom Line

Sketching with the iPad Architects have sketched for a long time and in locations other than the office. Being able to sketch in an intuitive fashion really helps get the creative juices flowing.

Master It Even though an iPad is a great schematic sketching tool, where else might it be helpful as you move from design to construction?

Designing with the Wacom Cintiq   Once you become accustomed to sketching directly on a screen, why would you give this up as the design progresses? Not only is it more elegant to work directly on-screen, our wrists didn't evolve to remain artificially rigid in order to manipulate a mouse.

Master It   What other roles could benefit from using touch screens and working directly on the screen rather than jumping between keyboard and mouse?

Navigating with 3Dconnexion Navigator Mice   Once you become accustomed to working directly on-screen with a stylus, you'll start looking for a more elegant way to navigate the model without constantly relying on the keyboard and a lot of keyboard shortcuts.

Master It   Constantly zooming in and out is distracting and disorienting during the design process when you're working on your own. But are there other times that you'll need to navigate the model and increase communication?

Chapter 25

Getting Acquainted with the API

If you've ever wanted to learn how to customize or extend the functionality of Autodesk® Revit® Architecture software but thought that learning to program might be too difficult or time consuming, I recommend that you give it a try. In this chapter you will learn the basics of the Revit API and even build and install your first add-in. As with anything, if you start out small and practice, the concepts become manageable and possible to master. The benefits obtained from even a basic understanding of programming can be limitless. In this chapter, you will build an add-in that will generate 3D masses from room elements.

In this chapter, you'll learn to:

♦ Understand the basics of the Revit API

♦ Write, debug, and install your own API projects

Introducing the Revit API

ABOUT THE CONTRIBUTING AUTHOR: DON RUDDER

Don Rudder is the CTO and director of software development for Case Design, Inc. He has extensive experience in .NET and web development for the AEC industry. His background, spanning over 15 years, is primarily in the MEP disciplines where he has served as designer, CAD manager, and customization consultant.

Don maintains a blog focusing on all things Revit and especially the API at www.RevitNet .blogspot.com.

An application programming interface (API) is a source-code-based specification intended to be used as an interface for other software components to communicate with each other. APIs are a common feature throughout successful software applications and are typically developed either by or under the direction of the original application developer. APIs serve as a means to expose core functionality through a collection of publicly exposed object classes along with fully functional properties and methods. It is easy to understand how impossible it is to generate a feature-rich application so robust that there is no need or request from its users to extend or customize it. This is the exact problem that an API is designed to solve. Companies typically spend enormous resources on their API development, and Autodesk is no different when it comes to its suite of BIM tools.

The Revit API is built on top of the Microsoft .NET Framework 4.0. In my personal opinion, this is one of the easiest programming frameworks to learn. The .NET framework has been around since 2002 and supports several languages, all with equal functionality. The two primary .NET languages that you will see used most commonly with the Revit API are Visual Basic .NET and C#. The best way to learn an API is obviously from great code examples and documentation, which leads us into our next topic, the Revit 2013 software development kit (SDK).

Revit 2013 Software Development Kit

Learning an API without proper samples and documentation can make for a very frustrating journey. There are over 25 working code samples contained in the 2013 SDK, some in VB.NET but most written in C#. The Revit 2013 Software Development (SDK) can be installed from the main installation media by clicking the Install Tools And Utilities button and then clicking Revit Software Development Kit, as shown in Figure 25.1.

FIGURE 25.1
Installing the Revit SDK

The Revit 2013 SDK is a valuable resource containing documentation and .NET sample projects that demonstrate how to do all kinds of things in the Revit API. The samples are updated fairly regularly on www.autodesk.com/revit and are an excellent starting point for getting your feet wet with the API. The Getting Started with the Revit API.doc document included with the SDK will help you understand the basic requirements to getting started with the Revit API. The SDK includes macro samples, point cloud indexing API samples, Revit Server SDK samples, and Revit Extensions samples (REX) as well as a couple of useful utilities. The Add-In Manager and the critical Revit Lookup utility are among these utilities.

The Revit Lookup Utility

After installing the Revit SDK, be sure not to overlook the Revit Lookup utility. The Revit Lookup utility is by far the most useful sample in the SDK. As you learn to develop in Revit, this tool will be your guiding light. It allows you to peek inside a model or family document and truly inspect the inner workings. This tool is great for identifying what elements and properties are accessible through the API and generally how to gain access to them. Revit Lookup also has a function that allows you to snoop through the current selection, making it easier than ever to see the data behind the elements that you are most interested in.

You will need to build the sample project (RevitLookup.dll) and copy it along with the included installation manifest file RevitLookup.addin included in the sample project into the .addins directory in order to use it in your Revit sessions. Once you have compiled and installed the utility, a ribbon drop-down menu to access the tool is available, as shown in Figure 25.2.

FIGURE 25.2
Accessing Revit Lookup from the ribbon

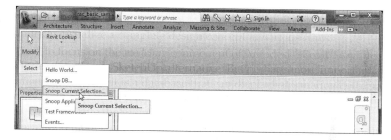

Revit API Project Types

There are basically three types of API projects you can develop with the Revit API: external commands, external applications, and database-level applications. The three types are distinct in lifetime and scope. All three project types are loaded in through an .addin manifest file. You can find everything you want to know about manifest files in the Getting Started with the Revit API.doc document in the Revit 2013 SDK.

External Commands

External commands are accessible by default from the Add-Ins tab under the External Tools drop-down button and have access to the Revit application and documents collection. Pseudo data generated by external commands will remain in memory only from the time the command is executed to when the command completes. Any objects in memory or references held by the command are destroyed upon completion of the command. This basically means that data will not persist in memory alone from one external command to another. If you need to share any kind of information from one external command to another, you have to employ a means to store this data either by parameters inside your model or by an external file of some sort.

The IExternalCommand interface is a required implementation for all external commands and must accompany a public function named Execute. This function requires three arguments — CommandData, Message, and Elements — and always returns either Result.Cancelled, Result.Succeeded, or Result.Failed:

CommandData   The CommandData parameter provides access to both the application information and the model database information. This is where you will get access to anything you need inside Revit.

Message   The Message parameter is used to report bad news to the user upon unsuccessful or canceled command executions. A meager limit of 1,023 characters exists for this message, meaning longer strings will be truncated. Don't worry; a failure message that is too long will not result in a failure within your failure.

Elements The Elements parameter is typically empty but can be used to highlight or display an element selection created by your command. This parameter can also be used to display related elements upon a returned command failure.

Empty boilerplate sample classes implementing this interface are shown here in both VB.NET (Listing 25.1) and C# (Listing 25.2).

LISTING 25.1:   VB.NET *IExternalCommand* example

```vbnet
Imports Autodesk.Revit.Attributes
Imports Autodesk.Revit.DB
Imports Autodesk.Revit.UI

<Transaction(TransactionMode.Manual)>
Public Class Command
    Implements IExternalCommand
    Public Function Execute(ByVal commandData As ExternalCommandData,
                        ByRef message As String,
                        ByVal elements As ElementSet) As Result _
                    Implements IExternalCommand.Execute

        Try
            ' Command Code Goes Here
            Return Result.Succeeded
        Catch ex As Exception
            message = ex.Message
            Return Result.Failed
        End Try
    End Function
End Class
```

LISTING 25.2:   C# *IExternalCommand* example

```csharp
using Autodesk.Revit.Attributes;
using Autodesk.Revit.DB;
using Autodesk.Revit.UI;

[Transaction(TransactionMode.Manual)]
public class Command : IExternalCommand
{
    public Result Execute(ExternalCommandData commandData,
                        ref string message,
                        ElementSet elements)

    {
        try
        {
            // Command Code Goes Here
```

```
            // Return Success
            return Result.Succeeded;
        }
        catch (Exception ex)
        {
            message = ex.Message;
            return Result.Failed;
        }
    }
}
```

External Applications

External applications are loaded when Revit starts and remain loaded until Revit shuts down. One of the biggest advantages that applications have over commands is that applications provide access to Revit document events. Applications are accessible from either the Add-Ins tab of the ribbon or a custom ribbon tab named whatever you want.

The IExternalApplication interface is a required implementation for all Revit API external applications and must accompany the OnStartup and OnShutdown events that fire off when Revit launches (OnStartup) and when it closes (OnShutdown). Empty boilerplate samples of this interface are shown here in both VB.NET (Listing 25.3) and C# (Listing 25.4).

LISTING 25.3:   VB.NET *IExternalApplication* example

```
Imports Autodesk.Revit.ApplicationServices
Imports Autodesk.Revit.Attributes
Imports Autodesk.Revit.DB
Imports Autodesk.Revit.UI

<Transaction(TransactionMode.Manual)>
Class Application
    Implements IExternalApplication
    ''' <summary>
    ''' Implement the external application when Revit starts,
    ''' before a file or default template is actually loaded.
    ''' </summary>
    ''' <param name="application">The Controlled Application</param>
    ''' <returns>Return the status of the external application</returns>
    Public Function OnStartup(ByVal application As UIControlledApplication) _
            As Result Implements IExternalApplication.OnStartup
        ' Add Your Application Code Here

        ' Return Success
        Return Result.Succeeded
    End Function

    ''' <summary>
```

```
''' This event happens as the session is ending,
''' All documents are closed by now
''' </summary>
''' <param name="application">The Controlled Application</param>
''' <returns>Return the status of the external application</returns>
Public Function OnShutdown(ByVal application As UIControlledApplication) _
            As Result Implements IExternalApplication.OnShutdown

    ' Add All Event Unsubscribe Code Here

    ' Return Success
    Return Result.Succeeded
End Function
End Class
```

LISTING 25.4: C# *IExternalApplication* example

```
using Autodesk.Revit.ApplicationServices;
using Autodesk.Revit.Attributes;
using Autodesk.Revit.DB;
using Autodesk.Revit.UI;

[Transaction(TransactionMode.Manual)]
class Application : IExternalApplication
{
    /// <summary>
    /// Implement the external application when Revit starts,
    /// before a file or default template is actually loaded.
    /// </summary>
    /// <param name="application">The Controlled Application</param>
    /// <returns>Return the status of the external application</returns>
    public Result OnStartup(UIControlledApplication application)
    {
        // Add Your Application Code Here

        // Return Success
        return Result.Succeeded;
    }

    /// <summary>
    /// This event happens as the session is ending,
    /// All documents are closed by now
    /// </summary>
    /// <param name="application">The Controlled Application</param>
    /// <returns>Return the status of the external application</returns>
    public Result OnShutdown(UIControlledApplication application)
```

```
        {

            // Add All Event Unsubscribe Code Here

            // Return Success
            return Result.Succeeded;
        }
    }
```

Database-Level Applications

Database-level applications were new to the 2013 API and are similar to external applications in that they both allow subscription to events and persist throughout the life of a Revit session. They are different from external commands in that they do not allow you to make any calls to RevitUI.dll. This includes adding any UI controls to the ribbon.

The IExternalDBApplication interface is a required implementation for all Revit API external database applications. External database applications must accompany the OnStartup and OnShutdown events that fire off when Revit launches (OnStartup) and when it closes (OnShutdown), similarly to standard IExternalApplication projects. Empty boilerplate samples of this interface are shown here in both VB.NET (Listing 25.5) and C# (Listing 25.6).

LISTING 25.5: VB.NET *IExternalDBApplication* example

```
Imports Autodesk.Revit.ApplicationServices
Imports Autodesk.Revit.Attributes
Imports Autodesk.Revit.DB
Imports Autodesk.Revit.UI

<Transaction(TransactionMode.Manual)>
Class DbApplication
    Implements IExternalDBApplication
    ''' <summary>
    ''' Implement the db application when Revit starts,
    ''' before a file or default template is actually loaded.
    ''' </summary>
    ''' <param name="application">The Controlled Application</param>
    ''' <returns>Return the status of the external application</returns>
    Public Function OnStartup(application As ControlledApplication) _
        As ExternalDBApplicationResult Implements IExternalDBApplication.OnStartup

        ' Add Your DbApplication Code Here

        ' Return Success
        Return Result.Succeeded
    End Function

    ''' <summary>
```

```
''' This event happens as the session is ending,
''' All documents are closed by now
''' </summary>
''' <param name="application">The Controlled Application</param>
''' <returns>Return the status of the external application</returns>
Public Function OnShutdown(application As ControlledApplication) _
As ExternalDBApplicationResult Implements IExternalDBApplication.OnShutdown

        ' Add All Event Unsubscribe Code Here

        ' Return Success
        Return Result.Succeeded
    End Function
End Class
```

LISTING 25.6:   C# *IExternalDBApplication* example

```csharp
using Autodesk.Revit.ApplicationServices;
using Autodesk.Revit.Attributes;
using Autodesk.Revit.DB;
using Autodesk.Revit.UI;

[Transaction(TransactionMode.Manual)]
class DbApplication : IExternalDBApplication
{
    /// <summary>
    /// Implement the db application when Revit starts,
    /// before a file or default template is actually loaded.
    /// </summary>
    /// <param name="application">The Controlled Application</param>
    /// <returns>Return the status of the external application</returns>
    public Result OnStartup(ControlledApplication application)
    {
        // Add Your DbApplication Code Here

        // Return Success
        return Result.Succeeded;
    }

    /// <summary>
    /// This event happens as the session is ending,
    /// All documents are closed by now
    /// </summary>
    /// <param name="application">The Controlled Application</param>
    /// <returns>Return the status of the external application</returns>
    public Result OnShutdown(ControlledApplication application)
```

```
    {

        // Add All Event Unsubscribe Code Here

        // Return Success
        return Result.Succeeded;
    }
}
```

External Utility Installation

Loading commands and applications into the Autodesk Revit UI is done solely through an
`.addin` manifest file. An `.addin` manifest file is an XML-formatted file that Revit reads on
startup and uses to register API applications into the current session. Manifest files are read and
processed by Revit from only the following two locations on your system:

Windows XP

> `C:\Documents and Settings\All Users\Application Data\Autodesk\Revit\`
> `Addins\2013\`
>
> `%USERPROFILE%\Application Data\Autodesk\Revit\Addins\2013\`

Windows 7

> `C:\ProgramData\Autodesk\Revit\Addins\2013\`
>
> `%USERPROFILE%\AppData\Roaming\Autodesk\Revit\Addins\2013\`

Loading multiple commands or applications within a single manifest file is possible by nesting AddIn elements into one .addin file between the `RevitAddins` tag. An example .addin file
showing how to nest a command and an application manifest is shown in Listing 25.7. This file
is the same as the `MARA2013.addin` file that you will use to load the sample add-in project into
Revit later in this chapter.

REVIT 2013 MANIFEST CONFIGURATION TIP

If you place your DLLs in the same directory as the `.addin` manifest file, you do not have to include
the path to your DLL file in the Assembly tag. Leaving the path off of the DLL file will also allow you
to debug the project without having to generate a second manifest file.

LISTING 25.7:   `.addin` manifest example

```xml
<?xml version="1.0" encoding="utf-8" standalone="no" ?>
<RevitAddIns>
 <AddIn Type="Command">
  <Assembly>MARA2013.dll</Assembly>
  <AddInId>b3719a2c-aa28-4331-a3a9-0e334d1a2653</AddInId>
```

```
      <FullClassName>MARA2013.Command</FullClassName>
      <Text>MARA2013 - Extrude Rooms to Masses</Text>
      <VisibilityMode>NotVisibleInFamily</VisibilityMode>
      <VendorId>MARA</VendorId>
      <VendorDescription>Mastering Autodesk Revit Architecture 2013
      </VendorDescription>
    </AddIn>
    <AddIn Type="Application">
      <Name>MARA2013 Sample</Name>
      <Assembly>MARA2013.dll</Assembly>
      <AddInId>356CDc5A-e6A5-412f-A9EF-B1233116B8C3</AddInId>
      <FullClassName>MARA2013.Application</FullClassName>
      <VendorId>MARA</VendorId>
      <VendorDescription>Mastering Autodesk Revit Architecture 2013
      </VendorDescription>
    </AddIn>
</RevitAddIns>
```

Selecting Your Development Environment

Just about any Microsoft .NET–compatible integrated development environment (IDE) can be used to generate custom commands and applications for Revit. Just remember that Revit 2013 now requires Microsoft .NET 4.0 for debugging your projects.

While there are several IDE options out there suitable for developing Revit add-ins, I recommend at least Visual Studio 2010. Visual Studio comes in many flavors that all range in price and features. Microsoft Visual Studio 2010 Professional is my personal favorite, but the Express versions are free and capable of hosting your Revit API development efforts.

Microsoft's free Visual Studio Express versions are available for download at www.microsoft.com/express. One of the downfalls with using an express version is that they each support only one .NET language, so if you need to work with C# as well as VB.NET, you have to download and install a version for each language. Express versions do not support customizations, nor do they contain an interface for configuring debug settings for a class library project. This just means that you have to use an ASCII text editor to manually make these adjustments outside of the express versions.

The Sample Add-In Project

Now that you have a basic grasp of the Revit API, let's build a project from scratch. The sample add-in project that you will be building contains both an external command and an external application. As you may be aware, rooms are not visible in 3D views, so the command you will build generates 3D masses from each placed room element in the current model document. The external application will add a tab to the ribbon where you can access the custom command.

GIT THE COMPLETE SAMPLE CODE

Don't worry if you get lost with the sample code in this section! You can download or fork it on github for free: http://github.com/rudderdon/MARA-2013-Sample.

Our add-in project will comprise one user form, a command class, and an application class. We'll start with the user form code and then work our way out to the command and application classes that implement the `IExternalCommand` and `IExternalApplication` interfaces.

The code samples in this section are all written in VB.NET using Visual Studio 2010 Professional. If you prefer to work in C#, you can translate the code by pasting it into `www.developerfusion.com/tools/convert/vb-to-csharp` (some cleanup will be required). See Figure 25.3.

FIGURE 25.3
Optionally converting VB.NET to C#

Open a fresh session of Visual Studio 2010 and select New Project to get started. Select Class Library as your project type and name the project **MARA2013** (Figure 25.4). This project will contain the code for both of our API samples. Be sure to save the project somewhere handy.

FIGURE 25.4
Creating the application project

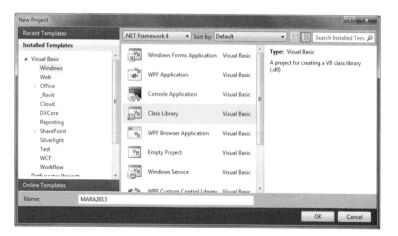

With the project created, the next thing to do is add the two required namespace references to `RevitAPI.dll` and `RevitAPIUI.dll`. All Autodesk Revit 2013 `IExternalCommand` and `IExternalApplication` interfaces require namespace references for these two libraries. Namespace references are added by right-clicking the title of the Visual Studio 2010 project name in the Solution Explorer and selecting Add ➢ Reference. Alternatively, you can select

Project ➢ Add Reference from the main menu. Navigate to the Program folder of your Revit installation (usually in C:\Program Files\Autodesk\Revit Architecture 2013\Program) and add these two references to your project, as shown in Figure 25.5.

FIGURE 25.5
Adding API references to your Visual Studio project

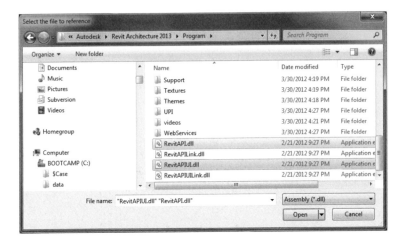

SETTING COPY LOCAL TO FALSE

The Copy Local property for the required Revit API DLL references default to True when added to a project. This property should be set to False so that you don't copy them unnecessarily with your project. Because an existing installation of Revit is always required to run your tool, you can just assume that these files already exist on the machine that will be running the add-in.

Select the RevitAPI.dll and RevitAPIUI.dll references and set their Copy Local property to False in the Properties palette, as shown here.

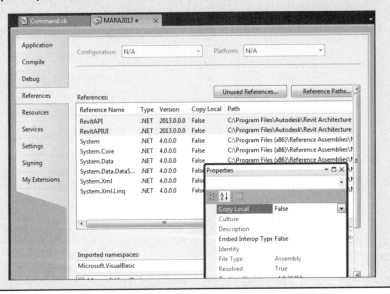

The `ExternalApplication` sample requires three additional references — to Presentation Core, `System.xaml`, and Windows Base — for the ribbon image functionality, so be sure to add these as well. Each of these references is available from the .NET tab of the Add References dialog box.

Visual Studio Debug Settings

Debugging a Revit command or application in Visual Studio 2010 Professional requires that you first enter the full path and filename to `Revit.exe` in the Start External Program field in the Debug tab of the Project Properties dialog box, as shown in Figure 25.6. Optionally, you can enter the full path and filename to a Revit document in the Command Line Arguments field to open Revit to a specific document while in debug mode.

FIGURE 25.6
Visual Studio 2010 Professional debug settings

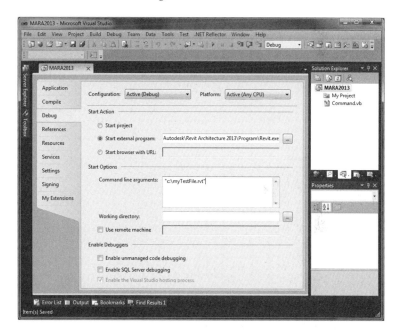

Debugging a Revit command or application in an Express version of Visual Studio 2010 requires that you manually edit either your `.vbproj.user` or `.csproj.user` file because there is no interface to add a startup application or document in the express versions. Adding a startup application is done by adding the information shown in Figure 25.7 into your user file.

FIGURE 25.7
Visual Studio 2010 Express debug settings

```
MARA2013.vbproj.user - Notepad
File  Edit  Format  View  Help
<?xml version="1.0" encoding="utf-8"?>
<Project ToolsVersion="4.0" xmlns="http://schemas.microsoft.com/developer/msbuild/2003">
  <PropertyGroup Condition="'$(Configuration)|$(Platform)' == 'Debug|AnyCPU'">
    <StartAction>Program</StartAction>
    <StartProgram>C:\Program Files\Autodesk\Revit Architecture 2013\Program\Revit.exe</StartProgram>
    <StartArguments>"c:\myTestFile.rvt"</StartArguments>
  </PropertyGroup>
</Project>
```

DEBUGGING ON A 64-BIT OPERATING SYSTEM

You will not be able to edit your code in break mode on a 64-bit operating system in Visual Studio 2010. Use a 32-bit operating system as your development station as a workaround.

Adding a User Form

You may find it easier to start designing your Revit API utilities from the user interaction point when there is one. I find that this approach helps keep my thoughts on track with what I'm trying to accomplish and less distracted with minor coding details. Add a new user form to the project by selecting Project ➤Add Windows Form from the main menu, name this form **form_Main**, and click OK. We will use a number of namespace objects on this form class, so you will need to add them all to the very top of the form above the class declaration, as shown in Listing 25.8.

LISTING 25.8: form_Main class code

```
Imports System
Imports System.Collections.Generic
Imports System.IO
Imports System.Reflection
Imports System.Windows.Forms
Imports Autodesk.Revit.DB
Imports Autodesk.Revit.UI
Public Class form_Main

End Class
```

CONTROLS LAYOUT

The final form controls layout is shown in Figure 25.8.

FIGURE 25.8
Form layout

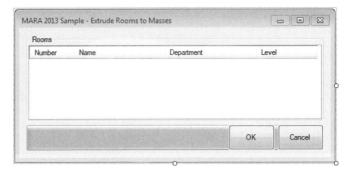

DataGridView control: `DataGridViewRooms`   The topmost control is a DataGridView control that we will use to display the list of rooms available in the model for extrusion to masses. After this control is placed onto the form, click the columns property so you can add the necessary text columns:

◆ UniqueID (Visible = False)

◆ Number

◆ Name

◆ Department

◆ Level

Progressbar control: `ProgressBar1`   This control is used to report progress information to the user at runtime. Place this control along the bottom of the form as illustrated earlier. Set the display so that it appears behind the two button controls.

FolderBrowserDialog control: `FolderBrowserDialogMass`   A `FolderBrowserControl` doesn't really get placed on the form, but it does get managed in the form designer. This is a helper control that will allow you to navigate to and select a directory for saving the mass families that will represent each room in the model. Name this control `FolderBrowserDialogMass` and set the Description property to "Select a Folder to Save the Mass Families."

Button control: `ButtonCancel`   The bottom-right button, named `ButtonCancel`, is used to close the command without performing any changes to the model. Set the text for this control to **Cancel**. Double-click the Cancel button and enter the code shown in Listing 25.9.

LISTING 25.9:   ButtonCancel code

```
''' <summary>
''' Cancel and Close the Command
''' </summary>
''' <param name="sender"></param>
''' <param name="e"></param>
''' <remarks></remarks>
Private Sub ButtonCancel_Click(sender As Object,
                               e As EventArgs) Handles ButtonCancel.Click
    ' Close the Form
    Me.Close()
End Sub
```

Button control: `ButtonOk`   The bottom-left button, named `ButtonOk`, is used to perform the mass extrusions from rooms. Set the text for this control to **OK**. Double-click the `ButtonOk` button and enter the code shown in Listing 25.10.

LISTING 25.10:   ButtonOk code

```
''' <summary>
''' Generate Masses from Rooms
''' </summary>
''' <param name="sender"></param>
''' <param name="e"></param>
''' <remarks></remarks>
Private Sub ButtonOk_Click(sender As Object,
             e As EventArgs) Handles ButtonOk.Click

    ' Form State Visibility
```

```
      SetFormViz(formViz.isProcessing)

      ' Browse to a Location to Save the Mass Families
      If Me.FolderBrowserDialogMass.ShowDialog = Windows.Forms.DialogResult.OK Then

          ' Was a Path Returned
          If Not String.IsNullOrEmpty(Me.FolderBrowserDialogMass.SelectedPath) Then

              ' Generate the Masses
              GenerateMasses(Me.FolderBrowserDialogMass.SelectedPath & "\")

          End If

      End If

      ' Close the Form
      Me.Close()

  End Sub
```

You may have noticed a few errors in the code that you just entered, and that's okay for now. We will build up the missing functions soon that will solve all of that. One of the functions that we can go ahead and take care of now is the SetFormViz function. I use this function to make it easier to toggle various form control visual states based on the state of the form. We use a private enumerator to manage the different form state options that we will use in the form. Enter the code shown in Listing 25.11 inside the form class to control the form visibility options.

LISTING 25.11: Form visibility code

```
  ''' <summary>
  ''' Visibility States
  ''' </summary>
  ''' <remarks></remarks>
  Private Enum formViz
      isProcessing
      isStandBy
  End Enum

  ''' <summary>
  ''' Change the form visibility based on state
  ''' </summary>
  ''' <param name="p_viz"></param>
  ''' <remarks></remarks>
  Private Sub SetFormViz(p_viz As formViz)
      Select Case p_viz
          Case formViz.isProcessing
              Me.ProgressBar1.Show()
              Me.ButtonCancel.Hide()
```

```
            Me.ButtonOk.Hide()
        Case formViz.isStandBy
            Me.ProgressBar1.Hide()
            Me.ButtonCancel.Show()
            Me.ButtonOk.Show()
    End Select
End Sub
```

THE FORM CLASS CONSTRUCTOR

The next step is creating the routine that constructs the form class before displaying it to the user. You need the constructor routine to widen the scope of the parameters that you pass to the class so that they are available to other functions in the form class. This is also a good place to crunch any preliminary needs that you may have. In this case, you will make sure that the required `Mass.rft` family template is in the same directory as well as save the mass category to a private variable.

The construction of your form class will require one argument of `p_App`, which in this case happens to be a `UIApplication` object that will allow you access to the Revit application and model data contained in the active document. Anytime you create a constructor for a form class, you must call `InitializeComponent()` immediately before any other code is entered. This function calls the default form construction preclass before running your custom constructor code on the form. The completed form class constructor code is shown in Listing 25.12.

LISTING 25.12:   The form constructor

```
Private m_Doc As Document
Private m_App As Autodesk.Revit.ApplicationServices.Application
Private m_AppCreate As Autodesk.Revit.Creation.Application
Private m_UiApp As UIApplication
Private m_FamFactory As Autodesk.Revit.Creation.FamilyItemFactory
Private m_massCat As Category
Private m_rooms As New List(Of Architecture.Room)
Private m_tPath As String = ""

''' <summary>
''' General Constructor
''' </summary>
''' <param name="p_App">The Revit Application</param>
''' <remarks></remarks>
Public Sub New(p_App As UIApplication)

    InitializeComponent()

    ' Document and Application Variables
    m_UiApp = p_App
    m_App = m_UiApp.Application
    m_Doc = m_UiApp.ActiveUIDocument.Document
    m_AppCreate = m_App.Create
```

```
' Mass Model Category
m_massCat = m_Doc.Settings.Categories.Item(BuiltInCategory.OST_Mass)

' Form State Visibility
Me.Text = "MARA 2013 Sample - Extrude Rooms to Masses"
SetFormViz(formViz.isStandBy)

' Find the Mass Template
m_tPath =Path.GetDirectoryName(Assembly.GetExecutingAssembly.Location) _
        & "\Mass.rft"
If Not File.Exists(m_tPath) Then
    ' Error, close
    MsgBox("Mass.rft was not Found!" & vbCr &
            "Expected to find it at:" & vbCr &
            "",
            MsgBoxStyle.Critical,
            "Cannot Continue")
    Exit Sub
End If

' Rooms
GetRooms()

End Sub
```

USER FORM CLASS SUBROUTINES

Depending on the complexity of your add-in, you may be able to get away with packing all of your functions and routines into your user form class. The form class utilizes two helper subroutines. GetRooms is a short and sweet subroutine called from the form class constructor subroutine and collects the rooms in the active document and then loads them into the DataGridView. GenerateMasses is used to perform the mass generation from the rooms.

The completed GetRooms subroutine is shown in Listing 25.13.

LISTING 25.13:   The completed GetRooms subroutine

```
''' <summary>
''' Load Matching Room Data into Data View
''' </summary>
''' <remarks></remarks>
Private Sub GetRooms()

    ' Clean Datagrid and Rooms List
    Me.DataGridViewRooms.Rows.Clear()
    m_rooms = New List(Of Architecture.Room)

    ' Get the Rooms Collection by Category
    Dim m_col As New FilteredElementCollector(m_Doc)
```

```vb
        m_col.OfCategory(BuiltInCategory.OST_Rooms)

    ' Process Each Room in the Collection
    For Each x As Element In m_col.ToElements

        ' Cast Element to Room
        Dim m_room As Architecture.Room = TryCast(x, Architecture.Room)

        ' Add to the List
        m_rooms.Add(m_room)

        ' Avoid Unplaced Rooms
        If m_room.Area < 1 Then Continue For

        ' Build and Add the Row
        Dim m_row As New DataGridViewRow
        Dim m_cell As New DataGridViewTextBoxCell

        ' UniqueID (This Column is not Visible)
        m_cell.Value = x.UniqueId.ToString
        m_row.Cells.Add(m_cell)

        ' Number
        m_cell = New DataGridViewTextBoxCell
        m_cell.Value = x.Parameter(BuiltInParameter.ROOM_NUMBER).AsString
        m_row.Cells.Add(m_cell)

        ' Name
        m_cell = New DataGridViewTextBoxCell
        m_cell.Value = x.Parameter(BuiltInParameter.ROOM_NAME).AsString
        m_row.Cells.Add(m_cell)

        ' Department
        m_cell = New DataGridViewTextBoxCell
        m_cell.Value = x.Parameter(BuiltInParameter.ROOM_DEPARTMENT).AsString
        m_row.Cells.Add(m_cell)

        ' Level
        m_cell = New DataGridViewTextBoxCell
        m_cell.Value = x.Level.Name
        m_row.Cells.Add(m_cell)

        ' Add the row
        Me.DataGridViewRooms.Rows.Add(m_row)

    Next

End Sub
```

With the room elements collected, the GenerateMasses subroutine has what it needs to create the mass extrusions. Since this routine has the potential of taking a while to run, we'll use a progress bar to show the user how far along the masses are. The maximum value for the progress bar will be set to the quantity of rooms collected. The progress bar will then increment on each room processed.

GenerateMasses will create a new file-based component mass family for each properly enclosed room in the model. The room boundary can include anything from walls to room separation lines. Ceilings will not be respected by this routine, nor will any complex features or slopes of the boundaries because this subroutine only analyzes the boundary at the floor level.

The started GenerateMasses subroutine is shown in Listing 25.14.

LISTING 25.14: Starting the *GenerateMasses* subroutine

```
''' <summary>
''' Generate the Mass Extrusions from the Room Elements
''' </summary>
''' <param name="p_path"></param>
''' <remarks></remarks>
Private Sub GenerateMasses(p_path As String)

    ' Progress Configuration
    With Me.ProgressBar1
        .Minimum = 0
        .Maximum = m_rooms.Count
        .Value = 0
    End With

    ' Random Number Helper
    Dim m_r As New Random

    ' Process Each Room
    For Each x As Architecture.Room In m_rooms

        ' Increment the Progress
        Me.ProgressBar1.Increment(1)

        ' Skip Unplaced and Non Enclosed Rooms
        If x.Area < 1 Then Continue For

    Next

End Sub
```

Now that you've got the basic iteration sequence setup for your mass generation routine, you can start to build up the parts that do the work that we're most interested in. First you will generate a subcategory representing the department of the room as well as a special material representation for each department. The code in Listing 25.15 shows the subcategory and material creation representing the department of each room. This code should go inside the main iteration sequence shown in Listing 25.14.

LISTING 25.15:   The department subcategory and material generation code

```
' Department Name for Subcategory
Dim m_SubCatName As String = "Mass_Rooms"
Try
    If Not String.IsNullOrEmpty(x.Parameter(BuiltInParameter.ROOM_DEPARTMENT)⏎
.AsString) Then
        m_SubCatName = "Mass_Rooms_" & x.Parameter(BuiltInParameter.⏎
ROOM_DEPARTMENT).AsString
    End If
Catch
End Try


' Create a New Family Using the Mass Template
Dim m_FamDoc As Document = m_App.NewFamilyDocument(m_tPath)


' Start a New Family Transaction
Dim m_TransFam As New Transaction(m_FamDoc, "Mass Family Transaction")
m_TransFam.Start()


Try
    ' Generate a Subcategory Representing the Department
    Dim m_subCat As Category = Nothing

    ' Map of Mass Subcategories
    Dim m_NameMap As CategoryNameMap = m_massCat.SubCategories

    ' Find the Subcategory by Name
    For Each x1 As Category In m_NameMap
        If x1.Name = m_SubCatName Then
            m_subCat = x1
            Exit For
        End If
    Next

    ' Create the Subcategory if it does not exist
    If m_subCat Is Nothing Then

        Try
            m_subCat = m_FamDoc.Settings.Categories.NewSubcategory(m_massCat,
                    m_SubCatName)
        Catch
        End Try

    End If

    ' Material to Represent Department
    Dim m_Material As Material = Nothing
    Dim m_colMat As New FilteredElementCollector(m_FamDoc)
```

```vb
    m_colMat.OfCategory(BuiltInCategory.OST_Materials)

    ' Find the Material by Name
    For Each m As Material In m_colMat.ToElements
        If m.Name = m_SubCatName Then
            m_Material = m
            Exit For
        End If
    Next

    ' Create the Material if Not Found
    If m_Material Is Nothing Then

        Try

            ' Name as Subcategory
            Dim m_matid As ElementId = Material.Create(m_FamDoc, m_SubCatName)

            ' Random Color
            Dim m_color As New Color(m_r.Next(1, 255),
                                     m_r.Next(1, 255),
                                     m_r.Next(1, 255))

            ' Apply the Color to the Material
            m_Material.Color = m_color

            ' Set 50% Transparency
            m_Material.Transparency = 50

            ' Assign the Material to the Subcategory
            m_subCat.Material = m_Material

        Catch

        End Try

    End If

    ' Extrusion Code (Later in the Chapter)

Catch ex As Exception

    ' Rollback
    m_TransFam.RollBack()

End Try
```

Now that the subcategory and material generation code for the room department is in place, you can get the boundary of the room that you will use to generate the mass form. Before you gather the boundary data, you will get the upper bound height of the room as well as the elevation height for the level that the room lives on. This is important so the room mass gets generated at the correct location in the Z direction.

The boundary data for each room is described by a series of BoundarySegment elements that parent the model curve elements that we are after. A required argument used to generate an extruded mass form is the profile described as a ReferenceArray. A ReferenceArray is an array of, you guessed it, Reference elements. You can get Reference elements from model curves, so you will iterate over each of the segments and trace a model curve matching the form of the segment. These new model curves are what you use to generate each Reference element that you collect to use as the boundary of your form extrusion.

The room boundary and form extrusion sequence shown in Listing 25.16 should be placed immediately beneath the End Try statements for the material and subcategory code from Listing 25.15

LISTING 25.16: The room boundary and form extrusion code

```
' Elevation and Upper Bounds of the Room
Dim m_RmHeight As Double = x.UnboundedHeight
Dim m_RmElevation As Double = x.Level.Elevation
If Not x.UpperLimit Is Nothing Then
    Try

        ' Make Sure there's a difference
        If x.UpperLimit.Elevation > x.Level.Elevation Then

            ' Get the Height from the Level Above
            m_RmHeight = x.UpperLimit.Elevation - m_RmElevation

        End If

    Catch

    End Try
End If

' Don't Allow 0 Height for Room
If m_RmHeight < 1 Then m_RmHeight = 9

' Get the BoundarySegment Collection
Dim m_sp_opt As New SpatialElementBoundaryOptions
Dim m_Boundary As IList(Of IList(Of BoundarySegment)) = x.GetBoundarySegments⤶
(m_sp_opt)

' Test for Valid Segment List
```

```
If m_Boundary Is Nothing Then Continue For

' Flat Sketchplane
Dim m_plane As Plane = m_UiApp.Application.Create.NewPlane(New XYZ(0, 0, 1),⤸
New XYZ(0, 0, m_RmElevation))
Dim m_skplane As SketchPlane = m_FamDoc.FamilyCreate.NewSketchPlane(m_plane)

' The Reference Array
Dim m_refArray As New ReferenceArray

' Iterate to gather the reference array objects
For i = 0 To m_Boundary.Count - 1
    Dim il As IList(Of BoundarySegment) = m_Boundary(i)
    ' Segments Array
    For ii = 0 To il.Count - 1

        Dim m_Seg As BoundarySegment = il.Item(ii)

        Dim m_mc As ModelCurve = Nothing

        ' Curve is Line
        If TypeOf m_Seg.Curve Is Line Then
            Dim m_cLine As Line = TryCast(m_Seg.Curve, Line)
            m_mc = m_FamDoc.FamilyCreate.NewModelCurve(m_cLine, m_skplane)
        End If

        ' Curve is Arc
        If TypeOf m_Seg.Curve Is Arc Then
            Dim m_cLine As Arc = TryCast(m_Seg.Curve, Arc)
            m_mc = m_FamDoc.FamilyCreate.NewModelCurve(m_cLine, m_skplane)
        End If

        ' Curve is NurbSpline
        If TypeOf m_Seg.Curve Is NurbSpline Then
            Dim m_cLine As NurbSpline = TryCast(m_Seg.Curve, NurbSpline)
            m_mc = m_FamDoc.FamilyCreate.NewModelCurve(m_cLine, m_skplane)
        End If

        Try

            m_refArray.Append(m_mc.GeometryCurve.Reference)
        Catch ex As Exception

        End Try

    Next
Next
```

```
Try

    ' The Extrusion Direction and Height
    Dim m_dir As New XYZ(0, 0, m_RmHeight)

    ' Extrude the form
    Dim m_form As Autodesk.Revit.DB.Form = m_FamDoc.FamilyCreate⤾
.NewExtrusionForm(True, m_refArray, m_dir)

    ' Assign the Subcategory
    m_form.Subcategory = m_subCat

Catch ex As Exception

End Try

' Commit
m_TransFam.Commit()

' Save and Close the Family, Options to Replace Existing
Dim m_opt As New SaveAsOptions
m_opt.OverwriteExistingFile = True
m_FamDoc.SaveAs(p_path & x.UniqueId.ToString & ".rfa", m_opt)
m_FamDoc.Close()
```

Now that the form family has been generated and saved to a location specified by the user, you can load it into the active document and place it at 0,0,0 so that the location of the mass will match up with the original location of the room that it is intended to represent.

The sequence of code used to place the family into the model will be enclosed in its own transaction and within its own try statement as a result. First, you'll create a new model transaction with the commit and rollback calls nested within a try statement. You will need to first load the family into the model and then gain a reference to it so you can place an instance of it in the model.

The code used to load and place the family form into the model is shown in Listing 25.17.

LISTING 25.17:   Code to load and place the family instance in the model

```
' Start a new Model Transaction
Dim m_Trans As New Transaction(m_Doc, "Extrude Rooms to Masses")
m_Trans.Start()

Try

    ' Load the Family
    Dim m_family As Family = Nothing
    m_Doc.LoadFamily(p_path & x.UniqueId.ToString & ".rfa", m_family)
```

```
' Get the Default Symbol from the Family
    Dim m_FamilySymbolSetIterator As FamilySymbolSetIterator = m_family⤸
.Symbols.
ForwardIterator()
    m_FamilySymbolSetIterator.MoveNext()
    Dim m_FamSymbol As FamilySymbol = TryCast(m_FamilySymbolSetIterator.Current,⤸
FamilySymbol)

    ' Place the Family at 0,0,0
    Dim m_FamilyInstance As FamilyInstance = m_Doc.Create.NewFamilyInstance⤸
(New XYZ(0, 0, 0), m_FamSymbol, [Structure].StructuralType.NonStructural)

    ' Commit the Model Transaction
    m_Trans.Commit()

Catch ex As Exception

    ' RollBack the Model Transaction
    m_Trans.RollBack()

End Try
```

That does it for the form generation code. The last thing to do is configure the command class used to run the add-in and the application for adding the ribbon button to access it.

The *Command* Class

Now with all of the main utility components basically built and ready to go, you can focus on connecting your utility up to function inside the Revit user interface. You will do this by adding a new command class that will implement the IExternalCommand interface. Add a new class to the project by selecting Project ➤ Add Class from the main menu, name this class **Command**, and click OK (see Figure 25.9).

FIGURE 25.9
Adding a new command class

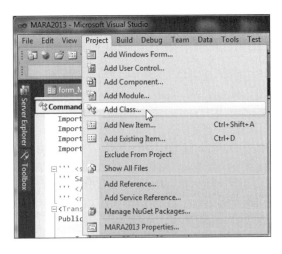

Open the Command class and add the namespace imports to the very top of the main class as shown in Listing 25.18 before we go any further.

LISTING 25.18: Adding the namespace imports to the top of the Command class

```
Imports Autodesk.Revit.UI
Imports Autodesk.Revit.DB
Imports Autodesk.Revit.Attributes
Imports System
```

With the namespace imports in place, the next step is to add the transaction attribute immediately above the class declaration and then add the implementation line for the IExternalCommand interface just inside the main class declaration as shown in Listing 25.19.

LISTING 25.19: Adding the IExternalCommand implementation and transaction attribute

```
Imports Autodesk.Revit.DB
Imports Autodesk.Revit.UI
Imports Autodesk.Revit.Attributes
Imports System

''' <summary>
''' Sample to Extrude Rooms to Mass Elements
''' </summary>
''' <remarks></remarks>
<Transaction(TransactionMode.Manual)>
Public Class Command

    Implements IExternalCommand

    Public Function Execute(commandData As ExternalCommandData,
                        ByRef message As String,
                        elements As ElementSet) _
                    As Result Implements IExternalCommand.Execute

    End Function

End Class
```

You may have noticed that after pressing the Enter key following the IExternalCommand implementation, a function named Execute with all required arguments and structure automatically appeared for you. If you are using a development environment other than Microsoft Visual Studio, you may not have the same result.

Now that the basic framework for your form code is all set up, you can construct and display the user form. The user form class requires a UIApplication object as an argument parameter, so you will need to pass that data over to the form constructor in your code. The now-completed Command class with all references to your settings class and user form is shown in Listing 25.20.

LISTING 25.20: The completed Command class

```vb
Imports Autodesk.Revit.DB
Imports Autodesk.Revit.UI
Imports Autodesk.Revit.Attributes
Imports System

''' <summary>
''' Sample to Extrude Rooms to Mass Elements
''' </summary>
''' <remarks></remarks>
<Transaction(TransactionMode.Manual)>
Public Class Command

    Implements IExternalCommand

    ''' <summary>
    ''' Command Entry Point
    ''' </summary>
    ''' <param name="commandData"></param>
    ''' <param name="message"></param>
    ''' <param name="elements"></param>
    ''' <returns></returns>
    ''' <remarks></remarks>
    Public Function Execute(commandData As ExternalCommandData,
                       ByRef message As String,
                       elements As ElementSet) _
                  As Result Implements IExternalCommand.Execute
        Try
            ' Construct and Display the Form
            Using m_Dlg As New form_Main(commandData.Application)
                ' Show the Dialog
                m_Dlg.ShowDialog()
            End Using
            ' Success
            Return Result.Succeeded
        Catch ex As Exception
            ' Failure
            message = ex.Message
            Return Result.Failed
        End Try

    End Function

End Class
```

The *Application* Class

The application class is simple in that it is used only to add a button to the Add-Ins tab of the Revit ribbon for gaining access to the sample command that we just wrapped up. Add a new class to the project by selecting Project ➢ Add Class from the main menu, name this class **Application**, and click OK. Open the Application class and add the namespace imports to the top as shown in Listing 25.21.

LISTING 25.21:   Adding the namespace imports to the Application class

```
Imports Autodesk.Revit.DB
Imports Autodesk.Revit.UI
Imports Autodesk.Revit.Attributes
Imports System
Imports System.IO
Imports System.Reflection
Imports System.Windows.Media.Imaging
```

The next step in setting up the Application class is to add the transaction attribute and implement the IExternalApplication interface. Open the Application class and enter the transaction attribute and IExternalApplication implementation as shown in Listing 25.22. Pressing the Enter key after the IExternalApplication implementation will automatically generate the two required OnStartup and OnShutdown functions for you.

LISTING 25.22:   Implementing the IExternalApplication Interface

```
Imports Autodesk.Revit.DB
Imports Autodesk.Revit.UI
Imports Autodesk.Revit.Attributes
Imports System
Imports System.IO
Imports System.Reflection
Imports System.Windows.Media.Imaging

''' <summary>
''' Class to Add a Ribbon Control to Access a Command
''' </summary>
''' <remarks></remarks>
<Transaction(TransactionMode.Manual)>
Public Class Application

    Implements IExternalApplication

    ''' <summary>
    ''' Fires off when Revit Session Starts
```

```
''' </summary>
''' <param name="application"></param>
''' <returns></returns>
''' <remarks></remarks>
Public Function OnStartup(application As UIControlledApplication) _
    As Result Implements IExternalApplication.OnStartup
    Try
        Return Result.Succeeded
    Catch ex As Exception
        Return Result.Failed
    End Try
End Function

''' <summary>
''' Fires off when Revit Session Ends
''' </summary>
''' <param name="application"></param>
''' <returns></returns>
''' <remarks></remarks>
Public Function OnShutdown(application As UIControlledApplication) _
    As Result Implements IExternalApplication.OnShutdown
    ' No Events to Unsubscribe From...
    Return Result.Succeeded
End Function

End Class
```

Now that the basic framework for your Application class is all in place, it is time to start on the code that will place the ribbon control that you will use to access your command. First you will generate a new ribbon tab named MARA and add a new push button to this tab. A new ribbon section named 2013 Sample will house your single push button. The push button will simply call your command class that just so happens to be in the same DLL file, but you could include commands from other DLL files if you wanted to. The now-final OnStartup function is shown in Listing 25.23.

LISTING 25.23: The completed *OnStartup* function

```
''' <summary>
''' Fires off when Revit Session Starts
''' </summary>
''' <param name="application"></param>
''' <returns></returns>
''' <remarks></remarks>
Public Function OnStartup(application As UIControlledApplication) _
    As Result Implements IExternalApplication.OnStartup
    Try
```

```
        Try
            ' First Create the Tab
            application.CreateRibbonTab("MARA")
        Catch ex As Exception
            ' Might already exist...
        End Try


        ' The Ribbon Panel
        Dim m_RibbonPanel As RibbonPanel = Nothing
        Try
            m_RibbonPanel = application.CreateRibbonPanel("MARA", "2013 Sample")
        Catch ex As Exception

        End Try


        Try
            ' The Execution Path
            Dim m_Path As String = Path.GetDirectoryName(Assembly⤶
.GetExecutingAssembly.Location) _
                                & "\"


            ' Add the Button
            Dim m_pb As New PushButtonData("MaraSample",
                                "Rooms to" & vbCr & "Mass",
                                m_Path & "MARA2013.dll",
                                "MARA2013.Command")
            m_pb.ToolTip = "Launches the Extrude Rooms to Masses Sample"

            ' Add it to the Ribbon
            m_RibbonPanel.AddItem(m_pb)

        Catch ex As Exception

        End Try

        Return Result.Succeeded
    Catch ex As Exception
        Return Result.Failed
    End Try
End Function
```

Setting Up the *.addin* Manifest Installation

Our sample application and command is all ready to go. It is now time to set up the `.addin` manifest file so you can run and debug the sample utility. Add a new manifest file to the project by right-clicking on the main project name in the Solution Explorer and selecting Project ➢ Add New Item from the main menu, select Class as the item type and name this item **MARA2013.addin**, and click OK.

You will use this single manifest file to load the sample command as well as your sample application. Fill in the manifest file with the code shown in Listing 25.24.

LISTING 25.24:   The completed MARA2013.addin installation file

```
<?xml version="1.0" encoding="utf-8" standalone="no" ?>
<RevitAddIns>
 <AddIn Type="Command">
  <Assembly>MARA2013.dll</Assembly>
  <AddInId>b3719a2c-aa28-4331-a3a9-0e334d1a2653</AddInId>
  <FullClassName>MARA2013.Command</FullClassName>
  <Text>MARA2013 - Extrude Rooms to Masses</Text>
  <VisibilityMode>NotVisibleInFamily</VisibilityMode>
  <VendorId>MARA</VendorId>
  <VendorDescription>Mastering Autodesk Revit Architecture 2013
  </VendorDescription>
 </AddIn>
 <AddIn Type="Application">
  <Name>MARA2013 Sample</Name>
  <Assembly>MARA2013.dll</Assembly>
  <AddInId>356CDc5A-e6A5-412f-A9EF-B1233116B8C3</AddInId>
  <FullClassName>MARA2013.Application</FullClassName>
  <VendorId>MARA</VendorId>
  <VendorDescription>Mastering Autodesk Revit Architecture 2013
  </VendorDescription>
 </AddIn>
</RevitAddIns>
```

Automating the Installation of the Manifest File

It is possible to have this .addin manifest file copied automatically for you from your development project directory into the required installation directory for Revit Architecture 2013, and here's how to do it.

Open the project's Properties palette and click the Compile tab. Click the Build Events button in the lower right and enter the following:

```
copy "$(ProjectDir)MARA2013.addin" "$(AppData)\Autodesk\REVIT\Addins\2013⤸
\MARA2013.addin"
```

Figure 25.10 shows the dialog box where custom build events are accessed and modified.

FIGURE 25.10

The Build Events dialog box, where you can build an event to copy the manifest file

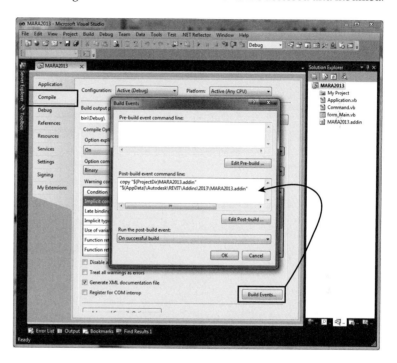

Running the Sample from the Debugger

You're almost ready to run the sample project. Press the F5 key to start the debugger. After Revit starts up, navigate over to the new MARA tab of the ribbon and you should now have a button that looks like the one in Figure 25.11.

FIGURE 25.11

The sample button

When you click the Rooms To Mass button, you will get a dialog listing the enclosed rooms found in your model. When you click OK, you will be prompted to select or create a directory to save the family files for each room. Upon completion, your model will contain the new 3D mass extrusions at the exact locations of your rooms, similar to Figure 25.12.

FIGURE 25.12
The resulting mass
extrusions

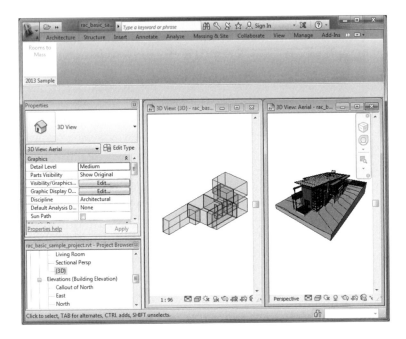

Additional API Resources

If you are interested in learning more about the Revit API, here are some online resources for
your viewing pleasure:

◆ DevTV: Introduction to Revit API Programming:

download.autodesk.com/media/adn/DevTV_Introduction_to_Revit_Programming_new

◆ Autodesk Developer Center and Developer Network (ADN):

www.autodesk.com/adn

◆ The Building Coder (a blog by Jeremy Tammik):

http://thebuildingcoder.typepad.com

◆ Autodesk Revit API Discussion Group:

discussion.autodesk.com/forum.jspa?forumID=160

The Bottom Line

Understand the basics of the Revit API.   The Revit software development kit (SDK) provides sample code and instructions for building add-ins for the Revit application.

   Master It   What are the three types of API projects you can develop for Revit?

Write, debug, and install your own API projects.   You can start to create your own custom applications and commands for Revit using either Microsoft Visual Studio Professional or a free tool such as Microsoft Visual Studio Express.

   Master It   How do you make the Revit API functions available in your developing environment?

Chapter 26

Revit for Film and Stage

Buildings may last for a long time, but film is forever! Autodesk® Revit® Architecture software provides extraordinary advantages for film and stage design professionals, from concept design to construction management. If you're in the film and stage industries (or interested in learning more about an incredibly creative and rewarding design environment), this chapter will give you some insight.

What's really important is learning how to quickly and easily communicate ideas much faster than using traditional 2D tools (which don't lend themselves to 3D) and far more efficiently than 3D tools (which don't lend themselves to construction documentation). Revit has the best of both worlds, and it provides an intuitive, integrated solution that helps everyone involved in the process of making the imagined real.

We'll profile how one set designer in the film industry, Bryan Sutton, has used Revit in his projects.

In this chapter, you'll learn to:

◆ Design scenically

◆ Use Revit in the design-to-production process

◆ Use Revit for previsualization

Revit in the Film Industry

Right up front, you should know that Revit does not have a widely established technical presence in the set design industry. Instead, this space is dominated by Autodesk® 3ds Max® and Autodesk® Maya® software as well as 3D, SketchUp, and Rhino. But Revit has begun making inroads in recent years.

ABOUT THE CONTRIBUTING AUTHOR: BRYAN SUTTON

Bryan Sutton is an incredibly talented set designer in Vancouver, British Columbia, Canada, who has been using Revit to design sets for major motion pictures since 2001. Vancouver is a center of commercial television and film production in North America.

One reason for the recent interest in using Revit in the film industry is Bryan Sutton and his initial posts in the Autodesk User Group International (AUGI) forums in fall 2004. When he posted a few renderings of the airlock door from the first *Fantastic Four* movie, he immediately grabbed the attention of the growing Revit community.

From that time, there has been a growing interest in using Revit in film and stage production. But of all the designers in that industry, Bryan is considered one of the most talented Revit users, not only in his industry but in the world. He has developed a style and approach to Revit that has moved beyond technical proficiency to a masterful art form. That's why we'll share his experiences using Revit with you in this chapter.

Bryan first began toying with computers primarily as a production tool but then quickly began to focus on parametric design technologies. All this was happening while he was working as a carpenter building sets for commercial productions. Some of the first tools he used were Autodesk® AutoCAD® software, 3ds Max, and Strata. Very soon he started doing production drawings and found he had an advantage in understanding both the set design and the accompanying construction processes.

In Bryan's industry, it's not enough to be technically or architecturally trained. What's important is that you understand how to design *scenically*. The design and documentation needs to be suggestive — and what lies beyond the façade should be taken into account.

Bryan's understanding of the importance of designing scenically quickly led him to look beyond the traditional 2D CAD tools. So, after starting with AutoCAD, Bryan began to experiment with other 3D tools, such as Rhino and IronCAD. It was IronCAD that opened his eyes to the realm of *parametrics* — the ability to build relationships and effect many changes at once. But the workflow was still lacking an integrated process: What was being designed in 3D was being exported for documentation. And design changes discovered during documentation required editing elsewhere: back to the 3D file, export, and so on.

Fortunately, Bryan discovered Revit from the same friend who had introduced him to IronCAD. He immediately realized that here was an integrated environment for doing architectural work that didn't care where you made the change: 3D, 2D, documents, and even schedules. Bryan was hooked. And he began using Revit 1.0 (just before version 2.0) on set designs for commercials.

In spite of his extraordinary and exceptionally aesthetic approach to using Revit, Bryan is the first to admit that, unfortunately, he can't draw himself out of a paper bag. His advice? Hand sketching is critical for the early design process. You need to be able to draw quickly and elegantly — and according to Bryan, sketching is the language of communicating design ideas.

You can find more information on Bryan at `www.imdb.com/name/nm1340613/`.

Using Revit in the Design-to-Production Process

Using Revit in the architectural profession involves unique processes and characteristics. The same is true in the production process of film and stage set design. Of course, there's going to be some overlap considering that both spaces need to be occupied by people. But you'd be surprised how little real architecture exists in the set design industry.

In this part of the chapter, we'll walk you through the process of using Revit in the film and stage industries. And if you're familiar with the industry, only Revit might be unfamiliar. But if you're an architect already familiar with Revit, the quality and craft of the film and stage industries is going to both impress and challenge you.

Understanding the role of a set designer is easier if you understand some adjacent roles in the production process. Roles that used to be distinct are now overlapping and merging throughout the production process. For one example, the director of photography and the director of visual effects used to have distinct roles. But because special effects are more computer-generated, the director of visual effects frequently works with or under the director of photography. Here's another example: The director of photography was traditionally in charge of the production filming, while the production designer was traditionally in charge of the overall look and feel of the production. But these two roles are also meshing together (again) because of computer-generated sets. Every role needs to understand both the real and virtual sets so that the digital environments have the same look and feel of the physical sets.

Digital tools have reinforced the need to have the entire production team working together in constant communication. Working in 2D can quickly lead to confusion. Even creative people struggle with reading 2D plans, sections, and elevations. Just as in traditional architecture, any miscommunication is expensive in both time and money. And just as with architecture, the production has a deadline — *the release date*. This deadline cannot move.

Revit offers the ability to provide so much communication in one elegant tool — you get 3D, 2D, visualization, and scheduling in a single environment. But what's compelling with Revit is its bidirectional nature. You can work directly from the production drawings to change the model; you can model in context with a production sketch as an underlay. Being able to quickly and easily create parametric content is key to a successful process.

At the end of the day, Revit is just better organized for creating buildings than using a generic 3D modeling tool like SketchUp, Rhino, or 3ds Max. According to Bryan, as a set designer he uses Revit for more than 95 percent of his job, with the occasional modeling in Rhino.

In the following sections, we'll walk you through the process of the overall workflow that takes a project from the earliest production sketches through fabrication and construction.

Design Interaction

As soon as the earliest sketches arrive from the art director, it becomes incredibly important to stay away from the coldness of computer renderings. They tend to be too hard and lack important emotive qualities — or may even look too finished. You need to focus on techniques to keep the design loose early on. This keeps the design open and tends to invite input from the director and others. In Figure 26.1, note how the materials are muted rather than literal representations. Although the glass is transparent, if you look carefully you'll notice there are hash marks on the glass. This is an important graphic gesture. It also communicates material-ness in elevation.

FIGURE 26.1
Muted materials and hash marks on glazing

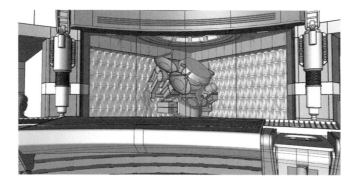

This same hand-sketchiness doesn't just apply to 2D plans, elevations, and sections. Even when rendering, you'll want to overdramatize lighting effects by placing geometry-less studio lights. The gaffer (who is in charge of lighting) and director of photography are keenly interested in lighting effects. So in many cases, you (or more likely, someone else) will need to take a rendering you've created in Revit or Maya and then work on it in Photoshop in order to exaggerate lighting or to soften it. The idea is that you're trying to bring more emotive qualities to the rendering than may be present (Figure 26.2).

FIGURE 26.2
Softened, emotive lighting effects

Lead Time and Production

Although design teams tend to work in their own silos (that are focused on different parts of the movie), expect to work in a collaborative environment. Everyone needs to understand how the vision of the art director will allow the movie to flow from one scene to the next.

Illustrators may or may not start with a 3D model. But if they do start with a 3D model, it'll likely be just enough to have provided context for their early design concepts and sketches. Lots of hand-drawing will go on top of these images. If you're provided with digital copies of the model and sketches, expect to remodel the geometry because it won't be useful in Revit for more than context. The same goes for the digital sketches. But at least it's a start!

Deadlines are likely going to be very, very tight. Where standard architecture practice allows for months, in the film industry you'll have weeks. And where standard practice allows for weeks, you'll have days. Expect to work 12-hour days, five days a week, and anywhere from four to eight months for a major motion picture (with a break of a few months between productions). That's *not* four to eight months for resolving design to documentation — it's for resolving *concept to construction*. And the detail to be resolved is going to have to be extraordinary, as shown in Figure 26.3.

Construction can start from a napkin sketch in cases when the design is not *too* complicated. On more complicated projects, it's likely that you'll be working on site and very near to the construction and other production teams — as in the same building, down the hall, or possibly in the same war room. Some pieces of your design may be repetitive and contain parts that have to fit together with a high degree of precision. When this is the case, it's likely these pieces will be prefabricated via computerized numerical control (CNC) and then assembled on site. Fortunately, you can export other formats from Revit that quickly lend themselves to fabrication (such as *.SAT or ACIS).

Bryan has worked on a number of third-act sets. Third-act sets are known for being large, complex, and/or highly themed because they'll be seen near the end of the movie and must leave a lasting impression. In the case of *Watchmen*, the Karnak set took months to create, and the Revit model was used to resolve issues ranging from design to camera angles to rigging for stunt work (Figure 26.4). Overall, remember that it's critical to stay a week or two ahead of the construction team because of the amount of lead time required by the set decorators after construction concludes.

FIGURE 26.3
Gritty realism in
*X-Men: The Last
Stand*

FIGURE 26.4
Detail of glazing in
Karnak

Even with all the early attention to detail during the design process, occasionally parts of sets will need to be pulled apart and rebuilt. But keep in mind that this is extremely disruptive to the entire production process. The deadline has been set years in advance, and the budget is inflexible. The tolerance for rebuilds is becoming more unlikely now that 3D is becoming so common in the design process.

Scheduling

While quantities are important, in the middle of all this design iteration and visualization production, some standard architectural techniques may not translate into designing for film and stage. For example, it's unlikely that you'll be creating discrete schedules as you normally would. So rather than noting quantities on schedules, you'll tend to note them on sheets. This makes it simple and keeps as much information in one place as possible. You'll also indicate spacing — but again not the hard numbers.

Details

In the same way that traditional architectural schedules aren't used (but rather, quantities are noted in context with documentation), details are shown in the context of the elements being detailed. So rather than segment your work into different groups (plans, elevations, sections, and so on), it's more likely that you'll be assembling your work in context, which is more like traditional architectural hand-drawing techniques. For example, being able to see both design intent and resolution at the same time is important. Plans, elevations, sections, and 3D views will likely be assembled together (not apart). This is particularly true because set builders can be given a lot of creative leeway, and you're often giving them enough information to get started. Prop builders, fabricators, and sculptors — they all love to have 3D representations! Taking an artist's sketch and putting it in context of the construction documents communicates the spirit of design intent (Figure 26.5).

FIGURE 26.5
Design intent and resolution on the same sheet

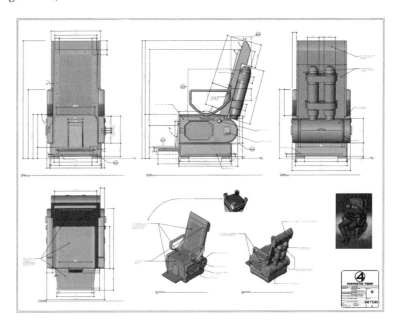

Dimensions

While we're discussing documentation, remember that dimensions in context with shaded views are better suited for resolving depth than mere hidden line views. Much of what you'll be designing in film and stage production involves curved, imaginative kinds of forms. These shapes aren't visualized well in black-and-white, 2D kinds of views. But if you change the views to shaded, curved elements are far more expressive. If you need to embellish 3D and perspective views, simply add the text and other notes outside the view once the views have been placed on the sheet.

Be sure to demonstrate finesse with regard to visualization that is suitable for communication as well as presentation — and sometimes these are different things. In other words, how you illustrate design intent comes in many styles and influences. But what's important is to be able to make deliberate design decisions while illustrating a certain aesthetic *lack* of resolution. Because so many people are going to influence the final product, you must visualize your work in a way that doesn't raise unnecessary objections while building consensus as quickly as possible.

Level of Detail

Level of detail is critical in the film and stage industries. Don't expect to model to the level of detail standard in architectural practice. In other words, you're *not* going to be able to model in 3D at a low level of detail and then document in 2D a greater level of detail. If the component calls for hardware, you'll probably model it. In this industry, geometric detail is vitally important. It'll be leveraged for documentation through visualization. What you model is what gets built — you're not going to be allowed to leave much, if anything, to guesswork or imagination (Figure 26.6).

FIGURE 26.6
Expect to model to a high level of detail

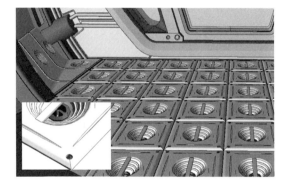

Fabrication

Fabrication is essential. CNC plays a large part in the set design industry and utilizes five-axis machining, laser cutting, and water cutting (which was used to create the latticework in Figure 26.7 and the door panels in Figure 26.8). Speed and accuracy are huge benefits and provide unmatched precision for preassemblage.

FIGURE 26.7
CNC latticework for pagoda from *Fantastic Four: Rise of the Silver Surfer*

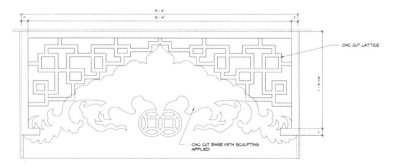

FIGURE 26.8
CNC door panel
detail for pagoda
from *Fantastic Four:
Rise of the Silver
Surfer*

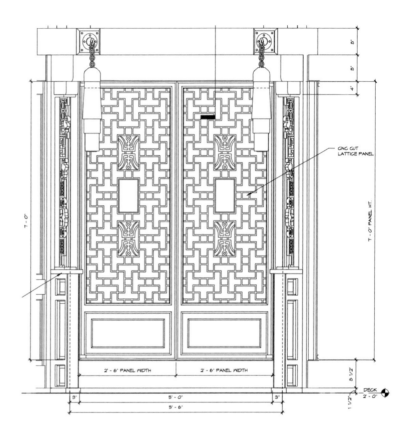

Five-axis tools usually mill high-density foam signboard if a more finished surface is required. If the surface needs to be less finished and a bit more porous, less-dense Styrofoam is used (typically used for simulating concrete).

But for *very* tight, automotive-quality finishes, CNC machines are used to make the molds, which are then treaded and used as negatives for fiberglass casting, a process that was used to manufacture the Fantasticar, as shown in Figure 26.9. And although Revit *wasn't* used to model the Fantasticar, it was used to model the dashboard elements that were used in the car — and its garage.

FIGURE 26.9
Fantasticar garage
and support
elements from
*Fantastic Four: Rise
of the Silver Surfer*

Geometry modeled in Revit will usually be taken to Rhino for *unfolding* a developable surface — like the airplane fuselage for *Snakes on a Plane*. But the structural ribs that were modeled in Revit were resolved by water cutting (Figure 26.10).

FIGURE 26.10
Cockpit interior of airplane fuselage from *Snakes on a Plane*

Construction

Some of the differences that you'll encounter in the film and stage industries compared to architecture will resonate when you get to construction. This is not to say that architectural projects aren't highly detailed — just that they're detailed differently. In film and stage production, you'll model not only what will be seen but in some cases what will *not* be seen. For example, when modeling, take into account the green screens beyond the actual sets, as in Figure 26.11. Being able to accurately previsualize their size and locations during the design standpoint is important.

FIGURE 26.11
Green screens surround the Karnak set from *Watchmen*

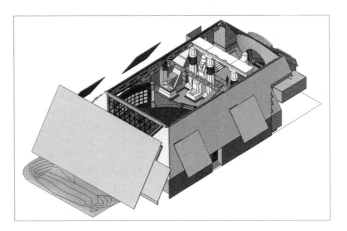

Previsualization in Revit

Remember that when you're designing scenically, you're going to be focusing on maintaining the emotive quality of the design without getting into too much detail. As the design progresses, geometric intent will give way to specific content. But even then, someone will take over what you've started and give the final look and feel to your work. You're not just trying to show the literal geometry of what needs to be constructed — you're also trying to maintain the emotive quality and connection to the earliest production sketches.

Form/Transparency

Concentrate on illustrating differences between what is solid and what isn't. The context of what is *beyond* the immediate space is important. Note the equipment in the room beyond the center space. For example, in Figure 26.12 the materials in Reed's science lab are muted and suggestive — but not too literal. Color is used to distinguish between different materials rather than to express specific materiality.

FIGURE 26.12
View through
Reed's lab from
*Fantastic Four: Rise
of the Silver Surfer*

TEMPLATE OR NO TEMPLATE?

Surprisingly, Bryan doesn't keep a project template. He says not starting from a template keeps it simple. However, details are often reused, and Bryan has created a set of custom line styles to indicate wild walls (where the walls have deliberately designed breaks so they can be opened for camera access).

Components and system families are *not* typically reused from project to project in the film industry — everything is highly customized from project to project (unless a sequel is being considered). Rather, Bryan uses a more elegant process of employing generic elements as placeholders during the early design stages. These component and system families are sufficient to indicate the design intent of placement, spacing, and locations — the big ideas of the design. As the design is refined, he'll swap out the placeholders with more-specific elements that share the same category and insertion point. Being able to swap out one idea for another quickly and easily is something that Bryan remarks "is what's really nice about Revit."

Lighting/Shadows

Even before materials are assigned, lighting plays an important role in adding emotive, dramatic context to the design. You have a couple of options because Revit allows shadows in real time but only a single light source, as illustrated in Figure 26.13. Beyond this you're going to need to render.

FIGURE 26.13
Real-time shaded view

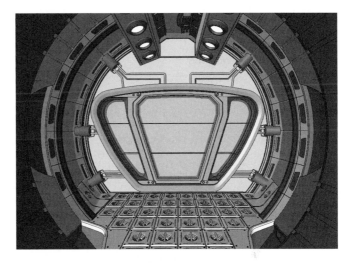

While the objects in Revit can contain the actual lights that can be controlled at time of rendering, this may not be enough. So keep in mind that studio lights (lights without lighting fixtures — just the light source) can be added to the project as well, a technique that was used to visualize Figure 26.14. These kinds of lights are useful for overdramatizing lighting effects and overcoming otherwise hard edges of shadows at the time of rendering.

FIGURE 26.14
Rendered view through the airlock, *Fantastic Four*

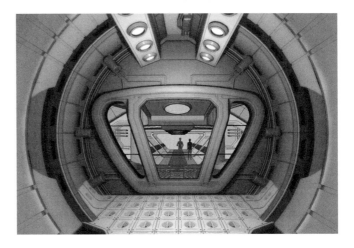

Materials

When materials are added, they're probably going to be understated during the design process. More detailed and specific materials assignments will be assigned by CGI artists (who will probably benefit from using your files as a starting point). In Figure 26.15, the horizon is being subtly suggested — but not as a hard, horizontal line in the distance that separates Earth from sky. Any more detail would be a distraction!

FIGURE 26.15
Rendering of walkway structure, *I, Robot*

Rendering and Visualization

Renderings are critically important to the design process in the film industry, and you'll have to communicate simultaneously with regard to form, space, lighting, material, opacity, transparency, and so on, as shown in Figure 26.16. But in some cases, you'll want to be able to render one theme at the exclusion of others.

FIGURE 26.16
Creating a matte-rendering filter

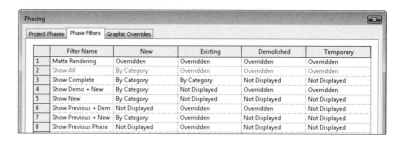

Rendering conceptually as any solid color is a quick way to rationalize and objectify the design. This can be quickly and easily done in Revit using phasing. All you need to do is create a new phase filter called Matte Rendering. Be sure all the phase filter assignments are set to Overridden. (To learn more about phasing, see Chapter 11, "Working with Phases, Groups, and Design Options.") This is shown in Figure 26.17, as phase filters are being overridden; Figure 26.18 illustrates material assignments associated with a particular phase.

FIGURE 26.17
Overriding phase
filters

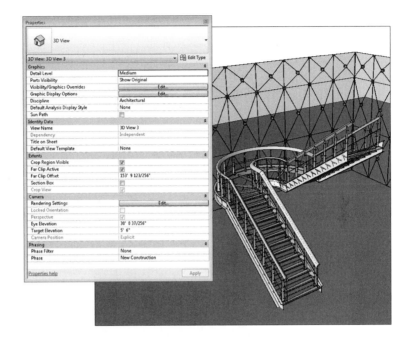

FIGURE 26.18
Applying material
assignments via
phasing

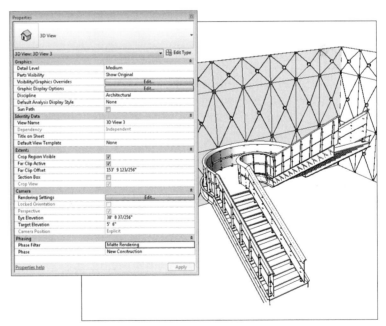

Using the Phasing dialog box, set the Graphic Overrides values of both shaded and rendered material assignments of the New phase to a solid, white (or off-white) matte material, as shown in Figure 26.19.

FIGURE 26.19
Overriding the surface and materials

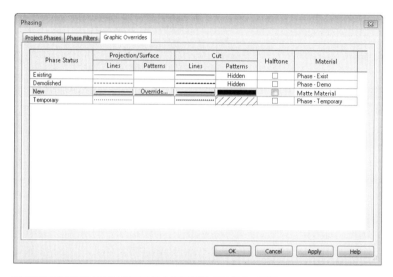

Create a 3D view, open the View Properties dialog box, and set Phase Filter to Matte Rendering. Figure 26.20 and Figure 26.21 show the results (before and after).

FIGURE 26.20
Rendered without glass

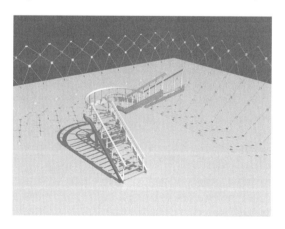

FIGURE 26.21
Rendered with glass

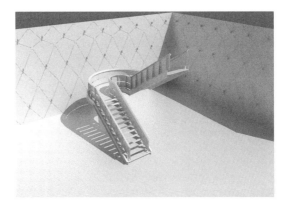

When you render with these settings, the result will be a monolithic scene that doesn't require you to manually manipulate the materials one by one for shaded views or renderings.

Keep in mind when using this technique that glass will render as opaque. If you want to render with glass as translucent, you'll want to render twice and create a composite view. First, turn off any glass via Visibility Graphics (Categories or Subcategories), and then render the view. Now create a composite view with the glass turned both on and off, and then set the transparency of the view with the glass turned on to around 20 percent. Figure 26.22 shows the final result.

FIGURE 26.22
Final composite view

Creating a hidden line composite view is just one more step beyond creating a composite rendered view (Figure 26.23). Hidden lines are helpful for distinguishing objects that are small, translucent/transparent, or at some distance from the viewer because they accentuate the edges of objects. In these cases you can export a hidden line view and then overlay with a rendered view in order to accentuate edges (Figure 26.24).

FIGURE 26.23
Hidden line export

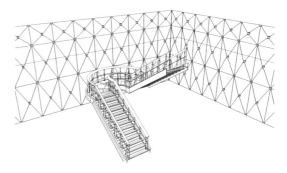

FIGURE 26.24
New composite
view

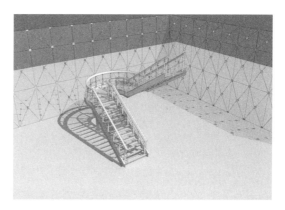

With this kind of composite view, it's easy to see why they're so effective and desirable. In Figure 26.25, it's apparent that important details are missing! But in the next image, the details are clearly visible through highlighting the edges of those objects from an exported hidden line view (Figure 26.26).

FIGURE 26.25
Detail before hid-
den line composite

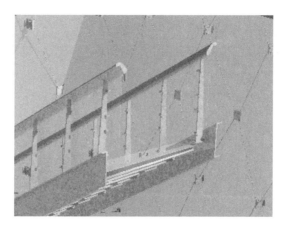

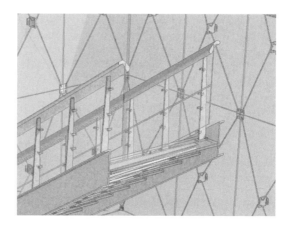

Photorealistic Renderings

Photorealistic renderings are certainly important to the design process for a set designer, but if your work is meant to resolve constructability, it may turn out that you're not responsible for creating highly emotive, finished views. Be aware that from within Revit, you are limited to the geometry that is in the Revit file.

But even if Revit were capable of creating any form imaginable, keep in mind that another person needs to render in their language of choice. And after years of fluency in one language, it's not likely that they're going to change languages to render in Revit. Additionally, they'll subject their renderings to significant postproduction in an image editor. So be prepared to work with the visualization specialist by exporting Revit to another format (DWG, 3DS, FBX, and so on).

Exploded Views

Live exploded 3D views can be quickly and easily assembled in a couple of ways. The first technique involves creating a section box around part of your project and then selecting and copying this section box (Figure 26.27). Copying a section box automatically creates another section box with the same view.

FIGURE 26.27
Real-time section
views through air-
lock, *Fantastic Four*

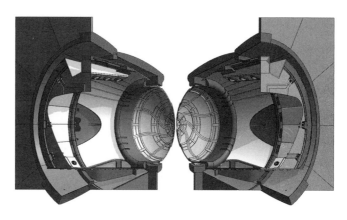

Another option is to isolate elements in duplicated views (with or without a section box). When you assemble the views together (on a sheet), you'll be able to pull them apart, creating the effect that the object is being pulled apart. This will help illustrate individual elements that will be prefabricated for assemblage.

Revit to CGI Workflow

According to Bryan, the film and stage industries in Vancouver overwhelmingly use Maya. And before FBX exporting, getting your file to a usable format wasn't always too successful. Fortunately, FBX has really helped. But in some cases you'll export to 3D DWG (and usually as ACIS solids). Autodesk® Mudbox® software is frequently used along with ZBrush for high-resolution close-ups.

Your Revit file is often a useful starting point for the CGI work that complements the physical sets, which can be exquisitely detailed, as in the Karnak main hall in *Watchmen* (Figure 26.28). What's nice is that everything should line up between the physical and digital designs. But don't be alarmed if much of your work needs to be rebuilt in Maya.

FIGURE 26.28
Karnak main hall,
Watchmen

First, people like to have full control in a familiar language (application) that they have used for years. The deadlines are demanding, and there's no room for unpredictable outcomes. Because Maya is being used extensively in the industry, it's likely that Revit files will get leveraged in Maya.

Second, the level of detail that you've produced in your Revit file (you know — the level of detail that is way beyond standard architectural practice) will likely be unnecessarily high for the CGI artist, as illustrated in Figure 26.29. Rendering is still incredibly expensive and time consuming. So any techniques that shorten rendering times (without sacrificing quality) are welcome. As a result, the CGI artists often use materials to represent granular geometric details — the kind of details that you've just modeled with geometry in Revit to resolve construction (Figure 26.30)!

FIGURE 26.29
Karnak glazing
detail

FIGURE 26.30
Karnak detail; note
the chamfering of
bolts

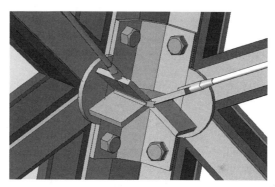

STACKING VIEWS

You should anticipate how the views should stack. It's not yet possible to reorder the front/back relationships of views *after* the views have been placed on sheets. So the views in the background need to be placed on the sheet *first* and the views that need to be in the foreground should be placed *last*. The image shown here displays the real-time exploded views through the airlock on *Fantastic Four*.

Best Practices for Film and Stage

Best practices for using Revit in the film and stage industries may have a lot in common with standard architectural practices, but sometimes they'll be significantly different. We'll cover both the similarities and the differences in the following sections.

Level of Detail

As mentioned earlier, the *level of detail* that you will model in these types of projects will greatly exceed what is customary in a standard architectural project, where a high resolution of detail is either not necessary for construction or is resolved in 2D with detail components during documentation. In this industry, modeling generically in 3D and then attempting to show more detail in 2D can be a distraction to an exacting art director. So don't be surprised if you're expected to model to less than an inch in detail — and expect what you model to be a fairly literal representation of what will be built.

Geometric Flexibility

Maintaining flexibility during design is critical to a successful project because once production starts, everything starts moving quickly. Use generic representations of an approximate size and category. As the design progresses, you can easily swap these design placeholders out for more specific elements.

Design Alternatives

In the film and stage industries, phasing and design options will also be used in 3D and documentation views to illustrate alternatives where pieces of the set need to convey some sort of movement — for example, if an object needs to be opened and closed or extended and retracted. In this case, simply assigning a unique phasing or design option to those elements will allow you to filter the views to show only one condition or another at a time.

In the case of the Comedian's (Eddie Blake's) apartment in *Watchmen*, phasing was used to illustrate the shattered curtain panel. The existing panel was unbroken, while the proposed panel was shown in the broken state (Figure 26.31).

FIGURE 26.31
Use phasing or design options to show alternatives.

Nesting Geometry

Nesting is extremely useful for creating a component once and then using it in many different components (Figure 26.32). The advantage is that it's significantly faster (more than 95 percent faster in some cases) to update family components rather than groups. Keep in mind that a lot of the elements you'll model will themselves contain nested components. This allows you to manage and update repetitive relationships quickly (Figure 26.33).

FIGURE 26.32

Nesting showing the door open in VIKI brain, *I, Robot*

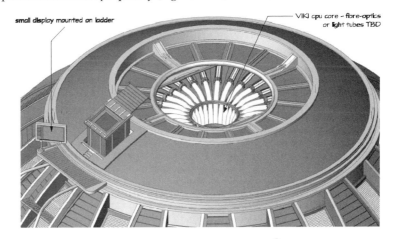

FIGURE 26.33

Nested components in VIKI brain, *I, Robot*

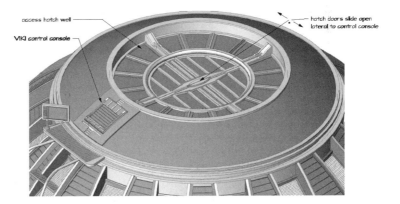

Family Category

Choosing the right family category is also important, but not in a way that often comes up in standard architecture practice ("Hmm . . . furniture or furniture system?"). Most of the time, the Generic Model category will suffice. But there remain a couple of subcategories that are really important.

First, you will have to select a Lighting category if you anticipate using the component to render lighting effects. Second, use face based rather than hosted.

Either face-based or hosted components can cut their host. With a face-based family, you need to model a void to cut the face, whereas with a hosted family you must add an opening or a void. That's not so much of a difference, right?

Wrong. If you select hosted, you need to also know what kind of host is going to be cut (Wall, Floor, Roof, or Ceiling). But in this industry, what is a floor one moment might be a ceiling the next. And what is a wall today may turn out to be a roof later! So specifically selecting a hosted category (which requires you to know what sort of host is going to be cut) can lead to disastrous results when the design changes (and it will…a lot)! Using a face-based family avoids this nasty consequence.

Another reason is that face-based families will easily orient themselves to the face of either component or system families, whether in the project or in a nested family environment.

Finally, a face-based family can cut the face of both system families (in a project environment) as well as component families (when nested). Overall, face-based families offer a lot of flexibility during the design process.

Keep in mind that in many cases nested components are likely to end up in multiple families as well as in the project environment. This adds another layer of complexity when you find yourself in the awkward situation of having to open and edit multiple families to make whole project changes to a nested component. This is where sharing the parameters of the nested components will save you a lot of time and trouble.

Here's how: If you expect that the nested family is going to be nested into other families — or used directly in the project — you'll want to consider setting the Family parameter of the nested family to Shared (Figure 26.34).

FIGURE 26.34
Select Shared in the
Family parameters.

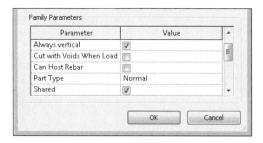

Simply select the originally nested component and edit its Category And Parameters setting. Select the Shared option and then reload this nested component in your family. The next time this family (containing the nested and shared component) is loaded into your project, both the component and the nested/shared component are loaded into the project. Whenever you edit this special shared/nested family (from either the project or one of the many families it's nested into), it will update everywhere in the project.

BE CAREFUL WITH SHARING

Remember, once an element is shared and loaded into the project, you cannot unshare that family!

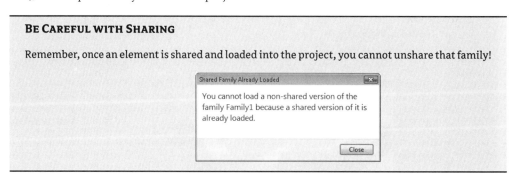

Advanced Geometry Creation

Modeling complex forms in Revit often differs from modeling in other 3D applications. Think of sculpture. First you can create something by building a formwork and then casting what you want within that form. This is an additive approach.

In Revit, the process, sculpturally speaking, is more subtractive. In other words, the complex form that you're trying to create is going to be accomplished by creating more geometry than necessary and then carving away the results with a void. This can be done by building up layers of geometry (and perhaps joining them). But when you add voids, selectively cut only certain layers of the geometry.

See Figure 26.35 for a simple example. Although the family looks complicated, it is composed of only *five* elements: two solids and three voids. This file is also available for download from the Chapter 26 folder as the c26 Complex Cube.rfa file.

FIGURE 26.35
Creating complex forms through layering geometry and voids

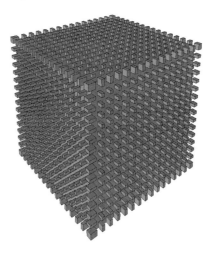

Carving geometry to resolve a desired shape is a simple technique but absolutely essential for being able to quickly create and (more important) to iterate complex forms in Revit, such as the airlock door in Figure 26.36. According to Bryan, nonlinear solid/void relationships give Revit the edge over other more generic modeling tools (Figure 26.37).

FIGURE 26.36
Single section of the airlock door

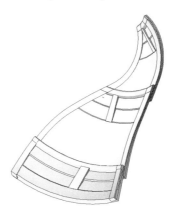

FIGURE 26.37
Completed airlock
door, *Fantastic Four*

The file of the airlock door (c26 Airlock Door.rvt) is also available for download from the Chapter 26 folder. It's a great example of using overlapping solids and selectively placed voids to cut away portions of geometry while leaving adjacent solid geometry intact. This technique was skillfully used to cut away the reveals that surround the airlock door (Figure 26.38).

FIGURE 26.38
Final rendering
of the airlock door
assembly, *Fantastic
Four*

Worksharing

Worksets are typically not needed in the film and stage industries unless the project is large or contains a campus-like collection of other Revit projects. Although this atmosphere is highly collaborative, it's also task-centric — one person dedicated to working on one part of the project or file is not uncommon. So using worksharing to distribute Revit files across multiple team members is not common.

Industry Examples

Having worked in the film and stage industries using Revit since 2003, Bryan has successfully managed a number of design challenges. The following are just a few production-related stories.

I, Robot

I, Robot was Bryan's first feature film and really quite special. After working for a number of years in set design at the scale of commercial production, it was trial by fire. The sets were much larger, as well as multistory, as shown in Figure 26.39.

Bryan had to take over from an architect, and in some cases, the drawings were hard to read. In other cases, one design view would not align with another view, and in this industry coordination is extremely important because of the short deadlines.

In Bryan's words, "Revit really saved the day." Views were always consistent and always agreed with each other. The precision was always there, even considering the detail in the access walkway and platform surrounding the computer core (Figure 26.40). Revit was used to count the number of spider brackets used for the railings and other hardware.

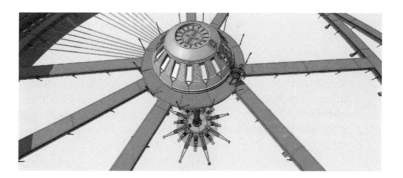

Ultimately, the VIKI brain that had been modeled in Revit for constructing the physical sets was leveraged for CGI work. This gave the CGI artists some great starting points (Figure 26.41). Again, precision was key.

FIGURE 26.41
Shaded detail perspective of VIKI brain, *I, Robot*

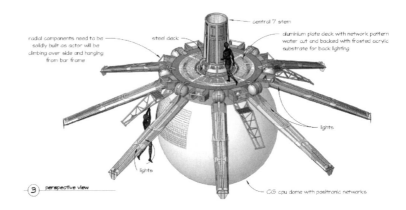

Fantastic Four

Fantastic Four was the next feature film that Bryan helped design in Revit. In this project, the level of detail increased because so many renderings were being done directly in Revit for this movie, starting with the interior of the space station (Figure 26.42).

FIGURE 26.42
Space station interior, *Fantastic Four*

Of course, these were the days of AccuRender — and many extra studio lights were placed in order to avoid the hard shadows that were common at the time. The shadows in AccuRender had hard edges and required a lot of artificial lights placed around the space, especially considering the detail and lighting of the ceiling (Figure 26.43). Fortunately, the implementation of Autodesk® mental ray® software has improved the process.

FIGURE 26.43
Space station ceiling, *Fantastic Four*

The ceiling was challenging to model, according to Bryan, because there were so few straight lines. But he was able to do it with Revit using a lot of built-up solid and void relationships. The sweeps going along the edges of the ceiling and down to the floor were particularly challenging, as shown in Figure 26.44.

FIGURE 26.44
Entry hall to space station, *Fantastic Four*

When you can't get the model just right, you have the geometry as context for documentation. This saves a lot of time over the back and forth compared to modeling in 3D, exporting, and then documenting in 2D.

X-Men: *The Last Stand*

This project built on the challenges of the previous projects. Bryan soon found himself selected to design the third-act set (see the section "Lead Time and Production" earlier in this chapter). The island of Alcatraz was going to be the third-act set and would be used for the big fight scene at the end of the *X-Men* film. It turned out to be an interesting challenge because it involved a lot of both indoor and outdoor sets, such as the exterior Alcatraz set (Figure 26.45).

FIGURE 26.45
Alcatraz set, *X-Men: The Last Stand*, looking toward prison complex

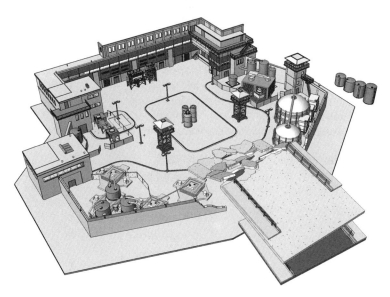

Fortunately for the third-act set, you're likely to be given a bit more lead time. It's got to be detailed — and it's going to be used for the big finale. For *X-Men*, it also had to include a debris field that was supposed to suggest the ripped-apart end of the Golden Gate Bridge (Figure 26.46).

FIGURE 26.46
Alcatraz set, *X-Men: The Last Stand*, looking toward collapsed bridge structure

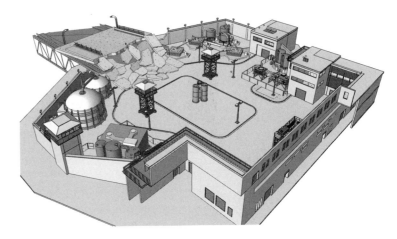

Snakes on a Plane

Originally, for *Snakes on a Plane*, actual pieces of aircraft fuselage were going to be used in context of other set pieces that remained to be built. So the new challenge was integrating pieces of actual planes into Revit for context. But in the end, the art directors and set designers decided to rebuild the plane from scratch and simply gutted the existing plane for parts and set dressing (Figure 26.47).

FIGURE 26.47
Airplane section, *Snakes on a Plane*

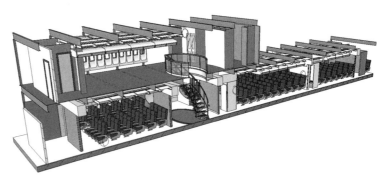

Some of the 3D shapes were a challenge. For instance, the fuselage consisted of complex shapes. But in the end, nearly the whole plane was designed in Revit, even the cockpit area (Figure 26.48).

FIGURE 26.48
Cockpit rendering,
Snakes on a Plane

Fantastic Four: *Rise of the Silver Surfer*

According to Bryan, this project was especially rewarding — the people working on the project were great. According to the production designer, Revit helped "save the movie." The set pieces, like the highly complex and detailed pagoda shown in Figure 26.49, required intricate structural elements and carefully cut screened panels.

FIGURE 26.49
Exterior of the
pagoda, *Fantastic
Four: Rise of the
Silver Surfer*

In the case of the pagoda, full-sized sheets were printed and used as stencils for cutting the lofted, structural ribs. In other cases, CNC machines were used to cut out the door and panel pieces designed in Revit (Figure 26.50).

FIGURE 26.50
Pagoda upper
screen detail,
*Fantastic Four: Rise
of the Silver Surfer*

Night at the Museum: Battle of the Smithsonian

For this movie, numerous set pieces were designed in Revit. But there was one particularly interesting challenge: a replica of the Wright Flyer, as shown in Figure 26.51, the world's first powered aircraft to achieve controlled, sustained flight. According to Bryan, there are companies that make very high-quality replicas for museums and other displays. In this case, though, the replica needed to be 85 percent smaller than the original. Oh, and the wings had to have proxy elements built of fiberglass so that the actor could walk on them during production.

FIGURE 26.51
Wright Flyer, *Night
at the Museum:
Battle of the
Smithsonian*

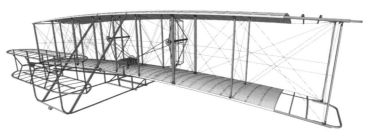

While reviewing copies of drawings originally from the Smithsonian, Bryan wasn't sure that it could be done in Revit. The detail in the drawings was extraordinary. But once he began to visualize and understand the parts that made up the whole — the ribs, the frame, and the engine — it all became quite clear. In the end, according to Bryan, it was great fun modeling the Wright Flyer in Revit.

In fact, in addition to the air and space set, even smaller details like the afterburner for the F104 were modeled in Revit (Figure 26.52).

Watchmen

Watchmen is a graphic novel (originally released as a limited series that included 12 comic books). It was created by writer Alan Moore, artist Dave Gibbons, and colorist John Higgins and published during 1986 and 1987. Although attempts to create a live-action film began shortly after the graphic novel's success, some deemed the complex narrative unfilmable.

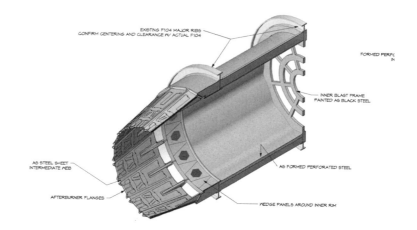

FIGURE 26.52

F104 Afterburner, *Night at the Museum: Battle of the Smithsonian*

Numerous production starts and stops continued until Warner Brothers brought in Zack Snyder (the director of *300*) and principal photography began in 2007. Snyder even created his own storyboard sketches to fill in the action between the key frames of the novel. According to Bryan, "It was fantastic working for the director who creates his own version of storyboards. He has a very visual approach. I actually used the sketches for reference within the context of the design and construction documentation."

Another detail that Bryan looked forward to during the *Watchmen* film and production was the opportunity to work with Alex McDowell, the production designer (www.imdb.com/name/nm0568273/). Bryan had long admired McDowell's work.

The Karnak set was the third-act set and would be extremely detailed. At the direction of McDowell, the bolt heads were modeled in Revit with chamfers (Figure 26.53).

FIGURE 26.53

Interior of Karnak, *Watchmen*

Once again, phasing was used extensively to turn off and on large portions of the model to visualize the various stages of construction and production. The glazing system was also extensive.

Ultimately, the model was so complex that major portions of it were done as large collections of nested families, as shown in Figure 26.54. This was done to manage the amount of highly detailed repetition.

FIGURE 26.54
Complex structure family for the Karnak set, *Watchmen*

Creating individual families and then nesting them into a single, large family maintained design iteration. This large family assemblage was then loaded and placed into the project (Figure 26.55). Admittedly, families of this scale might not be a standard architecture best practice because it would obviously affect scheduling. But the advantage to the exception in this case is pretty obvious. Rather than creating separate projects and linking them together, you're creating really large families and loading them into the project (Figure 26.56).

FIGURE 26.55
Support elements for Dr. Manhattan's lab, *Watchmen*

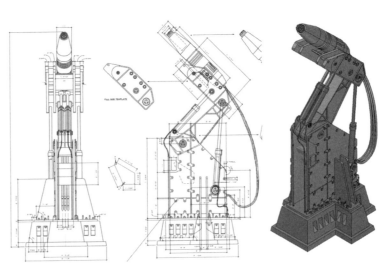

FIGURE 26.56
Tachyon corridor in
Karnak, *Watchmen*

Design iteration could then be managed by opening the master family and then drilling down to get to the single nested family, as in Figure 26.57. Next, the nested families would be reloaded into the master family. Then this master family would be reloaded into the project file, illustrated by the single cell in Figure 26.58.

FIGURE 26.57
Portion of Tachyon
panel

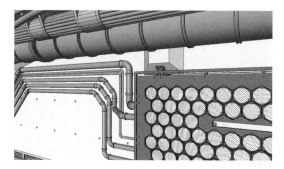

FIGURE 26.58
Detail of nested
Tachyon cell

Tron Legacy

With *Tron Legacy*, Bryan used Revit to design the kind of spaces that many architects seldom get to experience in their entire careers. The End of the Line nightclub in *Tron Legacy* is just another example of his extraordinary work. Few walls were parallel; nearly all were slanted (Figure 26.59). Because of the multitude of chamfered edge conditions, Rhino was sparingly used to model a number of intersections (Bryan still laments that Revit can't create these chamfered shapes natively). SAT files from Rhino were imported into Revit families before being placed in the Revit project. But overall, the vast majority of the project was done in Revit — from design through documentation.

FIGURE 26.59
Interior of End of
the Line bar

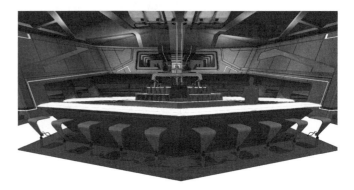

During the production process, significant design changes had to be accomplished in a very short time. In one case, the project had to be reduced to "85 percent of the previous design." Well, you can't just scale down the set! The set designers and art director had to rethink the design, and using phasing, Bryan was able to visualize which portions of the set would be built and which could be stitched in virtually.

In Figure 26.60, the lighter, outer geometries indicate the portions of the set that could be computer generated, distinguishing them from the portions that could be physically and practically built. FBX exporting from Revit has been a huge improvement in tightening the distinction between the physical and the digital. What we're seeing, suggests Bryan, is "more and more digital agility between the designers, builders, and visual effects artists."

FIGURE 26.60
Lighter, outer
geometry indicates
computer-gener-
ated portions of
the set

It was times like this that the scheduling features of Revit were invaluable. Material takeoffs were completed in Revit for the structural steel (by gauge) because so many custom elements had to be built.

According to Bryan, the set design and construction represented a well-honed design–build environment. The art directors and set designers were on site and nearly side by side with the construction crews. Information was delivered just in time. Using 3D was essential to communicating with everyone involved (Figure 26.61).

FIGURE 26.61
Blue screens beyond the construction of the physical set

Contextual documentation was the only way to communicate as much information as efficiently as possible. As much information is shown on the sheet as possible to avoid waiting for numerous sheets to be delivered to the construction crews. As you can see in Figure 26.62, the simultaneous slanted and curved nature of the design would make communicating the project in 2D impractical. But even when you can model in 3D, you still need to clearly dimension and document — and it's very important to have both! According to Bryan, Revit excels in both areas.

FIGURE 26.62
Slanted and curved walls

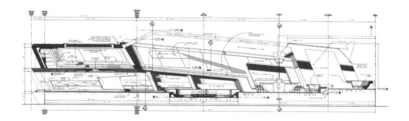

Real-time, shaded views were still used extensively to indicate different materials and finishes. Figure 26.63 illustrates the reveals in the walls and ceilings that would be used for lighting and lighting channels. But the shaded views also helped quickly communicate what the camera would see long before actual set construction was complete.

For more finished renderings, Bryan wanted to communicate materials with a more muted finish. But reflectivity and lighting was essential. The technique that he used was unique and elegant. Three views were exported from Revit: a rendered view, a real-time view with ambient lighting (no edges), and a hidden-line view.

These three views were composited in a photo-editing tool, where Bryan had control over the transparency of each image. The result allowed shadows and transparency while accentuating the edges and providing textured, gritty surfaces. Figure 26.64 shows the result: a polished, yet hand-illustrated, look and feel — almost a graphic novel artistic sensibility.

FIGURE 26.63
Lighting reveals in the walls and ceiling

FIGURE 26.64
Composited views of the End of the Line bar

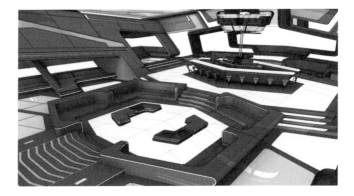

So what was one of the high points of the entire project? After the production wrapped, the talent and crew held a fantastic wrap party in the nightclub used in the movie!

Sucker Punch

With Rick Carter (www.imdb.com/name/nm0141437/) as the production designer, Bryan knew that the *Sucker Punch* project would be an amazing challenge. Among his other high-visibility projects, Carter received an Oscar for his work on *Avatar*. The director and screenwriter of the project was Zack Snyder, who was also the director of *Watchmen* (another award-winning project that Bryan had worked on). Bryan described the design-to-construction process as "all over the place — but in a good way!"

Sucker Punch is about a young girl who has been locked away in a mental institution by her stepfather. But rather than accept her fate, she envisions a fantasy world that is a parallel to her real one and uses these visions to plan her escape along with her fellow inmates. As a result, many of the set pieces needed to be reminiscent of both her real/institution and fantasy worlds.

Bryan worked on numerous sets for this film, including the B-25 bomber, the nurse station/ lounge bar, the Japanese temple, and the train car.

The bomber set was done in two separate parts: one for the nose and another for the main fuselage. Revit was essential to the success of this project and was used from design through documentation. Revit was also used to help fabricate the steel ribs used as the structure (Figure 26.65). After the separate sections were modeled in Revit, they were laser cut from sheet metal.

FIGURE 26.65
Structural ribs ready for laser cutting

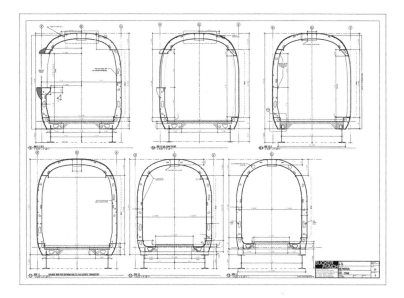

Because the model had been designed and assembled in Revit before laser cutting (Figure 26.66), the team was able to determine that the actual dimension of a B-25 bomber would not be adequate for filming. Bryan explained: "The real interior was far too small for the scene. In the actual plane there's only enough room to crawl on hands and knees to the tail gunning section. We had to enlarge it quite a bit."

FIGURE 26.66
Fuselage structure designed in Revit

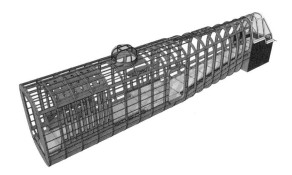

The nurse's station had to double as the lounge set in the film. Because one set was meant to reference another, both were created in the same Revit file, and Bryan used phasing to show either set in context with the other. Figure 26.67 shows the nurse's station, with its brick façade and surrounding chain link.

FIGURE 26.67
Nurse's station

FIGURE 26.67
Nurse's station

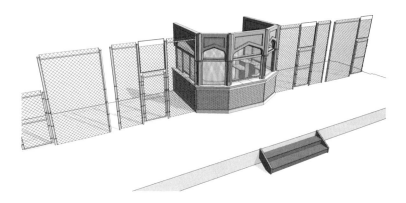

In another Revit phase and scene from the film, the nurse's station is shown from the same position — this time as a period bar (Figure 26.68).

FIGURE 26.68
Lounge set

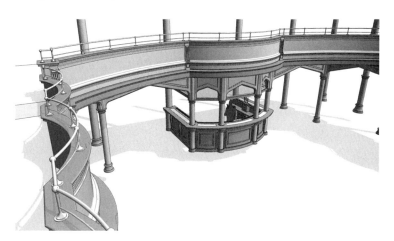

According to Bryan, Revit excels at creating highly illustrative documentation. A great example of this is the full-scale detailed section of the bar top (Figure 26.69). For these details, Bryan manually traced around the outer edge of the geometry with a hatch pattern to accentuate the edge for the construction crews, and he claims, "They really love these kinds of details."

For the Japanese temple set, only a small portion was physically constructed — the rest was a digital extension. The Revit file (Figure 26.70) was used to explore different roof possibilities for the digital set for the temple designed in Revit.

For the maglev (short for magnetic levitation) train portion, phasing played a major part in showing how the sets would need to be modified during the production of the film. In one phase, the roof is shown complete, whereas in another phase (Figure 26.71) the roof is shown blown open.

FIGURE 26.69
Detail section of
lounge

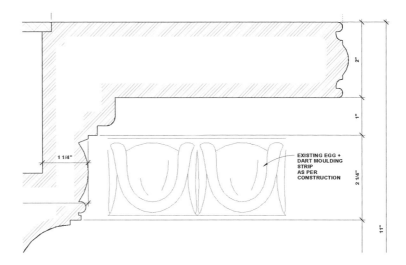

FIGURE 26.70
Japanese temple
options

FIGURE 26.71
Roof opening shown
through phases

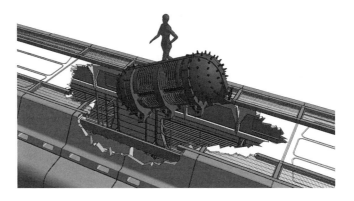

Once again, the rendering tools were used directly in Revit to visualize transparency, reflectivity, and artificial lighting (Figure 26.72).

FIGURE 26.72
Matte renderings of
the train's interior

FIGURE 26.72
Matte renderings of
the train's interior

Bryan used the same technique of merging both rendered and real-time images to give his images an illustrative, hand-drawn impression (Figure 26.73).

FIGURE 26.73
Montage of real-
time and rendered
view

Without this technique, it would be difficult to visualize the level of detail required by the production designer as well as the construction teams. Small details, like the chamfered bolt heads around the lower edges of the train car and welded seams of the bulkhead door (Figure 26.74), would barely be noticed — yet they add an important look and feel to the image.

All of these visual and phasing techniques really pay off for the first train car. The level of detail is extraordinary. Voids are used extensively to communicate the front of the rail car being completely destroyed (Figure 26.75).

Since *Tron Legacy* and *Sucker Punch*, Bryan has completed work on *Rise of the Apes* and the next *Mission Impossible* film. What's next? According to Bryan, it's likely to be with director Zack Snyder and production designer Alex McDowell on the next *Superman* movie or with the director of *Tron Legacy*, Joseph Kosinski (www.imdb.com/name/nm2676052/), on *Oblivion*.

We aren't sure how he's going to be able to choose between two great major motion pictures, but we know we can't wait to see the results!

FIGURE 26.74
Detail of "exploded"
roof looking into
rail car

FIGURE 26.75
End detail of rail car

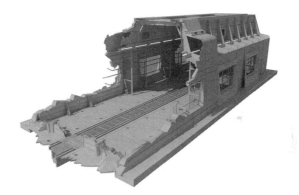

The Bottom Line

Design scenically.   According to Bryan Sutton, profiled in this chapter, designing scenically takes precedence over designing too literally. This might be different from standard architectural practice, but it's critical in the film and stage industries.

Master It   How would you design scenically, and how does this differ from standard architectural practice? What can you learn from the film and stage industries to keep the emotive quality high?

Use Revit in the design-to-production process.   While standard architectural practice entails design to documentation, the film and stage focus is from concept through construction.

Master It   With an emphasis on level of detail and tight, repetitive elements and finishes, what would you do to help maintain time and budget? How might you suggest creating intricate repetitive design elements in your next project?

Use Revit for previsualization.   When using Revit in the film industry, you need to keep the design loose during the early concept stages. You'll have to match the look and feel of the art director's vision. Keeping the materials muted will be far less distracting than being too specific. One of the great things about Revit is that you'll be able to emotively visualize in the same environment as you analytically rationalize. This will come in handy when the director, director of photography, and then art director all want a different question answered at the same time!

> **Master It**   How can you express constructability to a high level of detail, particularly when the object is going to be assembled from many individual parts? Why rely on standard architectural practice of documenting in plan, section, and elevation views?

Chapter 27

BIM in the Cloud

The AEC industry has come a long way in the last couple years since the chapter "Revit in the Cloud" in *Mastering Autodesk Revit Architecture 2011*. Since then, many firms have taken advantage of cloud-based hosting and computing to lower IT costs while increasing productivity. This update assumes you're generally familiar with cloud-based services as we consider how the technologies and services have matured. Gone are the days where we have to transfer large models around via FTP and wait days for design feedback. Clients expect almost real-time feedback, projects are moving faster, and firms are looking at tighter margins. All these things require maximum efficiency, and a BIM cloud provides just that.

In this chapter, you'll learn how to do the following:

- ◆ Realize practical, real-time collaboration with owner, design, and construction teams (IPD)

- ◆ Fit Autodesk's cloud into your BIM cloud collaboration

- ◆ Integrate a BIM cloud into your overall IT strategy

Understanding the Latest in BIM Cloud-Based Technology

Technology vendors Microsoft, Citrix, Oracle, VMware, nVidia, Teradici, Kaviza, and countless others are in a race to be the provider of virtual or remote desktop solutions because those are central to gaining all our cloud business. Because of this race, the technologies and approaches are changing rapidly. In the following sections, we'll look at some of the BIM cloud desktop building blocks. But keep in mind desktop virtualization or remote desktops were the last piece of the puzzle that enabled full migration to a *cloud*. In a broad sense, a cloud is nothing more than a datacenter. *Cloud* is an IT buzzword that means we are abstracting your IT — putting it in a black box. You don't know where your computing power is located and you don't care as long as it is there when you need it. Moving your desktops to the cloud successfully pulls the rest of IT with it. CIOs know this, as do the software vendors.

ABOUT THE CONTRIBUTING AUTHOR: CHRIS FRANCE

Chris France is the president of Advance2000 NC and leads the charge for private cloud computing services at his firm. He has been in the AEC industry for 11 years as the CIO of Little Diversified Architectural Consulting and a founding member of the AIA CIO Large Firm Roundtable. As an IT professional, he has worked for some very large companies (IBM, Bank of America, Wells Fargo) and uses information technology to increase firm value. It is from this toolbox of experience that he began experimenting with BIM clouds, which led to his January 2010 *AECBYTES* article. Chris saw huge opportunities to provide more IT value, facilitate real-time collaboration, and reduce costs, and he is doing just that at Advance2000 (www.advance2000.com). He resides in Charlotte, North Carolina, with his wife and three children. Please connect with Chris on LinkedIn at www.linkedin.com/in/christopherfrance.

As a reminder, a BIM cloud desktop is a concept whereby you shift the location of your desktop computer processing. Rather than buying a traditional workstation or laptop and locating it at your desk, you buy a larger server or desktop solution that can sit in one central location (like a datacenter). So rather than buying 10 $5,000 workstations and scattering them around, you buy 1 desktop server for $20,000 and centralize it next to the datastore. Firms that have done this are saving money as well as gaining mobility in their design process. And it doesn't take long to realize that if Autodesk® Revit® Architecture software works well in a BIM cloud, the same could be said for other applications. In effect, companies are building a Windows mainframe that allows people to run all their business and design apps in a centralized fashion.

There are basically two types of desktops you can run in a datacenter: virtual and physical. A *virtual* desktop means that you have a large amount of server resources (CPU, RAM, and so forth) and then install a desktop virtualization package like VMware or Citrix in order to create *instances* of a Windows Desktop on this server. To the end user, it looks just like a remote desktop, but to the IT department, it is a shared server. A *physical* desktop is very much like the one sitting on your desk. Rather than buying a tower unit with the required CPU, RAM, and video, you generally buy a rack-mounted workstation that can easily be supported in a datacenter. I commonly recommend a few IT maxims and here's one: *Virtual when you can, physical when you must.* Some applications perform better on physical hardware today, but in the next few months or years, that will likely change as the virtual software improves. If you're in IT, you'll recall the same thing happened with server virtualization. When VMware first came out, there were some servers that could not be virtualized. Today, there are very few servers than cannot be virtualized. The same is happening with desktops.

Virtual Workstations

Let's take a moment to consider virtual workstation technologies from two vendors. If you understand the pros and cons of these two, you'll be able to apply them to others. Autodesk has announced a partnership with Citrix to allow its products to run in a virtual workstation. This seems to indicate that Autodesk developers actually test the products using this remote desktop software. VMware users will likely benefit from the same testing environment.

But it's important to understand that moving to a virtual infrastructure is no trivial task. It requires a greater level of IT sophistication than most small and medium-size firms have available. If you decide to virtualize your infrastructure, you'll need the server and storage infrastructure, the virtualization software, plus a trained and certified IT staff to build it and keep it running.

Here are two good options:

◆ VMware

  ◆ VMware uses PCoIP protocol and is proving to be very good with high-performance graphics over high-latency networks.

  ◆ The latest version of VMware View (5.0) has many desktop and bandwidth performance improvements.

  ◆ VMware tends to have more of the processing on the remote end, with only screen images and mouse clicks traversing the network.

  ◆ The IT administration console and applications are very robust and easy to use.

◆ Citrix

  ◆ Citrix uses its proprietary ICA protocol, and enhancements to that protocol are catching up to the performance of PCoIP. Depending on your network infrastructure and applications, some might say Citrix performs better than VMware.

  ◆ Citrix adopted a hybrid strategy in which there is still some local client processing.

  ◆ Citrix is more challenging to administer compared to VMware. If you have a large infrastructure, you'll likely require more IT people than you would with VMware.

The bottom line is that you'll do okay with either of these technologies. But if you're already familiar with VMware on the back end, I'd recommend using VMware on the front end. The same is true with Citrix. Essentially, you want to avoid fragmenting your infrastructure because if you fragment your infrastructure, you'll pay more in licensing costs as well as IT labor and training. It is very difficult to maintain experts in both technologies.

TIP

For AEC applications, stay away from terminal server type applications. Currently the best practice is to virtualize using the desktop virtualization tools like VMware View or Citrix XenDesktop rather than Microsoft Terminal Services or XenServer. You'll have fewer conflicts with other users, environment variables, and more.

Physical Workstations

Perhaps you've tested your remote application on a virtual desktop but you're not satisfied with the performance when compared to your current physical workstation. If this is the case, then consider putting your workstation into the datacenter. There are technologies like Teradici's PCoIP protocol that can be implemented in hardware in addition to software.

Centralizing your workstations in a datacenter is pretty simple. Rather than buy a $5,000 workstation that sits on your desk in your office, you could buy a $4,000 workstation and mount it in the datacenter. Then you would buy a terminal-like device (like a Wyse P20 zero client terminal) and make sure there's about 1 Mbps of bandwidth between you and your remote workstation. Compared to desktop performance, it's likely as good or better than a typical workstation configuration. But the biggest advantage is that you are now able to centralize your data and access it at gigabit speeds.

In other words, you no longer have to bring data to the designers. Now you can bring the designers to the data. But keep in mind that this is not an all-or-nothing proposition. A firm might realize that 90 percent of its workers do just fine with a virtual desktop and the other 10 percent can be given a physical desktop. But in either case, everyone is working in the same datacenter right next to the data.

Collaboration with Owner, Design, and Construction Teams

Let's consider what you can do with cloud-based technologies to improve your business and provide better design services to clients. The present trends indicate that project collaboration is the biggest driver to the adoption of cloud-based technology. Even before the legal entity for an integrated project delivery (IPD) process is in place, it's likely that you are being asked by your contractors and owners to work together in real time on your model across project teams. This is similar to migration to Revit. Early adopters used Revit, and once they became proficient and saw the benefits, those design firms soon required their consultants to also work in Revit.

The same thing is starting to happen with cloud-based technology. Once a firm proves that it works for them, they quickly see the benefits of having their consultants in the same cloud to quickly collaborate across projects. But once you decide to embrace cloud-based technology to collaborate across teams, the next decision you face is *where* to put this collaboration infrastructure. In other words, the physical location of the data is important. Then once you decide on the locations of your data, you'll need to connect these locations using a single- or multiple-cloud scenario.

IPD TIP

IPD requires multiple firms working together in real time on a project model. A BIM cloud collaboration hub is basically a secure project sitting in a datacenter with access given to anyone on the team who needs to have access, be they an architect, engineer, consultant, contractor, facility manager, or owner.

There are three options to consider with regard to hosting your collaborative, cloud-based environment:

Location 1—HQ office or datacenter   A firm builds a *private cloud* and then begins giving access to its regional offices. Generally, this requires any existing data circuits to be upgraded to accommodate increased cloud traffic. This lays the foundation to allow all of the firm's offices to work together as if they were sitting in one location. If a firm using this strategy wanted to collaborate with outside firms, it would have to set up additional capacity (and security) to allow outside firms to come into its infrastructure to work projects. This causes issues with hardware, software licensing, and support, but it is possible.

Location 2—regional offices   Putting cloud technology in a regional office may provide some benefit as far as hardware reduction and improved mobility, but it does nothing for collaboration. Your data is still distributed in each office. The challenge is figuring out how to collaborate with an outside firm. In a regional office, you still have to set up the IT infrastructure and security to accommodate an outside firm. You'll want to contain employees of the outside firm to only the project they are authorized to see and not allow them to roam around your entire network. This is hard enough to do at the HQ location and therefore nearly impossible for regional offices.

Location 3—AEC collaboration hub   While I was a member of the AIA CIO Large Firm Roundtable, it concerned me that so many large firms would have their own collaboration sandbox for hosting projects. In order for this to work, a typical consultant would have to access many clouds to work on projects. But does a large firm really want to be the IT shop for all their consultants? Why not approach a hosting provider or service that could create a collaboration hub just once for everyone to use? This is the approach of Advance2000. As of March 2012, firms like Cannon Design, Moore-Lindner Engineering, Little Diversified Architectural Consulting, HDR, Heapy Engineering, Mashburn Construction, and many others are collaborating via Advance2000 cloud-based services. Creating a private cloud provides some benefits, but an ecosystem of private clouds provides a greater level of collaboration. Whether you create your own cloud or find a qualified service provider, you'll have to select one of two options: either a single- or multiple-cloud collaboration.

Single-Cloud Collaboration

It's important to walk before you run when adopting a cloud-based collaboration strategy. Begin collaborating in one cloud before you try joining together multiple clouds. Here are some important issues to consider:

Hardware   Be sure there is enough capacity to provide a good experience to the entire project team. This requires ongoing forecasting of CPU, memory, graphics, and storage needs.

Software licensing   Generally you have to BYOL (bring your own license) to the cloud for design software. Infrastructure software like VMware, Citrix, and Microsoft Windows Server will have to be purchased by the cloud provider.

Security   Ensure that team members have access to only their project because you don't want another firm trolling through all your client projects. You'll also need to make sure everyone plays nice within the project cloud; you may have to make some directories read-only.

Network bandwidth   Unless you have a long-term relationship with the outside firm, you probably don't want to install private circuits. In other words, you'll be working over the Internet. Make sure you have Internet capacity at each end—the hosting firm's cloud as well as on the end of the remote consultant.

IT support and help desk   This is a significant issue because if your project team has a problem, who do they call? These issues need to be addressed ahead of problems to successfully collaborate in the cloud. This category also includes the basic IT operations like backing up and replicating your data, changing the oil, rotating tires, tune-ups, and so on.

COLLABORATION HUB TIP

Be sure to have your IT department set up a collaboration hub so you can test it out before going live with a project. Not only is the technology new, but your design workflow will change. You will also manage the project, design, and communicate in new ways that may seem unfamiliar at first. All this needs to be worked out so you don't have chaos in the middle of a deadline.

Multiple-Cloud Collaboration

Don't paint yourself into a corner as cloud-based strategies grow in adoptions. Consider where your project data is today and where it will need to be in the future. If one firm has its own BIM cloud in Los Angeles and another firm has its own BIM cloud in Boston, you have a number of options:

◆ Replicate project data between clouds.

◆ The sub-firm agrees to work in the lead firm's cloud.

◆ You engage a third-party cloud provider to provide hosting for the project,

◆ Your firm's IT is already in the same datacenter as the third-party hosting service and the provider just does a cross-connect for the project collaboration to occur.

And by the way, you'll still have to address all the items listed in the section "Single-Cloud Collaboration" in this multicloud approach. I consider working in a multicloud environment *running*, and we'll see this happening in 2012.

How the Autodesk Cloud Fits into Your BIM Cloud Collaboration Strategy

In the last two years, Autodesk has decided to get into the cloud game. From the outset, it looks like the Autodesk cloud is a public cloud just like the Microsoft, Google, Salesforce.com, ADP, or Amazon cloud. These clouds are a new distribution mechanism for these companies' products. Microsoft sells Microsoft products in its cloud. Google sells Google products in its cloud, and Autodesk provides Autodesk products in its cloud (Figure 27.1). They all have good products, and you should look into them. But these clouds don't mitigate collaboration issues for AEC firms. Most firms employ products from many of these vendors, and if you're not careful, you can end up with unintended consequences.

FIGURE 27.1
Autodesk core cloud subscription services include rendering, optimization, and collaboration

A cloud is synonymous with a datacenter. Each public cloud you employ is creating a datacenter housing some piece of your enterprise data. As a result, you will need to figure out how

to integrate the data in all these clouds. Do you have the Autodesk cloud talk directly to the Microsoft cloud? Do you bring data from these clouds back to your cloud? If you don't have the in-house capabilities to do what the Autodesk cloud does, then this could be a first step toward using cloud-based services. It is a good first step in providing on-demand resources to small firms. But some have found there is still a distributed data strategy. And even if you have your own private BIM cloud, you can still interact with the Autodesk cloud. On the other hand, you cannot run non-Autodesk design applications in the Autodesk cloud (Figure 27.2). So you will be required to move stuff around.

FIGURE 27.2
Autodesk Select cloud subscription services include rendering, optimization, collaboration, energy analysis, and Autodesk® Green Building Studio®

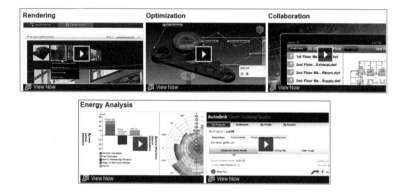

Integrating a BIM Cloud into Your Overall IT Strategy

Keep in mind that a firm owner or CIO doesn't look at a BIM cloud separately from the firm's IT infrastructure. Generally, an IT budget is made up of hardware, software, telecommunications, and IT labor. A BIM cloud is just part of these numbers.

Once firms build a BIM cloud for collaboration, it isn't long before the end users ask for more: Microsoft Office, Newforma, Deltek, even phone PBX systems. The following sections will address the issues to consider when your BIM cloud is wildly successful and you are collaborating.

Public Cloud Strategy

You'll want to consider the following steps for creating a public cloud strategy:

1. Set up a good infrastructure in your office. That will be the backbone on which to integrate all the various public clouds.

2. Implement Microsoft Office 365. As you employ this, consider how it will integrate with other applications. And you'll have to decide if you're okay with having this data stored in Microsoft's datacenter.

3. Implement Autodesk PLM360. Consider how you will get data to and from your storage locations.

4. Consider Google. You may have to decide between the Google and Microsoft clouds. You will also have to resolve how to directly exchange information between those clouds as well as if it needs to come back to your infrastructure for translation.

5. Implement Active Directory, which provides single sign-on capability. This is a problem that we've had forever in IT. Consider end-user experience bopping into public clouds—they generally cater to the masses and will not be hooked into your corporate directory. So when you log in to your corporate network, you'll need to also log in to each and every public cloud.

Consider all options of using public clouds. In Figure 27.3, a single datacenter of IT shared between two offices will be complicated by adding multiple public cloud datacenters. Begin with the end in mind.

FIGURE 27.3
Joining together public cloud datacenters can complicate collaboration

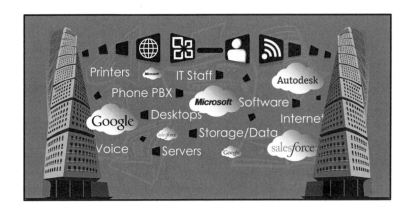

Private Cloud Strategy

Private cloud is a fancy term for a consolidated IT infrastructure sitting in a datacenter. If you have a distributed footprint, now is the time to start formulating your strategy to consolidate your IT. Many believe that in a few years, there will be no BIM clouds as such; rather, there will be private cloud and your BIM cloud will reside in your private cloud. There are a few options to create a private cloud:

♦ Make a private cloud (Figure 27.4).

   ◆ Build it yourself.

   ◆ Build it yourself but with some help from private cloud service providers.

FIGURE 27.4
Firms create a single private cloud to house all of the IT infrastructure

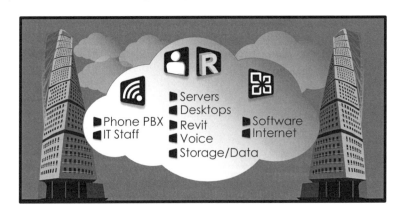

- Buy a private cloud.
  - Buy a cloud and have someone run it in your office.
  - Rent a cloud via a hosted service.

Hosted Private Cloud Strategy

A hosted private cloud is where this seems to be heading. The vast majority of firms will build an IT infrastructure that matches the size of their business. A 100-person firm does not build an infrastructure for 10,000 people. But when you look at the unit costs of computing of large firms versus small firms, you see a huge difference. It's like buying bulk at Sam's Club—the more you buy, the lower the unit costs.

The problem with Sam's Club is that if you don't use all the goods, they go bad and end up costing you more. But what if you could buy your goods in small batches at the same rate as the big batches? That's exactly what is happening with a hosted private cloud. A big infrastructure that can be leveraged over a larger user base will have much lower costs than if the same capabilities were mirrored on a small scale.

This economy of scale will allow hosting providers to do one of two things—drastically lower the costs of the same capabilities or lower costs of much better capabilities.

 **Real World Scenario**

UPGRADING TO PRIVATE HOSTING CLOUDS

Moore-Lindner is a small (less than 10-person) structural engineering firm based in Matthews, North Carolina. Typical of most firms its size, it had an in-house file server that was aging and needed to be replaced. On top of that, it relied on one of its structural engineers to keep its IT running, which took away from billable work. After researching and testing a private cloud over the course of a year, the firm decided to migrate to a hosted, private cloud rather than continue to spend money on local servers. Today, it is running in a hosted private cloud with Alcatel-Lucent IP telephony, integrated voice, Exchange/Outlook email, two virtual servers, 500 GB cloud storage, Revit® Structure desktops, 24/7 IT support, and enterprise-class security for what it used to have running locally without the IT capabilities, redundancy, or IT support. A small firm like this could have never afforded the technology it is running on if it did it themselves, but for roughly the same money as it was spending before, it got a whole lot of IT with fewer headaches. In this case, it migrated to the cloud before investing heavily.

Another firm, Little, had a different problem. With five offices nationwide and over 200 staff, it was looking for a better way to maintain its robust technology infrastructure to better serve its clients. All firms, sooner or later, have to upgrade their technologies. Rather than taking on a large capital expense for a new phone system, VMware server upgrades, and additional storage, Little moved to a hosted private cloud and avoided this outlay. While it is still migrating to the cloud as this goes to publication, Little is on track to reduce its annual IT spending by approximately 30 percent by leveraging cloud economies of scale.

As Figure 27.5 shows, a hosted private cloud provider is actually a multitenant IT high-rise that can leverage the economies of scale of desktop hardware, virtual servers, storage, PBX, voice and Internet circuits, datacenter space, and highly trained IT engineers. Another way to think of a hosted private cloud is as a Class A IT building that you can rent rather than buy. This is similar to the way many firms acquire office space. Owning a Class C IT building when you can rent a Class A IT building for less money seems to make far more sense.

FIGURE 27.5
A multitenant, hosted private cloud affords greater economies of scale and ability to scale up or down quickly

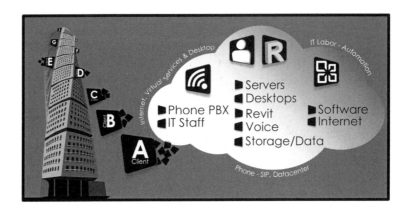

The Bottom Line

Realize practical, real-time collaboration with owner, design, and construction teams (IPD). Now that firms are Revit experts, they want to collaborate on projects in real time with any office in their firm as well as with outside firms. There was no practical, secure, and high-performing method for doing this until the BIM cloud.

    Master It How will you collaborate in real time with the entire design team no matter where they are located or for whom they work?

Fit Autodesk's cloud into your BIM cloud collaboration. Autodesk is providing additional benefit to its customers via its cloud-based design services. Any computing power that you can tap into at Autodesk might be that much less you have to build in your private cloud.

    Master It Can you use a private BIM cloud and the Autodesk cloud?

Integrate a BIM cloud into your overall IT strategy. A BIM cloud is a very specific solution for the AEC industry to facilitate working on design applications in a distributed footprint. It isn't long before a firm realizes that if it can put an architectural desktop into a datacenter, it can put all its firm technology into a datacenter.

    Master It What are the key strategies for integrating a BIM cloud into your overall IT strategy?

Appendices

In this section you will find:

- ◆ **Appendix A: The Bottom Line**
- ◆ **Appendix B: Tips, Tricks, and Troubleshooting**
- ◆ **Appendix C: Autodesk Revit Architecture 2013 Certification**

The Bottom Line

Each of The Bottom Line sections in the chapters suggest exercises to deepen skills and understanding. Sometimes there is only one possible solution, but often you are encouraged to use your skills and creativity to create something that builds on what you know and lets you explore one of many possible solutions.

Chapter 1: Introduction: The Basics of BIM

Leverage the model. Understanding the level of risk your firm is willing to take in new technologies will help you establish goals for your future use of BIM.

Master It Using the three areas of firm integration (visualization, analysis, and strategy), define how those areas overlap for your firm or project.

Solution Remember, there is no wrong answer in mapping a path forward for your firm or project. The important thing is to identify which areas are critical to the workflow of your firm to help you focus your future efforts.

Know how BIM affects firm culture. Not only is the transition to BIM from 2D CAD a change in applications, it's also a shift in workflow and firm culture. Understanding some of the key differences helps to ensure project and team success during the transition.

Master It What are some of the ways that BIM differs from CAD, and how does this change the culture of an office or project team?

Solution BIM shifts the level of effort in different phases of the project. This creates new responsibilities and workflows that the team needs to become aware of in order to maintain a level of predictability within the project workflow. Since BIM is also hosted out of a single file instead of several, isolated files, it changes the level of interteam communication on a project.

Focus your investment in BIM. One of the key elements to understanding BIM beyond documentation is simply to have an awareness of the possibilities. This allows you to make an educated decision as to what direction your firm or project would like to go.

Master It List some of the potential uses of a BIM model beyond documentation.

Solution Spatial validation, visualization, facility management, construction visualization, blast analysis, and whole-building analysis are all potential uses of a BIM model.

Chapter 2: Principles: UI and Project Organization

Understand the organization of the user interface. In addition to understanding how your project is organized, to use Revit software well you must understand how the user interface is organized. Once you grasp both of these concepts, you'll be ready to move ahead.

Master It The "big" areas of the user interface are the Ribbon, the Properties palette, the Project Browser, and the drawing area. How do these areas work together, and what tabs correspond to an iterative design process?

Solution The Home tab is where you'll turn in your early design process because it contains datum, system families, component families, and spaces. As the design develops, you'll establish your views from the View tab. When you start to get into documentation, you'll work from the Annotate tab. Having panels from the Modify tab pulled off and close at hand will keep you from having to go between one contextual tab and another.

Understand project organization. Revit software has been available for about 10 years, and yet after a decade, it remains unique in its approach to "whole-building BIM." The compelling advantage of being able to design, document, and manage your project across multiple disciplines — the architect, structural, and mechanical disciplines — is something that you can do only in Revit software, and understanding project workflow is key to getting off on the right foot.

Master It Thinking back to the Revit organization chart shown in Figure 2.32, what are the main components of a Revit project, and how can you apply them to your design process? How do these categories directly affect your design workflow?

Solution The top-level categories of a Revit project are datum, content, views, and management. They correspond to the design process of maintaining relationships, repetition, representations, and restrictions. Keep these corollaries in mind as you move sequentially from schematic design, design development, construction documentation, and construction management.

Chapter 3: The Basics of the ToolBox

Select, modify, and replace elements. There are many fundamental interactions supported by Revit software to select just what you need and to modify elements efficiently.

Master It How can you quickly select only the door tags in a plan view and switch them to another type?

Solution First, window-select around the entire plan. Then, using the Filter tool in the Modify Ribbon, select only the Door Tags category, close the Filter dialog box, and change the type in the Properties palette.

Edit elements interactively. The editing tools in Revit are similar to those found in other CAD and BIM software programs. Tools such as Move, Copy, and Trim are available on the Modify tab of the Ribbon.

Master It How do you create a parametric repetition of an element?

Solution   Select an element and activate the Array tool from the Modify tab of the Ribbon. Specify a linear array with the Group And Associate option and choose either Move To 2nd for specific element spacing or Move To Last for consistent overall length with varied element spacing.

Use other editing tools.   Beyond the basic editing tools are more advanced commands to help you consistently and intelligently populate a building model with content.

Master It   How do you copy model elements in the same location for a multistory building?

Solution   Select the required elements and copy them to the Clipboard (Ctrl+C). From the Clipboard panel in the Modify tab, select Paste ➢ Aligned To Selected Levels and then choose the levels to which you'd like to paste the copied content.

Creating site context for your Revit project.   The site tools allow you to create context for your building models, including topographic surfaces, graded regions, and property lines.

Master It   Describe the different methods used to create a topographic surface.

Solution   A topographic surface can be created by placing points at specific elevations relative to internal project coordinates, by using an imported 3D CAD file from a civil engineering software program, or by using a text file that contains the x-,y-, and z- coordinates of a field of points.

Chapter 4: Configuring Templates and Standards

Define settings for graphic quality and consistency.   The fundamental building blocks for any template are the customized settings to object styles, line styles, fill patterns, materials, and more.

Master It   How can a complex custom fill pattern be imported? Why create a custom template for your company?

Solution   Creating a custom template doesn't have to be done before you start your first Revit project. But eventually you'll want to evolve your company's graphic standards into a template that is the default starting point for a new project.

Organize views for maximum efficiency.   The project template can be used to capture a framework supporting your visual and organizational standards.

Master It   How can you customize the Project Browser to support your business needs?

Solution   Filtering folders based on view types and documentation helps the entire team quickly find what they're looking for in a project. Your project template can also exclude views that are not needed based on a specific task. For example, if you're in design development, you can exclude previous views and sheets that were part of a previous schematic design stage.

Create custom annotation families.   Developing a graphic style to match your standards will usually require you to edit some annotation families or create them from scratch.

Master It   Can a single label display more than one parameter?

Solution   A single label can show more than one parameter — and even custom parameters. Just remember to place the label with the Label tool (not adjacent the Text tool). Assign the label to report the desired parameter.

Chapter 5: Managing a Project

Understand a BIM workflow.   Understand how projects are completed in BIM and how the use of Revit software on a project can change how information within a project is created.

Master It   Explain one of the primary differences between a more traditional 2D CAD-based workflow and producing documents using Revit.

Solution   In a 2D CAD-based workflow, documents are created by team members by creating plans, sections, elevations, and details all as separate drawings and then manually coordinating that content for the project set. In a BIM or Revit workflow, the plans, sections, elevations, and perspectives are a by-product of creating the virtual building model and are coordinated through updates made to the model itself.

Staff a BIM project.   Since using Revit software is a change in workflow, it is also important to understand the change in staffing and who is needed to perform what roles on a project.

Master It   What are the three primary roles in a Revit project and what are the responsibilities of those roles?

Solution   Every successful Revit project will need three roles accounted for. These roles do not need to be individual people; one person can assume all three roles at any point in the project. The roles are architect, modeler, and drafter. These roles are responsible for understanding and articulating the design, creating model content, and laying out and annotating the documentation, respectively.

Work in a large team.   Many projects require multiple team members. Some require having a very large team assembled on a project. Working with a large team in the Revit environment is a matter of collectively managing a series of smaller models. Know how to manage these smaller models.

Master It   How many people is too many to have working in a single Revit file? What do you do when you reach that limit?

Solution   Typically, six to eight people is the realistic working limit for the number of separate users within a Revit file. When this number is hit, the team needs to decide on a good way to split the model up into smaller models that can then be linked back together.

Perform quality control on your Revit model.   Since you have several people using one file to create possibly hundreds of drawing sheets, it's important to keep a model clean of errors and functioning well. Performing regular maintenance on your model is essential to maintaining file stability and functionality. Should a file happen to become corrupted, you stand to lose the work of the entire team. Understand how to maintain a model and how to regularly check under the hood.

Master It   There are several ways to keep an eye on the model so it stays responsive and free of corruption. List some of these ways.

Solution   Here are some of the ways to maintain oversight of the model:

◆ Watch the file size. Jumps in file size or an excessively large file will point to possible problems or poor model performance.

◆ Schedules are a good way to track content within a model.

◆ Regularly check the Warnings dialog box and be sure to keep the overall error count low.

Chapter 6: Understanding Worksharing

Understand key worksharing concepts.   Once the team has created local files, it is necessary to understand how to keep both the local files and the central file up-to-date as changes occur on the project. Doing so ensures that everyone is working from an updated and recent copy of the model at all times.

Master It   Once you've begun working in your local file, how do you publish your changes to the central file? How do you download changes from the central file to your local file?

Solution   The easiest way to do this is by using the Synchronize With Central command, which is accessible from the Collaborate tab and is also accessible from the Quick Access toolbar.

Use worksharing in your project.   Knowing how to activate and utilize worksharing is indispensable to working in a team environment using Revit.

Master It   How do you transition a single-user Revit file to a multiuser environment using worksharing?

Solution   To activate worksharing, click the Worksets button on the Collaborate tab. This will initiate the worksharing feature and divide your model up into the two default worksets. To allow others to access the model, you will need to choose File ➢ Save As and save the file to a network location. After this, close the file. Each team member then makes a local copy of this network file and works exclusively within their local copy.

Manage workflow with worksets.   Once the central file has been created, you'll need to organize and structure the model into logical worksets to maintain workflow with Revit.

Master It   How do worksets differ from layers in 2D CAD? What are some logical ways to create worksets within a model?

Solution   2D CAD layers were logically divided around individual elements in isolated files. In Revit, because everything is in one file and you are working with 3D objects, not just model lines, you need to use worksets to divide the building in different ways. Some logical workset divisions would be Shell And Core, Interiors, FF&E, and Site.

Understand element ownership in worksets.   Editing elements in a central file means you have sole ownership over further changes to those elements. Understanding the permissions is critical to working in a team.

Master It   How do you edit an element in the model if someone has already taken ownership of it in a worksharing environment?

Solution   Trying to edit the element initiates a request for permissions in Revit. By alerting the other team member of your desire to have ownership of this element, they can grant your permission request using the Editing Requests button on the Collaborate tab.

Chapter 7: Working with Consultants

Prepare for interdisciplinary collaboration. Proper planning and communication are the foundation of effective collaboration. Although only some client organizations may require a BIM planning document, it is a recommended strategy for all design teams.

Master It What are the key elements of a BIM execution plan?

Solution An effective BIM execution plan will first list the goals and uses of building information modeling as well as the scope of the data to be developed. It will also list the software platforms to be utilized, information exchange process, delivery strategy, and technology infrastructure.

Collaborate using linked Revit models. The most basic tool for collaboration is the ability to view consultants' data directly within the context of your own model. Project files from other disciplines can be linked and displayed with predictable visual fidelity without complex conversion processes.

Master It How can worksharing complement the use of linked Revit models?

Solution Placing each linked model on a unique workset allows team members to choose when to load or unload the linked models without affecting their teammates. Worksets within linked models can also help manage graphic quality using the ability to load or unload worksets globally.

Use Copy/Monitor between linked models. The Coordination Monitor tools establish intelligent bonds between elements in a host file and correlating elements in a linked model. They also support a workflow that respects the needs of discrete teams developing their own data, perhaps on a different schedule than that of other team members.

Master It How can grids in two different Revit projects be related?

Solution The Copy/Monitor tool allows you to copy an element from a linked file into a host file and monitor the linked element for changes.

Run interference checks. Interference checking — also known as *clash detection* — is one of the most important components of building information modeling. It is the essence of virtual construction and has the greatest potential for cost savings during the physical construction process.

Master It How do you find interfering objects between two linked Revit models?

Solution On the Collaborate tab, locate the Coordinate panel and choose Interference Check ➢ Run Interference Check. If you are using linked models, select the desired linked project in the Categories From drop-down list while keeping the other column set to Current Project. Select the desired object categories in the left and right columns (for example, choose Structural Framing from a structural model and Ducts from an MEP model). Click OK to run the check. The results can be exported to a report for coordination with others.

Chapter 8: Interoperability: Working Multiplatform

Use imported 2D CAD data. CAD data can be integrated into your Revit project in a number of ways: as plans of existing conditions, as fixture layouts from consultants, or as standard details from your company's library.

Master It How can CAD details be used in a Revit project?

Solution Create a new drafting view for a single detail. From the Insert tab, choose Link CAD and select a DWG detail file. During linking, set the colors to Black And White. Make sure the scale of the drafting view matches the notation scale of the CAD detail. Use the Query tool to turn off unwanted layers within the linked file.

Export 2D CAD data. The ability to deliver quality 2D information to other constituents involved in your project is as important as importing it into the Revit environment. Appropriately formatted views, standardized layer templates, and proper coordinate settings will result in happy team members and a smooth coordination process.

Master It Does Revit software comply with the National CAD Standard?

Solution You have the ability to map Revit model categories to standardized layers in the Export Layers dialog box. Access this tool by clicking Application menu and selecting Export ➢ Options ➢ Export Layers DWG/DXF. Load industry-standard layer conventions using the Standard button.

Use imported 3D model data. Model data generated outside of the Revit environment can be integrated into your projects as whole-building systems, massing studies, or unique components.

Master It How can a building's structural model created with Bentley Structure be integrated into a Revit project?

Solution Create a structural framing family into which the DGN model will be inserted. When the family is finished, the DGN geometry will be displayed as any other Revit structural framing component.

Export 3D model data. Your modeled elements don't have to remain in the Revit environment forever. Data can be exported to 3ds Max, Google SketchUp, AutoCAD MEP, and more.

Master It How can I coordinate my architectural Revit model with an engineer using AutoCAD MEP?

Solution The engineer will likely require one DWG model per level for efficient coordination. Create duplicate floor plans for exporting and adjust the View Range settings for Top to Level Above, Offset: 0 and Bottom to Associated Level, Offset: 0. Create duplicate 3D views for each level, right-click the ViewCube, choose Orient To View ➢ Floor Plans, and find the corresponding floor plans. These 3D views can be batch-exported to DWG format and referenced by the MEP engineer in her designs.

Work with IFC imports and exports. Industry Foundation Classes (IFC) is a vendor-neutral model format designed to support interoperability in the AEC industry. It is widely used by some major BIM platforms available around the world.

Master It How is an IFC model integrated into a Revit project for coordination?

Solution You can open an IFC file by clicking the Application menu and selecting Open ➢ IFC. Once the file is open, the data can be saved as an RVT Revit project file and linked into another Revit file for continued coordination.

Chapter 9: Advanced Modeling and Massing

Create and schedule massing studies. Starting the design process with actual building elements can lead to a lot of unexpected frustration. Walls lead to rooms, which get room tags and eventually scheduled. But if you've failed to fulfill the client's program, you'll wonder where to start over!

Master It You're faced with creating some design studies of a large hospital complex. How would you go about creating a Revit project that would allow you to create a massing study and schedule it against the design client's program?

Solution Massing studies allow you to create schedules of the surface, floor areas, and volumes of a mass. This is incredibly helpful for resolving the design intent and client's program before committing to walls, floors, and other building geometry.

Know when to use solid masses and when to use surface masses. While solid masses and surface masses can both be used to maintain relationships to host geometry like walls and roofs, surface masses can't be volumetrically scheduled or contain floor area faces.

Master It You've been asked to create a complex canopy system for the entry to a hotel project. The system will consist of a complex wave of triangular panels. What kind of mass would you create?

Solution You're probably going to be better off not creating a solid mass because you don't need a solid — you only need a surface. It's best to use solids when you have to calculate the client's overall design program: floor areas, surface, and volume. For limited, surface-based relationships, just use surface massing. Surface masses will help you resolve the overall design idea first. Then you can move on to patterns and eventually component-level geometry.

Use mathematical formulas for massing. Not all massing is going to involve intuitive, in-the-moment decision making. By discovering the underlying rules that express a form, it is possible to create the formulas that can iterate and manipulate your massing study. So rather than manually manipulate the mass, you manipulate the formulas related to your mass.

Master It What's the best way to discover and create these formulas?

Solution Never stop sketching! Staring at a blank spreadsheet is a one-way road to frustration. Sketch the idea and try to discern the rules that make the form change and morph into your design idea. Once you think you've discovered the rules that contain the idea, start testing the rules. Once you find that the idea or principle is valid, it's simply a matter of scale.

Chapter 10: Conceptual Design and Sustainability

Embrace sustainable design concepts.   Understanding the concepts behind sustainable design is an important part of being able to perform analysis within the Revit model and a critical factor in today's design environment.

Master It   What are four key methods for a holistic sustainable design?

Solution   Four key methods for a sustainable solution are (1) understanding a building's climate, (2) reducing building loads, (3) using free energy when possible to power those loads, and (4) using efficient systems.

Leverage schedules.   Using schedules helps you track many of your design elements throughout the whole design process. These schedules can also be used to validate programmatic information during conceptual design.

Master It   Explain how to create a schedule from a conceptual mass that will show the programmatic areas for each floor level.

Solution   After the mass is created, insert it into the project. Select the mass, and from the Modify | Mass tab, click the Mass Floor button and apply floors to the mass. Finally, create a schedule of mass floors showing level and area.

Use sunshading and solar paths.   Understanding the effects of the sun on a building design is a critical way to create and form space. Revit has tools to help you identify how the sun will affect the design and where shade and shadow will fall inside and outside the building over the course of a year.

Master It   How can you use Revit tools to produce still and animated solar studies from interior and exterior views to understand shading and the sun's effect on the building and space?

Solution   Use the Graphic Display Options dialog box to set the global location of the project. Next, establish a time of day to view the effects of the sun. Create key interior and exterior views of the project and apply these sun settings to the new views. To see the effects of the sun at that time throughout the year, animate the solar study for each week throughout the year.

Prepare and export your model for energy analysis.   Being able to predict a building's energy performance is a necessary part of designing sustainably. Although Revit doesn't have an energy modeling application built into it, it does have interoperability with many applications that have that functionality.

Master It   Explain the steps you need to take to get a Revit model ready for energy analysis.

Solution   The steps are as follows:

1. The building has to have walls, floors, and roofs. Those all need to meet and join so there are no unrealistic gaps in the model.

2. Make sure each of the regions in the model has a room element inserted into it and the room element's height is set to the bottom of the floor above.

3. Under Area And Volume Calculations, turn on Room Volumes.

4. You're now ready to export the model to gbXML and import that into an energy analysis application.

Analyze your project for daylighting.   Not only can proper daylighting in a building save energy, it can make the inhabitants happier and healthier. Through analysis, you can now quantify the amount of light you're getting in any space and measure the footcandle readings before you begin building. This allows you to iterate the design-making modifications to maximize your daylight while balancing the amount of glazing against solar heat gain and mechanical needs.

Master It   Understand how much daylight you need to perform certain tasks. How much daylighting is needed for the following?

◆   Working in an office

◆   Reading a book

◆   Working on a detailed model or reading very small text for an extended period of time

Solution

◆   25 footcandles is the average needed as defined by the USGBC.

◆   15 to 40 footcandles, depending on the print size.

◆   200 to 2000 footcandles, depending on the size and task.

Chapter 11: Working with Phasing, Groups, and Design Options

Use the Phasing tools to create, demolish, and propose a new design.   Time is such an important element to the design process and nearly impossible to capture with traditional CAD tools. Don't use phasing for construction sequencing (there's a better way). Embrace phasing for *communication*, not just *illustration*.

Master It   How can you use phasing to communicate your design across a series of key stages? What kind of project is best suited to phasing?

Solution   From the Manage tab, you can access the settings for Phases. You can create phases for the major stages of work in your project as well as define filters and graphic overrides to illustrate the overall design approach. Use the Phase and Phase Filter view properties to customize project views including schedules. Set the Phase Created and Phase Demolished properties of model elements to adapt to the project phases. Any kind of project can utilize phasing, but tenant improvement projects benefit the most from the ability to document existing conditions and demolition.

Use the Groups tool effectively.   Groups are great for creating collections of both host and family component geometry. Just remember to apply best practices and you'll avoid a lot of common roadblocks. Individual model elements within groups will always appear properly in schedules, as you'd expect. And creating exceptions in groups allows you to make subtle changes without creating a new group.

Master It   Why shouldn't you mirror groups?

Solution Although mirroring works conceptually, it breaks down in implementation. Just because you can mirror something in Revit Architecture doesn't mean that it can actually be manufactured that way. And even more confusion can result if the mirrored object has to be powered, accessed, maintained, and so on in an impossible condition.

Mirroring groups has been known to create so much hassle that you are better off avoiding it. And we'll keep pushing Autodesk to restrict mirroring of family components (as well as groups) as a parameter.

Create and use design options to manage big design ideas. Like groups, design options work great when you follow the rules. Design options are intended for design iteration that is bounded and well defined — not for putting multiple buildings in one project file. Remember that links, groups, and phasing can exist within design options. Always keep hosted elements with their host when using design options.

Master It Suppose you have a multistory tower. How could you show multiple design options for the entire vertical exterior enclosure?

Solution Put each enclosure option in a different project file. You can link these files into one master project file. Then associate each of the links with a different design option. Eventually you set and accept the primary option. Then bind the link and the chosen enclosure model will become a group within your project. The group can be ungrouped to continue editing the final design.

Chapter 12: Visualization

Create real-time and rendered analytic visualizations. Analytic visualization is about communicating information about your project in a nonliteral way, and it's very important! It's not about showing real materials in the project but using filters to visualize important metadata.

Master It During the renovation of a space, you want to reuse the doors rather than throw them away. How would you illustrate this?

Solution Assign an instance parameter to the doors called Recycled. Then apply this value to all the doors fulfilling these criteria in your project. Now you can use this parameter to create a view filter to illustrate where these reused doors are being used.

Render emotive photorealistic visualizations. Photorealistic visualization is also about communicating design ideas but in emotive ways that are much closer to how the space will be experienced, including real lighting, materials, and entourage. Just remember that the time it takes to calculate and render your views will change dramatically based on the quality and resolution of your views.

Master It Would the rendering for a PowerPoint presentation differ from a rendering being printed for a marketing brochure?

Solution The rendering for the PowerPoint presentation needs to be only about 150 dpi, while the rendering for the printing needs to be 300 dpi. A 300 dpi image will take much longer to render than a 150 dpi image, even though they'll look the same on the screen.

Understand the importance of sequencing your visualization workflow. The sequence of design — building, content, materials, and cameras — is not the same as the sequence for visualization (geometry/cameras, lighting, materials). Lighting is far more important than materials of actual objects. Get the lighting right and the materials will look great, but not the other way around.

Master It How do you create a rendering environment that replaces the actual materials with matte materials in order to study the effects of lighting on your design?

Solution Until View Filters allow rendered materials to be overwritten in a view, use Phasing. Create a filter that overrides the materials and assign this analytic filter to the view that you're rendering with lights. After you achieve the desired lighting effects, start re-rendering the view showing the actual materials.

Chapter 13: Walls and Curtain Walls

Use extended modeling techniques for basic walls. Walls in Revit are made from layers of materials that can represent generic placeholders for design layouts to complete assemblies representative of actual construction.

Master It How can you customize the profile of a wall?

Solution A wall can be attached to another object such as a roof, floor, or reference plane. Select a wall, activate the Attach Top/Base tool, and pick the object to which the wall should be attached. You can also edit the profile of a wall in elevation by selecting a wall, activating the Edit Profile tool, and modifying the sketch of the wall.

Create stacked walls. Exterior walls are usually composed of several combinations of materials with varying thicknesses. These various wall types can be combined into a single entity called a stacked wall.

Master It How do you create a stacked wall?

Solution You must duplicate an existing stacked wall type within a project. In Type Properties, open the Edit Assembly dialog box and add any combination of basic walls into the stacked wall structure.

Create simple curtain walls. A curtain wall is an assembly of parts including curtain grids, panels, and mullions. They can be created in predefined types with regular horizontal and vertical spacing along with specific panel and mullion types.

Master It How do you add a door to a curtain wall?

Solution Use the Tab key to select a single panel in a curtain wall segment. If the panel is part of a predefined system, you must unpin the panel first. From the Type Selector, choose a curtain panel door family.

Create complex curtain walls. The Revit conceptual massing environment can be used to create complex curtain wall configurations. Pattern-based panel families can be loaded into the massing environment and populated on a divided surface. These populated surfaces can then be loaded and placed in a project model for documentation and scheduling.

Master It How do you create a complex divided surface?

Solution   From the Recent Files window, select New Conceptual Mass. Add a second level to the family and draw a curved line on each level. Select the two lines and click Create Form; choose the Planar Surface option. Select the new form and click the Divide Surface button on the ribbon.

Chapter 14: Floors, Ceilings, and Roofs

Understand floor modeling methods.   Floors make up one of the most fundamental, sketch-based system families used in a Revit model. You can customize them to accommodate a variety of assumptions at various stages of design.

Master It   How can you create a structural floor with integrated metal decking?

Solution   You can create a structural floor by going to the Architecture tab of the ribbon and clicking Floor ➤ Structural Floor. This tool activates the Structural parameter in a floor's instance properties. Once this is activated, edit the floor's type properties to add a Structural Deck layer and assign a deck profile.

Model various floor finishes.   Thick and thin floor finishes can be created to support tagging, scheduling, and quantity takeoffs.

Master It   How would you represent a thin finish material in your project such as carpet?

Solution   Activate the Split Face tool from the Modify tab of the ribbon, select a floor, and define the boundaries of the area to be assigned as the thin material. Activate the Paint tool, select the appropriate material, and click the split face you created within the floor.

Create ceilings.   Ceilings are sketch-based system families that can host objects such as light fixtures and HVAC diffusers.

Master It   What's the best way to model a ceiling within a space?

Solution   Ceilings are best created in a ceiling plan. Activate the Ceiling tool from the Build panel in the Architecture tab of the ribbon. Specify a value for the Height Offset From Level setting of the ceiling in the Properties palette, and use Automatic Ceiling to fill a bounded space with a ceiling object.

Understand roof modeling methods.   Roofs can be modeled as simple single-pitch shed roofs or complex extrusions of sinuous curves.

Master It   What is the best way to create a single vault roof?

Solution   That roof is best created with the roof-by-extrusion method. Go to the Architecture tab of the ribbon and click Roof ➤ Roof By Extrusion. Specify a wall or reference plane as the work plane and switch to an elevation, section, or 3D view. Draw the profile of a vaulted roof and click Finish Edit Mode. Adjust the extents of the extrusion as desired.

Work with advanced shape editing for floors and roofs.   A small but powerful toolset is available for extended editing of floor and roof objects. These tools allow you to create warped floor slabs and tapered layers of roof assemblies.

Master It How do you create a drainage point in a flat roof slab?

Solution Select a roof object and activate the Add Split Line tool from the Shape Editing panel in the ribbon. Draw two crossing lines from the four corners of the roof boundaries. Activate the Modify Sub Elements tool and select the point where the split lines cross. Change the value that appears to create a low drainage depression in the slab.

Chapter 15: Family Editor

Understand the Family Editor. Before you start modeling a piece of content in the Family Editor, take a moment to think about how you expect that piece of content to "behave" in your project. Don't be afraid to model a first pass quickly. But also be thinking ahead with regard to how it might change. The role of the Family Editor isn't just an environment to model geometry; it also determines how the content that you create will behave in the project environment.

Master It Choosing the right template is critical. You can convert from one family template to another, but this is not always the case. Why would you want to choose a door template rather than a Generic Model template?

Solution Balusters, curtain panels, detail components, and hosted elements all have specific, predefined behavior. Plan ahead when you're creating these categories. Objects that need to "cut" their host — like doors and windows — must be created in templates that are hardwired to contain a portion of the host that will be cut. This allows you to create the door and also cut the host in the way that it needs to cut in the project.

Choose the right family template. Some categories and parameters are more important than others. If you choose poorly, there's no backing up. You may simply have to start over and create the family correctly.

Master It Why are you concerned whether a family component should be hosted or not? What would happen if you selected a hosted template and then decided it should be non-hosted (or vice versa)?

Solution Hosted objects typically need to create an opening in their host and then maintain a particular relationship to that host. For example, if the host is deleted, the hosted family is deleted as well. If you choose a hosted template and need to convert the family to a nonhosted component, you'll essentially have to start over.

Create and test parameters. Reference planes, points, and lines are the "bones" of your component. Parameterize the bones and the geometry will follow along. Be sure to test the parameter and reference relationships before you start assigning geometry.

Master It Why build, parameterize, and test the references first? Why not just model the geometry?

Solution Testing the references and parameters before you add geometry keeps things simple and helps you troubleshoot parametric behavior before building the geometry. Remember to keep parameterized dimensions outside of Sketch mode so you and others can easily find them later. After you've tested the parameters and references successfully, you can be confident that your geometry will behave predictably.

Know why formulas are important. Sometimes parametric behavior will depend on the parameters that directly control it, but often these parameters will be expressed as a relationship to something else.

Master It Why are formulas so important? Why not just create the parameters you need and then modify them as needed in the project environment?

Solution Formulaic relationships help maintain rules within a family so that changing one rule can have an effect on many others. Using formulas therefore allows you to drive one parameter based on the value of another, and the result can drive a length, material, or other rules-based value. When you have many, many parametric-type permutations, it's better not to weigh your project down with a lot of options that you'll probably never use. Whenever this happens, don't load all the possible types in your project — just turn to a type catalog in order to select only the family types that you need. Since you don't want to have to remember all of these relationships manually, allow Revit to maintain them for you.

Chapter 16: Stairs and Railings

Understand the key components of stairs and railings. Having a complete understanding of the components of stairs is important. You don't want to set about breaking the rules until you understand how best (and when) those rules can be broken.

Master It What are the essential parts of stairs?

Solution Baluster posts, balusters, and baluster panels along with handrail profiles are the essential parts of any railing. Nosings, stringers, and treads are the essential parts of stairs. Having a firm understanding of how these components react to their respective dialog boxes is critical.

Design beautiful custom stairs with the default toolset. Designing in a spreadsheet is hard. Step back and consider what you're trying to accomplish. If you'll look at the components that make up stairs, you'll see some interesting opportunities.

Master It How would you create a continuous tread that wasn't monolithic? What would you do if you wanted to create a custom stringer? Are balusters always vertical and used to support handrails? What if your particular stair just can't be modeled in the Stairs tool?

Solution Try using the nosing profile to complement the shape of your tread. And don't forget that a handrail profile can be used to create a custom stringer profile with little trouble. Although balusters often support handrails, this is not always the case. Balusters may also consist of the support element that will support the tread. A complex baluster family associated with the railing as the start post can create the most complex railing conditions quickly and easily. But if all else fails, remember that there's still the Family Editor. Just model it the way you want it, and then put it in the project. It's probably more sculpture than stair at this point. Modeling it in the Family Editor means that you'll be able to move, elevate, rotate, and copy the results throughout the project. If you have to make changes (and you will), you'll simply open the component in the Family Editor.

Create elegant exceptions to the Stair and Railing tools. From model patterns to geometric intricacy, there's a lot that can be created with the Railing tool. When this doesn't work, look to the Curtain Wall tool for "railings" that can contain space and allow "balusters" to be conveniently unlocked.

> **Master It** Why would you not use a railing to manage repetitive relationships? What if you need to accurately distribute geometry along a path?

> **Solution** Modeling these railings as components in the Family Editor is often faster than creating groups and then copying them throughout the project. Railings are also helpful for creating geometry that needs to be distributed along paths, even if the results aren't actually railings. Finally, don't use geometry when a model pattern will do. This will keep your project light.

Implement best practices. There are specific best practices when creating custom stairs and railings. Pay attention to nesting geometry, maintaining the right level of detail, and filtering schedules so the metadata ends up in the right place.

> **Master It** Is it possible to create solutions that are too efficient? What's the big deal with detail levels? And finally, what's the most important thing to remember before creating an elegant workaround?

> **Solution** You're not the only person working on the project! Design is a team sport, and any out-of-the-box exceptions to the rules need to be understood by the entire team. "Overmodeling" is often misunderstood to mean "too much geometry," but geometry is critically important to understanding how your design is going to be assembled. So if you'll take the time to assign levels of detail to components, it'll help refresh views and printing. Finally, remember that the best solution is the one that is implementable. If your team doesn't understand your "custom hack," you're not playing a team sport and the project will ultimately suffer.

Chapter 17: Detailing Your Design

Create details. Details in Revit are a combination of 2D elements layered on top of 3D model elements or sometimes just stacked on top of each other. Creating good, easy-to-read details typically requires some embellishment of the 3D model.

> **Master It** What are the three primary categories of detail elements and how are they used?

> **Solution** Detail lines are used to create two-dimensional linework of various weights and styles. They are used for drafting, much as you would draft in a CAD application. Filled regions and masking regions are the two region types that are used to apply patterns (even if that pattern is a solid-white field) against your details. These can help to show context such as materiality. Components like detail components and detail groups are used to create 2D families that can be used and reused in a variety of details within the model. They are historically used to create elements like blocking, metal studs, metal deck, and so on.

Add detail components to families. You can make creating details in Revit easier by adding some of the detail elements directly to the family. In this way, when you cut sections, make callouts, or enlarge plan conditions, your "smart" details can begin to construct themselves.

Master It   Because you don't always want elements to appear in every scale of view, how can you both add detail elements to your families and still limit the amount of information that is shown in any given view?

Solution   Using the detail levels (Coarse, Medium, and Fine), you can control the visibility of any element within a family to show, or not show, at those settings. By controlling the detail level, you can keep the family simple in a Coarse view and add more detail as the drawing gets increasingly complex.

Learn efficient detailing.   As you master detailing in Revit, you'll begin to learn tips and tricks to make your process of creating details more efficient.

Master It   To help you assess how much effort you should be putting into your details, what are three questions you should be asking yourself before starting any detail?

Solution   Will I see or use this in other views in the project?

Will it affect other aspects of the project (like material takeoffs)?

How large is it?

Chapter 18: Documenting Your Design

Document plans.   With Floor plans you can create visual graphics that help to define how a space is laid out. However, Revit provides other tools such as area plans to help you describe space.

Master It   List the four types of area plans that you can create and note the two that Revit creates automatically.

Solution   The four types of area plans are rentable area, gross area, usable area, and BOMA area. The software provides automatic calculations to show rentable and gross areas.

Create schedules and legends.   Schedules are another view type; they allow you to show information about the model in a nongraphic format. Schedules can also be used to dynamically report quantities of elements inside the model.

Master It   Understand how to create schedules and report additional information about the elements in the model. How would you create a simple casework schedule showing quantities of types?

Solution   Here are the steps to create a schedule within Revit:

1. On the View tab, choose Schedule/Quantities from the Schedule button.

2. Choose Casework as a schedule category.

3. On the Fields tab, choose Family And Type followed by Quantity.

4. On the Sorting tab, choose to sort by Family And Type; make sure Itemize Every Instance is checked. When that's done, click OK.

Use details from other files.   In many project workflows, you will need to incorporate details from other projects. Reusing these details can aid in the speed and efficiency of project documentation.

Master It   There are several ways to reuse details from other projects. Name one and list the steps to perform the tasks necessary to quickly move a detail from one project to another.

Solution   Here are the steps to save views from one project for use in another project:

1. Start by opening the file with the views you want to save. Click the Application menu and select Save As ➤ Library ➤ Views.

2. The Save Views dialog box shows a list of view names on the left and a preview window on the right. Click the check box for each of the views you want to save into a separate file; click OK.

3. To import the views, open the project you'd like to import the views into and choose Insert From File from the Insert tab. Choose Insert Views From File.

4. In the resulting dialog box, you will have a list of the views you can import from the column on the left and a preview of those views on the right. Check the box for the views you want to import and click OK.

Lay out sheets.   Eventually in a project it will become necessary to create sheets that will become the documentation set. Knowing how to create a good sheet set provides you with another venue to communicate with contractors, clients, and other team members.

Master It   To properly create a sheet set, you need to understand the dynamics of adding views to a sheet. In the Revit environment, there is only one way to add views to a sheet. What is it?

Solution   Views can be added to a sheet by dragging them from the Project Browser and dropping them onto the sheet. From that point, they can be edited or manipulated to properly place them relative to other views that appear on that sheet.

Chapter 19: Annotating Your Design

Annotate with text and keynotes.   Although a picture is worth a thousand words, you will still need notes to make drawings understandable and be able to call out key elements in each view. Understand how to create and modify text and keynotes for a complete set of documents.

Master It   To properly utilize the keynoting feature, you'll need to understand what each of the three keynote types do and how they're used. List each and explain how they can be used in a project.

Solution   Element keynotes annotate assemblies such as walls, floors, and roofs. Material keynotes designate materials within Revit, such as concrete, gypsum board, or rigid insulation. User keynotes are not tied to an element or a material and can be used to note other aspects of the view or detail.

Use tags. Tags are text labels for elements such as doors, walls, windows, rooms, and several other objects that architects typically need to reference in a set of drawings. These tags typically refer back to other schedules or information in other portions of the drawing set and are unique to the view in which they are inserted.

Master It Inserting tags quickly can be a good way to make documentation time more efficient. How can you quickly tag a number of elements in the model at the same time?

Solution Use the Tag All tool. This tool allows you to load several tags for different elements at the same time and populate a view with all those tag types at once. You will probably need to manipulate the location of some of the tags, but most should be placed cleanly and accurately, saving you time for other portions of the project.

Add dimensions. Dimensioning is a critical part of the project documentation, allowing you to communicate the distance elements are from one another.

Master It Adding dimensions is a necessary part in any project. However, in a project workflow you will typically want to change the location of a dimension's witness line without having to re-create the entire dimension. How do you move a witness line without remaking the entire dimension?

Solution Highlight the dimension string and grab the blue grip that is below the text string. By clicking and holding this element, you can now select a new host for the witness line.

Set project and shared parameters. Revit Architecture lets users add as many custom parameters to an element as are needed to document the project. These parameters can be both tagged and scheduled, depending on how they are made.

Master It You need to add a custom parameter for your project to track the percentage of recycled content in materials. What's the best way to go about doing this?

Solution Since the items you want to track need to be scheduled but not tagged, it's easiest do to this with a project parameter. Add one to the project for a percentage of recycled content, and then track that in a Multi-Category schedule showing all the material types you want to track.

Chapter 20: Presenting Your Design

Add color fill legends. Color fills are a great way to illustrate data that otherwise might appear only in a schedule, such as department assignment, designed areas, and room finishes.

Master It There are a variety of ways to graphically display information using color fills. It can initially take a bit of time to get things organized, but once you create them, the legends can easily be transferred between views and projects. Describe how to add a color fill legend, once created, to your project template.

Solution To add a color fill legend from a project to your project template, add it to a view and add the view to a sheet. Legends can be transferred like schedules: once they are added to a sheet, they can be copied to the Clipboard and then pasted to the sheet in the project template. This will transfer all the colors, fonts, and other settings from the project to the template.

Use 3D model views in your presentation. Revit provides a variety of ways to help you visualize your designs — both while designing and during presentation. Understanding where these features are located and how and when to use them can help expedite the presentation process, depending on the look and feel you want to create with your images.

Master It Describe the process for creating an exploded 3D view of each level within your project.

Solution After adjusting the view range of your plan views to accommodate the actual bottom of the level up to the top, open a 3D view and right-click the ViewCube. Select Orient To View and choose the floor plan for each level.

Work with viewport types. Viewport types are simple to manage, but they are powerful when applied to the views you place on sheets. You can customize the view titles for any use case, from design presentations to construction documents.

Master It Describe the process for adding a new viewport type to your project.

Solution After placing a view on a sheet, select the view and click Edit Type in the Properties palette. Click Duplicate and create a uniquely named type. Once you have modified the settings, apply the new type to other views by selecting a viewport and picking the new type from the Type Selector.

Chapter 21: The Construction Phase

Add revisions to your project. You need the ability to track changes in your design after sheets have been issued. Adding revisions to a drawing is an inevitable part of your workflow.

Master It Add to your project revisions that automatically get tracked on your sheet.

Solution Use the Revision Cloud tool and the Revit Revision cloud tag family. Using those tools to create revision clouds ensures that they will automatically be tracked on the sheets on which they appear.

Use digital markups. DWFs provide a lightweight means to digitally transfer and mark up multiple sheets in a document set.

Master It Explain the workflow using DWF markups.

Solution Once your views are drawn and placed on sheets, export the sheets to a DWFx format. They can be shared with the quality assurance team for markup. QA will open the DWFx in Design Review and create the comments and then send the marked-up set back to the design team. This set is then linked back into the drawing set and the markups will be visible on the drawing sheets.

Model for construction. Parts and assemblies allow a design model to be used in more detailed ways for the construction process.

Master It Describe the method for breaking down a design-based model assembly into its individual components.

Solution   Select a wall, floor, roof, or ceiling and use the Create Parts tool. The view may need to be set to Show Parts. Once parts are created, they can be divided, merged, or excluded.

Chapter 22: Using Laser Scans in Revit

Plan for a LiDAR survey.   You'll need to understand the differences between the types of scanners and how they're best used between indoor and outdoor scan conditions.

Master It   For your project, select the right LiDAR scan equipment and estimate the number of survey points.

Solution   Choose your scanner type based on interior or exterior conditions. Each scanner type will have a set diameter for the amount of information it can collect in a single scan. Lay those scans out by drawing circles on your floor plans so you have complete coverage of the area to be scanned.

Create a BIM from the point cloud.   Once you've completed the LiDAR scan, you'll have a point cloud of the building. The next step is to get that point cloud into BIM.

Master It   Describe the steps needed to go from a LiDAR scan to a BIM model of an existing building.

Solution   With the point cloud established, the first step is to convert the cloud to a format readable by Revit. Open the PTS files in Revit to convert them to PCG files. Once that is completed for all the point cloud files, you can then begin to use Revit's link tool to link the point cloud files in and begin modeling over the top of them tracing the building geometry. When all of the PCG files have been linked and traced, the model will be complete.

Know the limits of LiDAR.   LiDAR creates a series of points within a file and many files create a scan set. These can range into the tens or hundreds of gigabytes in file size. Understanding how to store and use this information is critical to maintaining stability in your Revit files.

Master It   Describe the limits to LiDAR modeling in Revit.

Solution   The single largest limiting factor with LiDAR is RAM. Due to the fact that Revit will need to cache the entire point cloud to RAM when you import it, the number of scan points (PCG files) you can import at a time will be limited by the number of points in those files and how much RAM your computer has. By watching your RAM allocation (and Revit warnings) you can make sure your file continues to run smoothly.

Chapter 23: Revit in the Classroom

Use Vasari early.   Vasari makes it very easy to locate your building in the world and generate a quick context model. Even if you don't know the exact orientation and location, get it as close as possible during early design iteration.

Master It   How would you create various design options with some real-world context?

Solution   Use the import satellite image feature to get a properly scaled and oriented underlay that you can model over as a reference.

Utilize design options.   Don't be afraid to model many different configurations and run them through different analyses. Every exercise is a learning experience and you may discover a pattern or an opportunity to exploit on your specific site.

Master It   How would you create different options as massing studies within the same file?

Solution   Use design options to create multiple massing studies in the same file. Each massing study can live within its own option and views can be filtered to show only the desired option.

Leveraging Vasari files in Revit   Opening a Vasari file in Revit is perfectly fine because it's in the RVT file format, but you might notice that you don't have many components loaded; this is because the file was generated in Vasari. This may be a problem, especially if you'd like to use a custom template with all of your content preloaded.

Master It   How would you open a Vasari file so you could use the full suite of design tools available in Revit?

Solution   Don't open the Vasari RVT file in Revit. Instead, create a new Revit file using your template and link the Vasari RVT file in. Bind the link, ungroup it, and you'll have all Vasari geometry with the custom content of your template.

Chapter 24: Essential Hardware

Sketching with the iPad   Architects have sketched for a long time and in locations other than the office. Being able to sketch in an intuitive fashion really helps get the creative juices flowing.

Master It   Even though an iPad is a great schematic sketching tool, where else might it be helpful as you move from design to construction?

Solution   Time is money, a picture is worth a thousand words, and just *one* clarification or request for information can be more expensive than the cost of multiple iPads or other field-based tablets. The ability to quickly and easily request or clarify information during construction is essential. With an iPad you can quickly take a picture, annotate the results, and then email it to a team member for rapid review and response.

Designing with the Wacom Cintiq   Once you become accustomed to sketching directly on a screen, why would you give this up as the design progresses? Not only is it more elegant to work directly on-screen, our wrists didn't evolve to remain artificially rigid in order to manipulate a mouse.

Master It   What other roles could benefit from using touch screens and working directly on the screen rather than jumping between keyboard and mouse?

Solution   Marking up PDFs and DWFs during design reviews can benefit from being able to work directly on the screen. Rather than waste time constantly zooming in and out, the reviewer is able to zoom in to an appropriate level of detail and then pan around the sheet.

Navigating with 3Dconnexion Navigator Mice   Once you become accustomed to working directly on-screen with a stylus, you'll start looking for a more elegant way to navigate the model without constantly relying on the keyboard and a lot of keyboard shortcuts.

Master It   Constantly zooming in and out is distracting and disorienting during the design process when you're working on your own. But are there other times that you'll need to navigate the model and increase communication?

Solution   Being able to elegantly present your design by navigating in 3D can be a real challenge in walk-through situations: forward, back, left, right, zoom in and out gets confusing fast. 3Dconnexion navigators remove this barrier to presentations so you're always presenting what you need to present when you need to.

Chapter 25: Getting Acquainted with the API

Understand the basics of the Revit API.   The Revit software development kit (SDK) provides sample code and instructions for building add-ins for the Revit application.

Master It   What are the three types of API projects you can develop for Revit?

Solution   External commands are limited lifetime routines that have access to the current project as well as any elements selected. External applications are loaded when Revit starts and remain active until the end of the Revit session. Database-level applications are the same as external applications but do not make any calls to the Revit UI, such as to add buttons or tabs to the main ribbon.

Write, debug, and install your own API projects.   You can start to create your own custom applications and commands for Revit using either Microsoft Visual Studio Professional or a free tool such as Microsoft Visual Studio Express.

Master It   How do you make the Revit API functions available in your developing environment?

Solution   The Revit API namespace references must be added to every .NET project. In Visual Studio, right-click the title of the project name in the Solution Explorer and select Add ➤ Reference. Navigate to the `Program` folder where Revit is installed and select the files `RevitAPI.dll` and `RevitAPIUI.dll`.

Chapter 26: Revit for Film and Stage

Design scenically.   According to Bryan Sutton, profiled in this chapter, designing scenically takes precedence over designing too literally. This might be different from standard architectural practice, but it's critical in the film and stage industries.

Master It   How would you design scenically, and how does this differ from standard architectural practice? What can you learn from the film and stage industries to keep the emotive quality high?

Solution   Keep the materials suggestive. Concentrate on expressing transparency and opacity. Adding additional lights (that aren't part of any real light fixture) can soften shadows and sharp edges.

Use Revit in the design-to-production process.   While standard architectural practice entails design to documentation, the film and stage focus is from concept through construction.

Master It   With an emphasis on level of detail and tight, repetitive elements and finishes, what would you do to help maintain time and budget? How might you suggest creating intricate repetitive design elements in your next project?

Solution   CNC is being used more and more in the film and stage industries when repetitive elements need to be created quickly. CNC machines are essential to creating components that need to work together with a high degree of quality and fit.

Use Revit for previsualization.   When using Revit in the film industry, you need to keep the design loose during the early concept stages. You'll have to match the look and feel of the art director's vision. Keeping the materials muted will be far less distracting than being too specific. One of the great things about Revit is that you'll be able to emotively visualize in the same environment as you analytically rationalize. This will come in handy when the director, director of photography, and then art director all want a different question answered at the same time!

Master It   How can you express constructability to a high level of detail, particularly when the object is going to be assembled from many individual parts? Why rely on standard architectural practice of documenting in plan, section, and elevation views?

Solution   Live exploded views allow you to visualize the component parts and sequence of assemblage without exporting to another tool. Just create a 3D view and duplicate in order to isolate different parts of the assembly. All the duplicated views can be assembled together on a single sheet.

Chapter 27: BIM in the Cloud

Realize practical, real-time collaboration with owner, design, and construction teams (IPD).   Now that firms are Revit experts, they want to collaborate on projects in real time with any office in their firm as well as with outside firms. There was no practical, secure, and high-performing method for doing this until the BIM cloud.

Master It   How will you collaborate in real time with the entire design team no matter where they are located or for whom they work?

Solution   You will set up a secure, private BIM cloud; give appropriate login credentials to the design team; and then stand back to watch them work.

Fit Autodesk's cloud into your BIM cloud collaboration.   Autodesk is providing additional benefit to its customers via its cloud-based design services. Any computing power that you can tap into at Autodesk might be that much less you have to build in your private cloud.

Master It   Can you use a private BIM cloud and the Autodesk cloud?

Solution   Absolutely! Whether you access your private BIM cloud over the public Internet or a private circuit, you can tap into the Autodesk cloud from your BIM cloud.

Integrate a BIM cloud into your overall IT strategy.   A BIM cloud is a very specific solution for the AEC industry to facilitate working on design applications in a distributed footprint. It isn't long before a firm realizes that if it can put an architectural desktop into a datacenter, it can put all its firm technology into a datacenter.

Master It   What are the key strategies for integrating a BIM cloud into your overall IT strategy?

Solution   Four main strategies are (1) distributed IT, (2) public cloud (3) private cloud, and (4) hosted private cloud. The first two strategies involve some degree of data movement (bring data to designers). The last two centralize your data (bring designers to the data) and are what most firms are racing toward.

Appendix B

Tips, Tricks, and Troubleshooting

This appendix provides some tips, tricks, and troubleshooting to help keep your project files running smoothly. Listed here are some pointers to keep you from getting into trouble as well as a peppering of timesavers and other great ideas.

In this appendix, you'll learn how to:

◆ Optimize performance

◆ Use best practices

◆ Apply tips and shortcuts

Optimizing Performance

It should make sense that a smaller file on a good network will run the fastest. There is no "typical" project file size, and a file can range anywhere from 10 MB to over 300 MB. We've found that small, dense projects with a lot of geometry and detail (like a medical office building) can be larger in file size than a warehouse project (which is mostly full of space). Because documentation is often an indication of project complexity, we've found that for each documented sheet, your file will be about 1 MB. So a completed project of 100 full-size sheets will be about 100 MB.

Much of that variation depends on the level of detail in the model itself, the presence of imported geometry (2D CAD files, SketchUp, and so on), the number of views you have, and the overall complexity. Obviously, your hardware configuration will also be a factor in determining the speed and operation of your models.

You can optimize your hardware in a number of ways to get the most out of the configuration you have. You should first look at the install specifications and recommended hardware specs for a computer running Autodesk® Revit® Architecture software. Autodesk has published those requirements on its website, and they are updated with each new version of the software. You can find the current specs at www.autodesk.com/Revit; click Support, choose the link for Autodesk Revit Architecture, and then choose System Requirements under the Product Information heading.

Beyond the default specifications, you can do a number of things to help keep your files nimble. Here are some other recommendations:

Use a 64-bit OS. Revit Architecture likes RAM, and the more physical RAM it can use, the more model you can cache into active memory. Windows now offers several versions of a 64-bit OS. Windows XP, Windows Vista, and Windows 7 all have 64-bit capability. This allows you to bridge the 32-bit limit of Windows XP and earlier. The older operating systems were limited to only 2 GB of RAM per application. A 64-bit OS allows you to use as much as you can pack into your machine.

If you have a 32-bit OS, use the 3 GB switch. If you have a 32-bit OS such as Windows XP, need to get your project done, and don't want to deal with the upgrade, use the 3 GB switch. This setting allows you to grab an extra gigabyte of RAM from your computer for a maximum of 3 GB. To take advantage of this switch, you'll need to load Windows XP Service Pack 2 and follow the instructions found on the Autodesk support site at www.autodesk.com/support; choose Autodesk Revit Architecture, and then search for the term *3GB switch*. Of course, you need more than 2 GB of RAM in your workstation for this setting to be effective.

Figure out how much RAM your project will need. Before you email your IT department requesting 64 GB of RAM, figure out how much you're actually going to use on your project. Your OS and other applications like Outlook will use some of your RAM, but you can calculate how much RAM Revit Architecture will need to work effectively. The formula is as follows:

Model size in Explorer × 20 + Linked File Size(s) × 20 = Active RAM needed

Let's look at a couple of examples to demonstrate how it works. You have a Revit file with no linked files and your file size on your server is 150 MB. So you'll need 150 × 20 = 3,000, or 3 GB of RAM to operate effectively. In another example, you have a 120 MB file, a 50 MB structural model linked in, and four CAD files at 1 MB each. The calculation is as follows:

(120 × 20) + (50 × 20) + (4 × 20) = 3,480 MB or 3.5 GB of RAM

Once you've put as much RAM into your workstation as is practical, your next recourse for improving model performance is to reduce your file size so you're not using as much RAM. Here are some tips to do that and thereby improve your file speed:

Manage your views. There are two things you can do using views to help improve performance. First, the more views you open, the more information you will load into active RAM. It's easy to have many views open at once, even if you're concentrating on only a few views. Close windows you're not using to help minimize the drain on your resources. You can always close all the windows except your active one using the Close Hidden Windows tool. Choose the View tab and click the Close Hidden button (Figure B.1). You can map a keyboard shortcut to this command such as "XX" or you can find it in the Quick Access Toolbar. The Close Hidden Windows command will close the hidden windows in your active project as well as all other open projects and families in your current session of Revit.

FIGURE B.1
Closing hidden windows

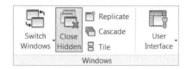

The other way to manage your views is to get rid of the ones you don't need. Revit allows you to make different views within your model quickly and easily. This can sometimes lead to having a lot of views (sometimes hundreds) that you aren't using in your document set and don't plan to use. Adding too many views can raise your overall file size even if you haven't added any geometry. Get rid of those unused views — typically views that are not on sheets — to help keep your file running smoothly. We discuss how to create a schedule to help identify the unused views in Chapter 5, "Managing a Project."

Delete or unload unused CAD files. There are many times in a project process you'll want to load content from another source as a background. This could be a client's CAD as-built drawings or a consultant's MEP design. You might link or import these files into your drawing and, during the busy course of the project, forget about them. As you've seen from the earlier tips on RAM use, all these small files add up. Getting rid of them can speed up your Revit project file and is just good housekeeping. If the CAD file is linked, you can remove it using the Manage Links button on the Insert tab. If the CAD files have been inserted instead of linked, right-click an instance of the CAD file in a view and choose Select All Instances from the context menu and then click Delete to remove all the instances in the entire model as opposed to only the active view.

Don't explode imported CAD files. A CAD file, when imported into Revit Architecture, is a collection of objects that is managed as a single entity. If you explode a CAD file, the single object immediately becomes many objects — and these all take up space in the file, requiring more resources to track and coordinate.

If you're importing DWG files, leave them unexploded as much as possible. If you need to hide lines, use the Visibility/Graphic Overrides dialog box to turn layers on and off. Explode only when you need to change the imported geometry, and start with a partial explode to minimize the number of new entities. Figure B.2 shows the tools available in the Options bar when you select an imported or linked DWG file. Also note that lines smaller than 1/32" [~1 mm] are not retained when CAD files are exploded. This can result in unusable imports.

FIGURE B.2
Explode options

A better workflow than importing your CAD files directly into the project is to import them into a family and then load that family into the project. This approach will also aid in keeping accidents from happening, like a novice user exploding the files. An example of this workflow is to import a SketchUp model in a mass family and then load the mass family into a project file. This workflow is covered in more detail in Chapter 8, "Interoperability: Working Multiplatform."

Turn on volume computation only as needed. Calculating the volumes on a large file can slow down your model speed immensely. This setting is typically turned on when exporting to gbXML, but sometimes teams forget to turn them back off again. Volumes will recalculate each time you edit a room, move a wall, or change any of the building geometry. Turn these off using the Area And Volume Computations dialog box found on the Room & Area panel on the Home tab (Figure B.3).

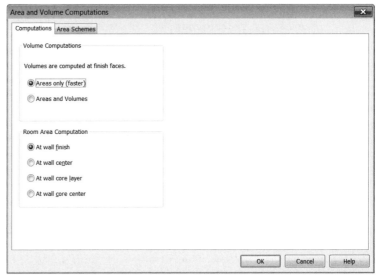

Using Best Practices

Good file maintenance is critical to keeping your files running smoothly and your file sizes low. Here are some best practices and workflows identified in other areas of the book but consolidated here as a quick reference. For more information on managing a Revit workflow, please refer to Chapter 5.

Manage the amount of information shown in views.   Learn to manage the amount of information needed in a given view. Minimize the view depth and the level of detail so you don't show more than you need to show in a view. Here are some simple tips to keep your individual views working smoothly:

Minimize the level of detail.   Set your detail level, found in the view control bar, relative to your drawing scale. For example, if you're working on a 1/32′ = 1′-0″ (1:500) plan, you probably don't need the Detail Level set to Fine. This will cause the view to have a higher level of detail than the printed sheet can show, and you'll end up with not only black blobs on your sheets but views that are slow to open and print.

Minimize view detail.   Along with the amount of detail you turn on in the view using the Detail Level tool, make sure you're not showing more than you need to. For instance, if you have wall studs shown in a 1/16′ = 1′-0″ (1:200) scale plan or the extruded aluminum window section shown in a building section, chances are it will not represent properly when printed. Turning off those elements in your view will keep things moving smoother as well as printing cleaner.

Minimize view depth.   View depth and crop regions are great tools to enhance performance. As an example, a typical building section is shown in Figure B.4. The default behavior causes Revit to regenerate all of the model geometry the full depth of that view every time you open the view. To reduce the amount of geometry that needs to be redrawn, drag the section's far clip plane (the green dashed line when you highlight the section) in close to the cutting plane.

FIGURE B.4
Minimizing the
view depth

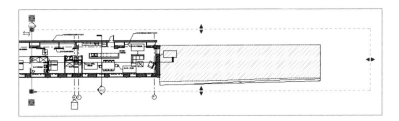

Model only what you need.   While it is possible to model to a very small level of detail, don't fall into the trap of overmodeling. Be smart about what you choose to model and how much detail you plan to show. If it's not conveying information about the project, maybe it's not really needed. The amount of information you do or do not model should be based on your project size and complexity, your timeframe, and your comfort level with the software.

How much to model: Use these three rules of thumb.   When trying to decide how much detail to put into a model or even a family, there are three very good rules of thumb to help you make the right decision for the particular element you're looking to create:

Scale   What scale will this detail be seen in? If it's a very small-scale detail, it might be simpler to just draw it in 2D in a drafting view.

Repetition   How many times will this detail appear in the drawing set? If it will appear only in one location or only one time, it might be easier to just draft it in 2D rather than try to model the element. If it will appear in several locations, modeling is probably the better solution. The more exposure an element has in the model (the more views it shows in), the more reason you have to model it. For example, doors are good to model. They show in elevations and plans all over the sheet set.

Quality   Be honest — how good at modeling families are you? Don't bite off more than you can chew. If you're new to the software, keep it simple and use 2D components. The more projects you complete, the better you'll understand the transition to a BIM workflow.

Don't overconstrain.   Embedding user-defined constraints into families and the model help keep important information constant. However, if you don't need to lock a relationship, don't do it. Overconstraining the model can cause problems later in the project process when you want to move or modify locked elements. Constrain only when necessary. Otherwise, let the model be free.

Watch out for imported geometry.   While you have the ability to use geometry from several other file sources, use caution when doing so. Remember that everything you link into a project or a family takes up around 20 times the file size in your system's RAM. So linking a 60 MB NURBS-based ceiling design will equal 2 GB of RAM and more than likely slow down your model. Deleting unused CAD files, using linking rather than importing, and cleaning up the CAD geometry before insertion will help keep problems to a minimum.

Purge unused files and family types.   You will find that you won't use every family, group, or material you create in your model. Revit Architecture has a tool that will allow you to get rid of those unused elements to help keep your file sizes down to a reasonable level. This tool, Purge Unused, can be found on the Manage tab in the Settings panel. If your file is very large, it can take several minutes to run, but eventually you'll be presented with a list (Figure B.5) of all the unused elements within your file.

FIGURE B.5
Use the Purge
Unused dialog box
to reduce file size.

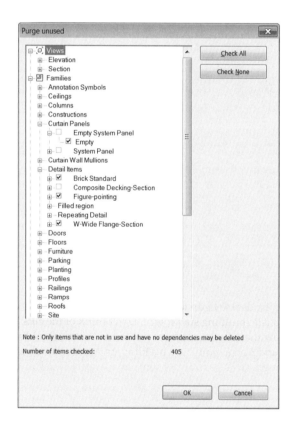

Using this tool is typically not recommended at the beginning of a project because you are still trying many design solutions and file sizes tend to be fairly small.

PURGE IMPORTED OBJECT STYLES

The Purge Unused tool will also remove any object styles from imported objects such as layers, line styles, and hatch patterns that are no longer in use. You won't see these styles listed in the Purge Unused dialog box, but they will be deleted. You can use this tool in both the project environment and the Family Editor.

Model correctly from the beginning.   As you refine your design, it's critical to model correctly right from the beginning, not taking shortcuts, so you don't have to fix things later. If you can begin by thinking about how your project will be assembled, it will save you a lot of time later in the process. It's good practice to plan ahead, but remember that the software will allow you to make major changes at any stage in the process and still maintain coordination. If you are still in an early phase of design and do not know the exact wall type, use generic walls to capture your design intent; changing them later will be simple.

Manage workshared files.   When employing worksharing on a project, there are additional tools and tips you'll want to follow. Check out Chapter 6, "Understanding Worksharing," for more details.

Make a new local copy once a week.   In a workshared environment, your local copy can begin to perform poorly or grow in file size while the central file remains small and nimble. If this is the case, it might be time to throw out the old local copy for a new one. As a general practice, if you're accessing a project on a daily basis, it's a good idea to make a new local copy once a week.

Divide your model.   For larger projects or campus-style projects, you can break up your model into smaller submodels that are linked together. You can also do this on a single, large building. Dividing a model up helps limit the amount of information you are loading into a project at one time.

This is a particularly good idea if your project is going to be delivered in separate phases or bid packages. As the project progresses and you complete each delivery, you'll start the next phase by creating a new project file and then linking in the previous project file as context. Doing so will greatly simplify your document set (because you'll be able to start over after each phase) and avoid inadvertently modifying the previous phase (since the geometry and documentation are in a linked file).

If you decide to divide your project, make your cuts along lines that make sense from a holistic-building standpoint. Don't think of the cuts as you would in CAD, but think about how the actual assemblies will interact in the building. For example, don't cut between floors 2 and 3 on a multistory building unless you have a significant change in building form or program. Here's a list of some good places to split a model:

- ◆ At a significant change in building form or massing
- ◆ At a significant change in building program
- ◆ Between separate buildings on the site
- ◆ At the building site

Fixing File Corruption

From time to time your project files will begin to experience duress and possible corruption. This can happen for any number of reasons — network problems, file size, too many errors, and so forth. If your file begins crashing, don't panic. There are a few things you can do before calling Revit Support. Here are some suggestions to help get you back on track:

Review warnings.   Each time you create something that the software considers a problem, a warning is issued. Warnings will accumulate if left unresolved. The software constantly checks your project against this live list of warnings waiting to be resolved. Think of all these warnings as unresolved math calculations. The more there are, the more your computer will have to struggle to resolve them, and eventually you will have performance issues or file instability. To review the warnings, click the Warnings button on the Manage tab in the Inquiry panel. You'll get a dialog box like the one in Figure B.6, which will allow you to search for and resolve the problem objects. Since the dialog box closes each time to resolve a warning, mapping a shortcut to open the Review Warnings dialog box helps move things along a bit faster. We're hopeful that in time warnings will simply be schedulable like any other model element. This should help project teams remember to review warnings before they get out of control.

FIGURE B.6
Resolving errors

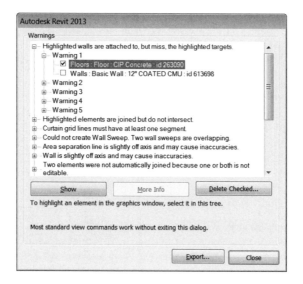

In addition to launching the full Review Warnings tool, you can observe and resolve warnings related to a selected model element at any time. When you select an element with associated warnings in a project view, you will see the Show Related Warnings button in the contextual ribbon (Figure B.7). This is a quick and easy way to resolve errors on the fly without viewing all the warnings accumulated in the entire project.

FIGURE B.7
Show warnings
related to a selected
element.

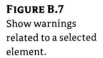

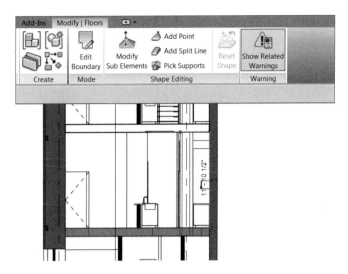

Reduce your file size. Sometimes when file corruption occurs, it's due to a file that has grown beyond capacity of the machines using it. Reduce your file size using the previous tips to make the model more manageable and resolve some of the errors.

Audit the file. Another way to deal with file corruption is to perform an audit on your file. You can find this tool in the lower-left corner of the File Open dialog box (Figure B.8). Auditing a file will review the data structures and try to correct any problems that have occurred. When the audit is completed, ideally you will have a fully functioning file again.

You can audit either a local file or the central file itself. Whenever you audit a file, make a new central copy and have all of your project team members create new local copies. The last thing you want is to have someone with file corruption in a local copy synchronize those problems back to your newly fixed central file.

FIGURE B.8
Auditing a file

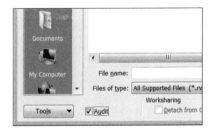

Applying Tips and Shortcuts

Beyond all the things you can do to hone your skills, you will begin to learn a number of tips and shortcuts as your experience grows using Revit Architecture. Here is a compilation of some of those tips and tricks:

Let the software do the math. Revit Architecture is like a big calculator, and it's very good at doing math correctly. Don't want to spend the time trying to figure out what your room size is after you subtract a 3 5/8″ and 5/8″ piece of gypsum board from an 11′–2″ room? Don't. If you need to modify a dimension, simply add an equal sign and a formula (Figure B.9) and Revit will calculate the value for you.

FIGURE B.9

Use an equal sign for performing calculations

Dimensions	
Thickness	=4' 5" - 2 13/16"
Height	7' 0"
Trim Projection Ext	0' 1"
Trim Projection Int	0' 1"

Make elevators visible in your plans. You want to create a shaft that will penetrate all the floors of your building and put an elevator in it that will show in all your plans. You could do that with an elevator family and cut a series of holes in the floors by editing floor profiles, but sometimes those holes lose their alignment. Fortunately, you can do both things at once using the Shaft tool found on the Opening panel of the Architecture tab. Here, not only can you cut a vertical hole through multiple floors as a single object, you can also insert 2D line work to represent your elevator in plan (Figure B.10). Every time the shaft is cut in a plan view, you will see the elevator line work.

FIGURE B.10

Adding elevators to a shaft

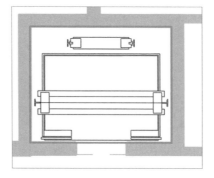

Orient to view. Creating perspective views of isolated design elements can be quick and easy in plan or section, but let's say you want to see that same element in 3D to be able to work out the details. Here's how:

1. Create a plan region or section cut isolating the area in question. If you're using a section, be sure to set your view depth to something practical.

2. Open the Default 3D view or any axon of the project.

3. Right-click the ViewCube®, select Orient To View, and select your view from the context menu.

4. Now, your 3D view will look identical to your section or plan region, but by rotating the view, you'll be able to see that portion in 3D.

— *Submitted by Mark*

Tune your shortcuts.   You can edit your keyboard shortcuts without the hassle of rooting through your hard drive looking for a TXT file. To edit your shortcuts, click the Application menu and select Options. Choose the User Interface tab and then click the Customize button. The Keyboard Shortcuts dialog box (Figure B.11) will allow you to edit those shortcuts. Consider making common shortcuts the same letter. So instead of pressing VG to get to your Visibility/Graphic Overrides dialog box, make the shortcut VV for quicker access.

FIGURE B.11

Editing your keyboard shortcuts

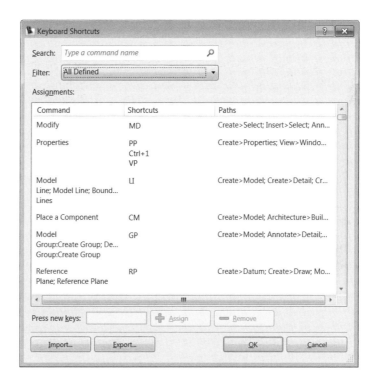

— *Submitted by John S. from St. Paul, Minnesota*

Drag and drop families.   You need to load a family into a project, you have the Explorer window open, and you know where the family is, but you don't want to go through the laborious effort of navigating across your office's server environment to get there. No problem. You can drag and drop families from Explorer directly into the project file.

— *Submitted by Tony D. from Kansas City, Missouri*

Copy a 3D view.   You made the perfect 3D view in your last project, and you can't figure out how to get it into your current project. Fortunately, there's a way to copy views from one project to another. Open both files in the same running instance of the software and then follow these steps:

1. In your perfect view, right-click the 3D view in the Project Browser and choose Show Camera from the context menu.

2. Press Ctrl+C to copy the selected camera.

3. In your new model, use Ctrl+V to paste the camera and your view and all its settings are now there.

Use a quick-cut poché.   Want to change everything that's cut in a view without having to select every family and change its properties? A quick-cut poché is, well, quick:

1. Open the view you want to modify.

2. Using a crossing window, select all the elements within the view.

3. Right-click and choose Override Graphics In View ➤ By Element from the context menu. As shown in Figure B.12, you can choose any filled region in the project and assign it to anything that is cut within your model.

FIGURE B.12
Using Override
Graphics for a
quick-cut poché

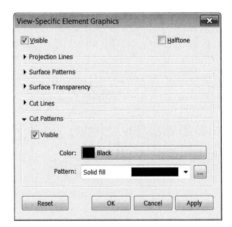

— *Submitted by Tobias H. from Boston, Massachusetts*

Move your ribbon.   Did you know that you can reorganize the tabs on the ribbon and place them in any order you'd like? Hold down the Ctrl key and select a tab (like Insert). You can drag it left or right to change the order in which they appear.

— *Submitted by Tobias H. from Boston, Massachusetts*

Additional Resources

A number of resources are available to help you along the way to improve your Revit Architecture skills, solve problems, or create new content. In our digital age, there is a wealth of information online to help you learn or communicate with users far and wide. So before you spend hours trying to solve a particularly challenging problem on your own, you might check some of these tools:

Help   Clicking the question mark icon in the upper-right corner of the application will take you to the Autodesk Wikihelp site at `http://wikihelp.autodesk.com/Revit`. This site will give you a basic synopsis of all the tools, buttons, and commands available in the application. As an online wiki, it also allows users in the global community to comment on the material and contribute new content. If you don't wish to use the online wiki help resource, you can switch to the traditional local help file by searching your computer for the 2013 version of the `Revit.ini` file. Find the variable called *UseHelpServer* and set it to 0.

Subscription Support   If you have purchased Revit Architecture on subscription, Autodesk offers web-based support. Autodesk's responses are speedy, the advice top-notch, and chances are your problem has been seen before. Subscription Support can be accessed online at `subscription.autodesk.com`.

AUGI   Autodesk User Group International (AUGI) is a source for tips and tricks as well as excellent user forums. The forums are free to participate in, and it's a great place to ask questions, find answers, or discuss project workflows. AUGI is located online at `www.augi.com`. Once you're there, look for Revit Architecture.

YouTube   Here's a great reason to tell your IT department you need access to YouTube. Autodesk has its own channel that has some great content, it's free, and it has hundreds of short videos showing you how to perform specific tasks in Revit. See `www.youtube.com/autodesk`.

AECbytes   AECbytes is a website dedicated to following the trends in the AEC industry, with a strong focus on BIM, technology, and the direction of the industry, put together by Lachmi Khemlani. See `www.aecbytes.com`.

Architecture-Tech   The authors of this book (Phil, Eddy, and James) maintain a popular blog at `www.architecture-tech.com`. A variety of posts related to Revit Architecture, other BIM software, and fun topics are available on a regular basis. You can also find links to many other blogs from industry experts.

Autodesk Revit Architecture 2013 Certification

Autodesk certifications are industry-recognized credentials that can help you succeed in your design career, providing benefits to both you and your employer. Getting certified is a reliable validation of skills and knowledge, and it can lead to accelerated professional development, improved productivity, and enhanced credibility.

This *Autodesk Official Training Guide* can be an effective component of your exam preparation. Autodesk highly recommends (and we agree!) that you schedule regular time to prepare, review the most current exam preparation roadmap available at www.autodesk.com/certification, use *Autodesk Official Training Guide*s, take a class at an Authorized Training Center (find ATCs near you here: www.autodesk.com/atc), and use a variety of resources to prepare for your certification — including plenty of actual hands-on experience.

To help you focus your studies on the skills you'll need for these exams, the following tables show each objective and the chapter in which you can find information on that topic — and when you go to that chapter, you'll find certification icons like the one in the margin here.

CERT OBJECTIVE

Table A.1 is for the Autodesk Certified User Exam and lists the section, exam objectives, and chapter where the information is found. Table A.2 is for the Autodesk Certified Professional Exam. The sections and exam objectives listed in the table are from the Autodesk Certification Exam Guide.

These Autodesk exam objectives were accurate at press time; please refer to www.autodesk.com/certification for the most current exam roadmap and objectives.

Good luck preparing for your certification!

TABLE A.1: Certified User Exam sections and objectives

TOPIC	LEARNING OBJECTIVE	CHAPTER
User Interface: Definitions	Identify primary parts of the user interface (UI): tabs, application menu, InfoCenter, ribbon, Elevation tag, Status bar, view control bar, Project Browser, context/right-click menus.	Chapter 2
User Interface: UI Navigation/ Interaction	Name the key features of the ribbon. Define how a split button works. Demonstrate the three ways the ribbon can be displayed: Full Ribbon, Min To Panel Tiles, Min To Tabs. Demonstrate how to detach a panel and move it on the screen.	Chapter 2
	Describe the hierarchy in the Project Browser for a new project.	Chapter 2
	Demonstrate how to add items to the Quick Access toolbar.	Chapter 2
	Describe why the Options bar changes.	Chapter 2
	Describe the function of the Status bar.	Chapter 2
	Describe what pressing the Esc key does.	Chapter 2
User Interface: Drawing Window	Describe what double-clicking an elevation view marker does.	Chapter 2
	Demonstrate how to turn on/off the 3D indicator.	Chapter 2
	Demonstrate how to change the view scale.	Chapter 2
User Interface: Navigation Control	Describe the functionality of the ViewCube®.	Chapter 2
	Describe what the ViewCube home icon does.	N/A
User Interface: Zoom	Describe how to zoom using the Navigation Bar.	N/A
	Describe the quickest way to zoom in or out.	N/A
	Describe the quickest way to pan.	N/A
File Management: Definitions	Define the acronym BIM and why it is important to Revit users.	Chapter 1
	Define a template file.	Chapter 4
File Management: Project Files	Identify the filename extension of a project file (.rvt).	N/A

TABLE A.1:   Certified User Exam sections and objectives   *(CONTINUED)*

TOPIC	LEARNING OBJECTIVE	CHAPTER
	Identify the filename extension of a template file (.rte). Create a template file for later project use.	Chapter 4
	Identify the filename extension of a Revit family file (.rfa).	Chapter 15
File Management: Open Existing Revit Project	Locate the Recent File window.	N/A (File menu drop-down)
	Demonstrate how to open a Revit file through Projects ➤ Open and through Application menu ➤ Open Documents icons.	N/A
File Management: Create New Revit Project	Demonstrate how to create a new Revit project folder and file through Application menu ➤ New ➤ Project.	N/A
	Change to a metric drawing.	N/A (Manage tab, Project Units, change Imperial to Metric)
	Add project information to a new drawing set.	Chapter 10
	Change system settings to create a new dimension style. Change arrows to architectural tick (obliques).	Chapter 19
Views: View Control and Properties	Navigate and change views using the view control bar.	Chapter 2, 12, 20
	Understand the view range of plan views and be able to change it.	Chapter 2
	Understand the purpose of view templates.	Chapter 18
	Change object visibility using temporary hide, hide category, and hide element.	Chapter 2
Views: View Types	Create section views including segmented ones.	Chapter 18
	Modify, crop, and place elevation views on a sheet.	Chapter 18
	Create and navigate 3D views.	Chapter 12
	Create callouts for details.	Chapter 18, 19

TABLE A.1: Certified User Exam sections and objectives *(CONTINUED)*

TOPIC	LEARNING OBJECTIVE	CHAPTER
	Create and annotate a drafting view.	Chapter 18, 19
	Use the section box to create a cutaway 3D view.	Chapter 12
Views: Cameras	Create a camera view, and modify its orientation.	Chapter 12
	Create and edit a walk-through.	Chapter 12
Levels: Definitions	Describe a level. Describe a use of a non-story level.	Chapter 2
	Understand how levels interact with intersecting views.	Chapter 2
	Create new levels.	Chapter 2, 9
	Understand level properties and characteristics.	Chapter 2
Walls: Home Tab ➤ Wall	Describe how to place walls.	Chapter 13
Walls: Options Bar	List options available when placing and modifying walls: Height, Location Line, Chain, Offset, Radius.	Chapter 13
Walls: Openings	Create a floor-to-ceiling opening in a given wall.	Chapter 14
Walls: Join	Demonstrate a join on crossing wall elements.	Chapter 13
Walls: Materials	Create a new wall style, and add given materials.	Chapter 13
Doors: Home Tab ➤ Door	Describe how to place doors.	N/A
Doors: Options Bar	Describe door options: Vertical/Horizontal, Tag On Placement, Leader, Leader Attachment Distance.	Chapter 19
Doors: Model in Place	Edit existing doors. Use Align to position a door.	Chapter 15
Windows: Home Tab ➤ Window	Describe how to place windows.	N/A
Windows: Options Bar	Describe window options: Vertical/Horizontal, Tag On Placement, Leader, Leader Attachment Distance.	Chapter 19
Windows: Model in Place	Edit existing windows.	Chapter 15

TABLE A.1:   Certified User Exam sections and objectives   *(CONTINUED)*

TOPIC	LEARNING OBJECTIVE	CHAPTER
Component: Options Bar	List options available when placing a component.	Chapter 15
Component: Component Host	Describe how to move a component to a different host.	Chapter 15
Component: Families	Navigate to find component families and load them.	Chapter 15
	Edit a family file and save.	Chapter 15
Columns and Grids: Definitions	Identify the uses of a grid.	Chapter 2
Columns and Grids: Home Tab ➢ Grid	Create an equally spaced grid pattern.	Chapter 3
Columns and Grids: Grid Properties	List the options available when placing and modifying grids.	Chapter 3
Columns and Grids: Home Tab ➢ Column	Place columns on a grid.	N/A
Columns and Grids: Column Properties	List the options available when placing and modifying columns.	N/A
Columns and Grids: Modify	List the tools you can use to modify columns and grids.	N/A
Stairs and Railings: Stair Types and Properties	Set the stair type.	Chapter 16
	Change the stair tread depth.	Chapter 16
Stairs and Railings: Stair Placement Options	Add a stair.	Chapter 16
Stairs and Railings: Railing Types and Properties	Set the railing to rectangular.	Chapter 16
	Set the railing properties.	Chapter 16
Stairs and Railings: Railing Placement Options	Add a railing.	Chapter 16
Roofs and Floors: Roof Types and Properties	Create a roof.	Chapter 14

TABLE A.1: Certified User Exam sections and objectives *(CONTINUED)*

TOPIC	LEARNING OBJECTIVE	CHAPTER
	Modify the roof properties.	Chapter 14
Roofs and Floors: Roof Elements	Create a fascia, a soffit, and a gutter.	Chapter 14
Roofs and Floors: Floor Types and Properties	Set the floor type (Sloped and Tapered). Create a floor.	Chapter 14
Sketching: Geometry	Sketch geometry and profiles using all sketching tools: Lines, Arcs, Polygons, Rectangles.	Chapter 17, 18, 19
Sketching: Fillet, Trim	Fillet objects.	Chapter 17, 18, 19
	Trim objects.	Chapter 3, 17, 18, 19
Sketching: Snaps	Describe the benefits of using snaps.	Chapter 3
	List the shortcuts to toggle snap on and off.	Chapter 3
Annotations: Text	Add model text to a floor plan.	N/A
Annotations: Dimensions	Add a dimension to a given floor plan. Create a wall section.	Chapter 19
	Add a spot slope to a roof on a given plan.	Chapter 14
Annotations: Tags	Add tags.	Chapter 19
	Tag untagged elements in a given floor plan.	Chapter 19
Schedules: Schedule Types	Create a door schedule.	N/A (While there is no specific coverage of a door schedule, creating schedules is discussed in Chapter 19.)
	Create a window schedule.	N/A
	Create a room schedule.	Chapter 20
Schedules: Legends	Create a Legend.	Chapter 19
Schedules: Keynotes	Add keynotes.	Chapter 19
Construction Document Sets: Sheet Setup	Create a title sheet with a sheet list.	Chapter 18

TABLE A.1:   Certified User Exam sections and objectives   *(CONTINUED)*

TOPIC	LEARNING OBJECTIVE	CHAPTER
Construction Document Sets: Printing	Create view/sheet sets for printing.	Chapter 18
	Print in scale. Print with percentage.	N/A
Construction Document Sets: Rendering	Render.	Chapter 12
	Place generic lights.	Chapter 12
	Set the solar angle.	Chapter 12

TABLE A.2:   Certified Professional Exam sections and objectives

TOPIC	OBJECTIVE	CHAPTER
Collaboration	Copy and monitor elements in a linked file.	Chapter 6, 7
	Use worksharing.	Chapter 6
	Import DWG files into Revit.	Chapter 7
Documentation	Create and modify filled regions.	Chapter 18
	Place detail components and repeating details.	Chapter 18
	Tag elements (doors, windows, and so on) by category.	Chapter 19
	Use dimension strings.	Chapter 19
	Set the colors used in a color-scheme legend.	Chapter 20
Elements	Change elements within a curtain wall: grids, panels, mullions.	Chapter 13
	Create compound walls.	Chapter 13
	Create a stacked wall.	Chapter 13
	Differentiate system and component families.	Chapter 13, 14, 15
	Create a new family type.	Chapter 15
	Modify an element's type parameters.	Chapter 15
	Use Revit family templates.	Chapter 15
Modeling	Assess or review warnings in Revit.	Chapter 5

TABLE A.2: Certified Professional Exam sections and objectives *(CONTINUED)*

TOPIC	OBJECTIVE	CHAPTER
	Create a building pad.	Chapter 7
	Define floors for a mass.	Chapter 10
	Create a stair with a landing.	Chapter 16
	Create elements such as floors, ceilings, or roofs.	Chapter 14
	Generate a toposurface.	Chapter 7
	Model railings.	Chapter 16
	Work with phases.	Chapter 11
	Edit a model element's material: door, window, furniture.	Chapter 12
	Change a generic floor/ceiling/roof to a specific type.	Chapter 13, 14
	Attach walls to a roof or ceiling.	Chapter 13, 14
Views	Define element properties in a schedule.	Chapter 18
	Control visibility.	Chapter 3, 12, 17, 18
	Use levels.	Chapter 2, 13, 14, 16
	Create a duplicate view for a plan, section, elevation, drafting view, and so on.	Chapter 18
	Create and manage legends.	Chapter 18
	Manage the view position on sheets.	Chapter 20
	Move the view title independently of the view.	Chapter 20
	Organize and sort items in a schedule.	Chapter 18

Index

Note to the reader: Throughout this index **boldfaced** page numbers indicate primary discussions of a topic. *Italicized* page numbers indicate illustrations.